Critical Acclaim for Andrew Collins'

GATEWAY TO ATLANTIS

"A bold and imaginative attempt to understand the destruction of the legendary city of Atlantis, the creation of Mesoamerican civilization, and the end of the last Ice Age."

—*Kirkus Reviews*

"Collins produces a tantalizing pattern of oral and written evidence that Atlantis not only existed but probably was destroyed by a comet some 10,000 years ago."

—*Boston Herald*

"Collins proves an engaging conductor of an exegetical tour of Plato's writings about a civilization in the Western Ocean that vanished when a natural catastrophe befell its homeland. His book [will] enamor imaginations sparked by the legend of lost Atlantis."

—*Booklist*

"This is the best book I have ever read on the subject of Atlantis. It is impressively researched and, in a fascinating story of discovery, accounts for data in a way no others have managed before. Buy it, read it, prepare to be amazed."

—Michael Baigent, author of
The Holy Blood and the Holy Grail

"Learned and erudite, but at the same time grippingly written and immensely readable. Probably the most substantial and well-researched book on Atlantis since Ignatius Donnelly. It will certainly become one of the classics of Atlantis."

—Colin Wilson, *Daily Mail* (London)

ALSO BY ANDREW COLLINS

From the Ashes of Angels
Gods of Eden

GATEWAY TO ATLANTIS

'Andrew Collins' *From the Ashes of Angels* is one of those books that comes along only once or twice a decade. Suddenly a whole new realm is opened up to us as we are invited on a hunt for our lost origins led by a voice that speaks clearly and forcefully. It is the kind of book that you can read and then read again and again and each time you will be rewarded. Andrew Collins is one of the key thinkers of a whole new generation of writers that have decided that the human past is much more interesting than we have all been led to believe.'

Rand Flem-ath, co-author of *When the Sky Fell*
and the up-coming book *The Atlantis Blueprint*

WHAT THE EXPERTS HAVE TO SAY ABOUT *GODS OF EDEN*

'In *Gods of Eden* Andrew Collins focuses his clear and steady eyes upon questions that haunt so many of us about ancient Egypt. Was the Egyptian civilisation a development or a legacy? Did the ancient Egyptians possess advanced knowledge of sonar technology? What was the complicated relationship between ancient Egypt and the Near East? Each of these questions are taken up with fresh and powerful insights that have elevated Andrew Collins above so many other feeble attempts to make sense of the past. Here is an author to watch. Here is someone who is really interested in the truth and will take us there at all costs. If science as a whole had a dozen more thinkers of this courage and tenacity then we would all be celebrating the millennium in the warmth of a new golden age.'

Rand Flem-ath, co-author of *When the Sky Fell*
and the up-coming book *The Atlantis Blueprint*

'The research and writing of Andrew Collins invariably refocuses our attention on the key points in current enigmas about the rise of civilisation and prehistory. Keenly sensing the challenge of what remains to be learned, Collins does not visit old ruts. Time and time again, he reaches beyond the known and pushes the envelope of inquiry, as is seen in *Gods of Eden*. The perspectives he is developing can contribute crucially to our common task of direction-finding in the uncertain future.'

John Lash, astrologer, mythologist
and author of *Quest for the Zodiac*

GATEWAY TO ATLANTIS

The Search for the Source of A Lost Civilization

ANDREW COLLINS

with an introduction by DAVID ROHL

CARROLL & GRAF PUBLISHERS
NEW YORK

Gateway to Atlantis:
The Search for the Source of a Lost Civilization

Carroll & Graf Publishers
An Imprint of Avalon Publishing Group Incorporated
161 William Street, 16th Floor
New York, NY 10038

Copyright © 2000 by Andrew Collins

First Carroll & Graf cloth edition 2000
First Carroll & Graf trade paperback edition 2002

All rights reserved. No part of this book may be reproduced in whole or in part without written permission from the publisher, except by reviewers who may quote brief excerpts in connection with a review in a newspaper, magazine, or electronic publication; nor may any part of this book be reproduced, stored in a retrieval system, or transmitted in any form or by any means electronic, mechanical, photocopying, recording, or other, without written permission from the publisher.

Library of Congress Cataloging-in-Publication Data is available.

ISBN: 0-7867-0963-4

Printed in the United States of America
Distributed by Publishers Group West

To the memory of the indigenous peoples of the Bahamas and Caribbean who died following the discovery of the New World, and to the black African population forced to replace them.

Also to the Abbé Brasseur de Bourbourg who, I realised only in the very final stages of writing this book, understood what I now know nearly 150 years ago.

CONTENTS

ACKNOWLEDGEMENTS

LET ME BEGIN BY THANKING Karen Deeley, for her loving support, patience, editorial suggestions and help under difficult conditions, and without whom my life would have been lost; David Southwell, for his exceptional inspirational insights, advice and support into all areas of the book's construction, and for acting as my 'lawyer' during very traumatic times; Graham Phillips, for pointing out the gate and urging me to go through it; David Rohl, for his continued support of my work and indispensable introduction; Amber McCauley, for her help on French and Spanish translations, particularly for the last-minute Brasseur de Bourbourg material; and Sue and Mark Foster, for their friendship and help in all fields.

My thanks also go to Geoffrey Ashe, for listening to my theories on Atlantis; David Aston, for scouting out Cuba on my behalf; Rose Blanchard and Norm Byers, for their insights into the mysteries of Andros island; Bob Bryden and Bernard G., for sharing insights into the history of the Knights Templar and other military orders; Simon Cox and Jacqueline Pegg of Quest Research, for their research and thoughts during the early stages of this project; Ann Deagon, for her invaluable Latin translations; William Donato, for supplying me with so much of his time and support in making sure that the Bimini chapters are as accurate as possible; David Eccott, for his research assistance on transoceanic contact and use of photographs; Lorraine Evans, for her assistance; Donnie and Maurice Fields, Mary Lomando, Vanda Osman, Pat Oren Purcell, Herb Sawinski, Anna Valentine, David Zink, the crew of the MV *Ocean Window*, for their help and support in connection with Bimini; Mel Fisher, for disclosing new insights into the Atlantis mystery and Taffi Fisher and Laura Pike for introducing me to him; Jo-Ann Hackett of Harvard University, for checking my insights into the Semitic languages; Catherine Hale, for her German translation work; Rodney Hale, for his continued support, time, maps and editorial suggestions; Heather Holden Brown, Celia Kent and Lindsay Symons of Headline, and Simon Trewin of Peters, Fraser and Dunlop, for continuing to support me during troubled times; Alan R. Kelso de Montigny, for sharing with me insights into his father's life; Gareth Medway and Mark McCann, for their help in research and checking my facts; Henk Meiyer, for the use of his photograph of the Naxos Gate; John Michell, for continued inspiration; Christian and Barbara Joy O'Brien, as well as Edmund Marriage, for thoughts and inspiration; Colin Wilson, for his quote and valued friendship; and Richard Ward, for his additional research.

Last but not least, I would like to thank Michael Baigent, Storm Constantine, Wayne Frostick, Johnny Merron, Chris Ogilvie Herald, Lisa Mundy and Matthew Adams, Niven Sinclair, John Sassoon, Emilio Spedicato, Pandora Stevens, Paul Weston, Caroline Wise, Steve Wilson, for their continued help, support and friendship during the preparation of this book.

Andrew Collins, 1999

Photo Credits

The author and publisher would like to thank those listed below for permission to use the following pictures included as numbered plates illustrations.

1. Stanze di Raffaello, Vatican/Scala, Florence; 4. Museo Pio Clementino, Vatican/Scala, Florence; 5. Sygma; 8. Cyrus H. Gordon; 10, 11, 12, 13, 23 & 44. David Eccott; 15. Park and Roche Establishment Archives, Schaan; 17 & 18. Trustees of the British Museum; 19. Topkapi Museum, Istanbul; 22. Museo Nacional de Historia, Madrid; 27. Fondo de Cultura Económica from *Historica Tolteca-Chichimeca*; 28. Estrella Rey and Ernesto E. Tabío; 32. Essex and Suffolk Water; 35. John W. White; 36, 40 & 41. Anna Valentine; 38. Joan Zink; 39. Ava Rebikoff; 42. William M. Donato; 43. Herb Sawinski.

Every effort has been made to trace and contact the copyright holders of all photographs which appear in this book. The author will be glad to rectify any omissions at the earliest opportunity.

The author would also like to thank Karen Deeley for the following line illustrations: Bimini Road, God L, Quetzalcoatl and God L/Votan; Rodney Hale for map texts and Chris Ollis and Ruby for the Atlantis groundplan.

INTRODUCTION

ATLANTIS – NEXT TO GOD THE most written about, debated, abused and ridiculed concept on our planet. Thousands of books and articles have been published over the years which set out to solve what is perhaps human history's greatest enigma. Most were written by non-academic 'freethinkers', many with their own agendas, few tackling the subject with dispassion, prepared to let the evidence alone guide them. Academia, on the other hand, has refused steadfastly to sully its hands with legendary tales of sunken civilisations and 'golden ages', preferring to deal with 'real history' based entirely on the archaeological evidence.

In some ways it is not difficult to understand why we have such polarised views. Extraordinary stories – we label them 'legends' or 'epics' – have always stimulated our collective imagination, unencumbered, as we tend to be, by the vagaries of evidence. This desire to believe in a legendary past – a primeval age – has recently been fed and nurtured by a new breed of popularist writer keen to promote the concept of a long-lost elder culture and its ancient wisdom. Their books are often stimulating and thought-provoking, sometimes exasperating in their inaccuracies and wilder claims, but always appealing directly to the human imagination and spirit. On the other hand, imagination has never been a major requirement within academia.

But what is it about this word 'Atlantis' in particular which tugs so violently at our emotions? Why do so many of us want to believe in an antediluvian civilisation reaching back into the mists of time? And why do historians and academics seize every opportunity to dismiss such beliefs as the ramblings of the lunatic fringe?

As with many great discoveries, academic resistance to radical revisionism is often based not so much on evidence but rather, ironically, on emotion. In a way, scholars are far more susceptible to such feelings than the general public. This is because they have vested interests and reputations which can often be undermined by revisionist scholarship. The simple truth is that they feel threatened by revolutionary ideas and argument. The image of the calm, methodical, open-minded historian is in reality more a myth than Plato's sunken island.

So on the one hand we have the 'amateur enthusiast' full of energy, not weighed down by facts, and on the other the 'stuffy academic', paranoid about his credibility and lacking the foresight to take his subject forward into new and intellectually stimulating territory. The two sides – New Age and conservative academic – stand utterly opposed, neither prepared to compromise their position.

As is often the case in such situations, a solution has to be found which takes a position in the middle ground between the opposing forces of dogma. Yes, facts and evidence are important and cannot be ignored in support of a pet theory – but, equally, imagination and intuition are invaluable assets in the tool-kit of a competent researcher. In the end it all boils down to a matter of balance and judgement.

But can the Atlantis enigma be resolved, at least in part, by adopting this more balanced approach? In the book you are about to read, author Andrew Collins, I believe, has found that elusive middle way. He has amassed a huge amount of data which sheds light on the mystery. Much of it consists of compelling evidence to show that the island of Atlantis did and still does (in part) exist. Some leaps of the imagination have been required in order for Andrew to complete his story – but this presents no real problem since his thesis does not directly contradict the evidence. This, after all, is part and parcel of good history-writing.

It is my task in this introduction to set the scene for the journey of discovery you are about to take. I must not give away all the secrets and revelations with which you will be confronted as you travel back in time through *Gateway to Atlantis;* I shall leave a few surprises and much of the detail to Andrew, your guide and travelling companion. But I can prepare you in part for what lies ahead.

Perhaps, then, we should start with some basic questions about the Atlantis enigma:

- Did Atlantis exist (in any shape or form)?

This is the first and foremost question of Atlantology which can be resolved only if we actually decide to climb out of our comfortable armchairs and go look for the place with open minds and divested of scholarly prejudice. If this is the basic challenge, we then find ourselves faced with a whole raft of other issues which must be addressed:

- Where might Atlantis have been located?
- What type of Atlantean culture should we be looking for?
- When could that culture have flourished?
- Can we confirm that Atlantis was destroyed in some form of natural disaster?

Following on from these major issues are fascinating subsidiary questions that have come to the fore in recent years and which directly impinge on any modern quest for the sunken kingdom:

- Given that conventional wisdom states that the Americas were not discovered until 1492, how do we explain recent claims involving the recovery of 2,000-year-old Mediterranean amphorae (storage jars) found in sunken wrecks off the coasts of Brazil in South America and Honduras in Central America?
- Why have traces of cocaine been detected in 3,000-year-old Egyptian mummies when we are informed that the only ancient source of this narcotic drug was South America – a region apparently unknown to the civilisations of the ancient world?
- Ditto tobacco.
- What do we make of the writings of Roman geographers in which it is specifically stated that 40 days' sail are required to reach the islands of the Hesperides, beyond the Western Ocean, once a ship departs from the African coast?
- Might these reports be connected with Plato's references to Atlantis – an island lying before or in front of a series of 'other islands' from which ancient voyagers could reach the 'opposite continent'?
- Moreover, why did the Spanish and Portuguese cartographers and navigators of the fifteenth century repeatedly send out maritime expeditions in search of a legendary island called Antilia, with which they associated an uncharted continent?
- And, finally, could this all explain why the newly discovered West Indies were so quickly identified with the lost island of Antilia – a name which they retain to this day in the forms of the Greater and Lesser Antilles?

These are only some of the intriguing questions that are examined and answered in this volume of Atlantological treasures. Your journey is going to be challenging – but the rewards will certainly be worth your effort.

★ ★ ★

In the years leading up to the end of the millennium we all witnessed a rush to exploit the Atlantis phenomenon. As our world approached its prophesied nemesis, the search for the Atlantean Hall of Records reached fever pitch – all in an attempt to prove the prediction of the 'sleeping prophet' Edgar Cayce that this repository of lost wisdom would be discovered by the end of the century. Add in Nostradamus's seventy-second quatrain from his *Tenth Century*, purporting to describe the impending appearance of the 'King of Terror' (incidentally a mistranslation), which would presage the end of our current existence in 1999, and we had a recipe for a psychotic soup of weird and wonderful Atlantean and end of the world/second coming theories. New Age authors had a field day, with publishers around the world signing up anything connected with catastrophism, ancient wisdom, doom prophecy and lost civilisations.

In an ironic conundrum of chronology, I am writing this introduction well before 31 December 1999. It is actually rather disorientating writing in the past tense when really in the present while trying to anticipate the future. In doing so I trust that I am not tempting fate. However, the simple fact that you are about to read *Gateway to Atlantis* in the year 2000 might encourage the belief that we are all still here. I am therefore delighted to see this book intentionally appear well after the no-show of the King of Terror, the not quite the end of the world (just yet) ongoing saga, and with the Hall of Records still awaiting discovery beneath the venerable Sphinx's right paw. Perhaps, now that we have finally got all this excitement out of our system for another thousand years, we can concentrate on the Atlantis legend in a more sober light and with an eye on the evidence currently available to us.

This leads me to an issue of methodology which is close to my heart. As a historian (academically trained as an Egyptologist and ancient Near East archaeologist), I believe absolutely in the foundation of evidence for historical interpretation. What I mean by this can be summed up in two thoughts.

(1) 'History' is not the past; it is merely our best interpretations of the archaeological and textual evidence handed down by our ancestors. 'The past' is what actually happened – and by definition we can never hope to know *exactly* what happened. We struggle with our differing historical perspectives of events even as recent as the two great wars of the twentieth century. It is not difficult to appreciate that the writings of the time were affected by political viewpoints (propaganda) and cultural bias (ethnicity). In addition, the writings of later historians can have diametrically opposing interpretations of the source material (evidence).

To take an extreme example: imagine how history would be

skewed if some archaeologist from Alpha Centauri were to dig up the long-hidden 'Hall of Records' of the Third Reich on a post-cataclysm planet earth of the twenty-fifth century – but then fail to find the equivalent contemporary archive of the Western Alliance. How would he write his history of human civilisation in the twentieth century? What would he make of the writings of the *Ahnenerbe* ('Ancestral Inheritance') – the Nazi academic institution that promulgated the ideas of an Atlantean super-race from which the German *Volk* were descended? The most respected archaeologists and historians of the 1930s were recruited by Heinrich Himmler to rewrite history in an attempt to show that Aryans were descended from the master race of Atlantis – with the implication that all other ethnicity was inferior and must be exterminated to keep the German race pure. If this were our extraterrestrial archaeologist's only documentary source for the twentieth century, he might be forgiven for believing that this dangerous nonsense was the historical reality simply because of the academic pedigree of its authorship. Without a second and independent perspective, historical truth can very easily become historical untruth.

This somewhat far-fetched analogy is intended to press home an appreciation of the problems modern historians have with the surviving evidence from our own distant past. Can that evidence be trusted? If it is written evidence, who wrote it? From what political and cultural perspective was it written? Can the facts be corroborated by different and disconnected sources? Could there be a crucial piece of missing evidence which, by its very absence, distorts the historical picture we have constructed? All these questions are the stuff of history-writing, and the ability to answer them directly impinges on the trustworthiness of the history being constructed. In that light, the last of the questions – do we have enough evidence to draw historical conclusions? – brings me to the second methodological point.

(2) 'Absence of evidence is not evidence of absence.' This is one of the most unfortunate methodological statements to be devised by the academic community. It is trundled out regularly by certain conservative scholars to defend their (often fundamentalist) positions. In my own field of research – Old World archaeology – we have a classic example of how this mantra is used to deny an overwhelming corpus of archaeological fact. It goes something like: absence of evidence for an invasion of the Promised Land by the Israelite tribes at the end of the Late Bronze Age is not evidence to conclude conclusively that the Israelites did not conquer the region later known as Israel. This flies in the face of archaeology, which shows clearly that none of the cities burned to the ground by Joshua, according to the Old Testament tradition, were destroyed at

this time. Indeed, the city of Jericho, itself one of the main focuses of the biblical narrative, did not exist at the end of the LBA. Yet renowned scholars such as Professor Kenneth Kitchen, formerly of Liverpool University, argue that the current absence of evidence for such an invasion may yet be resolved by future archaeology. The question which arises from such a standpoint has to be: how long do we have to wait before coming to an historical conclusion? Archaeological excavations in the Holy Land have been under way for the best part of two centuries, yet no evidence for an LBA conquest has come to light. Should we wait another hundred years before we decide the matter? Perhaps we need another thousand years to be absolutely sure?

One could also accuse certain New Age 'archaeologists' of employing this same methodological caveat. In recent decades the building of the pyramids at Giza has been attributed to both Atlanteans (John Anthony West) and extraterrestrials (Erich von Daniken, Zecharia Sitchin, Richard Hoagland, Alan Alford). Certain writers find it hard to believe that ordinary Egyptians, living in Old Kingdom times, could have accomplished such a task without the intervention of a more advanced scientific culture. The simple logic of such a view is superficially attractive. Yes, the pyramids represent an astonishing achievement which certainly defies our present understanding. You often hear researchers (even Egyptologists) saying that such a project could not be attempted today. We simply cannot understand the techniques used, the willpower needed or the chronology of such an operation. How did the workforce of Pharaoh Khufu cut, transport and place 2,300,000 two-and-a-half-tonne blocks of limestone on to the Giza plateau to construct the Great Pyramid in the space of just 23 years (the length of Khufu's reign as given in the Royal Canon of Turin)? Work it out for yourself: 100,000 blocks a year = 274 blocks a day = 11 blocks an hour = 1 block every 5 minutes – and that working 24 hours a day for every day of the year. With the more reasonable assumption that work stopped in the night hours, the daily figure would increase by at least a third. So there is clearly a puzzle here.

But should we really turn to lost civilisations or spacemen to find a solution to this mystery? Surely the answer must be sought in the available evidence. In spite of two centuries of exploration and archaeological endeavour on the Giza necropolis, no material has been unearthed which would suggest external forces were at work. The name of Khufu is associated closely with the Great Pyramid through quarry marks on building blocks inside the pyramid (not forgeries, as previously claimed), on fragments originating from the pyramid's causeway and in the tombs of the royal entourage surrounding the pyramid complex. On this basis we have to conclude that the Great Pyramid was indeed constructed as the final resting place of Pharaoh Khufu of the Fourth Dynasty and that the building of this awe-inspiring monument to one man's ego took place some time in the third millennium BC. This conclusion has somewhat reluctantly been accepted by both Graham Hancock and Robert Bauval, the doyens of New Age archaeology, even though they argue for a 12,500-year-old Sphinx and an alignment of the pyramid foundations dating to that same Atlantean era.

Recent research by Cambridge University Egyptologist Kate Spence has demonstrated that the north alignment of all the Old Kingdom pyramids shifted through time as the builders attempted to adjust for an observed shift in the relative position of the circumpolar stars. This tracking of the north celestial pole (relative to the stars) plots the known wobble in the earth's axis of rotation (referred to as precession), which can be dated using astronomical retrocalculations. Spence's analysis has produced a date for the building of the Khufu pyramid of *c.* 2470 BC, which is, in fact, some 114 years *later* than the orthodox date published in *Cambridge Ancient History* (Vol. I:2, p. 995). Interestingly enough, Robert Bauval's own calculations for the alignment of the Queen's Chamber shaft with Sirius produces a date of between 2400 and 2475 BC. The New Chronology date, retrocalculated from the fixed date of 664 BC (using both archaeological and eclipse evidence) and followed by myself and other researchers, gives a date of *c.* 2430 BC for the Great Pyramid. All this new research thus confirms an Old Kingdom dating for the construction of the Giza pyramids and rules out any prehistoric activity – at least in relation to these structures.

On the other hand there may be some merit in the proposal that the Sphinx itself is older than the pyramids of Giza. Primarily we have the water erosion features in the rock-cut enclosure surrounding the reclining leonine sculpture. These were undoubtedly formed by rainwater pouring off the plateau during heavy storms. But how old this makes the Sphinx is another matter. Geologist Robert Schoch originally gave an estimate of 5000 to 7000 BC. This date was elevated by Hancock and Bauval (and in agreement with Edgar Cayce's date for Atlantis) to 10,500 BC based on their star alignment theory (and their apparent desire to conform to Edgar Cayce's date for Atlantis). The reality could, however, be a great deal lower than both dates, given that the Neolithic Wet Phase (Nabtian Pluvial) lasted well into the fourth millennium BC and that the climate of Egypt was much wetter than it is today right up until the Fourth Dynasty, when the Giza pyramids took shape. The end of this wet phase was not sudden but rather a gradual process. As a result, rainfall on the Giza plateau was still relatively high during the Predynastic and Archaic Periods of early Egyptian history.

Perhaps it is appropriate at this point to make some fairly

straightforward observations about Hancock and Bauval's Sphinx alignment theory. They argue that the Sphinx was orientated not only to face the rising sun but also to the appearance of the constellation of Leo at the spring equinox. Again, they argue that due to the astronomical mechanism known as precession this occurred in around 10,500 BC – Edgar Cayce's Atlantean date. The *Keeper of Genesis* team have a well-reasoned case here but, as with most theories, there are clarifications and counter-arguments to consider.

First, there is the matter of their dating precision – a precision that, in my opinion, simply is not attainable in the prehistoric era. For example, the spring equinox dawn rising of Leo could have been observed at any time between 11,500 and 9000 BC, so Hancock and Bauval's 10,500 BC date seems a little too convenient. As we have seen, the period of erosion of the Sphinx and its enclosure has even greater margins. And the date range for the Great Pyramid shaft alignment with Sirius must be considered with similar flexibility (although in this case within a much narrower range).

But there is a more important point from an Egyptological perspective. Many Egyptologists would take issue with the basic assumption being employed by Hancock and Bauval for their calculations. The Egyptian climate is such that changes in the seasons are not as dramatic as in the northern European continent. The equinoxes may have been significant to ancient Europeans because they marked the birth and death of a year, but they were of no great importance to the Egyptians during the pharaonic era. It could be argued that Bauval and Hancock are taking what can only be described as a Eurocentric view of the ancient world. What really mattered in Egypt was the arrival of the inundation of the Nile, heralded by the heliacal rising of the star Sopdet (Greek Sothis, modern Sirius). This marked the Egyptian New Year, which began with the cleansing of the earth and the gift of rich, life-nurturing, waterborne silt from the East African highlands. The first appearance of Sirius each year fell in mid-July, fairly close to the longest day (i.e. the summer solstice). As a result, it is perhaps more appropriate to suggest that the Sphinx was approximately aligned to the appearance of a constellation at *this* time of the year. Conventional Egyptologists would then make much of the fact that the constellation of Leo appears on the eastern horizon at dawn on the summer solstice not in the eleventh but in the third millennium BC – the era of the early pharaonic dynasties and the pyramids of the Old Kingdom.

In mitigation of the Hancock and Bauval hypothesis, it is true to say that this situation might not have pertained in the pre-pharaonic era when the climate was a great deal wetter and the indigenous population was less dependent on the annual flood. It is not beyond the bounds of possibility that the peoples of prehistoric Egypt did regard the equinoxes as important calendrical events compared with their much later descendants. This view may be supported by the findings of Fred Wendorff concerning the prehistoric site of Nabta Playa (*c.* 6000 BC), located in the now bone-dry Sahara Desert west of Aswan. His study of the stone circles and lines at Nabta suggests that we are dealing here with a calendar site, the constructors of which were keen observers of seasonal astronomical alignments.

Then there is Hancock's and Bauval's most telling counter-argument to the suggestion of a solstice orientation for the Sphinx. The simple fact is that it faces due east, according to them precisely aligned to the point where the sun rises at the equinoxes. This is a major plus in their favour, with an adequate response from a conventional dating perspective hard to find.

But, then again, Egyptologists would argue that it is also an assumption on Hancock's and Bauval's part to suggest that the Egyptians recognised the stars that form the constellation of Leo as a representation of a lion. The Ramesside astronomical ceilings belonging to the royal tombs in the Valley of the Kings suggest that another group of stars was identified with the lion. In fact, we have no clear evidence to show that the constellations of the zodiac, as we know them, were introduced into Egypt before the Ptolemaic Period (*c.* 300 BC) with the arrival of the Greeks into the Nile Valley.

As a result of all these alternative understandings and interpretations, considerable doubt has recently been expressed over any connection between the construction and alignment of the Sphinx and the Atlantean date of 10,500 BC proclaimed by the followers of Edgar Cayce. The jury remains out.

However, another piece of evidence relating to the Sphinx suggests that it may predate the pyramids after all. The text of a small stela found in the Temple of Isis Mistress of the Pyramid (located on the east side of the southernmost satellite pyramid of the Khufu complex) does seem to confirm that the Sphinx was already standing when Khufu's architects set out the plan of the Great Pyramid. It mentions repair work undertaken by Khufu's workforce to the leonine sculpture itself – evidence of which (in the shape of Old Kingdom blocks attached to the natural rock of the Sphinx's body) has been revealed through archaeology. Admittedly, this 'Inventory Stela' appears to be a Late Period (Twenty-sixth Dynasty) copy of an original Old Kingdom decree, but there is no reason to suppose that its basic contents had been radically amended. Just because later writings of gods' names are used within the text does not automatically imply that the whole decree was made up by the priests of the late first millennium BC. Is it credible to believe that priestly officials at Giza, during any period of Egyptian history, could somehow have forgotten that the Sphinx was carved in the reign of and likeness of Khafre? If the text of the stela states that the

Sphinx was already in need of repair in the time of Khafre's father, then clearly we have to take this statement on trust until we find unambiguous proof otherwise.

The Sphinx and its temple do, therefore, appear to predate the pyramids of Khufu, Khafre and Menkaure – but by how much can only be guessed at. There is certainly no archaeological or astronomical requirement to push the date of its carving back 8,000 years before the pyramids. The weathering and water erosion patterns could have been produced during the late fourth to mid-third millennium – at the time of the foundation of the pharaonic state by the Followers of Horus and during the centuries which encompass Egypt's First to Fourth Dynasties.

So there is both positive and negative (the absence of) evidence which leads me to reject an Atlantean connection with the Giza monuments. It requires more than the revelations of a sleeping prophet to overturn the evidence we do possess in favour of evidence yet to be unearthed. That is the way of things in archaeology and ancient world studies. Wishful thinking is a poor counter-argument to established archaeological facts.

I will finish this discussion of the Giza monuments with an appropriate quotation from two well-known members of the 'alternative Egypt' community, Ian Lawton and Chris Ogilvie-Herald, who have recently re-examined the various Atlantean claims in far greater detail than I have been able to do here. In the introduction to their book *Giza: The Truth* (1999) they make the following rather damning but certainly accurate observation:

> . . . we do see a clear trend, which emerged almost as soon as exploration commenced at the Plateau, and which has become exacerbated in recent years – at least in part due to a combination of millennium fever and the ability of new Internet technology to spread rumours like wildfire, so that to many they become reality. What we have undoubtedly uncovered . . . is that much of the rumour mill surrounding the Plateau is at best misleading, and at worst complete garbage.[1]

Of course 'absence of evidence *is* evidence of absence' – it may not be *proof* of absence but it certainly is *evidence*. We can only work with the data at hand – not on what might be in the future. Otherwise how could we move forward? If we were to wait for future findings before coming to any conclusion, then no decisions would ever be made about anything. We have to deal with what we know, not what we might know. Time and continuing archaeological research has produced a general consensus about certain historical 'facts' which are unlikely to change with the passage of time and further archaeological discovery.

Ironically, in this respect Atlantis has a better claim than biblical archaeology or any quest for the Hall of Records – simply because the search for the sunken civilisation is still in its infancy as far as archaeological endeavour is concerned. Underwater investigations for submerged landmasses and lost civilisations are relatively new to archaeology. The equipment to undertake such searches has only recently become available. Underwater archaeology is a new science which has a long way to go before it catches up with land-based archaeology. The lands of the Bible have been dug, dissected and delved into for generations – but that certainly cannot be said for the vastness of the Atlantic Ocean and its underwater shelves. In this case (and this case alone) one might be justified in saying that absence of evidence is not evidence of absence – but probably only for the next 20 years or so. With modern sonar techniques, magnetometry and water-penetrating photography, any lost cities or sunken kingdoms will surely be revealed within our lifetimes. If they fail to appear, then – and only then – we can be satisfied that the Atlantis legend is nothing more than a myth.

The saga of Atlantis is almost as old as time itself. The genesis of the story can be traced back to Plato who, in the fourth century BC, wrote his two philosophical treaties the *Timaeus* and the *Critias*. However, in these accounts of the fallen Atlantean utopia, the celebrated poet and philosopher informs his audience that the story had been passed down from his ancestor – the Athenian archon (chief magistrate) and legislator, Solon. The latter had visited Egypt when Amasis (570–526 BC), the last great pharaoh of the Twenty-sixth Dynasty, was on the throne. There, in the delta capital of Sais, Solon had learned about the sunken island of Atlantis from a temple priest. The old Egyptian (Plutarch names him as Senchis, probably a Greek form of Sinku, a hypocoristicon of Susinku = Shoshenk) claimed that the destruction of this earliest of civilisations was brought about by earthquakes and floods some 8,000 to 9,000 years before the Athenian's visit to Sais. By our reckoning, this would be between 9570 and 8570 BC.

This alone of all the fabulous 'facts' about Atlantis has given cause for its complete dismissal by historians who know full well that the earliest city civilisations cannot be dated before around 4000 BC on current archaeological evidence. Moreover, the Atlantis legend tells of a conflict between the island empire and the founding fathers of the city-state of Athens – but Athens itself was not 'founded', as we understand the term, until the Mycenaean Late Bronze Age, conventionally dated to around 1550 BC.

If there had been an Atlantic culture in the tenth and ninth millennia BC which had been destroyed in a great cataclysm, how did knowledge of it survive through 5,000 years of darkness before the 're-emergence' of civilisation in the fifth millennium ancient Near East? And how could its technology and 'wisdom' have spanned the intervening millennia? These basic questions lie at the heart of the recent attempts to redate the Giza pyramids and Sphinx to a much earlier era than the mid-third millennium BC when Egyptologists have placed the Fourth pharaonic Dynasty.

Of course, the anomaly of the dark period between the golden age of Atlantis and the rise of Egyptian civilisation is only significant if another of Plato's claims is taken seriously – that Atlantean culture was technologically, militarily and artistically comparable with the Athens of Plato's own time (or even of Old Kingdom Egypt). Indeed, Plutarch in his *Lives* suggests that Plato had greatly elaborated and exaggerated the original story brought back to Athens by Solon. If the Atlantean culture we seek is rather seen as an advanced Neolithic, perhaps even Megalithic, civilisation, and which had no direct influence over the much later Giza monuments (or anywhere else in the ancient world for that matter), then most of the dating difficulties are eased. It is therefore extremely important to look again at Plato and the genesis of the Atlantis epic. This, quite rightly, is the starting point for *Gateway to Atlantis*.

However, what has amazed me is how much post-Platonic material on Atlantis has come to light as a direct result of Andrew's thorough detective work. He introduces us, through the writings of Proclus Daidochus (AD 412–485), to heated debates in the hallowed halls of the Platonic Academy attached to the Alexandrian Library – debates that, even with the resources available in those days, failed to reach a consensus as to whether Plato's Atlantis had definitely once existed. But then so much evidence comes to light from a very different library of knowledge – reports of the earliest seafarers who plied the Atlantic eastern seaboard routes and the writings of classical scholars such as the geographer Strabo, the historian Diodorus Siculus, the biographer Plutarch and the naturalist Pliny the Elder.

We are left with a real dilemma here. Yes, it would be perfectly reasonable simply to reject Plato's Atlantean tale as fiction – a literary device to put across his philosophical message. But, if this is the case, then why do we find so much other material, outside Plato's treaties, concerning a place variously called Atlantis, Atlantides, Atulliae, Antilia, the Hesperides, Aztlan and Tulan, which lay somewhere out in the Atlantic Ocean?

At the beginning of this introduction I mentioned that professional historians had, for the most part, shied away from the Atlantis debate. Over the years, and as more and more exotic theories were being propounded from outside the ivory towers of academia, the very word Atlantis itself became a sort of profanity or blasphemy.

The 'A-word' could not be uttered for fear of ridicule or even ostracism. All this changed in the 1950s when a 'respectable' Atlantis theory came to the fore and took root in the 1960s, following the excavations of Professor Spyridon Marinatos on the Aegean island of Santorini.

Marinatos had unearthed an ancient Bronze Age city near the village of Akrotiri, on the southern coast of Santorini, which had been destroyed by an earthquake and then buried in volcanic ash to a depth of tens of metres. It had long been known that the central volcano of the island of Santorini (ancient Thera) had blown its top towards the beginning of the Late Bronze Age (*c.* 1500 BC), but now the Greek professor of archaeology had located the principal city of the island destroyed in the cataclysm. It was also apparent from the recovered artefacts that the peoples of ancient Akrotiri were culturally closely related to the Minoans of Crete.

Marinatos and his academic colleagues were not slow to recognise a solution here to the Atlantis enigma. In a series of papers and books, they announced to the world that the eruption of Thera/ Santorini had been the historical model for Plato's sunken kingdom of Atlantis. Initially, many archaeologists and historians accepted this proposal. After all, Thera had partially sunk beneath the waves just like Atlantis; the Minoan peoples were bull-worshippers just like the Atlanteans; Minoan Crete had been oppressing the Greek mainland and in particular Athens (according to the Theseus and the Minotaur legend), which again paralleled Plato's story of the conflict between Athenians and Atlanteans; moreover, it appeared that the civilisation of Crete had been destroyed by a great tidal wave resulting from the eruption of Thera, leaving the Greeks free of the yoke of Minoan oppression.

No wonder the academic community embraced this Atlantis theory in preference to all others. It was based on archaeological evidence and neatly fitted many elements of the Platonic narrative. However, even before Professor Marinatos' tragic death while excavating at Akrotiri in 1974, doubts were beginning to surface. Subsequent archaeological analysis had revealed that Crete had not succumbed in the era when Thera exploded (Late Minoan IA). It rather continued to flourish for a further century before falling to what seems to have been a military invasion and occupation of the island by Mycenaean Greeks (Late Minoan IB).

But even more damaging to the Mediterranean Atlantis theory were the elements of Plato's narrative which simply did not fit with an Aegean model for the legend. Not least of these was the fact that Plato's Atlantis lay beyond the Pillars of Hercules, which, since time immemorial, had been identified with the Strait of Gibraltar. The location of Plato's Atlantis was unquestionably stated to be in the Atlantic Ocean and not the Mediterranean.

In his *Timaeus* Plato refers to the existence of an 'opposite continent' beyond Atlantis which clearly appears to be an allusion to the Americas. He also writes of 'other islands' located in front of this great continent. Another detail is also intriguing. Mention is made of a 'shallow sea' which stands between seafarers and the opposite continent. This place, treacherous because of its shoals of mud, was once above sea-level and formed part of the Atlantean landmass. As you will discover from the evidence presented in this book, Plato appears to have been referring to the shallows of the Sargasso Sea and, perhaps, the shoals surrounding the Bahaman islands. Plato was not the only early writer to refer to this mysterious region. Aristotle, Theopompus, Pseudo-Scylax, Strabo, Marcellus and Plutarch variously allude to an opposite continent, a sea of weeds and islands in the far west.

None of this remotely fits a Mediterranean location for Atlantis. The political and catastrophic history of the fall of Atlantis may seem superficially to support the Theran model – but the geography and chronology clearly do not. As a consequence, the academic solution manages to explain only part of the Atlantis enigma. Sadly, most scholars are content to live with this half-solution.

However, these matches and mismatches between the Atlantis tradition and the archaeological evidence from the Aegean need not lead us to reject entirely either the Mediterranean or Atlantic elements. A more reasoned approach to the problem would be to see Plato's tale as an amalgam of historical events, intentionally brought together to create a story which his Athenian audience could readily understand and relate to. We might then envisage this Platonic version as the colourful adaptation of an original tale purported to have been handed down from the author's ancestor, Solon, or perhaps from some other source which Plato came across during his own visit to Egypt. This core story was then heavily embellished in the *Timaeus* and the *Critias* with other traditions – including the memory of the destruction of Thera and the subsequent demise of Minoan Crete in a conflict with Mycenaean Athens and its mainland allies.

But if we peel away this late secondary layer from the original legend we are once again left with the kernel of the tale – an Atlantic island civilisation which existed in remote antiquity beyond the Pillars of Hercules. This original story clearly has no historical precedent in the Mediterranean environment and its exceptional elements – islands beyond the Western Ocean, a sea of mud and seaweed, a far continent – are unlikely to have been Platonic invention.

The Atlantis legend continued to be debated and argued over well beyond the pagan era and the burning of the Alexandrian Library by the early Christians. It remained a powerful idea even in the late Christian era. There can be little doubt that the search for Atlantis was a dominating factor in the age of discovery. In their search for the lost island of Antilia – as Andrew argues almost certainly a variant spelling of Atlantis – the Spanish and Portuguese pushed further and further westwards until Columbus made his famous landfall on the islands of the West Indies in 1492. The search was then on to find the fabled 'Seven Cities' of Antilia and the now infamous El Dorado.

Then came the Austrian Jesuit scholar Athanasius Kircher who, in the seventeenth century, first re-promoted in his writings the idea of an independent Atlantean landmass within the Atlantic Ocean.

It is generally accepted that the modern revival in Atlantology began with a book entitled *Atlantis: The Antediluvian World*, written by the former US Congressman, Ignatius Donnelly. This remarkable volume fired the imaginations of great swaths of the American and European public. *Atlantis* came out in 1882, towards the end of a century of great discovery. Over the previous 60 years, the Egyptian civilisation had gradually been revealed to the western world thanks to the decipherment of hieroglyphics in 1822. A year before the publication of *Atlantis*, the mummies of the great New Kingdom pharaohs had been recovered from the Royal Cache in western Thebes. A decade or so before, Heinrich Schliemann had begun his excavations of Priam's 'Windy Troy' (1870) and then, six years later, Agamemnon's 'Golden Mycenae' (1876). It appeared that Homer's fictitious age of heroes was turning into historical fact. In this atmosphere of nineteenth-century discovery and enlightenment, finding answers to the Atlantis legend remained a laudable and achievable aim. In my view the passing of a second century of archaeological endeavour has not significantly changed that position. The door to a potentially amazing discovery still remains open for those brave enough to cross the threshold.

But what should scholars and archaeologists be looking for? Unfortunately, the whole problem of identifying the cultural remains of Atlantis has been coloured by romantic fiction. The modern birth of this aspect of the Atlantean myth came with Jules Verne's classic science-fiction adventure *Twenty Thousand Leagues Under the Sea*, first published in 1869. There the submerged antediluvian city of Atlantis is modelled on the classical Greek or Roman world. The crumbling ruins of temples and palaces with fluted columns and sculptured architraves lie scattered across the seabed:

> There, indeed, under my eyes, ruined, destroyed, lay a town – its roofs open to the sky, its temples fallen, its arches dislocated, its columns lying on the ground, from which one could still recognise the massive

> character of Tuscan architecture. Further on, some remains of a gigantic aqueduct, here the high base of an Acropolis, with the floating outline of a Parthenon; there traces of a quay, as if an ancient port had formerly abutted on the borders of the ocean, and disappeared with its merchant vessels and its war-galleys. Further on again, long lines of sunken walls and broad deserted streets – a perfect Pompeii escaped beneath the waters. Such was the sight that Captain Nemo brought before my eyes!
>
> Where was I? Where was I? I must know, at any cost. I tried to speak, but Captain Nemo stopped me by a gesture, and, picking up a piece of chalk stone, advanced to a rock of black basalt, and traced the one word – Atlantis.

This image has been with us ever since, reinforced by Hollywood movies (*Atlantis: The Lost Continent*) and more recent popular fiction. This has led to some extraordinary archaeological 'proofs' of the Atlantis legend over the years. Divers searching the shallows of the Bahaman shelf have reported finding isolated stone blocks of non-indigenous materials and what appear to be the drums of columns. Precisely because of the classical model of Atlantis spawned by romantic fiction, these vestiges of ruined 'monuments' have been proclaimed as evidence for the existence of the lost civilisation. However, reasonable explanations for such unusual finds are there for those who want to look for them. The drum sections of stone pillars turned out, on subsequent examination, to be made of modern concrete. The admittedly more interesting 'foreign' blocks of granite and other hard stones unfortunately also have a mundane explanation. Sailing ships which once plied these waters carried stone ballast which was often 'quarried' from archaeological sites in the Old World. Before the ancient cities became protected, it was not uncommon for bits of classical ruins to be sequestered for such purposes. These would then be dumped in the shallows of the New World as the empty outward-bound vessels were loaded up with the exotic produce of the Americas. I suppose one could reasonably argue that this practice does not satisfactorily explain every instance of such finds. However, what is required to resolve the matter is the identification of a whole series of blocks, *in situ* and forming a recognisable structure or at least the foundations of such a structure. We are still awaiting an unambiguous archaeological discovery of this kind or confirmation of a number of vaguely reported finds in the recent past. It never ceases to amaze me how often we read of just such submerged buildings on the Bahaman shelf, but then, when it comes to checking the discovery, the location of the site has conveniently been lost beneath the waves once more.

In more recent years, as millennium fever took hold, the exploitation of the Atlantis legend reached its apogee. Millions of copies of books have been sold and devoured by 'ancient wisdom' aficionados – a huge readership crossing all social and cultural boundaries. This informal, unstructured, even anarchic movement has become a refuge for those seeking alternative answers to what is on offer from conventional religious teaching. In a sense ancient wisdom has become a world faith, the religious tenets of which are disseminated in the writings of its high-priestly authors and their internet gurus, spreading the new gospel through the World Wide Web.

The passion and fervour for Atlantean research remains an international phenomenon. We have seen American Atlantologists scouring the Bahaman shelf (Association for Research and Enlightenment, J. Manson Valentine, Marine Archaeology Research Society, David Zink, Alan Landsburg); searches for Atlantis in the eastern Atlantic seaboard and Mid Atlantic Ridge with Russian submarines plumbing the depths off Cornwall and the Azores (Viatscheslav Koudriavtsev, Ignatius Donnelly, Nikolai Zhirov, Christian O'Brien); and the grand master of ancient wisdom researchers, Graham Hancock, diving in just about every nook and cranny of our oceans looking for evidence of sunken civilisations. Yet in spite of all this effort nothing really tangible has, as yet, come to light – no submerged cities, no 12,000-year-old civilisations.

Similar searches have been running in parallel on dry land. In recent years we have heard of one eccentric British explorer searching the Peruvian/Bolivian plateau for evidence of an Atlantean city (John Blashford-Snell); other, better-qualified researchers traipsing across Anatolia in search of the lost city of Tantalis (Peter James & co.) based on not much more than a similarity of names, in spite of some interesting historical research; and Rand Flem-ath and Graham Hancock (once again) suggesting we take a look under the icecap of Antarctica. A German archaeologist (Eberhard Zangger) has also attempted to link another legendary tale to the Plato story, identifying Homer's Troy with the kingdom of Atlantis (unsuccessfully, in my opinion). And, finally, we are constantly being fed stories concerning international teams of pseudo-archaeologists wanting to dismantle the Giza plateau block by block or dig up fields and villages in its environs in search of that infamous Hall of Records (the Schor Foundation, Nigel Appleby's Hermes Foundation). Again, nothing has surfaced to confirm the Atlantis legend – no Atlantean remains to support the candidature of Peru or Anatolia, and certainly no Hall of Records at Giza or nearby. Indeed, as I noted earlier, from out of the same New Age archaeology stable we are now beginning to see books (of varying quality) which are seeking to debunk much of what has been written about Atlantis and the Hall of Records over the last decade (*The Stargate Conspiracy*, *Giza: The Truth*). It seems that the shiny new ideas on the Giza connection with Atlantis are beginning to look more than a little tarnished.

That said, *Gateway to Atlantis* adopts a much more refreshing approach to Atlantean research which gets us back to the pre-Cayce facts. Meticulously collating and analysing all the ancient source material currently available to researchers, Andrew Collins has come to the conclusion that the folk traditions of the lost kingdom are based on a real geographical entity once known as Atlantis (and its variants). However, the physical evidence is not so much lying submerged at the bottom of the sea but buried in the writings of historians, geographers and chroniclers, and in the myths and legends of ancient peoples. Brought together, these sources paint an extraordinary picture of a lost island culture – not quite as Plato described it but, nevertheless, an ancestral homeland beyond the Pillars of Heracles, between what we know as the Old World of the Mediterranean and the New World of the Americas. It was this Atlantic island and its people which formed the basis of the Atlantis saga and Plato's elaborate story of a golden age.

And my opinion, for what it is worth? Well, herein lies the dichotomy of the Atlantis phenomenon which reaches deep within us all. I have just expended considerable effort in arguing the case of evidence over emotional speculation. So the historian in me has to say that there is, as yet, no conclusive archaeological evidence for a lost Atlantean kingdom. But the human spirit in me equally expects that something is out there somewhere, waiting to be discovered. Andrew Collins has produced tantalising oral and written evidence from the last 2,500 years to support the existence of a lost island culture in the Caribbean, remembered in both Old World and Mesoamerican tradition. His book reinforces in me the very human belief in an Atlantis of distant memory.

I look forward to the adventure that awaits us all over the coming decades.

David Rohl, Kent

THE QUEST BEGINS

Thursday 2 September 1998

IT HAD TAKEN ME NEARLY 20 years of research to get this far. Having reached this mosquito-infested isle, following a nail-biting flight as the sun rose slowly above the eastern horizon, I found myself amid a crowd of well-meaning local people. Each one seemed intent on offering advice and services.

In pidgin Spanish my colleague and I were able to convey to them the purpose for our visit, which was to reach the Punta del Este caves located in the south-west corner of this subtropical island. We had hoped to persuade a taxi driver to take us the 40 or so kilometres to our destination, but this appeared to be out of the question. Not one was willing to drive us that far. It was clear that we would have to attempt to hire a vehicle in Nueva Gerona, the only town, which we reached quickly in a bashed-up old taxi that would have been illegal on the streets of Europe.

With some idea of the complexity of the road journey ahead, we decided to secure the services of not only a four-wheel drive vehicle with driver but also an archaeologist from the local museum. Johnny Rodriguez, a stocky, ponytailed man in his twenties, could speak almost no English but was familiar at least with the caves in question.

Where we were going, no tourist ever ventured. This military-controlled zone contained some remarkable archaeological sites, but access was denied to anyone not in possession of the correct papers. Unfortunately, our guidebooks had neglected to mention this fact, and so the whole success of the visit was now in the hands of Johnny and the driver, who insisted that they could get us past the armed guards at the checkpoint. They said there would be no problem, and they were right. After just a brief conversation with the two cigar-smoking soldiers, the barrier was raised and we were through. From here on in it was a single unmade track across hostile terrain notorious for its crocodiles and poisonous flora.

It was one of the bumpiest, most nerve-racking journeys I had ever experienced. Yet eventually, after several kilometres of hard driving, we quite literally reached the end of the road.

With the harsh late-morning sun now beating down on our exposed skin, and black and white vultures gliding ominously overhead, the party left the vehicle on the edge of the tangled swamp. In front of us was a group of abandoned concrete buildings, erected during the Cold War as a telecommunications centre. Despite their dilapidated state, one building still appeared to be home to a small contingent of men who may or may not have been soldiers, for they wore no uniforms. Why these individuals should have had to remain in this unbearable climate was not made clear. Yet by default they had become the guardians of Punta del Este's sacred caves, and without their consent we would be going nowhere. So we offered bottled water and cigarettes as Johnny and the driver, whom they seemed to know, laughed and joked with them.

I had been told that this was the worst spot in the entire country for insects, and so there was no way on earth that I was going to spend even one night in this godforsaken place. We needed to be back at the local airport by dusk to catch the plane out, and no other option would be considered.

Yet for so many months I had yearned to be here. I had even visited the cave in my dreams. I almost felt as if some unseen *genius loci* was calling me to its lair. However, my reasons for coming to this place were based on sound historical and archaeological fact, which had led me to conclude that the answer to one of the world's greatest mysteries might lie inside one of the caves.

Very little was known about the cave. Even though various Hispanic archaeologists had visited the site, very few articles had ever been written on the subject. Despite this lack of background information, I knew instinctively that it was important. The cave's walls and ceilings were covered with strange petroglyphs, which perhaps expressed the indigenous people's myths and legends concerning the emergence of humanity at the beginning of time. I needed to see them and understand their meaning.

We kept to the narrow path, which was infested by large sand crabs that did not seem pleased by our intrusion into their territory. The uneasy nature of the place made me question my motives for coming here.

Finally we entered a clearing, and in front of us lay the gaping mouth of a large open cave. A metal plaque on the wall announced that we had reached the goal of our quest – Punta del Este's Cueva # 1. Unexpectedly, my stomach started to churn. What if I was wrong and there was nothing here of any significance?

No supernatural guardian stood before us as we passed into the cave's unwelcoming interior, home only to bats and countless mosquitoes.

Instantly we were confronted by the sight of faded red and black petroglyphs, composed in the main of whole series of rings and other geometric forms. Overhead were two roughly circular skylights cut out of the soft rock by ancient hands, allowing sunlight to penetrate the cave interior. On the ground I could see broken pieces of conch shell discarded hundreds of years ago by Amerindian occupants.

In Spanish, Johnny explained that beneath the skylight there would originally have been a stone dais, around which tribal ceremonies would perhaps have taken place. In its place today was a crude concrete copy, which ably allowed us to visualise what the setting might have been like in prehistoric times. He also told us that the rear skylight, now obscured by a small mountain of earth, was thought by some archaeologists to have been used to mark the transit of the planet Venus. However, he shook his head when we asked him if any academic paper had been written on the subject.

Johnny also drew our attention to the central feature of the cave, a huge multifaceted petroglyph consisting of a series of concentric rings, some sets overlapping each other, giving the impression of falling raindrops making ever widening ripples on a surface of water. Piercing its target-like rings was the drawing of a long arrow-like dart.

While trying to translate Johnny's views on the symbolic meaning of the cave art, I carefully examined individual petroglyphs. Some seemed very familiar indeed. They were like the megalithic art found carved at certain Neolithic and early Bronze Age sites in Brittany and the British Isles, and curiously enough these examples were from a very similar time period. It was also difficult not to see them in terms of either the orbit of planets or the revolution of stars.

Once I became accustomed to the low light and persistent mosquitoes, I began to realise something important. Preserved on the walls and ceilings of this prehistoric Sistine Chapel was what appeared to be a symbolic language conveyed in abstract picture form. It seemed to tell of archaic events which had occurred in the western hemisphere before the dawn of history. More than this, I began to realise that here might be the key to understanding the final fate of lost Atlantis. Yet before sharing the excitement and exhilaration I experienced in the wake of my visit to Punta del Este on the Isle of Youth, we must return to the beginning – to ancient Athens, where the legend of Atlantis was born around 2,350 years ago.

PART ONE
DISCOVERY

CHAPTER I

THE OLD PRIEST SPEAKS

Sometime around the year 355 BC, the Athenian poet and philosopher Plato (429–347 BC) evoked the inspiration of the Muses before writing what is arguably one of classical literature's most enigmatic works. Already he had completed a book entitled the *Republic,* which set out his vision of Athens as an ideal state. This was based to some degree on the philosophical teachings of Pythagoras (born *c.* 570 BC) who was a major influence on Plato's life. His new work would be called the *Timaeus* and, like its predecessor, it would take the form of a drama, or dialogue, enacted by four historical figures in the year 421 BC, when Plato would have been just eight years old. The participants, the same as those who featured in the *Republic,* were Socrates, Plato's great mentor and friend, who died of poison by his own hand in *c.* 399 BC; Timaeus, an astronomer of Locri in Italy; Hermocrates, an exiled Syracusan general; and Critias, who was either Plato's great-grandfather or his maternal uncle (see Chapter Three).

This style of writing, common in Plato's day, was intended to establish, in an informative and readable manner, the principal themes of the book. In this new dialogue, which was meant as a sequel to the *Republic,* subjects to be discussed included the mechanics of the universe and the nature of the physical world. Yet instead of Socrates assuming the role of chairman, as he had done in the *Republic,* this honour would go to Critias.

It is almost at the beginning of the *Timaeus* that Plato introduces the world to the subject of Atlantis. Critias (styled 'the Younger') relates to Socrates and those present how, when only a child, his elderly grandfather, also named Critias (styled 'the Elder'), had told him a fascinating story. This he had gained from Dropides, his father, who in turn had learned it from a friend and relative named Solon. Like the participants in the dialogue,

Solon (*c.* 638–558 BC) is also a historical character – a celebrated Athenian legislator spoken of by Plato as one of Athens' seven great sages.

Hoary with Age

The *Timaeus* informs us that Solon obtained what he knew of the story while at Sais, 'the city [in Egypt] from which King Amasis came'. This Amasis, who is more correctly identified as Aahmes II, ruled Egypt from his seat at Sais from *c.* 570 BC onwards for a duration of 44 years.[1] Although Solon was alive at this time, the text does not specify that Solon was in Egypt during his reign. Indeed, Plato's pupil, the philosopher Aristotle (384–322 BC), tells us that Solon visited Egypt at the beginning of a ten-year sojourn overseas, following his time as the archon, or chief magistrate, of Athens. Since this is believed to have occurred in *c.* 594–593 BC, some 22 or 23 years before Amasis' reign, there is a possible discrepancy here. Yet we know that Solon did indeed visit Egypt around this time because the Greek historian Herodotus (484–408 BC) in his *History* informs us that: 'It was this king Amasis who established the law that every Egyptian should appear once a year before the governor of his canton, and show his means of living . . . Solon the Athenian borrowed this law from the Egyptians, and imposed it on his countrymen, who have observed it ever since.'[2]

It implies therefore that Solon must have visited Egypt towards the end of his life and thus after Amasis had become pharaoh in *c.* 570 BC (see also Chapter Two).

Critias tells us that on entering the temple dedicated to the worship of Minerva (the Greek name for Neith, the patron goddess of Sais), Solon engaged in conversation one of the priests, who was said to have been 'a very old man'.[3] He spoke about the destruction of the human race in former ages, a matter the Athenian statesman felt he knew something about from his own education in these subjects. Yet in response the priestly elder chastised Solon for knowing *so little* about the true history of mankind, saying: '. . . you Greeks are always children; in Greece there is no such thing as an old man . . . You are all young in your minds . . . which hold no store of old belief based on long tradition, no knowledge hoary with age.'[4]

After enlightening Solon in respect of the 'many and divers destructions of mankind, the greatest by fire and water',[5] the priest went on to explain the nature of those catastrophes that destroy everything memorable of the past. These traditions were, he said, preserved only in the registers belonging to the temple, for they 'are the oldest on record'.[6]

Solon is told that the history and genealogies of Athens, which he

recited, 'are little better than nursery tales'.[7] It is also explained 'your people [i.e. the Athenians of Solon's age] remember only deluge [of the Greek flood hero Deucalian], though there were y earlier; and moreover you do not know that the bravest and est race in the world once lived in your country'. It was rently from this race that the Athenians of Plato's day were ended.[8]

e elderly priest – identified by the Greek biographer Plutarch 0–120) as 'Senchis the Saite'[9] – then spoke of how before the test of all destructions by water', the citizens of Athens were most valiant in war', their exploits and government being the est under heaven'.[10]

on is informed that the 'great exploits' of the noble race of na are recorded in the temple's sacred registers, and that perhaps should reconvene to 'go through the whole story in detail er time at our leisure, with the records before us'.[11] Yet one great it that Solon does learn from his conversations with the old man w the Athenian nation 'once brought to an end' an almighty r that 'insolently advanced against all Europe and Asia, *starting he Atlantic ocean outside* [author's emphasis]'.[12]

edless to say, it is at this juncture in the dialogue that the of Sais reveals to Solon the story lying behind the destruction antis, the homeland of this almighty power. In most English ations of the *Timaeus* this all-important textual account takes out 50 lines. However, each one is loaded with compelling regarding this sunken kingdom. Plato goes on to recount r details of his Atlantean nation in the unfinished sequel to naeus entitled the *Critias*. We must, however, never forget that gh the *Timaeus* actually contains a wealth of astronomical ientific knowledge, more or less unparalleled in its day, the thing was written as a fictional narrative.

An Almighty Landmass

iest of Sais relates next how the great force that rose up to the mighty nation of Athens came from an 'island' situated t of the Pillars of Hercules.[13] This was the name given in l times to the pillar-like rocks that stood on either side of the f Gibraltar and marked the entrance to the Atlantic Ocean. l man justifies the placement of this 'island' in the Atlantic aling that 'in those days' the 'ocean could be crossed'.[14]

t might Plato have meant by 'crossed'? As we might imag- mplies that the Atlantic 'island' from which this aggressor d was not only accessible in past ages, but that it was also by ocean-going vessels able to *cross* the Atlantic Ocean.

here did Plato have in mind when he first considered the

idea of an Atlantic 'island' on which lived a warlike race that opposed the might of earliest Athens? Could it have been based on early maritime knowledge of the Madeiras? One of the Canary Islands, perhaps, or even the Azores? All these island groups are located on the eastern Atlantic seaboard and were unquestionably known to ancient mariners during the first millennium BC (see Chapter Five).

Yet Plato does not seem to be referring specifically to any of these islands, for the old priest informs Solon that the Atlantic 'island' was larger than 'Libya and Asia put together'.[15] This is a quite fantastic statement. In Plato's day, Libya was seen as the entire North African continent west of Egypt – a landmass comparable in size to Europe today. Asia, on the other hand, was considered to stretch between Egypt in the west, the Caucasus Mountains of southern Russia in the north, Arabia in the south and India in the east. The Asia of Plato's day might be compared in size with North America. This therefore suggested the former existence of an almighty landmass of gigantic proportions, too big even to fit in the North Atlantic Ocean!

Since an island continent of the extent implied by Plato in his *Timaeus* could not possibly have existed at any point in the earth's geological history, scholars understandably dismiss Plato's account of his colossal island as mere fiction. Most Atlantologists are very much aware of this problem and often attempt to shrink down the size of Plato's Atlantic island by proposing that by Asia the author in fact meant only Asia Minor, i.e. modern Turkey. Yet there is no reason to make this assumption based on Plato's existing text. He does not imply this in any way. Indeed, it would appear that in comparing the size of Atlantis with that of Libya and Asia when placed together, he was simply attempting to convey the immense size of Atlantis in the absence of any true geographical knowledge.

Other scholars have assumed that if Plato really was alluding to a landmass of the size suggested in the *Timaeus*, then he must have been referring to the American continent. The Americas *do* match the proportions of his Atlantic 'island'. Indeed, the idea that either North or South America could be Atlantis was first proposed by Spanish explorers and scholars, such as Francesco Lopez de Gomara, shortly after the discovery of the New World.[16]

If Atlantis did once exist, and it really was of the immense size proposed in the *Timaeus*, there is no better solution. So when referring to his Atlantic island, had Plato been alluding to the American mainland – an opinion that has received considerable attention again in recent years?[17]

In actuality, this solution has a significant drawback, for after relating the size of the Atlantic island, the old priest of Sais tells Solon that 'from it [i.e. Atlantis] the voyagers of those days could reach the other islands, *and from these islands the whole of the opposite continent* [author's emphasis]'.[18]

This last statement should be seen in the context of the age in which it was written. To put it bluntly, there *was* no 'opposite continent' in the classical age! According to the official history of the world, the American mainland was not 'discovered' until Christopher Columbus' third voyage to the New World in 1498. This is, of course, if we ignore the Viking settlements established in Newfoundland around the year AD 1000, or indeed the indigenous peoples that have inhabited the continent for the past 15,000 years.

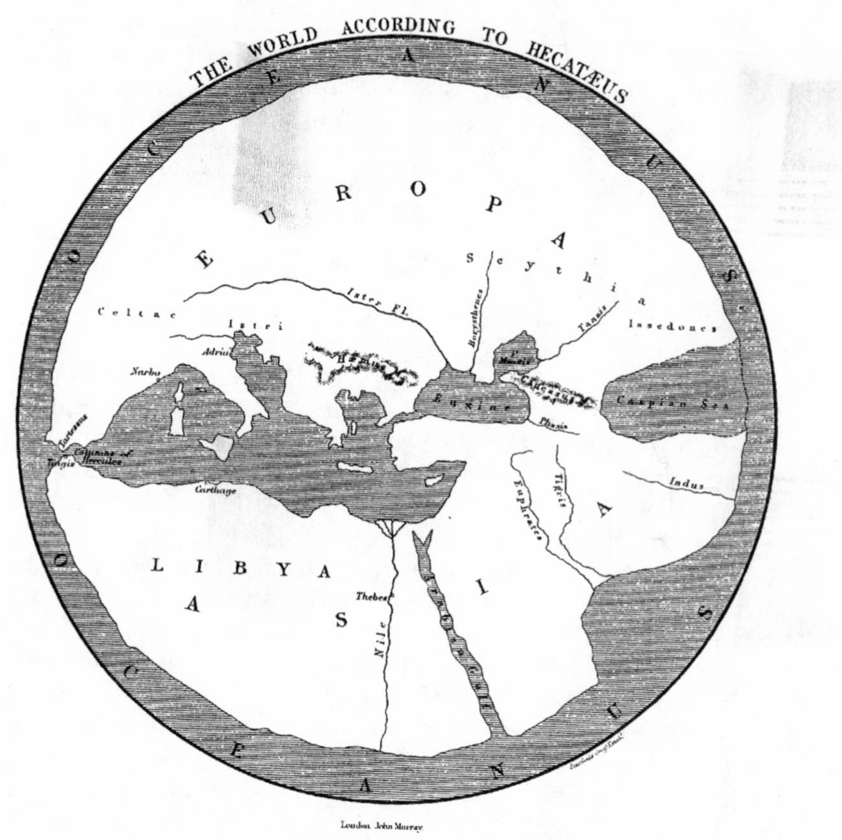

The ancient world according to Hecataeus of Miletus, *c.* 500 BC. Notice the absence of any 'opposite continent' beyond Oceanus, the Ocean River - a topic that became the subject of rumour and speculation in the age of Plato and Aristotle.

Yet Plato seems, quite clearly, to be referring to the Americas, suggesting therefore that he was somehow aware of this continent's existence on the other side of the Western Ocean. Oddly enough, there is evidence that by 300 BC other classical writers were also aware of a separate landmass beyond Oceanus, the ocean river once thought to encircle the ancient world. A work entitled *De Mundo*, written around 300 BC and falsely attributed to the philosopher Aristotle, talks about the known world as being a 'single island round which the sea that is called Atlantic flows'.[19] The text's author – who was very possibly a pupil of Aristotle[20] – goes on to speculate in the following, quite revealing manner:

> But it is probable that there are many other continents separated from ours by a sea that we must cross to reach them, some larger and others smaller than it, but all, save our own, invisible to us.[21]

Pseudo-Aristotle ends his musings by stating poetically that 'as our islands are in relation to our seas [i.e. the Mediterranean], so is the inhabited world in relation to the Atlantic, and so are many other continents in relation to the whole sea; for they are as it were immense islands surrounded by immense seas'.[22]

Land of the Meropes

Further evidence in support of the view that early classical writers were very much aware of the American continent comes from the writings of a younger contemporary of Plato named Theopompus of Chios – a Greek historian born around 378 BC. Only fragments of his writings survive today, and these are found in a work entitled *Various Anecdotes*, written by a second-century Roman naturalist and historian named Aelian.

Theopompus relates how during one fateful journey through Phrygia, a country of Asia Minor (modern Turkey), Silenus, a satyr and teacher of the god Bacchus, became drunk and fell asleep in the rose gardens belonging to the legendary King Midas. On waking up he found himself under the charge of the king's gardeners, who promptly marched him off to the royal palace. Having been placed under guard, Silenus was given his freedom only after suitably amusing his host with various anecdotes.

One of the tales told by Silenus is of particular interest, for he informs the king that: 'Surrounding the outside of this world' is a 'continent' that is 'infinitely big'.[23] Here you could find 'men twice the size of those who live here. Their lives are not the same length as ours, but in fact twice as long', and they possess 'various styles of life'.[24] There are also 'two very big cities'; one called Machimus, or 'Warlike', and the other Eusebes, or 'Pious'.[25] In addition to those who lived in these cities, Silenus tells Midas that on the continent is a race called Meropes, 'who live among them in numerous large cities'.[26] At the edge of their territories is 'a place named Point of No Return [Anostus], which looks like a chasm [gulf] and is filled neither by light nor darkness, but is overlaid by a haze of a murky red colour'.[27] It is said that 'two rivers run past this locality, one named Pleasure and the other Grief. Along the banks of both stand trees the size of a large plane.'[28]

According to Theopompus, the peoples of the distant continent once planned a voyage to 'these islands of ours'. No fewer than 10 million of them are said to have sailed the ocean (thus supposing that they had seafaring capabilities) and came upon Hyperborea, an unknown island usually identified as the British Isles (see Chapter Seven). On coming ashore, the visitors from another continent felt that the Hyperboreans were 'inferior beings of lowly fortunes, and for that reason dismissed the idea of travelling further'.[29]

Lucky Guesses

In addition to the accounts presented above, the Greek geographer Strabo (60 BC–AD 20) makes reference to an unknown continent that can only have been America. It comes during a discussion on the opinions of a Greek geometer and astronomer named Eratosthenes (276–196 BC), who claimed that 'if the immensity of the Atlantic Sea did not prevent, we could sail from Iberia [ancient Spain] to India along one and the same parallel'.[30] In response to this statement, Strabo voiced the opinion that: 'we call "inhabited" the world which we inhabit and know; though it may be that in this same temperate zone there are actually two inhabited worlds, or even more, and particularly in the proximity of the parallel through Athens that is drawn across the Atlantic Sea'.[31]

It would be easy to dismiss these apparent references to the American continent as either misconceptions on the part of authors like myself or lucky guesses on the part of well-informed classical figures such as Plato, Pseudo-Aristotle, Theopompus and Strabo. Yet if we can accept that knowledge of the existence of an 'opposite' continent was available to a select few during Plato's age, might this information have been deliberately withheld from the outside world? Perhaps there were stories and rumours circulating Greece, and/or Egypt, regarding the existence far beyond the Pillars of Hercules of another continent. Yet beyond maritime circles no one was aware of the full picture, leading to the sort of speculations voiced by Plato in his *Timaeus*.

It seems certain that Plato was somehow aware of America, the so-called 'opposite' continent, and so incorporated this idea into a dialogue on the nature of the universe. Where exactly this knowledge might have come from need not detain us here. What seems more important is that this theory is strengthened considerably if we now consider Plato's assertion in the *Timaeus* that from the Atlantic island, i.e. Atlantis, '. . . the voyagers of those days could reach the other islands, and from these islands the whole of the opposite continent'.[32]

Atlantic Voyagers

This all-important statement should be read again and again until it sinks in as to what Plato is implying. He is suggesting that Atlantis was located in front of, or before, 'other islands' that acted like stepping stones for maritime voyagers wishing to reach 'the opposite continent', which we will take to be the Americas.

Does this information make sense in geographical terms? From the time of Columbus' first landing on the island of San Salvador in 1492, the Bahaman and Caribbean archipelagos have been used in precisely this manner – as stepping stones for seagoing vessels journeying to the American mainland, either via the coast of Florida or the Gulf of Mexico. Moreover, the chain of islands known as the Lesser Antilles that connect Puerto Rico – the most easterly of the three main Caribbean islands – with the northern coast of South America might also be viewed in a similar manner.

Was it this island-hopping process to and from the American mainland that Plato is alluding to in his account of the Atlantic island? It seems as good a solution as any put forward by Atlantologists and scholars alike. Yet how might a Greek philosopher and poet have come across such precious nautical information, which was supposedly unavailable during his own day? Plato himself seems to supply us with the answer, for his account suggests that this knowledge was derived from Atlantic 'voyagers', who in ancient times 'crossed' the Atlantic Ocean and visited these islands en route to the American continent.

In itself this is a startling revelation – one that has often been overlooked by scholars simply because it is considered inconceivable that mariners might have reached the Americas prior to the age of Columbus. So if Plato really had become aware of journeys made by transatlantic 'voyagers' before his own time, how might this information affect our understanding of Atlantis? Did it really exist as an Atlantic island, and if so where exactly might it have been located?

Although the *Timaeus* does not say exactly where Atlantis was to be found, there seems little doubt that the island lay in the outer ocean. Repeatedly we find references in classical literature to similar island paradises under a variety of names, most important the islands of the Hesperides (see Chapter Six). Almost without exception they are said to have lain either in or beyond the *Western* Ocean, the domain of the hero-god Atlas, and so this is where we must start our own search for Plato's Atlantic island.

Turning back to the account given in the *Timaeus*, the old priest tells Solon:

> Now on this Atlantic island there had grown up an extraordinary power under kings who ruled not only the whole island but many of the other islands and parts of the [opposite] continent . . .[33]

There seems to be no vagueness in this statement. Atlantis, we are told, was ruled by a monarchy that Plato insisted held dominion over 'other islands', seemingly those referred to in connection with 'the opposite continent'. These kings would also seem to have held sway over 'parts of the [opposite] continent' itself. What sort of kingdom might we be dealing with here? Was the Atlantean nation really an island-based culture with seafaring capabilities that enabled it to control not only vast areas of the Western Ocean but also parts of the American continent?

More difficult to understand is Plato's next assertion that these same Atlantean kings held sway 'within the straits', in other words *inside* the Mediterranean basin.[34] He informs us that they were 'lords of Libya [i.e. North Africa] so far as to Egypt, and of Europe to the borders of Tyrrhenia [modern Tuscany in Italy]', and 'attempted at one swoop to enslave your country and ours and all the region within the strait'.[35] There are no easy explanations for this statement, and it might seem easier to dismiss Plato's words as mere fiction. An Atlantic culture of the description given to us by Plato controlling towns and ports in both Europe and Libya seems nonsensical.

Sacred Registers

This brings us perhaps to what is arguably the most controversial aspect of Plato's Atlantis narrative: the dates given for these supposed events in the Atlantic Ocean. A little earlier in the text, the old priest of Sais has informed Solon that the city of Athens was founded a full 1,000 years before the 'institution' of Egypt's sacred registers.[36] Since these are said to contain a record of events spanning a period of 8,000 years, and Solon visited Egypt in *c.* 570 BC, it implies that Athens was founded in *c.* 9570 BC. Almost in unison, classical historians will inform us that in 9570 BC civilisation had not yet begun, and that Athens was not even a twinkle in the eye of its founding goddess Athena.

We know that humanity's transformation from nomadic hunter-gatherer to settled Neolithic farmer did not occur in the Near East until sometime after the cessation of the last Ice Age, *c.* 9000–8500 BC. In the opinion of archaeologists, there was nothing whatsoever happening around Athens in 9570 BC. Indeed, it is only with the arrival of the first settlers from Asia Minor and the Levant in *c.* 1500 BC that a city was established there. So it seems that Plato got it wrong.

Yet if we examine his words a little more closely we can determine how he arrived at these dates, and in so doing understand their meaning in the context of what he has to say in the *Timaeus*.

The Myth of Dates

The old priest of Sais informs Solon that 'the age of our institutions is given in the sacred records as eight thousand years'.[37] This might seem a fantastic statement which, if we presume that he visited Sais in *c.* 570 BC, implied that Egyptian civilisation began in *c.* 8570 BC. Quite naturally, historians suggest that Plato must have been mistaken in this respect or that the time-frame he provides in the *Timaeus* is meaningless. Yet in Plato's final work, *The Laws*, one of the characters known only as 'the Athenian' attempts to explain the establishment of Egypt's legislation. During this speech he refers to the arts of the Egyptians in the following manner: 'If you examine their art on the spot, you will find that ten thousand years ago (and I'm not speaking loosely: I mean literally ten thousand), paintings and reliefs were produced that are no better and no worse than those of today.'[38]

Even though there is a 2,000-year difference between the figure given in the *Timaeus* and the one cited in *The Laws*, it is apparent that Plato fully believed that these dates related to real time. Such enormous time-spans are considered mythical by Egyptologists. However, they appear with frequency in king-lists such as the fragmentary Royal Canon of Turin, which dates to the Nineteenth Dynasty of Egyptian history, *c.* 1308–1194 BC. This tells us how a semi-divine race known as the Shemsu-hor, the Followers of Horus, reigned for a period of 13,420 years (although the end character is missing, meaning that as many as 1,350 years can be added to this figure) before the rise of the first pharaoh in *c.* 3100 BC.[39] The Royal Canon also gives a total of either 33,200 or 23,200 years for the various dynasties of divine or semi-divine beings.[40] Other similar canons contain equally extravagant time periods, leaving us to conclude that both the 8,000 years quoted in the *Timaeus* and the 10,000 years given in *The Laws* derive most probably from now lost Egyptian king-lists.[41]

It becomes clear therefore that by suggesting the Athenians are 1,000 years older than their Egyptian rivals, Plato is merely attempting to define the even greater antiquity of his own race. Certainly, there is no historical precedent to suggest that this was in fact the case. Indeed, there is overwhelming evidence to show that some of the greatest wisdom and philosophy taught at the Athenian schools was derived from the mystery schools of Egypt. The Greek philosopher Pythagoras, for instance, was educated in Egypt, where, according to the fourth-century Latin grammarian Ammianus Marcellinus (*fl.* AD 353–390), the priests 'taught him to worship the gods in secret'.[42] Solon is also said to have visited Egypt so that he might become acquainted with the wisdom of the ancients (as did Plato himself – see Chapter Two).[43] Perhaps Plato saw the fact that Egypt had a much more ancient heritage as a national embarrassment, and so in the *Timaeus* he attempted to redress the balance by bolstering up the antiquity of the Athenians, who were presumably his intended readership.

Having established a date of around 9570 BC for the foundation of Athens, Plato has the old priest of Sais explain to Solon that it was *following* this time that the Atlantic nation rose up against his country. For he states: 'Many great exploits of your city [i.e. Athens] are here recorded for the admiration of all; but one surpasses the rest in greatness and valour.'[44] Indeed, since the kings of Atlantis are said to have risen up against Egypt also, the clear inference is that the war with Athens occurred sometime *after* the Egyptian sacred records were begun in *c.* 8570 BC. As we shall see, this is a statement blatantly contradicted in the text of the *Critias*.

With this in mind, we are next informed that thereafter the Atlantic kingdom attempted 'at one swoop to enslave your country [i.e. Athens] and ours [Egypt] and all the regions within the strait [of Gibraltar]'.[45] According to the *Timaeus*, the Athenians were then 'forced by the defection of the rest' of the Mediterranean nations to move against the aggressor.[46] Furthermore, since the Athenian fleet was deemed to be the 'foremost of all in courage and in the arts of war', it vanquished 'the invaders' and freed 'all the rest of us', including Egypt, from the threat of bondage and slavery.[47]

Crucially, the text of the *Timaeus* then reveals that:

> *Afterwards* ['*At a later time*' in the Loeb edition] there was a time of inordinate earthquakes and floods; there came one terrible day and night, in which all your men of war were swallowed bodily by the earth, and the island of Atlantis also sank beneath the sea and vanished [author's emphasis].[48]

This is a loaded statement, and one that appears incredible. It is alleged that both the Atlantic island and the Athenian 'men of war' were lost during an almighty cataclysm involving 'earthquakes and floods' that can only have occurred post 8570 BC. So what are we to make of this stupendous event, clearly unrecorded in conventional history? Did it really happen, and what can it tell us about the true location of lost Atlantis?

CHAPTER II

EGYPTIAN HERITAGE

SOME 400 YEARS AFTER PLATO wrote his Atlantis dialogues, the Greek biographer and moralist Plutarch referred to Solon's visit to Egypt, stating that his account of the Atlantic island had been gained during philosophical conversations with 'Psenophis the Heliopolitan and Senchis the Saite, the most learned of the Egyptian priests'.[1] He also spoke of Solon's assumed role in bringing the story to light, for according to him:

> Solon moreover attempted, in verse, a large description or rather fabulous account of the Atlantic Island, which he had learned from the wise men of Sais, and which particularly concerned the Athenians; but by reason of his age, not want of leisure (as Plato would have it), he was apprehensive the work would be too much for him, and therefore did not go through with it . . . Plato, ambitious to cultivate and adorn the subject of the Atlantic Island, as a delightful spot in some fair field unoccupied, to which also he had some claim by his being related to Solon, laid out magnificent courts and enclosures, and erected a grand entrance to it, such as no other story, fable, or poem ever had.[2]

Despite this testimony, no other classical source before the age of Plutarch seems to recognise that Solon was responsible for the core material behind Plato's Atlantis account. All we can say for certain is that, following his time as Athens' archon, or chief magistrate, Solon left Greece and spent part of his ten-year absence in Egypt.[3]

Plutarch goes on to say that, because the elderly statesman was unable to do the story justice during the remaining years of his life (he died *c.* 558 BC, a minimum of 12 years after his visit to Sais), it was taken up by Plato, who transformed it into the fabulous story presented in his dialogues.

Once again there is no independent evidence to confirm this was ever the case.

If it were not for Plutarch's own account of Solon's meeting with the Saite priest, it could be argued that Plato merely used the historical memory of Solon's visit to Egypt in order to lend weight and credibility to his narrative. It is even possible that Plato borrowed his Saite setting for Solon's meeting with the old priest from the works of the fifth-century BC Greek historian Herodotus, who provides the reader with a vivid description of its temple in a section of his *History* on the reign of King Amasis.[4] More damning still is that Solon's borrowing of the sacred laws of Amasis for use in his own country is noted by Herodotus in the very next paragraph after his account of the Saite temple.[5] It is certain that Plato would have been very much aware of Herodotus' work when he came to write the *Timaeus*. In this knowledge, Plato's account of Solon's meeting with the old priest of Sais is, at best, suspect. Only the correlations between the chronology of the Egyptian king-lists and the dates supposedly preserved in the sacred registers of the Saite temple prevent us from completely abandoning any connection whatsoever between Plato's story of Atlantis and Solon's celebrated visit to Egypt.

Unfortunately, there is an equally plausible source for Plato's knowledge of Egypt's mythical chronology. It is known that he himself spent some time in Egypt visiting its mystery schools and ancient temples. Plutarch, in another of his works entitled *Isis and Osiris*, tells us that like the 'wisest of the Greeks', who apparently included Solon, Thales, Eudoxus and Pythagoras, Plato 'came to Egypt and consorted with the priests'.[6] Here, too, he is said to have 'acquired his glorious wisdom', according to Ammianus Marcellinus, the fourth-century Latin grammarian and author of a history of the Roman world.[7]

It is conceivable therefore that Plato learned of the Atlantis story – or at least found confirmation of it – during his own stay in Egypt. If this was true, he might then have used it as the basis for his famous dialogues. Yet how much of his narrative might be seen as fact, and how much of it is merely fiction? What have scholars said about the texts of the *Timaeus*, and where have others sought a historical Atlantis?

The Aegean Answer

One solution is to assume that Plato was alluding to historical events that took place in an entirely different time-frame from the one suggested by the fabulous dates presented in his Atlantis account. For instance, it has been suggested that he was referring not to solar years but to lunar months of 28 days.[8] If this was indeed the case, it would mean that instead of 9,000 years having elapsed since the foundation of Athens, the true time period was just 690 years, providing a date in the region of *c.* 1260 BC. Historically speaking, this takes us into a more reasonable time-frame, since it was during this age that the eastern Mediterranean began to suffer repeated attacks by a mixed-race, seaborne confederate remembered as the 'Peoples of the Sea'.[9] Their ships terrorised Egyptian, Palestinian and Syrian ports before being repelled by the forces of the pharaoh Merenptah in *c.* 1219 BC, and finally defeated by the army of Rameses III in *c.* 1170 BC.

Who exactly this confederacy might have been is still a matter of conjecture. There is, however, mounting evidence to suggest that their crews were led by displaced peoples originating from the coastal and island cultures which inhabited the Aegean-Anatolian world in the aftermath of the volcanic eruption that completely devastated the island of Thera (modern Santorini) in the Aegean in either *c.* 1628 BC, *c.* 1450 BC, or possibly even *c.* 1380 BC, depending on the source consulted.[10]

This catastrophic event undoubtedly influenced the entire history of the Aegean world. So great was the final explosion that an estimated 114 cubic kilometres of debris was ejected outwards to leave a water-filled crater with an area of 51 square kilometres.[11] Indeed, it has been suggested that the magnitude of the blast was the equivalent of 6,000 nuclear warheads.[12]

By far the most important empire to suffer from this almighty cataclysm was that of the Minoans, whose cities and ports were to be found on Thera and, more important, on the island of Crete, which lay 96 kilometres south of the blast's epicentre. It is suggested that the huge eruption created enormous tidal waves, which advanced southwards and obliterated not only the Minoan fleet, stationed on the northern coast of Crete, but also the towns and cities that lay in the same vicinity.[13] These enormous waves, which are estimated to have been as much as 100 metres high, reached the eastern Mediterranean coast and struck coastal towns over 1,120 kilometres from Thera.

How the total annihilation of Thera might have affected the coasts of Greece, Asia Minor and Egypt is still a subject of fierce debate. Whatever the answer, such a catastrophic event would unquestionably have been remembered during the classical age. As a consequence, there seems little doubt that Plato's Atlantis account *could* have been influenced not only by the destruction of Thera but also by the subsequent tidal waves that resulted in the destruction of the Minoan fleet and the devastation of Crete's coastal towns and cities. Moreover, in 426 BC a severe earthquake had shaken Greece, causing an almighty tidal wave which devastated the town of Orobia on the Aegean island of Euboea (modern Negropont) and wrecked ships in the neighbourhood of the island of Atalante, near Opuntian Locris, where it also carried away an Athenian fort. Such a natural catastrophe must equally have affected Plato's account of Atlantis' destruction by earthquakes and floods.

Plato's writings are also likely to have been tainted by a memory of the Minoans' brutal oppression of the Greek mainland during this same period, conjuring the idea of the Atlantean aggressor versus the Athenian nation. In addition to this, the memory of Rameses III's defeat of the Peoples of the Sea might additionally have influenced the contents of the story. This great battle is commemorated on the exterior walls of the temple at Medinet Habu in southern Egypt, and it has been suggested that these reliefs carved in stone could have been viewed by Solon during his visit to the country in *c.* 570 BC.[14]

Conclusions such as these have led some scholars to champion what has become arguably the most academically accepted solution to the Atlantis mystery, and this is the view that either Crete or Thera *was* the Atlantic isle spoken of by Plato. Since the theory was first proposed in an anonymous article that appeared in *The Times* newspaper on 19 February 1909, and was subsequently found to have been written by a young Belfast scholar named K. T. Frost, several popular books have been published expounding this theory. All of them have attempted to compare our knowledge of the Minoan civilisation of either Crete or Akrotiri, a Minoan town excavated on Santorini, with the description of Atlantis as given in the *Critias.*[15] Yet all attempts to confirm this view have led its supporters, many of them academic writers, to adopt and accept a number of fundamental misconceptions about Plato's Atlantis narrative.

For example, it was suggested, initially by Greek geologist A. G. Galanopoulos, that the dates and dimensions given in the *Timaeus* and *Critias* are wrong, due to a mistranslation of the assumed Egyptian texts shown to Solon by the old priest of Sais.[16] In the process, the Greek statesman somehow managed to confuse the hieroglyph that denotes the number 100 with the character that represents a figurative value of 1,000.[17] If this were so, it would change the date implied for the foundation of Athens from 9,000 years before Solon's visit to just 900 years, providing a revised date of *c.* 1470 BC, close to the traditional date of *c.* 1450 BC for the Thera eruption. At first this might appear to offer a neat and logical solution to both the problem posed by the very early time-frame suggested for the destruction of Atlantis and the unimaginable dimensions of Atlantis' city and plain as outlined in the *Critias* (see Chapters Three and Four).

The Aegean answer to Atlantis is, however, seriously flawed, for according to those Egyptologists who have taken time to examine the problem, no such confusion can have occurred. The hieroglyphs used to denote the numerical values of 100 and 1,000 are visually quite different. Solon – or anyone else for that matter – could not have made such a mistake. This is made clear in an important essay on the links between Egypt and Atlantis by J. Gwyn Griffiths, who points out:

> If we assume a hieroglyphic form of the prototype, there seems to be very scanty ground for the proposal, since the normal forms for 100 and 1,000 are so sharply distinguished.[18]

So the idea that Solon, or indeed Plato, could have misread what was shown to him in Egypt is unfounded. Since it is also totally untenable that lunar cycles were meant instead of solar years, there seems to be no viable reason for altering the time-frame connected with the events featured in Plato's Atlantis account.

Movable Pillars

Another gross misconception assumed by the Cretan-Atlantis theorists is that Plato's sunken kingdom lay *within* the Pillars of Hercules, something that neither the *Timaeus* nor the *Critias* implies in any way. Surely Plato would not have referred to Atlantis as an Atlantic island if he had meant it to be located anywhere else but *in* the Atlantic Ocean. Clear statements such as the Atlantic fleet 'advanced against all Europe and Asia, starting from the Atlantic ocean outside'[19] should be enough to convince anyone that Plato's Atlantis was not located in the Mediterranean Sea. As writer James Guy Bramwell, the author of *Lost Atlantis,* so eloquently put it in 1937: 'Either Atlantis is an island in the Atlantic ocean or it is not "Atlantis" at all.'[20]

In addition to changing the dates and location of Atlantis, those scholars who have supported a Mediterranean solution to the problem attempt to prove that the Pillars of Hercules referred to by Plato were nowhere near the Strait of Gibraltar. For instance, A. G. Galanopoulos and Edward Bacon, in their 1969 book *Atlantis: The Truth Behind the Legend,* proposed that since some of Hercules' famous 12 labours were set in the Peloponnese region of southern Greece, his so-called 'Pillars' might have been originally the eastern and western promontories marking the waterway between the Gulf of Lakonia and the Mediterranean Sea.[21]

All I can say is that Galanopoulos and Bacon should perhaps have considered Hercules' tenth and eleventh labours which were performed, respectively, at Gades in south-west Spain and Mount Atlas on the Atlantic coast of Africa. Indeed, the last mentioned labour involved him having to journey to the Atlantic isles known as the Hesperides in order that he might steal Hera's golden apples (see Chapter Six). Not only are all of these locations situated *beyond* the Strait of Gibraltar, but it was because of Hercules' association with the Atlantic realm that the waterway between the Mediterranean Sea and the outer ocean became known as the Pillars of Hercules.

An even wilder idea proposed in 1992 by professional geoarchaeologist Eberhard Zangger is that there were originally two locations known as the 'Pillars of Hercules'. One pair he placed at the entrance to the Atlantic and the other at the entrance to the narrow straits of the Dardanelles which connect the Mediterranean Sea with the Black Sea. He came to this conclusion after reading a single, rather debatable, line in Servius' commentary on Virgil's *Aeneid*, which reads: 'columnas Herculis legimus et in Ponto et in Hispania' ('We pass through the Pillars of Hercules in the Black Sea as well as in Spain').[22] Having established this fact, Zangger went on to decide that Plato had been alluding to the Pillars of Hercules at the entrance to the Black Sea, and *not* those standing on either side of the Strait of Gibraltar. This allowed Zangger to identify Plato's Atlantis as the legendary city of Troy in south-west Turkey.[23]

All these ideas I find quite fantastic, especially as every classical historian and geographer who mentions the Pillars of Hercules places them first and foremost at the entrance to the Atlantic Ocean. Even if the Pillars of Hercules also stood at the entrance to the Black Sea, why should Plato have wanted to allude to these instead of those that marked the exit to the ancient world, beyond which he placed his Atlantic island?

I hope that by now most readers will agree that connecting Atlantis with Crete, Thera or indeed Troy is very misleading indeed. This same sentiment is now shared by many respectable scholars of ancient history. For instance, in 1978 a blistering attack was launched against the persisting Cretan-Atlantis theory by American historian J. Rufus Fears of Oklahoma University in a prestigious work entitled *Atlantis: Fact or Fiction*, edited by Edwin S. Ramage and published by Indiana University Press. In his view:

> It is disturbing that, in the last quarter of the twentieth century, serious scholarship is still called upon to debate the possibility that Plato's Atlantis is a remembrance of Minoan Crete. Even at a superficial glance, the equation of Atlantis with Minoan Crete is revealed as a tissuework of fabrications, a flimsy house of cards, constructed by piling dubious hypothesis upon pure speculation, cementing them together with false and misleading statements and with specious reasoning.[24]

I could not agree more. Even though I accept that there is every likelihood that much later historical events and places may well have *influenced* the development of Plato's Atlantis account, there is no reason whatsoever to suppose that his sunken kingdom lay anywhere else but beyond the Pillars of Hercules in the Atlantic Ocean.

The Shallow Sea

As we have determined already, the *Timaeus* seems to preserve a primitive knowledge of ancient voyages both to and from the Americas, Plato's 'opposite continent'. It also seems to allude to the Bahamas, the Caribbean and the Lesser Antilles, the 'other islands' said to have lain beyond Atlantis. With these thoughts in mind, we find that the apparent location of the sunken Atlantic isle is given in the sentence which follows the reference to the island's destruction by 'earthquakes and floods':

> Hence to this day that outer ocean [i.e. the Atlantic] cannot be crossed or explored, the way being blocked by mud, just below the surface, left by the settling down of the island.[25]

This is a truly remarkable statement. To begin with, it contains elements of the type of misinformation that was spread by the Carthaginians of North Africa, in an attempt both to throw a smokescreen over their own voyages beyond the Pillars of Hercules and to prevent any unauthorised exploration of the outer ocean by rival nations. These stories suggested that the seas beyond the Pillars of Hercules were impassable due to otherworldly hazards such as clouds of darkness, dangerous shoals, deathly mists and great monsters.[26]

It is, however, Plato's reference to the Atlantic Ocean being 'blocked by mud, just below the surface' that is most revealing, for this same idea is repeated in the works of other writers from the same era. For example, an author named Scylax, who was in fact an imposter of Scylax of Caryanda, a famous Greek geographer of the fourth century BC, states in his work the *Periplus* that at a distance of 12 days' sail 'from the Pillars of Hercules' was the Phoenician island settlement of Cerne.[27] Yet he also asserted that: 'The parts beyond the isle of Cerne are no longer navigable because of shoals, mud, and sea-weed. This sea-weed has the width of a palm, and is sharp towards the points, so as to prick.'[28]

More significantly, Aristotle records in his work the *Meteorologica*, that 'the water outside the Pillars of Hercules is shallow because of the mud but calm'.[29]

What exactly might these three notable authors of the classical age have been alluding to by these enigmatic statements? What was this region of the outer ocean renowned for its shoals, its mud, its seaweed and its 'calm'? Any knowledge they might have had regarding what lay beyond the Pillars of Hercules would have been second, third or even fourth hand, and very likely it was derived from Carthaginian sources. This conclusion can be determined from a secondary account of the Atlantic voyages of a Carthaginian navigator of the fifth century BC named Himilco, preserved in the *Ora Maritima* of Rufus Festus Avienus, a Latin historian of the fourth century AD. According to him:

> . . . the inhabitants of Carthage and the people living between the columns of Hercules used to approach these waters [i.e. those beyond the Pillars of Hercules] which the Carthaginian Himilco asserts can barely be crossed in four months, as he reported himself to have proved the matter sailing, so widely no breezes propel the ship, so sluggish the liquid of the lazy sea stagnates.
>
> And he adds this: that among the shoals much seaweed sticks up and often in the manner of a thicket holds back the ship. He says moreover that here the back of the sea does not go down deep, and the [ocean] floor is barely covered over by a small amount of water. The wild creatures of the sea are always appearing here and there, and among the slow ships languidly creeping along, sea monsters swim.[30]

Historians can only guess at the location of this shallow sea of weed, which, according to Himilco, could 'barely be crossed in four months'. Where exactly this accomplished Carthaginian navigator might have reached on his own celebrated voyage, or voyages, remains a mystery. It is known that on one occasion he left his home port of Carthage on the Mediterranean coast of North Africa and then sailed out through the Pillars of Hercules. After that it is anybody's guess. What does seem clear, however, is that Avienus' report of Himilco's maritime experiences preserves a somewhat better picture of the shallow sea alluded to by Plato, Aristotle and Pseudo-Scylax a century later. So can we determine the location of this impassable sea of mud, shoals, seaweed and calm, where Plato believed that Atlantis had sunk beneath the waves?

There seems to be little question that what all these writers allude to, knowingly or otherwise, is the Sargasso Sea. This Atlantic region, marked by a vast expanse of free-flowing seaweed roughly the size of Europe, stretches between the Azores and the Bahamas. The exact origin of this seaweed – called gulfweed, sea holly or, more correctly, *Sargassum bacciferum* – is still a matter of conjecture. It was once believed to break away from the coast of North America and gather in the calm and silent waters that fall between the various transatlantic currents and trade winds which encircle the North Atlantic Ocean. Yet today marine biologists accept that the seaweed is indigenous to the region, and reproduces without any connection with the mainland coastline.[31]

It was Christopher Columbus who first officially discovered the Sargasso Sea on his initial voyage to the New World in 1492. An account of the journey recorded by his son Ferdinand states that on Sunday 16 September – 27 days prior to his celebrated landing in the Bahamas – the surface of the water became 'covered with a great mass of yellowish green weed, which seemed to have been torn away from some island or reef'.[32] The next day they continued to encounter these 'mats of weed' which were said to resemble 'star grass, save that it had long stalks and shoots, and was loaded with fruit like the mastic tree'.[33] The existence of this peculiar sea caused Columbus to believe that his vessels were nearing land, for he saw within the seaweed a live crab and noted also that the water was 'less salty by half than before'.[34]

Scholars find it impossible to accept that Himilco could have been alluding to the Sargasso Sea.[35] However, the description he gives of the languid sea that 'can barely be crossed in four months' is almost perfect – a mass of seaweed, deathly calm and the rich aquatic life viewed as 'wild creatures of the sea' or even 'sea monsters'. Columbus himself apparently encountered large fish here that included huge tuna which 'swam about the ships, coming so near that the Nina's people [the crew of one of the boats] killed one with a harpoon'.[36]

There are, of course, no shoals or mud banks lurking beneath the surface of the Sargasso Sea. However, the fact that this was so readily accepted by ancient mariners is extremely important to our understanding of Plato's statement regarding the former site of Atlantis. If he was not simply basing his story on the misconceived ancient association between the Sargasso Sea and shallow waters, it is intriguing that his words also describe very well the shoals and shallows which *do* exist in the vicinity of the Bahamas. These stretch for several hundred kilometres between Great Bahama in the north and Cay de Sal in the south. Indeed, the Bahamas are not only notorious for their shallow banks, but they also take their name from the Spanish 'baja mar', meaning 'shallow sea'.[37] Is it possible that in addition to the Sargasso Sea, some knowledge of the Bahamas' shoals and shallows was being alluded to by early classical writers such as Plato, Aristotle, Pseudo-Scylax and even Himilco?

Suggesting that Plato might have been referring to actual geographical locations on the western Atlantic seaboard might seem difficult to comprehend, especially as the Cretan-Atlantis theory is the most widely accepted solution to the mystery. Yet these conclusions are on offer to anyone making an in-depth study of Plato's works, and I would certainly not be the first to draw such a conclusion. As early as 1875, L. M. Hosea, in a remarkable article entitled 'Atlantis: A Statement of the "Atlantic" Theory Respecting

Aboriginal Civilisation', which appeared in the scholarly *Cincinnati Quarterly Journal of Science*, made the following statement:

> Without presuming to determine whether in fact the Sargasso sea or shoal is a subsided island or an eddy of the ocean, it is sufficient for the purposes at hand to observe that in the spot designated by the Atlantic tradition [of Plato], there exists and has existed for an indefinite period an impediment to navigation which may by fair intendment relieve the ancient Egyptians and Greeks of the geographical ignorance imputed to them.[38]

We shall meet again with Hosea's writings on Atlantis. Yet in accepting the supposition that Plato was alluding in the *Timaeus* to the Sargasso Sea, and perhaps even the Bahamas, we are left with one inescapable conclusion. Whether by accident or design, Plato located his sunken 'island' somewhere on the western Atlantic seaboard.

So is it possible that Atlantis was once situated in the region of the ocean now occupied by the Sargasso Sea? Unfortunately not, for hydrographic surveys have revealed that the watery depths beneath this region of the North Atlantic Ocean vary between 1,500 metres and 7,000 metres.[39] No lost island continent awaits discovery at this location; it was simply never there in the first place.

It seems more likely that in singling out the Sargasso Sea as the position of the Atlantic island, Plato was merely drawing his readership to the *approximate* area once occupied by the sunken landmass. His reference in the *Timaeus* to 'other islands' placed beyond the Atlantic island, which enabled ancient 'voyagers' to reach the 'opposite continent', is perhaps the greatest clue. As I have already suggested, Plato seems to be describing the manner in which the island chains of the Bahamas, the Caribbean and the Lesser Antilles were used like stepping stones by ancient sailing vessels attempting to reach the American continent. If this were truly the case, we must look for Atlantis in this part of the Atlantic Ocean, for it is clear that Plato believed that it lay within easy reach of these 'other islands'.

Curiously enough, in 1130 a writer named Honorius of Autun wrote that the 'curdled sea' – seemingly another reference to the Sargasso Sea – 'adjoins the Hesperides and covers the site of lost Atlantis, which lay west from Gibraltar'.[40] The Hesperides are legendary isles thought to have been located in the Western Ocean and, as we shall see, are very much linked with the West Indies, the name given to the Bahamas and Caribbean during the age of discovery.

Whether or not Honorius simply read Plato and realised that the 'curdled sea' was one and the same as the impassable sea 'blocked

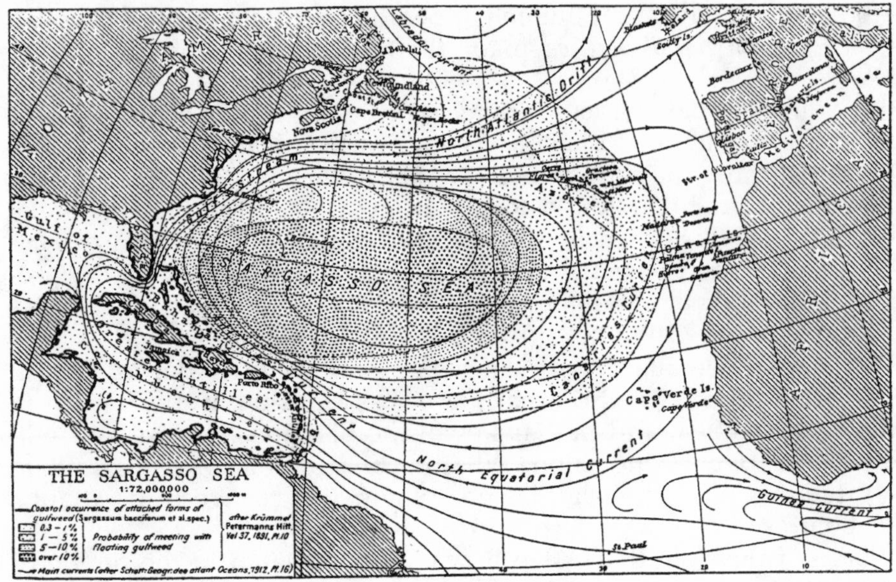

Stories circulating Plato's world concerning the existence of the Sargasso Sea helped perpetuate the idea of an impassable expanse of mud shoals and shallows that existed beyond the Pillars of Hercules.

by mud, just below the surface, left by the settling down of the island'[41] cannot now be determined. However, since Honorius asserted that further mythical islands lay in the same vicinity, there is every reason to believe that these are synonymous with the 'other islands' Plato suggests lay in front of the 'opposite continent'.

Beyond Britain

Quite recently, it has been proposed that Atlantis was once located in the proximity of the British Isles, which possesses rich legends of lost lands that lay beyond its western coastline.[42] Should this be so, it would imply that Plato's 'other islands' were those encountered by ancient mariners who used the so-called Northwest Passage to reach New England.[43] If a vessel were to leave, say, the northern coast of Ireland or Scotland, it could very easily make a transatlantic crossing via the Faeroe Isles, Iceland, the tip of Greenland, Newfoundland and finally Nova Scotia. It was then just a short sea crossing to Cape Cod, Massachusetts.

There is ample evidence that fishing vessels from England and the Basque country of Spain were secretly using the Northwest Passage to exploit the abundant cod grounds off Labrador, Newfoundland and New England long before the age of Columbus. It is a case convincingly argued in an intriguing book entitled *Cod: A Biography of the Fish that Changed the World* by American writer and journalist Mark Kurlansky. He has pointed out that when in 1534 the Frenchman Jacques Cartier 'discovered' the mouth of the St Lawrence, west of Newfoundland, he was confounded by 'the presence of 1,000 Basque fishing vessels'.[44]

It is also a fact that a large number of Old World artefacts have turned up at various locations in New England. These have included Roman and Carthaginian coins, Iberian and Carthaginian amphorae, as well as an assortment of inscribed stones in various Old World languages (examples are cited in Notes and References).[45] If these finds are to be seen as genuine, it implies ancient contact with North America up to 1,800 years before the arrival of the Norse seafarers in the tenth and eleventh centuries. Did some knowledge of these early oceanic crossings filter through to the Mediterranean world in Plato's day?

The most recent scholar who has attempted to demonstrate that Atlantis lay off the west coast of Britain is Russian scientist Viatscheslav Koudriavtsev of the Institute of Metahistory in Moscow.[46] He is convinced that evidence of the island's former existence will be found on the shallow banks that lie beyond Cornwall's Isles of Scilly, traditionally the site of lost Lyonesse. One problem with this theory is that the Sargasso Sea is literally thousands of kilometres south-west of Britain. Moreover, there is no similar oceanic debris off the British Isles that might account for the impassable sea alluded to, not just by Plato but also by Aristotle, Pseudo-Scylax and, most important of all, Himilco.

In the Azores

Another, equally plausible solution to the Atlantis mystery is that Plato's Atlantic island was located in the vicinity of the island group known as the Azores. As we have seen, Honorius of Autun wrote that the islands of the Hesperides were adjoined to the 'curdled sea' that covers the site of lost Atlantis. Since the Sargasso Sea lies to the west of the Azores, and the Hesperides have occasionally been identified with this island group,[47] Atlantologists argue that the sunken landmass must have been situated in this part of the ocean.

The cluster of nine main islands that make up the Azores group are located amid a chain of underwater mountains which rise to heights in excess of 9,000 metres. They form part of the Mid-Atlantic Ridge that defines the division between tectonic plates, running roughly north–south beneath the ocean floor for a distance of around 17,600 kilometres. It is the tips of the very highest of these subterranean mountains that protrude from the ocean floor as the principal islands of the Azores, which are themselves endowed with sizeable mountains that soar to a height in excess of 2,100 metres.

One of the first writers to suggest that the Azores are the remnants of an Atlantean island continent was Ignatius Donnelly, author of the seminal classic *Atlantis: The Antediluvian World,* first published in 1882. This American congressman set down the foundations for the thousands of books and articles that have been written on this subject over the past 120 years or so. Although Donnelly's book has seen countless reprints and is still available today, much of what he had to say about Atlantis being an antediluvian motherland for the diffusion of civilisation on both sides of the Atlantic has since been proved incorrect. However, Donnelly's original thesis of a central Atlantean landmass has been perpetuated by a number of well-respected scholars of the Atlantis mystery.

Perhaps the most authoritative writer to develop the theory of a sunken continent in the vicinity of the Mid-Atlantic Ridge was the Russian academic Nikolai Zhirov. During the 1960s he wrote a series of papers on the subject, as well as a definitive book entitled *Atlantis – Atlantology: Basic Problems,* published in England during 1970. Like Donnelly, he argued that the former Atlantean landmass lay in the vicinity of the Azores and that, before it sank without trace, it acted as a land-bridge for the migration of flora and fauna between Africa and the Americas.[48]

Christian O'Brien, a retired industrial geologist, archaeologist and historical writer, has also tackled the concept of a mid-Atlantic continent having once existed in the vicinity of the Azores. In his 1997 book *The Shining Ones* – co-authored with his wife Barbara Joy – he proposed that the Azorean landmass, as he sees it, suffered immense cataclysms and eventually sank into the earth's liquid magma, leaving only the Azores as hard evidence of its former existence.[49] The discovery of six fields of hot springs in the vicinity of the Azores is, he postulates, firm evidence of this hypothesis. They can be seen as typical of the effects caused by cold seawater that percolates down through the lava before being forced upwards to the ocean floor by rising heat.[50] During explorations off the island of São Miguel, the largest island in the Azores group, in 1971 Christian and Barbara O'Brien found clear evidence of an underwater river bed filled with water-worn boulders.[51] By applying detailed contouring methods to hydrographic charts, the O'Briens discerned that rivers draining off the southern slopes of São Miguel once converged together in a huge valley, now situated some 64 kilometres out from the present coastline.[52] Other islands in the Azores group have yielded similar hydrographic anomalies, and in one case the O'Briens even traced a series of river valleys that extended for a distance of 288 kilometres before converging together in a much larger river basin.[53]

Using this knowledge of ancient river systems, the O'Briens were able to reconstruct a land profile that revealed an Azorean landmass 'about the size and shape of Spain', with high mountain ranges rising over 3,655 metres above sea-level, as well as impressive rivers that run 'in curving valley systems'. Furthermore, they have pointed out that:

> In the southeast, a feature which we have called 'The Great Plain' covered an area in excess of 3,500 square miles [9,065 square kilometres], and was watered by a river comparable in size to the River Thames in England. It has, as we shall see, points in common with a great plain described by Plato in his *Critias*, as being a feature of the island of Atlantis.[54]

The conclusion drawn from these findings is that the Azores once formed part of a much greater landmass which sank beneath the waves and is now situated 'many thousands of feet' below the current sea-level.[55] To obtain a more substantial insight into this fascinating subject, the O'Briens have proposed that a scientific team extract a series of core samples from their proposed river channels. They confidently predict that these will show evidence not only of ancient river beds, but also of freshwater flora and fauna that once thrived on the former Azorean landmass.[56]

In this theory we are presented with another attractive role model for sunken Atlantis, supported in this case by the knowledge that on the island of São Miguel a local legend tells of seven cities now submerged beneath two volcanic lakes, one of blue water and the other of green (see Chapter Thirteen).[57] Unfortunately, there are fundamental problems in accepting the theory of a former Azorean landmass. It is now known, for instance, that the volcanic mountains that constitute the Mid-Atlantic Ridge are of relatively recent composition. In many ways they can be seen as enormous geological scars on a gaping wound that never properly heals. The north–south-orientated tectonic plates produce an upward flow of magma which constantly creates new underwater mountain systems that could never have formed part of a geological landmass in the manner described.

In addition to these problems, we must also acknowledge that there is now wide-scale acceptance of the so-called continental drift theory, first proposed in 1915 by the German meteorologist Arthur Wegener. In simple terms, this asserts that many millions of years ago the American and African landmasses were joined together, yet ever since they have been slowly moving apart. Just by making paper cutouts of the different continents and slotting them together we can see they fit snugly, suggesting that the continental drift theory is real. Furthermore, the fact that the American and African continents were once joined together explains much of the flora and fauna they have in common.

More damning still is the fact that when the first Portuguese navigators reached the Azorean islands in 1427, they found them completely devoid not only of human life but also of any animals. Even though some evidence has emerged to suggest that sometime in the third century BC Carthaginian vessels from North Africa reached Corvo, the westernmost of the Azorean islands (see Chapter Five), no archaeology has come to light to suggest that the archipelago ever supported an indigenous culture.

Even if the O'Briens' proposals regarding prehistoric river beds, located off the coast of São Miguel, do prove to be correct it seems unlikely that Plato's Atlantis is based on a memory of a high culture which once thrived on any proposed Azorean landmass. Admittedly, if we look again at our global jigsaw made of paper cutouts, we can see that there *are* slight gaps. However, these fall not in the vicinity of the Azores but around the Gulf of Mexico and the Caribbean Sea. Could it be possible that Atlantis awaited discovery somewhere in this region of the globe?

Everything points towards Atlantis having once existed somewhere off the east coast of the American continent, plausibly in the vicinity of the Bahamas and Caribbean. Yet it is also clear that there are major problems with this theory, not least of all in respect to the supposed size of Plato's Atlantic island, which would hardly fit in the gaps of our global jigsaw. How might we justify these curious anomalies? A more definite indication that I was on the right track would come from a careful examination of the *Critias,* the second of Plato's dialogues on the mysteries of Atlantis.

CHAPTER III

THE ATLANTICUS

PLATO SAT DOWN TO WRITE his second and final version of the Atlantis legend some five years after the completion of the *Timaeus*. How exactly the original story of a sunken Atlantic isle was received among his contemporaries is unclear (although see Aristotle's comment on the matter in Chapter Four). Whether they applauded it, condemned it or were merely indifferent to it remains a matter of speculation. What we do know is that peculiar stories began to circulate in Greece within a century or so of Plato's death. One rumour put about by Timon the Pyrrhonist (*c.* 279 BC) suggested that the *Timaeus* was based on primary material borrowed by Plato from earlier authors.[1] Another accused him of having stolen the book from a rival, while still another spoke of Plato paying someone for an existing manuscript that he later claimed as his own![2] None of these allegations is likely to have been based on any real truth, and no similar accusations were levelled against the *Critias*.

This clearly unfinished second text, which features the Atlantis theme exclusively, was either Plato's penultimate work (the last of his dialogues being *The Laws*), or even the final literary offering he wrote before his death in around 347 BC. It is possible that since he knew he was nearing the end of his life (he was around 79 in 350 BC), he had nothing to lose by committing to writing all that he knew about the fabled Atlantean empire.

As in Plato's earlier works, the *Republic* and the *Timaeus*, the *Critias* features the same assembly of four: Socrates, Timaeus, Hermocrates and Critias, after whom it is titled. Curiously, there is evidence to suggest that the work also possessed a rather intriguing second title. Proclus Daidochus (AD 412–485), a philosopher, poet and scientist, in his *Commentaries on the Timaeus of Plato*, written *c.* 432–440 AD,[3] refers specifically to the *Critias* as the *Atlanticus*. For instance, at one point he states: 'Hence in the

Atlanticus, Critias having assembled the Gods, as consulting about the punishment of the Atlantics, he says, "*Jupiter thus addressed them*".'[4] Proclus is here describing the last lines of the *Critias*, showing that he is alluding to it under this title. Later in the text, Proclus discusses the chronological order of the dialogues: 'Conformably to this congruity, the *Republic* has an arrangement prior to the *Timaeus*; and the *Timaeus* to the *Atlanticus*',[5] confirming that he is referring to the *Critias*. Whether Proclus himself named it the *Atlanticus* or whether it was a title already in existence is unclear.

The Dialogue Recommences

Following an introduction to set the scene in which Hermocrates invites the presence of the god Paean, the goddess Memory, and the Muses, Critias provides the reader with a brief recap of the Atlantis story told so far. The participants of the dialogue are first reminded that 'it is in all nine thousand years since a general war . . . between those who dwelt without and those who dwelt within the pillars of Heracles'.[6]

Instantly a gross inconsistency has crept into the account, for although Critias affirms that Athens' aggressor came from 'without' the Pillars of Hercules, the actual war is here said to have taken place 'nine thousand years' before the date of the dialogue, *c.* 421 BC. This implies a date in the region of 9421 BC, which is not what was stated in the *Timaeus*. Here 9,000 years is the time that has elapsed between the foundation of Athens and Solon's visit to Sais *c.* 570 BC. Since Egypt was said to have been founded a full thousand years later, and the 'aggressor' rose up against both Athens *and* Egypt, it provides a date post 8570 BC. These widely differing dates leave us with a glaring anomaly that defies explanation. The only obvious solution is to accuse Plato of a certain amount of sloppiness when compiling the text. Obviously, this is not a good start to what must be seen as a sequel to the original Atlantis account contained in the *Timaeus*.

Those who came from beyond the Pillars of Hercules are confirmed as the 'kings of the island of Atlantis', which 'as you will recollect, was once . . . an island larger than Libya and Asia together'.[7] The assembly is also reminded that the landmass was 'engulfed by earthquakes [there is no mention of floods] and is the source of the impassable mud which prevents navigators from this quarter from advancing through the straits into the open Ocean'.[8] These words seem to affirm Plato's belief that the Atlantic Ocean was once accessible to 'voyagers' from his own world, although in his day this passage was impossible due to the presence of the shallow sea.

The *Critias* then proceeds with a brief review of the origins, past deeds and deluges of the Athenian nation as recounted in the *Timaeus.* Finally, Critias turns his attention to the defeated Atlantean aggressor, saying: 'As for the condition and early history of their [i.e. the Athenians'] antagonists, if my memories of the tale I heard as a boy do not play me false, I will now impart the story freely to you as friends.'[9]

Using Critias the Younger as the dialogue's storyteller enables Plato to insinuate, quite cryptically, that he, too, is merely recalling a story passed on to him when just a boy by this same Critias. He is identified as either Plato's uncle or great-grandfather, depending on the genealogy consulted. Both are claimed to have had grandfathers called Critias and great-grandfathers called Dropides. Which one is being alluded to in the text is of no special relevance. All we need to presume is that Critias the Younger is suggesting that the account was inherited from his own great-grandfather, Dropides, who acquired it originally from Solon, a friend and relative.

Critias then explains why, in the narrative he is about to relate, the Atlantic 'barbarians' bear Greek names. He tells us that:

> Solon had a fancy to turn the tale to account in his own poetry; so he asked questions about the significance of the names and discovered that the original Egyptian authors of the narrative had translated them into their own speech. In his turn, as he learned the sense of a name, he translated it back again, *in his manuscript,* into our own language. His actual papers were once in my father's hands, and are in my own, to this day, and I studied them thoroughly in my boyhood [author's emphasis].[10]

There is much of interest in these statements. First, it is suggested that, as the biographer Plutarch was later to repeat, Solon had intended to publish the Atlantis story, but never got around to doing it, even though he had already completed 'his manuscript' on the subject. This remained in the family until eventually it came into the possession of Critias the Younger. Secondly, the reader is told that the names that feature in the *Critias* were first changed from their native language by the Egyptian priests before being transferred into Greek by Solon for poetic purposes: hence the next line of the text, which reads: 'So if you hear names like those of our own countrymen, you must not be surprised.'[11]

These few facts alone hint at the former existence of an original *Atlanticus* – one that was authored by Solon and passed on in some form or another through successive generations of Plato's family. If correct, might this have been the original source material behind Plato's own knowledge of the subject? The problem here is that there is no contemporary evidence to suggest that Solon ever wrote such a manuscript. We have only Plato's own fictional account of the supposed events that led him to gain knowledge of the story, and, as we have already discovered, there are ample grounds to treat these claims with some suspicion.

Gods of the Outer Ocean

Returning to the text of the *Critias*, the reader learns next that the 'long story' of Atlantis 'began much in this fashion'.[12] When the gods of old divided up the earth, Poseidon (the Greek form of Neptune) received as his lot 'the isle of Atlantis'.[13] It goes on:

> By the sea, in the centre of the island, there was a plain, said to have been the most beauteous of all such plains and very fertile, and, again, near the centre of this plain, at a distance of some fifty furlongs [10 kilometres], a mountain which was nowhere of any great altitude.[14]

'In this mountain [i.e. within a cave]', the reader is told, there lived a mortal being named Euenor and his wife Leucippe. She bore a daughter named Clito, who, following the death of her parents, was desired by Poseidon. To possess her the sea-god built a fortified 'fence of alternative rings of sea and land, smaller and greater, one within another'.[15] Two of these 'wheels' were of earth and three were of water, making the centre island inaccessible to 'man', for 'there were as yet no ships and no seafaring'.[16]

From these words we can view these events as having taken place during the age of the gods, a time when humanity still inhabited caves and civilisation had not yet been born.

Critias tells us that two fountains were to be found on the main island – one warm and the other cold. Furthermore, the soil thereabouts produced an abundance of 'food-plants of all kinds'.[17]

Poseidon and Clito went on to produce ten children, described as 'five twin births of male offspring'. Atlantis was then divided into ten portions to accommodate each of the ten sons.[18] The first-born, Atlas, was granted the land in the middle of the island, where his mother was born, as well as the 'lot of land surrounding it'.[19] Through his birthright, Atlas was also appointed to be the first king of Atlantis.[20] The rest of the princes were granted sovereignty over 'a large population and the lordship of wide lands'.[21]

Atlas, of course, is a name integrally linked with both the antediluvian island kingdom named by Plato and the ocean in which it was located. 'Atlas', 'Atlantis' and 'Atlantic' are considered by language scholars to derive their origin from the Greek word *tlâo*, meaning 'to ensure' or 'to bear', recalling Atlas' role as bearer of the vault of heaven. The name Atlantis has a female determinative and is generally rendered 'daughter of Atlas'.

As one of the Titans, Atlas was said to have married either Pleione, a daughter of Oceanus, or Hesperis, by whom he produced seven daughters known as the Atlantides, or the Hesperides in some accounts. He was also a legendary king of Mauritania, an ancient kingdom of Libya which originally embraced Morocco, Algeria and the Western Sahara. The Greek hero Perseus, fresh from his pursuit of the Gorgons, was said to have turned Atlas into a mountain using the head of Medusa.

Today the Atlas Mountains of North Africa are considered to be the location of Atlas' petrification. Forming a crescent on the north side of the Algerian Sahara, they stretch right across to the north-west coast of Africa. There is even a Mount Atlas, the appearance of which gave rise to the belief that it is in fact a stone giant supporting the vault of heaven on his shoulders (and plausibly the origin behind the myth of Atlas – see Chapter Fourteen).

Traditionally, Atlas' connection with Libya and the Western Ocean came about because, to the Hellenic Greeks, his kingdom was seen as the most westerly point of the known world. Beyond Mauritania was an uncharted region that even accomplished mariners would not dare to navigate unless they first gained the blessings of its patron, Atlas, who presided over the depths of the sea. This, then, is why Plato's Atlantic isle, Atlantis, became the exclusive dominion of Atlas, whom Plato makes a half-mortal son of Poseidon.

In Greek mythology, Poseidon was the son of Cronus, the Greek form of Saturn, who was said to have devoured his son immediately after birth. Yet Poseidon was then restored to life by means of a magic potion provided by Metis, one of the Oceanides. On the death of his father, Poseidon divided up the world with his brothers, and received for himself dominion over all waters. These included the seas, rivers, fountains, springs and, of course, the outer ocean. He was also said to have been able to 'cause earthquakes at his pleasure, and [to] raise islands from the bottom of the sea with a blow of his trident'.[22] As in the case of Atlas, the veneration of Poseidon was said to have been especially strong among the peoples of Libya, who saw him as the first of all gods.[23]

These, then, are the key Greek gods in Plato's Atlantis narrative. Their role here is perhaps apt, and yet their pre-existing myths are expanded in the text almost beyond recognition. Poseidon is made to desire a mortal woman, Clito, who bears him five sets of male twins, the first being mighty Atlas. Although this paternal link between the two gods is unknown outside the *Critias*, it does not necessarily invalidate Plato's story. Myths and legends are merely vehicles for the conveyance of ancestral memories of age-old events across countless generations. Plato simply exploited this same literary vehicle for his own purposes.

Princes of Numerous Islands

Next in the *Critias* we find that, whereas Atlas becomes Atlantis' first king and so gains control over the central portion of the island, his twin brother is bestowed 'the extremity of the island off the pillars of Heracles, fronting the region now known as Gadira'.[24] His name in Greek is Eumelus, 'but in the language of his own country [it is] Gadirus, and no doubt his name was the origin of that of the district'.[25]

Plato was no geographer. Neither was he a historian, or a navigator. However, as we have already established, there is every reason to assume that he did have access to garbled maritime knowledge concerning supposedly unknown Atlantic islands, and in particular their proximity to 'the opposite continent' and the Sargasso Sea. It is therefore with some interest that he makes reference to a region fronting Atlantis called Gadira.

There can be little doubt that the reference to Gadira alludes to the ancient Phoenician city-port of this name situated on the Atlantic coast of south-west Spain, ancient Iberia. In Plato's day it thrived under the control of the Carthaginians, even though it still acted independently to their main city-port of Carthage on the Mediterranean coast of Tunisia. In later Roman times the Iberian port became known as Gades, from which the modern Cadiz takes its name (although it is not located on the same spot). In the style of many other Phoenician and Carthaginian city-ports, Gades grew up around an offshore island. Here stood a temple dedicated to the Phoenician god Melqart, who in Greek tradition was associated with Hercules.

Gades was said to have been located just 40 kilometres beyond the Pillars of Hercules,[26] and yet in the *Critias* Plato implies that one of the princes of Atlantis, the twin of Atlas, held dominion over the portion of the Atlantic island that lay closest to this city-port. It is difficult to determine exactly what he might have meant by this statement. If, however, Plato truly believed that Atlantis was the size of Libya and Asia together, it is conceivable that he saw its eastern extremities as extending so far across the outer ocean that it almost reached the coast of Spain. On the other hand, his inclusion of Gades in the Atlantis story has led some authors to conclude that either the Atlantic island lay off the Spanish coast, or that Gades (or more precisely the neighbouring city-port of Tartessos) was itself Atlantis.[27] Such ideas make little sense of Atlantis' geographical placement as defined in the *Timaeus*, and, as we shall see, Gades may have played a quite different, yet equally important, role in the construction of the Atlantis myth (see Chapter Twelve).

The *Critias* provides the reader with the names of the other four sets of male twins born to Clito, before adding that:

> All these and their descendants for many generations reigned as princes of numerous islands of the ocean *besides* their own, and were also . . . suzerains of the population of the hither or inner side of the straits, as far as Egypt and Tyrrhenia [author's emphasis].[28]

There is further confirmation here that Atlantis lay somewhere in the Western Ocean, and that the Atlantic empire consisted of a series of islands ruled over by the princes of the main island. This is a statement found originally in the *Timaeus*, which also says that the kings of Atlantis held dominion over 'other islands and parts of the [opposite] continent'.[29]

Very possibly, these are the same islands that Plato informs us were used by ancient voyagers to reach 'the opposite continent', i.e. the American mainland. What is more, the suggestion that Atlantis also gained control of lands within the Pillars of Hercules clearly implies that the empire established itself in both Europe and Libya. All this would indicate some kind of connection between the supposed Atlanteans of the Western Ocean and the 'voyagers' from within the Mediterranean, whom Plato tells us were able to reach 'the opposite continent' via a series of 'other islands', before the final destruction of Atlantis.[30]

Marvels of Atlantis

The *Critias* then informs the reader that the descendants of Atlas were able to retain the throne of Atlantis for many generations, creating a city on the main island which possessed immense natural resources.[31] Mining is said to have taken place, and one of the most precious metals 'excavated in various parts of the island' was 'orichalc', or ' orichalcum'.[32] Plato tells us that it 'gleamed like fire'[33] and was second only in value to gold.[34] Various attempts have been made to identify orichalc. The name itself appears in other classical writings and seems to translate as 'mountain copper', or even 'mountain brass'. Russian Atlantis scholar Nikolai Zhirov argued convincingly that orichalc was a bronze-zinc alloy produced in ancient times and known also as 'tombac'. Since it contained 18 per cent or less of zinc, it appeared red in colour and lent 'itself to cold forging, flattening and drawing'.[35]

In addition to the mining of metals, stone was quarried in Atlantis and timbers felled for use in the construction of buildings. Wild and domesticated animals were found in abundance; 'even elephants', we are told, 'were plentiful'.[36] This last statement has often been used by sceptics to demonstrate the incredible nature of Plato's account. No evidence that elephants ever roamed any Atlantic island has ever come to light. Furthermore, no elephants were found when the first conquistadors penetrated the tropical heartland of the American continent.

What we can say is that various species of mammoth and mastodon inhabited the American continent prior to the cessation of the last Ice Age, *c.* 9000–8500 BC. Conceivably, such enormous beasts could have been construed as elephants, invoking the possibility that they might have existed on Plato's Atlantic island. In support of this theory Atlantologists cite the fact that mammoth and mastodon bones have been trawled up from the sea bottom by vessels fishing off the Atlantic shelf, close to the Mid-Atlantic Ridge.[37] Despite such inexplicable curiosities, there is no hard evidence whatsoever to lend credibility to the idea of elephants in Atlantis.

Yet is it elephants that Plato refers to in the *Critias*. What might have caused him to introduce this noble beast into the Atlantis account? Elephants were obviously known to traders and navigators of the ancient world, particularly those who travelled through Libya, where a now extinct species once thrived. Furthermore, ancient Egyptian kings, such as Thutmosis III (*c.* 1490–1436 BC), embarked on hunting expeditions in pursuit of the elephant,[38] while the now extinct Syrian elephant, with its characteristic small ear, is depicted on an ostracon located in the tomb of Rameses III (1182–1151 BC).[39] Since we know that both Solon and Plato visited Egypt to gain instruction in philosophy and wisdom, is it possible that they learned of the existence of elephants while in this country? Both men also travelled widely throughout the Mediterranean world and might have chanced on stories that spoke of elephants living in lands beyond the Pillars of Hercules (plausibly along the West African coast – see the account of Hanno the Carthaginian general's sea-voyage in Chapter Five). On this basis alone, either Solon or Plato could thus have added this unusual element to the Atlantis story.

Strange Fruit

After recalling the beasts present on Atlantis, the *Critias* goes on to describe the various fruits of the earth grown and cultivated on the main island, one of which makes very interesting reading indeed:

> . . . the soil bore all aromatic substances still to be found on earth, roots, stalks, canes, gums exuded by flowers and fruits, and they throve on it. Then, as for cultivated fruits, the dry sort which is meant to be our food-supply and those others we use as solid nutriment – we

> call the various kinds pulse [e.g. peas and beans] – as well as the woodland kind which gives us meat and drink and oil together, the fruit of trees that ministers to our pleasure and merriment and is so hard to preserve, and that we serve as welcome dessert to a jaded man to charm away his satiety.[40]

Something very significant is made clear here – the cultivated product used as 'solid nutriment' that is said to give 'meat and drink and oil together' has a familiar ring to it. It is surely the coconut, which does indeed contain a nutritious 'drink' as well as fleshy white 'meat', from which is extracted a highly prized 'oil'. So can Plato have been alluding to the coconut, an exotic fruit so obviously tropical in origin?

Everywhere from Florida to the Bahamas, the Caribbean and the Lesser Antilles coconuts grow in abundance. Yet before the discovery of the New World, it is not known exactly how widespread the distribution of the coconut palm might have been in the western hemisphere. In the opinion of nearly all botanists the coconut genus originated on the islands of Melanesia in the western Pacific and spread gradually westwards until it entered Southeast Asia and eastwards until it reached the Pacific coast of the Americas.[41] Good evidence exists to show that it was to be found from Panama right down to Colombia and Ecuador on the Pacific coast of South America *before* the time of Conquest.[42]

In theory coconuts were unknown on the western Atlantic seaboard until after the discovery of the West Indies in 1492, which, if so, would make nonsense of Plato's statement to this effect. This is not, however, the full story.

The great sea-adventurer and historian Thor Heyerdahl has made a special study of the coconut and proposed that the official attitude towards its worldwide distribution derives from biased preconceptions concerning the presumed isolation of the Americas before the time of 'discovery'. He has shown that the coconut palm, *Cocas nucifera*, evolved not in Asia or in the western Pacific but in the Americas, where various members of its subfamily (*Cocoinae*) occur naturally (only in its hybrid form does it exist in Asia).[43] Heyerdahl further points out that the old belief in ripe green coconuts falling on to beaches and being transported by the tide to distant lands, where they then germinate, is fraught with problems. Experiments carried out in 1941 on Hawaii demonstrated conclusively that during long sea journeys 'fouling organisms' enter through the eyes of the fruit and destroy its ability to germinate properly.[44] Thus there is no way that the coconut could have spread across the Pacific in such a casual fashion. More likely is that the fruit was carried across the ocean not by the actions of water but on board vessels making transpacific journeys (compelling evidence to suggest that contact between cultures in Southeast Asia and the Americas occurred with frequency in pre-Columbian times is presented in Chapter Nine).

So if the coconut genus originated in the Americas, is there any evidence to suggest that it was present either in the Bahamas or Caribbean before the age of Columbus?

No early Spanish chronicler who visited the Caribbean ever makes mention of a tree or fruit which matches the description of the coconut, certainly not until enough time had elapsed for it to have been introduced to the western Atlantic seaboard by colonial settlers. Yet the enormous distribution of the coconut throughout the entire Caribbean world makes it a little difficult to accept this solution. Furthermore, deluge stories connected with 'the natives of Haiti', and the Caribbean in general, claim that 'the earth was repopulated by a lone survivor who threw coconuts into the air which came down as men and women'.[45] If this account originated among the indigenous tribes, it would suggest that coconuts really were present in the archipelago during the prehistoric age.

A Marvel of Civilisation

After describing food production in Atlantis, the text of the *Critias* explains that '. . . the kings employed all these gifts of the soil to construct and beautify their temples, royal residences, harbours, docks and domain in general on the following plan'.[46] What follows is a highly conceptualised description of Atlantis' mighty city at the height of its power. Having already been informed that Poseidon constructed a series of three water-filled rings around the foundation point of the Atlantean royal dynasty, the reader is then told that a road was built across these furrows to the central islet. Here was constructed a palace, as well as a great temple dedicated to the island's gods and great ancestors. Each new king added to these buildings until they were a marvel to behold.

Other construction projects included the cutting of a roofed canal that began at the sea and broke through each of the rings of land until it reached the innermost ring of water which surrounded the all-important central islet. In all, the canal was said to have been in length 50 furlongs (10 kilometres), in breadth 300 feet (91.5 metres) and in depth 100 feet (30 metres). Towers and gates were erected on the bridges at either end of the canal to ensure the safe passage of the great seagoing vessels that continually navigated this covered waterway.[47]

Stones in three colours were employed individually or together in patterns to enhance the beauty of the Atlantean citadel. These were quarried either from beneath the central islet or from the construction sites of the various circular canals. In addition to this, the walls of the buildings were said to have been coated each with a different coloured metal. Those of the outer land ring were covered in copper; those on the inner land ring were coated in 'melted tin', while the walls of the buildings on the central islet were lined with orichalc, 'which gleamed like fire'.[48]

Surrounded by golden railings in the heart of the great temple was an untrodden inner sanctum sacred to the memory of Poseidon and his spouse Clito. It thus symbolised 'the very place where the race of the ten princes had been first conceived and begotten'.[49] This enormous building is said to have had a roof of ivory, ornamented with gold, silver and orichalc, and walls lined with silver.[50] On pediments were statues covered in gold, including one of Poseidon on a chariot, drawn by six winged horses and accompanied by a hundred Nereids riding dolphins. So large were these figures that their heads virtually touched the ceiling. All were focused around an altar of gigantic proportions.[51]

Outside the temple were to be found statues in gold of all the wives of the ten founding princes of Atlantis, as well as many other grand statues commissioned by both kings and private individuals. There were also dual springs (the same as the two fountains mentioned earlier?) – one hot and the other cold – the virtues of which are described as truly remarkable.[52] Around these were buildings and basins into which the waters were channelled. These provided warm baths in winter, and after their use the waters flowed into the grove of Poseidon, where there were also trees of every kind.[53] Here, too, were temples, dedicated to other gods, as well as gardens and a gymnasium.[54] On the other island rings were more buildings, including stables for horses. In the centre of the largest ring was a racecourse that completely circumnavigated it. Barracks for bodyguards and dockyards full of seagoing vessels also occupied the island rings.[55]

Some 50 furlongs (10 kilometres) distant from the outer ring of water was built a great wall. It began by the sea at the mouth of the canal and surrounded the entire city.[56] Within its boundaries were a multitude of houses, while into the canal came 'merchant-vessels and their passengers arriving from all quarters, whose vast numbers occasioned incessant shouting, clamour and general uproar, day and night'.[57]

This is the vivid picture of Atlantis' fabulous city painted for us by Plato some 2,350 years ago. Such a marvel of civilisation exists nowhere in our memory of humanity's great achievements in the prehistoric age. Never has the spade of an archaeologist, or the explorations of a diver, ever uncovered any shred of evidence to support the popularly held belief that this fabled city once existed. This is not to say that the description offered by Plato does not bear

Fantastic conception of Plato's Atlantean city, complete with step pyramids (after Russian academic Nikolai Zhirov and R. Avotin). Why has the archaeological world failed to discover ruins that might confirm the former existence of this utopian realm?

similarities to known cities of both the ancient world and the Americas: only that at the present time we have nothing whatsoever to compare it with directly. Should we therefore dismiss Plato's description of the Atlantean city as mere fiction conceived of by his rich and fertile imagination?

At this point in many of the more popular books on the Atlantis mystery, the author will refer the reader to the discovery in 1872 of ancient Troy by German scholar Heinrich Schliemann. They will say that prior to his age this legendary city was thought by historians and classicists alike to be just a fable conjured to life in the pages of Homer's *Iliad*. Yet Schliemann thought otherwise. After following up certain clues regarding the possible location of Troy, he began excavating an occupational mound near Hissarlik on the Aegean coast of southern Turkey, and very soon turned myth into reality.

The moral of the story is that some legends *are* based on truths, and that we should never dismiss out of hand Plato's account of Atlantis. His fabulous city might await discovery somewhere in the depths, or indeed shallows, of the Atlantic Ocean. Let us hope that, one day, a city of the description provided by Plato is found; it would be the greatest archaeological discovery of modern times. For the moment, however, it is essential to stick wholly with the available evidence and look not for a city of fable but the historical source material *behind* his conception of the Atlantic island. Only then can we begin to piece together all the various strands of evidence that seem clearly to indicate the existence in the outer ocean of a forgotten world that thrived long before the classical age. It is in this spirit that we must now move on to examine Plato's proposed geography for his lost island paradise.

CHAPTER IV

THE VIEW OVER ATLANTIS

I HAVE NOW GIVEN YOU a pretty faithful report of what I once learned of the town and the old palace, and must do my best to recall the general character of the territory and its organisation.[1]

With these words Plato, through the voice of Critias, concludes his account of the Atlantic island's fabulous citadel before going on to describe the more 'general character' of the island and its inhabitants. Just how much of what he says really is a 'pretty faithful report' of historical information will be up to us to decide. Only after we have examined the final section of the *Critias* can we go on to gain a more reliable picture of what was truly thought to lie beyond the Western Ocean.

Returning to the narrative we find Critias explaining the island's geography and terrain, about which he informs us:

> . . . the district [of Atlantis] as a whole, so I have heard, was of great elevation and its coast precipitous, but all round the city was a plain, enclosing it and itself enclosed in turn by mountain ranges which came right down to the sea. The plain itself was smooth, level, and of a generally oblong shape; it stretched for three thousand stadia [552 kilometres] in one direction, and, at its centre [i.e. a line drawn north–south *through* the centre of the plain – see below], for two thousand [368 kilometres] inland from the coast. All through the island this level district faced the south and was thus screened from the cold northerly winds.[2]

We are told that the 'oblong' plain was sheltered from the 'cold northerly winds' by 'mountain ranges which came right down to the sea'. For this to have been possible, the plain must have orientated east–west, and not north–south as some writers have assumed. The citadel was itself situated on the plain, just 50 furlongs (10 kilometres) from the shoreline, implying that it was most probably located on the southern coast. It could not have been situated on its northern shoreline, as this was occupied by the 'mountain ranges' that purportedly offered protection from the northerly winds.

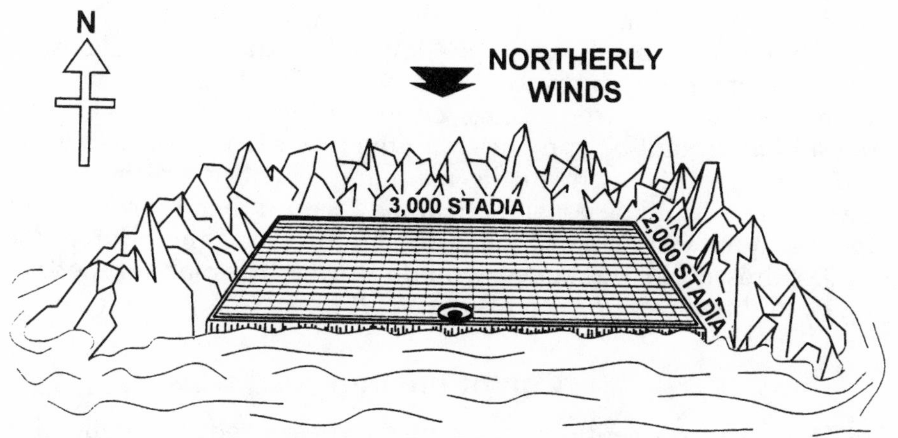

The Atlantean world according to the description given in Plato's *Critias*, *c*. 350 BC. This view is not found in his earlier Atlantis dialogue the *Timaeus*.

Thus affirmed, we are informed that the 'mountains contained numerous villages with a wealthy population, besides rivers, lakes and meadows which provided plentiful sustenance for all sorts of animals, wild or domestic, and timber of different kinds in quantities amply sufficient for manufactures of every type'.[3] The rain that fell on the northern mountain range was directed down into an enormous 'fosse', or trench, constructed around the entire plain. This was said to have had a perimeter of 10,000 stadia (1,840 kilometres) and a width of 2,000 stadia (368 kilometres). The enormous channel was itself crisscrossed by a series of irrigation channels, perhaps like a chessboard, which allowed the plain to be well nourished with any excess water being discharged into the ocean.[4]

Next in the *Critias* is a detailed account of the lands allotted to the peoples that inhabited the various districts and villages that made up the Atlantic island. The ruling princes of the various territories (and individual islands) would come together to carry out and obey the commands of Poseidon as prescribed of old on 'a column of orichalc preserved in the sanctuary of Poseidon in the centre of the island'.[5]

At this ancient column the princes were accustomed to assemble alternately every four or five years. On such occasions they discussed common affairs and judged whether any of their number had transgressed the holy laws.[6] These periodic rites of sovereignty involved the capture of one of the sacrificial bulls allowed to roam freely in the sanctuary of Poseidon. This ritualistic act was conducted using 'wooden clubs and cords only but no implement of iron', and afterwards the victim was brought to the pillar of orichalc and there slaughtered, the blood being allowed to run down its inscription.[7]

The bull's 'members' were then 'devoted' to the god, while drops of blood – one for each prince – were mixed in a bowl of wine. One by one they would scoop out a cupful using a gold beaker and, after a libation had been made on to the fire, each would swear an oath to exact judgement in the manner prescribed on the pillar.[8] The mixture would be consumed, and all would then retire to join a great banquet.[9] After dark, when the bonfires had died down, the princes, dressed in blue robes, would return to the place of sacrifice to give and receive judgement until daybreak.[10]

Cult of the Bull

This idealised conception of sacrificial rites, used in conjunction with the swearing of oaths and laws, has often been cited by scholars as evidence for the Aegean answer to the Atlantis mystery. In this respect they cite the legend of Minos, Crete's legendary king whom the Athenian general and historian Thucydides (471–402 BC) accredits with having created the first navy.[11] He is said to have asked Poseidon to provide a white bull so that he might sacrifice it in his honour. A beast was duly provided, but because the king liked it so much he sought out a substitute animal and sacrificed that one instead. As punishment for his disobedience, Poseidon caused Minos' wife Pasiphaë to fall in love with the white bull. Her unnatural desires were fulfilled through the help of Daedalus, and as a result she gave birth to a beast, half-man and half-bull. Known as the Minotaur, it was confined to an underground realm built by Minos and known as the Labyrinth. It was decreed that the defeated Athenian nation should offer as a yearly tribute seven boys and seven girls in order that the beast's sanguine appetite might be satisfied. This barbarity continued until the Minotaur was finally slain by the hero Theseus.

The above story is only a fable. Yet after Sir Arthur Evans began his famous excavations on Crete in 1895, it quickly became clear that by far the greatest cult practised by its Minoan inhabitants 3,500 years ago was that of the bull. In the royal palace at Knossos he discovered walls adorned with enormous frescoes that depicted in vivid detail young men and women performing the dangerous act of bull-leaping, while elsewhere bull motifs and symbols were found in profusion.[12]

To some archaeologists and historians this alone was enough to convince them that Plato's statements concerning bull sacrifices in Atlantis were based on a memory of the Cretan bull cult. Moreover, tapered stone pillars, discovered among the Minoan ruins of Akrotiri on the remaining fragments of Thera, were likewise seen as evidence of the former existence of columns like the inscribed pillar of orichalc at which the chosen bull was sacrificed during the covenants attended by the princes of Atlantis.[13]

Is it possible that Minoan bull ceremonies on the island of Crete really did influence the development of the Atlantis legend? Strangely enough, there is every possibility that this might have been the case, and yet not for the reasons suggested by the Cretan-Atlantis supporters. Ancient writers tell us that bulls were sacrificed regularly in honour of the sea-god Poseidon. The gall, or bile, of the victims was especially favoured as an altar offering since its taste was considered to resemble 'the bitterness of the sea water'.[14] It is therefore conceivable that Plato introduced the idea of bull sacrifices on Atlantis simply because the animal was sacred to Poseidon. There seems no reason to link these taurine ceremonies with Minoan Crete, purely on the basis that its young men and women performed the act of bull-leaping and bull motifs litter its ruins.

One respected Atlantis author who made a serious study of the bull-worship in Plato's *Critias* was L. Sprague de Camp. In his essential work *Lost Continents: The Atlantis Theme in History, Science, and Literature,* first published in 1954, he found the connection with Cretan bull ceremonies 'suggestive'. He added that 'perhaps they entered the Atlantis story as fragments which Plato picked up and which his subconscious wove into his Atlantean fiction'.[15] Yet having admitted this much, de Camp also pointed out the total implausibility of the Cretan-Atlantis hypothesis by adding that 'the Egyptians [as the presumed creators of the myth] are unlikely in a matter of 600 years or so to have moved Crete clear out of the Mediterranean, enlarged it a hundred-fold, and predated it by 8,000 years'.[16] It is easier therefore to assume that the link between Crete and Atlantis was not a common origin to their bull ceremonies but a shared sea-god in Poseidon who presided over the waters that encircled such islands.

End Times

After reviewing the sacred rites and holy laws adhered to by the princes of Atlantis, Critias turns his attention to the civil liberties and legal requirements adhered to by the Atlantic island's inhabitants.

These are outlined in some detail before we are at last told the plight of the kingdom prior to the island's final destruction. It is said that the Atlanteans' love of material wealth, combined with their loss of spirituality, was the true cause of their downfall. Thus corrupted, they 'began to behave themselves unseemly'. Furthermore:

> To the seeing eye they now began to seem foul, for they were losing the fairest bloom from their most precious treasure, but to such as could not see the true happy life, to appear at last fair and blest indeed, now that they were taking the infection of wicked covet and pride of power. Zeus, the god of gods, who governs his kingdom by law, having the eye by which such things are seen, beheld their goodly house in its grievous plight and was minded to lay a judgement on them that the discipline might bring them back to tune. So he gathered all the gods in his most honourable residence, even that stands at the world's centre and overlooks all that has part in becoming, and when he had gathered them there, he said . . .[17]

Here the text simply cuts off in mid-stream, leaving the reader to assume that Zeus, having gathered together the gods in council, made the decision to allow Athens to rise up against this mighty aggressor from the outer ocean. Once the Atlantean fleet had been defeated, 'earthquakes and floods' would then have been unleashed in an attempt to wipe out the wickedness that had spread throughout the island.

Why Plato left the text unfinished has been a matter of speculation for hundreds, if not thousands, of years. Is some part of the book missing? Did Plato lose interest in the Atlantis legend just prior to the commencement of his final work, *The Laws*, apparently written just years before his death in *c.* 347 BC? Or could it be that this was the ending that Plato had always intended? Perhaps he wanted to leave the whole story on a cliffhanger so that he could expand the plot in some later work, perhaps a third and final volume of his Atlantean trilogy.

The fact remains that the sudden termination of the *Critias*, without even so much as a return to the dialogue in progress, deprives us of any further information regarding the true nature and locality of the Atlantic island. However, in some ways this might be a good thing, for it is quite clear that the writing style of the *Critias* differs greatly from that of its predecessor, the *Timaeus*. It seems to paint an entirely different picture of the Atlantic island, tinged clearly with flawed idealistic principles of a utopian world, while the two dialogues are also contradictory in respect to the pseudo-history they each present.

It is as if, in creating the Atlantis story as presented in the *Critias*,

Plato has in mind somewhere else – somewhere known to him very well, which he saw as stagnating and falling into a state of decay during his own age. Might it be that he merely utilised the existing Atlantis legend as a warning of what could happen to a country or state if it does not adhere to the political and legislative laws outlined previously in his *Republic*?

Plato's Warning

So where might Plato have had in mind when he created his vision of an idealistic island kingdom that finally fell from grace? Some writers have proposed that he based the Atlantean empire on his home city of Athens. A century and a half before Plato wrote his dialogues, the Greek nations had come together to oppose the might of the Persian Empire at the same time that they were also at war with the Carthaginians. These twin conflicts came to an end in 480 BC, when the mainland Greeks defeated the Persians in a decisive naval battle near the island of Salamis and the Sicilian Greeks defeated the Carthaginians in a land battle at Himera.

The virtues of the Greek confederacy, led by Athens, can be compared with the role played in Plato's dialogues by the Athenians in their decisive war against the might of Atlantis. Yet although in the 50 or so years that followed the defeat of the Persians and Carthaginians Athens experienced a golden age of growth and expansion, this same period saw its decline into a state of decadence, reminiscent of that which befell the Atlantean nation.

Athens began to increase its wealth and power by invading neighbouring states and islands that had previously been under autonomous control. The Greek nations viewed this tyranny with great disdain, and so accused Athens' ruling authority of being little better than their great enemies, the Persians, who had carved out their own empire in a similar manner. These events led eventually to the Peloponnesian War (431–404 BC), in which a Greek confederacy, headed by Athens, was finally defeated by Peloponnesian forces during a decisive naval battle that once again reminds us of the war waged between Athens and the Atlantean aggressor.

Following Athens' surrender, its harbour was seized by the Peloponnesian forces, who then took control of the city, ironically on the day that the Athenians annually celebrated the defeat of the Persian navy off the coast of Salamis some 76 years earlier. Quite understandably, the Athenians were left totally demoralised by this humiliation. Athens' defeat marked the end of its dominion over the other Greek nations, leaving it to plunge into a long period of civil strife, political unrest and economic decay.

Whereas Athens was once seen as the greatest and most influential Greek nation, the ineptitude and barbarity of its political leaders now became a subject that Plato strived to highlight and rectify with a heartfelt passion. Moreover, Plato had a far more personal reason to despise and loathe its ruling authority. In 399 BC it sentenced to death his close friend and mentor Socrates, who was later to play the leading role in his various philosophical dialogues. A terrible incident such as this must have left a lingering emotional scar – one that Plato unquestionably bore for the rest of his life.

Plato's warning to Athens' ruling authority was therefore quite clear: either dispense with your wicked ways and return to the ideals that made you a great nation in the first place or suffer the wrath of Zeus and the gods of Olympus, the consequences of which would be ultimate destruction.

As the great American geographer and historical writer William H. Babcock concluded in respect of Plato's Atlantis narrative:

> Atlantis may fairly be set down as a figment of dignified philosophic romance, owing its birth partly to various legendary hints and reports of seismic and volcanic action but much more to the glorious achievements of Athens in the Persian War and the apparent need of explaining a supposed shallow part of the Atlantic known to be obstructed and now named the Sargasso Sea.[18]

In my opinion, these comparisons are realistic, and any scenarios introduced into the Atlantis narrative by Plato simply for political purposes will need to be stripped away before we can go on to assess the real source material behind the Atlantis legend.

Sources of Inspiration

Other authors have attempted to demonstrate that Plato based his conception of Atlantis on Sicily, and in particular its celebrated city of Syracuse. Following the death of Socrates in 399 BC, he travelled abroad visiting Egypt, mainland Greece and finally reaching Megara in Syracuse in 388 BC. On his return to Athens in 386 BC, Plato founded the school of philosophy known simply as the Academy, which occupied his time for the next 20 years. In 367 BC he returned to Syracuse as a personal adviser of the ruler Dionysius II. Yet he became embroiled in political wrangles and power struggles, forcing him to leave once more for his native Athens. His third and final visit to Syracuse was in 361–360 BC.

There is little question that the city-plan of Syracuse provided one or two ideas for his description of the Atlantean city as presented in the *Critias*.[19]

In addition to these facts, the Sicilians' celebrated repulsion of the Athenian naval fleet during the Peloponnesian War might also be compared with Plato's account of the Atlantean aggressor's defeat at the hands of the Athenian navy.[20] This comparison is strengthened in the knowledge that it was the historical Hermocrates, a general of Syracuse and one of the four participants in Plato's philosophical dialogues, who had helped the city repel the Athenian fleet during an all-important sea battle in 415 BC.[21] This avenue of investigation is convincingly argued by Phyllis Young Forsyth in her book *Atlantis: The Making of Myth*.[22] Yet Sicily is an island inside the Pillars of Hercules so, like Crete, cannot have been the original inspiration behind Plato's concept of an Atlantic island.

Comparisons have also been made between Plato's Atlantis and other major cities of the ancient world that flourished during the classical age. These include Carthage,[23] Babylon[24] and Ecbatana, modern Hamadan, the ancient capital of the Medians in western Iran. According to the much-travelled Greek historian Herodotus, Ecbatana was built on a hill and surrounded by a series of concentric walls, seven in all, each one represented by a different colour.[25] Did this knowledge influence Plato to ascribe each of Atlantis' ringed islands with different coloured metals? It is certainly possible.

No one can deny these clear comparisons between Plato's Atlantean realm and the ancient world in which he lived. Yet in attempting to find contemporary explanations for the Atlantis legend it is all too easy to lose sight of the fact that his famous dialogues are supposed to be *fiction*. He had every right to expand upon any existing knowledge he might have possessed regarding some unknown island that lay beyond the Pillars of Hercules with his own ideals of life.

Plato meant his works to be read by statesmen, politicians and aristocrats, as well as by philosophers, in the hope that they would take heed of his warnings and build a sound future for their citizens or subjects. It is an explanation shared by many classical scholars. Yet as I have outlined in earlier chapters, the knowledge contained in both Atlantis dialogues points overwhelmingly to one conclusion. It is that Plato drew his initial inspiration for the Atlantis legend from secondary maritime sources available to him at the time. In summary, it would appear that, stripped of its political and fantastic overtones, Plato's Atlantis narrative preserves a knowledge of an island kingdom or empire that:

(a) thrived in the Atlantic Ocean thousands of years before recorded history;
(b) was linked via a series of 'other' islands to an 'opposite continent', identified tentatively as the Americas;
(c) was accessible to ancient 'voyagers' who were once able to cross the outer ocean (and thus may have been responsible for introducing knowledge of the Atlantic realm to the ancient world);

(d) was destroyed by a natural cataclysm involving 'earthquakes and floods', and, finally;
(e) that an 'impassable sea' of mud and shoals (identified either as the Sargasso Sea or the shallow waters of the Bahamas, or both) occupies the former position of the sunken island, preventing any further navigation to 'the opposite continent'.

All these facts were gleaned initially from the *Timaeus*, the first of Plato's two accounts of the Atlantis legend, suggesting therefore that it was this work, and not the *Critias*, which contains most of the original inspiration for the story. This does not mean that we now relegate the *Critias* to a position unworthy of consideration; only that the *Timaeus* appears to contain more historical data than its unfinished successor.

The Dimensions of Paradise

What, then, can we say about Plato's description of the Atlantic island as outlined in both the *Timaeus* and the *Critias*? Is it purely symbolic, the creation of the author's own mind, or does it hold important clues to our overall understanding of the real Atlantic island? Let us look again at the passages of the *Critias* containing a detailed description of the island's geography. Plato speaks clearly of a vast irrigated plain that 'stretched for three thousand furlongs [603 kilometres] in one direction, and at its centre, for two thousand [402 kilometres] inland from the coast'.[26] In the original Greek text the great plain's measurements are specified as 3,000 by 2,000 stadia (552 by 368 kilometres).

Beyond the plain to the north was an extensive mountain range 'that came right down to the sea', creating a 'precipitous coastline' that 'sheltered the city from cold northerly winds'.[27] The citadel itself was said to have been situated on the edge of the plain, apparently on the site of the 'mountain which was nowhere of any great altitude', where Euenor, the mortal ancestor of the kings of Atlantis, had previously lived in a cave with his wife and daughter.[28] Rivers and streams that began in the mountains were said to have flowed down into a fosse or trench that helped irrigate the fertile plain. At a distance of 50 furlongs (10 kilometres), or 50 stadia (9.2 kilometres) in the original account, from the outer edge of the final ring of water was a great circular wall that started and finished at the mouth of the deep canal which emptied into the sea.[29]

It does not take a genius to work out that these simple facts and figures convey the idea of a much smaller island than Plato would have us believe. Only the northerly placed mountains appear to divide Atlantis' rich fertile plain from its precipitous northern shoreline. No mention is made of the extent of this mountain range, although surely this cannot have covered an area of land equal to that proposed by Plato when he tells us that the island was the size of Libya and Asia combined. Even the mighty Himalayas of central Asia, although around 2,400 kilometres in length, are only between 160 and 240 kilometres in width. Atlantis' northerly placed mountain range cannot have been any wider than the Himalayas, implying that at its greatest extent the island was no more than 600 kilometres from north to south, and probably even smaller still. Indeed, if the mountain range really was only a few kilometres in thickness, it would suggest that Atlantis was no more than 400 or so kilometres from coast to coast.

Once again we must be careful not to take Plato's measurements too literally, as they are unlikely to preserve accurate dimensions carried across several millennia. Furthermore, there is every reason to believe that some, if not all, of the numbers recorded by Plato in connection with Atlantis possess some kind of symbolic or sacred value, derived most probably from Pythagorean philosophy. These points considered, the given measurements must be taken as at least an indication of the island's overall size.

Can Plato have been so negligent as to include two entirely different sets of reference in respect to the Atlantic island's overall size? I feel that we cannot ascribe such incompetence to arguably one of Athens' most celebrated writers, even if there are still discrepancies in the dates provided for the war between Athens and the Atlantean aggressor. So how are we able to reconcile these blatant contradictions in his Atlantis dialogues?

Having carefully reviewed the relevant passages, I feel that we are left with four possible options:

(i) Plato's Atlantis dialogues have been altered or changed, either accidentally or deliberately, by later copyists and translators of his works.

(ii) Plato inadvertently created confusion in his texts by featuring age-old lore that related not simply to one single island but to two or more inhabited Atlantic islands either visited or known to ancient mariners. These he haphazardly blended together to create the memory of one key island referred to by him under the name of Atlantis.

(iii) The description and dimensions of Atlantis as cited by Plato in the *Critias* are basically correct, and his statement alluding to the island being as large as Libya and Asia combined is somehow wrong.

(iv) The entire Atlantis account is pure fiction and in creating his imperfect Atlantean kingdom Plato did not intend its dimensions to be seen as anything other than meaningful symbolism derived most probably from Pythagorean philosophy.

The final solution cannot be dismissed, and yet it still implies that Plato was an incompetent writer who included facts and fancies in his dialogues without any care for consistency. The other three proposed solutions look far more promising and perhaps they should be reviewed not individually but together.

Kings of the Islands of Atlantis

It was the American author Ignatius Donnelly, the great nineteenth-century pioneer of Atlantean research, who first questioned the validity of Plato's statement about Atlantis being the size of Libya and Asia together. His version of the *Critias*, included for reference purposes at the beginning of *Atlantis: The Antediluvian World*, departs from the usual translation of the text when it comes to the size of the Atlantic island. In this we find the passage quoted as follows:

> . . . the combatants on the other side [of the war with Athens] were led by the kings of the islands of Atlantis, which, as I was saying, once had an *extent* greater than that of Libya and Asia; and, when afterward sunk by an earthquake, became an impassable barrier of mud to voyagers sailing from hence to the ocean [author's emphasis].[30]

Realising the obvious significance of this statement, I immediately made an attempt to track down the English translation of Plato's dialogues used by Donnelly for his own purposes. To this end I called on the assistance of Canadian Atlantis scholar Rand Flem-ath, co-author, with his wife Rose, of the 1995 book *When the Sky Fell: In Search of Atlantis*. He made enquiries on my behalf but was unable to identify the translation quoted by Donnelly. However, after consultation with Rand, we concluded that since it was popular in the nineteenth century for writers to make their own copies of classical texts, it is possible that Donnelly composed his English translation from an authentic Greek text available to him at the time.

Whether or not Donnelly's translation of the *Critias* is accurate remains to be seen. However, this new variation of the well-known quotation concerning Atlantis' immense size throws a completely new light on what Plato might have meant to convey by these words. Is it possible that he was attempting to tell us that the rulers of the Atlantic island, and indeed its 'other' islands, held sway over an *area* of the ocean *equal in size* to that of Libya and Asia? Certainly, it makes perfect sense of Donnelly's reference to the 'kings *of the islands* of Atlantis [author's emphasis]', for it confirms once again that the supposed Atlantean empire was not a single landmass but a *series* of islands.

Central to the whole story was one great island, orientated east–west, several hundred kilometres in length and dominated by a northerly mountain range that shielded an open plain to the south. Somewhere close to its southern shoreline was its hypothetical 'city', constructed on a raised plateau and symbolising the emergence point of the Atlantean dynasty. This island was the jewel of Atlantis.

Such a location is easy to imagine. It could fit the description of any one of a number of Atlantic islands. Yet did the Atlantis of Plato really exist, or was it simply a composite creation born out of the memory of two or more unknown islands situated in the Western Ocean? If it did exist, was it really home to a powerful maritime empire that was either destroyed by earthquakes and floods or forced to abandon its homeland following a series of terrible cataclysms?

CHAPTER V

ISLES OF THE BLEST

THE STORY OF THE RISE, fall and ultimate destruction of Atlantis appears only in the dialogues of Plato, and as we shall see shortly there seems to be no other ancient source that describes this same island empire. It is an unfortunate situation frequently highlighted by detractors of the Atlantis legend, and since the very beginning they have been in good company, for it was Aristotle, Plato's own rational-thinking pupil, who first derided the story for its obvious absurdity. In his opinion, 'Its inventor caused it to disappear'.[1] In other words, it was inconceivable that Plato could ever have believed that his readership would be fooled by such ludicrous fiction.

In addition to this rather disconcerting situation, we know that the subject of Atlantis was openly debated during the third century AD among the philosophers in the Platonic Academy attached to the famous library and university at Alexandria. This fact is recorded in the writings of Proclus (AD 412–485), a Greek Neo-Platonic scholar and commentator on Plato's *Timaeus*.[2] As Russian scholar Nikolai Zhirov was forced to admit: '. . . the Academy did not have [at its disposal] the pertinent documents' to resolve the matter one way or another.[3]

Before its tragic destruction by fire at the hands of, initially, Julius Caesar in 48 BC and then later by mobs loyal to the Christian fanatic Bishop Cyril in AD 391, the library at Alexandria was estimated to have housed some 490,000 individual items.[4] Among these must have been many thousands of manuscripts that are now lost to the world. Yet to consider that it contained nothing whatsoever that might have validated Plato's story is worrying to say the least. If he were the only source for this tradition, we would be on uneasy ground supporting the case for a historical Atlantis.

To take the matter further it will be necessary to review what other classical writers have had to say about legendary islands of the Western Ocean. Although none of these early sources ever uses the name Atlantis in the same manner as Plato employs it, they do offer a glimpse of very similar island paradises, some of which may well have links with Plato's own Atlantic island.

Hanno's Journey

We begin our investigations by examining a maritime journey made down the west coast of Africa by a Carthaginian general and navigator named Hanno, sometime around *c.* 425 BC. An account of this event was supposedly recorded in the temple of Saturn (actually Baal-Hammon) at his home port of Carthage.[5] Although the original work is now lost, a version of the text was mercifully preserved in Greek.[6]

With a reported fleet of 60 ships, called 'penteconters', loaded with '30,000' crewmen, Hanno began exploring the north-west coast of Africa. Almost immediately he founded a temple to 'Poseidon' on a 'Libyan promontory covered with trees'.[7] Afterwards, he is said to have encountered a great lake full of 'tall reeds, where elephants and many other wild animals fed', making us recall Plato's words regarding the elephants supposedly found on Atlantis.[8] His fleet sailed on, founding a total of five cities before it came to a river named Lixos, generally taken to be the river Draa, which borders the region between Morocco and the Western, or Spanish, Sahara.[9] Here a race called the Lixitae 'pastured their flocks'.[10] These peoples are identified by scholars as the so-called Berber tribes that inhabit the region to this day.[11]

Hanno hired interpreters from among the Lixitae, who were, it seems, already familiar with the topographical features witnessed by Hanno on his long voyage. Moreover, they could also communicate with other tribes encountered along the way, strongly hinting that the Lixitae were themselves mariners, or that they were employed regularly as pilots and interpreters by Phoenician and Carthaginian sea-captains.

Hanno explored inland and there encountered 'inhospitable Ethiopians [i.e. native Africans] in a land ridden with wild beasts and hemmed in by great mountains'.[12] Among these sprang the source of the Lixos, and here, too, lived a race of troglodytes 'of strange appearance', whom the Lixitae said were able to 'run more swiftly than horses'.[13] It is clear that they were in fact exploring the western extremities of what are today the Atlas Mountains, which formed part of the ancient kingdom of Mauritania.

Leaving behind this region, they sailed south for two days and then eastwards for another day. It is at this point that they came upon a small island at the 'farther end of a gulf'; said to have had a circumference of just five stadia (920 metres).[14] Here they established a settlement, which they called Cerne (as previously mentioned, the Phoenicians and Carthaginians made a point of founding ports on small offshore islands). All Hanno tells us about this island is that it lay 'directly opposite Carthage, for a voyage from Carthage to the Pillars and from there to Cerne seemed alike'.[15] The Carthaginian general is said to have then taken an exploratory party 'up a big river called Chretes', until it reached a lake 'in which were three islands bigger than Cerne'.[16] After exploring another great river (seemingly located beyond the lake), 'teeming with crocodiles and hippopotamuses', they returned to Cerne, before continuing the journey southwards for another 14 days and entering 'an immense gulf'.[17] Here they encountered further islands, smoking volcanoes, lava flows, scorching heat and primitive peoples,[18] before the fleet eventually turned for home after exhausting its supplies.[19]

Piecing together Hanno's exact journey is beyond the scope of this book. Some scholars have suggested that he reached as far as Sierra Leone.[20] Others say that he entered the Gulf of Guinea and travelled eastwards as far as the Cameroons, or even Gabon.[21] Nobody really knows. The only island location mentioned in Hanno's account that historians have attempted to pinpoint with any degree of accuracy is the settlement of Cerne. Donald Harden, who has made a special study of Phoenician and Carthaginian voyages beyond the Pillars of Hercules,[22] felt Cerne must be 'an island, not exactly identified, near the Senegal delta'.[23]

Other scholars have placed Cerne further north, identifying it with either Herne Island, which lies on the southern edge of the Western Sahara, or Arguin Island, located about 320 kilometres further south.[24] Hanno himself said that Cerne was located at the same distance from the Pillars of Hercules as the Pillars themselves were from Carthage.[25] If this distance is loosely projected out from the Strait of Gibraltar, it brings us not to Senegal but to somewhere in the vicinity of the Western Sahara, which suggests that Herne Island was the original settlement of Cerne. Yet as Harden conceded in proposing the mouth of the Senegal as the true location of Cerne: 'It looks as if we must abandon Hanno's distances.'[26] Support for this theory comes from the writings of Pseudo-Scylax, which date to the mid-fourth century BC. He recorded that at Cerne 'the traders here are Phoenicians. When they arrive at the island of Cerne, they anchor their cargo-boats, and pitch tents for themselves on Cerne. Then they unload and ferry their merchandise in small boats to the mainland. They are Ethiopians on the mainland; and it is with these Ethiopians that they trade . . . They have also a great city, to which the Phoenician merchants sail.'[27]

We must also not forget that Pseudo-Scylax spoke of Cerne Island as lying at a distance of 12 days' sail from the Pillars of

Hercules.[28] He further recorded that the 'parts beyond the isle of Cerne are no longer navigable because of shoals, mud, and seaweed',[29] a tentative reference to the Sargasso Sea. Since we know that this same shallow sea was said to have marked the site of lost Atlantis, might Cerne have been confused with the memory of Plato's Atlantic island? Is it possible that stories concerning the existence of Cerne, as a prosperous island settlement that lay beyond the Pillars of Hercules, could have reached the Mediterranean world and influenced Plato's composition of the Atlantis account? It is a matter dealt with in Chapter Twelve.

Pseudo-Aristotle

We move on now to the writings left to us by Pseudo-Aristotle. This imposter of the famous Greek philosopher, who is thought to have been one of his own pupils, wrote a work entitled *On Marvellous Things Heard, c.* 300 BC. His text is important in that it speaks of a 'desert island' situated 'in the sea outside the Pillars of Heracles'. It is said to have been discovered by Carthaginians who 'frequented it often owing to its prosperity',[30] and spoke of it as just 'a few days' voyage away'.[31] Some Carthaginians are 'even [said to have] lived there', for here was 'wood of all kinds' as well as '*navigable* rivers [author's emphasis]' and 'all other kinds of fruits'.[32] Any non-Carthaginian who ventured within sight of this island was caught and put to death. Moreover, its inhabitants were likewise massacred so that they 'might not tell the story, and that a crowd might not resort to the island . . . and take away the prosperity of the Carthaginians'.[33]

No idea of the island's location is given in the account, although it would appear to have been within easy reach of the Pillars of Hercules. Most probably it was Madeira, the larger of the two main islands that make up the Madeiras (even though they were found to be uninhabited when discovered by the Portuguese in 1427). This island group is certainly mountainous and rich in vegetation and forests and was known about in ancient times. Pliny the Elder (AD 23–79), the celebrated Roman naturalist, seems to refer to them as the *Purpurariae*, the Purple Isles, after the manufactory of purple dyes said to have been established there by King Juba II (died *c.* AD 18) of Mauritania.[34]

Due also to its mild climate, Madeira produces a variety of different fruits that are especially prized in the European spring market. The only thing that prevents us from properly identifying Madeira as Pseudo-Aristotle's 'desert island' is its lack of navigable rivers. Indeed, if it were not for its extensive system of post-Conquest irrigation channels, which enable highland water to flow down into the valleys below, Madeira would be a virtual desert.

I would not be the first person to pick up on this glaring anomaly in Pseudo-Aristotle's account. The American historian Cyrus H. Gordon similarly reviewed the evidence of Carthaginian contact with this Atlantic island and concluded: 'The element of navigable rivers is significant because west of Africa there are no navigable rivers until Haiti, Cuba, and the American mainland.'[35]

Could it be possible that, in addition to the island of Madeira, the author of the work was alluding to another Atlantic island, plausibly one that really did possess navigable rivers and a native population? Yet in accepting this proposition we have to conclude that Pseudo-Aristotle was recalling one of the islands in the West Indies, perhaps Cuba or Hispaniola, both of which possess navigable rivers.

Pseudo-Aristotle goes on to speak of an Atlantic journey made by Iberic-Phoenician sailors from Gades.[36] They are said to have travelled for four days with an east wind behind them until they reached 'desert' islands full of 'brushes and seaweed'.[37] Here they were able to catch 'a quantity of tuna of incredible size and weight'.[38] On being brought ashore, the fish were pickled and jarred and taken to Carthage, where they were consumed by the inhabitants and not exported to other countries.[39] Once again, this appears to be a reference to Madeira, where tuna were found in great abundance until comparatively recent times.

Diodorus Siculus

One of the best known of the Greek historians is Diodorus Siculus, or Diodorus of Sicily (*c.* 8 BC). He was the author of an extensive and partially extant work known as *Bibliotheca Historica*, the *Library of History*. Originally it consisted of some 40 books, although today only 15 of these survive, some merely as fragments. Their pages feature the legendary history of many countries of the ancient world, including Libya, Egypt, Persia, Syria, Media, Greece, Rome and Carthage. Diodorus was unquestionably a very learned man, familiar with many other classical writings – a fact that might well have influenced his apparent knowledge of Atlantic islands which lay beyond the Pillars of Hercules.

Beginning with Book III of his *Library*, we find Diodorus writing about a race of fierce women known as Amazons. They are said to have been warlike and to have lived at the very edge of the inhabited world, somewhere 'in the western parts of Libya'.[40] Accordingly, their homeland was an island called Hespera that lay in the 'marsh Tritonis', identified as an ancient salt lake connected with the Lesser Syrtis, modern Sebkah-el Farauun, in what is today the Northern Sahara. Marsh, or Lake, Tritonis is said to have gained its name from 'a certain river Triton which emptied into it'.[41] The island itself was said to be of 'great size' with 'fruit-bearing trees of every kind'.[42]

Having subdued the peoples that inhabited the country around Marsh Tritonis, the Amazons moved against other nations, the first of whom were the Atlantioi, who were said to have been the 'most civilised men among the inhabitants of those regions'.[43] They 'dealt in a prosperous country and possessed great cities', among which 'mythology places the birth of the gods'.[44] These Atlantioi were said to inhabit 'the regions which lie along the shore of the ocean'.[45]

The Atlantioi appear to be synonymous with another race known as the Atlantes, the people of Atlas, who were referred to four centuries earlier by Herodotus in his *History*.[46] He claimed that they lived in the Western Sahara, did not eat any living thing and never experienced dreams.[47] Clearly the Atlantioi of Diodorus were likewise the indigenous peoples of this same region. Yet now, some 400 years later, these sons of Atlas were seen as the 'most civilised men among the inhabitants of those regions'.[48]

Myrina, the queen of the Amazons, then gathered together 30,000 foot soldiers and 3,000 cavalry and marched into the city of Cerne where, in a pitched battle, she defeated the Atlantioi.[49] In order that they might continue their existence, the fallen race offered to do anything for Myrina.[50] The Amazon leader acted honourably, and on the site of the former city of Cerne she built another that bore her name. The peoples of Cerne lived on, and yet from time to time their territories were invaded by a terrible race known as the Gorgons that resided on the borders of their lands (presumably from the mythical Atlantic islands known as the Gorgades – see Chapter Six). Myrina was asked to intervene on behalf of the Atlantioi to rid them of this enemy. This she did, going against the Gorgons and quickly 'gaining the upper hand'.[51] Myrina and her fellow warriors promptly seized 3,000 prisoners and tried to burn out the rest.[52] Yet in this pursuit ultimately she failed and was forced to retreat. The Gorgons were defeated eventually by the hero Perseus, a son of Zeus, during his own travels through the kingdom of Mauritania.[53]

Diodorus also informs us that Marsh Tritonis 'disappeared from sight in the course of an earthquake, when those parts of it which lay towards the ocean were torn asunder'.[54] Afterwards, he mentions once again the Atlantioi and suggests that 'it will not be inappropriate in this place to recount what their myths relate about the genesis of the gods'.[55]

This is the second time that Diodorus alludes to the genesis of the gods in connection with the Atlantioi, for in an earlier passage he tells us they possessed 'great cities', among which 'mythology places the birth of the gods'.[56] Remember, he is including in this list the Carthaginian settlement of Cerne. Furthermore, why should he place the birth of the gods in the Far West – on the very edge of the known world? Does this hint at the former existence of a much earlier civilisation somewhere in the vicinity of the ancient kingdom of Mauritania, where localised forms of the god Poseidon, his son Triton, the goddess Athena and the hero-god Atlas were venerated long before the advent of the classical age? More important, might the Atlantioi, or the Atlantes, and their city of Cerne have some bearing on Plato's Atlantis narrative?

The Atlantides

Diodorus goes on to present us with an account of the history of the gods. He says that following the death of Hyperion, one of the mythical Titans, the world was divided into portions and shared among the sons of Ouranus. Of these, the most renowned were Cronus and Atlas, who received the regions bordering the ocean. It was in his memory that the inhabitants of this country were known as the Atlantioi and Mount Atlas bore his name.[57] He tells us also that Atlas was gifted in the art of 'astrology and was the first to present to mankind the doctrine of the sphere', for which reason he is said to have supported the vault of heaven on his shoulders (in some accounts this was his punishment for the part he played in the wars between the Titans and the gods of Olympus).[58]

Diodorus also provides the reader with an account of the Atlantides, the seven daughters fathered by Atlas. They are said to have lain with the most renowned gods and heroes, because of which they became the first ancestors of the 'larger part' of the human race, by whom they achieved 'immortal honour', and 'were enthroned in the heavens and endowed with the appellation of Pleiades'.[59]

The story of the seven Atlantides is also found in the writings of a much earlier Greek historian named Hellanicus of Lesbos (died *c.* 411 BC). He composed a work intriguingly entitled *Atlantis*, which sets out the genealogy of the Atlantides. Despite its compelling title, this *Atlantis* had nothing whatsoever to do with the Atlantis of Plato's dialogues. Here it denoted only the 'daughters of Atlas'. Hellanicus' work records that the mother of the seven daughters fathered by Atlas was Pleione, one of the Oceanides (Diodorus gives her name as Hesperis – see Chapter Six). Poseidon, the god of the sea, mated with two of them. One of them, named Celaeno, gave birth to a son named Lycus, whom the sea-god made to live in the 'Isles of the Blest'.[60]

Even though Diodorus tells us that the Atlantides were born at Cyllene in Arcadia, their associations with both the star constellation of the Pleiades and the 'Isles of the Blest' is our first indication that their story might hold a significance beyond that implied by these basic mythological concepts. We know, for instance, that the name Pleiades is derived from a Greek word meaning 'to sail', because 'that constellation shows the time most favourable to navigators, which is in the spring'.[61] Add to this Diodorus' assertion that Atlas was the first 'to present to mankind the doctrine of the sphere', and it would appear that we might well be dealing with some kind of arcane maritime knowledge preserved in mythological form.

Identifying the true location of the Isles of the Blest, or the Fortunate Isles, is a tricky business, since there are no hard-and-fast answers. They were thought to be a group of otherworldly islands that lay in the Far West.[62] The concept of a blessed isle, or indeed isles, situated on the edge of the known world, where the dead are received in the afterlife, is age old. It is found in Egyptian myth; it is also present in Sumerian myth, and it formed part of the religion of the Minoan peoples of Crete, after whom some believe the Greeks adopted the idea.[63] Before it became widely known that islands lay outside the Pillars of Hercules, most Mediterranean cultures were happy to place their blessed isles merely beyond the western horizon. For instance, Diodorus asserted that the island of Lesbos was 'blessed',[64] while Pliny the Elder stated that Crete was likewise an 'Island of the Blest'.[65]

On his discovery of the Canary Isles at the end of the first century BC, the Mauritanian king Juba II believed that he had at last found the true Blessed Isles.[66] His announcement to this effect caught the popular imagination of the classical world, and thereafter these legendary islands became associated with the Canaries.

Book V

These are thought-provoking considerations as we move from Book III to Book V of Diodorus' *Library*, in which he informs the reader that what he is now about to deliver is 'an account of those [islands] *which are in the ocean* [author's emphasis]', implying that those mentioned previously were still considered to be part of the ancient world.[67] He begins by noting the existence of a 'fruitful' island of 'considerable' size that lay 'a number of days'' sail to the west of Libya. It was mountainous, possessed a 'plain of surpassing beauty' as well as 'navigable rivers' that were used for irrigation. Here were to be found 'parks planted with trees of every variety and gardens in great multitudes', traversed by 'streams of sweet water'.[68] Here, too, were 'private villas', along with 'banqueting houses' in settings of flowers as well as excellent hunting for 'beast and wild animal'.[69] The climate on the island was mild all the year round, enabling it to produce an abundance of fruit – a virtue that made it seem like a 'dwelling-place of a race of gods and not of men'.[70]

In this description of a mountainous Atlantic isle with a fertile plain and a sophisticated ancient society, we are nearing Plato's description of lost Atlantis. Yet it really does seem as if Diodorus borrowed at least part of this account from Pseudo-Aristotle. As we have seen, in his work *On Marvellous Things Heard* he spoke of a 'desert' island colonised by Carthaginians that lay just a 'few days' voyage' beyond the Pillars of Hercules. It was said to possess 'wood of all kinds', 'navigable rivers', and 'all other kinds of fruits'.[71]

Diodorus next recounts the story of how Phoenician mariners, while sailing along the shores of Africa, were driven off course by strong winds 'a great distance out into the ocean'. After being 'storm-tossed for many days', they were put ashore on 'the island we mentioned above',[72] i.e. the one with 'navigable rivers' already described. As a consequence of the island's 'felicity and nature', the 'Phoenicians [of Gades] . . . caused it to be known to all men'.[73] This great announcement apparently prompted the Tyrrhenians, the people of Etruria, or Tuscany, as masters of the sea, to dispatch ships to colonise the island. However, the Carthaginians called a halt to this plan since they wished to keep the island for themselves, due both to its excellence and because it could be used as a refuge should a disaster ever befall Carthage.[74]

Since the Iberic-Phoenician sailors of this story were journeying along the West African coast when they were blown off course, it really does seem that the island alluded to in both accounts preserved by Diodorus is Madeira, a conclusion also drawn by Donald Harden.[75] Yet still we have the problem of 'navigable' rivers. None are to be found on any island between Africa and the Caribbean, suggesting that, like Pseudo-Aristotle before him, Diodorus combined together traditions concerning two or more Atlantic islands. One of these was, very possibly, Madeira. The other one, with 'navigable' rivers, if it existed independently, can only have been one of the islands of the West Indies.

The Lives of Plutarch

We move on now to Plutarch (AD 50–120), the noted Greek moralist and biographer. Among the wealth of material in his monumental work entitled *Lives* is an intriguing story concerning a Roman general named Sertorius who, while governor of Iberia between 80 and 72 BC, learned of the accidental discovery of two Atlantic islands. This information came from two Iberic-Phoenician sailors who had just returned to Gades. Apparently, their vessel had been blown off course by northerly and easterly winds until finally they had come across them.[76]

The two islands, seen as the Fortunate Isles, were 'separated only by a narrow channel'.[77] Furthermore, 'rain seldom falls there, and when it does, it falls moderately: but they [the islands] generally have soft breezes, which scatter such rich dews'.[78] In addition to this, Plutarch asserts 'that the soil is not only good for sowing and planting, but spontaneously produces the most excellent fruits, and those in such abundance, that the inhabitants have nothing more to do than to indulge themselves in the enjoyment of ease'.[79]

The seasonal changes are described as an 'insensible transition into each other'. More curiously, Plutarch also states that 'it is generally believed, even among the barbarians, that these are the Elysian Fields, and the seats of the blessed, which Homer has described in the charms of verse'.[80]

The islands' mild climate and abundant fruit seems to be the hallmark of so many of the Atlantic paradises discovered either by Phoenician or Carthaginian mariners. Yet this time we have a quite specific distance connected with the story, for the islands mentioned by Plutarch are said to have lain 400 leagues (1,920 kilometres) from the African coast.[81] If we assume that the Phoenician vessel began its journey from Gades, it might be proposed that the islands discovered were members of the Azores group, rediscovered by the Portuguese in 1427. This theory is strengthened in the knowledge that these islands are located approximately 1,850 kilometres to the west of Spain, just slightly less than the distance provided by Plutarch. Certainly, the Azores have a mild climate, and evidence of a Carthaginian presence on the islands came with the discovery on Corvo in 1749 of a broken black clay vase containing a caked mass of coins, minted either in Carthage or in the Greek North African colony of Cyrene during the fourth and third centuries BC.[82]

Whatever the identity of the two islands in the Life of Sertorius we find that, in addition to being designated the Isles of the Blest, they were also equated with the so-called Elysian Fields, otherwise known as Elysium. In classical tradition, this otherworldly realm was said to have been an island that lay in the Far West. Tradition asserts that it was covered with never-ending green bowers, as well as 'delightful meadows with pleasant streams'.[83] Here, too, the air was always 'wholesome, serene and temperate', while 'the birds continually warbled in the groves, and the inhabitants were blessed with another sun and other stars'.[84] According to some classical writers, Elysium was also considered to be one of the Fortunate Isles.[85] As with the other paradisical isles of the Atlantic, traditions surrounding the Elysian Fields seem to be of Phoenician origin. Although Greek historians have long considered that Elysium means 'coming', as in a place to which the pious come, the name is now thought to derive from a Semitic root meaning 'field of El', with El being the principal god of the Phoenicians.[86]

So far we have found that several writers of the classical age refer specifically to ancient contact, usually by Iberic-Phoenician and Carthaginian sailors, with Atlantic island groups that lay within relatively easy reach of the Pillars of Hercules. With names such as Cerne, Elysium, the Fortunate Isles and the Isles of the Blest, these accounts point to a basic knowledge of the Madeiras, the Canaries and even the Azores.

We can also say that certain elements among the many tales of Atlantic islands preserved by the classical writers so far cited do not conform with the geography, topography and location of the various archipelagos on the eastern Atlantic seaboard. This is especially so of the Atlantic islands with 'navigable rivers' mentioned by Pseudo-Aristotle and Diodorus Siculus, making us recall Cyrus Gordon's statement that 'west of Africa there are no navigable rivers until Haiti, Cuba, and the American mainland'.[87]

Could it be possible that both accounts preserve a knowledge gained from Atlantic voyagers of one of more of the principal islands of the West Indies? In the next chapter we shall see that a memory of ancient voyages to islands on the western Atlantic seaboard would also appear to have been preserved by key geographical writers of the Roman period.

CHAPTER VI

FORTY DAYS' SAIL

GAIUS PLINIUS SECUNDUS WAS A noted Roman naturalist of the first century AD, better remembered under the name Pliny the Elder. In a 37-volume work entitled *Natural History*, he included sections on everything from the stars, the heavens and the winds, to all manner of other aspects of nature such as rain, hail, minerals, trees, flowers and plants. In addition to this wealth of material, his books contained a detailed knowledge of ancient geography. Moreover, like Diodorus Siculus before him, Pliny the Elder had much to say about legendary islands of the Western Ocean. We also know that he was fully acquainted with Plato's Atlantis narrative, for he accepted without question that 'cases of land [were] entirely stolen away by the sea', including '. . . [if we accept Plato's story] the vast area covered by the Atlantic'.[1]

Among the Atlantic locations recorded by Pliny were 'a number of islands opposite to Celtiberia [i.e. Spain]', called by the Greeks the *Cassiterides*.[2] This was unquestionably a reference to either the Isles of Scilly off Cornwall, or the British Isles as a whole, exploited by the Phoenicians and Carthaginians for their rich resources of tin.

Pliny also spoke of 'six islands of the Gods' that face the *Arrotrebarum promunturi*, and which are known as the 'Isles of Bliss [*insulae . . . Fortunatas*]'.[3] According to other ancient writers, these lay west of Mauritania, and are unquestionably to be identified with the Canary Isles.[4] Juba II himself managed to discover only six out of seven of the islands, and so this became the standard figure connected with the archipelago.

Pliny also informs us that aside from the Fortunate Isles, there is another island 'off Mount Atlas'. Its name, he says, is 'Atlantis'.[5] Yes, *Atlantis*. He gives no details whatsoever about it, and states simply:

> From which [i.e. Atlantis] a two days' voyage along the coast reaches the desert district in the neighbourhood of the Western Ethiopians [*Aethiopas Hesperio*] and the cape mentioned above named the Horn of the West [*Hesperu Ceras*], the point at which the coastline begins to curve westward in the direction of the Atlantic. Opposite this cape also there are reported to be some islands, the Gorgades, which were formerly the habitation of the Gorgons, and which according to the account of Xenophon of Lampsacus are at a distance of two days' sail from the mainland. These islands were reached by the Carthaginian general Hanno . . . Outside the Gorgades there are also said to be two Islands of the Ladies of the West [*duae Hesperidum insulae*, i.e. the islands of the Hesperides].[6]

As can be determined from any detailed map of Africa, the only islands that lie in the vicinity of the Atlas Mountains are the Canaries group, which seem to be synonymous with the 'Isles of Bliss'. Yet Pliny now informs us that one island 'off Mount Atlas' actually went by the name of *Atlantis*. So exactly *where* was Pliny's Atlantis?

Unfortunately there is not enough information for us to draw any clear conclusions. Pliny fails to tell us how large it is, how far the island is from the shore, or whether it is part of an island group. The only slight clue is his statement that from it a 'two days' voyage along the coast reaches the desert district in the neighbourhood of the Western Ethiopians' and the promontory *Hesperu Ceras*. Since the journey Pliny describes is clearly an anticlockwise circumnavigation of the West African coast, in the manner of Hanno, it is likely that he is alluding to one of the small coastal islands. These might include Harden's Cerne Island in the mouth of the Senegal river, or perhaps Herne Island or Arguin Island, which have also been proposed as sites for the Phoenician or Carthaginian settlement of Cerne.

Islands of the Gorgons

Attempting to identify the other locations referred to in the above passage quoted from Pliny's *Natural History* will now lead us into a minefield of possibilities. He says that somewhere in the vicinity of the desert are the 'Western Ethiopians' and beyond that a place known as *Hesperu Ceras*, generally translated as 'Horn of the West'. Pliny specifically refers to it as a 'cape', even though the term 'horn' was anciently taken to mean a gulf. This fact has led geographers to assume that the Horn of the West was a large bay in the vicinity of either the Gambia or Sierra Leone. Yet bays are not capes and, as we shall see, *Hesperu Ceras* is almost certainly to be identified with the jutting headland named Cape Verde, near

Dakar, in Senegal. If a mariner voyages south along the West African coast he passes Mount Atlas on his port side. After this there is very little until the shoreline begins to curve out towards Cape Verde, the westernmost tip of Africa, which obviously made it an important point of reference for ancient navigators.

Pliny states that 'opposite' *Hesperu Ceras* were the Gorgades, the islands of the Gorgons. Paul T. Keyser, a classical historian at the University of Alberta, has tentatively identified the Gorgades as either the Bissagos Islands, south of the Gambia river, or the Sherbro Isles, in Sierra Leone.[7] Yet in my opinion they are more likely to have been the Cape Verde Islands, which are located some 640 kilometres west-north-west of Cape Verde. Even though there is no evidence of contact with this island group before its rediscovery in 1460, this solution is by no means new. In 1563 the Portuguese historian Antonio Galvão wrote in his *The Discoveries of the World from their first originall unto the yeere of our Lord 1555* that the Cape Verde Isles were anciently known as the Dorcades, Hesperides and the Gorgades.[8] Dorcades is probably just a corruption of Gorgades, while the reference to the Hesperides is, as we shall see shortly, completely erroneous.

In 1587 the English geographer and writer Richard Hakluyt produced a map that illustrated the work of the early Spanish chronicler Peter Martyr d'Anghiera, who wrote at the beginning of the sixteenth century. On this chart the Cape Verdes are marked both as the 'Gorgades vel Medusiae' and, once again, the Hesperides.[9] Since the words of Pliny the Elder make it extremely unlikely that the Cape Verdes are the Hesperides, Galvão and Hakluyt's identification of this island group as the Gorgades is very important, as the so-called Mecia de Viladestes map of 1413 shows, lying off the coast of Africa at a latitude consistent with Cape Verde, a pair of elongated islands marked with the legend 'les jles de gades se oseiruen asi p salario hi p ysidolu' ('the islands of Gades are observed here according to Salario and Isidore [of Seville]').[10] The name Gades is so similar to Gorgades that this cannot be coincidence, showing that the island group was anciently thought to have been located at a position corresponding to the Cape Verdes. This connection between the 'jles de gades' and the Cape Verdes was noted by the cartographical scholar Armando Cortesão in 1954.[11]

The 'Salario' mentioned in the inscription on the Mecia de Viladestes map is the lesser-known Roman grammarian, historian and geographer named Caius Julius Solinus,[12] who lived in the first century AD. His works are said to have had a great influence on Isidore of Seville, or Isidorus Hispalensis, a Spanish bishop of Seville who died in AD 636. He was the author of several books on worldly matters, including an encyclopaedia of the arts and sciences entitled *Origines*. What all of this implies is that knowledge of the 'jles de gades', in other words the Gorgades and very possibly the Cape Verdes, came via an interpretation of Solinus' works by Isidore of Seville during the seventh century.

Garden of Delight

Yet if Pliny really was alluding to the Cape Verde Islands when he spoke of the Gorgades, why should he go on to state that beyond these 'are also said to be two Islands of the Lady of the West [*duae Hesperidum insulae*, i.e. the two Hesperides]'? The origin of the Hesperides as islands is very important and needs to be examined in some detail. They take their name from the Greek root *hesper*, or *vesper*, meaning 'setting sun', indicating very clearly the direction in which they were thought to lie.[13] The islands of the Hesperides were seen as the residence of celebrated nymphs (three, four or even seven in number) of this name whom Diodorus saw as synonymous with the seven Atlantides, through their mother Hesperis.[14] According to legend, the Hesperides were appointed to guard the beautiful golden apples that Hera entrusted into the care of Zeus. These were kept in a garden of delight that abounded in the most wonderful fruits of every kind, but which was guarded by a fearsome dragon that never slept. It was the Greek hero Hercules who was finally able to steal these golden apples as the penultimate of his 12 labours.

In one version of the story, Hercules went to Africa and demanded from Atlas three of the golden apples. Accepting the challenge, the giant unloaded on to Hercules his burden of supporting the heavens on his shoulders. Atlas then set off for the Hesperides and returned with the divine fruit. Hercules then tricked the giant into taking back the burden and promptly stole the golden apples, which had been cast to the ground. In another version, Hercules himself goes in search of the golden apples. On arriving in the Hesperides, he mortally wounds the dragon and steals away the precious fruit. Since the only place in which they could be preserved was the Hesperides, the goddess Athena returned the fruit to the garden.

The story of the golden apples is a myth integrally linked with both the western limits of the known world and the outer ocean. It brings together Hercules, whose name is attached to the entrance to the Atlantic; Atlas, whose petrified form was seen as the mountain that bears his name in Mauritania, and the Hesperides themselves, which were both nymphs of great distinction *and* islands situated in the Atlantic Ocean. The image of abundant fruits and a verdant paradisical garden located on the Hesperides brings to mind the verdant islands described in a similar manner by classical writers such as Pseudo-Aristotle and Diodorus Siculus. Were these Greek legends based on ancient memories of distant islands reached in antiquity?

Curiously enough, Hercules' tenth labour – the one prior to stealing the golden apples – had been to kill the monster Geryon, king of Gades, and steal his precious cattle. Gades, as we know, was a Phoenician city-port in south-west Spain, from which Iberic-Phoenician vessels sailed on their voyages of discovery to unknown Atlantic islands.

Did this show some kind of connection between Gades, Mount Atlas, Atlantic islands and Phoenician mariners? Might they have been responsible for introducing these stories to the Mediterranean world?

That the islands of the Hesperides lay in the Atlantic Ocean does not seem to have been in doubt. The Greek poet Hesiod, who lived in the eighth century BC, spoke of the 'clear-voiced Hesperides' that lay 'beyond the famous ocean',[15] while Apollodorus, the Athenian grammarian of the second century BC, saw them as located in the proximity of the Atlas Mountains of Mauritania.[16] As we also saw in Chapter Two, in the twelfth century Honorius of Autun wrote that the 'curdled sea', apparently a reference to the Sargasso Sea, 'adjoins the Hesperides and covers the site of lost Atlantis, which lay west from Gibraltar'.[17]

Secret Recesses of the Sea

Returning to Pliny, we learn that the two islands of the Hesperides lay *even further out* in the ocean than the Gorgades. Yet beyond the Cape Verde Isles is only open sea and the pull of the North Equatorial Current, which will carry a vessel directly to the West Indies. Since we know that the Hesperides take their name from the linguistic root *hesper*, or *vesper*, meaning 'setting sun', we can be sure that they were thought to be located in the Far West, *beyond* the ocean river.

I am not alone in realising the significance of the Gorgades and their geographical relationship to the islands of the Hesperides. In his 1962 book *Land to the West: St Brendan's Voyage to America,* historical writer Geoffrey Ashe noted:

> Martianus Capella, who practised law at Carthage in the fifth century, was the author of a philosophical work in which – besides affirming the Earth to be round [like Plato before him] – he repeated Pliny's statements about the three groups of Atlantic islands, but with the unexpected addition that the Hesperides lie beyond the Gorgades 'in the most secret recesses of the sea' . . . This rearrangement of Pliny's island-groups into a chain stretching away from

> Africa – to Madeira? to the Azores? – becomes still more explicit in Dicuil [Irish monk and writer of *c.* AD 800], who says that the Gorgades are farther out than the Canaries and . . . the Hesperides are farther out than the Gorgades.[18]

The Azores are located directly in the path of the Gulf Stream, some 1,850 kilometres west of the Portuguese coast. This powerful ocean current comes in from the west, then passes around the island group on an easterly course before heading off in the direction of first the Madeiras and then the Canary Isles. The Azores seem a most unlikely candidate for the Gorgades, and in this knowledge I feel justified in identifying them with the Cape Verde Islands. Yet where, then, were these 'most secret recesses of the sea', where Martianus Capella says the Hesperides could be found? Were they on the other side of the Atlantic Ocean, among the West Indies perhaps? I would not be the first to draw this conclusion, not by a long way.

The Authority of Statius Sebosus

Searching further I came across the claims of Statius Sebosus, a Roman geographical writer who lived *c.* 50 BC, and thus was a contemporary of Diodorus Siculus. He composed a book called *Periplus,* which is no longer extant, as well as another work entitled the *Wonders of India.* According to Ferdinand Columbus, the son and biographer of Christopher Columbus, Sebosus stated that 'certain islands called the Hesperides were *forty days' sail* west of the Gorgonas Islands [author's emphasis]'.[19] Columbus points out this fact in order to show the 'tall tales' that the Spanish traveller and historian Gonzalo Fernándaz de Oviedo y Valdéz (1478–1557) 'spins' in his work *Historia general y natural de las Indias* of 1535. It seems certain that this important statement regarding the sailing time between the Gorgades and the Hesperides was derived from the writings of Pliny, who quotes Sebosus as an authority on Atlantic geography. The passage in question appears in Book VI of his *Natural History,* and in fact follows directly after the reference to the two islands of the Hesperides which are said to lie beyond the Gorgades, information that was also supplied by Sebosus. According to the English translation of Pliny, made by H. Rackham and published as part of the Loeb series in 1938, it reads:

> . . . and the whole of the geography of this neighbourhood is so uncertain that Statius Sebosus has given the voyage along the coast from the Gorgons' Islands past Mount Atlas to the Isles of the Ladies of the West [i.e. the Hesperides] as forty days' sail and from

> those islands to the Horn of the West as one day's sail.[20]

If I am correct in proposing that the Hesperides were perhaps islands of the Caribbean, while the Gorgades were the Cape Verde Isles, this passage makes very little sense. A mariner could not possibly have passed Mount Atlas on his way from the Cape Verdes to the West Indies, while the journey time between the Hesperides and the 'Horn of the West', most probably Cape Verde in Senegal, would not have been one day's sail. Something had to be wrong, especially as Oviedo clearly believed that the Hesperides lay 40 days' sail 'west' of the Gorgades and were synonymous with the islands of the West Indies.

First, I turned to another summary of Oviedo's assessment of Sebosus' Atlantic sailing times: those found in Antonio Galvão's *The Discoveries of the World*, first published in 1563. Here it states:

> In the 650th yeare after the flood there was a king in Spaine named Hesperus, who in his time as it is reported went and discovered as far as Cape Verde, and the Island of S. Thomas, whereof he was prince: And Gonsalao Fernandes of Oviedo the Chronicler of Antiquities affirmeth, that in his time the Islands of the West Indies were discovered, and called somewhat after his name Hesperides: and he alleageth many reasons to prove it, reporting particularly that in 40 daies they sailed from Cape Verde unto those Islands.[21]

The legend concerning the Spanish king named Hesperus has no precedent and seems to be an Iberian variation of the Greek myth surrounding Hesperus, the father of Hesperis, who married Atlas and was the mother of the Atlantides or Hesperides. Confusingly, Galvão goes on to assert that Oviedo reported that between the Hesperides and 'Cape Verde' it was 40 days' sail. This does not appear to have been what Sebosus, Pliny or Oviedo actually stated, showing an error on the part of Galvão. What the Portuguese writer does appear to confirm, however, is that Pliny's *Hesperu Ceras*, the Horn of the West, *was indeed* Cape Verde – and moreover that its supposed connection with King Hesperus derives from the name *Hesperu Ceras*, which can also be translated as the 'Horn of Hesperus' (see below).

To determine what exactly Pliny had stated on this matter, I turned to the original Latin text of his *Natural History*, and saw that it read as follows:

> . . . ultra has etiamnum duae Hesperidum insulae narrantur; adeoque omnia circa hoc incerta sunt ut Statius Sebosus a Gorgonum insulis praenavigatione Atlantis dierum XL ad Hesperidum insulas cursum prodiderit, ab his ad Hesperu Ceras unius.

Even at a glance I could see that the original text differed slightly from the English translation consulted during the preparation of this book. With the invaluable help of Ann Deagon, the Professor of Classical Languages Emerita at Guildford College, Greensboro, North Carolina, a new translation of the vital passages was made. This reads:

> The two islands of the Hesperides are said (to be) even beyond these [i.e. the Gorgades]. And all things surrounding this are so uncertain that Statius Sebosus has stated the voyage from the islands of the Gorgons by sailing past Atlas to the islands of the Hesperides (to be) of 40 days, from these to the Horn of Hesperus of one (day).[22]

From this new translation it is clear that Pliny obviously accepted that an ancient voyager would pass 'Atlas', i.e. Mount Atlas – *Atlantis* in the original Latin text – on a journey between the islands of the Gorgons and the Hesperides. This really makes no sense, as Pliny himself has only just told us that the Hesperides lie 'outside' the Gorgades, which were themselves beyond the Horn of the West, i.e. Cape Verde in Senegal. Since it also seems certain that the Cape Verde Isles are the Gorgades, I can conclude only that Pliny mistakenly confused this mythical island group with the Phoenician island settlement and city-port of Gades in south-west Spain. This theory is strengthened if we consider that early sources, such as Isidore of Seville and the Mecia de Viladestes map of 1413, allude to the Cape Verde Isles as the 'jles de gades', the Islands of Gades. As previously noted, Gorgades and Gades are similar-sounding words and may even stem from the same linguistic root.

This confusion I believe led some medieval scholars to assume wrongly that Sebosus, through Pliny's words, was referring to a maritime journey from Gades in Spain past Mount Atlas to the Cape Verdes. This included Antonio Galvão and Richard Hakluyt, who both confusingly named this island group as the Gorgades *and* the Hesperides – a sheer impossibility!

Yet I feel that none of this is what Sebosus originally intended to say. It is my opinion that Pliny added confusion to the matter by assuming that a vessel would have to pass Mount Atlas on a voyage between the Cape Verde Isles and the West Indies. If this assumption proves to be correct, it also brings into question the statement found in the Loeb translation of Pliny's passage to the effect that the Hesperides lay just one day's sail from the Horn of the West, i.e. Cape Verde. How might we rectify this additional discrepancy?

The answer appears to lie in our understanding of Pliny's use of other people's geographical views. We know, for instance, that immediately before Pliny cites Sebosus' claims, he informs us that

'Opposite this cape [i.e. the Horn of the West] also there are reported to be some islands, the Gorgades . . . [and] according to the account of Xenophon of Lampsacus [they] are at a distance of two days' sail from the mainland'.[23] When Pliny makes such statements, he is merely quoting the opinions of others whom he considers to be authorities on these subjects. Xenophon of Lampsacus recorded the journey time between the Gorgades and the 'cape' as two days' sail. Does it not then make sense to conclude that what Pliny was trying to say is that in the opinion of Sebosus it was one day's sail from the Gorgades (i.e. the Cape Verde Isles) *back* to the Horn of the West (i.e. Cape Verde)? If we look again at the more direct rendering of the original Latin passage by Professor Ann Deagon we can see that this solution is totally plausible.

Whether or not Sebosus' sailing times are correct, and where exactly he might have come by this information, remains unclear. Yet if I am correct in my identification of the geographical locations to which he alludes, then we have a very rare discovery indeed. I say this because the words of Sebosus, as Oviedo obviously realised in the sixteenth century, appear to confirm that transatlantic journeys had taken place between Cape Verde on the African coast and the West Indies in ancient times. Evidence that this is indeed the case comes from the 40 days' sailing time Sebosus gives for the voyage between the Gorgades and the Hesperides.

On his epic journey to the New World, Christopher Columbus departed from the island of Gomera in the Canaries group on 6 September 1492, 'which day may be taken to mark the beginning of the enterprise and the ocean crossing'.[24] In order to reach the Bahamas, Columbus is considered to have picked up the Canary Current which, with a little help from the north-easterly trade winds, will carry a vessel south-westwards towards the Cape Verde Islands. Only after having passed a point coincident to this archipelago could his ships have gone on to pick up the North Equatorial Current, which would have carried them on to the northern limits of the Caribbean. Yet on his celebrated journey, Columbus somehow managed to miss the Caribbean altogether and instead made first landfall on the island of San Salvador in the Bahamas on 12 October 1492. This means that it took his three vessels 37 days to travel from Gomera to the Bahamas.

Assuming that the sailing time between Gomera and the Cape Verdes was two to three days, this would have left him with 34 or 35 days to journey on to the West Indies. This figure makes Sebosus' purported 40 days' sail for a voyage between the Cape Verdes and the West Indies uncannily accurate. Moreover, on Columbus' second journey to the New World in 1493, he left Gomera on 7 October and finally reached Espanola (Hispaniola), after brief stopovers in the Lesser Antilles, on 22 November, a period of 46 days.[25] If we subtract two or three days for the fleet to pass a position due north of the Cape Verdes, it provides us with a sailing time of 43 to 44 days. We must therefore conclude that Sebosus' sailing times appear to be based on a genuine knowledge of transatlantic journeys that must have taken place either during or prior to his own age. More important, it strongly supports the view that the Hesperides were the key islands of the West Indies, suggesting perhaps that some knowledge of their existence circulated the Roman world.

Pliny's Ape

Yet why end here, for we have even further confirmation that not only is the above interpretation of Statius Sebosus' statements correct, but also that the West Indies are indeed the Hesperides. As we have seen already, the writings of Caius Julius Solinus greatly influenced the seventh-century Spanish bishop and writer Isidore of Seville. It was from him that the anonymous compiler of the Italian nautical chart of 1413 apparently learned of the Roman geographical writer's knowledge of the 'jles de gades', the islands of Gades, which appear to be synonymous with both the Gorgades and the Cape Verde Isles.

Solinus is the author of a work entitled *Polyhistor: De Memoralibus Mundi*, which highlights the most celebrated places of the ancient world, very much in the style of Pliny. Indeed, Solinus has been called 'Pliny's ape', since his work is generally looked on as a mere copy of Pliny's *Natural History*.[26] Unfortunately, this little-known classical work has only rarely appeared in printed form, the last time being a limited edition published in Venice during 1498. One person who would appear to have consulted a copy is the great explorer and navigator Sebastian Cabot (1476–1557). He was the son of the Venetian explorer and navigator Giovanni Caboto (1455–1498/9), who as 'John Cabot' sailed under the English flag during the reign of King Henry VII. In June 1497 he rediscovered the Northwest Passage to Newfoundland – the first person to do so in the wake of Columbus' more famous landfall in the West Indies just five years earlier. His son Sebastian accompanied him on this celebrated journey.

We know of Sebastian Cabot's interest in Solinus' work from official documents relating to the claims and representations made in a Seville courtroom between 1535 and 1537 by the descendants of Christopher Columbus. These were in respect to 'offices and awards due to them as heirs of the "Discoverer of America"'. Cabot had been summoned as a witness by the Spanish Crown due to his maritime experience as an explorer and navigator of the New World.

According to court proceedings dated 31 December 1536, Sebastian Cabot:

> Declared that Solinus, an historical cosmographer, states that from the 'Fortunate Isles', now called the Canary Isles, journeying or sailing westwards in the ocean for the space of thirty days, are the Islands named the 'Hesperides'; and that these islands, the witness presumes, are the islands which were discovered in the time of the Catholic kings of Glorious Memory; which he [Cabot] had heard said by several people, in this city of Sevilla, had been discovered by the said Cristobal Colón [i.e. Christopher Columbus].[27]

If we accept the authenticity of this statement – and I see no reason to doubt the translation of the case documents or the word of Cabot – we have here yet another allusion to the anciently known journey time between the eastern Atlantic seaboard and the West Indies. Admittedly, Solinus' 30 days' sail between the Fortunate Isles (unquestionably the Canaries) and the Hesperides is somewhat shorter than Sebosus' proposed sailing time between the Gorgades and the Hesperides, but this does not matter. A vessel leaving the Canary Isles might pick up the north-easterly trade winds and be blown east-south-east until it reaches the westerly flowing North Equatorial Current, which would then carry it directly towards the West Indies. In this way it would avoid the Canary Current, reducing the overall sailing time by many days.

There is a problem, however. I was able to read a 1498 copy of Solinus' work in the Whipple Library, Cambridge, and subsequently had the chapter on the Fortunate Isles, the Gorgades and the Hesperides translated by Professor Ann Deagon. Nowhere does it state that the sailing time between the Fortunate Isles and the Hesperides is 30 days. So whether Cabot either misinterpreted Solinus or was privy to writings by the Roman author that are no longer extant may never be known. All we can say is that Cabot quite obviously believed that, for whatever reason, the Hesperides lay 30 days' sail west of the Canary Isles. What also seems clear is that he understood the West Indies to be synonymous with the islands of the Hesperides. Since Cabot was an accomplished explorer and navigator of great renown, his statements made, presumably under oath, in a Spanish courtroom should not be taken lightly.

What Solinus does repeat in his work is Sebosus' assertion that the Hesperides lay 40 days' sail beyond the Gorgades. His exact words are: 'Beyond the Gorgodes [*sic*] are the islands of the Hesperides. Sebosus affirms that they went back into the innermost limits of the sea by a voyage of 40 days.'[28] The significance here is that there is no mention whatsoever of having to pass Mount Atlas on the journey from the 'Gorgodes' to the Hesperides, which seems to affirm that Pliny's statement to this effect is erroneous.

All this is good news, for I now feel we can safely conclude that the Hesperides *were indeed* the West Indies, and that a sketchy knowledge of this island group's existence persisted into Roman times. It was information such as this that writers including Pliny, Sebosus and Solinus would seem to have picked up on and used as geographical anecdotes in their respective works. In turn, much later writers such as Isidore of Seville, Dicuil and Honorius of Autun included this information in their own works, which were much later consulted by medieval cartographers prior to the age of discovery. In this way ancient maritime lore, perhaps thousands of years old, came into the possession of European explorers and chroniclers in the wake of Columbus' first voyage to the New World. Historians such as Oviedo and navigators such as Cabot realised correctly that the islands of the West Indies had been anciently known as the Hesperides, a magnificent insight that was as controversial then as it remains today.

CHAPTER VII

CLUES TO CATASTROPHE

IN THE FIFTH CENTURY AD, the Neo-Platonist, poet and scientist named Proclus took it upon himself to write a commentary on the *Timaeus* of Plato. History tells us that he was one of the last teachers of the Academy before the subject of philosophy was outlawed in an edict passed by the Emperor Justinian in AD 529. In addition to the extraordinary achievements he made in philosophy and science, Proclus practised religious universalism. This was his belief that a true philosopher could attain enlightenment by paying homage equally to the gods of all faiths, and not just those of his own country.

Even though Proclus was writing some 800 years after Plato described his sunken kingdom (a time-frame of AD 432–440 is suggested for the construction of the work),[1] his commentary cites much earlier sources to create an open forum for the philosophers of Alexandria to give their own comments on the historical validity of the Atlantis story. These primary sources include the testimony of a student of Plato named Crantor (*c.* 340–275 BC), styled the 'first interpreter of Plato', who is supposed to have visited Egypt and confirmed the authenticity of the 'history about the Athenians and Atlantics [i.e. those of the Atlantic island]'.[2] This he apparently achieved by speaking with 'the prophets of the Egyptians, who assert that these particulars [i.e. those narrated by Plato] are written on pillars which are still preserved'.[3] Unfortunately, this is all Proclus has to say about Crantor's alleged visit to Egypt, other than to mention these same pillars again later in the text ('But the history [obtained by Solon from Sais] is from pillars, in which things paradoxical and worthy of admiration, whether in actions or inventions, are inscribed').[4]

Modern supporters of the Atlantis legend have consistently cited Proclus' statement regarding the inscribed pillars to confirm that Solon did indeed gain his account of the Atlantic island and its war with the Athenian nation from the old priest of Sais. Yet Proclus does not make clear who exactly went to Egypt in order to confirm Solon's testimony. The only published English translation of Proclus' *Commentaries on the Timaeus of Plato* is the one produced by classical scholar Thomas Taylor in 1820. In his edition the crucial paragraph reads as follows:

> With respect to the whole of this narration about the Atlantics, some say, that it is a mere history, which was the opinion of Crantor, the first interpreter of Plato, who says, that Plato was derided by those of his time as not being the inventor of the *Republic*, but transcribing what the Egyptians had written on this subject; and that he so far regards what is said by these deriders as to refer to the Egyptians this history about the Athenians and Atlantics, and to believe that the Athenians once lived conformably to this policy. Crantor adds, that this is testified by the prophets of the Egyptians, who assert that these particulars are written on pillars which are still preserved.[5]

Yet as classical scholar Alan Cameron and Atlantis author Peter James have been at pains to point out, this is not how it reads in the original Greek text.[6] Taylor made an error in his translation, for Proclus said only that '*He* adds that this is testified to by the prophets of the Egyptians . . .', implying that the author was in fact referring not to Crantor but to Plato, who is the subject of the sentences immediately preceding this all-important statement. Read the whole paragraph again and decide for yourself. In my opinion, the passage can be read either way. Yet whether it was Plato or Crantor who visited Egypt, what seems more important is the supposed presence in that country of 'pillars' on which the 'particulars' of the Atlantis legend were said to have been 'still preserved'. Did they really exist, or were they merely hearsay? The honest answer is that no one really knows. No evidence of their existence has ever been unearthed, either at Sais or indeed anywhere else in Egypt. No reference to these pillars, or to the Atlantis account, is found in any Egyptian text, and no other classical writer seems to mention them. All we can say with any certainty is that Proclus obviously believed in the existence of these inscribed pillars, otherwise he would not have included them in his *Commentaries*.

In reference to the Atlantis story, Proclus goes on to say that 'some refer to the analysis to the fixed stars and planets: so that they assume the Athenians as analogous to the fixed stars, but the Atlantics to the planets'.[7] In support of his case, Proclus cites the opinion of the 'illustrious Amelius', an obscure third-century Neo-Platonist and follower of the Alexandrian philosopher Plotinus (AD 205–270). We are told that Amelius 'vehemently contends that this must be the case, because it is clearly said in the *Critias*, that the

Atlantic Island was divided into seven circles. But I do not know of any other who is of the same opinion.'[8]

This is a curious statement, for nowhere in the *Critias* does it suggest that the Atlantic island was divided into 'seven circles'. We can assume only that the 'illustrious Amelius' must have been referring to the divisions of the city, which according to Plato consisted of a central islet surrounded by three circular waterways, two ringed portions of land and beyond that the plain itself. Are we to believe that Plato intended these seven divisions to signify the seven planets of Pythagorean philosophy, i.e. the sun, moon, Mercury, Venus, Mars, Saturn and Jupiter? All we know is that Plato possessed a brilliant knowledge of ancient astronomy, unquestionably gained from his exposure to the teachings of Pythagoras. Not only was he aware of the correct order of all the known planets, but he also knew their approximate distance from the earth and the fact that they rotated in their own orbits.[9] He was also seemingly aware that the earth itself was a globe, which hung suspended in space.[10] These are remarkable achievements for 350 BC, yet even with such a profound knowledge of the solar system, there seems to be no independent evidence to link the concept of the seven planets with the design of the Atlantean city, so why should the 'illustrious Amelius' have made such a bold assertion? Did the number seven have some hitherto unrealised significance in the development of the Atlantis legend? Was this knowledge still dimly preserved among the Neo-Platonists of Amelius' day, and, most important of all, did it relate to the concept of the seven planets, or to something else perhaps? It is a matter we shall return to in due course.

After relating the opinions of various other scholars for and against the former existence of Atlantis, Proclus at last draws his readership's attention to the writings of one Marcellus. That Proclus unwittingly preserved for posterity this precious piece of evidence is a miracle in itself, for it might just provide us with an accurate fix not only on the true location of lost Atlantis but also the whereabouts of the seven Atlantides.

Islands Afar

Not very much is known about Marcellus. He would appear to have been a geographer of the Roman world who lived *c.* 100 BC.[11] He was the author of a now lost work entitled *Ethiopic History*, and it is this that Proclus paraphrases to lend support to the view first proposed by Plato to the effect that 'so great an island [as Atlantis] once existed'. For this is evidenced, he says:

> ... by certain historians respecting what pertains to the external sea. For according to them, there were seven islands in that sea, in their

> times, sacred to Proserpine, and also three others of an immense extent, one of which was sacred to Pluto, another to Ammon, and the middle of these to Neptune [the Roman name for Poseidon], the magnitude of which was a thousand stadia [184 kilometres]. They also add, that the inhabitants of it preserved the remembrance from their ancestors, of the Atlantic island which existed there, and was truly prodigiously great; which for many periods had dominion over all the islands in the Atlantic Sea, and was itself likewise sacred to Neptune. *These things, therefore, Marcellus writes in his Ethiopic History.*[12]

This passage is like a puzzle waiting to be unravelled. What are we to make of these statements based on the knowledge of Atlantic islands already in our possession? Where exactly were these 'seven islands in that sea'? Can we identify them with a known island group? The only clue we have is that 'in their times' they were sacred to the goddess Proserpine, or Persephone. She was the daughter of Jupiter (or Zeus) and Ceres, who was abducted into the underworld by the god Pluto (or Hades). Her mother was so distraught by this tragedy that she asked Jupiter to intervene, and after much persuasion he consented to allow Proserpine to live a third of the year on earth and the remaining part in the underworld as Pluto's wife. The importance of this familiar legend is that the underworld over which she ruled as queen was synonymous with the otherworldly realm known as Elysium, or the Elysian Fields. We have seen already how Plutarch in his *Lives* linked this mysterious place with two Atlantic islands, discovered by Phoenician merchants and thought to have been members of the Azores group.

Before we can go on to determine the location of the seven islands sacred to Proserpine, we must first identify Marcellus' three islands of 'immense extent', dedicated to Pluto, Neptune and Ammon (the Greek form of Amun, the Egyptian ram-headed god).[13] Only the central island, sacred to Neptune, is elaborated on in any way. It is said to have had a magnitude of 1,000 stadia (184 kilometres), and, if we take this to mean its size (and not its circumference), this would suggest that it was some 184 kilometres from coast to coast. Such a measurement hardly seems fitting with the statement that all three of the islands were of 'immense extent', even by classical standards. Despite this fact, the reported size of Marcellus' island sacred to Neptune makes it three times larger than any individual island in the Azores, Canaries, Madeiras or Cape Verdes.

On the eastern Atlantic seaboard only the British Isles can be construed as being of 'immense extent'. Yet in this case there are just two principal islands – Ireland and the landmass that includes England, Scotland and Wales. Furthermore, there are no traditions that link the British Isles with Pluto, Neptune or Ammon. Indeed, it would seem that in classical times the British Isles were seen as sacred to the sun-god Apollo. Hecataeus of Abdera, a Greek writer of fiction who lived in the fourth century BC, is quoted by Diodorus Siculus as having said that the race known as the Hyperboreans (the inhabitants of Hyperborea, or Britain) worshipped Apollo 'above all other gods' and were classed 'as priests of Apollo', because his mother Leto 'was born on this island'.[14] Furthermore, he says that on this same 'island' was 'both a magnificent sacred precinct of Apollo and a notable temple which is adorned with many votive offerings and is spherical in shape'.[15] It has long been considered that this temple, 'spherical in shape', might in fact be Stonehenge, Britain's most famous megalithic site, or indeed some other sacred monument of these isles. If this is correct, it confirms both Britain's identification as the 'island' of Hyperborea and its much-celebrated connection with the sun-god Apollo.

A further complication is that Marcellus, through Proclus' words, tells us that those who inhabited the central island preserved 'the remembrance from their ancestors, of the Atlantic Island, which existed there'. Although this sentence, as well as the ones that follow, clearly imply that Marcellus was drawing on Plato's Atlantis account, his words are extremely important. They suggest that its inhabitants believed that there had once existed an all-encompassing landmass – sacred to Poseidon, their own patron-god – which had disappeared in the manner Plato described. Moreover, Proclus implies that this former landmass actually was Atlantis which, as our own enquiries have determined, 'for many periods had dominion over all the islands in the Atlantic Sea', i.e. either over local or more widespread island groups.[16]

If the historical knowledge taken by Proclus from Marcellus' *Ethiopic History* is in any way representative of the original text, it would suggest that these three islands were seen as the *surviving portions* of the former Atlantean kingdom. If this was correct, the discovery of these key islands could provide us with an actual location for lost Atlantis. Moreover, we might be forced to conclude that parts of the island empire *existed today*.

So how might we go about identifying these three great islands? Having decided that they are not members of any of the more obvious island groups to be found on the eastern Atlantic seaboard, we must continue our search on the other side of the ocean, in the same vicinity as the Hesperides.

The Island of Cronus

There is one classical reference that might well aid us in identifying Marcellus' three islands of 'immense extent'. It is found in a work entitled *The Face of the Moon* by Plutarch, the much-celebrated biographical writer. It features a lively discourse on astronomical matters, including a debate between Plutarch's grandfather Lamprias and a Carthaginian named Sextius Sulla on whether or not men exist on the moon.

The Carthaginian relates a story concerning the moon and the destiny of the soul which he had gained from a stranger in Carthage. He, in turn, had learned of it during a visit to a mysterious western isle. On being pressed as to its location, Sulla spoke only of pilgrims who periodically made long journeys to this unknown island. Eventually, he asks that he might be permitted to quote from the *Odyssey*, written by the Greek poet Homer, who flourished in the ninth century BC. On being given permission to do so, he recounts the following line: 'An isle, Ogygia, which lies far off in the sea.'[17]

Sulla then goes on to state:

> [the island is] a run of five days off from Britain as you sail westward; and three other islands equally distant from it and from one another lie out from it in the general direction of the summer sunset. In one of these, according to the tale told by the natives, Cronus is confined by Zeus, and the antique (Briareus), holding watch and ward over those islands and the sea ['gulf'] that they call the Cronian main, has been settled close beside him. The great mainland ['continent'], by which the great ocean is encircled, while not so far from the other islands, is about five thousand stades from Ogygia, the voyage being made by oar, for the main is slow to traverse and muddy as a result of the multitude of streams.[18]

In this key passage Plutarch speaks of an Atlantic isle named Ogygia, alluded to in the *Odyssey* and said to be located 5,000 stadia (920 kilometres) west of the British Isles. At an equal distance beyond this island, in the direction of the 'summer sunset' (i.e. west-north-west), are three further islands. These are said to be situated 'not so far' from the great 'continent' that encircled the ocean, the ocean river, a theme already familiar to us from Plato's Atlantis dialogues, where his 'opposite' continent is also imagined as having encircled the known world. In fact, it has been suggested that Plutarch borrowed the idea directly from Plato in an attempt to raise discussion on the concept of a sunken Atlantean landmass.[19] This theory is further implied, say scholars, by Plutarch's reference to the ocean being 'slow to traverse and muddy', echoing Plato's shallow sea that he saw as having resulted from the submergence of Atlantis. Yet this idea, as we have seen, was mentioned by various classical writers, such as Aristotle, Pseudo-Scylax and Rufus Avienus in respect of Himilco's voyages in the outer ocean. Moreover, we may safely conclude that these references are very probably distorted recollections of both the Sargasso Sea and the shallows that thwart shipping in the Bahamas (see Chapter Two).

The geography described by Plutarch, who was hardly a navigator, is virtually meaningless. There are no obvious islands situated 5,000 stadia (920 kilometres) west of Britain, and no group of three islands is to be found at a further distance of 5,000 stadia. In view of his reference to the British Isles, the easiest solution would be to propose that Plutarch had gained some knowledge of the Northwest Passage. If this was the case, were the three islands located in the vicinity of either Hudson Bay or Labrador?[20] It is just possible. However, this theory fails to identify the three islands. They could be any one of a whole range of large islands in this cold, remote region of the American continent.

What does seem likely is that Plutarch possessed some knowledge of the Northwest Passage. Did he confuse this vague geographical knowledge with tales he had heard, perhaps from Carthaginian sources, regarding what lay on the other side of the ocean river? Looking again at Sextius Sulla's words, Pliny has him say that on one of the three islands the 'natives' assert that Cronus, the Greek god of time (synonymous with the Roman Saturn), had been confined for all eternity by Zeus. Here, too, the 'antique' Briareus was said to watch and ward over the islands and the 'gulf' that 'they call the Cronian main'.[21] Classical scholars usually identify the Cronian 'main' with the Adriatic Sea,[22] while the 'great mainland' (the Greek actually translates as 'continent') is generally dismissed as the lands beyond the Caspian Sea, which was once believed to be a gulf that joined the outer ocean. Even Plutarch himself adds confusion by speaking of a 'gulf' that 'lies roughly on the same parallel as the mouth of the Caspian Sea'.[23]

Yet there can be no mistake concerning Ogygia's placement in the Atlantic Ocean. It supposedly lay west-north-west of the British Isles, while the three islands were said to be located 'not so far' from the 'great' continent. Moreover, the imprisonment of Cronus by Zeus, following their paternal wars, was intimately connected with the Western Ocean. Prior to their association with Hercules, the Pillars of Hercules are said to have borne the name of Cronus' guard, Briareus, and even of Cronus himself.[24]

So what are the identities of the three islands alluded to by Plutarch? If they are not to be found either in the vicinity of Hudson Bay or Labrador, might they be the three islands of 'immense extent' referred to by Marcellus? If so, then it made more sense to search for them not in Newfoundland but further south, in the direction of the Caribbean, where the islands of the Hesperides would appear to have lain in the 'secret recesses of the sea'.

Such a conclusion might at first seem premature. However, it is important to remember that from Cape Cod, Massachusetts, along the Atlantic coast to Florida, there is a single, relatively uninterrupted shoreline with southerly flowing waters placed conveniently between the beach and the more powerful, northerly flowing Gulf Stream. This would have allowed any vessel a relatively easy passage to the Bahamas and Caribbean, while on the homeward journey a ship could have picked up the Gulf Stream to sail north back to Cape Cod. Before this clockwise-flowing ocean current veers eastwards towards the most westerly isles of the Azores, it is said to have a width of around 64 kilometres.[25]

If we are to look towards the West Indies for a solution to this problem, Plutarch's somewhat confusing geography now makes better sense. Trying to comprehend the placement of Caribbean islands in the context of an extremely baffling long-distance transoceanic journey to the 'great' continent without the aid of a world map would have been virtually impossible. Yet this seems to be exactly what Plutarch managed to achieve – an account that contained knowledge of the existence not only of the Northwest Passage but also the shallows of the Bahamas *and* three islands in the proximity of the West Indies.

Even if Plutarch really *was* alluding to the West Indies, could we go on to identify these three islands, perhaps synonymous with those spoken of by Marcellus? At first this seemed like an impossible task, but then I found that somebody else had beaten me to it in a most convincing manner.

The 'Real' Atlantis

Geoffrey Ashe is a much-respected historical writer of several books on subjects that have included King Arthur, Glastonbury, sacred wisdom and ancient cosmology. In 1962 he produced a thought-provoking work on the voyages of St Brendan the Navigator, a legendary Irish monk of the sixth century who, tradition asserts, discovered various islands in the Western Ocean. Entitled *Land to the West: St Brendan's Voyage to America*, Ashe's book also deals with the problem of Atlantis.

Even though more than 2,000 books and publications on the subject of Atlantis had preceded his own, Ashe made a careful examination of the facts and evidence at hand and provided the reader with a unique insight into this age-old mystery. He, too, saw as significant Marcellus' paraphrased material on the ten Atlantic islands, as quoted in Proclus' *Commentaries on the Timaeus of Plato*, and, after due consideration, had felt inspired to write:

> . . . if only we could admit that his islands were the Antilles [i.e. the Caribbean], the main chain of the West Indies. Seven is a fair round number for the principal Lesser Antilles: the islands intended could be

> Guadeloupe, Dominica, Martinique, St Lucia, Barbados, St Vincent and Grenada. The three greater members of the chain are Cuba, Haiti and Porto Rico, all big by Mediterranean standards; Haiti, the middle one, is approximately a thousand stadia – i.e. a hundred miles [160 kilometres] or a little over – from side to side.[26]

Cuba, Hispaniola and Puerto Rico. Could these really be the three islands of 'immense extent' alluded to by Marcellus in his now lost work the *Ethiopic History* and by Plutarch in *The Face of the Moon*? Had Geoffrey Ashe been the first person to recognise the true location of Atlantis? Was he justified in assessing the available evidence in such an unorthodox manner? In an attempt to quantify his bold assertions, Ashe went on to cite instances of catastrophe legends found among the indigenous peoples of the Caribbean:

> . . . the Spanish discoverers of the Indies learned that the natives of this area had an unusual Deluge legend. Instead of saying, like most nations, that the floodwater subsided, they said it stayed where it was, in possession of the ground it had swallowed. Many of the Antilles in fact had formerly been joined into a single mass, but a disaster in ancient times had split it into fragments with sea between. Such a tradition was recorded among the Caribs and among the tribes of Haiti itself, the very island to which Proclus's assertion would seem to point.[27]

These are quite extraordinary statements. Proclus, with a little help from Marcellus, had somehow managed to provide a key to unlocking the mysteries of Atlantis. Geoffrey Ashe had then used this key to open the door. I found it quite amazing that no other author in the field of Atlantology had *ever* picked up on these same ideas, first proposed by Ashe in 1962, especially as he has gone on to cite the same interpretation of Marcellus' paraphrased statements in two further books.[28]

Everything pointed towards the fact that Marcellus had knowingly recorded that three Caribbean islands, tentatively identified as Cuba, Hispaniola and Puerto Rico, stood in the proximity of Plato's former Atlantic island and were thus surviving portions of its renowned island empire. Moreover, Plutarch had associated these same islands with a tradition suggesting that Cronus had been imprisoned on one of them.

Intrigued by Ashe's assertions regarding an ancient cataclysm that had split apart the Caribbean, I checked out his primary sources for these references. One of them was taken from a book entitled *Histoire de la découverte de l'Amérique*, written in 1892 by French historian Paul Gaffarel, a professor of the Faculty of Letters at Dijon. He states that on arrival in the Lesser Antilles, the first

Spanish explorers were told by the native Caribs that 'the Antilles had at one time formed a single continent, but they were suddenly separated by the actions of the waters'.[29] Gaffarel also recorded that a legend found among the indigenous population of Haiti spoke of the islands of the Antilles being created during a sudden flood.[30]

Ashe's other reference source came from a volume of *Folk-lore in the Old Testament*, written by nineteenth-century mythologist Sir James Frazer, who recorded that:

> The Caribs of the Antilles had a tradition that the Master of Spirits, being angry with their forefathers for not presenting to him the offerings which were his due, caused such a heavy rain to fall for several days that all the people were drowned: only a few contrived to save their lives by escaping in canoes to a solitary mountain. It was this deluge, they say, which separated their islands from the mainland and formed the hills and pointed rocks of sugar-loaf mountains of their country.[31]

The stories presented by both Gaffarel and Frazer were taken from even earlier works by Spanish explorers and chroniclers who had visited the West Indies shortly after the time of the Conquest. Yet the brief accounts provided by these two historians would suffice to demonstrate how the indigenous Amerindians of the West Indies would appear to have preserved rich myths and legends concerning catastrophic events that apparently befell the Caribbean before the dawn of history. Moreover, since these stories were obviously told to the first Spanish explorers who reached these islands, is it possible that similar tales were recounted to ancient voyagers who visited the Caribbean prior to Plato's age? Did these unknown mariners return to the Mediterranean world not simply with accounts of strange tropical islands that lay beyond the Western Ocean but also with stories and rumours concerning a great landmass that formerly existed in the same vicinity as these islands?

That Plato's Atlantic island might have been located in the Caribbean was an intriguing possibility. As we know, in the *Timaeus* he tells us that it was situated within easy reach of 'other islands' which acted like stepping stones for ancient voyagers wishing to reach 'the opposite continent', or the American mainland. Such terminology could not describe the island chains of the Caribbean more accurately. Archaeologists José M. Cruxent and Irving Rouse, who spent many years examining the migration routes of early cultures arriving in the Caribbean, spoke of the islands, banks, reefs and cays that stretch from Central America towards the Greater Antilles, in the following manner: 'When the sea level was lower a few thousand years ago, the chain formed a nearly continuous series of stepping-stones leading to the Greater Antilles.'[32] Similarly, they describe the Bahamas as providing 'the best stepping-stone route between the mainland to the north and eastern Cuba and Hispaniola to the south'.[33]

What we can also say is that up until around 5,000 years ago a great many of the Bahaman islands formed part of two enormous landmasses known as the Great and Little Bahama Banks, which were gradually submerged as the sea-level rose following the melting of the ice fields at the end of the glacial age.[34] Hydrographic surveys of the largest of these underwater platforms, the Great Bahama Bank, have indicated that this inundation process began as early as *c.* 8000 BC and continued through until *c.* 3000 BC.[35] Very slowly this whole landmass was flooded by the rising sea-level to leave the many thousands of islands and cays which make up the Bahaman archipelago today.[36] Similar processes resulted in the drowning of other low-lying regions in the Caribbean, some much quicker than others. For instance, marine geologists consider that Cay Sal Bank, located between Cuba and Andros, the largest of the Bahaman islands, was flooded relatively rapidly between *c.* 10,000–8000 BC and *c.* 6000 BC.[37]

Do the Caribbean catastrophe myths unearthed by Ashe suggest that these former landmasses were submerged during more violent cataclysms involving a devastating flood of the sort hinted at both by Marcellus and Plato? Is it possible that these landmasses once supported not just indigenous flora and fauna, but also human life? If so, could the cessation of this human occupation have gone on to influence the legends found among the native peoples of the Caribbean, which in turn influenced the construction of Plato's Atlantis narrative?

Mr Clarke's Comment

These are tantalising possibilities concerning the origins of the Atlantis legend, and they will be fully explored in due course. Yet as revelatory as they might seem, I can take no credit for locating Atlantis in the region of the Bahamas and Caribbean, nor can I award this prize to Geoffrey Ashe. Leaving aside the claims by Atlantologists, such as nineteenth-century Mayan scholars Augustus le Plongeon and the Abbé Brasseur de Bourbourg as well as the celebrated Scottish mythologist Lewis Spence, who all saw the Antilles as surviving remnants of an enormous Atlantean continent, we must applaud American historian Hyde Clarke for making this same connection. In a ground-breaking paper entitled 'Examination of the Legend of Atlantis in Reference to the Protohistoric Communication with America', delivered to the Royal Historical Society in June 1885, he speculated on the seven

Atlantides, or Pleiades, being individual Atlantic islands.[38] This was an insight in itself, and yet he went on to comment on Plato's assertion in the *Timaeus* that the kings of Atlantis had subdued the Atlantic island 'together with many others [in that vicinity], and parts also of the [opposite] continent'.[39] His address to the assembled audience continued as follows:

> My comment on this is that the head seat of the great king [of Atlantis] was possibly in the Caribbean Sea; it may be in St Domingo [i.e. Hispaniola]. It is to be noted, however, that at the Spanish invasion this island was under the Caribs, whose language is traced there. Consequently the relics of the former civilisation in this and other islands were lost.[40]

These are extremely perceptive observations which at the time could not have been fully appreciated, due to the publication three years earlier of Ignatius Donnelly's *Atlantis: The Antediluvian World*. As previously mentioned, this book proposed the former existence of an enormous Atlantic landmass in the vicinity of the Mid-Atlantic Ridge. Nobody wanted to consider the possibility that, in creating his Atlantic island, Plato might in fact have been alluding to a much smaller landmass which once existed in the vicinity of the West Indies – one that was linked via a series of island chains to the American mainland. For this reason Hyde Clarke's important paper was lost to the academic world until mercifully it was discovered during the preparation of this book. As we shall see, this same theory has now been independently resurrected by, among others, Emilio Spedicato, the Professor of Operations Research at Italy's Bergamo University, who has written a well-argued paper suggesting that Hispaniola matches the description of Plato's Atlantic isle (see Chapter Eighteen).[41]

All of this quite disparate evidence suggests that we should take very seriously the possibility that, in Ashe's words, when Marcellus proposed that the three islands of 'immense extent' occupied the approximate position of the former Atlantean landmass he was 'on the right track'.[42] Yet before exploring the matter further, we must first take to task Ashe's view that the seven other islands mentioned by Marcellus, and said to be sacred to Proserpine, were actually members of the Lesser Antilles. Even though this is a wholly original idea, is there any reason to assume it is correct? Their number, and the fact that they seem to be linked with traditions concerning Elysium, suggests an association with a more accessible island group, plausibly the Canaries or the Azores. Moreover, Proclus, in his *Commentaries on the Timaeus of Plato*, makes further reference to Marcellus' *Ethiopic History* in which he provides details of 'the Atlantic mountain', i.e. Mount Atlas, which is located fairly close to the Canary Islands.[43]

At face value there seems to be no reason to conclude that Marcellus' seven islands were situated on the opposite side of the Atlantic Ocean. Only the three islands of 'immense extent' appear synonymous with Caribbean islands. It was a matter I put to Geoffrey Ashe after tracking him down for a brief conversation at his home in Glastonbury, Somerset, on New Year's Day 1999. Having listened to my queries he re-emphasised that there are seven notable islands in the Lesser Antilles. So if Marcellus really had been alluding to the three main islands of the Greater Antilles, why should we assume that he was referring to the Canaries or the Azores? If we take Marcellus' three islands of immense extent to be Cuba, Hispaniola and Puerto Rico, surely it makes better sense to identify his seven islands, sacred to Proserpine, with principal members of the Lesser Antilles.

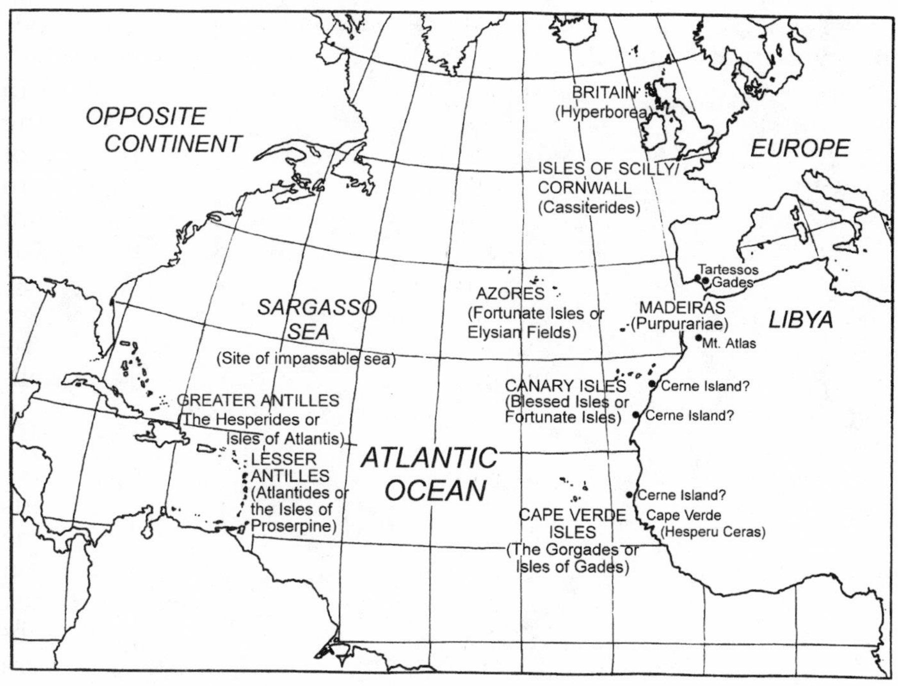

Suggested locations for the various legendary islands of the Western Ocean. The Roman geographer Statius Sebosus spoke of the Hesperides as lying 40 days' sail from the African coast.

The mention here of a group of seven islands also brings to mind the idea, first proposed by Hyde Clarke, that the seven Atlantides, or daughters of Atlas, were mythical islands, each connected with one of the seven stars of the Pleiades. Theopompus, the younger contemporary of Plato, wrote that the inhabitants of the opposite continent were known as the Meropes.[44] In the knowledge that Merope was one of the Atlantides, or Pleiades, could this name have been attached either to one of the islands of the Lesser Antilles or to the American mainland itself?

Everything points towards the conclusion that the seven Atlantides, or Pleiades, were synonymous in some way with Marcellus' seven islands, sacred to Proserpine and tentatively identified as the Lesser Antilles. Quite obviously, these astonishing revelations create fresh questions and extraordinary implications that might well provide us with important clues which will help unravel the mystery behind the supposed destruction of Atlantis. Yet before jumping ahead too far, we must first determine whether or not there could have existed a line of transmission between the Pre-Columbian Amerindians of the Caribbean and the Mediterranean world in which Plato lived some 2,350 years ago. Our greatest lead comes not from any evidence in the Americas but from the contents of Egyptian mummies.

PART TWO
CONTACT

CHAPTER VIII

DEALING IN DRUGS

On 26 September 1976, under the full gaze of the international media, the body of the Egyptian king Rameses II, styled 'the Great', was shipped from the Cairo Museum to Paris for a seven-month 'state visit'. Its purpose was to determine why deterioration had been noticed in the skin and around the neck of the dead pharaoh. Some 20 of France's leading scientists had offered their services in an attempt to find out what might have occurred (the problem was found to be beetle invasion).

One of these scientists was Dr Michelle Lescot of the National History Museum in Paris. She used an electron microscope to determine whether any form of bacteria or virus was present in the wrappings, and was stunned to find herself staring through the lens at tiny samples of the tobacco plant. Confident of her findings, Dr Lescot went public and was immediately attacked and ridiculed by her fellow academics. In their opinion, there was absolutely no way that tobacco could be present in the wrappings, unless through contamination. It was suggested that the Egyptologists who in 1881 had found the mummy among the so-called 'royal cache' in a tomb at Deir el-Bahri, in southern Egypt, must have been smoking pipes at the time. If so, they could have inadvertently dropped some tobacco which managed somehow to find its way into the wrappings.

In an attempt to counter these claims, Dr Lescot was allowed to conduct further tests using samples taken from deep inside the body. Once again the microscopic examinations produced exactly the same results. Tiny traces of tobacco were found to be present in these samples, completely dispelling the initial belief that its presence was due to tobacco falling from a pipe.

These new results made it even more likely that tobacco had been introduced to the wrappings during the funerary procedures that followed the death of the king, who ruled for an incredible

66 years, *c*. 1290–1224 BC. Even more tests revealed that where the internal organs of the body had been removed for placement in canopic jars, there was a stuffing of vegetable matter that, aside from plantain, stinging nettles, flax, black pepper seeds, camomile and wheat, included *chopped tobacco leaves*. Since this mixture was introduced into the mummy in order to help preserve its body tissue, it has been speculated that the tobacco was used in the embalming process as both an insecticide and to prevent putrefaction.[1]

The presence of tobacco in Rameses' mummy wrappings and body interior came as a complete surprise to Egyptologists and botanists alike for one basic reason – the plant was not known in the ancient world. It made no sense whatsoever, and although the chance find has been mentioned in a few popular books on strange mysteries of the past, no mainstream Egyptologist has been willing to embrace or explain this intrusion into an otherwise well-attested Egyptian history. The much greater problem that the tobacco plant is considered to be indigenous only to the Americas has been quietly swept aside by all.

The Cocaine Mummies

There the matter rested until 1992 when a German doctor of toxicology named Svetlana Balabanova, working with the Institute of Forensic Medicine at Ulm, began conducting a series of unique tests on samples taken from Egyptian mummified remains preserved at the Munich Museum. They came from one complete body, one incomplete body and seven detached heads of unknown provenance.[2] The preserved body was that of Henuttawy, a priestess and singer in the temple of Amun at Thebes, *c*. 1000 BC. Her tomb had been uncovered in a necropolis set aside for those of priestly rank at Deir el-Bahri, close to modern Luxor, in southern Egypt. The early history of her mummy remains uncertain. Records show that in 1845 an English traveller named Dodwell sold Henuttawy's mummy to Ludwig I, the king of Bavaria. He and his family built up a large collection of antiquities, and these subsequently formed the basis of the museum's own collection, housed today in the old royal palace.[3]

From the mummified remains examined at the Institute of Anthropology and Human Genetics at Munich University, Dr Balabanova took bone and skin tissue, as well as samples of head and abdominal muscle. The results she produced were extraordinary – so extraordinary that she felt it necessary to send similar samples to three other laboratories, which quickly confirmed her original findings. What all the tests appeared to show was that the mummified remains contained large quantities of drugs. In all nine cases hashish was present, although this was not so much of a surprise since scholars accept that it was freely available to the pharaonic Egyptians in the form of hemp. Adding still further to the mystery was the presence in eight of the nine bodies of nicotine, the narcotic ingredient of the tobacco plant. What really stunned the scientists, however, was the presence, in each and every one of the bodies, of cocaine, a psychoactive alkaloid present in the leaf of the coca plant.[4]

Dr Balabanova knew instantly the implications of her findings. Tobacco was difficult enough to explain, but cocaine was quite another matter for it was produced for the first time only in 1859 and did not circulate among the high society circles of Europe until the late nineteenth century. Its origins are exclusively South American. In the years following the conquest of Peru by Pizarro in 1532, Spanish travellers in the Andes of Peru and Bolivia recorded that the native population seemed to be constantly chewing dried leaves called 'coca'.[5] This they rolled into a ball and placed in their mouth with a little ash or lime (caustic earth), a process that unlocked the cocaine content. It apparently relieved hunger, thirst and fatigue, and was also used as a mild stimulant, which induced euphoria and anaesthesia, factors that eventually led to its use and abuse in the Western world. During the American Civil War cocaine was taken by injured soldiers to relieve pain.

Partially digested remains of coca leaves have been retrieved from rubbish tips of ancient Peruvian cultures that go back as far as 2500 BC, while the extended cheeks of the coca chewer appear on stone idols from Colombia that date to *c.* 1500 BC.[6] Indeed, much evidence of this habit has recently come to light during the excavation in Peru of a number of graves that contain the bodies of mummified individuals dating to between 200 BC and AD 1500.[7] When subjected to tests similar to those conducted by Balabanova and her colleagues on the Munich mummies, these, too, proved positive for cocaine.[8] Furthermore, many of these Peruvian bodies were found buried with bunches of coca leaves still in their cheeks, presumably in the belief that the deceased would benefit from their effects in the afterlife.[9]

Calls of Incompetence

Dr Balabanova is no maverick. She is a forensic toxicologist who has been frequently called upon by the police to test suspect bodies for evidence of the presence of drugs or poisons. The results obtained from such tests are acceptable as legal evidence in court, and so any serious doubts about her techniques, methodology or findings must bring into question the whole subject of toxicological evidence. Furthermore, whilst conducting her tests on the mummies she ensured against rogue readings by backing up her findings with chromatography. This is a process that reveals the individual signatures and metabolites (biochemical breakdown products produced by the body) present in the chemicals isolated from individual samples.[10]

Dr Balabanova subjected the mummified remains to the so-called hair shaft test, based on the knowledge that if a person uses or has been subjected to drugs or poisons before their death, tiny traces are absorbed into the hair protein. These remain in a living person for some months before gradually dissipating away. It is this same procedure that allows employees, sportsmen or members of the military services to be checked for possible drug abuse. These separate tests also produced positive results.

Since the original trials were conducted on the samples taken from the mummified bodies at Munich Museum, Dr Balabanova and her colleagues have conducted up to 3,000 similar tests on other preserved bodies from countries such as Germany, China, Sudan and Egypt.[11] A high level of these samples has also shown the presence of nicotine and/or cocaine. Date-wise, these specimens have ranged between 800 and 7,000 years, making some of them even older than the original samples taken from the Munich mummies. There seems very little chance that either the procedures or the equipment used by Balabanova were in any way flawed.[12]

Finding Fakes

Another criticism levelled at Svetlana Balabanova and her results is that the mummified bodies preserved in Munich Museum, and used in the initial tests, were in fact forgeries purchased from Arab racketeers by European travellers eager to obtain genuine antiquities. Since carbon-14 testing of the organic materials relating to such remains can produce spurious and contradictory results, scientists are always eager to determine the provenance of artefacts used for testing. In the case of the mummies housed at the Munich Museum, some were, as we have seen, simply detached heads. However, other samples were taken from one whole body, that of Henuttawy, and the partial remains of another. These were investigated by Rosalie David, an Egyptologist from Manchester Museum who was asked to verify Balabanova's claims by the makers of a Channel 4 Equinox documentary which featured the cocaine mummies. She found evidence of complex embalming methods having been employed in their preservation, along with packages of viscera, amulet inscriptions and wax images bearing impressions of the Egyptians gods.[13] As a consequence, it seemed unlikely that these mummies were modern forgeries.

Rosalie David had initially been sceptical of Dr Balabanova's results, but during the preparation of the documentary, screened in Britain for the first time in 1996, she agreed to check for evidence of drugs on a number of mummies preserved at Manchester Museum. The results astounded her. Three of the bodies examined contained substantial traces of nicotine. None, however, proved positive for cocaine.[14]

One final criticism of Dr Balabanova's findings in respect to the mummified remains examined is that there is no archaeological, historical or pictorial precedent to suggest that the ancient Egyptians were familiar with drugs such as cocaine and nicotine for either recreational or medical purposes. Certainly it is true that no wall relief, tomb painting or ancient text alludes to the use of such substances. However, many of the herbs and plants referred to in medical texts remain unidentified, while there is substantial evidence to show that the ancient Egyptians were habitual drug-users. Furthermore, there is the clear presence of tobacco leaves inside the mummy wrappings and body of Rameses the Great. In addition to this, Dr Balabanova's findings strongly suggest that the ancient Egyptians somehow absorbed nicotine into their bodies, either through smoking, chewing or injecting tobacco in some manner currently unknown to us. Even though Egyptologists have found no evidence of smoke inhalation in Egypt before Arab times, there is tantalising evidence of this practice in a Middle Eastern country that had very close ties with the pharaonic world.

Incense in Syria

In 1930 Near Eastern scholar Stefan Przeworski wrote a useful article for the scholarly journal *Syria* about the discovery at various archaeological sites in northern Syria of a number of curious objects that might well turn out to be smoking pipes.[15] He catalogued ten in all that have been tentatively dated to between *c.* 1200 and *c.* 850 BC.[16] Each one takes the form of a bowl carved from hard stone, usually blue-green steatite. They have a short stem, centrally perforated through to the bowl itself and tapered at the end so that they can be inserted into a hollow tube, probably made of wood or metal.[17]

The bowls themselves are modelled into distinctive forms, such as couched lions[18] or hands that clasp their convex exteriors.[19] Often the undersides have additional decorative patterns, such as stylised lotus flowers.[20] Sizes vary between 8.1 and 13.5 centimetres in length, 5.2 and 7.7 centimetres in diameter and 2.1 and 6 centimetres in height.[21]

The purpose of these curious, and little understood, stone bowls has been largely ignored by Near Eastern scholars. Sir Leonard

Woolley, the famous English archaeologist who discovered the treasures of the city of Ur in southern Iraq during the 1920s, was inclined to label them as 'libation bowls' due to their general appearance.[22] Przeworski, on the other hand, admitted that their 'purpose remains quite obscure'.[23] He dismissed Woolley's view that they were libation bowls and instead favoured the idea that they might be a unique form of incense burner. In his opinion:

> . . . the Syrian tube was not only used to handle the incense burner, it was also used as a pipe, through which one blew into the bowl, via the small communicating hole. Thus making it easy to maintain the glowing embers, and release the perfume.[24]

Syrian priest with smoking pipe, *c.* 1000 BC. Did the Phoenicians learn the art of smoking during trading expeditions beyond the Pillars of Hercules? Compare this image with the cigar-smoking figure of God L/Votan from the Maya city of Palenque (see plate pages).

Przeworski illustrated the point by reproducing the outline of a Syrian relief that shows a male priest with a long pipe to his lips, smoke emerging from its bowl.[25] If this carved relief were to be found on the wall of a temple in Mexico there would be little doubt as to what it represented. Yet the same image in northern Syria is interpreted quite differently. Since oral smoking is not attested in western Asia until the Arab period, scholars can only conclude that the figure must be exhaling instead of inhaling smoke!

That these curious objects from northern Syria are not incense burners but smoking pipes is an intriguing possibility, and one that was proposed originally by American prehistorian Cyrus H. Gordon in his 1971 book *Before Columbus*.[26] He pointed out that, following the publication of Przeworski's article in 1930, more of these bowls came to light during excavations. One specimen was found in 1932 at a Judaean archaeological site named Tell Beit Mirsim, where Gordon was present as a member of the field staff.[27] In his opinion, they bore all the hallmarks of smoking pipes and could be compared with the decorated stone pipes used by native American Indians, many of which also have 'animal heads on the bowl' and 'a hand (with all five fingers) carved in relief on the bottom of the bowl'.[28] He added that:

> The heads indicate that the bowls were personified, while the hands not only suggest that the fragrant smoke was being offered, but also that the whole cultic object was called a 'hand' (*kaf*, 'hand', is the name of such an object in Hebrew). Since such smoking bowls appear during Old Testament times in the Near East, it is possible that the American peace pipes are an adaptation of Near East *kaf* pipes.[29]

There is no clear indication of exactly what kind of substance the Syrians might have used in the pipes. It could have been opium or hemp. However, the presence of such pipes between *c.* 1200 and *c.* 850 BC is strange in itself, particularly as this time-frame coincides exactly with the rise of the Phoenicians, the undisputed merchants of the high seas whose city-states were to be found on the Lebanese and Syrian coasts (see Chapter Ten).

Curiously enough, Przeworski proposed that the Syrian pipes developed, via a now lost intermediary, from more conventional incense burners used in Egypt during the second millennium BC.[30] It is an interesting idea, although there exists no hard evidence to support this theory, other than a basic comparison in styles between the couched lions some of the bowls resemble and the sphinx-like leonine form so familiar to Egyptian art. It seems far more likely that Phoenician seafarers adopted the idea of inhaling smoke, as opposed to exhaling incense fumes, from one of the many diverse cultures they encountered on the fringes of the ancient world. Yet where exactly and from whom? And what might the connection be between the Syrian smoking pipes and the presence in ancient Egypt of tobacco and cocaine?

On the Case of Tobacco

In America the two oldest attested smoking pipes date from *c.* 1500 BC. One comes from Marajo Island, situated at the mouth of the Amazon in Brazil, while the other was found at Poverty Point, Louisiana.[31] Central American cultures, such as the Maya of the

Yucatán, the Aztecs of central Mexico and the islanders of the Caribbean, are also known to have used pipes to smoke tobacco. Yet these examples were little more than conical tubes, made out of silver, stone or wood, into which they would place tobacco and rolled-up pieces of grass. These acted as filters to prevent fragments of leaf going into the mouth. In the Caribbean, the first Spanish explorers came across *caciques*, or tribal leaders, using a form of Y-shaped pipe made of reed that was inserted up both nostrils in order to inhale smoke. Pipes, however, were only for the elite. Less important members of the community would have to make do with rolling up the leaves and smoking them as a cigar.

The virtues of tobacco smoke were seen as manifold. It was used in America as a cure against asthma, nasal congestion, headaches, snakebite, boils, toothache and complications during childbirth.[32] For more priestly or shamanistic purposes, nicotine could be ingested by first extracting a resin from the tobacco and then using it as an enema. The absorption of such high concentrations meant that the user would quickly experience an altered state of consciousness. In other cases, it could be rolled into a ball and chewed, something that, similar to coca-chewing, was done to stave off hunger. What we know as recreational smoking bears very little resemblance to the use of tobacco among Mesoamerican cultures.

It is a common belief that there was no tobacco in the ancient world until after it was introduced from the Americas during the age of discovery. This, however, is a complete misnomer, for there is ample evidence to show that a form of wild tobacco, called *Nicotiana rustica*, as opposed to the New World variant designated *Nicotiana tabacum*, was widely known in parts of Africa, including the western Sudan, long before Columbus.[33] It is thought to have been used as an Arabic smoke medicine,[34] while black African cultures ingested tobacco fumes to attain meditational states and 'tranquillising pleasure'.[35] The act of smoking was known as *tubbaq*, and it was under this name that it filtered into a number of African dialects as variations such as *taba*, *tawa* and *tama*.[36]

In order to use tobacco as a medicine, Afro-Arabians would first cure or dry fresh leaves, which would then be pressed together to make compact bricks.[37] Afterwards, the resulting compound would be applied to the body in some manner, or mixed with other substances, such as charcoal, so that it could be burned to produce smoke. This is in contrast to the Americans, who first dried and then crushed their tobacco leaves.[38] They could then be administered as a powder, a juice, a leaf poultice or rolled into a ball and chewed, a method of ingestion that might possibly have been used in Egypt.[39]

The African tobacco plant is also mentioned in a medical treatise written by a medieval Arab physician named Ibn al-Baitar. He referred to it as 'a species of tree growing upon the mountains of Mekkah, having long, slender, green leaves, which slip between the fingers when squeezed'.[40] Apparently, 'it attains the size of a man . . . lives in groups . . . one never finds one alone'.[41] Furthermore, we are told 'it is beneficial as an antidote against poisons, taken internally or applied as a dressing, and as a remedy for the mange or scab, and the itch, and fevers of long continuance, and colic, and jaundice, and obstructions of the liver . . .'[42]

Additional evidence that tobacco was not only present in Africa prior to the age of Columbus but was also utilised as a smoke medicine by the Arabs comes from the writings of the nineteenth-century explorer Captain G. Binger. He found it being used in Africa as money, and said that 'the inhabitants of the Darfur [in Sudan] call it in their language *taba* . . . In Fezzan and at Tripoli in Barbary it is called *tabgha*. I have read a kasidah or poem, composed by a Bakride or descendant of the Khalif Abu Bakr, to prove that smoking is no sin. These verses, I think, date back to the ninth century of the hegirah.'[43]

This suggests a date of AD 1450, over 40 years before Columbus' celebrated journey. Furthermore, the use of the terms *tubbaq*, *taba* and *tabgha* for smoking leads us to question the origin of the word 'tobacco', employed by the pre-Columbian peoples of the Caribbean to denote both the act of smoking and the instrument used in the smoking process.[44] That Afro-Arabian variants of the word existed before the age of Columbus seems too much of a coincidence. Could it be that there are common origins for these word variations which all denote the same thing – smoking tobacco?

The similarities between these root words for tobacco smoking only deepen the mystery and strongly suggest that either the tobacco plant was introduced into Africa via transatlantic contact before the age of Columbus or it was taken to the Americas by visitors from the African continent. If this is possible, it could mean that tobacco was present on both sides of the Atlantic as early as *c.* 1500 BC, the date attributed to the earliest known smoking pipes found in the Americas.

Since we know that a species of the tobacco plant was present in Sudan before the age of Columbus, and samples taken from mummified remains in western Sudan also reveal high quantities of nicotine, it is possible that tobacco entered Egypt via Nubia. Yet when can we say this might have taken place? It could have occurred as early as pharaonic times or as late as the mid-fifteenth century. However, knowledge that cocaine has also been detected in Egyptian mummified remains suggests that the picture is a little more complex. Even though we might attempt to explain the presence of tobacco in ancient Egypt in terms of an indigenous African variety, we cannot do this with cocaine. As we have seen, the coca leaf, and coca chewing, is native only to the Americas.[45]

As fantastic as this proposal might seem, the only realistic solution to explain the discovery of cocaine in Egyptian mummies is to suggest trading contact between the two continents.[46] Furthermore, if the coca leaf was really being exported in this manner, there has to be a possibility that tobacco from Central America was also being shipped to the ancient world. The presence of tobacco and cocaine in the same Egyptian individuals would tend to support this supposition. Moreover, the strange relationship between the names used for tobacco smoking on both sides of the Atlantic implies a cross-fertilisation of terminology, techniques, and quite possibly even plants and produce centuries before the age of Columbus. Only by establishing this ancient trade route can we go on to propose a means by which knowledge of the Caribbean islands, and the cataclysms they would seem to have suffered in some past age, can have reached the Mediterranean world prior to the age of Plato.

Continent to the South

One tantalising piece of evidence that suggests the true source of Africa's trade in drugs comes from the following, quite extraordinary account. The year after Columbus' triumphant return from the New World in 1493, King Ferdinand and Queen Isabella of Spain signed a treaty proposed by Don Juan, the king of Portugal, that effectively divided up the Atlantic Ocean, and the lands within it, between the two great powers. Spain would have everything found to the west of the demarcation, including all the territories Columbus had so far claimed in the names of the sovereigns of Castile and Aragon. Portugal, on the other hand, would receive all lands discovered east of the line, an agreement that effectively gave it only the Azores, the Madeiras and the Cape Verdes. Yet in reality there is good reason to suppose that the king of Portugal was already privy to knowledge which spoke of the existence of a southern continent that lay within the territories allotted to him.

We are, of course, talking about South America, Brazil in particular, the existence of which would appear to have been common knowledge among the black African and Arab populations of West Africa. In time, this information became known to Portuguese navigators and merchants, who in turn carried it back to their native country.[47] Having already missed out on the discovery of the West Indies, the king of Portugal was not about to make the same mistake again. It was for this reason that he devised the agreement between the two nations.[48]

Before signing the so-called Treaty of Tordesillas in 1494, Isabella and Ferdinand had employed spies to seek out new information regarding the rumoured southern continent. Yet somehow the Spanish sovereigns greatly misjudged what these advisers had to say. Although Columbus did indeed discover the mainland on his third voyage to the New World in 1498, he never set foot on land, leaving the Portuguese navigator Pedro Ãlvares Cabral to lay claim to Brazil in the year 1500. As predicted, its coast lay east of the demarcation, meaning that, according to the treaty, it rightly belonged to Portugal.

This was undoubtedly a crushing blow for the Spanish sovereigns, who realised that they should never have signed the agreement. Moreover, one of the advisers who reported back on what was known about the continent to the south had earlier provided both them and Columbus with more than just confirmation of its existence. In a letter to Columbus dated 8 August 1495, Jaime Ferrer de Blanes, a distinguished Spanish geographer and trader in precious stones, stated that he had heard from 'Hindooes and Arabs and Ethiopians [i.e. black Africans]' and from 'many conversations I have had in the Levant, in Alcaire and Domas' that 'within the equinoctial regions there are great and precious things, such as fine stones and gold and spices *and drugs* . . . [author's emphasis]'.[49] Furthermore, that 'the inhabitants are black or tawny . . . when your Lordship finds such a people, an abundance of the said things will not be lacking'.[50]

What kind of 'drugs' had Ferrer in mind when he announced that they would be found in 'abundance' within the 'equinoctial regions'? Were they simply medicinal drugs, or were they something more exotic, such as tobacco and cocaine? We shall never know the truth of the matter, although this information really does open up the possibility that an age-old transatlantic trade route could well have existed between the West African coast and the Americas. More important, it would appear that one of the principal commodities that travelled between the two continents was drugs – drugs that could have found their way into Egypt by the beginning of the first millennium BC.

Yet if the pharaonic Egyptians were indeed dealing in drugs such as tobacco and the coca leaf, who might have been responsible for these transatlantic shipments? Was it a seafaring culture of American origin, or were these precious commodities shipped into either the Mediterranean or Red Sea by a known seafaring culture of the ancient world? Since there seems to be no hard evidence whatsoever to substantiate the idea that any pre-Columbian culture of the Americas paid regular visits to the Old World, we must look for another solution to this mystery. In which case, we must ask ourselves this: were the Egyptians themselves in a position to establish trading links with the American continent or were they merely receivers of class-A drugs that would appear to have originated in a tropical paradise that lay beyond the Western Ocean? It is with these thoughts in mind that we must take a closer look at the maritime capabilities of the ancient Egyptians.

CHAPTER IX

OLMECS AND ELEPHANTS

On the southern side of the Great Pyramid there is a long, slim, glass-fronted building known as the Boat Museum. Inside is one of the two large funerary vessels discovered in stone-lined pits located at the base of this wonder of the ancient world, built by the pharaoh Khufu around 4,500 years ago. Made of Lebanese cedar, this enormous boat is over 43.3 metres long, 5.9 metres wide, with an estimated weight displacement of 45 tonnes.

Egyptologists tell us that the purpose of these vessels was to enable the soul of the dead pharaoh – in this case Khufu – to make his final voyage into the afterlife. Such funerary practices were common in ancient Egypt. For example, up to 12 even older boat burials, all 18 to 21 metres in length, have been uncovered within the North Cemetery at Abydos in southern Egypt. These examples, discovered in 1991 and still only partially excavated, date to the formative years of Egyptian history known as the Early Dynastic, or Archaic Period, *c.* 3100–2700 BC.[1] Other boat pits have been found in Early Dynastic necropolises at places such as Saqqara and Helwan.[2]

Gazing up at this proud ancient form is a breathtaking experience. Its high prow, sturdy oars and central cabin all exude an impression of great confidence, coupled with a profound understanding of maritime knowledge spanning not hundreds but many thousands of years. It is easy to imagine it on the high seas, cutting through crashing waves towards some distant land.

This view, however, is extremely misleading since Khufu's boat was never intended for the high seas. The whole structure is stitched together using rope, with lines of mortise and tenon joints across the hull. It would have leaked badly and eventually disintegrated in the calmest of waters. Such realisations have led scholars to assume that Egypt simply borrowed its maritime expertise from foreign cultures. This might be so, but there *is* good evidence to show that the Egyptians really did possess large seagoing vessels that embarked on immensely long sea journeys.

There is, for example, the story of a Persian navigator named Sataspes, who in *c.* 470 BC was set the task of circumnavigating Africa by King Xerxes. Accepting the challenge, Sataspes proceeded to Egypt, where he acquired a ship and crew and sailed out beyond the Pillars of Hercules.[3] He passed the Libyan headland, 'known as Cape Soloeis', without incident, and then continued southwards. After 'many months' of journeying, and 'finding that more water than he had crossed still lay ever before him, he put about, and came back to Egypt'.[4] On his return to the Persian court Sataspes claimed he had not been able to complete the journey 'because the ship stopped, and would not go any further'.[5] Xerxes, however, was not impressed, and so promptly had him impaled!

The plight of Sataspes was recorded by the Greek historian Herodotus, who said he had gained the story from the Carthaginians. If this was correct, we must see in it another attempt by this seafaring nation to promote rumours concerning shallow waters and treacherous seas in the hope of preventing any further foreign exploration of the outer ocean.[6] Regardless of this fact, the account does seem to confirm the obviously well-attested seaworthiness of Egyptian vessels at the time of the Persian empire. Furthermore, there is good evidence to indicate that this capability had existed in Egypt for at least 1,500 years prior to this age.

Tale of the Shipwrecked Sailor

Among the Egyptological items found in the Imperial Museum of St Petersburg is a papyrus of unknown provenance. Labelled as P. Leningrad 1115, it tells the story of the Shipwrecked Sailor, an ancient account that has been linguistically dated to the Middle Kingdom of Egyptian history, *c.* 2135–1796 BC.[7] If based on historical reality, it preserves the memory of long sea voyages undertaken by Egyptian mariners during, or even prior to, this distant epoch.

The account tells of a high official returning from a sea journey, during which he has failed to procure whatever the vessel was dispatched to find. He therefore dreads the reception that awaits him at the royal court. An attendant consoles the official, saying that he must celebrate the fact that he has returned to his homeland safe and well. The attendant then informs him of a time when he himself came near to death on a similar long voyage, and it is the finer details of this section of the story that are important here.

According to the attendant's story, he and the rest of the crew were dispatched to the king's mines; located in some foreign land, on a vessel 120 cubits (54 to 66 metres) long and 40 cubits (18 to 22 metres) wide.[8] These measurements, if accurate, speak of an enormous boat, larger than the ceremonial vessels found at Giza, and far greater than the merchant ships and caravels on which Christopher Columbus and his crews reached the New World.

The crew of 120 were said to have been 'the pick of Egypt', and to confirm this statement the text states that 'looked they at sky, looked they at land'[9] – 'seen the heavens and seen the earth' in another translation[10] – implying that they had made similar long voyages before and were familiar with the art of celestial navigation. In addition to this, the crew could 'foretell a storm before it came; a tempest before it struck',[11] suggesting that they possessed a sound knowledge of maritime weather prediction.

The story relates how the attendant was shipwrecked after the vessel had encountered waves eight cubits (3.6 to 4.4 metres) high. All the crew except for him were killed, and after being cast on to the 'island of the *ka*', he remained alone for three days before encountering a huge bearded serpent 30 cubits (13.5 to 16.5 metres) in length. It addressed the sailor, telling him that it was the surviving member of a family of 75 serpents that had lived on the island before a 'star fell, and they [the serpents] went up in flames through it'.[12]

The monster said that a vessel would come to take the shipwrecked sailor back to his native land. On its arrival the Egyptian told his host that he would dispatch great riches to the island as a sign of his appreciation for the kind assistance he had received. The story continues:

> Then he [the serpent] laughed at me for the things I had said, which seemed foolish to him. He said to me: 'You are not rich in myrrh and all kinds of incense. But I am the lord of Punt, and myrrh is my very own. That *hknw*-oil you spoke of sending, it abounds on this island. Moreover, when you have left this place, you will not see this island again; it will have become water.'[13]

The above passage is often quoted by ancient mysteries writers to lend weight to the theory that the pharaonic Egyptians possessed their own concept of a paradisical island – abundant in fruits, game and riches – that was destroyed through fire and flood. Yet from our knowledge of Egyptian geography, we know that the mysterious land of Punt lay to the south of Egypt, beyond Ethiopia. In this knowledge, it has been suggested that the mythical 'island of the *ka*' might have been located on the east coast of Africa, plausibly in the vicinity of what is today Somalia.[14]

The nature of the island's destruction will be dealt with in a separate chapter. However, the importance of the story is that it would appear to confirm that the kings of Egypt regularly initiated daring maritime expeditions in an attempt to seek out and bring back mined commodities that presumably included rare metals and precious minerals. The Tale of the Shipwrecked Sailor also confirms that during the Middle Kingdom of Egyptian history, enormous seagoing vessels, like the ones described both in this text and by Herodotus in the story of Sataspes, were crewed not by foreigners but by skilled Egyptians.

We also know from wall inscriptions that in the reign of the Egyptian female king Hatshepsut (1490–1468 BC), a flotilla of ships was dispatched to the fabled land of Punt. In the Deir el-Bahri mortuary temple of Hatshepsut in western Thebes, inscriptions speak of this celebrated expedition and record that, along with a large collection of exotic animals, 31 live myrrh trees were brought back to Egypt for transplantation.[15] Lavish scenes depicting the wealth of this distant land are displayed on the walls of the temple, despite the fact that it still remains unclear where the fleet might have reached on its long sea voyage.

Elliot Smith and the Egyptians

Having established the maritime capability of the Egyptians, we must go on to ask whether its vessels were in a position to have sailed the Western Ocean. If so, could they have reached the Americas? It is an extraordinary thought, and one that has captured the imaginations of scholars and mystics alike since the theory was first proposed during the seventeenth century by the German Jesuit scholar and physicist Athanasius Kircher (1602–1680) in his work *Oedipus Ægyptiacus*. This book postulated the Egyptian colonisation not only of the American continent but also of India, China and Japan.

Among the more adventurous scholars to have tackled the problem was Australian-born brain anatomist and Egyptologist Grafton Elliot Smith. In a book entitled *Elephants and Ethnologists*, published in 1924, he argued for the diffusion of Egyptian culture into the Americas via India and China, citing as primary evidence of his theory a carved relief on a commemoration stela found in the Mayan city of Copan in Honduras. To him Stela B, as it is catalogued, showed the heads of two elephants, back to back, each with its own rider.[16] More conventional scholars have, however, demonstrated that they are not elephants at all but macaws, an apparent error of judgement that made Smith a laughing stock. The truth is that nobody really knows whether or not they are macaws. As we shall see, evidence of ancient contact between Southeast Asia and Central America has come thick and fast in recent years.

The Olmec Heads

The prospect of ancient Egyptians trading with, or at least reaching, the Americas was given a huge boost at the commencement of the

1970s by explorer Thor Heyerdahl, following the success of his Ra II expedition from Morocco to the Caribbean island of Barbados. He opened the way for further speculation and discovery with respect to transatlantic contact in the distant past, a subject that was taken up by Indian writer Rafique Ali Jairazbhoy. Between 1974 and 1992 he penned three books that cite cultural, architectural, artistic and religious parallels between the pharaonic Egyptians, China and early Central American cultures, in particular the Olmec civilisation that thrived in Mexico between *c.* 1200 and 400 BC. It is their culture that produced the famous colossal stone heads regularly cited as proof positive of African contact with the Americas in prehistoric times. In all, some twelve of these colossal heads exist: four at the great Olmec centre of La Venta in the state of Tabasco,[17] seven at San Lorenzo, on the Rio Chiquito,[18] and another at Tres Zapotes, near Hueyapan, in the state of Vera Cruz.[19] They are fashioned from single pieces of basalt that weigh up to 20 tonnes apiece.

Of those present at the Parque-Museo de La Venta in Villahermosa (the original La Venta site having been destroyed during commercial exploitation of the region), one stands 2.55 metres high and is 6.6 metres in circumference. Another, 2.7 metres high, has the top of its head flattened, showing that it was once used as an altar. A speaking tube runs from its ear through to its mouth, which enabled it to function as an oracle during ceremonies. The heads also bear strange headdresses, described variously as resembling a 'helmeted dome',[20] an upturned kettle or an American football helmet.[21] Some also have individual teeth, as well as earplugs on which feature designs, such as carved crosses. Curiously, on their discovery, the heads at La Venta were found to be facing east, towards the direction of the rising sun.[22]

Their broad faces, wide cheeks, rounded jaws, full lips and flattened noses give them an uncanny resemblance to black Africans. More intriguing still is that their sheer size and weight, along with their prominent position at cult centres such as La Venta and San Lorenzo, tell us that they represented individuals with an extremely high status in Olmec society.

Foreign visitors first noted the Olmec heads' African features as early as 1862. A traveller by the name of José María Melgar y Serrano was passing through the province of San Andrés Tuxtla (the state of Vera Cruz) when he learned of the recent discovery at a site named Tres Zapotes, near Hueyapan, of a monolithic human form. He ordered it to be fully cleared of undergrowth and was amazed by what he saw. In the bulletin of the Mexican Geographical and Statistical Society, Serrano recorded that the colossal head was:

> ... a work of art ... without exaggeration, a magnificent sculpture ... but what most amazed me was that the type that it represents is

> Ethiopian [i.e. black African]. I concluded that there had doubtless been blacks in this region, and from the very earliest ages of the world.[23]

No other type of person is represented by the Olmec in a similar fashion, leading us to conclude that the individuals portrayed by the stone heads were either great leaders or revered ancestors. Furthermore, a number of smaller, terracotta statues that also seem to represent black Africans have been found at various sites, belonging not just to the Olmec but also to other early Mexican cultures.[24] Like the giant heads themselves, they bear distinctive features such as broad faces, thick lips and flattened noses. In addition to these traits, many of them also have tight curly hair and tribal scars. Further evidence of the presence among the Olmec of black Africans has come from the study of 98 skeletons found in the pre-classical cemetery of Tlatilco. A Polish craniologist named Andrzej Weircinski determined that 13.5 per cent could be directly compared with the skeletons of African peoples.[25] A collection of 25 skeletons from a much later Olmec cemetery at Cerro de la Mesas produced a figure indicating that only 4.5 per cent of those examined bore African traits, implying that in the intervening period intermarriage with the indigenous population had significantly reduced the number of foreign males present in the community.[26] The only conclusion to be drawn from this slender evidence is that black Africans appeared among the Olmec very early on in the development of their culture, but that in later times their presence had dwindled considerably.

It was not until the 1950s that carbon-14 testing of organic materials was conducted in connection with the La Venta site. A joint expedition by the National Geographic, the Smithsonian Institution and the University of California provided dates with an average reading of 814 BC (+/−134 years).[27] It is now known that construction began at La Venta as early as *c.* 1100 BC and ceased abruptly sometime around *c.* 400 BC.[28]

If therefore the colossal heads and terracotta statues do represent black Africans, as so many writers have suggested, it would imply that some kind of transoceanic contact existed between Africa and the Gulf of Mexico as early as *c.* 1100 BC and as late as *c.* 400 BC. Understandably, scholars have tended to shy away from tackling this problem, although Jairazbhoy and others, such as the noted linguist, anthropologist and author Ivan Van Sertima of Rutgers University, have concluded that black Africans arrived in Mexico from Egypt. In Jairazbhoy's case, he believes they journeyed here during the reign of Rameses III (1182–1151 BC), who spoke of a maritime journey upon the 'inverted waters' bound for a mountain named Manu, said to have been situated 'in the Far West at the edge of the Underworld'.[29] He saw this as signifying a sea voyage across the Atlantic Ocean to Mexico in '1187 BC', around the time of the foundation of the Olmec civilisation.[30] Van Sertima, although agreeing with many of the points raised by Jairazbhoy in his books, considers that the stone heads represent Nubian kings, who ruled Egypt between *c.* 751–656 BC and established Olmec cult centres such as La Venta and Tres Zapotes.[31]

These are all bold and noble assertions that might eventually prove to be correct. Yet they all suffer from inherent problems that must be addressed if conclusions of this type are to be made. First, there is no reason to take Rameses III's legendary journey to the mountain in the 'Far West' as a historical event. The story is far more likely to represent some kind of symbolic voyage to the *duat*-underworld, the subterranean domain through which the sun was said to pass from sunset to sunrise each night. In the religion of the ancient Egyptians the deceased pharaoh had to navigate this dark realm travelling on a solar barque from west to east before he could fully enter the afterlife. Furthermore, although it was once thought that the genesis of the Olmec civilisation was around 1200 BC, the time-frame of Rameses III's reign, it is now known that its first beginnings could have been as early as *c.* 1500 BC. Quite clearly, this revised chronology brings into question Jairazbhoy's assertions, a problem he himself admitted in his 1974 book *Ancient Egyptians and Chinese in America*.[32]

Van Sertima's ideas fare little better. First, there is no reason to assume that the colossal heads at La Venta date from the time-frame of the Nubian Egyptian dynasty of kings, *c.* 751–656 BC. These dates fall somewhere within construction phases III and IV at the site, which took place between *c.* 800 and 400 BC. It is far more likely that they date from building phase II, *c.* 1000–800 BC, when the greatest amount of construction work took place at La Venta. It is even possible that the heads date from the earliest building phase, *c.* 1100–1000 BC. It was during this period that the foundations of the great court were laid out and work began on La Venta's famous ten-sided pyramid, which is also cited by Van Sertima as evidence of Nubian contact with the Olmec. In addition to this, the Nubian kings of Egypt are not known to have made long sea journeys to distant lands in the distant west. Furthermore, no obviously Egyptian item has ever turned up at an Olmec site, and no Olmec artefact has ever been found in Egypt.

Lastly, there is the enigma of the heads themselves. Even though Mesoamerican scholars accept that they are lifelike representations of either great leaders or highly revered ancestors, they are unable to accept that the heads show Negroid features. In their opinion, they depict the Olmec themselves, whose distinctive features are still to be observed among those who inhabit the same regions today. This might seem like denying the blatantly obvious, for whatever the colossal heads represent, it certainly isn't the indigenous population. Yet do the heads *really* depict black Africans?

Baby-Faced Visitors

In addition to the clearly Negroid reliefs and statues in stone and terracotta, excavations at Olmec sites in Mexico have revealed a large number of figurines that clearly bear distinctive Mongoloid, or Oriental, features. Many of these so-called 'baby-faced' items, such as the famous bearded figurine known as the Wrestler of Uxpanapa, bear an uncanny resemblance to Chinese or Japanese individuals. Betty J. Meggers, a Research Associate of the Department of Anthropology at the Smithsonian Institution's National Museum of Natural History, has argued the case for contact between China's Shang dynasty and the Olmec culture. She has demonstrated that a large number of traits belonging to the Shang of *c.* 1750 BC closely parallel those found in connection with Olmec sites currently dated to *c.* 1200 BC. They include writing, the carving of jade, the use of batons as symbols of office, similarities in styles of settlement and architecture, as well as several other comparisons relating to art and religion.[33]

Unexpected support for her theories came in 1996, when it was announced that two Chinese specialists on the Shang dynasty, Dr Mike Xu and Han Ping Chen, had found that they could 'read' markings carved on stone celts unearthed at Olmec sites.[34] Amid the inevitable publicity that surrounded this announcement, Xu and Chen were severely criticised by scholars, and yet they stood their ground and did not retract their initial statements on the matter. In the opinion of the Chinese scholars: 'Recent discoveries of ancient relics from both Olmec land and Shang sites, plus intensive new studies on the Olmec and Shang writings and DNA testing, have proved Meggers' original ideas to be even more relevant, visionary, and correct.'[35]

Strengthening the link between Southeast Asia and Mexico are the close parallels in the production of bark-cloth and paper-making techniques, a subject adequately investigated in the 1960s by Paul Tolstoy. He found that of 121 traits peculiar to this industry, 92 of them were shared by both Southeast Asia and Mexico. He further pointed out that no fewer than 44 of these traits were employed only to increase the overall effect, and so were therefore not essential to the main production of the material.[36]

In addition to this evidence, there is also the case of the eclipse calendar included in a Mayan astronomical work known as the Dresden Codex (the Maya of the Yucatán inherited aspects of their calendar system from the earlier Olmec culture). Not only does it work on precisely the same basis as an eclipse calendar used in China during the Han dynasty, *c.* 202 BC–AD 220, but both incorporate exactly the same errors![37] A common origin seems to be the only explanation.

Then there is the discovery at an archaeological site in the Valdivia region of Ecuador, close to the Pacific coast, of very distinctive pottery 'virtually identical' in design to that found in association with the Jomon culture of Japan, *c.* 3000 BC.[38] Work on the Jomon–Valdivia relationship has also been championed by Betty Meggers. She feels that there is enough evidence of a correlation between the two cultures on opposite sides of the Pacific to imply direct contact in prehistoric times.[39]

More significantly, recent studies in human lymphocyte antigens (HLAs) – proteins found in white blood cells – have revealed a direct correlation between certain peoples in Southeast Asia (as well as certain Afro-Arabian tribes) and native peoples of the Americas, such as the Ramah Navajo, the Mapuche, the Araucano and the Nahua or Uto-Aztecans of the Mexican plain.[40] Since this link is purely genetic in nature, it can have stemmed only from cross-fertilisation between these different cultures divided by the Pacific Ocean.

All this evidence suggests that if we are to look east for a solution to the colossal heads, we should also consider the possibility that a transpacific trade route existed between Southeast Asia and the Americas. Indeed, this is the one solution that the academic community is more open-minded towards. My own opinion is that, in addition to black Africans, some of the colossal heads display clear Polynesian features of a racial type present among the island cultures of the mid-Pacific.

Even though most people scoffed at the theories proposed by G. Elliot Smith, history is now proving him correct. There is hard evidence to suggest transpacific contact between Mexico and ancient China and Japan. Yet if he was correct in this respect, could he also have been right when he proposed that the Egyptian influence among the Mexican cultures had come not from across the Atlantic Ocean but via Southeast Asia? The answer seems to be yes. However, there are also good reasons to consider seriously the possibility of contact between the Olmec civilisation and the peoples of the eastern Mediterranean.

A Bearded Mystery

In addition to the colossal heads and multifaceted pyramid that were once located at La Venta, the cult centre also possessed a number of curious stone reliefs that seem in stark contrast to the images of typically Olmec individuals. They show figures with pronounced Semitic, or at least eastern Mediterranean, features that include aquiline noses, high cheekbones, extended jaws, bushy moustaches and full beards. Similar reliefs are to be seen at the Olmec site of Monte Alban.[41] Moreover, in addition to the statues and figurines that seem to resemble either black Africans or Orientals, many other examples in stone and terracotta appear to portray Semitic individuals with characteristic long faces and pointed beards, something highly irregular in Olmec art.[42] Moreover, it is a fact that the native peoples of Central America were incapable of growing substantial facial hair.

American archaeologist George C. Vaillant made a study of bearded faces in Mexican art and found several primary examples from various different cultures of the pre-Columbian era.[43] Although he was not prepared to accept that this evidence demonstrated the presence of individuals from an ancient world culture, he did admit that: 'We are left in the perplexing position of having the same physical traits portrayed by artists of several different tribal groups, who evidently recognised a people different from themselves.'[44]

One stone relief with apparent Semitic features found at La Venta has been nicknamed 'Uncle Sam' by archaeologists. American writer Constance Irwin paid special attention to this relief, as well as another example found at the site, in her book *Fair Gods and Stone Faces*, first published in 1963. In this landmark work she pointed out that, in addition to the obvious Semitic face, trimmed beard and Mediterranean-style dress, the individuals seen in the reliefs appear to be wearing 'shoes with odd pointed upturned toes', something completely alien to conventional Olmec art.[45] Irwin noted that only three Mediterranean civilisations wore such shoes: the Etruscans, the Hittites and the Phoenicians.[46] The Etruscans, she concluded, 'would seem the least likely to have found their way to American shores',[47] while the Hittites of Anatolia (modern Turkey) were a 'land-bound' peoples.[48] This left only the Phoenicians, whom she proposed conducted sea journeys to the Gulf of Mexico and were responsible for introducing black Africans into Mexico.[49]

This conclusion on the part of Constance Irwin is incredible. Yet how else might we explain the presence at Olmec sites of statues, figurines and reliefs that appear to show individuals with quite obvious eastern Mediterranean and black African features? As there seems to be no hard evidence to suggest that the Egyptians themselves ever reached the Americas, surely we must begin to look towards another culture altogether in order to discover those responsible for the hypothetical transcontinental drugs trade. As we saw in Chapter Six, the most obvious navigational route across the Atlantic other than the Northwest Passage is to follow the

North Equatorial Current from the Cape Verdes across to the Caribbean. Evidence suggests that both black Africans and Afro-Arabians were very much aware of the existence of the South American landmass long before the Portuguese navigator Pedro Ãlvares Cabral 'discovered' Brazil in the year 1500. Furthermore, tobacco smoking seems to have been practised on both sides of the Atlantic before Columbus, and one of the oldest known smoking pipes was found on Marajo Island, which lies at the mouth of the River Amazon in Brazil. It has been dated to *c.* 1500 BC, the suggested foundation date of the Olmec civilisation and just 300 years before the artisans of northern Syria began fashioning stone smoking pipes.

Could all these facts be linked in some way? Could those renowned navigators the Phoenicians have been trading with the Olmec civilisation, perhaps acting in concert with black African tribes that inhabited the Atlantic coast of West Africa? Could it really be the faces of Phoenicians that stare out from the carved stone reliefs found at cult centres such as La Venta, Monte Alban and Tres Zapotes? If so, was it really possible that the true trans-atlantic dealers in exotic drugs, such as cocaine and tobacco, were not the Egyptians but the Phoenicians? Who exactly were the Phoenicians, and how far did their maritime capabilities extend?

CHAPTER X

THE MUREX MERCHANTS

THE LAND OF THE PHOENICIANS was made up of a series of city-states located on the Mediterranean Levant coast in what is today Syria and the Lebanon. In the Old Testament, those who inhabited these territories were known collectively as the Canaanites, the peoples of Canaan, the 'land of the purple'; a title that translates into Greek as Phoenicia. It was an appellation derived from the deep crimson or purple dye extracted from the murex and purpura shellfish and used to colour the expensive textiles so prized in the ancient world. Indeed, this dyed cloth was considered a luxury fit for royalty, surely the reason for the age-old connection between aristocracy and the colour purple.[1]

The Phoenician nation evolved originally from a fusion of existing races that inhabited the Middle East in the second millennium BC. They included Semitic-speaking peoples from northern Syria and Iraq, as well as an indigenous Neolithic culture that had established a sea-port at ancient Gebal, or Byblos, on the Lebanese coast sometime around 4500 BC.[2] This same Byblos, or Proto-Phoenician, culture was trading raw materials and other commodities with both Egypt and Crete as early as 3000 BC.[3] How much further afield its trade routes extended is a matter of speculation, although it is likely that they were familiar visitors to coastal ports throughout the Mediterranean (see Chapter Twenty-six).

The earliest known Phoenician historian is the priest Sanchoniathon of Berytus (Beirut). He lived during the twelfth century BC, and his important work, entitled the *Theology of the Phoenicians*, is preserved in the writings of a first-century historian named Philo of Byblos. Despite its fragmentary form, Sanchoniathon's textual account provides us with some fascinating insights into the origins of the Phoenicians, who, he asserts, inherited their maritime capability from a dynasty of gods that founded Byblos during some bygone epoch.[4] These mythical individuals are said to have introduced civilised society and to have given birth to many sons and daughters who bore the names of later countries and city-states throughout the eastern Mediterranean. More curiously, it is said that one god named Taautus, a Phoenician form of the Egyptian moon-god Thoth, was granted the land of Egypt, where he created its first civilisation.[5]

This tentative understanding of Levantine prehistory, from both archaeology and mythic tradition, enables us to understand why the later Phoenicians were able so easily to pull ahead of their neighbours in Egypt, Assyria and Babylon to become the undisputed masters of the high seas. For unlike any other nation of the first millennium BC, as experienced merchants and seafarers, they established city-ports and settlements, many based around offshore islands that stretched from one end of the Mediterranean to the other. They also had a port named Ezion-geber (modern Pharaoh Island, near Eilat) on the Red Sea, from where they set out on long journeys as far afield as Somalia on the East African coast, ports in the Arabian Gulf and plausibly even India. Every type of raw material and commodity, from textiles to herbs, incense, spice, fish, timber, fruit, metals, jewellery and trinkets, were all traded from one port to another throughout the ancient world.

With the foundation in *c.* 1100 BC of major city-ports at Gades and Tartessos in Iberia, the Phoenicians were able to spread their influence beyond the Pillars of Hercules. This position was strengthened greatly with the foundation in *c.* 814 BC of a sister colony at Carthage on the Mediterranean coast of Libya (modern Tunisia). As a nation it grew with such strength that, following the submission of the Phoenician city-states of Tyre and Sidon to the Babylonian king Nebuchadnezzar in the early sixth century BC, Carthage seized the Phoenician trading ports in Iberia, which thereafter came under its control. Despite this takeover, most ancient writers continued to refer to Gades and Tartessos as ports belonging to the 'Phoenicians'.

In the centuries that followed, the Carthaginians and Iberic Phoenicians explored the outer ocean and established island settlements, such as Cerne and Mogador on the Morocco coast, in order to allow further exploration and trading exchanges with native peoples. Together they pushed out as far as the British Isles in search of tin and the Baltic coast of Germany in search of amber.[6] We have also seen how the Carthaginian general Hanno explored the West Coast of Africa all the way down to the Gulf of Guinea, founding five cities along the way. We also know for certain that the Carthaginians traded with indigenous peoples of West Africa, and how such trade exchanges were made.

Herodotus tells us that in Africa at least, when Carthaginian vessels arrived at the determined place of trading, the cargo would be transferred to the shore. Here the merchants would spread out their wares before lighting a fire and retiring to the ships. The smoke would mark out the spot, prompting local tribesmen to approach. They would place next to the goods an amount of gold deemed appropriate as payment, and then retreat. In due course the Carthaginians would return to see whether the offer in gold was sufficient enough. If it was, then they would take the payment and go; if not, they would once more withdraw, allowing the tribesmen to add further gold to the existing offer. This bartering process would continue until the Carthaginians were satisfied that the correct price had been paid – the whole exchange taking place without any form of communication or misconduct between either party: hence the term 'dumb commerce'.[7]

Around the Cape

Only the Phoenicians and the Carthaginians would seem to have been in a position to trade directly with the Americas during the first millennium BC. Moreover, the maritime influence of the Phoenicians on Egyptian history is well attested. Herodotus tells us that in an attempt to find a means of transferring vessels from the Red Sea to Egypt's Mediterranean ports, the pharaoh Necho II (*c.* 610–595 BC) commissioned a group of 'Phoenician men' to circumnavigate the African continent. This they accomplished by first departing from Ezion-geber, and then journeying south along the East African coast until they reached the Cape of Good Hope. From here the vessels sailed in stages along the West African coast until, in the third year of their journey, they finally entered the Mediterranean. It is said that the fleet was able to sustain itself on the long voyage by setting up temporary settlements in the autumn and sowing and harvesting their own corn.[8]

As a footnote to the story, Herodotus tells us that: 'They declared – I for my part do not believe them, but perhaps others may – that in sailing round Libya [i.e. Africa] they had the sun upon their right hand.'[9] This is in fact the one thing that proves that the Phoenicians really did make the journey. We know this because the peoples of the ancient world would not, in theory, have known that the solar orb is seen to spend most of its year in the northern sky when viewed from a position below the Tropic of Capricorn.

If the Phoenicians were able to achieve such extraordinary feats of seafaring ingenuity 2,100 years before Portuguese navigators would again make the same journey, just how far were they willing to go? If we might draw a comparison with Hanno's recorded exploration of the African coast in *c.* 425 BC, the Phoenicians' circumnavigation of the same continent 175 years earlier was not for the purposes of seeing their names in the history books.

Unquestionably, their own agenda was to establish settlements in order to enhance further their own trading capability, seemingly under the sponsorship of Egyptian kings such as Necho II. The Phoenicians were clearly seeking to exploit potential new sources of raw materials and saleable commodities that could be transported with relative ease to sea-ports both in the Mediterranean and on the Red Sea.

Transoceanic Contact

In Chapter Five we saw how evidence of the various island groups on the eastern Atlantic seaboard was known to the ancient world. We also saw how the Phoenician and Carthaginian mariners would appear to have established settlements in the Madeiras, and also on the island of Cerne, which lay either on the edge of the Western Sahara or near the mouth of the Senegal river. We also know that they reached the Azores and the British Isles. Yet did they get any further? Did they reach the other side of the Atlantic Ocean? The answer would appear to be yes.

We have, for example, the writings of Pseudo-Aristotle and Diodorus Siculus, who both speak of Carthaginians settling on Atlantic islands with mild climates and navigable rivers. If these are not greatly exaggerated references to the Madeiras, they are allusions to Caribbean islands, very probably Cuba or Hispaniola. Not only do they have major navigable rivers, but, as we saw in Chapter Six, they would seem to have been synonymous with the mythical Hesperides, said by Statius Sebosus and others to have lain even beyond the Gorgades,[10] a mythical island group identified with the Cape Verdes.[11] If the Carthaginian settlement of Cerne really did lie at the mouth of the Senegal river, as historian Donald Harden has proposed,[12] it would have been in an ideal position to act as a staging post for transatlantic journeys. Here Iberic-Phoenician or Carthaginian vessels could have taken on board supplies, interpreters, pilots and even a fresh crew before embarking on long journeys to the Caribbean.

Sir Edward Herbert Bunbury, a nineteenth-century Cambridge geographer and Fellow of the Royal Geographical Society, was of the opinion that the legend surrounding the Hesperides, as originally recorded by Hesiod in his *Theogony*, *c.* 700 BC, was 'almost certainly of Phoenician origin'.[13] This lends weight to the view that it was their seafarers who first introduced a knowledge of these islands to the ancient world.

In addition to the above accounts, we also have the testimony of Himilco, the Carthaginian general whose oceanic voyages and maritime lore are mentioned in the writings of the fourth-century Roman historian Rufus Festus Avienus. As detailed in Chapter Two, there is every reason to believe that Himilco was very much aware of the Sargasso Sea and described it in extraordinary detail, saying that it could 'barely be crossed in four months'. If this was so, there seems little doubt that this distinguished Carthaginian navigator journeyed across the Atlantic Ocean and he may thus have been familiar with the West Indies.

In all likelihood the Phoenicians and Carthaginians kept secret what they knew, not just about Atlantic trade routes but also the nature of the materials and commodities to be found in these tropical lands. Neither do we have to see the Phoenicians' circumnavigation of Africa under the Egyptian king Necho II in *c.* 600 BC as the first time that they might have undertaken such a fantastic journey. Remember, this account has been preserved for posterity by Herodotus, who almost certainly learned of the story during his famous visit to Egypt. If this was the case, we have only the Egyptians' testimony that this event took place. From the Phoenicians and Carthaginians themselves there is merely a wall of silence when it comes to any knowledge of exactly where or how far their trading routes might have extended.

A perfect example of the great lengths to which the Iberic Phoenicians would go to prevent any knowledge of the Atlantic trade routes becoming known to the outside world is demonstrated in a story told by the Greek geographer Strabo of a vessel outbound from the Iberic coast. Its destination was evidently the Cassiterides, which we will take to be either the Isles of Scilly or the south-west coast of England. Here they were to exchange pottery, salt and copper utensils with the tin and lead mined at no great depth by the inhabitants. Yet having taken to the open sea, the Phoenician ship's captain noticed that a Roman boat was tailing his vessel. Realising that its intention was to learn the nature and destination of their voyage, he made the decision to alter course and head into 'shoal water', probably the treacherous waters off the Isles of Scilly. Consequently, both vessels were wrecked, although the Phoenician ship captain apparently survived by clinging to a piece of wreckage. On his return to port, he was handsomely compensated by the state for the value of his lost cargo. It is said, however, that by trying many times, the Romans did eventually learn the whereabouts of this trading market, as they probably did with many of the other routes used by the Phoenicians and Carthaginians.[14]

In the face of such extreme measures to protect their trading interests, it is very possible that shipmasters selected black African pilots, interpreters and maybe even deck hands from among the Lixitae to accompany vessels on transatlantic journeys. In this way they could ensure that rumours or stories concerning the opposite continent did not spread among the Iberic or Semitic inhabitants of city-ports in Spain and Africa. However, like any good secret it is eventually going to be lost to the outside world, and this is very likely what happened during the early classical age.

The Paraiba Controversy

One of the most often cited examples of Phoenician contact with the Americas is the so-called Paraiba inscription. According to the story, on 11 September 1872 Viscount Sapucahy, the President of Rio de Janeiro's Instituto Historico, received a package that, on being opened, was found to contain a sheet of curious handwritten characters and a covering letter. This told of the discovery of a carved stone by black slaves working on a plantation owned by one 'Joaquim Alves da Costa' of Pouso Alto, near Paraiba. Understanding its possible significance, da Costa had carefully copied the unusual inscription before duly dispatching it to the viscount.

A member of the institute named Ladislau Netto was given the task of translating and validating the written script, which was quickly identified as Phoenician. To this end he called on the expertise of the Brazilian emperor, Dom Pedro II, since he was the only person in the country with sufficient knowledge of the Semitic languages to even attempt a translation. Having made only partial progress in this respect, the two men decided that they should seek foreign assistance from a more formidable authority on such matters. It was the great French savant and historian Ernest Renan that they contacted. He had conducted excavations in the Lebanon and was an expert in Semitic languages. In an attempt supposedly to safeguard the full potential of the discovery, Netto decided to release only small sections of the text at any one time. Inevitably this aroused suspicion on Renan's part, and after having examined only part of the text the Frenchman decided that he was being duped, and so dismissed the whole episode as a hoax. As a result Dom Pedro withdrew his support, forcing Netto to admit to Renan that he had been mistaken in presuming the inscription genuine. The supposed perpetrator of the fraud, 'Joaquim Alves da Costa', was never traced, adding weight to the conclusions drawn by Renan.

There the matter rested until 1967 when Cyrus H. Gordon, the Director of Mediterranean Studies at Brandeis University in Massachusetts, decided to take up the case of the Paraiba inscription. One of his colleagues, a former graduate student in Hispanic studies, had chanced on a whole scrapbook containing material that related to the early history of the supposed stone, including a more accurate rendition of the inscription. Copies were sent to Gordon, and with some enthusiasm the two men engaged in a full investigation, which seemed to pay remarkable dividends. They were able to ascertain that it was written in a form of Semitic script apparently unknown in 1872.[15] After some difficulties a full translation was finally made. According to them it read as follows:

> We are Sidonian Canaanites from the city of the Merchant King. We were cast up on this distant island, a land of mountains. We sacrificed a youth to the celestial gods and goddesses in the nineteenth year of our mighty King Hiram and embarked from Ezion-geber into the Red Sea. We voyaged with ten ships and were at sea together for two years round Africa. Then we were separated by the hand of Baal and were no longer with our companions. So we have come here, twelve men and three women, into 'Island of Iron'. Am I, the Admiral, a man who would flee? Nay! May the celestial gods and goddesses favour us well.[16]

The text speaks of a 'Canaanite', or Phoenician, vessel that had apparently left the Red Sea port of Ezion-geber bound for the Cape of Africa, the same route taken by the Phoenician mariners who circumnavigated Africa on behalf of the Egyptian king Necho II in *c.* 600 BC. Yet instead of then turning north to sail along the West African coast, the vessel continued on a south-westerly course until finally it reached Brazil. As unlikely as this story might seem, the text matches what we know about the Phoenicians, including their unhealthy appetite for infant sacrifice.[17] Of more interest, however, was the reference in the inscription to the 'hand of Baal', a saying similar to our own expression 'hand of fate'. According to Gordon, its use was unknown before the discovery on Cyprus in 1939 of a Phoenician inscription which contained this very same wording.[18]

After due consideration, Gordon decided that the 'King Hiram' alluded to in the Paraiba inscription was Hiram III, who ruled the Phoenician empire *c.* 553–533 BC.[19] In his book *Before Columbus*, published in 1971, he thus concluded: 'The king can only be Hiram III', meaning that '. . . the voyage from Ezion-geber began in 534, and ended in Brazil in 531'.[20] These dates implied that the voyage must have taken place some two generations after the recorded circumnavigation of Africa by Phoenician mariners in *c.* 600 BC.

Since the 1970s Cyrus Gordon has had a change of heart in respect of the authenticity of the Paraiba inscription.[21] Following considerable criticism from his contemporaries, he at last accepted that the king alluded to in the inscription was not Hiram III but Hiram of Tyre, the biblical king who assisted King David in building his 'house'.[22] The Old Testament also tells us that Hiram of Tyre entered a similar alliance with David's son Solomon, whom he helped to complete the temple in Jerusalem, *c.* 970 BC.[23]

As a legendary biblical character, Hiram of Tyre is accepted to be the master mason of Solomon's Temple, the architecture and design of which is thought to embody the secrets of Freemasonry. In this role, the Phoenician king is revered by Freemasons as the spiritual founder of the Craft. It is therefore now believed that the Paraiba inscription was a fraud perpetrated by Brazilian Freemasons, connected with either the Instituto Historico at Rio de Janeiro or the emperor Dom Pedro II.

With the Paraiba inscription's only academic ally having openly withdrawn his support, it can no longer be cited as reliable evidence of contact with the Americas. There are, however, quite separate indications that the Phoenicians and Carthaginians reached the Americas.[24]

Ancient Artefacts

It is a fact, for instance, that as early as 1787 workmen employed in the construction of the Cambridge to Malden road in Massachusetts are said to have unearthed a hoard of Carthaginian coins. Since none of the navvies present could identify them, they were given away to passers-by who had gathered to marvel at the spectacle. Mercifully, the Revd Thaddeus Mason Harris brought them to the attention of the enlightened American president John Quincy Adams. Harris had happened to chance by on his horse when the discovery was made. Surviving specimens of the copper and silver pieces were finally identified as coins minted in the third century BC. They bore short inscriptions in Kufic, a script used by the Carthaginians.[25]

Further coins, unquestionably minted in Carthage, were unearthed in more recent times by Frederick Gastonguat, a landowner from Waterbury, Connecticut.[26] Barry Fell, a leading epigrapher (the study of ancient inscriptions) and prehistorian, recognised them as belonging to 'the earliest issue of Carthage'. He translated their short inscription in Punic, the language of the Carthaginians, as reading OMMQNI, signifying the term 'in camp', a reference to the fact that they were minted for military usage. They also bore the image of a horse's head, the motif of Carthage.[27] Although conventional American historians have been able to confirm the coins' North African origin, they are unable to accept them as evidence of a Carthaginian presence in the Americas. In their opinion, the coins must have been lost, discarded or deliberately buried during colonial times, and so do not constitute archaeological evidence of any kind.

I find this assumption difficult to understand. A hoard of Carthaginian coins found in 1749 on Corvo has been cited by historians as evidence of this nation's contact with the Azores, even though no other evidence has ever come to light to confirm this supposition. Why, one might ask, have Carthaginian coins found under similar circumstances in the United States not been treated in a similar way? It just does not make sense, other than to assume that there is some kind of political motive for denying evidence of transatlantic contact with the Americas in ancient times. Furthermore, it is not just coins that have suggested a Phoenician presence in New England.

In 1948 an eastern Mediterranean oil lamp, dated to the third century BC, was found at an Amerindian site in Elm Street, Manchester, New Hampshire,[28] while in 1870 at Concord, New Hampshire, an ancient Iberian short iron sword blade was uncovered by Lyman Fellows as he helped dig the foundations for a railroad station. Its wooden knob-hilt had decayed, although an etched inscription was just about visible. Barry Fell identified this as Iberian, and translated it as: 'Hand wrought death dealing steel, able to cut through armor'.[29] In 1993 the item appeared in an exhibition of pre-Columbian artefacts at Jamestown, Virginia.[30]

In addition to the discovery in North America of numerous ancient coins and out-of-place artefacts, there exists a whole range of inscribed stones that are seen as evidence of transoceanic contact with the ancient world. Too many of them exist to list individually, but some are incontestable and imply that foreign visitors from various different cultures travelled to the Americas and left their mark in a number of different ways. What these items, all found in New England, do not do, however, is provide us with any further confirmation of a Phoenician presence in Central America. To continue this line of enquiry we must go on to examine the evidence behind what is arguably one of the most politically sensitive and controversial cases of alleged pre-Columbian contact in the whole of the Americas – the discovery of actual wrecks from the ancient world.

CHAPTER XI

SHIPWRECKS AND SAILORS

IN 1976 A YOUNG DIVER named José Robert Teixéira was spear-fishing by rocks at Ilha do Gobernador, in the Bay of Guanabara, some 24 kilometres outside the busy port of Rio de Janeiro. Searching the clear blue waters for prize fish to sell in the local market, his eyes caught sight of something unfamiliar protruding from the murky seabed. On closer examination he could see that it was three huge jars, each over a metre long, with double-handled necks. Curious to see what they were, he pulled one free from its resting-place. As the fine sand fell away from its curved form, he saw that it was covered in crustaceans, and so knew that it must have lain undisturbed for a very long time.

José retrieved all three of the giant vases that day in the Bay of Guanabara.[1] They fetched a better price than the fish would have done, and so his labours had not been in vain. The antiques dealer who was lucky enough to have purchased these jars knew full well their real value and so took them along to the Brazilian Institute of Archaeology for examination. For too long the scientists pondered over the huge terracotta containers before admitting, somewhat cautiously, that they were ancient 'Greek' amphorae, used to transport commodities such as olives or dates from one port to another in the ancient world.[2]

News of the find spread rapidly through Rio de Janeiro, and soon it seemed that every scuba-diver in the city was heading out to Guanabara Bay to see if they, too, could find ancient jars. As might be expected, Brazilian scholars attempted to explain away their presence by proposing that the amphorae were merely disgorged cargo from a colonial vessel inbound from the Mediterranean.[3]

It was not until five years later that the director of Rio de Janeiro's Maritime Museum decided that they should take a closer look at the site where the amphorae were being discovered. They knew very well that ever since the 1960s a number of similar jars had been located by fishermen in the same general area, so it was quietly speculated that an ancient wreck might lie somewhere in the bay.[4] As a consequence, the director of the museum decided to bring in the expertise of world-renowned underwater archaeologist, shipwreck historian and treasure salvor Robert F. Marx.

Having learned of the discovery of the amphorae, Marx remained a little sceptical. Yet after being introduced to one local diver who had no fewer than 14 of the great jars in his garage, he began to think seriously about the matter. First, he determined that they were not Greek in origin. They were of a design known to have been manufactured around 2,000 years ago at Kouass, near Tangiers, on the Atlantic coast of Morocco.[5] Marx borrowed one of the amphorae and showed it to oceanographers at two of Brazil's leading marine institutes. He was half expecting that they would confirm the thick encrustation to be of Mediterranean origin, showing that the jars had travelled to the New World in colonial times. Instead, the scientists explained that the encrustation was of a type unique to the waters around Guanabara Bay, meaning that it had built up *in situ* over thousands of years. So the answer was clear: the amphorae jars were unquestionably spilled cargo from a vessel that had travelled to Brazil when the Roman Empire was at the height of its power.

Sea-growth removed from the broken amphorae found in the Bay of Jars was sent by Marx to Dr Ruth Turner of Harvard University's Museum of Comparative Zoology, and Dr Walton Smith of the University of Miami's Marine Laboratory. Not only were they able to confirm the findings of the Brazilian scientists, but they also ascertained through carbon-14 testing that the encrustation was at least 1,500 years old.[6] Dr Elizabeth Will of the Department of Classics at the University of Massachusetts, and her colleague Dr Michael Ponsich both concurred with these findings, yet suggested that the jars were of a type manufactured in the Moroccan port of Zilis (as opposed to Kouass), sometime during the third century AD.[7]

Italian Pizza Vendor

Initially, Robert Marx was given the go-ahead by the Brazilian authorities to search for the exact location of the presumably Roman wreck. Although his expedition found no intact amphorae, it did manage to retrieve a large number of shards that included necks and handles, as well as a huge stone disc, perforated at its centre. This, he concluded, could have been a weight anchor from the vessel.[8] Marx also called on the services of Harold E. Edgerton of the Massachusetts Institute of Technology who conducted extensive sonar surveys in the vicinity of the hoped-for wreck. He quickly located two sunken targets on underwater reefs that were

1. The philosopher Plato and his pupil Aristotle, c. 350 BC. In their age rumours and stories abounded regarding an opposite continent, an impassable sea and unknown islands that lay beyond the Pillars of Hercules. One of these islands was Atlantis.

2. The Athenian poet and chief legislator Solon (c. 638–558 BC), whom Plato asserts learnt of the story surrounding the destruction of Atlantis from a priest at the temple of Sais in the Nile Delta. Yet there is every reason to believe that Solon's role in Plato's Atlantis dialogues is not what it seems.

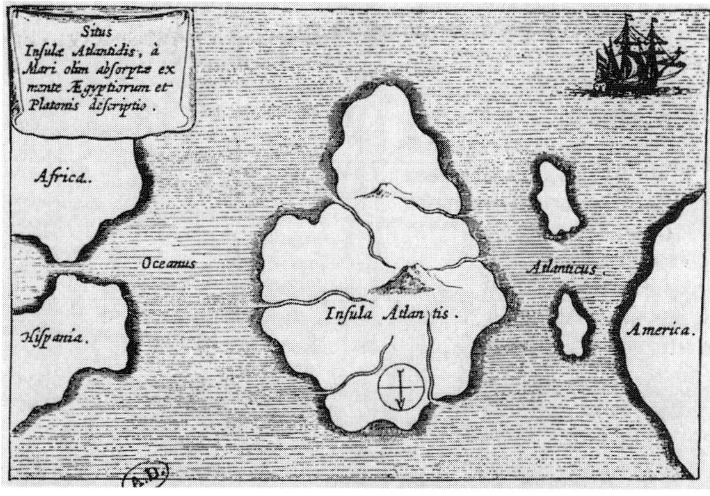

3. Map of Atlantis by seventeenth-century German Jesuit scholar and physicist Athanasius Kircher.

4. Atlas, the Greek god who supported the heavens on his shoulders and gave his name to a mountain range in North Africa. New evidence shows that his legend, integrally connected with the Atlantis story, derives from either Phoenician or Carthaginian sources.

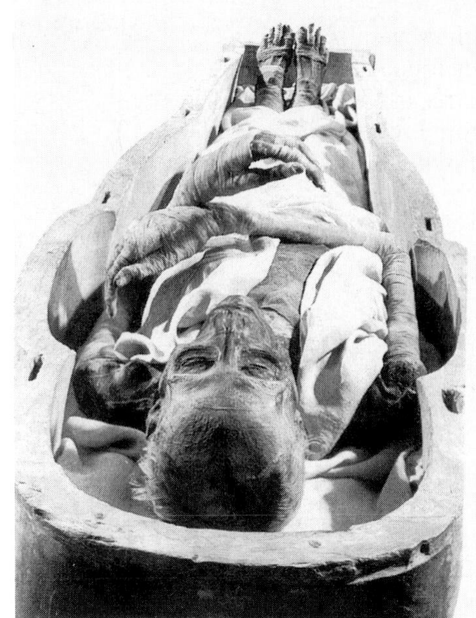

5. An examination of the mummified body of Rameses the Great (pictured) in 1976 revealed that it contained significant traces of the tobacco plant. More recently, Egyptian mummies studied by German toxicologist Svetlana Balabanova have revealed the presence not only of nicotine but also of cocaine, a powerful drug derived from the coca plant native to the Americas.

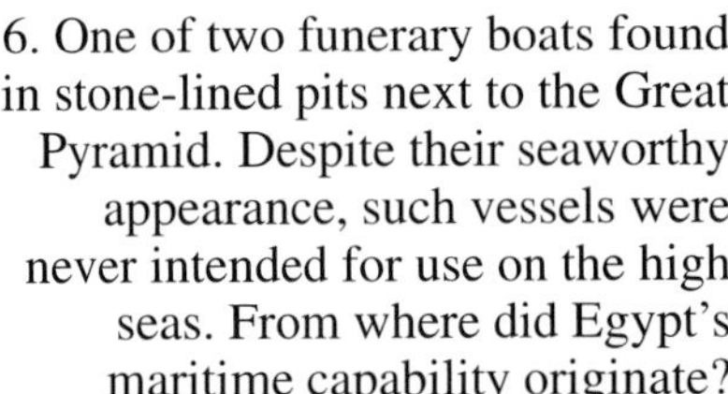

6. One of two funerary boats found in stone-lined pits next to the Great Pyramid. Despite their seaworthy appearance, such vessels were never intended for use on the high seas. From where did Egypt's maritime capability originate?

7. One of the several great stone heads found at key Olmec centres in Mexico, this one from La Venta in Tabasco province. Their resemblance to African individuals is irrefutable, but who were these noble ancestors and what role did they play in the introduction of the Atlantis legend?

8, 9 & 10. African-style head (right) from Vera Cruz, oriental-like statue known as 'The Wrestler' (far right) from Uxpanapan, Vera Cruz, and a ceramic head of Mediterranean appearance (below) with beard and moustache from Tres Zapotes, Vera Cruz. Why did Mesoamerican cultures such as the Olmec and Maya depict individuals with such contrasting racial features?

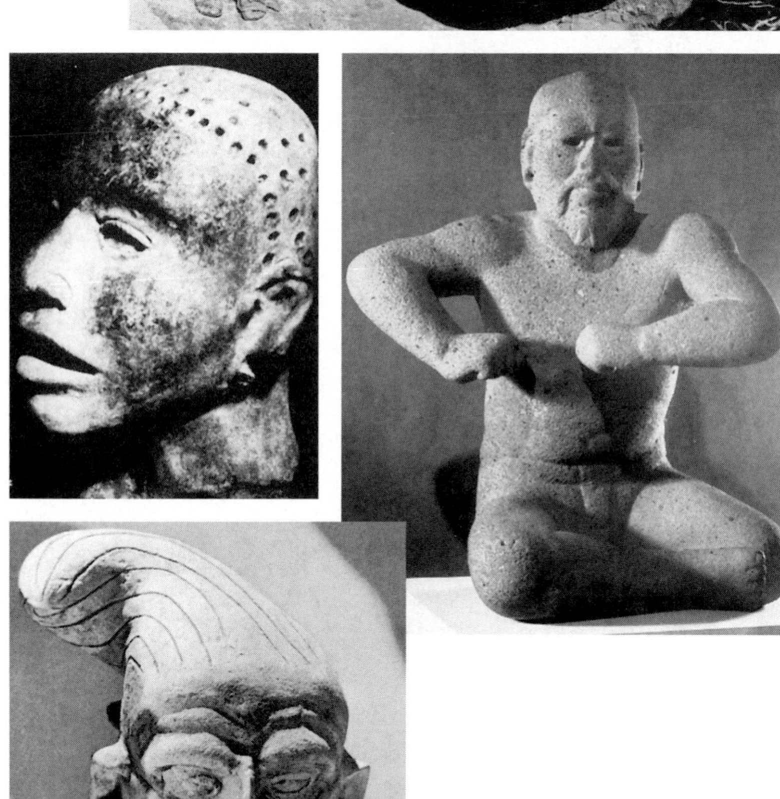

11. Relief from Stela #21 at the Olmec site of La Venta showing the bearded figure nicknamed 'Uncle Sam'. American writer Constance Irwin argued that this carving showed a Phoenician seafarer from the eastern Mediterranean.

12. Exterior wall of fired clay brick belonging to the Palace at the Maya centre of Comalcalco, near Villahermosa, in Tabasco province. Much of the city is constructed from fired brick, some of which bear marks that resemble an archaic script developed in the Indus Valley, where fired bricks were also used.

13. Ceramic head of Afro-Arabian appearance from the Maya site of Comalcalco. Who does it represent? Certainly, it is not a member of the indigenous population as they were incapable of growing substantial facial hair.

14. Cyclopean masonry photographed in the 1920s at Niebla, south-west Spain, by English archaeologist Elena Whishaw. In her opinion this wall formed part of an extensive seaport that thrived as early as 2500 BC.

15. Bust of Christopher Columbus (1430?–1506), the discoverer of the New World, in the Capitoline, Rome. His crew from Palos in south-west Spain only consented to join the Genoese navigator on his celebrated voyage because they fully expected him to find the legendary island of Antilia.

16. Woodcut by the sixteenth-century French traveller André Thevet showing indigenous peoples of the West Indies smoking tobacco in the form of a cigar. Smoking was first encountered by members of Christopher Columbus' crew on the island of Cuba in October 1492.

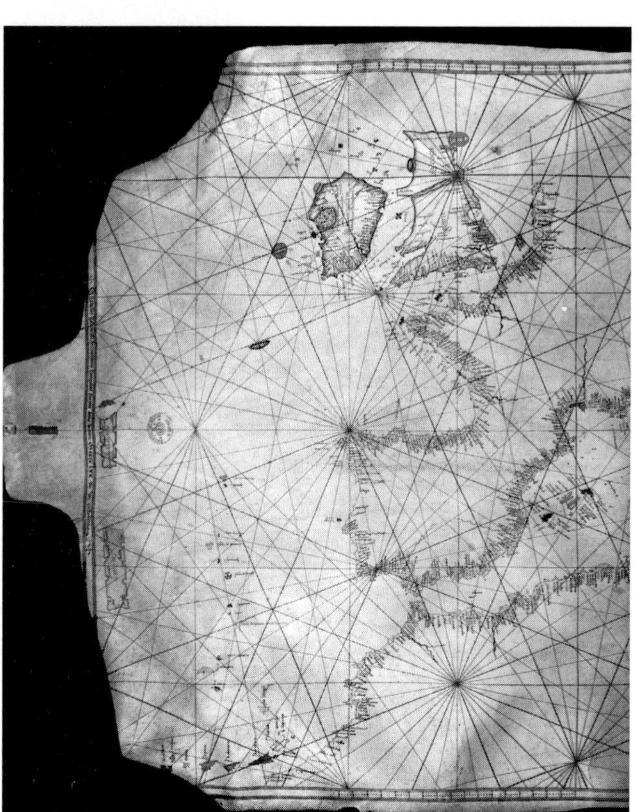

17. Benincasa map of 1476 showing Antilia (bottom left). Knowledge of its existence would seem to have been preserved by the Phoenicians, Carthaginians and Moors long before this legendary Atlantic island began appearing on medieval sea-charts.

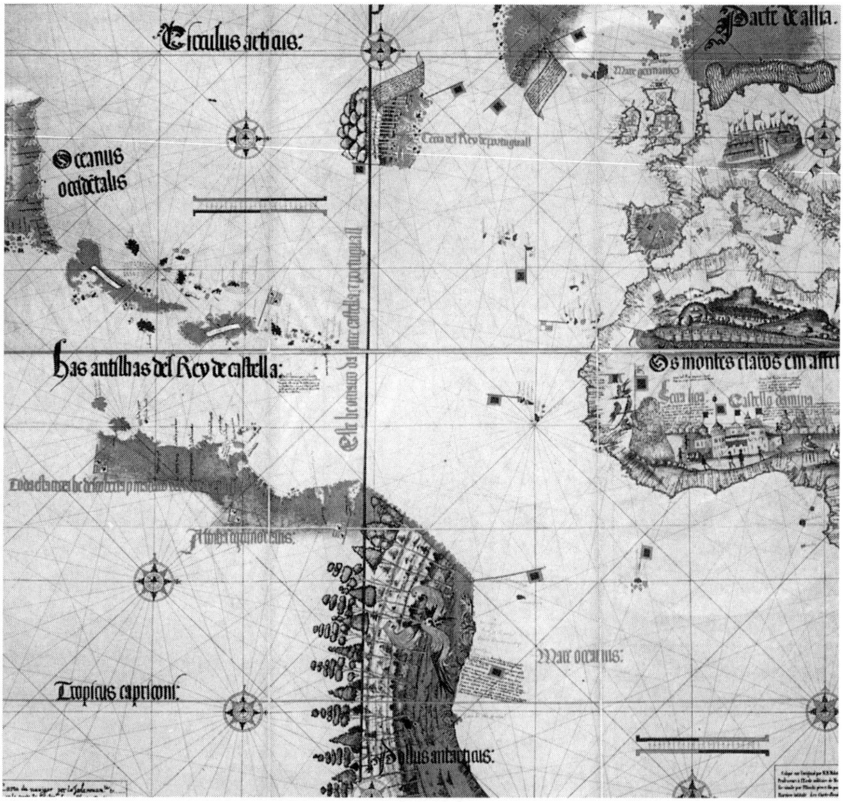

18. The Marine World Chart of Nicolo de Canerio Januensis of 1502, identifying the main islands of the West Indies as the 'Antilhas del Rey de Castella' (Antilles of the King of Castille). It confirms their association with the four islands of Antilia just ten years after Columbus' first voyage to the New World.

19. The Piri Reis map of 1513. Professor Charles Hapgood of Keene College, New Hampshire, concluded that its truncated representation of Cuba was drawn using an ancient source map, supporting the theory of ancient sea journeys to the West Indies in pre-Columbian times.

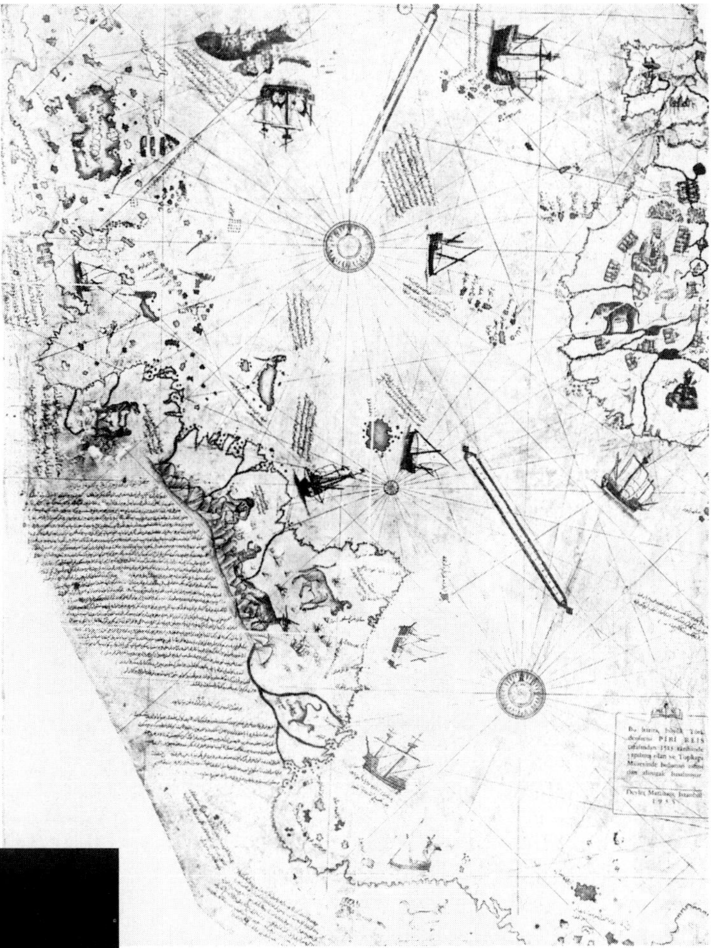

20. Martin Behaim (left) (1459–1507), the German scientist, navigator and Portuguese knight of the realm. It was on his famous globe of 1492 that the legend surrounding the Island of the Seven Cities appears for the first time.

21. Prince Henry the Navigator (right) of Portugal (1394–1460). More than anyone else he spearheaded the quest to discover the New World through his attempts to find Antilia and its legendary Seven Cities.

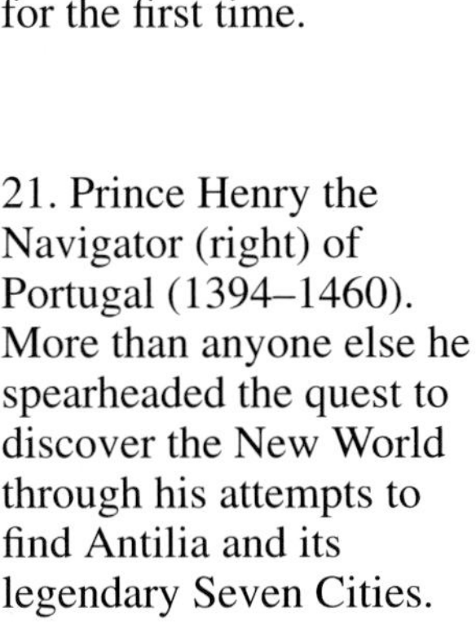

22. Hernando Cortés meets Montezuma, the Great Speaker of the Aztec nation, on his entry into Tenochtitlan in November 1519. What was the origin behind the ancient prophecies that led to Cortés being mistaken for the returning god Quetzalcoatl?

23. The ancient Mexican city of Teotihuacán, looking along the Avenue of the Dead towards the Pyramid of the Sun. Beneath this monumental structure archaeologists have uncovered a series of chambers corresponding to Chicomoztoc, the Seven Caves of the Mexica.

almost certainly the remains of one, and possibly even two wrecks lying on the sea bottom. However, following requests by Marx to explore the site more fully, the Spanish and Portuguese governments suddenly intervened and persuaded the Brazilian authorities to cease any further involvement in the affair.[9] They considered that confirmation of a Roman wreck in Brazilian waters would bring into question the validity not only of Pedro Ãlvares Cabral's claim to have 'discovered' Brazil on behalf of the Portuguese sovereign in 1500, but also Spain's own claim to have 'discovered' the New World in 1492.

With Brazil's upcoming quincentenary coinciding with the millennium celebrations, it seemed unwise to unlock a whole can of worms that might spoil Rio de Janeiro's heavily publicised 2000 party. As a consequence of this extraordinary decision, Robert Marx was refused permission to conduct any further investigations into the mystery of the amphorae found in Guanabara Bay.

The furore surrounding these events in Brazil eventually led to public slogans, such as 'Cabral Sí, Marx No', as well as protests and marches against what was seen by the Brazilian people as Marx's wish to rob them of their national heritage. One Brazilian archaeologist who was asked by Marx to examine possible Phoenician jewellery rings found in Brazil not only confiscated these items but added rather indignantly: 'Cabral discovered Brazil, and let's leave it like that.'[10] More incredibly, the then Brazilian Minister of Education apparently took Marx to one side at a Christmas party and said to him: 'Every plaza in Brazil has a statue of Cabral, the real discoverer of Brazil, and we are not going to replace these with monuments to some anonymous Italian pizza vendor just because you have invented a Roman shipwreck where none exists.'[11] In the wake of this fiasco, Marx accused the Brazilian government of deliberately suppressing vital information and materials which could confirm diffusion from the ancient world prior to the age of Cabral.[12]

As may be seen, the whole Bay of Jars affair degenerated into a sensitive issue of international and political concern that has now ruined any chances we have of confirming the presence of Roman wrecks on the seabed outside Rio de Janeiro. This appalling situation makes me wonder just how many times national politics have stood in the way of truth when it comes to presenting evidence of pre-Columbian contact with the supposed 'New World'.

Scholars rarely dispute evidence such as the Moroccan amphorae found in Guanabara Bay. How can they? Yet they explain their presence in American waters by admitting that every once in a while a seagoing vessel from the ancient world might just have been blown off course during storms and bad weather. Having reached the American coast, it would probably have ended its days either floundering on uncharted shoals or rocks, or being abandoned when the crew could go no further. It is pointed out that Cabral himself discovered Brazil only after his vessel rounded the Cape of Africa and was inadvertently carried across the ocean as he attempted to find the passage to India. Apparently, in the past century alone no fewer than 600 African vessels have ended up being cast on to the South American coast, due either to bad weather or poor navigation.[13] This might well be true, but just how many vessels in past ages were able to make the return journey *back* to Africa? How many of their mariners were able to tell their people of this great continent that lay beyond the Western Ocean? How many of these stories prompted others, such as the Phoenicians and Carthaginians, to initiate their own voyages of discovery? This is the real enigma that must be addressed by historians.

The Comalcalco Conundrum

Despite the cautious attitude towards ancient world contact with the Americas shown by academics, evidence does exist to suggest some form of contact between the Old World and certain Maya sites located close to the Gulf coast of Mexico. For example, on a plain in the state of Tabasco, around 55 kilometres north-west of Villahermosa, we find the great Maya centre of Comalcalco, which in the language of the Nahua peoples of central Mexico means 'houses of the clay pans'.[14] This curious title derives from the fact that instead of employing limestone as the main source of building material, those responsible for its enormous structures used fired clay bricks, the shape of which resemble the clay pans made by the Nahua.

Simply by looking at the towering walls that make up its North Plaza and Great Acropolis, there is a sense of recognition for those familiar with Roman architecture. These structures are made almost entirely of fired bricks, resembling those used en masse during Roman times. In addition to this, some of the buildings possess buttresses, wing-walls and large, square windows, all of which 'are relatively unknown in Maya architecture'.[15] Yet similarity does not necessarily mean contact. We would need far more than comparisons to suggest that an ancient world culture had introduced the Maya to fired bricks and new forms of architecture sometime around AD 200.[16]

Amazingly, there *are* other connections between the buildings at Comalcalco and the ancient world. Two of the many temple mounds excavated by field archaeologist Neil Steede have revealed more than 4,500 fired bricks that bear marks incised on the wet clay before they were sun-dried. Many of these symbols are unquestionably of Maya origin, yet a small percentage resemble signatures that appear on bricks and tiles from the Roman world. Furthermore, similar markings have been found on adobe bricks used to construct the

Huaca Las Ventanas pyramids of north-west Peru, which epigrapher Barry Fell identified as a form of alphabetic Libyan script.[17] These structures are accredited to the Mochica, or Moche, culture and are dated to somewhere between 300 BC and AD 800.

So could Romans have visited Maya sites such as Comalcalco?

Neil Steede conducted an extensive study into this subject and initially concluded that a Roman presence in Mexico might well explain the use of fired clay bricks at Comalcalco.[18] He also found a number of other parallels between the two cultures, including similarities in architectural design, artistic styles and proposed astronomical alignments.[19] Furthermore, even though other local Maya sites, such as Bellote and Jonuta, have brick structures, this particular building technique is unique to the area and is not found anywhere else in pre-Columbian America.[20]

Surely these factors alone are strongly indicative that the presence of kiln-baked bricks at Maya sites is evidence of intervention from the ancient world. Indeed they are, and yet curiously the real answer might lie outside the influence of the Roman Empire. In spite of his earlier announcements, which have appeared in professional journals, Neil Steede has conceded that since no Latin inscription has ever been found at Comalcalco, there is no reason to assume that Romans ever reached Mexico.[21] In addition to this, English transoceanic specialist David Eccott, who has also made an extensive study of the evidence available at Comalcalco, considers that the knowledge regarding the use of fired clay bricks may have come from an altogether different location in the ancient world, the key being the maker's marks. Working alongside other colleagues in this field, he has determined that certain inscriptions found at Comalcalco indicate that the technology, and maybe even the expertise, behind the brick-making could be part of a long tradition stretching back hundreds, if not thousands, of years. In his opinion, certain of the signs represent a form of ancient script familiar to Mesopotamia and the Indus Valley culture of northern India, *c.* 3000 BC. This is thought to have spread gradually eastwards to China, Sumatra, Easter Island and then, finally, through transoceanic contact to Peru, Panama and Mexico.[22] Examples of this Indus Valley script have been identified both at Comalcalco and on the adobe bricks found at Huaca Las Ventanas in north-west Peru.[23] Yet regardless of the controversy surrounding the brick-maker's marks, there is still the lingering suggestion of a Roman presence in Mexico.

Roman Crossings

Although a full 24 kilometres from the coast, Comalcalco is located on the Rio Seco, a now silted tributary of the Rio Grijalva that flows into the Gulf of Mexico. Once a vessel could sail all the way to Comalcalco, and this is indeed what the Spanish conquistador Hernando Cortés attempted to do on his arrival on the Gulf coast in 1519.[24] I can therefore find no reason why Roman vessels inbound from Africa should not have reached the region by first entering the Caribbean Sea and then following the Gulf coast to the mouth of the Rio Grijalva. Furthermore, other indications of a Roman presence in Mexico also exist. Take, for instance, the tiny sculpted Roman head professionally excavated in 1933 at a site named Calixtlahuaca, 72 kilometres west of Mexico City. This fascinating artefact is in the form of a terracotta pot, just two centimetres high. It is fashioned into the features of a Roman head which appears to be wearing a Phrygian cap, like the one worn by the god Mithras. A scientific process known as thermoluminescence, which dates ceramic objects with some accuracy, has determined that the pot was manufactured around AD 200. It was, however, found as a funerary offering, along with other grave goods, in a truncated pyramid structure dating to the twelfth century. This suggests that the Roman pot could have been in Mexico for up to a thousand years. Those experts who have studied this sculpted head agree that it derives from the Hellenistic/Roman world.[25]

In addition to the Roman head of Calixtlahuaca, there is the case of the jar containing several hundred Roman coins found washed up on the northern coast of Venezuela. Their ages span an immensely long period from the reign of Caesar Augustus (63 BC–AD 14) to around AD 350. Since the hoard includes many duplicates, there seems very little likelihood that it could have been a discarded or buried collection of colonial origin, or that it might have been part of a national treasure trove on its way either to or from the New World. What seems more likely is that it is the wealth of a Roman trader lost overboard when his ship was wrecked sometime around AD 350. Remember, a vessel that follows the North Equatorial Current westwards from the Cape Verdes will be carried directly to the northern coast of Venezuela, almost precisely where the hoard was found. The coins are now in the possession of the Smithsonian Institution.[26]

Lastly, and somewhat more significantly, in 1972 scuba-divers searching in waters off the coast of Honduras found an ancient hull with a cargo of 'Punic' amphorae, suggesting that the vessel was of Carthaginian origin.[27] An accidental journey to the Americas might account for the apparent presence of a Roman vessel in Guanabara Bay, Brazil, or even one off the coast of Venezuela. Yet knowledge of a presumably far older wreck in the Gulf of Honduras, formerly a stronghold of the southern Maya, does not immediately suggest a chance, accidental journey across the North Atlantic Ocean. To have ended up at this location the vessel would have had to sail through the Lesser Antilles and Caribbean Sea, a voyage that must have been deliberate and not accidental. Exactly how old the wreck might be is unfortunately unclear, for it could date to either before or after the destruction of Carthage by the Romans in *c.* 146 BC. Since the Romans reoccupied ports such as Carthage and Mogador on the Atlantic coast of Morocco, they would have unquestionably reused old amphorae left behind by the Carthaginians. If the wreck dates to before the fall of Carthage, its discovery could constitute proof of Carthaginian journeys to the Americas in exactly the manner proposed in this book.

Unfortunately, as would be the case a decade later in Brazil, the Honduran government stepped in and refused to grant anyone, including Robert Marx, the right to investigate the site of the wreck.[28] The underlying motive behind this decision was once again the fear that the discovery of an Old World vessel in American waters would undermine the achievements of Christopher Columbus. How many more wrecks might await discovery off the Atlantic coast of America? How many more times will they be ignored in the name of political expedience and national embarrassment on the part of the Hispanic world?

Yet if the Romans really were making transatlantic journeys to the Mesoamerican world, why did they not formally record such maritime ventures? It can only be that, like the Phoenicians and Carthaginians before them, they wished to keep secret this lucrative trading market. Since the amphorae found in both Brazilian and Honduran waters are of North African manufacture, it is possible that the Romans gained their knowledge of transatlantic trading routes from the inhabitants of former Carthaginian ports, and from the Lixitae – the nomadic Berber tribes of Morocco.

Was it through such voyages that the Romans came into contact with the Maya of Central America, in the same way that Phoenician and Carthaginian merchants would appear to have come into contact with the Olmec who inhabited the very same region several hundreds years beforehand?

In the next chapter we will return to the mysterious presence of psychoactive drugs in pharaonic Egypt. For I feel we now have enough evidence to point a finger at those responsible not only for initiating the transatlantic trade in tobacco and coca but also for providing Plato with the source material behind the story of Atlantis.

CHAPTER XII

ATLANTIC VOYAGERS

FROM THE EVIDENCE PROVIDED IN the preceding chapters, it seems clear that at the beginning of the first millennium BC the Olmec territories of Mexico were the destination of trans-oceanic voyagers. To the west lay Japan and the Chinese Empire, while to the east were the Iberic Phoenicians of Gades and Tartessos and the Carthaginians of North Africa, all of whom would appear to have left their mark on the pre-Columbian civilisations of Mesoamerica. Yet is it even realistic to suggest that the Olmec might have had a hand in supplying tobacco and coca to oceanic traders, who in turn would carry these valuable commodities halfway around the world for the pharaonic Egyptians to consume at their leisure? Let us look first at the problem of tobacco.

No Smoke without Fire

There is no known evidence to suggest that the Olmec practised smoke inhalation, using either tobacco or any other kind of narcotic substance. This, however, proves nothing, since we know that tobacco smoking was widespread among the Olmec's successors the Maya who, according to conventional chronology, first established key centres in Mexico's Yucatán Peninsula and in other parts of Mesoamerica around *c.* 100 BC. Indeed, our word 'cigar' actually derives from the Mayan 'sikar', signifying either a cigar or tobacco.[1] Moreover, the Maya also depicted some of their gods wearing large hats and smoking fat cigars.[2] One such god, the black jaguar-headed God L, was the patron of merchants, in which role he was shown with a cigar in his mouth and a bundle of merchandise on his back.[3] The origins of these gods are unknown. However, it is possible that they represent Olmec forebears, since we know that much of the Maya's cultural knowledge was inherited from the Olmec, who were probably seen as divine ancestors. If this was so, it seems inconceivable that the Olmec were not smokers, and if they were then they become the prime suspects in our case to identify those who supplied this valuable commodity to the ancient world.

God L of the Maya pantheon smoking a cigar. Does this illustration imply that the earliest ancestors of the Maya introduced smoking to Central America?

If the Olmec *were* responsible for trading tobacco, might they also have introduced ancient world mariners to the delights of smoke inhalation? Remember, it must have been in this very manner that smoking was adopted by the first Spanish explorers and crewmen to reach the West Indies during the age of discovery. As previously mentioned, one of the oldest attested smoking pipes was found on Marajo Island, situated at the mouth of Brazil's Amazon river. It dates to *c.* 1500 BC, just 300 years before the northern Syrians began fashioning stone pipes made of hard stone. Since it seems likely that these pipes were used for smoke inhalation, there has to be a chance that the Phoenicians adopted the art of smoking from a Mesoamerican culture such as the Olmec. If this was the case, it must have been the Phoenician merchants who introduced the virtues of nicotine ingestion to the ancient Egyptians as early as *c.* 1200 BC. Yet 1200 BC is 100 years before the foundation of Iberian ports such as Gades and Tartessos, and many hundreds of years before the official foundation date of Cerne on the West African coast. Can we really account for the presence in ancient Egypt of tobacco simply by supposing that it was supplied by Phoenician and Carthaginian traders?

It is a difficult question, and the most sensible solution is to suggest that the tobacco present in Egypt *c.* 1200 BC was either indigenous to Africa or was traded via some other route, plausibly between America and Southeast Asia. Yet a Pacific route of this sort would mean that, after its arrival in Asia, the tobacco would either have had to be carried overland or transported via a series of sea routes around the continent's entire southern coastline until it reached the Middle East. Only the second possibility makes any practical sense, and yet this would imply some kind of exchange cooperative between cultures not only in Southwest Asia, but also in Indonesia, India, Arabia and finally the Red Sea. If this really was the case, we should expect to find a considerable amount of cross-cultural contact between the different peoples that inhabited these different regions of the Asian continent. In many ways it brings us back to the ideas of transpacific contact suggested as early as the 1920s by Grafton Elliot Smith in his curious yet compelling book *Elephants and Ethnologists*. He proposed that the earliest civilisations of Mesoamerica were trading with the Chinese Empire, which was in turn trading with India and Egypt.

I have no problem in accepting that some kind of trading network existed between the Americas and the peoples of Southeast Asia. I also have no problem in accepting that tobacco might have been introduced to the Asian continent via this same transpacific route. What I do query is who exactly might have been trading tobacco to the ancient Egyptians as early as *c.* 1200 BC. Since we know that the Phoenicians had established ports on the Red Sea as early as 1000 BC, and probably even earlier still, they might have traded with Asian merchants at ports in the Arabian Sea, who were themselves importing American tobacco via India and Southeast Asia. No other nation was in this same privileged position. Yet if this was so, why do we not see more evidence of the presence of tobacco among the cultures that inhabit these regions? This comes only from Africa, where a wild form of the plant is known to have grown since time immemorial. From West Africa through to Sudan and Egypt there is evidence of pre-Columbian tobacco medicine and smoke inhalation on a scale that appears nowhere else outside America. Furthermore, the linguistic comparisons between the word 'tobacco' in both Africa and Mesoamerica point towards some kind of pre-Columbian relationship involving transatlantic communication. It is therefore far more likely that the tobacco entering Egypt as early as *c.* 1200 BC came via transatlantic trade involving Phoenician merchants using ports in either Libya or Iberia.

Ports of Spain

Even though the Phoenicians are not considered to have begun Atlantic voyages until around the time of the foundation of Carthage *c.* 814 BC, evidence for the presence of Bronze Age Iberic Celts in North America as early as *c.* 1500 BC[4] hints strongly at transatlantic contact by this time. Since we know that these same Iberic territories were in the hands of Phoenicians by *c.* 1100 BC, there is every likelihood that the peninsula's earliest ports were established by a much earlier race of Mediterranean origin. Indeed, at Niebla, close to the former site of Tartessos, a complex of Neolithic galleried dolmens, temples, fortresses, hydraulic systems and harbour works was unearthed during the 1920s by Elena M. Whishaw, the Director of the Anglo-Spanish-American School of Archaeology.[5] Since they were contextually placed alongside Copper or Bronze Age artefacts considered to date to something in the region of 2500 BC, Mrs Whishaw concluded that a seagoing maritime culture had occupied the Iberian peninsula during this early epoch. More intriguingly, since she concluded that no Mediterranean culture was making Atlantic journeys during this early age, those who founded the earliest port at Niebla were part of a trading colony belonging to the Atlantean empire described by Plato in the *Timaeus* and *Critias*.[6] This extraordinary assumption led Mrs Whishaw to believe that the very earliest stone structures found here were in the region of between 10,000 and 15,000 years old.[7] Her views were expounded in an essential book entitled *Atlantis in Andalucia*, first published in 1929.

Who might have built harbour works of stone in south-west Spain thousands of years before the arrival of the Phoenicians in *c.* 1100 BC remains unclear (although see Chapter Twenty-six). What we do know, however, is that Strabo recorded that the Turdetans, the inhabitants of Tartessos, possessed records that went back 6,000 years,[8] a fact that cannot have failed to influence the extraordinary theories of Elena Whishaw.[9]

If we can assume therefore that transatlantic voyages took place as early as the second millennium BC, I see no problem in accepting that the tobacco found in the mummy of Rameses II was supplied by proto-Phoenician mariners who traded with Central American cultures, such as the Olmec. Strengthening this view still further is our knowledge of coca production and distribution in the first millennium BC.

As we saw in Chapter Eight, coca chewing was practised in Peru as early as *c.* 2500 BC, while the extended cheeks of the coca chewer

Scene from a pottery vessel belonging to the Moche culture of Peru showing coca chewers (right) summoning the spirit of the divine plant (left). Did the cocaine found in Egyptian mummies come from Peru?

appear on Colombian stone idols that date from around *c.* 1500 BC.[10] By this time the presence of coca was widespread throughout the Andes Mountains, from Colombia in the north right down to Chile in the south.[11] In Ecuador, for instance, traces of the lime used to unlock the cocaine content of the coca leaf have been found in gourd-like vessels unearthed at sites belonging to the Machalilla culture of Manabi province. These items have been dated to between *c.* 1500 and *c.* 1000 BC.[12]

Despite the extensive distribution of coca throughout the Andes region, could it have found its way as far north as Mexico, where the Olmec thrived between *c.* 1200 and *c.* 400 BC? If so, what possible culture might have been responsible for its transportation from the Andean highlands to Mexican cult centres such as La Venta, Monte Alban and Tres Zapotes? Is there any evidence that the Olmec might have been in contact with a South American culture that traded in coca?

Land of the Chavín

The answer is likely to be yes, for it has long been speculated that the Olmec could have had some form of contact with the Chavín, an important Peruvian culture which thrived between *c.* 1000 BC and *c.* 200 BC. Various parallels exist between the two tropical forest cultures, most spectacularly the pre-eminence they each gave to the cult of the jaguar, which included the use of extensive feline iconography.[13] In itself this might not seem like compelling evidence, especially as the jaguar motif is found among many Andean cultures during the same time period. However, it is the cult's presence among the Olmec that must be explained, for its form is strikingly similar to that of the Chavín. More significantly, it was during the formative years of the Chavín that maize was introduced to Peru from Central America, an undeniable fact that has prompted some scholars to suggest some form of cross-cultural contact with the Olmec civilisation.[14]

As the American writer Constance Irwin observed in this respect:

> It is indeed conceivable that . . . Mesoamericans, possibly Olmec, had ventured down to Peru bearing not only maize but also less tangible cultural gifts: architectural skill, some knowledge of astronomy, a feline deity, and possibly even an account of a bearded Fair God.[15]

So if the Olmec introduced maize to Peru, might we also conceive of some form of trade exchange in coca leaves via a relay route employing trains of llamas across the highlands of Ecuador and Colombia?

The Chavín produced a very distinctive art style using stone, pottery and obsidian, and this has been identified at sites all over Peru.[16] Even though their main cult centre at Chavín de Huántar is situated in the central highlands, Chavín artefacts have been found as far south as the plains of Nazca, showing that they were accomplished long-distance traders.[17]

Yet did the Chavín also trade in coca?

In many parts of the Andes coca was a highly valued crop produced in mid-valley zones, called *yunga*, which rise between a height of 500 and 2,500 metres and provide an ideal environment for cultivation.[18] Two main forms of Erythroxylon, the genus of the coca plant, were domesticated and grown in these specialised zones – truxillense, which thrives between a height of 200 and 1,800 metres, and another variant known simply as coca, cultivated between a height of 500 and 1,500 metres.[19] There is no doubt that coca was an important commodity in Peru's local and regional economy, especially among the Chavín. It was either exchanged for other bulk goods as part of an inter-zone trading network, or it was received at major ceremonial centres as tributes to local deities from worshippers belonging to outside communities.[20]

The main cultural and religious centre of the Chavín in the central highlands of Peru was Chavín de Huántar, situated in the bottomlands between two mountain ranges – the Cordillera Blanca and the Cordillera Oriental, where the Huachecsa river converges with the larger Mosna river. This in turn flows north-north-eastwards into the much larger Marañon river, which is itself a branch of the Amazon. Although Chavín de Huántar was not the largest Chavín centre, it was certainly the most impressive, with its extraordinary Old Temple complex and accompanying settlements, which thrived between *c.* 1000 BC and *c.* 500 BC, a time-frame known to archaeologists as the Late Initial Period.[21] As a key commercial centre it became an important crossroads for the exchange of bulk goods.[22]

Even though the Cordillera Blanca acts as a natural barrier to the parallel-running coast for a distance of around 180 kilometres, there are a number of passes that converge at Chavín de Huántar to form the meeting point of various pan-regional trade routes.

The Coca Cartel

The presence in settlements of refuse pits that have been found to contain forms of pottery from the south-central and northern highlands makes it clear that produce was received at Chavín de Huántar from all over Peru.[23] As a commercial centre it must have acted as a clearing house, where commodities were received before being transported onwards using natural corridors of trade.[24] As Richard L. Burger concludes in his impressive work *Chavín and the origins of Andean Civilisation*: 'Thus, the early settlement of Chavín de Huántar was in an excellent position to gain access to exchange networks linking distant production zones, and to profit by regulating or controlling the use of these routes by other groups.'[25]

It is known that one of the most important commodities that featured in Chavín de Huántar's trading network was coca, even though the site's elevated position would have made it impossible for the plant to have been grown locally.[26] So if coca really did form such a significant trading commodity and yet was not cultivated at Chavín de Huántar itself, where might it have come from?

One of the most well-known areas of coca production during the Initial Period was Bagua, located in the northern highlands of Peru on a tributary of the Marañon river. At a height of 522 metres, the agricultural lands around Bagua proved to be ideal for cultivating coca. Furthermore, since its settlements were situated at a crossroads of communication routes west to the coast of Peru, north to the highlands of Ecuador and east into the Amazonian lowlands, it was itself a very important commercial centre.[27] Exotic pottery found at Bagua demonstrates the extent of this trading network, which linked various different economic zones inhabited by the Chavín.[28]

It is therefore conceivable that at least some of the coca received and subsequently exchanged at Chavín de Huántar, the cultural and ceremonial centre of the Chavín, came from Bagua. Yet Bagua's own strategic position suggests that coca produced here could have been transported northwards without it needing to pass first through Chavín de Huántar. In other words, coca could have been transported directly from Bagua via Ecuador and Colombia to the Central American territories of the Olmec.

All we can say for certain is that in the time-frame suggested the most likely Andean culture to have traded directly with the Olmec were the Chavín. Only they have been linked through clear cultural similarities with this ancient Mexican culture. In turn, the Olmec would appear to have established trading connections of their own with transatlantic traders such as the Phoenicians and Carthaginians.

It could, of course, be that the Phoenician merchants cut out the middleman and dealt directly with a South American culture such as the Chavín. On this subject Constance Irwin felt inclined to comment: 'if early mariners were, like later ones, seeking a westward passage, the Amazon would surely have beckoned, luring the traveller westward ever farther, until at last he reached its unnavigable headwaters, not far from Chavín de Huántar [or indeed Bagua]'.[29] This remains a distinct possibility, as might some kind of direct or indirect contact between Southeast Asia and coca-producing cultures in Peru, Ecuador and Colombia. However, my own suspicions lead me to conclude that a three-way trading cartel existed between the Chavín of Peru, the Olmec of Mexico and the Phoenicians of the ancient world. This multicultural trading network probably included not only the supply of coca but also the knowledge of how to extract purple dye from tiny shellfish, a matter firmly developed in its entirety by the Phoenicians, and how to spin and weave cotton to make garments (see Appendices I and II).

Another tantalising avenue of research concerns the pre-Columbian distribution of the coca plant in other regions of the Americas. Not only was it cultivated in countries such as Chile, Bolivia, Peru, Ecuador, Colombia and Brazil, but some species were to be found in Guiana, Panama and even in North Mexico and Cuba.[30] Evidence of chewing coca has also come to light among pre-Columbian cultures in countries such as Costa Rica, Nicaragua, Panama and the Atlantic coast of South America.[31]

Is it possible that the Olmec, or indeed the proposed transatlantic trading cartel, obtained its coca not from the Chavín of Peru but from a Central American country? Could one or more of the pre-Columbian cultures in countries such as Costa Rica, Panama or Nicaragua have received coca from Peru before exchanging it on to more northerly tribes such as the Olmec? What about Mexico and Cuba, where species of Erythroxylon grew naturally – was coca chewing practised in these countries as well?

Until further evidence of cocaine ingestion comes to light both in the Americas and in the ancient world, this is as far as we can go on the subject. In conclusion, it would appear that those responsible for supplying tobacco and coca to the Egyptian royal courts and temples from around 1200 BC onwards were in all probability the Phoenicians and Carthaginians. With their thirst for open commerce, their sense of exploration and their accomplished marine capability, no other nation would have been in the same unique position. Yet if the Phoenicians and Carthaginians really were responsible for introducing Caribbean catastrophe myths to the Mediterranean world prior to the age of Plato, could these nations be linked directly to the Atlantis legend? Incredibly, the answer is yes.

Map showing the extent of coca chewing and coca distribution in the Americas in pre-Columbian times. Did the trade in coca extend to the Olmec territories and also to West Indian islands such as Cuba, where species of the plant are known to have thrived before the discovery of the New World?

The Language of Atlantis

In Chapter Three we saw how, in Plato's dialogue the *Critias*, Atlas – the first-born of the five twins of Poseidon – became the first king of Atlantis, while his twin brother was bestowed 'the extremity of the island [of Atlantis] off the pillars of Hercules, fronting the region now known as Gadira'.[32] We also learnt that in Greek this twin's name was Eumelus, but 'in the language of his own country [it was] Gadirus, and no doubt his name was the origin of that of the district'.[33]

These words contain very important facts. To begin with we can now assume that the immense size accredited to Atlantis, equal to that of Libya and Asia combined, does not relate to the extent of the landmass, but to the dominion over which the kings of the Atlantic island were seen to hold sway. Secondly, Gadira, or Gades, was, of course, the Phoenician city-port of this name founded in south-west Spain *c.* 1100 BC. Interestingly enough, Gadira is the *only* location, other than the Pillars of Hercules, singled out in connection with Plato's Atlantic island, a fact made doubly important when we read that 'in the language of his [Eumelus'] own country [i.e. Atlantis] Gadirus' was his name. In other words, Plato believed that both 'Gadira' and 'Gadirus' derived from the Atlantean language. So how might we explain this apparent relationship between Gadira and Atlantis?

Gadira, or Gadeira, are Greek variations of the original Phoenician or Carthaginian name for the city-port. Pliny refers to it in the first century AD as 'Gadir', which he says is Punic (i.e. Carthaginian) for 'a fence',[34] a name derived from the three-letter Semitic root *g-d-r*, meaning an 'enclosure', or 'an enclosure of stones'. This can be interpreted to mean the 'walled city', or the 'city of walls', as in Geder, an unidentified Canaanite town mentioned in the Bible,[35] and Gedor, a town in the highlands of Judah.[36] Both derive their names from the same root as Gades.

Since the names Gadira and Gadirus are clearly Semitic in origin, it tells us that 'the language of his [i.e. Eumelus' or Gadirus'] own country' was not Atlantean, as Plato thought, but *Punic*. In other words, the original language of the Atlantean tradition was Carthaginian. As well as this revelatory conclusion, it would seem that those responsible for introducing the Atlantis legend to Plato used Gadira as a geographical reference point in order to explain better the extent of the Atlantean kings' oceanic dominion. Yet in naming Gadira, these storytellers have more or less given away their identity, for the most likely seafaring nations to have cited this Spanish city-port as a geographical reference point were the Phoenicians and Carthaginians.

Even though Gadira, or Gades, is the only location singled out in connection with the extent of the Atlantean kings' influence, there *are* indications that other Carthaginian settlements also feature in the Atlantis narrative. For instance, Carthage itself has long been compared with the description given by Plato of his Atlantean city. Both were situated on low fortified hills, while

Carthage's arrangement of docks and waterways has occasionally been likened to those that surrounded the Atlantic citadel.[37] We have also seen how there appears to be a close similarity between the concept of Plato's Atlantic island and the Carthaginian settlement of Cerne, situated off the West Coast of Africa. This small island, thought to have been located either in the proximity of the Western Sahara or close to the mouth of the Senegal river, was linked by Pseudo-Scylax with 'parts' of the ocean 'no longer navigable because of shoals, mud, and sea-weed', an allusion almost certainly to the Sargasso Sea.[38] Why associate Cerne with this region of the ocean if the ancient mariners who reported these hazards had not either commenced or ended their journeys in this island?

Nineteenth-century French geographer Felix Berlioux even came to the conclusion that Cerne actually *was* Plato's fabled Atlantic island. Using Diodorus Siculus' account of the Atlantioi (the Atlantes of Herodotus), among whom 'mythology places the birth of the gods',[39] Berlioux imagined an almighty Atlantean nation that arose out of Cerne and grew to become a huge Libyan empire.[40]

It seems more likely that Cerne's association with the Atlantis legend came about not because Plato's Atlantis was located off Africa but simply because this Carthaginian island settlement became confused with other stories concerning distant islands to be found many days' sail beyond the Pillars of Hercules. In all probability it was under these circumstances that the stranger aspects of Atlantic voyages became entangled with the core Atlantis legend, including perhaps the idea that elephants were present on the island. Remember, elephants had been witnessed in reed-swamps by Hanno, the Carthaginian general who partially circumnavigated the African coast, around *c.* 425 BC. Furthermore, it was on this same journey that he is alleged to have founded the island settlement of Cerne. Did such stories become so confused that eventually the African elephants to be found beyond the Pillars of Hercules were transferred out of the reed-swamps of Mauritania and actually on to the celebrated Atlantic island, which by then included certain elements exclusively gained from Carthaginian contact with the African coast?

There can be no certainties in this business. Yet if we are to point a finger at those responsible for introducing the Atlantis legend to Plato's world, we need look no further than the Iberic Phoenicians and their partners in crime, the Carthaginians. In them we have determined a much *earlier* source for the legend of the sunken island that lay beyond the Western Ocean. The enigma surrounding the submergence of the Bahaman landmass and the fragmentation of the Caribbean islands now cries out for further investigation if we are fully to understand what might have occurred in this tropical region thousands of years before recorded history. Yet before we can go on to do this, we must move forward in time and find out what the medieval world, immediately prior to the celebrated journeys of Christopher Columbus, might have known about the true identity of lost Atlantis.

PART THREE
CONQUEST

CHAPTER XIII

THE RETURN TO PARADISE

EIGHTEEN YEARS BEFORE THE GENOESE navigator Christopher Columbus set out on his historic journey to the New World, he received a letter and sea-chart from the Florentine astronomer and mathematician Paulo del Pozzo Toscanelli (1397–1482). Included in this correspondence was the transcript of a letter Toscanelli had sent to the canon of Lisbon cathedral, Fernão Martins, who at the time was attempting to convince the king of Portugal to give his blessing to an exploratory voyage around the Cape of Africa. Although the authenticity of this document has been challenged, there seems to be no point in ignoring its contents, for it alludes to what a navigator might expect to encounter on a sea-voyage across the Atlantic Ocean:

> From the city of Lisbon due west there are twenty-six spaces marked on the map, each of which contains two hundred and fifty miles [400 kilometres], as far as the very great and noble city of Quinsay [now Jangchow in China]. This city is about one hundred miles [160 kilometres] in circumference, which is equal to thirty-five leagues, and has ten marble bridges. Marvellous things are told about its great buildings, its arts, and its revenues. That city lies in the province of Mangi, near the province of Cathay [the northern part of the Chinese Empire], in which the king resides the greater part of the time. And from the island of Antillia, which you call the Island of the Seven Cities, to the very noble island of Cipango [i.e. Japan], there are ten spaces, which make 2,500 miles [4,000 kilometres], that is two hundred and twenty-five leagues. This land is most rich in gold, pearls, and precious stones, and the temples and royal palaces are covered with solid gold. But because the way is not known, all these things are hidden and covered, though one can travel thither with all security.[1]

It is perhaps pertinent to point out that when Columbus set out on his own epic voyage of discovery, very little was known about the western limits of the Atlantic Ocean. Although some cartographers and geographers accepted that ancient philosophers, such as Pythagoras, Plato and Aristotle, had got it right when they suggested the world was in fact a sphere, what they believed lay beyond the uncharted waters of the Western Ocean was the Asian continent. Almost the only knowledge of the Orient circulating the Mediterranean world during medieval times was the writings of the Venetian traveller Marco Polo (1254–1324), who had journeyed overland to Mangi and Cathay, and from whose book *The Description of the World* Toscanelli drew his own account of these exotic locations.

Despite this rather poor understanding of world geography, a number of navigational charts appeared during the fourteenth and fifteenth centuries which showed various mythical, or semi-mythical, islands that were thought to lie far out in the Western Ocean. They bore names such as Hy-Brazil, St Brendan's Isle (after the legendary travels of an Irish monk of this name in *c.* AD 520–577/8), the Isle of Demons, the Hand of Satan and, most significantly, Antilia. It was this island that Toscanelli identified in his letter with the so-called 'Island of the Seven Cities'. So where exactly was 'Antillia', and what were the Seven Cities?

The Emergence of Antilia

The first allusion to Antilia is on a nautical chart compiled in 1367 by two Venetian brothers named Domenico and Francesco Pizzigani, or Pizzigano. In the proximity of where the Azores group should be placed is a legend that reads: 'Here are statues which stand before the shores of Atulliae and which have been set up for the safety of the sailors, for they serve to show how far it is possible to navigate in these seas, and beyond these statues is the vile sea which sailors cannot navigate.'[2]

Controversy has raged over exactly what, or where, 'Atulliae' might have been. Originally geographers took it to be a variation of the name Antilia. Yet this solution is now dismissed in favour of the all-important line reading 'ante ripas Getuliae', or 'ante ripas A(r)cules', with the last word being seen as a misspelling of Hercules.[3] This solution allows scholars to conclude that the legend relates merely to the 'shores' of the Strait of Gibraltar, where anciently the Pillars of Hercules had once stood.[4] Yet simply by examining the all-important inscription on the original map one can see that the word in question is 'Atulliae', and not 'Getuliae', or 'A(r)cules'. Moreover, it is clear that the legend relates not to the Pillars of Hercules but to the furthest limits a navigator could journey in the outer ocean before he encountered a shoreline on which were statues of warning. Beyond this island were only uncharted waters and the impassable sea that had to be avoided at all cost.

I prefer to align myself with the study made of the 1367 Pizzigani map by the noted German cartographic specialist Konrad Kretschmer. After making a careful examination of the original map at the end of the nineteenth century, he concluded that the key name reads 'Atulliae', a conclusion which has been accepted by some of the greatest geographers in the world.[5] Other suggested variations of the name are 'Atilae' or 'Atulae'.[6]

Since the legend on the Pizzigani map of 1367 is in the exact spot where the Azores would later be discovered by Portuguese mariners, it has been suggested that Atulliae might have been an ancient name attached to one of the islands.[7] Support for this theory is found in the *Historia del Reyno de Portugal* of Manuel de Faria y Sousa (1590–1649), published in 1628. He recounts the supposed discovery on Corvo, the westernmost island in the Azorean archipelago, of a strange equestrian statue that just might be one of the statues of warning alluded to on the Pizzigani map. According to this Portuguese historian:

> . . . on the summit of a mountain which is called the mountain of the Crow [i.e. Corvo], they found the statue of a man mounted on a horse without saddle, his head uncovered, the left hand resting on the horse, the right extended toward the west. The whole was mounted on a pedestal that was of the same kind of stone as the statue. Underneath, some unknown characters were carved in the rock.[8]

It was not until the appearance in 1424 of a nautical chart compiled by a Venetian cartographer named Zuane Pizzigani, possibly a descendent of the Pizzigani brothers who compiled the Venetian map of 1367, that Antilia appears for the first time under its more familiar name. On this map, which bears an assortment of place-names that belie its heavy Portuguese influence,[9] the island is shown as a rectangular landmass orientated approximately north–south – a form it takes on all subsequent charts of the fifteenth century. In size, it is approximately 450 kilometres by 100 kilometres, and in distance it is around 800 kilometres from Portugal (although later maps place it at least 1,600 kilometres' distance from the shores of the ancient world).[10] Along its extended coasts is a series of seven bays, four on one side and three on the other, with a much larger eighth bay located at its southern end. Seven only of the bays are identified by name. These are: Asay, Ary, Vra, Jaysos, Marnlio, Ansuly and Cyodue.[11] Many of the subsequent maps that appeared in the wake of the 1424 Venetian chart, and which show Antilia, contain variations of these seven place-names.[12] Not one of these names appears to derive from real locations known in antiquity. Yet, as we shall see, the association of the number seven with the island of Antilia is of paramount importance to our investigations.

Even though the 1424 Venetian chart fixes the island name as 'Antilia', in a legend that appears alongside the landmass it is written 'Antlylia',[13] demonstrating that at the time there was no fixed spelling. If the compiler of this chart was indeed a descendant of the earlier Pizzigani brothers, it seems likely that 'Antlylia' was simply a modification of 'Atulliae', the form it takes on the 1367 map.

From the 1424 chart onwards until the end of the fifteenth century, Antilia formed part of an island group, composed of Saya, Satanazes, Antilia and Ymana, which eventually became known to geographers and historians as the islands of Antilia.[14] Their names also vary considerably on later maps, with Saya becoming Taumar, Satanazes becoming Saluagia and Ymana becoming Roillo.[15] Always these four islands were located far out in the Western Ocean on a latitude that corresponds very well with the West Indies.

It is certain that Christopher Columbus would have been familiar with this somewhat sketchy knowledge of the Western Ocean prior to his initial voyage to the New World, particularly as his brother Bartholomew was a cartographer in Lisbon.[16] Since we also know that Christopher Columbus was aware of Antilia's supposed existence, there can be little doubt that he expected to encounter this island on his intended journey to Cipango and Cathay. Despite this knowledge, there is no real evidence to suggest that he might have been aware of the existence of the American continent before his arrival in the West Indies, nor that he ever considered he had discovered the island of Antilia.

Curiously enough, the four islands of Antilia on the Battista Beccario map of 1435 are marked with the legend 'Insulle a Novo Repte (newly reported islands)'.[17] This statement unquestionably relates to the discovery of the first of the Azores group in 1427.[18] Yet a further map made by the Venetian cartographer Andrea Bianco in 1436 confirms that Antilia was located far to the west of the Azores. Here the island is positioned to the west of this more familiar archipelago, between which is a gap that bears the inscription 'Questo xe mar. de baga', the Berry Sea, a reference to the berry-like bladders of the *Sargassum bacciferum*, the species of seaweed that dominates the Sargasso Sea.[19] Since the word 'baga' is Portuguese, it implies that Portuguese navigators explored the outer ocean as far as the Sargasso Sea, and perhaps even beyond it, and thus provided the core information for some of the earliest nautical charts of the fifteenth century.

It was shortly after the discovery of the West Indies (i.e. the

Indies reached by the westward passage) that they became associated with the legendary Antilian islands for the first time. The Marine World Chart of Nicolo de Canerio Januensis, produced just ten years after Columbus' first voyage, identifies the three main islands of the West Indies as the 'Antilhas del Rey de Castella [Antilles of the king of Castille]'.[20] Another, similar chart dating from around the same time also collectively identifies the islands of 'Newe Spain' as 'Antilie', i.e. the Antilles,[21] while in 1511 Peter Martyr d'Anghiera, the Spanish chronicler, stated that they were known as 'the islands of Antilia'.[22] This, of course, is the name they retain to this day.

Yet how did early Spanish explorers come to identify the West Indies as 'the islands of Antilia', especially as Columbus remained adamant that he had reached either Cathay or Cipango, even after his return to Spain? The answer would appear to lie in the fact that it was the Spanish crews that accompanied him on his voyage of discovery – and not Columbus – who came to believe that they had encountered the fabled islands of Antilia. These men originated in the main from the Iberian port of Palos, from which Columbus' three vessels had set sail for the New World in the summer of 1492. Its local seamen possessed a long tradition of maritime experience that stretched back to the time of the Phoenicians and Carthaginians. Indeed, Palos was just a few kilometres' distance from the sites of ancient ports such as Tartessos, Niebla and Gades.

According to an obscure book entitled *Historia de la Rabida*, written by Fray Angel Ortega, a Franciscan monk at the famous Monastery of La Rabida at Palos, local seamen preserved the memory of a great island called Antilia that lay across the Western Ocean.[23] Apparently, it was their belief in the existence of this world across the water, visited by their Iberic-Phoenician forefathers, that convinced them to join Columbus's expedition.[24] Among those who belonged to this seafaring community at Palos was Martin Alonso Pinzón, an experienced navigator who went on to captain one of the two caravels that accompanied Columbus' merchant vessel the *Santa Maria*.[25] In this knowledge, it is easy to understand why the seamen of Palos should have become convinced that they had relocated Antilia on their arrival in the West Indies.

Fray Ortega arrived at these extraordinary conclusions after consulting a considerable amount of contemporary documentation on the subject. In his opinion:

> these Andalucian adventurers had already frequently set forth to seek Antilia because they knew and applied in their navigation all the science and progress of their time. It is the height of injustice to describe these men, as so many historians of the Discovery have done,

as poor ignorant fishermen, and still more to suggest that their skill at sea was due to their pursuing the profession of pirates.[26]

Search for the Seven Cities

In 1492, the year in which Columbus set sail for the New World, a German geographer and navigator named Martin Behaim (1459–1507) produced the first geographical globe. Yet unlike modern examples, Behaim's able attempt to draw the entire earth lacked the presence of three major landmasses – Antarctica, Australia and America. Instead, a huge segment, taking up around a third of the globe, was filled with an enormous ocean containing literally dozens of small islands of different sizes, shapes and colours. More important, at a latitude just north of the equator, close to the centre of the vast Atlantic Ocean, he placed the familiar, rectangular-shaped island of Antilia which, when compared with the infinitely larger island of Cipango to its west, was small indeed. Next to Antilia is a legend which insists that in '1414 a ship from Spain got nighest it without being endangered'.[27] If this was true, it perhaps bears out the claims made by the seamen of Palos who seemed convinced that their forebears had discovered Antilia many years before Columbus' own landfall in the West Indies.

There is nothing out of the ordinary about Antilia's appearance on the Behaim globe. By this time it had become standard practice to include it on navigational charts. What is significant, however, is that next to the island is an extraordinary legend that makes compelling reading:

> In the year 734 of Christ, when the whole of Spain had been won by the heathen (Moors) of Africa, the above island Antilia, called Septe citade (Seven cities), was inhabited by an archbishop from Porto in Portugal, with six other bishops, and other Christians, men and women, who had fled thither from Spain, by ship, together with their cattle, belongings and goods.[28]

What exactly were these Seven Cities that had earlier been alluded to in the Toscanelli letter of 1474, and how did they relate to the island of Antilia? It is the so-called Weimar map of 1461/2 that first shows the 'Septe citade' in association with Antilia.[29] Yet it is Martin Behaim's globe that contains the oldest reference to the legend of the Seven Cities, which had apparently been the impetus for various Portuguese expeditions to find Antilia in the years leading up to the discovery of the New World.

A curious account of a vessel reaching the Seven Cities is given by the Portuguese historian Antonio Galvão in his book *The Discoveries of the World*. He records that in 1447 a Portuguese ship was driven westwards by storms and eventually found its way to the Island of the Seven Cities. Its inhabitants, speaking in Portuguese, asked 'if the Moores did yet trouble Spaine',[30] a reference to the conquest of Spain and Portugal by the Moors of North Africa at the time of the flight of the seven bishops. He also states that: 'The boateswaine of the ship brought home a little of the sand, and sold it unto a goldsmith of Lisbon, out of the which he had a good quantitie of gold.'[31] Galvão's inscription concludes with the words:

> There be some that thinke, that those Islands whereunto the *Portugals* were thus driven, were the *Antiles, or Newe Spaine,* alleaging good reasons for their opinion, which here I omit, because they serve not my purpose. But all their reasons seem to agree, that they should be that countrey, which is called *Noua Spagna*.[32]

It is clear that the English also had their sights set on the discovery of Antilia. In a letter received by the sovereigns of Castille and Aragon from the Spanish ambassador to England dated July 1498, he states that the 'Merchants of Bristol have for the last seven years annually sent out ships in search of the island of Brazil and the Seven Cities'.[33] Where exactly these vessels might have reached is not recorded, although the crowning glory of these uncertain ventures on behalf of the English Crown was the rediscovery in 1497 of the Northwest Passage by the Venetian navigator Giovanni Caboto, better remembered under the anglicised name 'John Cabot'. According to a document discovered in 1896, Cabot's principal sponsor was one Richard Amerycke, the High Sheriff of Bristol,[34] which at the time was England's leading port.

One writer who took it upon himself to record instances of supposed attempts to find Antilia and the Island of the Seven Cities was Ferdinand Columbus, the son and biographer of Christopher Columbus. He not only included the Toscanelli letter in the introduction to the annotated diaries of his father, but he also recorded the following information in respect of the same archaic tradition:

> Aristotle in his book *On Marvellous Things* reports a story that some Carthaginian merchants sailed over the Atlantic to a very fertile island (as I shall presently relate in more detail); this island some Portuguese showed on their charts under the name of Antillia, but in a different situation from Aristotle, though none placed it more than two hundred leagues [960 kilometres] due west of the Canaries and the Azores. And they hold it for certain that this is the Island of the Seven Cities, settled by the Portuguese at the time the Moors conquered Spain from King Rodrigo, that is, in the year AD 714. They say that at that time seven bishops embarked from Spain and came with their ships and people to this island, where each founded a city: and in order that

> their people might give up all thought of returning to Spain they burned their ships, riggings, and all else needed for navigation. Some Portuguese who speculated about this island conjectured that many of their nation had gone thither but were never able to return.[35]

The Atlantic island referred to by Pseudo-Aristotle in *c.* 300 BC (and again by Diodorus Siculus in *c.* 8 BC), we will recall, is the one said to have been settled exclusively by Carthaginians. It had 'wood of all kinds', 'navigable rivers', 'all other kinds of fruits' and an indigenous population.[36] We must presume that this same knowledge had also been available to Ferdinand's father Christopher before he embarked on his own journeys of discovery. Yet the fact that Ferdinand goes on to dismiss the theory that this island with 'navigable rivers' could ever have been one of the West Indies is wholly understandable. The thought that this island group could have been discovered thousands of years beforehand by Carthaginians undermined the great achievements of his father.

It is further stated by Ferdinand that 'in the time of the Infante Dom Henrique of Portugal [most probably in 1447, making this a variation of the account told by Galvão] there arrived at this island of Antillia a Portuguese ship, driven there by a storm'.[37] On going ashore the crew joined the islanders for a church service, but being afraid that they might be detained once knowledge of their presence became more widely known, the Portuguese seamen returned to their own country. It is said that when Prince Henry the Navigator learned of this voyage to the Island of Seven Cities, he ordered the crew to embark once again for the island, at which they all promptly disappeared! Like Galvão, Columbus informs us that sand taken for use in the ship's 'firebox' was found to contain a third part gold.[38]

That the island of Antilia with its Seven Cities was believed to exist during the Middle Ages does not seem in doubt. Whether it be in legends surrounding its initial discovery by the Portuguese following the Moorish conquest of Lusitania (ancient Portugal), or in stories concerning its supposed rediscovery by Spanish and Portuguese mariners during the fifteenth century, there is enough evidence to show that it was a popular subject among cartographers, geographers and navigators of the day.

Antilia was very much a Portuguese enigma. This can be determined if we examine the derivation of its name. In Latin *ante* means 'counter', 'before' or 'in front of', while *illa*, or *ilha*, is Portuguese for 'island'. When placed together, Antilia thus implies an island located before, or in front of, something else, perhaps even a great continent. In March 1487 the Portuguese king João II had granted two sea-captains, Fernão Dulmo and João Affonso, permission to seek 'a great island or islands or coast of a continent which presumably is the island of the Seven Cities'.[39] Since Spanish and Portuguese historians of the sixteenth century were happy to identify the islands of Antilia with the West Indies, there is no reason why we should not conclude that this 'great island or islands' was believed to lie in the proximity of the then unknown American continent.

Yet was Antilia really to be found in the West Indies, or did it lie elsewhere in the Western Ocean?

Seven Cities in the Azores?

Some medieval cartographers and navigators unquestionably viewed Antilia, and thus the Seven Cities, as connected with the Azores. This idea was drawn from the island's positioning on certain charts and the knowledge that it supposedly possessed statues of warning similar to the one said to have existed on Corvo. Furthermore, as we saw in Chapter Two, a legend found on the island of São Miguel speaks of the Seven Cities as lying at the bottom of two volcanic lakes separated from each other by a narrow causeway – one with water that appears emerald green and the other with water of turquoise blue.[40] There are even seven villages situated near the shores of the two lakes that bear the name 'Sete Cidades', the Seven Cities.[41] Yet not one of these points in favour of Antilia being found among the Azores holds any weight. We know, for instance, that the island moved around on the navigational charts, which we must not forget were drawn by cartographers who had little, if any, maritime experience of the outer ocean (Martin Behaim being the one notable exception).

We can also be quite sure that the association between the Azores and both the legendary statue of warning on Corvo and the supposed existence of the Seven Cities on São Miguel evolved only after the first Portuguese and Flemish settlers began colonising the archipelago during the 1460s. We know this because when the earliest Portuguese navigators reached the Azores in 1427 they were found to be devoid of both fauna and human life. This is despite the fact that the archipelago appears on an old chart purchased in Venice by the Portuguese in 1428, as well as on an even earlier Genoese map from 1351.[42] It therefore seems certain that these stories sprang up only after the Portuguese began exploring the islands. The volcanic lakes mentioned in connection with the legend of the Seven Cities were probably singled out for this distinction because of the eerie quality they exude. Their waters reflect the image of the nearby rim of a volcano, and so give the impression that a hidden landscape awaits discovery within the lakes' unseen depths – a perfect setting for any lost city.

That the islands of Antilia were not the Azores group but

representations of islands much closer to the American mainland is a conclusion that some more open-minded geographers have been willing to accept over the past century. For example, in 1954 Portugal's celebrated University of Coimbra published a scholarly work on the then newly rediscovered Venetian chart of 1424. Entitled *The Nautical Chart of 1424 and the Early Discovery and Cartographical Representation of America*, it was authored by Armando Cortesão, a former counsellor for the History of Science at UNESCO and Vice-President of the International Academy for the History of Science. Accompanying the text was a foreword by Professor Dr Maximino Correia, the university's rector.

As an expert on medieval nautical charts, Cortesão was specifically requested to make an examination of the 1424 chart, which had originally formed part of the Phillipps Collection, assembled by the Englishman Sir Thomas Phillipps (1792–1872). Following a five-year study of the map, Cortesão felt he was ready to announce some staggering conclusions in respect of the identification of the islands of Antilia, for as he notes in the introduction to the book:

> I began my study with an entirely open mind, without any preconceived idea or prejudice; I have tried never to depart from scholarly honesty, to be guided only by scrupulous scientific method, and to base my reasoning on facts whenever possible. I have come to the conclusion that Antilia and the other westernmost isles figured on the 1424 Chart are intended to represent the easternmost part of the American hemisphere, but I fear that general agreement will never be reached on this controversial question; I know it only too well, alas.[43]

In the book's summary, Cortesão adds that in his opinion: 'there are many and good reasons for concluding that the Antilia group of four islands shown for the first time in the 1424 Chart should be regarded as the earliest cartographical representation of any American lands'.[44] I am sure that Armando Cortesão expected his remarkable discoveries to shock the academic world. Unfortunately, it was simply not ready for such announcements, and neither is it today.

Island in the Sea

Finding the true geographical location of Antilia, and thus the Island of the Seven Cities, was also the challenge taken up by American geographer William H. Babcock, the author of *Legendary Islands of the Atlantic: A Study in Medieval Geography*, first published in 1922. To this end, he concentrated on the Battista Beccario map of 1435, which clearly defines the four islands of Antilia. These Babcock identified finally as Jamaica, the Florida peninsula, the

Bahaman islands and, in the case of Antilia, Cuba.[45] So having ignored Hispaniola and Puerto Rico as possible candidates for Antilia, Babcock chose instead Cuba, the largest of the three main islands of the Greater Antilles. Sprague de Camp, in his critical work *Lost Continents: The Atlantis Theme in History, Science, and Literature*, acknowledged Babcock's assertions in respect of Antilia, saying that the legendary island:

> . . . corresponded so closely in size, shape, and direction with the real Cuba that when the latter and its neighbors were finally found they were promptly named the Antilles . . . Babcock the geographer thought that the pre-Columbian Antilia was evidence of a pre-Columbian voyage that actually touched Cuba – not, perhaps, entirely impossible.[46]

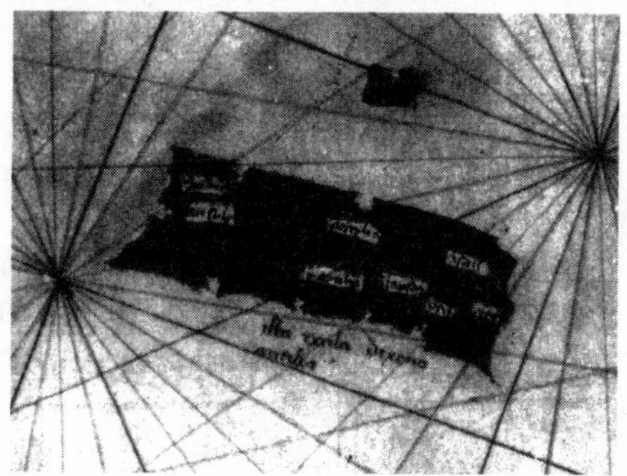

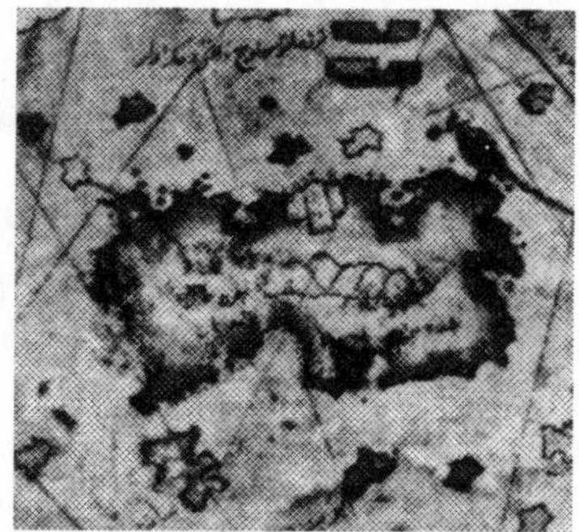

The island of Antilia from the Venetian chart of 1424 alongside the truncated form of Cuba as found on the Piri Reis map of 1513. Is the pre-Columbian memory of these islands one and the same?

Further support for Babcock's theory comes from the famous Piri Reis map of 1513, produced in Turkey some 21 years after Christopher Columbus first reached the West Indies. Here Cuba appears as a rectangular-shaped island that is strikingly similar to how Antilia is shown on navigational charts of the fifteenth century. A number of coastal and inland features on the Piri Reis map match exactly the known topography of Cuba, and yet other quite obvious features of the island are clearly missing. Professor Charles Hapgood of Keene College, New Hampshire, realised that the Piri Reis map showed only the eastern part of Cuba – the western half simply did not appear at all. This fact led him to conclude that the mapmaker in question must have been working from an ancient source map that showed only half of the island.[47] Believing perhaps that this alone was the complete outline of the island, the Turkish cartographer had gone ahead and drawn a truncated form of Cuba in its approximate geographical position.

For Professor Hapgood this was a very exciting discovery. He knew full well that by the date attributed to the Piri Reis map, i.e. 1513, nearly all nautical charts showed the *entire* Cuban coastline based on early maps made by the first scholars and navigators to visit the West Indies. None of these charts displayed any kind of major fault in their detail of Cuba. Since the Piri Reis mapmaker had quite obviously been unaware of the very latest cartographic knowledge reaching the Mediterranean world, it suggested that his sources were pre-Columbian in origin. As a consequence, Hapgood concluded that Cuba must have been 'well known in Europe before the first voyage of Columbus'.[48]

Does the island of Antilia's distinctive rectangular shape denote that it, too, represents a truncated form of Cuba, perhaps derived originally from the same age-old source maps? More important, if Cuba really was the role model for Antilia, how did it relate to the legends surrounding the Island of the Seven Cities?

The Lust for Gold

After exploring several small Bahaman islands during his initial voyage to the New World in October 1492, Christopher Columbus was directed by the local Lucayan Amerindians to search for a much larger island known as Colba, or Cuba.[49] This, he concluded, must be Cipango, where he would find the 'city of gold' belonging to the Great Khan.[50]

It was on Sunday 28 October that his vessel came within sight of Cuba for the first time. After surveying one of its navigable rivers, Columbus sent a party of envoys into the island's interior with a letter of introduction from the Spanish sovereigns. Yet when the search party returned several days later it reported that neither the Great Khan nor the 'city of gold' could be found. Instead, his envoys had been directed by the Amerindians they encountered to a local cacique, or tribal chief, to whom they showed samples of cinnamon, pepper and other spices, which, of course, they hoped to find in abundance. In response, the cacique explained that none of these commodities were to be found here. He suggested that they search further south, perhaps even on another island altogether.[51]

Having failed to find gold in the quantities desired, Columbus lost interest in Cuba. Instead, he set his sights on another large island that the indigenous peoples knew as Bohio. It turned out to be Hispaniola, or La Espanola as it was originally christened by Columbus.[52] It was here that he would later found La Navidad, the first city of the New World.

Columbus returned to Spain and basked in the glory he felt he justly deserved before setting sail again for the West Indies, this time with mass colonisation in mind. In all he made four voyages to the New World, in 1492, 1493, 1498 and 1502. His brother Diego was eventually made governor of La Espanola, while Cuba, which was christened Juana, after a Spanish prince of this name, was at first left relatively untouched.

Yet in 1511 Cuba's peace was shattered for ever as the conquest of paradise began in earnest. For it was in this year that Diego Columbus appointed as its first governor a maniacal Spaniard named Diego Velasquez, who had sailed with Columbus on his second voyage to the West Indies in 1493. His task was to initiate colonisation at any cost,[53] and it was a challenge he took up with an unimaginable zeal.

With a contingent of 300 fully armed conquistadors, Velasquez departed La Navidad with four caravels in November 1511. As the Spaniards pushed further and further into Cuba's mountainous interior they were surprised to encounter fierce resistance from the indigenous peoples. Led by a cacique named Hatuey, the native peoples managed to hamper Velasquez's progress for many months. Yet despite their fighting spirit, the Indian warriors, with their wooden spears and near-naked bodies, were simply no match against the armour, halberds, muskets and swords of the conquistadors, and amid some of the most gruesome barbarity ever inflicted on humankind one by one the tribal provinces fell. Hatuey was caught and burned alive. Before his death, a Catholic friar who accompanied the expedition offered to redeem Hatuey's soul by allowing him to renounce his faith and convert to the Church of Rome. In response to this bizarre request, Hatuey purportedly had called out that he would rather go to hell than 'to a place where he would ever meet again such cruel and wicked people as Christians'.[54]

Blood-soaked and unrepentant, Velasquez marched on, ever pursuing his lust for gold. He, too, never quite found what he was looking for, and yet the genocide he initiated resulted, within a matter of ten short years, in the annihilation of almost the entire native population of Cuba. Those who did not submit to the sabre-blade, musket or cannonball committed suicide, either by strangulation or by eating poison squeezed from the roots of the yucca plant.[55] It is estimated that around 200,000 individuals were either put to death or died through malnutrition, exhaustion, hunger, suicide, European diseases or through standing in rivers up to 12 hours a day, panning the sand for gold.[56] By 1521 there were so few inhabitants left on Cuba that it had been necessary to import thousands of black African slaves, who on their arrival were dispatched to work either on the sugar plantations or in the gold mines opened by the Spaniards.[57]

Leaving aside the hideous crimes against humanity he was unquestionably responsible for in the name of colonisation, it is quite clear that Velasquez believed he would encounter far more than fierce opposition from the indigenous population in the heart of Cuba. Everything suggests that he was searching for the Seven Cities and their gold-bearing sand. There is no proof of this supposition. However, during the 13 years that he spent as governor of Cuba prior to his death in 1521, Velasquez laid the foundations of exactly 'seven cities',[58] each with its own province which still exists today. This alone makes it clear that he considered Cuba to be the original Island of the Seven Cities, recalled so vividly in the legend of the seven bishops who managed to escape the persecution of the invading Moors some 800 years beforehand.

El Dorado – Land of the Golden Man

Inevitably there were those who could not come to terms with the idea that the West Indies were the islands of Antilia, and thus contained the legendary Seven Cities. As a consequence, navigational charts of the sixteenth century began placing them in new locations. The Seven Cities were shown, for instance, in the heart of Brazil, which was by then in the hands of the Portuguese. Other maps placed them further west in Colombia, Peru and even in Ecuador.[59] Still others located them in North America, generally in the region of either Florida or California.[60] Between 1538 and 1542 various Spanish expeditions departed Mexico in search of the legendary 'Seven Cities of Cibola', which were thought to be located somewhere in the vicinity of the Colorado river. None of them succeeded in achieving anything other than bloodshed and misery.

The Seven Cities were never found, and yet the mystery surrounding their whereabouts not only lingered but also transformed into a quite different quest altogether. For it is fair to say that during the 1530s the search for the Seven Cities, or the 'golden cities' as they became known, was responsible for the rapid emergence of rumours regarding the existence of a fabled empire of immense wealth attached to the legend of El Dorado, 'the Golden Man'.[61]

In the wake of the discovery in 1519 of the Aztec Empire by Hernando Cortés (1485–1547/54) and the conquest in 1532 of the Inca Empire by Francisco Pizarro (1475–1548), it was believed that an even greater empire awaited discovery somewhere in the heart of South America. Legends spoke of a sacred lagoon, or lake, on which great heaps of gold and emeralds were offered to the water's presiding deity. Apparently, during the inauguration of a zipa, or supreme monarch, the chosen heir would be escorted to this sacred lake and there his garments would be removed. His body would be coated with a gluey earth, following which a pipe would be used to blow gold on to his skin, giving him the appearance of a sun-god. Remaining perfectly still, the heir would then be floated out on to the lagoon on a raft of rushes. With him would go a company of four subject chiefs wearing gold finery. When the raft finally reached the centre of the lagoon, the priests would make offerings of gold to the water deity, throwing out each item in turn until the raft was empty.[62]

In another version of the story the Golden Man would dive into the water, allowing the gold dust to fall from his body until he was totally cleansed. The zipa's return to the surface marked his transition from chosen heir to supreme monarch, the point at which large quantities of gold would be cast into the water.[63] Quite obviously, the sediment at the bottom of the lagoon was considered to contain a thick layer of gold as well as unimaginable treasures made as offerings to the god of the lake over hundreds, if not thousands, of years.

Among those who searched in vain for the golden city was the Elizabethan navigator Sir Walter Raleigh. Having become convinced that it awaited discovery deep inside the interior of Guiana (modern Venezuela), following the capture of certain Spanish reports which spoke of 'Nuevo Dorado' and the lost kingdom of 'Manoa', he set out in search of El Dorado in 1595.[64] After journeying up the Orinoco river for a distance of around 400 kilometres and finding nothing, he turned back content that he had accumulated enough evidence to convince the English sovereign, Elizabeth I, to give her blessing to a more substantial expedition. Yet the queen was not amused when he arrived back in England empty-handed, forcing him to abandon any plans that he might have had of returning to Guiana. Instead, he spent his time writing a book based on his adventures which was published in 1596 under the title *The Discoverie of Guiana*. It became an instant bestseller, with three impressions in the first year alone and immediate translations into German, Latin and Dutch.

Seven years later Raleigh was accused of taking part in a plot to overthrow the new monarch, James I. As a result he was promptly made a prisoner in the Tower of London and sentenced to death. Yet he ever dreamed of making a fresh attempt to find the lost empire of Manoa, and in 1617 he was finally able to convince the king to allow him to mount a second expedition. Once again he failed to find El Dorado, and this time all that awaited Sir Walter on his return to London was the chopping block!

In the meantime, Spain claimed sovereignty of the as yet undiscovered 'province of El Dorado', while the search for the lagoon began to focus on a lake high up in the Colombian Andes, not far from Bogotá. Known as Guatavita, it was thought to match the description of the lagoon into which the gold had been offered to the presiding deity by the Golden Man. Moreover, local tradition asserted that the lake contained the wealth of a powerful kingdom ruled by a people known as the Chibcha, who worshipped its presiding deity.[65] Yet despite high expectations, all attempts to retrieve the supposed gold that lay at the bottom of the lake failed.

The whereabouts of El Dorado still eludes the world. Yet what seems certain is that the search to discover this unknown empire was originally inspired by much earlier traditions surrounding the legendary Seven Cities. For instance, an Italian world chart of 1510 actually shows 'Antiglia', undoubtedly an allusion to Antilia and the Seven Cities, in north-west Venezuela, close to the location of the Guatavita lake.[66] Moreover, Antilia's gold-bearing sand might easily be compared with the gold dust that was said to have been scooped up from the ground and used to cover the body of the Golden Man as part of his inauguration ceremony.

In conclusion, it would seem that the transference of the Sete Cidades out of the ocean and on to the mainland became the impetus for the creation of fresh legends, concerning the existence of mysterious golden cities deep in the interior of the American continent. Rumours and stories told by coastal Amerindian tribes of sacred and forbidden ruins must have spurred on European explorers to mount fresh expeditions of discovery, yet all the time in vain. Their vision of finding a lost city of gold was fictitious, a creation of their own sense of adventure. Yet whether the object of their quest was Antilia, El Dorado, Cibola or Manoa, there must have been a common thread to these stories that obviously convinced them of the existence of this lost golden empire. Perhaps the indigenous peoples of these regions preserved the memory of a former high culture that saw the number seven as playing a significant role in their society, probably through its importance in their creation myths. Yet every time this sacred number cropped up in the tales and stories told by native peoples to Europeans, it was eagerly seized on as evidence that the Indians had some knowledge of the whereabouts of the Seven Cities. If this was correct, it might well explain why their location moved around so frequently on nautical charts of the Middle Ages.

Encircled Islands

So if the Seven Cities have never been found, are we to assume that they never existed in the first place? Was their existence merely the product of medieval fantasies born out of the naivety of the earliest European cartographers and explorers in respect of what lay on the other side of the Western Ocean?

It is a fact that some medieval world charts would occasionally show, far out in the Western Ocean, a ring of land surrounding a body of water. Inside it would appear a collection of tiny islets, like boats enclosed within a circular dock. On a Catalan map of 1375, nine are shown, while on other variations of the same basic map, seven can be counted.[67] On this subject, geographer William H. Babcock commented: 'These miniature islands have sometimes been thought to represent the seven cities of the old legend; but islets are not cities, and there seems no reason why each city should require an islet. However, the coincidence of number, exact or approximate, is suggestive.'[68] Islands, or islets, are certainly *not* cities, although the link is a real one, with the clear connection being the number seven. Remember, too, that Antilia is quite separately shown with seven lobed bays along its elongated eastern and western coastlines, and seven place-names positioned on the island itself, facts that cartographical scholar Armando Cortesão believed were linked to the tradition of the Seven Cities.[69]

If Babcock's observations were accurate, it suggests that knowledge of Antilia and the legendary Seven Cities might originally have been detached from the story of the seven Portuguese bishops fleeing the Moors in the eighth century AD. Then towards the end of the fourteenth century these separate traditions, which probably derived from the same root source, were combined to become one single island with a preponderance of the number seven.

All the evidence points towards the fact that the legends surrounding Antilia and the Seven Cities predate the exploration of the Western Ocean during the age of discovery by many hundreds, if not thousands, of years. Where exactly the earliest European cartographers and explorers might have obtained this valuable information of unknown Atlantic islands is more difficult to ascertain. It is, however, a subject that we must now address in our attempt to find the true origins behind the story of Antilia and its legendary Seven Cities. Only by doing this can we go on to comprehend the island's relationship to Plato's Atlantis.

CHAPTER XIV

THE EXALTED ONE

THE DATE IS 2 JANUARY 1492. The scene is the famous Alhambra palace, built chiefly in the fourteenth and fifteenth centuries and unquestionably the finest remaining example of Arab architecture in the whole of Spain. Blood-soaked bodies litter the ground, most of them Moorish soldiers and civilians, some Christian Crusaders. This ancient citadel, the last stronghold of Islamic occupation, has fallen.

Crowds begin to gather. A group of Christians climb the roof and tear down the building's crescent-tipped pinnacle which shimmers in the sunlight above the gilded dome. It is wrenched out of its socket and crashes to the ground, the faith of the infidel banished from Spanish soil, for ever.

It is an imagined scenario based on very real events. Yet somehow there is a strange irony in the fact that the fall of Granada took place the same year as the discovery of the New World. For it now seems certain that without the great wisdom and enlightenment of the Moors there is every likelihood that the Americas might have lain undisturbed for many years to come. The departure of the Moors from Western European soil was indeed a tragic affair. Not only did they help initiate the age of discovery, and thus catalyse the Renaissance, but their presence in Spain and Lusitania, the ancient name for Portugal, would also appear to have been instrumental in the emergence of legends surrounding Antilia and the Island of the Seven Cities.

The End of Andalucia

The Moorish occupation of al-Andalus (Andalucia), the name they gave to Spain, had begun almost 800 years earlier. In the seventh and eighth centuries the Arab armies pushed forward from Persia across to the Atlantic coast of Africa, and with them had come new ideas in culture and religion. Among the races that embraced the ways of Islam was the Lixitae, the Berber tribes of Mauritania.

Known to Europeans as the Moors, this Afro-Arabian culture advanced across the Strait of Gibraltar in AD 711 and began the conquest of Spain, which at the time was ruled by a Germanic tribe known as the Visigoths. They had seized control of the country following the collapse of the Roman Empire. The Moors pushed forwards as far as France, but in 732 were forced to withdraw to Spain following a decisive defeat against an army led by France's great cultural hero, Charles Martel. Four years later, in 736, they established the Umayyad emirate (later a caliphate), which took as its capital the ancient city of Córdoba. Other great Arab centres included Toledo, Seville, Merida and, of course, Granada.

For four whole centuries the Moors ruled supreme in Andalucia. Yet power struggles among the contenders for the caliphate weakened their grip on the country. Steadily the Christian armies began to take back Spain. First they gained control of its northern territories, and by the summer of 1139 they held Lusitania, a decisive victory which led to the inauguration of Alfonso I (1096–1185) as the first king of Portugal. Then in 1236 the Crusaders took Córdoba, the Moorish capital. Some 13 years later the Christians regained the Algarve with the assistance of the military fighting machine known as the Knights Templar. For another 242 years the Crusade continued until one day in 1492 the Moors lost Granada, their final stronghold.

Portugal's Golden Age

As an independent kingdom Portugal thrived. In the reign of King João I (1385–1433), it began to expand its influence overseas, following an extensive series of maritime expeditions under the charge of an enlightened figure named Prince Henry the Navigator (1394–1460). In 1418 and 1420 Portuguese navigators João Gonçalves Zarco and Tristão Vaz Teixeira rediscovered the islands of Porto Santo and Madeira. In 1427 Diogo de Silves, the pilot of the Portuguese king, reached the Azores, although it would be another four years before the Portuguese explorer Gonçalves Velho Cabral would make landfall on the islands.

In Africa, the Portuguese journeyed along its western coast until they reached the Gulf of Guinea, where they established innumerable settlements. From here they advanced westwards, and in 1460 the Venetian navigator Alvise Cadamosto, sailing on behalf of Prince Henry, discovered the Cape Verde Islands, some 640 kilometres out from Cape Verde in Senegal. Furthermore, in 1488 navigator Bartolomeu Diaz succeeded in rounding the Cape of Good Hope, while exactly ten years later another Portuguese vessel under the command of Vasco da Gama (1450–1524) not only circumnavigated Africa but also climbed the East Coast and established a passage to India. Curiously enough, it is a fact that in 1420 an Indian junk had been successful in crossing the Indian Ocean and then rounding the Cape of Good Hope in search of islands that were said to have been inhabited separately by men and women. This legend is inscribed on a map produced between 1457 and 1459 by a Venetian priest named Fray Mauro at the request of Portuguese king Alfonso V.[1]

It is clear that long before Columbus' monumental journey to the New World, expeditions commissioned by Prince Henry the Navigator regularly explored the Western Ocean beyond the Azores. Here they encountered, like every vessel before them, the 'Mar de Baga' (the Berry Sea), the name by which the Portuguese referred to the Sargasso Sea.[2]

It even seems possible that Diogo de Teive, one of Prince Henry's most able sea-captains, very nearly discovered the island of Newfoundland in 1452, 55 years before it was claimed in the name of the English sovereign Henry VII by John Cabot. Having set out on a north-westerly course from the Azores, de Teive managed to sail across the Gulf Stream before entering a region where harsh cold winds blew in from the north. Realising that the vessel was heading into dangerous waters, he set a south-easterly course back to the Azores. It was only afterwards that geographers realised that, against all odds, he had reached a latitude of 50 degrees and had therefore come within just a few hundred kilometres of the east coast of Newfoundland.[3] This account, given by de Teive himself, is in stark contrast to the alternative version of what is presumably the same journey recounted by Ferdinand Columbus. He records that the main objective of de Teive's expedition was to discover the Island of the Seven Cities.[4]

Prince Henry had every reason to commission expeditions to relocate the lost Seven Cities. Their discovery would have enabled Portugal to claim sovereignty over the island, not only through conquest, but also through the right of inheritance. This would have been of paramount importance when it came to convincing other countries, such as Spain and England, that Portugal could rightfully lay claim to such territories. For example, the Spanish chronicler Gonzalo Fernández de Oviedo y Valdéz claimed that if the West Indies really were the Hesperides, they rightly belonged to the Spanish sovereign. This was because the Roman writer Statius Sebosus had said that the Hesperides were the daughters of Hesperus, a legendary 'Spanish' king, whom Oviedo saw as a distant ancestor of the Spanish monarch.[5]

Britain, on the other hand, attempted to lay claim to the Americas by asserting that they had been discovered in the year 1170 by

Madoc, the seafaring son of a Welsh king named Owen Gwynedd. Dr John Dee, the mathematician, mapmaker and court astrologer to Queen Elizabeth, promoted this idea during the 1570s in an attempt to establish a firm foundation for what he termed the 'Brytish Empire'. In summary, he believed that Madoc's journey enabled the British to lay claim to 'all the Coasts and Islands beginning at or abowt Terra Florida . . . unto Atlantis going Northerly', and beyond that to all the islands as far as Russia.[6] The mention of the all-important 'A' word is not without significance, for Dr Dee became convinced that North America was Atlantis, and even marked it thus on navigational charts he produced during this period.

Prince Henry the Navigator

There is no doubt that by the end of the fifteenth century Portuguese navigators were among the most capable in Europe. Yet so many of their naval achievements can be accredited to the extraordinary leadership and foresight of Prince Henry. In 1419 he had founded an academy, or school, of navigation within the confines of his polygonal stone fortress at Sagres in the Algarve. Located on a desolate promontory overlooking the Atlantic, it stood on the very edge of the known world. Here Prince Henry advocated an education in cartography, geography and physics, and set up as its first director a Majorcan named 'Master Jacob'.[7] Under the influence of the Catalans, Majorca had thrived during the thirteenth and fourteenth centuries as a maritime centre with an extensive trading network. Prince Henry had therefore wanted to capitalise on its ancient traditions, which included the production of high-quality nautical charts and instruments.[8]

In an attempt to create the greatest, and most cosmopolitan, seagoing nation of all time, Prince Henry invited to Portugal expert sailors, cartographers, cosmographers, navigators and astronomers from all over the Mediterranean world. He can be said to have succeeded in this aim, for there is little doubt that his efforts paved the way for the greatest discovery of all – the relocation of the New World. According to tradition, Vasco da Gama, Ferdinand Magellan, Bartolomeu Diaz, Pedro Álvares Cabral and even Christopher Columbus all passed through Sagres' school of navigation.

Prince Henry was not afraid to push new boundaries when it came to oceanic exploration. He unquestionably knew about the undiscovered southern continent spoken of by Moorish pirates and black African seafarers. He would have known, too, that Antilia and the Island of the Seven Cities lay beyond the Mar de Baga. He must also have been aware that a nautical chart produced in 1448 by Andrea Bianco, who had spent time in Portugal, showed south-west of Cape Verde a mysterious land next to which was a curious inscription that read 'authentic island [that] is distant 1,500 miles [2,400 kilometres] to the west'.[9]

According to the chronicle of Diogo Gomes, one of Prince Henry's captains and close associates: 'The Prince wishing to know about the far away regions of the western ocean, whether there were any islands or continent (*terra firme*) besides those described by Ptolemy [a well-known Alexandrian astronomer and mathematician of the second century AD], sent caravels to discover.'[10] It is even clear from a letter dated 14 July 1493 to King João of Portugal from a doctor of Nuremberg named Hieronymus Monetarius that Prince Henry had attempted during his lifetime 'to demonstrate the sphericity of the earth'.[11]

What motivated Portugal's wish to explore the outer limits of the ocean during the fifteenth century? Was it simply to expand their trading network and sovereignty, or could Prince Henry have been privy to knowledge unavailable to the rest of the maritime world? If so, did it concern the whereabouts of Antilia and the Island of the Seven Cities?

Emergence of a Legend

According to the tradition surrounding the foundation of the Seven Cities, it was in AD 714 that the advancing Moorish army laid siege to the city of Merida, the old capital of the Roman province of Lusitania (which is today a town over the border in Spain). As a result, seven bishops and their flocks decided to escape persecution by securing a fleet of ships and setting sail into the unknown. They traversed the Western Ocean until one day the fleet came upon an island known as Antilia, where they established Sete Cidades, the Seven Cities.

This is the basic story as told by cartographers, historians and navigators of various nationalities during the late fifteenth and early sixteenth centuries. Yet as we have seen, there are basic problems in accepting these accounts as straightforward historical fact. No evidence of a pre-Conquest Portuguese colony has ever come to light on any Atlantic island. There is not one scrap of evidence to suggest the former existence of the Seven Cities either in the West Indies, or anywhere else for that matter. So why were the Portuguese so eager to mount long-distance maritime voyages in an effort to find them?

The only answer is that they considered these stories to be actual history. Yet if this was so, why exactly did they believe in them so fervently? Were they transmitted to the Portuguese by those who could rightly claim that their most distant ancestors had some knowledge of these events, which had supposedly taken place in their country several hundred years beforehand? If so, who might this have been? Since the kingdom of Portugal did not exist in the eighth century, and the Visigoths who occupied these territories at the time of conquest had long since been vanquished, the only people in a position to have recounted these legends were the Moors.

Such a solution might seem at first like an odd one, especially as the Moors were quite obviously being evicted from a land that they felt could easily be called their own. However, it is a fact that throughout the Moorish occupation of Spain and Lusitania a considerable amount of contact existed between Arabs and Christians. Many Europeans clearly recognised the wisdom to be gained from the secret teachings of Islamic mysticism and philosophy which thrived in the Moorish centres of learning, such as Córdoba and Toledo. New knowledge which included algebra, astronomy, cartography, geography, geometry, mathematics, navigation and classical philosophy was accessible to those willing to put aside racial and religious intolerance. There is no question that the Moors introduced many of these key sciences to the medieval world.

Islamic cities also became the focus of alchemists, occultists, mystics and freethinkers who descended on Spain in the hope of gaining ultimate enlightenment not only from the established schools of learning but also from back-street opportunists who at the right price would reveal their own brand of the forbidden sciences.

The Knights Templar

Among those who recognised the importance of the Moorish centres of learning were members of clandestine military orders such as the Knights Templar. According to the stories, they had frequently trafficked with the Saracens during the Crusades in the Holy Land. The Order of the Knights of Christ and the Temple of Solomon, as they were more correctly titled, was founded in 1128 to protect pilgrim routes in and out of the Holy Land. Yet in a matter of a few short years they grew to become the most powerful fighting force in the whole of Christendom. With preceptories, tithes and estates in virtually every country of Europe, they gained the favour of kings, protecting their wealth and instituting the first international banking system. Yet they also became a law unto themselves, owing allegiance to no one but the Pope, and worse still they dabbled in forms of Christian mysticism which turned out to be their undoing.

By the beginning of the fourteenth century, the French king Philip the Fair owed them vast sums of money. So with the aid of the Pope, Clement v, he had every Templar in France arrested at dawn on Friday 13 October 1307. At the same time other monarchs were ordered to arrest their Templars and bring them to justice. They were accused of blasphemy, heresy and denying the divinity of Christ. Many were tortured into giving false confessions, and when the knights were finally brought to trial in France they were found guilty of the charges made against them. Many were put to death, including the Grand Master, Jacques de Molay, who was burned at the stake in March 1314.

The Pope officially dissolved the Order in 1312, and all Templar lands reverted to the sovereign of the countries in question. Yet the results of the trials outside France varied considerably. In Scotland, for instance, the evidence against the Templars was deemed inconclusive, so the case against them was dropped, while in Spain, Portugal, Germany and Switzerland they were fully acquitted of all charges.

The trials themselves lasted for several years and produced literally thousands of official documents which contain some fascinating insights into the apparent relationship that existed between the Templars and their Arab adversaries. One account speaks of the 'Master of The Temple and the other chiefs of the Order' paying homage to Saladin (1137–1193), the sultan of Egypt and Syria when Jerusalem fell to the Saracens in 1187.[12] Another witness testimony states that at times of truce, when no battles were being fought, Templars paid serviture to the 'Soldan', i.e. the Sultan, and also 'kept them friendly'.[13] In another case a witness confessed that: 'He had heard that the Christians had suffered much from the great familiarity that existed between Bello Joco, then Master of the Order, and the Soldan and Saracens, but he believed the contrary.'[14] Lastly, it came to light during the trials that Item No. 119 of the Order's regulations prescribed that the Master of the Order should take a 'Saracen scribe' as an interpreter.[15]

Although much of what the Templars were accused of can be dismissed as fabricated charges, the trial documents show how strong the rumours were regarding their connection with the Arab world. There seems little question that this relationship extended to the Moors, particularly at their great centres of learning in Spain and Portugal. So what did the Templars learn from the Moors, and how much of this knowledge might have passed into the hands of the military orders that succeeded them?

Knights of Christ

The Knights Templar led the crusading armies to victory in the Portuguese Algarve and were rewarded in this respect by being given estates and tithes right across the country. After the departure of the Moors, it is likely that the Templars became the custodians of at least some of the libraries that existed in the Arab centres of learning. Exactly how this curious relationship might have influenced their development or interests remains uncertain, although it is what happened to the Templars of Spain and Portugal after the dissolution of the Order that is of key importance here.

As previously stated, the ruling councils in both countries acquitted them of all charges. Despite this, the Order was disbanded, and so, to fill the gap, new orders were set up. The Spanish sovereign created the Knights of Santiago, a key chivalric order greatly influenced by Templar tradition. In Portugal the king, Dionysius I, announced the creation in 1317 of an order to be called the *Christi Militia*, or the Knights of Christ, which was given a bull of approbation by Pope John XXII in 1319. Curiously enough, it was also in 1317 that the Portuguese king appointed the Genoese navigator Emmanuel Pezagno as hereditary admiral of the country's fleet, an act that marked the commencement of a new era in Portuguese naval power. All former estates, tithes and properties belonging to the Order of the Temple were henceforth handed over to the Knights of Christ, and quite naturally the Portuguese Templars flocked to join its ranks. It is said that only a candidate with four generations of hereditary nobility was eligible for investiture, ensuring that the Order consisted only of hand-picked brethren who could be trusted implicitly by the aristocracy.[16]

Like the Templars before them, the Knights of Christ outwardly opposed the Moors. Having decided that the Order would take to the high seas, they launched a series of naval expeditions against Moorish pirates under the command of Prince Henry. The Order's decisive victory at the battle of Ceuta on Africa's Mediterranean coast in 1415 signalled the beginning of Portugal's overseas exploration. Two years later, Prince Henry was appointed Grand Master of the Order, a post he was to hold until his death in 1460. Chivalric rites of initiation and enlightenment unquestionably took place in his remote castle fortress at Sagres. We can only guess at the relationship there might have been between investiture into the different grades of the Order and the advancement of maritime scholarship.

Under Prince Henry's influence, Pope Leo X granted the Knights of Christ the right of presentation to all bishoprics overseas, meaning that the Order was to be given full status in whatever country its cavaliers might enter. Can we see in this right Prince Henry's desire to present his order to the seven bishoprics that were assumed to exist on the Island of the Seven Cities?

There seems little doubt that by the middle of the fifteenth century the Knights of Christ, under the patronage of Prince Henry, had grown to become one of the most powerful military organisations in Europe. Yet in many ways the Order was merely a reconstituted form of the Knights Templar, with its centre now in Portugal instead of France. The familiar red cross ensign of the Templars was borne on the sails and flags of the Order's hundreds of vessels, while everywhere they went the Knights of Christ established military commanderies – 454 in all, with 37 in Africa alone.[17]

Some of the most famous Portuguese navigators were members of the Knights of Christ. Even Christopher Columbus' name has been linked to the Order. His vessel the *Santa Maria* is said to have sailed under the Order's red cross ensign, an enigma that has perplexed historians to this day. It has even been suggested, without any kind of substantiation, that Columbus was himself a member of the Knights of Christ, and that the Order supplied him with navigational charts and maps on Atlantic trade routes.[18] There are no official records to this effect, even though it is a fact that following the death of his Portuguese father-in-law, Bartolomeu Perestrello, the first governor of Madeira and a knight of the realm, Columbus received as part of his inheritance 'writings and sea charts'. These told of the different voyages of discovery in which Portugal was currently engaged.[19] Indeed, it is quite clear that Columbus' frequent journeys to Portuguese settlements on the Guinea coast helped him to become a proficient navigator in his own right.

Behaim's Investiture

There seems to be an integral relationship between the Knights of Christ and Portugal's interest in the rediscovery of the Island of the Seven Cities. This can be determined if we examine the life of Martin Behaim, the German navigator and merchant who in 1492 produced the world's first globe. His expertise as a scientist and navigator brought him to Lisbon in 1484, where he continued to live periodically until his death in 1507. Almost immediately after his arrival in Lisbon Behaim joined two separate maritime expeditions to West Africa. The Behaim family archives state that in between these long voyages he was invested as a knight of the realm on 18 February 1485 by King João II.[20] This important ceremony, which took place in the Church of St Saviour in the town of Alcaçovas, was sponsored not only by the king but also by three key members of the aristocracy. Moreover, the event was said to have been conducted 'in the presence of all the Princes and Knights [of the Order], and of the Queen'.[21]

It is not specified which military order Behaim embraced as a cavalier, although the fact that so many knights, dignitaries and members of the royal family attended the ceremony strongly suggests that it was the Knights of Christ. This same conclusion has been drawn by various historians, although it has, however, been questioned by Behaim's biographer E. G. Ravenstein in his book *Martin Behaim: His Life and His Globe*, published in 1908.[22] Despite such shortcomings, what we do know is that just a few months after the date given for his investiture, Behaim would appear to have been asked to join an expedition to go in search of the Island of the Seven Cities. Under the joint command of two Portuguese sea-captains named Fernão Dulmo and João Affonso, it was scheduled to leave Terçeira in the Azores during March 1487. Moreover, a deed of partnership, sanctioned by the king and dated 12 July 1486, states that the two sea-captains were to be joined by a 'cavalleiro alemão [German knight]'.[23] Since the only German knight to whom this description could at the time have applied was Martin Behaim, it was almost certainly him who was being considered for this prestigious role on behalf of the Portuguese Crown.[24]

The eventual fate of this bold venture is not recorded. Furthermore, it seems certain that Behaim played no part in it. Yet what we can say is that just five years later his famous globe bore an inscription that outlined for the very first time the story behind the foundation of the legendary Seven Cities on the island of Antilia.

This catalogue of events is strangely suggestive of some kind of connection between Behaim's investiture as a Portuguese knight of the realm, his apparent invitation to join a vessel bound for Antilia, and his subsequent knowledge of the legend surrounding the Island of the Seven Cities. Might it have formed part of some kind of secret discourse to which a cavalier in, say, the Knights of Christ became privy on his investiture? Once again, there is no proof of this supposition, although the tantalising evidence surrounding the apparent relationship between the Knights Templar and the Arab world makes this possibility extremely attractive indeed. Yet if this was the case, where might the Moors have obtained knowledge of this island in the west?

The Lisbon Wanderers

Shortly after their conquest of Spain and Lusitania, the Moors began their own exploration of the Western Ocean, the fruits of which were recorded by an Arab geographer, El Idrisi (*c.* 1099–1164). In his celebrated work entitled *Geography*, *c.* 1154, he detailed the discovery of several Atlantic islands.[25] In fact El Idrisi believed there to be an incredible 27,000 islands located in the Western Ocean, some of which he attempted to highlight on a world map wrought in silver made for Robert, the king of Sicily. Sadly, this extraordinary item has not survived.

El Idrisi also spoke of the Al-Khalidat, or the Fortunate Isles, on which he said were bronze statues on tall columnar pedestals that faced out towards the west. Curiously enough, El Idrisi spoke of there being six of these statues, with one of them being located at Cadiz, ancient Gades.[26]

This information alone confirms the role that the Moors must have played in introducing a knowledge of Atlantic islands to the medieval world, for it is not until some 200 years later that any reference to these alleged statues of warning reappears. As we have seen, similar statues are mentioned in the legend on the Pizzigani map of 1367 in connection with an Atlantic location named as 'Atulliae', very probably an early form of Antilia. Since this is also the oldest known reference to the island's existence, might it be seen as further evidence that the Moors were instrumental in bringing Antilia to the attention of the medieval world?

El Idrisi also tells us of the amazing exploits of the eight Maghrurins ('deceived men'), also known as the 'Lisbon Wanderers', who undertook a maritime journey of discovery to find out 'what is it that encloses the Ocean, and what its limits are'.[27] They are said to have departed from the port of Lisbon, then obviously under Moorish rule. After a number of days' sail, the ship is said to have entered the 'Sea of Darkness and Mystery', almost certainly the Sargasso Sea.[28] Afterwards, the expedition discovered various Atlantic islands, including one known as Al-Ghanam, the 'Isle of Sheep', thought possibly to be Madeira.[29] Later, the Moorish vessel is said to have changed its course and come across a further island group, very probably the Canaries. Having disembarked on one of its islands, the Moorish sailors were imprisoned by the local population. Yet after securing their release, the Maghrurins were able to navigate their way to the African coast, before eventually setting a course back to Lisbon.[30]

The Moors certainly possessed the capability to explore the outer regions of the North Atlantic Ocean. They discovered key island groups, such as the Azores, the Canaries and possibly even the Cape Verdes, which they knew as the 'islands of the two wizards'.[31]

Is it possible that the Moors, as the descendants of the Lixitae, gained at least some of their maritime knowledge and capability from the Carthaginians, as well as the Spanish descendants of the Iberic Phoenicians who occupied the coastal regions of Andalucia? Could the original inspiration for the legends surrounding Antilia and the Island of the Seven Cities have come from the Phoenicians and Carthaginians? If this was so, then the Moors might therefore have been the caretakers of oceanic knowledge and lore that stretched back for at least 1,700 years before the Arab conquest of

Spain and Portugal. To take the matter further we would have to take a closer look at the origins of the name Antilia.

To Endure, or not to Endure

Scholars suggest that the name Antilia derives from the Latin *ante,* 'in front of', and the Portuguese *ilha,* meaning 'island'. Yet this translation is based on its final form only. On the Pizzigani map of 1367 it appears as 'Atulliae', which seems to have been its more formative spelling. Other, later variations of this same basic spelling include 'Atilhas', found on a map dated 1518,[32] 'Ateallo', from a Catalan map dated *c.* 1448,[33] and 'Attiaela', which appears on another Catalan map of the fifteenth century.[34] If this is the more correct spelling, the name does not derive from *ante-ilha,* but comes from a much older variation of uncertain origin. Since it has been proposed that detail on Catalan maps like the ones mentioned here may well have been taken from Moorish sailing-charts,[35] could it be possible that the original form of Antilia was Afro-Arabian in origin?

In the 1830s Alexander von Humboldt (1769–1859), the celebrated German naturalist, traveller and statesman, proposed that 'Antillia' and its variations were derived from 'Al-tin', Arabic for 'the dragon'.[36] If this was correct, it would perhaps imply that the island was home to a fabulous beast of this description (bringing to mind the dragon that guarded the golden apples on the islands of the Hesperides). Support for this theory comes in the knowledge that at least one mythical island in Arab folklore was actually known as the Island of the Dragon.[37] So was this the answer? Almost certainly not, for the transition from Al-tin to Antilia is far too severe for it to make linguistic sense.

If not obviously Latin, Portuguese or Arab, from where might the name Antilia have originated? Could it be either Phoenician or Punic, the language of the Carthaginians? With this prospect in mind, I made a search of known place-names in common usage during biblical times and came across something very interesting indeed. My eyes were drawn to an entry in a biblical dictionary for 'Attalia', or 'Attaleia', a port at Pamphylia in Asia Minor, now Turkey, built by Attalus II, the king of Pergamon (159–138 BC). The first syllable was sufficiently close to the formative spellings of Antilia for a comparison to be made. The origin of the word 'Attalia' is unknown, although it could be Greek. However, what intrigued me most about this place-name is that it later altered to Antalya, the form by which this Turkish port is known today.[38]

The purpose of this exercise is to demonstrate how easily the name Antilia could have evolved from the earlier spelling of 'Atulliae', or 'Atilae'. Moreover, when stripped of its inferred vowels, and the superfluous second letter 'l', the linguistic root of the formative spellings of Antilia is composed of just three consonants: a-t-l. As we saw in Chapter Three, the root *atl*, as in Atlas, Atlantis or Atlantic, is commonly thought to derive from the Greek *tlâo*, 'to endure' or 'to bear'.

The controversy surrounding the origin of the linguistic root *atl*, so crucial to our understanding of the Atlantis mystery, is one that has raged for a century and a half. Seven years before the American congressman turned historical detective Ignatius Donnelly launched his monumental work *Atlantis: The Antediluvian World* on to an unsuspecting public, a scholarly article appeared in *The Cincinnati Quarterly Journal of Science.* Entitled 'Atlantis: A Statement of the "Atlantic" Theory Respecting Aboriginal Civilisation', the paper, penned by American historian L. M. Hosea, addresses the linguistic origin behind the proper name Atlas, which he acknowledges is thought by language scholars to derive from the Greek word *tlâo*.[39] In his words:

> This derivation, however, appears hardly reasonable, since the name would seem to have existed before the duty [of supporting the heavens] was imposed upon the god, and was no doubt imported into the Greek through maritime intercourse with the African nations. It is more probable that the original signification of Atlas . . . was gradually lost as commerce declined and the tradition of the existence of the islands [under his domain] became indistinct, and was ultimately merged in the secondary idea of 'keeper of the pillars which hold heaven and earth asunder' – which stood upon the western horizon where the eye would naturally turn in looking toward the fabled islands, and thus became crystallised in the mythology of the day. It is, therefore, more reasonable to suppose that the few Greek words, and there are but few, which contain the radical *atl* or *tl*, all of them involving the idea of supporting a burden, are themselves derived from this secondary signification of Atlas.[40]

What Hosea is saying here is that the root *atl* cannot have stemmed from a memory of Atlas' punishment, or vice versa, since one or other of them must have existed in the first place. But is there a suitable solution to this problem, one that might be acceptable to the scholarly world?

Raised on High

Greek belongs to a family of languages known as Indo-European, which is derived from some of the earliest written and spoken languages of western and southern Asia. So in theory the origin behind the name Atlas should be found in one of the core Indo-European languages, such as Sanskrit. Although native to India, it is one of the oldest forms of this language group. I therefore put the matter to Clifford Wright, Professor of South Asian studies at the School of Oriental and African Studies. In his opinion, the only word in this language that resembles the linguistic root *atl* is the Sanskrit 'tul' or 'tol' which means 'to weigh'.[41] Since this implies an act whereby an item is lifted to determine its weight, Professor Wright could understand how a Greek language scholar might conclude that the world *tlâo*, 'to bear' or 'to endure', might stem from this Indo-European root. Furthermore, he pointed out that this same Sanskrit word was the root behind the Latin 'tollo', 'to lift', 'to raise' and 'to weigh'. Yet to Professor Wright, the act of weighing implied by this word did not fully explain the idea of bearing or enduring a heavy weight suggested by Atlas' penance of having to support the heavens on his shoulders.[42] Furthermore, the name begins with the letter 'a', which when used as a prefix in Greek words reverses the original meaning. So *tlâo* prefixed with an 'a', as in *atlâo*, becomes 'to not endure' or 'to not bear', making complete nonsense of how Atlas is supposed to have gained his name. Lastly, the Latin 'tollo' obviously dates to a slightly later period and might have been influenced by the Greek word *tlâo*. So was there an alternative linguistic root for 'Atlas'?

It is accepted that certain proper names found in the Greek language are in fact West Semitic in origin. This is a language branch that includes Arabic, Hebrew, Phoenician and Punic. It is Herodotus who informs us that 'writing' was first introduced to the Greeks by the Phoenicians. It was they who 'shaped their letters' using their existing 16-character alphabet. Furthermore, that: 'afterwards, in the course of time, they changed by degrees their language, and together with it the form likewise of their characters'.[43] Could the *atl* root behind both Atlas and Antilia therefore be of West Semitic origin?

Extraordinarily enough, an examination of this language group does provide some answers. The word root *atl* appears in the vowel-less language of the Hebrews, where it means 'exalted', as in 'elated' or 'raised' on high. For example, it is present in the Hebrew name 'Atalyah', meaning 'Yah is exalted'. This is composed of the root *atl*, 'exalted', and *yah*, meaning 'god'.[44] The same word root *atl* is also present in the Arabic language, where it also means 'exalted' or 'raised'. More significantly it is found in Akkadian, an East Semitic language that thrived in ancient Iraq as far back as the third millennium BC.[45]

Most important of all, the *atl* word root appears as a proper name in Punic. Jo Ann Hackett, the Professor of Biblical Hebrew at Harvard University, informed me that it appears on a dedication stone from Carthage written as ATLA.[46] However, it is not recorded whether or not this personal name actually means 'exalted' or 'raised', yet there is every reason to assume that it does. Even though the exact age of this dedication stone is unknown, it was probably manufactured sometime between the fourth and second centuries BC.[47]

This is where it starts getting interesting, for in addition to meaning 'exalted', the Hebrew word *atl*, and indeed its variations, can also mean 'elevated', which a standard English dictionary tells us means 'raised; at or on a higher level; lofty in style'.[48] This adjective is, of course, derived from the noun 'elevation', which denotes 'the act of elevating; the state of being elevated; an elevated position or ground; height above sea-level; the height of a building' and, lastly, 'the angular altitude of a heavenly body above the horizon'.[49]

If we turn now to Lemprière's standard classical dictionary and look at the entry for 'Atlas', we find it reads:

> The fable that Atlas supported the heavens on his back arises from his fondness for astronomy, and his often frequenting *elevated* places and mountains, whence he might observe heavenly bodies [author's emphasis].[50]

Since we know that Mount Atlas was deemed to be the petrified Titan supporting the heavens on his shoulders, Atlas' name is therefore intrinsically linked with his action of having elevated or raised up these misty heights. Clearly, then, this connection strongly suggests that the name Atlas does not derive from the Indo-European language of the Greeks but from the Punic language of the Carthaginians – furthermore, that the word root *atl* does not mean 'to bear' but 'to elevate' or 'to raise'. The mountain must therefore take its name from the fact that its 'heavens' are 'elevated' above ground level, an act seen as having been performed by the mighty stone giant. In this respect, Atlas thus becomes the personification of this act, in a sense the one who raises or elevates the heavens into the air. If this was the case, it tells us that, as a noun, Atlas, and indeed ATLA, might well translate as 'the elevator', 'the exalter', or indeed 'the exalted one'.

Homer and Hesiod

So if Atlas derives his name from the Carthaginians, it now seems certain that both Atlantis and Antilia stem from the same linguistic root. Yet as the *atl* root is also found in ancient texts written in the East Semitic language of the Akkadians, this tells us that its usage long antedates the first references to the hero-god Atlas in classical literature. Such works include Homer's *Odyssey*, composed *c.* 800–

600 BC,[51] which speaks of Atlas upholding the heavens, and Hesiod's *Theogony*, written *c.* 700 BC,[52] which tells of Atlas' association with the Hesperides.

Unfortunately, there is still no way of telling which came first, Atlas the Titan or Atlas the mountain. All we can say is that both were associated with ancient Mauritania, the land of the Moors and Carthaginians, and that Atlas was additionally connected with astronomy, navigation and the watery depths that lay in the direction of the setting sun. It is almost certainly due to this connection that the Greek islands located in the Western Ocean were considered to be 'daughters' of Atlas, or Atlantides, their existence being preserved either in mythical form or as speculative maritime lore. Even as late as the sixteenth century, Atlantic islands were still referred to as 'Atlantides'. Antonio Galvão in his *The Discoveries of the World* states that in the *Timaeus* Plato records that there existed 'in ancient times in the Ocean sea Atlanticke certaine great Islands and countries named Atlantides'.[53]

There can now be little doubt that it was the Carthaginians, and not the Greeks, who introduced the *atl*-derived names, such as Atlas, Atlantis and Antilia, to the ancient world. Support for this theory comes from Sir Edward Herbert Bunbury, the nineteenth-century Cambridge geographer and Fellow of the Royal Geographical Society, whose book *A History of Ancient Geography* remains a standard bench-mark in all major universities. Having made an exhaustive study of the Greek myths exposed to the world for the first time by the likes of Homer and Hesiod, he became convinced that those which feature Atlas and the Hesperides were 'almost certainly of Phoenician origin'.[54] He further added that: '. . . we find in the earliest Greek records many vague and dimly-traced ideas as to the wonders of "the far west", which are in all probability derived from Phoenician sources'.[55]

Adding still further weight to this argument is the knowledge that the concept of the Elysian Fields or Elysium, the mysterious isle of the dead located in the Western Ocean, is Phoenician in origin.[56] The same might also be said of Oceanus, the Ocean River, first found mentioned in Homer's *Iliad*.[57] In the words of noted nineteenth-century Swedish geographer A. E. Nordenskiöld 'the name οχεανοζ [*okeanos*] is probably of Phoenician origin'.[58]

It is my opinion that some semblance of this legendary maritime knowledge remained in the possession of the ancient Lixitae, who as the Moors carried this understanding of Atlantic islands into Spain and Portugal sometime between the eighth and fourteenth centuries. Among their traditions was a fragmentary knowledge of a mysterious Atlantic island called Atulliae. Somehow this tradition came to the attention of the medieval cartographers and navigators of Portugal, who updated the name of this island to Antilia, *ante-ilha*, the island 'before' or 'in front of' something else, most probably the unknown American continent.

This is not to say that the concept of the Seven Cities was the creation either of the Moors or the Portuguese, only that the true origins of this tradition had somehow been lost along the way. Seven is the number that predominates in the legend of Antilia, and the islands of the Western Ocean in general. Seven cities, seven named bays, seven bishops, seven islets, seven Atlantides, seven Pleiades, seven islands sacred to Proserpine (after Marcellus) and seven divisions, or 'circles', of the Atlantean city as envisaged by the Neo-Platonist named Amelius.

Were the Seven Cities simply an elaboration of some much more archaic tradition connected directly with the core legends behind both the Atlantis myth and the medieval traditions of Antilia? It is a tantalising possibility, and one that we begin to explore in the next chapter.

Yet for the moment we return briefly to the pioneering work of American historian L. M. Hosea. Having queried the linguistic root of the name Atlas, he went on to propose that: 'If . . . we can find a country, in the spoken language of which the word Atlantis has an indigenous root, there it is said we are justified in seeking traces of the long lost race.'[59]

Yet having made this statement Hosea went on to suggest that the 'country' in question was the 'lovely vale of Anahuac', the pre-Conquest name for Mexico. Quoting the Abbé Brasseur de Bourbourg, an accomplished nineteenth-century French philologist and language scholar who made an in-depth study of Mesoamerican religion and mythology, he informs us: 'Here, too, we find the radical *tl* or *atl*', meaning 'water', and from which was 'derived Atlan, *on the border or in the midst of water*'.[60]

Is there any way that a language spoken by the indigenous peoples of Central Mexico could have any connection with the naming of the West Indies by Phoenician and Carthaginian traders? As we shall see, exploring this fascinating although linguistically difficult line of enquiry will reveal some remarkable insights into the possible origins of the Sete Cidades.

CHAPTER XV

FAIR GODS FROM AFAR

THE DATE IS 18 NOVEMBER 1519. After months of daring exploits rivalling anything the pages of history had ever seen, the Spanish conquistador Hernando Cortés entered Tenochtitlan, the gleaming island metropolis of the Aztec Empire. Tens of thousands of Aztec citizens, brightly attired in colourful robes, lined either side of the long causeway into the city. Advancing between them was a column of several hundred fully armed Aztec warriors in animal skins and plumed headdresses. They were the royal guards of the Aztecs' Great Speaker Motecuhzoma II – better known to the world as Montezuma – who was being carried on a golden litter by four attendant noblemen moving at a slow, deliberate pace.

Cortés, dressed in full armour, was mounted on a well-groomed horse. He was accompanied by a trusted band of cavaliers, and in file behind them was a company of no more than 300 disciplined foot soldiers marching to the sound of pipes and drums. Some carried colourful banners, including Cortés' own by now tattered standard, which had united his motley army on so many occasions since they had landed in New Spain.

Trailing behind the Spaniards were 4,000 fierce, feather-clad warriors from the eastern province of Tlaxcala. Having been defeated no fewer than four times by the Spaniards, they had become Cortés' greatest allies in his plan to seize outright control of the Aztec nation.

There is no question that this was the latest, and greatest, act of sheer lunacy orchestrated by Cortés and his noble company. At any moment Montezuma could have given the signal for the entire population of Tenochtitlan to attack his army. Those not killed outright would have been captured and offered up as human sacrifices in the temples already stained with the blood of thousands upon thousands of victims. Yet Cortés was no ordinary Spanish general.

Hernando Cortés was born in 1485 at Medellin, a town in the province of Estremadura in western Spain. From an early age he displayed a fighting spirit, able wit and good intelligence that his father had wanted to channel into the study of law. Yet the young cavalier had other ideas. Having already shown a fondness for military action, he seized the opportunity in 1504 to depart for the New World. Seven years later he accompanied Diego Velasquez and his vicious conquistadors on their brutal colonisation of Cuba. Later he was to become Velasquez's secretary. Yet Cortés disagreed fundamentally with the governor's ill-conceived and bloody policies which in 1518 he attempted to bring to the attention of the ruling council on Hispaniola. He and his co-conspirators were arrested, although he managed to escape and claim sanctuary in a church. Eventually, the two men settled their dispute and Cortés was granted an estate with arable lands in the neighbourhood of St Jago, and for a short while he adopted an agricultural lifestyle.

Discovery of New Spain

Yet fuelled by reports reaching Cuba of a great empire in New Spain, the name given to the American mainland, Cortés set his sights on conquest. His motives are said to have been gold, glory and the conversion of the people in the name of the Church of Rome. Expectations had been raised by the return from the Yucatán of an expedition led by Hernandez de Cordova in 1517. His vessel had been blown off course from Cuba en route to the Bahamas, and by chance it had made landfall on the coast of the Yucatán. Here the Spanish crewmen encountered hostile inhabitants, unquestionably Maya warriors, who were much better equipped than the peoples so far encountered in the West Indies. Moreover, they constructed buildings and temples made of stone, something that had not been seen on any of the islands of the West Indies. Most curious of all, Cordova was of the opinion that 'thereabouts were the Seven Cities',[1] a point that cannot have gone unnoticed by the Cuban governor Diego Velasquez and his young secretary Hernando Cortés.

A second expedition under the command of Juan de Grijalva left Cuba bound for the Yucatán on 1 May 1518. It, too, experienced an unfriendly welcome from the local Maya, although Grijalva pushed on and reached as far as the modern province of Tabasco on the Gulf of Campeche, close to the site of the Maya city of Comalcalco. He then journeyed north along the Gulf coast and came across two offshore islands. One of them he named the Isla de los Sacrificios, following the discovery there of skeletal remains and a blood-stained temple that could only have been used for human sacrifice – the first time this practice had been encountered in the New World.[2]

Fired by such reports, Cortés planned an entire mission to New Spain, complete with a fleet of 11 vessels, 100 shipmasters, pilots and sailors, an army of around 500, 16 horses and sufficient quantities of arms and armour, all without the knowledge of Velasquez. Despite the governor's late attempts to prevent the expedition from leaving Cuba, the fleet departed Cape St Antonio bound for the Yucatán on 18 February 1519. After successfully defeating the Maya in various skirmishes, Cortés sailed south-westwards and finally reached the Gulf coast on 21 April 1519. With the help of the local population, he built an extensive settlement as a base camp as well as a place of refuge should it be needed in the months to come. On the site of this encampment grew the modern city of Veracruz.

The events that were to follow Cortés' first landing in New Spain are quite remarkable. Having decided to burn his ships, so that there might be no going back, he decided to make his advance towards the Aztec capital, even though Montezuma had forbidden it. Cortés had also ordered the Totonac of nearby Cempoalla to arrest Aztec tribute collectors, and then had them secretly released in order to gain the respect and admiration of the Great Speaker. Cortés had also torn down pagan idols inside sacred temples in front of frantic crowds and replaced them with wooden crosses and images of Mary and the Infant Saviour. Moreover, he had led his troops against armies of 100,000 or more Tlaxcalan warriors as if it were a simple skirmish, and yet he had always won the day. Now Cortés seemed intent on tearing the heart out of the Aztec Empire in the name of the Spanish sovereign Charles I. All that stood in his way was the god-like Montezuma and every Mexican subject still loyal to him.

The Great Speaker

The Great Speaker's personal army came to a halt as the golden litter, its canopy of green feathers bedecked with gold, silver, pearls and green stone, was slowly lowered to the ground.[3] Montezuma, aided by his brother and nephew, went to greet the white strangers, as noblemen strew cotton mats before him so that his feet would not make contact with the bare earth. As he passed, all eyes lowered, for it was forbidden to look directly into those of the monarch. Others, overawed by the Great Speaker's presence, prostrated themselves.

Montezuma was about 40 years of age. He was tall and thin, with a long dark face, straight black hair that covered his ears, and groomed stubble. On his head he wore an elaborate plumed headdress that consisted of a green fan of feathers taken from the sacred quetzal bird. It trailed down his back and was worn as a symbol of kingship and to denote that he had been a great military commander in his earlier days.

For over 150 years the Aztecs had been fighting to carve out an empire that embraced all the tribes and peoples of Anahuac. After the fall in *c.* AD 1200 of the Toltec Empire, the entire country had been plunged into conflict and chaos. Yet since the founding of Tenochtitlan in 1345, the Aztecs gradually won the day and the country had finally begun to stabilise. The Great Speakers saw themselves as descendants of the Toltec ruling dynasty. Their empire had risen to power around AD 900, and for a period of some 300 years they had reigned supreme from the ancient city of Tula, which lay to the north-east of Tenochtitlan (on which Mexico City was eventually founded). Even earlier, Anahuac had been ruled by an unknown race that built the sacred city of Teotihuacán, located north of modern Mexico City, and left as a legacy the awesome Pyramid of the Sun and Pyramid of the Moon. Officially, this extraordinary cult centre thrived somewhere between the dates AD 300 and 900, although its foundations were infinitely older and more mysterious. Now the land of Anahuac was under the rule of the Aztecs, the last of the great Mesoamerican civilisations.

For the intended meeting with Cortés, Montezuma wore a cotton girdle and square-cut blue cloak clasped at one shoulder. On his feet were sandals of solid gold, decorated with sparkling emeralds. His approach towards Cortés, in the company of several nobles who walked in front of him, was with a sense of dignity and trust. This was despite the fact that he had made repeated attempts to outwit and slay these white men from the east ever since their arrival on the shores of his world. In many ways he considered Cortés his nemesis and that the fate, not only of himself and his family, but also the entire Aztec nation, now lay in the hands of this man in shining metal who sat on an animal that resembled a great deer.

On seeing Montezuma's approach, Cortés dismounted and handed the reins to a page before slowly advancing in the company of his most trustworthy companions. Finally, he said in some haste: 'Is this not thou? Art thou not he? Art thou Montezuma?'[4] To which Montezuma replied in his native language: 'Indeed, yes: I am he.'

Following cordial greetings, Cortés took hold of a gold cord containing a series of margarita stones in many colours and slowly placed it around Montezuma's neck. Instinctively, the general moved to gently hug his adversary but was immediately rebuked and restrained from doing so by the shocked attendants, since it was protocol not to make physical contact with the Great Speaker.[5] Montezuma accepted the gift from Cortés as garlands of flowers and gifts of gold were showered on Cortés and his entourage.

There then followed an address from Montezuma to the Spanish general, of which the following is considered to be a faithful report:

> O our lord, thou hast suffered fatigue, thou hast endured weariness. Thou hast come to arrive on earth. Thou hast come to govern thy city of Mexico; thou hast come to descend upon thy mat, upon thy seat, which for a moment I have watched for thee. For thy governors are departed . . . who yet a very short time ago had come to stand guard for thee, who had come to govern the city of Mexico . . . I have been afflicted for some time. I have gazed at the unknown place whence thou hast come – from among the clouds, from among the mists. And so this. The rulers departed maintaining that thou wouldst come to visit thy city, that thou wouldst come to descend upon thy mat, upon thy seat. And now it hath been fulfilled; thou hast come; thou hast endured fatigue, thou hast endured weariness. Peace be with thee. Rest thyself. Visit thy palace. Rest thy body. May peace be with our lords.[6]

Following a return speech from Cortés, the Spanish general seized Montezuma's hand as if to reassure him, after which the Spaniards were led away to the quarters that had been prepared for them during their uneasy stay in the capital city.

Montezuma's Speech

Why had Montezuma made such a curious speech? Why had he been in such reverence of Cortés, the man he had attempted to capture or kill for so many months? Why did the Great Speaker insist that they had always known he would one day return 'to govern thy city of Mexico' and descend 'upon thy seat', kept warm for him by Montezuma's ancestors, almost as if the Great Speakers had merely prepared the way for his coming?

The answer came the following day when Cortés and his knights paid Montezuma a visit in his great Hall of Audience. Having removed their boots as a sign of respect, the Spaniards were ushered forward by nobles. Montezuma graciously received them, and after formal pleasantries and a further exchange of gifts, Cortés got down to the main purpose of the meeting – the conversion of the Aztec nation to the faith of Rome. It was his intention to convince Montezuma that his subjects should desist from conducting their barbarous rites to mere pagan idols, which bore the likeness of devils. Everywhere they had seen evidence of the mass slaughter of human individuals, whose hearts were wrenched from still-writhing bodies and offered up to demons of hell.

Through his interpreter Doña Marina he explained the mysteries of the Catholic Church. Montezuma – who was himself a priest of the god Tezcatlipoca, in his form of the fire-god Huitzilopochtli – listened attentively to the account of the white god said to have died on a cross and arisen from the dead after three days. He even accepted that this Jesus must indeed be a powerful god to have protected the Spaniards against the wrath of the gods whose idols the Spaniards had destroyed both in his country and in the land of the Maya. Only after Cortés had finished his own address did Montezuma deliver his return speech. Thankfully, it is preserved among the famous 'Letters from Mexico', written by Hernando Cortés to the Spanish sovereign in 1519. What he said is of great importance:

> For a long time we have known from the writings of our ancestors that neither I, nor any of those who dwell in this land, are natives of it, but foreigners who came from very distant parts; and likewise we know that a chieftain, of whom they were all vassals, brought our people to this region. And he returned to his native land.
>
> And we always held that those who descended from him would come and conquer this land and take us as their vassals. So, because of the place from which you claim to come, namely, from where the sun rises . . . we believe and are certain that he is our natural lord . . .[7]

Another version of the speech is more revealing and alludes specifically to the identity of the great leader who it was believed would one day return:

> In a word, we believe that the great Prince to whom you pay obedience, is a descendant of Quetzalcoatl, Lord of the Seven Caves of the Navarlaques, and lawful sovereign of the 7 nations that gave rise to the Mexican Empire. For from the tradition he left these countries to conquer new regions in the east, with a promise that in the process of time his descendants should return to new-model our laws and reform government. We have therefore already determined that everything shall be done for the honour of a Prince who is the offspring of such an illustrious progenitor.[8]

Cortés was fully aware that Montezuma, the Aztec nation and all the other tribes of New Spain held him in awe because he supposedly resembled a god who had arrived with his followers on a boat that had come from the direction of the rising sun. He had brought civilisation to Anahuac. His homeland was known as Tlapallan, the 'red land',[9] and it was to here that he had departed after his ministry. The name Quetzalcoatl derives from two words in the Nahuatl language: *quetzal*, 'feathered' or 'plumed', and *coatl*, 'snake', more specifically the rattlesnake. According to Aztec tradition he was the seventh son of his father Itzac-Mixcohuatl, whose name means White Grass Snake Nebula.[10] The term 'nebula' alludes to the river of stars known as the Milky Way. Quetzalcoatl's celestial form is determined by the second syllable of his name, *coatl*, which can mean 'twin', a reference to his role as Venus personified as the Morning Star. His dark twin, Xolotl, was seen as Venus in its form as the Evening Star.

Quetzalcoatl was originally a great culture hero of the Toltec peoples and was still revered in many parts of Mexico at the time of the Conquest. According to the earliest Spanish chroniclers, who made a point of learning about this Quetzalcoatl, in his earthly form he was said to have been tall in stature, with long dark hair and a flowing beard.[11] Many also assumed that he possessed white skin, although this assertion is dismissed by scholars as a creation of the Spaniards who wanted to see themselves as fulfilling the prophecy of Quetzalcoatl's return.[12]

The Toltec god Quetzalcoatl atop a teocalli pyramid temple. His cloak bears crosses that might just preserve the memory of pre-Columbian journeys to Mexico by members of medieval military orders.

The Cross and Tunic

More difficult to understand was Quetzalcoatl's connection with the cross, which supposedly adorned his black tunic.[13] For 500 years Christian writers and historians have seized on this religious symbolism to suggest that Quetzalcoatl was an early Christian seafarer, such as the apostle Thomas, whom the Spanish clerics of the sixteenth century were convinced reached the Americas.[14] Yet white crosses on black tunics do not bring to mind an apostle of Jesus but a knight belonging to a medieval military order, such as the Knights Templar or the Knights of St John.

One medieval knight who *is* considered to have reached Mexico prior to the voyages of Christopher Columbus is Henry Sinclair, Prince of Orkney. There is convincing evidence to show that in 1398 he sailed with a fleet of 12 ships, under the charge of the Venetian navigator Antonio Zeno, to Nova Scotia using the Northwest Passage.[15] Some historical writers also believe that he continued on down the east coast of the United States and eventually made landfall somewhere in the Gulf of Mexico.[16] Curiously enough, this fantastic hypothesis is supported by some inexplicable stone carvings in Rosslyn Chapel, an unfinished collegiate church near Edinburgh built in the mid-fifteenth century by Prince Henry's immediate successors. Among the mystical imagery that adorns its interior walls and barrel-roofed ceiling are open maize cobs, as well as a species of aloe cactus. There is also a series of scenes that depict skeletal figures like those featured in the Mexican festival known as the Day of the Dead.[17]

Lord of Tlapallan

Quetzalcoatl was said to have appeared on the Gulf coast, close to where Cortés made his own celebrated landfall in 1519. Like Cortés, Quetzalcoatl protested against the barbaric ways of the native peoples and preached against human sacrifice. He was said to have taught of a divinity called Opu, the Invisible, or Yohalli Ehecatl, 'night wind', who was to be offered oblations in the hours of darkness in a sacred enclosure removed from all noise even on the coldest of nights. Furthermore, every 20 days, large conch shells would be used to announce the commencement of a ceremony in which devotees would present on an altar an aloe spine stained red with their own blood.[18]

For 20 years Quetzalcoatl stayed in the ancient city of Cholula instructing the Toltec in the arts of metalworking, agriculture and government administration, all things that were apparently unknown before this time.[19] He also founded the Toltec city of Tula, or Tollan (another name for Tlapallan), in honour of his homeland.

Yet there had been those who looked on Quetzalcoatl's presence in the land of Anahuac with great disdain. Among them was a vengeful magician named Tezcatlipoca, who in place of one foot had a circular mirror fashioned from the black volcanic glass known as obsidian – hence his name, 'Smoking Mirror'. This black-faced god, the patron of Tenochtitlan and the Aztec nation, craftily persuaded Quetzalcoatl to consume a draught of an alcoholic beverage known as 'pulque'. It so intoxicated him that he forgot his oath of chastity and slept with his sister Quetzalpetlatl. As self-punishment for this misdeed, the Feathered Serpent decided to abandon Tollan – a decision that was to have grave consequences. On his departure, Quetzalcoatl is said to have razed the houses and buildings built by him. He also buried his treasure of gold and banished all birds of rich plumage.

At a location named as Coaapan, Quetzalcoatl was met by some of the gods of Anahuac, who asked him: 'Where do you go?'

'I go to Tlapallan whence I came.'[20]

'For what reason?'

'My father the Sun has called me thence.'

'Go, then, happily,' they bade him, 'but leave us the secret of your art, the secret of founding in silver, of working in precious stones and woods, of painting, and of feather-working, and other matters.'[21]

Quetzalcoatl refused to hear their words and continued his journey eastwards, until he reached Tabasco on the Gulf coast.[22] From here he departed for Tlapallan on a raft made of snakes.[23]

After this time, the dark lord Tezcatlipoca reigned supreme and was worshipped by Toltec and Aztec alike. So that Smoking Mirror might continue to permit the sun to rise each morning, and thus allow the empire to prosper, this grim god gorged on the steaming hearts of countless human sacrifices, offered up daily on the altars of Tenochtitlan's Great Temple.

Yet because Quetzalcoatl was not killed, but simply went away, those who followed him firmly believed that one day he would return to the land of Anahuac. He would punish those who had turned their back on him – a threat that hung like a sword of Damocles over the Aztec Empire. Its priests and ruling dynasty knew full well that their bloody allegiance to Tezcatlipoca would thus ensure their downfall and at the same time plunge the world into chaos and disorder.

Montezuma considered it possible that Cortés was an incarnation of Quetzalcoatl. So much so that after the Spaniards had established their settlement at Veracruz, he dispatched, in addition to a welcoming party, a proficient artist, whose task it was to paint an accurate picture of the general. When Montezuma beheld Cortés' image for the first time and saw for himself the pale face, black beard and metal helmet, like the conical hat worn by Quetzalcoatl, he must have been tempted to admit that this was indeed the returning god. Even stranger was the fact that Cortés bore on his chest a white shell set in gold which greatly resembled the so-called 'wind jewel' worn by Quetzalcoatl.[24] This took the form of the cross-sectioned whorl of a conch shell, which regularly features in Aztec art and sculpture as the insignia of the god.

Prophecies of Doom

If all this was not enough to unnerve the Great Speaker, a series of rather unusual portents and signs had already suggested that the return of Quetzalcoatl was imminent.[25] For instance, in 1510 Lake Tezcuco, on which Tenochtitlan was built, became violently agitated without any form of tempest or earthquake. As a consequence its banks had overflowed, flooding the streets of the city. The following year the turrets of the metropolis's Great Temple, sacred to Tezcatlipoca in the form of the fire-god Huitzilopochtli, spontaneously caught fire and continued to burn despite frantic attempts to subdue the blaze. In the years that followed no fewer than three comets were seen in the skies, while shortly before the arrival of the Spaniards a mysterious 'sheet' or 'flood' of fire appeared in the sky. According to one account the luminous mass had eventually become 'thickly powdered with stars'.[26] Most bizarre of all was the rumour that spread quickly through the Aztec capital to the effect that Montezuma's sister had returned to life four days after her death to warn the Great Speaker of the dark cloud that now hung over the future of his empire![27]

In addition to these supposed supernatural events, it was considered by Aztec priests and astronomers, including Montezuma, that Quetzalcoatl would return to wreak destruction when the year Ce Acatl (One, Arrow Reed), his name as the Morning Star, coincided with the day Chiconaui Ehecatl (Nine Wind), the birth date of the first Quetzalcoatl.[28] This moment occurred only once in every fifty-second year, and by strange fate, if indeed this is what it might be called, these two calendar events combined during the spring of 1519, shortly before Cortés made his landfall at Veracruz.

Yet the age-old prophecies and strange portents did not preclude the idea that Quetzalcoatl might arrive on the shores of Mexico with a group of companions who also bore a similar resemblance. Nahuan peoples encountered by Cortés and his men during his toilsome journey to Tenochtitlan in 1519 spoke of the return of 'white' men in plural. For example, the Tlaxcala, whom Cortés beat decisively, came to accept that 'the Spaniards might be the white and bearded men foretold by the oracles'.[29]

Who were these 'white and bearded men foretold by the oracles'? What part did they play in the rise of Mesoamerican civilisation and the development of its mythic traditions?

Whether or not Montezuma truly believed that Cortés was an incarnation of Quetzalcoatl, and his fellow Spaniards fair gods from afar, is impossible now to say. Neither can we be sure about the authenticity of Montezuma's famous speech (of which there is more than one version and differences of opinion regarding when and where it was given).[30] It has been suggested that what he had to say about the returning god was falsified by Spanish historians in order to justify the conquest of Mexico, something I find difficult to comprehend. All that can be said with any degree of certainty is that Montezuma believed Cortés to be of the same lineage as himself,[31] while it was debated whether or not the Spaniards were of the 'family of Quetzalcoatl'.[32] These facts are recorded by the earliest Spanish chroniclers who either accompanied Cortés during the conquest of Mexico or wrote of these matters shortly after this time.

The greatest enigma is why Montezuma did nothing to save his empire once Cortés and his army were firmly within his grasp. From the moment that the Spaniards first set foot in Tenochtitlan, Montezuma could have just clicked his fingers and they would have been seized and killed by the royal guard. Indeed, following Montezuma's subsequent arrest at the hands of Cortés, the emperor was transported through the streets on his royal litter escorted by attendants and Spanish soldiers. Crowds began to gather, roused by the thought that the white men were carrying off their Great Speaker by force. There is little question that the Spaniards would have been lynched had not Montezuma 'called out to the people to disperse, as he was visiting his friends of his own accord; thus sealing his ignominy by a declaration which deprived his subjects of the only excuse for resistance'.[33]

Had Montezuma been too proud to act, or had he in some way come to accept that the hand of fate was on him and that nothing he could do would save his empire? If this was the case we must return to the sheer potency of the prophecy of Quetzalcoatl's return and attempt to understand why one of the greatest rulers of history succumbed so easily to superstitious fear and belief.

Why *did* Cortés' arrival become confused with the prophecy of Quetzalcoatl's return? Who exactly was Quetzalcoatl, and, indeed, what did he really represent? More important, where was Tlapallan, his ancestral homeland, to which he departed at the end of his ministry? Answering these questions will permit us to understand the Mesoamerican vision of an original homeland which parallels exactly Old World traditions of Atlantis, Antilia and the Island of the Seven Cities.

CHAPTER XVI

PEOPLE OF THE SERPENT

According to the creation myth of the Mexica, before the first dawn there had been four previous suns. Tezcatlipoca had been the chief god of the first sun, and those who lived on earth were giants devoured in the last days by jaguars. Ehecatl, the wind-god (and a form of Quetzalcoatl), had watched over the second sun, although this world was destroyed by wind and its inhabitants became monkeys. The rain-god Tlaloc presided over the third sun, but this one was obliterated by fiery rain and its inhabitants became butterflies, dogs and turkeys. The water-goddess Chalchiuhtlicue controlled the fourth sun, Nahui Atl (Four Water), although this world was engulfed by a flood and its inhabitants became fish (i.e. they drowned).

Afterwards there came a fifth sun, or age, jointly initiated by Tezcatlipoca and Quetzalcoatl, who elevated the heavens by transforming themselves into great trees. The two gods then slayed the caiman (or crocodile), from whose body they fashioned the present world.

Quetzalcoatl, in the company of his twin Xolotl, then descended into the underworld in search of the bones of those who drowned in the previous world age. Having fooled Mictlantecuhtli, the god of death, into giving up these remains, the twins proceeded to Tamoanchan, which means the Place Where the Serpent People Landed. Here the bones were ground like corn into a fine meal, before being mixed with blood to produce the first human beings, whose descendants ruled Anahuac as the Aztec nation.

There exist important variations of this story which might help us to locate the ancient homeland of the Feathered Serpent. They speak of the ancestors of the Mexica emerging from a place called Chicomoztoc, the Seven Caves, generally thought to be situated beneath Colhuacán, the Crooked Mountain. One version speaks of a lightning staff being struck on the Seven Caves, while another describes their escape from inside the earth only after the sun had fired an arrow of sunlight into the House of Mirrors, another name for this seven-fold cave.[1]

During the sixteenth century a Mexican chronicler named Don Fernando de Alva Ixtlilxóchitl wrote a mythical history of the Nahua peoples entitled *Relaciones*. He recorded that human beings emerged into the world only during the third age. Chief among them were two tribes – the Olmec ('rubber people') and Xicalanca – who were said to have made landfall in the land of Papuhá.[2] Where they came from is not stated, although Ixtlilxóchitl records that afterwards the two tribes founded the city of Cholula and settled in the province of Tabasco. The land of Xicalanco extended from Campeche in the Yucatán south to the mouth of the Tabasco river, although the ancient town of this name stood on the point of an island, situated between the sea and the immense Lagoon de Terminos.[3] Tradition asserts that it was also in this same region that Quetzalcoatl departed for Tlapallan after quitting the land of Anahuac. It is interesting therefore that Ixtlilxóchitl placed the coming of Quetzalcoatl during the same epoch as the arrival of the Olmec and Xicalanca.[4]

The concept of the Feathered Serpent was unquestionably known to the Olmec, for its form has been detected among the formative architecture at La Venta in the province of Tabasco. Monument 19 contains a sculpted image of a rattlesnake bearing an avian beak and a plumed crest, which scholars consider to be an early representation of Quetzalcoatl.[5]

After the first Quetzalcoatl came many more, for it became a title applied to at least one Toltec lord, who is remembered as Ce Acatl Topiltzin Quetzalcoatl. Moreover, the successors of the Toltecs, the priest-kings or Great Speakers of the Aztec Empire, also adopted the title Quetzalcoatl.[6] In this way they saw themselves as lineal descendants of the Feathered Serpent, the reason perhaps why Montezuma was willing to consider that Cortés and the Spaniards were also of the 'family of Quetzalcoatl'.

Faces of the Serpent

The Feathered Serpent also appears in the mythology of the Quiché of Guatemala. They are one of a whole group of mountain tribes known collectively as the southern Maya because they adopted the language, lifestyle, architecture, administration and sophistication of the Yucatec Maya. The Quiché's creation myths and early history are preserved in a remarkable work known as the *Popol Vuh*, or 'Council Book'.[7] Here Quetzalcoatl becomes the 'Sovereign Gucumatz', or 'quetzal serpent', one of the seven creator-gods who were thought to have fashioned the first human beings from a ground mixture of white and yellow maize.[8] Dennis Tedlock, the translator and editor of what is arguably the most definitive version of the *Popol Vuh*, said that these gods were located either 'on or in the sea in the primordial world'.[9]

Later in the *Popol Vuh*, Gucumatz reappears as 'a true lord of genius' who ruled the Cauec, the first-ranking Quiché lineage, during the fourth generation of their historical period. He possessed three companions who were also seen as 'lords of genius', and together they are described in the following quite revealing manner:

> They knew whether war would occur; everything they saw was clear to them. Whether there would be death, or whether there would be famine, or whether quarrels would occur, they knew it for certain . . . But it wasn't only in this way that they were lords. They were great in their own being and observed great fasts. As a way of cherishing their buildings and cherishing their lordship, they fasted for long periods, they did penance before *their* gods [author's emphasis].[10]

The expression 'their gods' implies that these lords of the Quiché were not native to the tribe but came from elsewhere with foreign customs and beliefs. Could the Quiché's Feathered Serpent have belonged to the tribe spoken of in the *Popol Vuh* as the Gumatz, or 'serpents', who along with 12 other tribes, including the Quiché, arrived out of the east before the first dawn?[11] What we can say is that in the language of the Quiché the name Gucumatz is identical to that of Quetzalcoatl, suggesting that originally these two culture heroes were one and the same. Yet the concept of founding civilisers in the guise of walking serpents was not exclusive to the Nahua and Quiché, for it reappears once again among the Maya tribes of the Yucatán.

Serpent of the East

According to *The Sixteen Books of Chilam Balam*, or 'Jaguar Translator', written in the Roman alphabet by priestly scribes wishing to preserve the sacred history of the Maya following the conquest of the Yucatán, the peninsula's original inhabitants were known as Ah-Canule, the 'People of the Serpent'. Their priestly elite were known as Chanes, 'Serpents', Canob, 'Serpents' Wise Men', or Ah-Tzai, 'People of the Rattlesnake'.[12] This race was said to have come out of the east on boats in the company of a great leader named Zamna, or Itzamna, who bore the title Lakin-Chan, Serpent of the East.[13] One account speaks of him arriving in the company 'of a considerable number of priests, warriors and artists of all professions, apparently chosen from among those most capable of helping their leader in his noble enterprise of initiating the barbarians'.[14] He also introduced the people to the arts and sciences, as well as legislative laws and the characters of writing.[15] Like Quetzalcoatl, he and his companions 'did not make human sacrifice', 'had knowledge of only one God, Hunal (or Hunab)-Ku, who created heaven and earth and all things', and made offerings only of flowers and fruit.[16] The first town that he built was Mayapan, situated on the slopes of the Mani Mountains.[17] Itzamna went on to found many other cities, each with its own province, before at the end of his days he went to live by the sea. At the place where Itzamna died, the great centre of Izamal grew up.[18] Maya from all over the peninsula would come here to offer up prayers and gifts at his shrine, where miracles and cures were frequently reported. His hand, known as Kab-ul, the 'guiding hand', became the symbol of his faith, and this alone could be used as a protection against the evil eye.[19]

The *Chilam Balam of Chumayel* states that the People of the Serpent, whom it names as 'the First People', were said to have made landfall on Cozumel Island, which lies beyond the east coast of the Yucatán. From here they spread to other parts of Mexico, where they founded various cities, including Chichén Itzá, which means 'the Mouth of the Wells of the Itzaes'.[20]

Here, of course, we find the pyramid temple known as the Castillo, noted for its amazing lighting effects. On the two equinoxes each year the triangular shadows cast on the northern stairway, which terminates at ground level in serpents' heads, appear to undulate with the movement of the sun, giving the impression of a snake ascending at the spring equinox and descending at the autumn equinox.

Yet this city was equally celebrated as the cult centre of Kukulcan, the Mayan form of the Feathered Serpent, who, according to the sixteenth-century Spanish historian Bartolomé de Las Casas, arrived in the Yucatán 'from the east' in the company of '20 illustrious leaders'[21] who were 'dressed in long, flowing clothes and had big beards'.[22]

Itzamna was not the same person as Kukulcan, who would appear to have been the Maya equivalent of Quetzalcoatl or Gucumatz. Indeed, Kukulcan's descendants, the priest-kings known as the Cocomes (*cocom* is the plural of 'snake' in Nahuatl), were direct rivals of the Itzaes, the descendants of Itzamna, from whom they seized control of the Maya territories shortly before the time of the Conquest.

The Itzaes' priesthood, the Chanes, venerated the rattlesnake and saw as particularly sacred a species known as *Crotalus durissus durissus*, which has a distinctive crisscross design along the entire length of its back.[23] This pattern is replicated on the exterior façades of a number of key Yucatec temples, including Chichén Itzá. The rattlesnake is also connected with calendrical cycles, since it is commonly thought to shed its fangs every 20 days, a time period amounting to one *uinal* in the Maya calendar system.[24] Moreover, in Maya astrology, the rattlesnake was represented as a starry constellation whereby the seven stars of the Pleiades formed its seven-fold rattle.[25] Indeed, *tsab*, the rattles of the snake, is listed in Maya dictionaries as the name of the Pleiades.[26]

Where the Serpent People Landed

Edward H. Thompson, the celebrated US consul and explorer, wrote a book entitled *People of the Serpent: Life and Adventure Among the Maya*. Published in 1932, it contains some remarkable insights into the religious beliefs of the native Mexican peoples. He asserted that the People of the Serpent landed on the Gulf coast at Tamoanchan, the Place Where the Serpent People Landed. This mythical location was thought to lie at the mouth of the Panuco river, south of Tampico in the province of Tamaulipas.[27] Remember, it was also to Tamoanchan that Quetzalcoatl and his twin Xolotl brought the bones of those who had died in the floods which destroyed the third sun or age.

Thompson presents a rather flamboyant account of the Chanes' arrival on 'strange craft' that 'shone like the scales of serpents' skins, and to the simple natives who saw them approaching they appeared to be great serpents coming swiftly toward them'.[28] He goes on to describe the appearance of the individuals:

> In these craft were light-skinned beings, and some of the traditions have it that they were tall of stature and blue-eyed. They were clad in strange garments and wore about their foreheads emblems like entwined serpents. The wondering natives who met them at the shore saw the manner of their coming with the symbol of the Sacred Serpent, which they worshipped, on their brows, and knew the strangers to be their gods come down from their home in the sun to teach and guide them.[29]

Thompson wrote that the local inhabitants of Mexico and the Yucatán accepted the Chanes as their guides and teachers, through whom civilisation arose in these regions.[30] He also believed that they probably separated into two distinct groups 'in the furtherance of a concerted plan', one moving northwards to lead the peoples of the land of Anahuac and the other moving southwards to Chiapas and Guatemala in order to unite the mountain tribes there. He was also convinced that the People of the Serpent were the founders and ruling dynasty of the Olmec and Toltec civilisations, which gave rise to great Maya centres such as Chichén Itzá.[31] His conclusion was that the People of the Serpent conquered 'not by force and strange weapons, but by binding the primitive peoples to them by force of their power and wisdom'.[32]

What we see here is the arrival among the indigenous peoples of Mexico of what appears to have been an elite group, remembered as being serpentine in nature or appearance. They used their knowledge, organisational skills and great wisdom to unite tribal communities with a common cause – the foundation of civilisation. In return, these priest-kings, lords or rulers were seen as divine and remembered by later generations as gods or great wisdom-bringers.

It therefore becomes crucial to establish the whereabouts of their original homeland, and the most immediate clue appears to be Quetzalcoatl's link to Tamoanchan. Since it was thought to have been located on the Gulf coast, it suggests that Chicomoztoc, the Seven Caves, where Quetzalcoatl and Xolotl obtained the bones of the former human race, lay beyond here in the direction of the rising sun.

Indeed, we find that it was at Panuco, where Tamoanchan was traditionally situated, that the Nahua tribes are said to have arrived following a journey across water on seven boats which the early Spanish chronicler Fray Bernardino de Sahagún said were collectively known by the name 'Chicomoztoc'.[33] On this journey they were accompanied by wise men, known as Amoxoaques, a name which suggests they had extensive knowledge of sacred texts.[34] According to Bartolomé de las Casas, their leader was Quetzalcoatl himself, implying that the region around the Panuco river was where the Nahua first established themselves on the mainland after leaving Chicomoztoc.

In Search of Chicomoztoc

The only known representation of Chicomoztoc is the one found in a codex known as the *Historia Tolteca-Chichimeca*, which dates from the sixteenth century. Here it is shown as a seven-lobed cave with an entrance corridor. Sitting on top of it is the curled form of Colhuacán, the 'Crooked Mountain'. Inside each bay, and in the earth that surrounds them, are the bones of the former inhabitants, along with various tribal symbols such as birds' heads, hands, reeds and feathers. These show that Chicomoztoc is the place of the ancestors of the seven tribes (sometimes eight or even thirteen clans/tribes) that emerged from here at the beginning of the present world age.

Unfortunately, Nahua tradition does not give a precise location for Chicomoztoc. Moreover, there appears to be confusion as to where it was thought to have been situated in the mythical world. One version of the story reads:

> This is the beginning of the record of the coming of the Mexicans from the place called Aztlan. It is by means of the water that they came this way, being four tribes, and in coming they rowed in boats. They built their huts on piles at the place called the grotto of Quineveyan. It is there from which the eight tribes issued . . . It is there where they were founded in Colhuacán [the 'Crooked' or 'Curved Mountain']. They were the colonists of it since they landed there, coming from Aztlan.[35]

The 'grotto of Quineveyan' is a form of the Seven Caves, and it is to here that the Mexica embarked on a journey across water from Aztlan, which translates as 'Place of Whiteness', 'Place of Herons'[36] or 'Place of Reeds'.[37] It is from this place-name that the Aztecs derived their own appellation. They were the 'People of Azt', just as the Toltecs were the 'People of Tol', after Tollan, or Tula, the name given to both their capital city and Tlapallan, Quetzalcoatl's homeland.

In drawings, Aztlan is shown as an island surrounded by water, over which a single person rows a canoe towards the shore. Located on the island is a teocalli, or stepped pyramid, around which are six further temples, making seven in total – an allusion to the symbolism of the Seven Caves.

Illustration recording the flight of the Mexica from Aztlan, their legendary island homeland, from an Aztec codex in the Boturini collection. What is the true relationship between Aztlan and Plato's Atlantis?

Despite the reference to the 'grotto of Quineveyan' being located on the mainland, the sixteenth-century Spanish historian Diego Durán recorded that it was anciently believed by the Aztecs that their forefathers had come from 'that delightful place' Aztlan. Here could be found 'a great hill in the midst of the waters' called Colhuacán, as well as the 'caves or grottoes' called Chicomoztoc. More important, he recorded that the Mexica abandoned this homeland 'and came to the mainland'.[38]

This shows that some traditions placed the Seven Caves in Aztlan, which was itself located overseas. However, Mesoamerican scholars have other ideas about the Mexica's former homeland. For instance, Dr Paul Kirchhoff identified Colhuacán, the 'Crooked Mountain', beneath which Chicomoztoc was located, as San Isidro Cuilacán, which lies 270 kilometres north-west of Mexico City.[39] He therefore concluded that Aztlan was nearby and that the Seven Caves must lie slightly to the east.[40]

Professor Wigberto Jiménez Moreno accepted that the Seven Caves lay to the north-west of the Valley of Mexico, but proposed that Aztlan was once located in a lagoon at Mexcaltitlan, on the north-west coast of Mexico.[41] In its waters is a small island which Moreno felt corresponded with the pictorial representations of Aztlan. He also pointed out that on the banks of the Mexcaltitlan is a site known locally as Aztatlan, which might once have been surrounded by water.[42] This he felt was the true origin behind the mysterious island homeland of the Mexica.

Other scholars have had different ideas. For instance, Rudolph Van Zantwijk proposed that if Aztlan signified the 'White Island', then it had to be Cuitláhuac (modern Tlahuac) in northern Mexico, which even to this day is known locally as the White Island.[43]

Such views have allowed scholars to perpetuate the view that the earliest nomadic peoples to reach Central Mexico came originally from North America. Here they are considered to have lived hunter-gatherer lifestyles since crossing the Bering Strait land-bridge, which connected Siberia with Alaska until it was swallowed up as the sea-level rose at the end of the last Ice Age. I do not contest that some of the earliest inhabitants of Mexico arrived from North America. Yet the religious beliefs and creation myths of the Mesoamerican peoples suggest that the real picture is more complex. The development of these various tribal cultures resulted most probably from the emergence of an elite group that arrived not overland from North America but by boat from across the water. Moreover, we can say that their totemic symbols, or distinguishing features, were the quetzal bird and the rattlesnake.

In the Midst of the Sea

Returning to the question of the Mexica's mythical homeland, Mesoamerican scholar Nigel Davies was prepared to admit that the various theories concerning its suggested whereabouts raised 'the question of whether there were, perhaps, two Aztlans'.[44]

Or indeed three, four or even five? All the indications are that those sites proposed on the mainland were merely symbolic representations of an ancestral homeland that existed somewhere out to sea. Although the Aztec codices speak only once of Aztlan's placement beyond 'the mainland', there does exist an ancient folk tale that throws considerable light on the matter. It records that the Aztecs' former homeland might be likened to a great disc surrounded by 'the water of heaven', in that it 'touched the sky at the horizon'.[45] The story in question additionally says that: 'from across those waters came the people in canoes or on the backs of huge turtles. The dead too had to be carried over them by dogs as they had no boats.'[46]

In my personal opinion, 'the water of heaven' is a reference to the infinite reaches of the sea, since an island that lies beyond sight of land will be in waters that, in every direction, touch 'the sky at the horizon'. Moreover, the ancient idea that some of the 'people' arrived 'on the backs of huge turtles' is suggestive of sandbanks, cays or islands which might have acted as stepping stones to reach the mainland.

In the knowledge that Aztlan might have been located overseas, is it not possible that this is simply another allusion to Tlapallan, or Tollan? Linguistically, Tollan can be written variously as *tulan*, *tlan*, *atla* or even *atlan*.[47] Aztlan, on the other hand, is a word made up of just two glyphs – the heron feathers, which denote the sound 'azt', and another glyph that evokes an 'a' sound.[48] The linguistic root of this word was a matter discussed by American historian William H. Prescott in his monumental work *History of the Conquest of Mexico*, first published in 1843. He pointed out that Tollan was derived from *tolin*, meaning 'reed', thus signifying, like Aztlan, the 'place of reeds'.[49]

As we have already established, the *atl* word root features prominently in the Nahuatl language, where it signifies 'water', 'war' and, more curiously, the top of the head.[50] From these derivations the French philologist and language scholar l'Abbé Brasseur de Bourbourg determined that the Nahuatl *atlan* meant 'on the border of' or 'amid the water'. In this respect, he pointed out that a 'city named Atlan existed when the continent was discovered by Columbus, at the entrance of the Gulf of Uraba, in Darien [on the northern coast of Colombia], with a good harbour; it is now reduced to an unimportant pueblo named Acla'.[51] We might also cite Professor Wigberto Jiménez Moreno's Aztatlan, the place-name attached to an area of land next to a lagoon at Mexcaltitlan, on the north-west coast of Mexico. From the above exercise in Nahuatl linguistics, it would imply that the name Aztatlan can be translated as 'herons/whiteness/reeds on the border, or in the midst, of water'.

What all this suggests is that memories were preserved among the tribes of Mesoamerica regarding a single island landmass from which came a displaced peoples who formed the ruling dynasties of the earliest races to inhabit the region. This view is easily confirmed if we now take a closer look at the creation account of the Quiché-Maya tribe of Guatemala, for they also preserved the memory of an exodus from a former homeland containing a seven-fold cave of emergence.

The *Popol Vuh*

The Quiché text known as the *Popol Vuh* speaks of seven creator-gods, one of whom, as we saw, was known as the Sovereign Gucumatz. They agreed to make four men from a ground paste of yellow and white maize, and once this had been done their creations were allowed to fall asleep. Four women were then placed beside the men.[52] Afterwards the ancestors of the Quiché were led in the darkness before the first dawn to find a place called Tulan-Zuyua, in which was Wucub-pek, the Seven Caves. Here each of the men was allotted the patronage of an individual god, who was carried out of the cave in the form of an idol. This idea of a movable god is also found in Aztec myth, which speaks of 'an idol called Huitzilopochtli' being 'borne by four guardians [*teomamas* – 'bearers of the god']',[53] who came out of Aztlan in the company of the seven clans of the Mexica.

The *Popol Vuh* tells us that it was in the Seven Caves that the four men and the four women suddenly found that they were unable to comprehend each other's words, since they now spoke different tongues.[54] Amid this confusion, they departed Tulan-Zuyua and went in search of a more favourable region in which they could worship the sun-god Tohil. He was the patron deity of Balam-Qitzé, the first leader of the Quiché. Constantly it poured with rain, putting out the sacred fires lit in Tohil's honour. Somehow they were able to cross a great sea, a matter that the authors of the *Popol Vuh* attempt to explain in the following manner:

> They crossed over as if there were no sea. They just crossed over on some stones, stones piled up in the sand. And they gave it a name: Stone Courses, Sand Banks was their name for the place where they crossed through the midst of the sea. Where the waters were divided, they crossed over.[55]

Still in perpetual darkness, the ancestors of the Quiché came upon a mountain named Hacauitz.[56] Here the god Tohil informed them that they would soon see the sun, which at last appeared. Very gradually, the face of the earth, which had been both 'soggy' and 'muddy', was dried by the unbearable heat, and it was here, on this sacred mountain, that they built the first citadel.[57]

These are the basic elements of the Quiché creation myth. As to the direction of the Seven Caves, this is made quite clear. In Book Four of the *Popol Vuh* we read:

> Their hearts [i.e. those of the first four men] did not yet harbor ill will towards the gods who had been taken up and carried away when they all came from Tulan Zuyua, there in the east, and who were now in the forest.[58]

Further on in the text the descendants of the first ancestors of the Quiché decide to go in search of Tulan-Zuyua, with the words: 'We are going to the east, where our fathers came from.'[59] Later, those who embark on this long journey tell us: ' "We're not dying. We're coming back," they said when they went, yet it was these same three who passed over the sea.'[60]

So in the knowledge that the Mexica also located the Seven Caves overseas, there can be little doubt that we are dealing *with one place of emergence for the two quite separate tribes*. Obviously, this is not the conclusion of Quiché scholars who associate Tulan-Zuyua with the ruined city of Utatlàn, west of the modern town of Santa Cruz del Quiché.[61]

Annals of the Cakchiquels

Despite such conservative attitudes, a belief that the Seven Caves was located on a landmass beyond the sea is also present in the creation myths of the Cakchiquel, a Guatemalan mountain tribe related to the Quiché-Maya. In the *Popol Vuh* the Cakchiquel are one of the 13 tribes, along with the Serpents and Quiché, that departed in the darkness from Tulan-Zuyua following the confusion of tongues in the Seven Caves.[62] Yet *The Annals of the Cakchiquels* speaks of their departure from the same ancient homeland, which was known to the tribe as either 'Pa-Tulán, Pa-Civán',[63] or Civán-Tulán:

> We came to the shore of the sea. There were gathered warriors of *the Seven Cities*, and many perished before our eyes. 'How shall we cross the sea?' they said. 'Who will help us?' There was a forest there of red-trunked trees [pines]. We made some poles and, pushing off with them, went out to the open sea, into the boundless waters [author's emphasis].[64]

Here it is stated that the 'warriors' must 'cross the sea' and enter 'the boundless waters'. Elsewhere in the same text it states that the Cakchiquel came originally 'from the other side of the sea to the

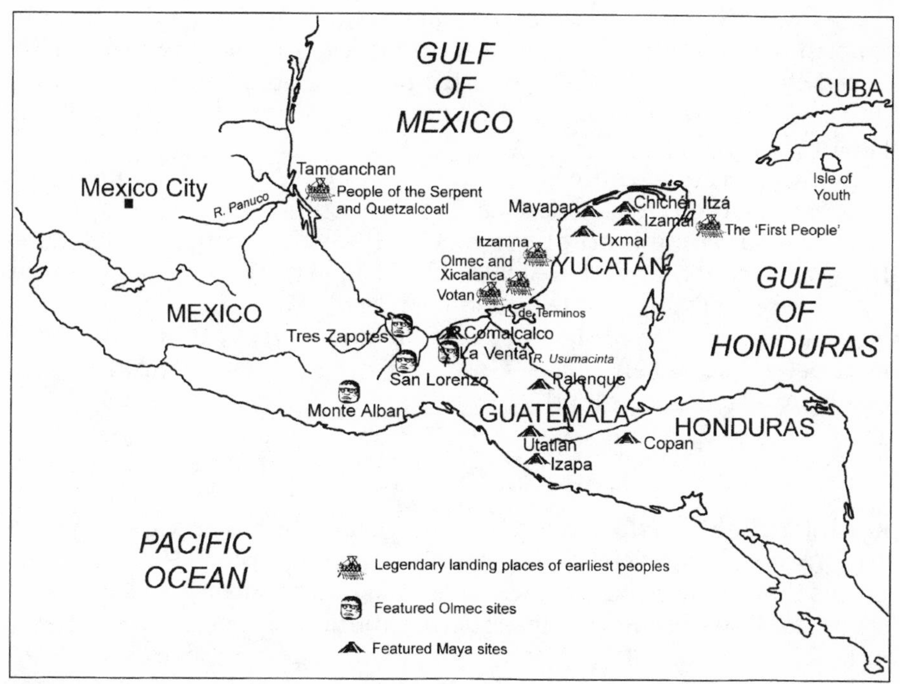

Map of Central America showing principal Olmec and Maya sites as well as the legendary places of landfall attributed to early civilisers such as the Feathered Serpents. These sites generally took the form of offshore islands close to key river estuaries on the Gulf coast.

place called Tulán',[65] not to be confused with the otherworldly location of the same name. Furthermore, we learn from another sixteenth-century Cakchiquel text known as the *Title of the Lords of Totonicapán* that, along with the rest of the 7 tribes and 13 clans, the tribe's first ancestors departed 'from the other part of the sea, from the East'.[66] So there is no mistake as to where this homeland lay, the text also states: 'When they arrived at the edge of the sea, Balam-Qitzé [the first elected leader in both Cakchiquel and Quiché tradition] touched it with his staff and at once a path opened, which then [after they had reached the other side] closed up again.'[67] Since it also says that Balam-Qitzé achieved this Moses-like feat because the Cakchiquel were 'sons of Abraham and Jacob', I feel it is safe to assume that the text's construction has been corrupted by Christian influences. Despite this, the Cakchiquel quite obviously believed that, similar to all other Mesoamerican tribes, their ancestral homeland lay across 'the boundless waters' to the east.

More significantly, the Cakchiquel believed that Civán-Tulán was the ancient homeland of the tribe's own Feathered Serpent, whose name was Nacxit.[68] Before their departure, this great 'Lord' is said to have given Balam-Qitzé a 'gift' known as Giron-Gagal,[69] a name denoting a powerful stone kept wrapped up in a bundle. This sacred item, probably fashioned from either obsidian or rock crystal,[70] is said to have been used during incantations in order to instil fear in rival tribes.[71]

In addition to learning that the Cakchiquel's 'ancient homeland' lay 'on the other side of the sea',[72] we also find that there appears to have been some kind of urgency to their departure, almost as if they were being forced to leave in haste. What is more, like the account preserved in the Quiché's *Popol Vuh,* the Cakchiquel's departure was in total darkness.[73] Did this suggest that some kind of disaster had taken place – one that necessitated a rapid departure from this foreign land?

Crossing the Causeway

So where might we start looking for this island homeland spoken of in so many creation myths of the Mesoamerican peoples? The *Popol Vuh* tells us that the 13 tribes crossed 'over on some stones, stones piled up in the sand', which were subsequently named: 'Stone Courses, Sand Banks'. We are further told that: 'Where the waters were divided, they crossed over.'[74] As Dennis Tedlock has pointed out, the original Quiché words used in this passage give the impression of a causeway across a body of water.[75] The Cakchiquel likewise spoke of having crossed through the sea, almost as if it had parted before them. Moreover, *The Annals of the Cakchiquels* speaks of the tribes passing 'over the rows of sand, when it widened below the sea and on the surface of the sea'.[76] Is it possible that these accounts record a migration route that took in a series of small islands, sandbanks and cays which acted like stepping stones from the proposed island landmass across to the mainland?

As anthropologists José M. Cruxent and Irving Rouse commented in respect of the islands, banks, reefs and cays that today stretch between the Greater Antilles and the Honduran coast: 'When the sea level was lower a few thousand years ago, the chain formed a nearly continuous series of stepping-stones leading to the Greater Antilles.'[77] We also know that, up until a matter of 4,000–5,000 years ago, the Mosquito Coast of Honduras and Nicaragua extended out in the direction of Jamaica for a further 250 kilometres, although this, too, was submerged by the rising sea-level. Was the ancestral homeland of the Mesoamerican peoples in the Caribbean?

Seashells and Serpents

There is a major clue to be found on the exterior walls of the Temple of Quetzalcoatl at Teotihuacán. Its façades are adorned with stone heads of the plumed serpent attached to serpentine bodies that undulate in and out of various types of seashell. The problem here is that Teotihuacán is 320 kilometres away from the Gulf coast, and, as Mesoamerican scholar George C. Vaillant realised, the seashells shown on the temple walls are unique to the Caribbean.[78] Vaillant could make no sense of this curious mystery, although his observations were noted by American writer Constance Irwin. In her opinion: 'It is almost as if the builders who bestowed such infinite care on this temple were trying to convey the message that Quetzalcoatl had come to these parts out of the Caribbean.'[79]

The identity of those who constructed the great city and religious centre of Teotihuacán in the final centuries before the Christian era remains a mystery. Yet this distinction was claimed by the Totonac peoples of eastern Mexico in their own sacred history.[80] More significantly, these annals speak of their race arriving in the land of Anahuac from Chicomoztoc, the Seven Caves. I was therefore intrigued to discover that in 1971 archaeologists uncovered 'several' hewn chambers directly beneath the Pyramid of the Sun at Teotihuacán. They are described as forming a virtual clover-leaf arrangement, which, when seen in concert with a long entrance chamber, gives them the seven-fold symbolism of the cave of emergence so familiar to Mesoamerican tradition.[81]

If the chambers uncovered beneath Teotihuacán's Pyramid of the Sun do represent Chicomoztoc, we can be pretty sure that they are copies of an earlier structure which signified the true place of emergence of those who built this magnificent city. This is confirmed by the fact that the familiar teocalli, or pyramid temples of Mexico, are accepted to be physical representations of world mountains, such as Colhuacán, the Crooked Mountain, beneath which the Seven Caves were thought to have been located.[82]

Since the Seven Caves symbolism appears to be present at Teotihuacán, the clear connection between the Temple of Quetzalcoatl and the Caribbean cannot be ignored. Did the founders of this race come, as the Totonac annals imply, from an overseas landmass in the vicinity of the Caribbean Sea? Was this where we would now have to continue our search for the ancestral homeland of the Feathered Serpents? This surmise was cannily predicted by American historian Robert B. Stacy-Judd, the author of *Atlantis – Mother of Empires*, originally published in 1939. Having reviewed all available material on the origins of Quetzalcoatl, Itzamna, Kukulcan and Gucumatz, he concluded: 'As the traditions of the Aztecs frequently refer to their original homeland as "on a great water" perhaps we may assume, as fact, that Tollan-Tlapallan, the land from which Quetzalcoatl came, was situated in ancient Antillia, of which the present Greater and Lesser Antilles are now all that remains.'[83] By 'ancient Antillia' he was alluding to the theory proposed by early-twentieth-century Scottish mythologist Lewis Spence that the final portion of a much greater Atlantean continent existed in the region of the West Indies. To this smaller landmass Spence had allotted the name Antillia, after the legendary island of this name. Yet how might we better pinpoint this original homeland?

Beyond Cozumel

The *Chilam Balam of Chumayel* tells us that the First People, or the People of the Serpent, came out of the east in boats and made landfall on the small island of Cozumel, located off the east coast of the Yucatán. This would have been the most obvious spot for any vessel to have landed following a journey from the east. Indeed, in 1518 the expedition led by Juan de Grijalva left the Cuban port of St Jago de Cuba and, having been blown slightly off course, finally came upon Cozumel Island. He followed its western coastline before moving on to the Gulf of Campeche, where the Olmec and Xicalanca were considered to have first made landfall. The same thing happened a year later when Cortés set out on his own monumental expedition to conquer Mexico. He, too, visited Cozumel Island before continuing his journey on to the Gulf coast and making landfall at what is today Veracruz.

Where might vessels belonging to the People of the Serpent have come from before they reached Cozumel Island?

Due east of the Yucatán at a distance of no more than 250 kilometres is Cuba, where both Grijalva and Cortés had set out on their own respective voyages to New Spain. Was it possible that the founders of the Mesoamerican tribal dynasties had come originally from Cuba?

In his *History of de Nuestra Señora de Izamal,* the Spanish historian Lizana included a detailed look at the early history of the Yucatán. He collected memories which suggested that the earliest inhabitants of the peninsula had come originally from Cuba, where they had settled after leaving Haiti.[84] Other Spanish authors concluded from stories related to them by the Nahua that Chicomoztoc could be found either in Florida or on the island of Cuba.[85]

Clearly, there appeared to be differences of opinion among the early Spanish commentators on the subject. Had the People of the Serpent come from Cuba, Haiti, Florida, or some other location altogether?

One possible way of rectifying the situation was to find the Seven Caves. There had to be an outside possibility that, if such a place once existed, it might have continued to be revered even after the ancestors of the Mesoamerican ruling dynasties had departed their homeland. Was there any sacred place or archaeological site that matched the description of the Seven Caves anywhere in Florida, the Bahamas or the Caribbean?

Just one site fits the description perfectly, and this is Cueva # 1 (Cave No. 1), found among a group of 'seven caves'[86] at Punta del Este on the Isle of Youth, which lies some 100 kilometres south of the Cuban mainland.

The caves in question were discovered by accident in 1910 after a French vessel was wrecked in the vicinity of the island.[87] A surviving sailor named Freeman P. Lane found himself on the shores of Punta del Este and, on entering the nearby swampland, quite literally stumbled across the complex. Inside he found that the walls and ceiling of the main cave were covered in petroglyphs, described today as 'paintings of a celestial and tribal nature'.[88]

Could this obscure grotto be the place of emergence spoken of with such reverence in the creation myths of the Mesoamerican peoples? If so, what might it tell us about the origins of the elite group described as 'feathered serpents', who brought civilisation to the various indigenous tribes, and how might this knowledge affect our understanding of Cuba's role in the Atlantis legend?

CHAPTER XVII

THE OLD, OLD RED LAND

THE AMERINDIANS WHO CAME OUT to greet Christopher Columbus and his crew when the *Santa Maria* approached the north-east coast of Cuba on 28 October 1492 belonged to a culture known today as the Taino. In contrast to the peoples of Mesoamerica they were fairly primitive, with a basic lifestyle comparable to the Neolithic farming communities of Eurasia.

The Taino were, however, accomplished fishermen and regularly journeyed between islands in their dugout canoes. They made decorated pottery, cultivated plants such as maize, cotton, yucca and tobacco, and lived on a diet of fish, crab, conch, birds, reptiles and small mammals. Their native religion included the worship of celestial deities and communication with ancestral spirits, which they represented in the form of personal idols, or 'zemis', carved from stone, shell and clay. The Taino lived for the most part in communal settlements, which would often consist of up to 3,000 individuals. Like the great cult centres of Mesoamerica, each village would have its own ball court in which members of the community played a rubber-ball game.[1]

The Taino's earliest ancestors had arrived on Cuba from South America, via a long and arduous migrational course that had taken in the Lesser Antilles and Puerto Rico. Each step had involved settling on one or more islands before they embarked on the next stage of their ceaseless journey to find the ultimate homeland. Estimates suggest they first left the region surrounding the mouth of the Orinoco river, in Venezuela, sometime around the time of Christ and arrived on Hispaniola around AD 250.[2] They are thought to have made the final crossing to Cuba sometime in the region of *c.* AD 450–600. Traces of Taino culture are also found on the Bahamas, which they reached in *c.* AD 600–700,[3] although here the indigenous population were known as the Lucayans.

There is very little to connect the Taino with the development of

Mesoamerican civilisation. As we saw in Chapter Fifteen, when the Spaniards arrived in the West Indies they found no evidence that the native people built stone structures, even though they unquestionably travelled as far as the Yucatán. When Bernal Díaz, an early Spanish chronicler, landed on the Yucatec coast with a group of conquistadors in the sixteenth century, he was met by a young Indian woman who spoke to them in a language native to Cuba (it was probably Arawak, the language of the Taino). On being asked where she came from, the woman related how, two years previously, she and ten others had been fishing in a canoe off Jamaica when it had been carried out to sea by strong currents. Finally, they had reached the land of the Maya.[4] If nothing else, this story demonstrates just how easy it is for a small vessel, such as a canoe, to use prevailing currents to travel from the Greater Antilles to the coast of Central America.

In spite of the easy means of contact between Cuba and the Yucatán it would seem that the lifestyle, sophistication and culture of the highly advanced Maya had no lasting effect on the Taino, who were content to be little more than fishermen and farmers. Yet the Taino were not the first inhabitants of Cuba. In the early years of colonial rule, explorers penetrated deep into the country's interior and reported seeing all manner of strange monuments, as well as grotesque carvings and stone idols which were utterly alien to Taino culture.

This same sentiment was voiced by the Abbé Brasseur de Bourbourg in 1857 when he wrote: 'Modern travellers assure that they have seen sculpted rocks and ruined buildings around Havana indicating the presence of ancient civilised populations on this Island.'[5]

Little by little it emerged that Cuba had been occupied by a much earlier, and far more advanced, culture that had left its mark in entirely different ways.

The Black Idol

A century ago, Daniel G. Brinton, the Professor of American Archaeology at the University of Pennsylvania, wrote an important paper for the journal *American Anthropologist* entitled 'The Archaeology of Cuba'.[6] He drew on information contained in much earlier articles which described curious finds made in several parts of the island. Among the strangest of these was the discovery by Cuban archaeologist Don Miguel Rodriguez-Ferrer of a black marble idol found among the mountains in the eastern province of Santiago. It stood a metre high and was carved into 'the upper portion of a human figure, the face bearing a mild expression'.[7] Rodriguez-Ferrer subsequently presented the statue to the University of Havana, 'where it yet should be'.[8]

It goes without saying that this black idol had nothing whatsoever to do with the Taino, who did not use stone in this manner and almost exclusively occupied coastal regions of the island. Furthermore, since marble was not indigenous to Cuba, it meant that the stone used to fashion the idol must have come from elsewhere, plausibly neighbouring Hispaniola, where marble is found in the southern part of the island.[9] It is even possible that it came from further afield, perhaps from the Central American mainland. To this day the origin of the black idol remains a mystery.

Brinton also referred to two localities in the eastern part of Santiago province, one known as Pueblo Viejo, the other being La Gran Tierra de Maya, where Rodriguez-Ferrer had discovered 'circles, squares, mounds and enclosures'. These were said to resemble the general character of earthworks in the Mississippi Valley of the United States.[10] The use of the word 'Maya' does not necessarily relate to the civilisation of this name for, as Rodriguez-Ferrer made clear to Brinton, it was also a word that featured in the native Arawak language.

More interesting was Rodriguez-Ferrer's suggestion that the earthen monuments in Cuba's Santiago province resembled those found along the Mississippi Valley. The great river of this name rises in streams which empty into Lake Minnesota before flowing south to the Gulf of Mexico. Some of the earthen monuments that litter the valley in various states of preservation are of an extraordinary nature and date to as early as *c.* 4000–3000 BC.[11]

Aside from these curious archaeological enigmas, Brinton spoke also of the discovery of huge anthropomorphic forms carved on rock faces in the river valleys of central Cuba, as well as 'monolithic statues' which seemed to have had no obvious connection with the Taino.[12]

The Jade Celt

Then there is the remarkable jade axe or celt, found within a cave located in the extreme eastern limits of the island.[13] At 19 centimetres in length, it is perfectly symmetrical, highly polished and beautifully finished. Daniel Brinton said that at the time of its discovery it was acknowledged to be 'the finest object of its kind from America the members [of the Berlin Anthropological Society] had seen'.[14] The cave in question was one of a number that overlooked the sea and were found to be 'particularly rich in bones, pottery and stone implements'.[15]

Jade is not indigenous to the Caribbean. It was, however, used extensively by Mesoamerican cultures from the time of the Olmec civilisation through to the time of the Conquest. The exact age of the celt found on Cuba remains unknown, although similar examples made of blue-green jade have been found in Costa Rica.[16] The fashioning of jade artefacts was also a speciality among the artisans of Vera Cruz and Tabasco – provinces on the Gulf coast of Mexico linked not only with the Olmec and Xicalanca but also with traditions concerning the departure of Quetzalcoatl to Tlapallan.

History of the Ciboney

Clearly there had been a much earlier culture present on Cuba – one that sculpted in stone, built earthen monuments, possessed a more sophisticated religion and penetrated deep into the country's interior. So who were these people?

The first clue appears to be the enormous number of natural caves found in many parts of Cuba, most of which contain clear evidence of both domestic and ritual usage from the prehistoric age onwards. Cut out of limestone or 'reef rock' by the action of water tens of thousands of years ago, these caverns seem to have held an enormous importance for a pre-Taino culture known as the Ciboney.

The history of the Ciboney is not easy to understand, although they are considered to fall into two quite separate cultures defined by the time-frames in which they thrived on the island. One is the Cayo Redondo, who inhabited Cuba from around AD 200 until the time of the Conquest. They are classified by archaeologists as Meso-Amerindians, in that their culture is considered to have reached a stage of development comparable with the Mesolithic peoples of Eurasia who thrived between *c.* 9000–4500 BC. The Cayo Redondo are seen as a transitional phase between the Neolithic-style farming communities of the Taino and the more primitive Palaeo-Amerindians who occupied Cuba between *c.* 5000 BC and AD 200.[17]

Known as the Guayabo Blanco, Cuba's Palaeo-Amerindians are thought to have occupied caves and temporary settlement sites. They are considered to have reached a stage of development comparable to that of the Palaeolithic hunter-gatherers who inhabited Eurasia *c.* 40,000–9000 BC (although some anthropologists categorise them as Meso-Amerindians). The Guayabo Blanco also fashioned tools and artefacts of flint, bone and shell. Yet, as we shall see, some of the Guayabo Blanco, or at least those who would seem to have lived alongside them, developed a high culture with a level of sophistication beyond that attributed to the Cuban Palaeolithic Amerindians.

Interestingly enough, the Guayabo Blanco were not the earliest inhabitants of Cuba. Recently, tantalising evidence has come to light of an even earlier Palaeo-Amerindian culture. At this stage, very little is known about them, although they are thought to have been present on the island as early as 6000 BC.[18] Archaeologists have labelled them the Levisa.[19] What relationship they might have to later cultures is at present unknown. It is likely, however, that the Levisa were absorbed into the Guayabo Blanco culture sometime after the latter's arrival in *c.* 5000 BC.

Megalithic Monuments

Even though anthropologists and archaeologists have assigned neat appellations and timescales to the earliest peoples of Cuba, something is clearly amiss. As previously noted, nineteenth-century Cuban archaeologist Don Miguel Rodriguez-Ferrer came across a series of 'circles, squares, mounds and enclosures' in Cuba's Santiago province at the eastern end of the island. Since they were not the work of the Taino, these structures must have been built either by the Meso-Amerindians or the Palaeo-Amerindians of Cuba. Sadly, we have no dates for these sites, and so the identity of those who constructed them remains undetermined. However, as we shall see, it is likely that they date from an era when only the most primitive peoples are thought to have inhabited the island.

At a 4,000-year-old occupational site, linked with a cave named Cueva Funche at Guanahacabibes in the western province of Pinar del Río, archaeologists working in 1966 uncovered two upright stone pillars which formed part of a large earthen structure.[20] It showed that those responsible for the mounds of Cuba thrived at least 4,000 years ago and, more significantly, erected standing stones like those so familiar to the Neolithic and Bronze Age cultures of Europe.

This was a staggering discovery, and one that has made archaeologists reconsider earlier documented accounts of earthworks found in other parts of the island. Were these monuments constructed by this same faceless culture that must have lived alongside the Palaeo-Amerindians of Cuba some 4,000 years ago? Might they also have been responsible for the carving of the black marble idol or, indeed, the jade celt and the monolithic statues discovered on the island by early explorers and archaeologists? Who exactly were the Cuban mound-builders, and how might they relate to the Guayabo Blanco?

Previously Established Culture

During their research to find the original homeland of the prehistoric peoples of Hispaniola, archaeologists José M. Cruxent and Irving Rouse realised something of immense importance concerning the origins of Cuba's earliest inhabitants. In their opinion a direct comparison could be made between artefacts found at Guayabo Blanco sites and a mound-building Amerindian culture that thrived near the headwaters of the St Johns river in Florida, *c.* 2000 BC.[21] At a number of sites in the St Johns river area, one of the principal scraping tools found in abundance was the shell gouge, made by breaking off a triangular section from the outer part of a conch whorl and then grinding one edge of it.[22] They pointed out that very similar shell tools are found in abundance at occupational sites attributed to Cuba's Guayabo Blanco culture. This led Cruxent and Rouse to conclude that 'Cuba's early Paleo-Amerindian complex was derived from Florida, although we know too little about the pre-pottery cultures of Florida to state this as a certainty'.[23]

Cruxent and Rouse were not the only ones to realise the apparent relationship between the Guayabo Blanco and the Neolithic Amerindians of the mainland. Cuban archaeologists Ramón Dacal Moure and Manuel Rivero de la Calle, in their 1986 book *Arqueologia Aborigen de Cuba* (*Aboriginal Archaeology of Cuba*), drew comparisons between the burial customs of the Mississippi mound-builders and the funerary mounds of Cuba. This followed a detailed study of earthworks located in Camaguey and Ciénaga da Zapata.[24] More intriguingly, they pointed out that the configuration and design of the earthen structures found on the island suggested that they were the handiwork of 'a previously established culture'.[25] Even more controversial was Moure and de la Calle's conclusion that burial customs associated with Cuba's mounds demonstrated the presence on the island of a sophisticated Neolithic culture which far exceeded the state of development of its Meso-Amerindian and Palaeo-Amerindian inhabitants.[26]

The Caves of Cuba

Further evidence of the presence on Cuba of a prehistoric culture of immense sophistication is the remarkable cave art and, indeed, the caves themselves. These have been found to contain a rich variety of quite unique petroglyphs (i.e. abstract forms) and pictographs (animal and human forms) which adorn their walls and ceilings in either ochre-red or charcoal-black.

Dating the cave art is dependent on the recognition of a certain style. For instance, all the stickmen, animals and fish found drawn on the walls in some caves are considered to be fairly recent and were probably executed by Taino artists prior to the time of the Conquest. There are even depictions of what appear to be black-skinned individuals, which are thought to have been painted by African slaves who took refuge in the caves after escaping from either the sugar plantations or mines founded by Spanish colonists.

More intriguing are the abstract geometric designs that adorn the walls and ceilings of some of the caves. These include concentric rings, spirals, triangles, boxes and diamonds. This style is recognised as being much older, and is usually accredited to the Guayabo Blanco people. Where caves are filled with geometric forms, it is clear that they were the domain, almost exclusively, of the earliest inhabitants of the island. Moreover, where geometric designs are found, circular skylights are often cut into the cave ceiling, allowing shafts of sunlight to penetrate their dusty interiors. Cuban archaeologists have recognised the magico-religious significance of these deliberately fashioned light holes and relate them directly to the presence of the petroglyphs, which become illuminated on certain dates in the solar calendar.[27]

In many ways the Cuban cave skylights resemble the holes cut into underground rooms by the Olmec civilisation. These so-called 'zenith tubes' permitted rays of sunlight to penetrate the darkened interior at midday on the vernal and autumnal equinoxes. One example can be found among the mountaintop ruins of Monte Alban, an Olmec site in the Valley of Oaxaca.[28] The idea of the emergence of human life from caves was an important religious concept to the Olmec.[29] If, as Edward H. Thompson has suggested, the Olmec priest-kings were descended from the People of the Serpent, it is possible that their magico-religious understanding of sunbeams penetrating the darkness of caves was inherited from their island ancestors on Cuba.

Art of the Ancients

More of a mystery is the exact age of the earliest prehistoric cave art on Cuba. Since much of it is accredited to the Guayabo Blanco culture, it could be several thousand years old. There seems to be no evidence that it might date any earlier than this period. That said, several caves on Mona, a small island which lies in the Mona Passage between Puerto Rico and Hispaniola, were found to contain a whole series of petroglyphs and pictographs similar to those on Cuba. They include 'finger paintings' that represent 'human figures, and heads, serpents, geometrical figures and undulating lines', all of which are 'depicted with great subtlety and elegance'.[30]

Most scholars accept that these paintings belong to an unknown culture that preceded the arrival of the Taino in *c.* AD 250 and were remembered by them as the Arcaicos, the 'ancients'.[31] They are thought to have come originally from Cuba and thus are most probably linked to the Guayabo Blanco. If this is true, the cave art on Mona probably dates back to somewhere between *c.* 5000 BC and AD 250. What is infinitely more puzzling are the conclusions made in respect of the cave art on Mona by Professor Pedro Santana Vargas of the Humacao Regional College at the University of Puerto Rico. Rather surprisingly, he is of the opinion that the designs, 'the first found outside Europe', could be as much as

30,000 years old![32] Assuming that the printed date should not read 3,000 instead of 30,000, I can only assume that Professor Vargas' assessment of the petroglyphs is based on their apparent similarity to the well-known Upper Palaeolithic cave art found in France and Spain, some of which may well be 30,000 years old.

Since there is no evidence whatsoever for the presence of early man in the Greater Antilles before *c.* 6000 BC, it is perhaps safer to conclude that its earliest cave art dates to between *c.* 5000 BC and AD 250.

In Search of the Red Land

All the evidence presented by the mythological traditions of the early cultures of Mesoamerica points toward the islands of the Greater Antilles being the original homeland of their earliest ancestors and wisdom-bringers, described repeatedly as 'serpents' or 'feathered serpents'. What I needed, however, was confirmation of this hypothesis from Cuba itself. I had yet to visit Punta del Este's Cueva # 1, and before I did so it seemed a worthy exercise to explore the possible relationship between Cuba and mythical locations such as Aztlan, Tulan and Tlapallan. In their mythical form, all were said to have been landmasses which were thought to have been located in the sea. More curiously, Tlapallan, as we know, means the 'red land', a name that may have been connected with the island's overall appearance.

Some scholars might argue that, in Mesoamerican tradition, the colour red had a symbolic value alone. We know, for instance, that in the religion of the Maya, red was connected with the east.[33] In addition to this directional colour coding, the Maya believed that a spirit named Ah Musen Cab, 'The Secret Red of the Earth', governed the 'eastern section of the subterranean world'.[34] For 'subterranean world' substitute either the otherworld or simply the primordial world, strengthening the view that a sacred land beyond the sea was associated with the colour red.

Can we look towards Cuba for an explanation to this mystery?

If we make an examination of the three principal islands of the Greater Antilles, the first point we realise is that Cuba's geology is unique. Whereas Hispaniola and Puerto Rico are almost entirely rugged and mountainous, Cuba is noted for its vast plains, which are often at a height just above sea-level. Moreover, climatic weathering, coupled with the underlying geology of the island, has produced a lateritic or oxidised soil which is quite literally *blood red* in colour. It is found in many parts of the island but is most visible on the rich and fertile plains that stretch westwards between Havana and the western tip of the island, on which grows the tobacco for Havana's famous cigars. It also once produced more sugar cane than any other country.[35] With the help of Cuba's rich soil, its cane yields a higher content of sugar than anywhere else other than Mexico.[36]

It must be pointed out that iron-enriched soil of the type found on Cuba is not exclusive to the island. It can also be found in other parts of the Antilles, although the nature of their geology means that it appears only sporadically and in very isolated patches. Of all the islands only Cuba is well known for its distinctive red earth.[37] It is therefore conceivable that a memory of Cuba's fertile plain could have reached Mesoamerica, making it an obvious candidate for the title 'huehue tlapallan', the 'old, old red land'.

If Cuba *was* Tlapallan, I found it strangely ironic that Cortés, seen by Montezuma as a virtual incarnation of Quetzalcoatl, should have departed on his quest to conquer Mexico from the Feathered Serpent's ancient homeland. It might even be suggested that Cortés unconsciously acted out an archetypal role set in motion by a highly superstitious nation – one that became convinced its world was about to be destroyed by an avenging angel named Quetzalcoatl. Such is the potency of self-fulfilling prophecies.

The Isle of Cranes

Moving from Tlapallan to Aztlan, we find certain descriptive features that seem to make sense of Cuba's identification as the Mexica's ancestral homeland. As we have seen, the name Aztlan is composed of two glyphs – the heron feathers and the sign for land, implying among other variations the 'Place of Reeds' or 'Place of Herons', or more correctly cranes. Is it not coincidental that, although various species of sandhill crane inhabit North America, only one subspecies is found in the Antilles, and this is the endangered Cuban sandhill crane.[38] There are now thought to be just 300 birds left in the country, with most of these being found in the pine-palmetto savannas and swamps on the Isle of Youth.[39]

Strangely enough, the sighting of Cuban sandhill cranes on the Isle of Youth by Columbus' crewmen in May 1494 may have led to the belief that Christian holy men inhabited the island. The story goes that, having anchored off its coast, Columbus sent in a group of crossbow-men to hunt game in the pine forests.[40] On their return they declared that their party had encountered 'light-complexioned natives wearing white tunics which reached to their knees'.[41] For some bizarre reason, Columbus concluded that they were Christians of 'Ethiopia'.[42]

A search party was sent to investigate, although all they found were cranes 'twice the size of those of Europe'.[43] The discovery led the crewmen to presume that the crossbow-men had mistaken these huge birds for pious holy men![44] Despite this illogical conclusion, the incident would appear to have had a profound effect on

Columbus, for he went on to christen the island La Evangelista (The Evangelist).[45]

In the light of this information, there seems good reason to suppose that the presence on the Isle of Youth of sandhill cranes remained strong in the racial memory of the ancestors of the Mexica, or Aztecs, following their proposed migration to the mainland. The fact that these cranes were once common on the island singles it out for special attention and begins to make sense of why Chicomoztoc, the Seven Caves, might indeed have been located here.

The Spanish historian Diego Durán related the story of how Montezuma I attempted to establish the whereabouts of Chicomoztoc. To this end he consulted an ageing historian named Cuauhcoatl who spoke of the Great Speaker's ancestors as having come from Aztlan. Here was to be found ' "a great hill in the midst of the waters, and it is called Colhuacán because its summit is twisted . . . In this hill were caves or grottoes [i.e. Chicomoztoc] where our fathers and grandfathers lived for many years . . . However, after they abandoned that delightful place and came to the mainland, everything turned against them." '[46]

It is difficult to conceive of Colhuacán as 'a great hill in the midst of the waters' unless we identify it as an offshore island close to Aztlan. Can this account be describing the Isle of Youth, which does indeed contain great hills beyond which is the most likely candidate for the site of Chicomoztoc, the Seven Caves?

Isle of Pines

Turning to the creation account of the Cakchiquel, we read that on the departure from the original homeland, the warriors of the 'Seven Cities' debated on how they might cross the 'boundless waters' of 'the open sea'.[47] To this end they entered 'a forest there of red-trunked trees' and from these were made 'some poles' which they used to push out their vessels, presumably rafts, into deeper waters.[48] The 'red-trunked trees' would seem to have been pines.

Today two species are known on the Isle of Youth, *Pinus caribaea* and *Pinus tropicales*. More important, there are only two areas of Cuba where pines proliferate – Pinar del Río in the west of the country and on the Isle of Youth, which used to be known as the Isle of Pines. Pines do exist on some of the Bahaman islands, such as Andros, the largest of the group, as well as on Hispaniola. However, their preponderance on the Isle of Youth is strangely significant and adds further support to my belief that this island and its caves played a special role in the creation myths of the Mesoamerican peoples.

These might all seem like slender pieces of evidence in favour of

Cuba's role as the mythical homeland of both the Feathered Serpents and ruling dynasties of Mesoamerica. Yet when seen in the context of proposed migrations from the Greater Antilles in prehistoric times, they take on a greater role when we recall that the various tribes which emerged from the Seven Caves are supposed to have built 'Seven Cities'. Although this cannot have referred to cities of mortar and stone, the fact that the Cakchiquel promoted this view of their creation account implies that they themselves believed in the existence of actual cities built by their earliest ancestors.

That Portuguese maritime tradition preserved the memory of an Atlantic island, called Antilia, on which stood the Seven Cities is too much of a coincidence. In Chapter Fourteen we traced back this age-old tradition through the Moors to the Carthaginians and the Iberic Phoenicians. We have also seen how the etymological root of Antilia appears to be identical with that of Atlantis, and that both names derive from the Semitic word root *atl*, and, quite possibly, the Punic proper name ATLA.

Cuba emerges as the most likely identity not only of Antilia, but also of one of the surviving remnants, along with Hispaniola and Puerto Rico, of Plato's Atlantean empire. Since it also seems likely that Cuba was the island homeland of the Mesoamerican races on which the Seven Caves or Seven Cities are said to have been located, I feel that there has to be a direct relationship between these seemingly quite separate traditions.

I propose that the Mesoamerican creation myths involving the Seven Caves may have existed as early as the second or first millennium BC and that they were made known to early Atlantic voyagers. They in turn carried these abstract mythological ideas back to Spain and North Africa, where they gestated for many hundreds of years before emerging as the legend of the Septe Cidades. As the Seven Cities were assumed to be located on the island of Antilia, and Atlantis possessed a city divided into seven divisions, there had to be a reason why these place-names were so similar to *atlan*, a variation of 'Tollan' or 'Tulan'. This word, as the Abbé Brasseur de Bourbourg was at pains to point out, translated as 'on the border of' or 'amid the water', a perfect appellation for an island landmass located in the open sea.[49]

The sheer fact that these similar-sounding names all seem to relate to the same island, i.e. Cuba, does suggest some kind of shared phonetic usage, most obviously through the Semitic root *atl*. If this surmise should prove to be correct, it could imply that only when these names entered separate languages did they take on individual spellings and meanings.

In advance of travelling to Cuba with the express purpose of visiting the Isle of Youth, I wanted to explore one other possibility –

that certain elements of Plato's Atlantis account referred specifically to the country. However, I knew that, in this respect, I had serious competition, for shortly before my intended visit to the island I became aware that a world-renowned scientist was making similar claims in respect of the island of Hispaniola. I felt sure I could embrace this heavyweight challenge. I knew very well that Hispaniola *was* important to the Atlantis story, and had every right to stake its claim as the shining jewel of Plato's island empire. So, as I readied myself to jet off to the Caribbean, it became clear that I was about to enter an important academic battle, the consequences of which would be recognition of either Cuba or Hispaniola as the true site of lost Atlantis.

CHAPTER XVIII

HISPANIOLA VERSUS CUBA

IN AN IMPORTANT PAPER DELIVERED to members of the Royal Historical Society in June 1885, American historian Hyde Clarke proposed that the Atlantean empire's 'head seat', or island, was Hispaniola.[1] At the moment he made this curious statement, he could not have been aware of its true import. We can now be pretty sure that the three islands of 'immense extent' spoken of by the Roman geographical writer named Marcellus as surviving portions of Plato's Atlantis are in fact the three principal members of the Greater Antilles. Moreover, that the inhabitants of the central island, sacred to Poseidon (also the patron god of Atlantis) and identified as Hispaniola by Geoffrey Ashe, preserved a memory of the disaster and flood which led to the submergence of this landmass.

From these points alone I could understand why the smart money was already on Hispaniola being the true site of lost Atlantis. This placed Cuba somewhat at a disadvantage, even before my pro-Hispaniola contestant had been introduced. Yet I still felt confident that I could make a convincing argument. The American geographer William H. Babcock had proposed that Cuba was Antilia. Since Antilia appeared to be a medieval form of Atlantis, and both derived their names from the same Semitic word root, I felt Cuba, and not Hispaniola, was being singled out as the island of special importance.

I knew, too, that Antilia was the Island of the Seven Cities, and that this tradition echoed Mesoamerican legends regarding a mythical homeland containing Seven Caves. This, too, I had identified as Cuba. Furthermore, the Atlantean city was said to have displayed a seven-fold division focused on a cave of emergence, located in a 'mountain' surrounded by water. This also echoed the seven-fold symbolism expressed in Mesoamerican creation myths.

Having already studied the geology, geography, history and

topography of the Greater Antilles, I felt in a strong position to counter any points put to me in favour of Hispaniola. Despite this confidence, there were also natural feelings of hesitation. In some ways it seemed like a dangerous exercise attempting to make direct comparisons between Plato's description of his Atlantic island, as outlined in the *Critias*, and actual Atlantic islands. Many others had already tried and failed to win the crown of Atlantis because they wrongly considered as fact much of Plato's very visual description of his Atlantean city. There was always a chance that either I, or indeed my opposite number, would deliver statements that had no geographical or historical validity, and so would only help to throw the whole thing into confusion.

Background Form

My opponent was a formidable one. Indeed, he is a leading authority in his chosen field of study. His name is Emilio Spedicato. As the Professor of Operations Research, a mathematical discipline, at the University of Bergamo in Italy, he lectures on theoretical physics in some of the greatest universities of the world. Emilio is most celebrated for his pioneering work into the mechanics, historical framework and effects of impacts with so-called Apollo, or earth-crossing, objects, most usually asteroids.

For his insights into this compelling subject, Emilio Spedicato has gained the admiration and respect of other pioneers in this field. They include Victor Clube and Bill Napier, as well as great thinkers such as transatlantic seafarer and author Thor Heyerdahl. Above and beyond his work on Apollo objects, Emilio has proposed astounding new theories regarding the origins of stellar and planetary systems, which are also now challenging mainstream science.

That so renowned an authority should come forward to advance the theory that Hispaniola, one of the islands of the Greater Antilles, was Plato's Atlantis is in itself quite extraordinary. As we know, the usual academic line on Atlantis is that it is a memory of the Aegean island of Thera, or indeed Crete, devastated by a volcanic eruption some 3,450 years ago. If Spedicato is being proved correct with respect to his scientific theories on Apollo impacts, his proposal that Hispaniola was Atlantis would not have been made lightly.

I first became acquainted with Emilio when he contacted me after having read my earlier work *From the Ashes of Angels*. He applauded me on my own controversial theories and discoveries in respect of the genesis of civilisation, for which I felt most gratified. It was shortly afterwards that a copy of his all-important paper on Apollo objects and the Atlantis theory arrived by post from Italy.

This was despite the fact that he had no idea I considered Cuba to be the principal island of the Atlantean empire. Entitled 'Apollo Objects, Atlantis and other Tales: A Catastrophical Scenario for Discontinuities in Human History', Emilio's lengthy article was originally published in 1985, although it has been revised and expanded since that time.[2]

The Case for Hispaniola

This then would be Emilio's main line of attack as he attempted to forward Hispaniola's role as the crowning jewel of Atlantis. Like me, the Italian professor had fully realised that Plato's Atlantis dialogues related not to a single landmass the size of Libya and Asia together, but to the *extent* of the proposed island empire. He had also concluded that the geographical account of the Atlantic island given in the *Critias* appeared to describe an actual location that could not have been submerged simply through earthquakes and floods. In other words, it still existed today. More important, he realised that Plato had left a trail of clues suggesting that his Atlantic island stood in front of an ocean continent, accessible in the past to voyagers from his own world. With all this in mind Emilio had focused his attentions on the islands of the Great Antilles and had concluded, finally, that Hispaniola matched Plato's description of Atlantis. His reasoning ran as follows:

(1) The coasts of Atlantis are said to have been particularly precipitous, a description which applies very well to Hispaniola's entire coastline. Moreover, since there have been no major changes to the shoreline since the termination of the glacial age, geologists can safely say that this is how the island would have looked in the time-frame proposed by Plato for the destruction of Atlantis.[3]

(2) Plato states that the Atlantean city was built in a central position on a large rectangular plain. On Hispaniola a roughly rectangular-shaped plain exists in the south-eastern corner of the island. Similar to the irrigated plain described in the *Critias,* it is shielded to the north by a range of hills.[4]

(3) One possible candidate for the location of the Atlantean city would be the lowland region of Hispaniola known as the Plaine de Cul-des-Sac. It is bordered north and south by mountains. Moreover, it possesses several lakes, including Lake Enriquillo, the surface of which is currently below sea-level. There is every reason to suggest that the lake might contain coralline structures, today covered by sediment, which might well help to explain the red, white and black stone said

by Plato to have been used to construct the city.[5]

(4) Plato asserts that the size of the Atlantean plain is 600 by 400 kilometres. This comes close to matching the overall size of Hispaniola, which is oriented east–west and measures approximately 650 by 300 kilometres.[6]

(5) The Taino of Hispaniola referred to the island as Quisqueya, the 'mother of lands'. Did this denote its importance as a mythical homeland to the peoples of the Caribbean archipelago during prehistoric times?[7]

(6) If Hispaniola is Atlantis, then the other islands said by Plato to have formed the Atlantean empire would constitute the principal islands of the Greater Antilles, namely Cuba and Puerto Rico.[8]

These then were Emilio Spedicato's points in favour of Hispaniola being the principal island of Plato's Atlantean empire. Even though he seemed unaware of the earlier findings of Hyde Clarke or Geoffrey Ashe, he had produced some serious ideas which now challenged Cuba's claim to the same title. Yet having read and absorbed the various statements made by Emilio, I felt in a commanding position to counter his proposals.

The date for the encounter was set for 21 May 1998, with the venue being the Department of Theoretical Physics at Cambridge University. Emilio was to lecture there during the early afternoon and afterwards we had agreed to meet. The day came, and during the early afternoon we settled down in an empty canteen on the ground floor, a pocket cassette recorder on the low table before us.

Before we even had a chance to commence our conversation, I became aware that the whole episode would have an unwitting witness. As I turned my head, I saw Stephen Hawking, arguably one of the most outstanding scientists of the twentieth century, being guided to a table just a few paces away. Here he was to remain for the larger part of our lively debate.

In a firm position to respond suitably to each of Emilio's points, we got on with the matter at hand.

Mountains and Plains

First, I fully appreciated that Hispaniola's coastline is particularly precipitous in a manner described by Plato in the *Critias*. However, Plato alludes to this rugged coastline only beyond the mountain range that embraced the Atlantean plain on its northern, western and eastern sides. To the south, where Emilio also accepted that the Atlantean plain and city was situated, the coastline must have been either at or very close to sea-level. We are told, for example, that a roofed canal was built from the sea through to Atlantis' central islet. This waterway was in length 50 furlongs (10 kilometres), in breadth 300 feet (91.5 metres) and in depth 100 feet (30 metres). As explained in Chapter Four, from the description given by Plato it would seem to have entered the island from the south, showing that there could not have been any mountains or precipitous cliffs between the southern shoreline and the city. So if we assume that the 30-metre-deep canal was half-filled with water, it would mean that the great plain could not have been any more than 15 metres above sea-level. This does not fit the description of Hispaniola's southern coastline. Moreover, since we know that the sea-level has risen at least 60 metres since 9500 BC,[9] it means that the Atlantean plain must now be deep under water.

Cuba, on the other hand, is much better suited to Plato's description of the island's fertile plain as outlined in the *Critias*. If we examine its coastline we find that, except for the south-west, it, too, can be described as 'precipitous'. Furthermore, if we focus on western Cuba we can see that its northern limits are dominated by the Cord de Guaniguanico mountain range. This completely shields the rich and fertile plain that stretches from Havana westwards to Pinar del Río, a distance of around 540 kilometres. More significantly, until some 10,000–8,000 years ago, it extended south to the Isle of Youth, giving it an estimated breadth of 160 kilometres. What is more, if Plato's Atlantis account contains a memory of a real fertile plain on one of the islands of the Greater Antilles, we must assume that he was alluding to an island renowned for its plains. If so, then the only island that makes any sense is Cuba. Hispaniola cannot be described in a similar manner.

Emilio's proposal that the Atlantean city might have been located on Hispaniola's Lake Enriquillo is an interesting theory. Yet Plato does not say the city was built on a lake, only that constructed waterways encircled its central islet where once had been 'a mountain which was nowhere of any great altitude'.[10] Although I accept that the idea of the Atlantean city being located on an island within a lake is appealing, it is not to be found in Plato's narrative.

As to the suggestion that coralline structures currently buried beneath Lake Enriquillo's sediment might account for the supposed presence of red, white and black building blocks, said by Plato to have been used to construct the Atlantean city, this must remain an unsubstantiated theory. What is more, the hope of finding coralline structures in three different colours seems doubtful.

Mother of Lands

I was initially intrigued to learn that the Taino had referred to the island of Bohio, their name for Hispaniola, as Quisqueya, meaning the 'mother of lands' or the 'mother of islands'. This did indeed suggest that the island held some special significance in the minds of its inhabitants. We must not forget, however, that the Taino arrived on Hispaniola only in *c.* AD 250, and so their understanding of its sacredness probably relates not to its connection with Atlantis but to the fact that it was the first major island they reached after departing Venezuela.

In 1497 Christopher Columbus dispatched the Jeronymite Friar Ramón Pané to make a record of the religious beliefs of the Taino who inhabited the Macorís territory of north-central Hispaniola.[11] He discovered that the villagers spoke of a sacred mountain called Cauta which lay in a region of the island known to them as Caonao.[12] Here were two caves, one named Cacibajagua. 'Cave of the Jagua', and the other Amayaúna, 'Without Importance'.[13] From the former emerged 'most of the people who inhabit the island',[14] while from the latter came all other races.[15]

Creation myths of this order are not unusual in any part of the world. The idea of humanity's emergence from caves in sacred mountains is a universal one, reflecting the rebirth of life from the swollen womb of the earth. Yet mythological concepts such as this always become localised to the landscape into which a tribe or culture emerges. This means that the Taino could only have adopted a local mountain as the place of emergence of its people *after* their arrival in Hispaniola. Yet once achieved, this association would have satisfied the spiritual needs of the various communities. On being asked 'where do we come from?' the storyteller could justifiably allude to a distant mountain and say that their first ancestors emerged from there. As much as this might be true, it does not preclude the possibility that the Taino carried the basic theme behind this myth from their own original homeland, which would appear to have been the region at the mouth of the Orinoco river.

Unfortunately, no similar survey of the religious beliefs of the native Cuban cultures was carried out before Diego Velasquez was given free rein to decimate the local population in 1511. So even though Cuba is the largest island of the Greater Antilles, we know very little about the myths and legends of those indigenous peoples present when Columbus arrived off its northern coast in October 1492. What we do know is that the Spanish chronicler F. X. de Charlevoix spoke of the inhabitants of Cuba as believing the world to have been created jointly by three celestial personages. Afterwards the island was devastated by a universal deluge in which everything drowned except for one old man.[16]

The only likelihood that the name 'mother of lands', used to describe Hispaniola, might have had anything to do with the Atlantean tradition is that the incoming Taino preserved the memory of an island homeland once occupied by their most distant ancestors. For this to be right, we would have to accept that the original inhabitants of the Greater Antilles were forced to migrate on to the mainland, before much later making a return journey to the islands. Even if this was the case, and I do agree it is an attractive proposition, we have no way of knowing whether they returned to the correct island landmass.

Atlantean Plain

With all due respect to the proposals put forward by Emilio Spedicato as to the identity of Atlantis, I could see no convincing evidence that would sway my interest away from Cuba in favour of Hispaniola, despite the initial findings of Hyde Clarke and Geoffrey Ashe. Indeed, Cuba's counterclaim for the same title seemed to highlight the immense significance of its own western plain, surrounded on the northern and western extremes by the Cord de Guaniguanico mountain range. We also know that it once extended southwards, across what is today the Bay of Batabanó, to the Isle of Youth, the proposed site of the Seven Caves. Here then is evidence of a vast plain, originally 540 by 160 kilometres in extent, which may well have been drowned, in part at least, during the timeframe allotted by Plato.

Using his own interpretation of Plato's Atlantis narrative, Emilio was proposing that Hispaniola's precipitous coastline had remained unchanged over the past 11,500 years. However, I do not feel that we can simply ignore Plato's assertion that Atlantis, or at least some part of its island landmass, sank beneath the sea. Since the low-lying Atlantean plain would have been the first part of the island to submerge, the fact that we have a location of this description on one of the islands most likely to be a surviving part of Atlantis cannot be ignored.

Cuba's Cord de Guaniguanico can also be compared with the mountain range that Plato tells us shielded Atlantis' great plain from northerly winds. As we know, Cuba, and the Greater Antilles as a whole, is subject to the cool, moist breezes that accompany the north-easterly trade winds blowing in from the Atlantic Ocean. They affect vegetation, rainfall and public health. Without them, life on the islands would be more or less intolerable. In Cuba's case, they provide the necessary moisture to generate cultivation on its vast fertile plains.

Yet between November and February each year, Cuba is also subject to north winds, known as 'los nortes', or 'northers', which before they arrive in the Caribbean bring intense blizzards to the eastern United States.[17] Although these cold fronts reach exposed regions of the Cuban landmass, the Cord de Guaniguanico completely shields the western plain from these harsh winds, which would otherwise damage winter crops. This situation fits exactly Plato's statement to the effect that: 'All through the island this level district [i.e. the plain] faced the south and was thus screened from the cold northerly winds.'[18]

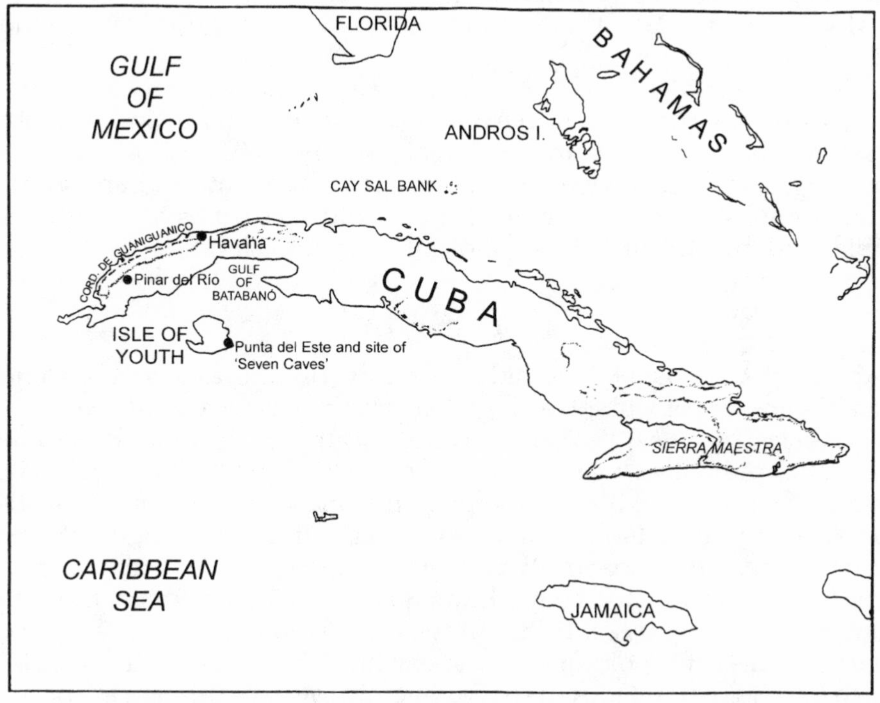

Map of Cuba showing the position of the Punta del Este cave site on the Isle of Youth. Ancient traditions found on both sides of the Atlantic Ocean strongly hint at Cuba's role in the development of the Atlantis legend.

Finding Dead Centre

In the knowledge that Cuba's Batabanó plain might be compared with Plato's Atlantean plain, what then could I say about Plato's description of his marvellous citadel? Prior to the inundation of the Bay of Batabanó, the Isle of Youth would have been an elevated, mountainous landscape located in the middle of the southern extreme of Cuba's extended plain. Curiously enough, the Punta del Este caves, which are positioned on a headland at the south-east end of the island, would have been placed exactly halfway along the plain's southern shore. Indeed, they would have occupied a position very similar to today, just a few hundred metres from the beach. Plato, we shall recall, placed the city in the centre of the plain close to the island's southern shoreline.

If this might be considered a reasonable comparison, then the Isle of Youth would match the position of the Atlantean citadel, while the Punta del Este caves would serve as the grotto wherein Leucippe gave birth to Clito, the progenitor of the Atlantean royal dynasty. As vague as these basic comparisons might seem, they could well reflect some element of the core Atlantis legend originally transmitted to the Mediterranean world by Phoenician and Carthaginian traders.

Sadly, no evidence of a true Atlantean city has been found in the Bay of Batabanó. More important, we have no Atlantean kings, no circular hydraulic systems, no canals and no evidence of maritime activity before the arrival of the earliest Palaeo-Amerindians sometime around *c.* 6000 BC. Yet absurdly enough we do have unfathomable evidence for the presence of bulls on the island.

Bovine Art

Among the books I was able to study on the archaeology and prehistoric art of Cuba was *Arqueologia Aborigen de Cuba* (*Aboriginal Archaeology of Cuba*) by Ramón Dacal Moure and Manuel Rivero de la Calle, published in Havana during 1986. Spread throughout its pages are line drawings of the primitive art to be seen on the walls and ceilings of different caves in Cuba. Yet among them are two pictographs that contradict everything we know about pre-Columbian Cuba, for they show, quite clearly, stickmen hunting large bovine creatures. In the first example, we see two men – one carrying a knife, pole or short spear and the other with a similar weapon held point downwards. Facing towards him is a horned creature that is unquestionably a long-coated bull. Unfortunately, the picture is not captioned, so there is no note on where this remarkable scene might be viewed.[19]

The other example in Moure and Calle's book shows the thick body of an enormous horned bull facing towards an unarmed stickman, who appears to be on the other side of a barrier made of sharp poles, angled towards the approaching beast.[20] The picture is enlarged on the preceding page and bears a caption informing the reader that it is a pictograph from the Ceuva del Aguacate at Guara in the province of Havana.[21]

Both images seem to show bovine creatures being hunted or provoked by humans in a manner that might be compared with, on the one hand, Spanish bullfights and, on the other, prehistoric art connected with the cult of the bull. For instance, some of the Upper Palaeolithic cave art in Spain and France shows very similar bovine creatures being hunted, while on a wall in the sub-surface city of Çatal Hüyük in southern Turkey we see a striking mural that

Pictographs showing bull baiting from two Cuban caves. Top, from an unknown cave site on the island, and bottom, from the Ceuva del Aguacate at Guara in the province of Havana.

depicts a bull-hunt in *c.* 5800 BC.[22] With these thoughts in mind, we are, of course, reminded of Plato's statement concerning the presence of bulls in the Atlantean citadel's sanctuary of Poseidon. These, we learn, were periodically captured using 'wooden clubs and cords only but no implement of iron', before they were slaughtered as sacrificial victims.[23]

I am simply at a loss to explain the presence of bovine imagery in the caves of Cuba. The *only* logical explanation is to assume that the pictographs are the work of Taino artists and that they depict bulls introduced to the island in the wake of the Spanish Conquest. Certainly there was a bullring at Regla, a suburb of Havana, although surely this was built *after* Cuba's native population had been annihilated by the forces of Diego Velasquez. Indeed, Havana itself was not founded until *c.* 1519, eight years after he began colonising the island.[24] Yet if the pictographs are representations of bullfights, perhaps done by black African slaves, why do we rarely find similar representations of other colonial features and activities such as men riding horses, galleons sailing into port and the outlines of stone buildings? Why might the bullfight have been singled out for special attention? Admittedly, there is a Christian priest stickman depicted next to a Calvary cross in the Cueva de Ambrosio, located close to what is now the holiday resort of Varadero. However, the style in which it is drawn suggests that it was executed by a Christian pilgrim and not by a Taino or African artist.

If, however, these pictographs do not represent Spanish bull-fights, we have a major problem on our hands. It would imply that, at some point in the past, large bovine creatures were either present on the island or they were witnessed by the cave artists on the American mainland. Since no remains of bulls or bison have ever surfaced during excavations at occupational sites belonging to the Taino, we can take the matter no further. If, however, Cuba's bovine cave art does turn out to be pre-Columbian it would be very significant indeed.

The three largest islands of the Greater Antilles would appear to have been known to the ancient world as the Hesperides, as well as surviving remnants of lost Atlantis. However, only Cuba and Hispaniola, the two largest members of the group, would appear to have played a more significant role in the memory of Plato's principal island landmass, and of these it is Cuba that I feel most resembles Atlantis' overall description.

Cuba's memory as the mythical homeland of the Mesoamerican peoples must also not be forgotten, for its significance in this respect may also have influenced the part it played in the development of the core Atlantis legend, plausibly at the hands of Phoenician and Carthaginian traders.

Even though I consider Cuba, and not Hispaniola, to be the Atlantean flagship, the sheer fact that an academic of Emilio Spedicato's calibre is willing to accept that Plato's Atlantic island was one of the Greater Antilles is itself remarkable.

I feel I have adequately supported Cuba's claim to be the true site of lost Atlantis, and Emilio Spedicato has done the same for Hispaniola. The final judgement must now be the responsibility of the individual reader. Yet nothing I have reviewed so far in connection with the Greater Antilles explains key elements of Plato's Atlantis account. There is no evidence yet of a sunken kingdom and, more pressingly, there are unanswered questions concerning the supposed fate of the Atlantean island empire. Both matters would have to be dealt with sufficiently before anyone could accept that Cuba, or indeed Hispaniola, deserved to take the crown of Atlantis.

That a major cataclysm occurred in the Caribbean during prehistoric times had been alluded to by Geoffrey Ashe, following his assessment of the statements made by Marcellus with respect to the three islands of 'immense extent'. Yet myths of cataclysm and flood are universal. They are preserved in the folk memories of indigenous peoples all around the globe. Literally thousands of legends exist which speak of a time before the current world age when the waters rose up and drowned every earthly inhabitant, save for a chosen few who either climbed mountains, ascended trees or built ark-like vessels to escape the all-encompassing deluge.

Whether or not flood myths have any basis in historical reality is still a matter of conjecture among scholars. Yet in this case we are dealing with one single story which speaks of the supposed submergence of an island landmass that once occupied the Caribbean. For the folk memories of the Taino of Hispaniola and the Carib of the Lesser Antilles to have any real meaning, we would need to determine whether or not a catastrophe really did befall the region in prehistoric times. A gut feeling told me that a key to this mystery awaited discovery in the Seven Caves.

PART FOUR
DESTRUCTION

CHAPTER XIX

THE OLE MOON BROKE

NEVER BEFORE HAD I VENTURED so far in pursuit of the truth. In the fume-filled time warp that is Havana, I found myself wasting time, money and effort trying to purchase air tickets to the Isle of Youth. Once this had been achieved, my travelling companion and I got out of the capital and headed towards Pinar del Río, the great cigar-manufacturing centre where the cost of living would be cheaper. The journey was pleasing in that we had a chance to survey Cuba's great western plain from one end to the other. I was particularly interested in the Cord de Guaniguanico mountain range, which includes a number of peaks that are strangely truncated or curved in the style of Colhuacán, the Crooked Mountain, of Aztec myth. Regularly, I stopped to take photographs of these sugar-loaf mountains, which border the northern and western limits of the plain.

Just as curious was the plain's distinctive red soil, which penetrates to a depth of at least two to three metres. I often pulled the vehicle over on to the hard shoulder in order to gather samples, much to the amusement of the local population. At one point on the motorway, while examining a layer of red earth, I was stunned to see a man emerging from the nearby field of sugar cane carrying a crocodile! It was a metre in length and had presumably been caught in the swamplands that border the Bay of Batabanó to the south.

Almost every available acre of cultivated land between Havana and Pinar del Río is covered with sugar cane, although the nearer we got to our destination the more the fields contained tobacco. By the time that we reached Pinar itself, there were tobacco plantations virtually everywhere.

I needed to know what I could expect to find inside Punta del Este's Cueva # 1 on the Isle of Youth. From the few pictures available in archaeological books, I had become convinced that it held major clues regarding the origins of Mesoamerican civilisation.

The quality and character of its petroglyphs was simply outstanding. More important was the fact that two Cuban archaeologists, doctors Ernesto E. Tabío and Estrella Rey, had stated that, in their opinion, the complexity of the cave art in Cueva # 1 did not conform with the known styles of the Guayabo Blanco culture.[1]

Yet if the cave art in Punta del Este Cueva # 1 was not the handiwork of the Guayabo Blanco, then who had been responsible for creating this veritable Sistine Chapel of the prehistoric world? Could it have been the Levisa, the relatively unknown culture who were present on Cuba in *c.* 6000 BC? Or was it the more enigmatic mound-builders who would appear to have lived alongside the Guayabo Blanco and had links with the Mississippi Valley and St Johns river cultures of the United States?

A Sudden Separation

If the site of the original Seven Caves was to be found on the Isle of Youth, could there be a connection between the knowledge of a flood preserved in Aztec tradition and the cataclysm recalled in the folk memories of the Taino of Hispaniola and the Caribs of the Lesser Antilles, as originally proposed by Geoffrey Ashe?

French historian Paul Gaffarel in his *Histoire de la découverte de l'Amérique*, published in 1892, stated that native Caribs of the south Caribbean islands told the Spanish chroniclers that 'the Antilles had at one time formed a single continent, but they [the islands] were *suddenly* separated by the actions of the waters [author's emphasis]'.[2] Gaffarel also recorded that the indigenous population of Haiti spoke of how the islands of the Antilles were formed during a *sudden* flood.[3]

In addition to the work of Gaffarel, Sir James Frazer's *Folk-lore in the Old Testament* recorded that:

> The Caribs of the [Lesser] Antilles had a tradition that the Master of Spirits, being angry with their forefathers for not presenting to him the offerings which were his due, caused such a heavy rain to fall for several days that all the people were drowned: only a few contrived to save their lives by escaping in canoes to a solitary mountain. It was this deluge, they say, which separated their islands from the mainland and formed the hills and pointed rocks or sugar-loaf mountains of their country.[4]

Clearly, these legends do not appear to convey the idea of the gradual submergence of low-lying islands and landmasses in the manner prescribed by marine geologists. Furthermore, in the creation account of the Cakchiquel, the tribe's departure from Civán-Tulán exudes a note of desperation and a sense of urgency, almost as if they were being forced to leave their original homeland.

Is it really possible that there is a major piece of information missing from our knowledge regarding the final submergence of the low-lying regions of the Bahamas and Caribbean so many thousands of years ago? Did an almighty cataclysm really wreak havoc in the western hemisphere in the manner described by the indigenous peoples of the Greater and Lesser Antilles? Were the survivors those who either reached higher ground, entered caves or abandoned their original homeland before the catastrophe took place?

Prior to embarking on my quest to find the Seven Caves, I had attempted to locate other flood myths related by the Amerindians of the Bahamas and Caribbean. My search had not gone unrewarded, for I turned up some important new evidence. For instance, the Spanish chronicler Peter Martyr d'Anghiera in his book *Decades of the New World or West Indies*, published in 1511, recorded the following:

> . . . the natives themselves declare that there is such a tradition transmitted to them by their ancestors. [They say that] little by little, violent tempests submerged the lands, and separated them one from another by arms of the sea.[5]

These words seem clearly to contain the memory of climatic and oceanic events that caused destruction in the West Indies at some point in the distant past. Is it really possible that such poignant information might have been passed down from generation to generation, and from one culture to another, across many thousands of years?

Tales from Tobago

Another curious tradition of a very similar nature was preserved among the Afro-Caribbean community on Tobago, an island situated at the southern end of the Lesser Antilles. As unlikely as it might seem, they would appear to have inherited stories regarding a localised catastrophe from the native Carib population, who survived on some of the islands of the Lesser Antilles until at least the end of the sixteenth century. For example, those on neighbouring Trinidad helped Sir Walter Raleigh in his search for lost Manoa, following the English sea-captain's capture of its Spanish garrison in 1595. This knowledge makes some sense of why at the beginning of the twentieth century the people of Tobago considered that in past ages 'very, very big men' lived on the islands. '*But there wasn't no sea then*', they said, for, as their story relates:

> Then everything got smashed up . . . the ole moon broke . . . the sea rushed in. After a time Tobago came dry again, but very small, small. How long ago was it? It was long before anybody's grandfather could remember. No, not British white men, these BIG MEN who lived in these days so long, long ago. But *not* black men, either![6]

This quaint old tale emphasises the lingering presence in the Caribbean of archaic memories concerning the sudden drowning of lands – an event that can only be linked to the final submergence of the low-lying islands, reefs and banks in the Antillian chain. This accepted, we must also ask ourselves who the 'very, very big men' might have been, and what the islanders could have meant when they said that 'the ole moon broke'.

First, the 'very, very big men'. Obviously, we can only but speculate on such statements. However, I am reminded of the stories surrounding the People of the Serpent, who in Maya tradition arrived out of the east in boats. According to the American archaeologist Edward H. Thompson, these individuals were said to have been 'light-skinned beings . . . tall of stature and blue-eyed'.[7] If this statement is correct it suggests that those who were believed to have inhabited the Lesser Antilles at the time of this alleged cataclysm, and afterwards moved on to the Central American mainland, were unlike any known Mesoamerican racial type.

With such thoughts in mind, we move on to the use of the curious phase 'the ole moon broke'. What could this mean? It is a quite specific statement, and one that we must assume has an importance relative to the story being told. In other words, there is a connection here between the 'ole moon' breaking and the catastrophe that splits asunder, or at least sinks, parts of the Antilles.

One last statement in the folk account from Tobago drew my attention. This was the suggestion that 'the sea rushed in', and *then receded again*, leaving behind only part of the island land-mass that had formerly occupied the same position. Does this not suggest that the catastrophe included a massive *tsunami* ('harbour-attack'), the familiar Japanese term for a tidal wave. Although the connection here with a *tsunami* seems plausible enough, they are themselves secondary effects of geological events such as earthquakes, volcanic eruptions and landslides. More important, after engulfing everything in their path, a *tsunami* will recede to leave low-lying regions covered in a thick sediment and the sea-level very much as it was beforehand.

Something was therefore amiss in the folk story preserved by the islanders of Tobago, suggesting that it related to more than one event – one a catastrophe involving a super-*tsunami* and the other being the consequences of the more permanent drowning of the low-lying regions of the Caribbean.

The Eagle-Serpent People

Moving to the American mainland for a moment, we find that among the Amerindian tribes who preserve a memory of the destruction of a previous world age by floods and devastation are the Yuchi tribe of Oklahoma. They migrated from the Gulf coast of Alabama to their present home in the nineteenth century. Yet it is the knowledge that their original homeland lay across the sea that could well hold vital clues regarding a cataclysm which overtook the Bahamas and Caribbean in prehistoric times.

Joseph B. Mahan, who until his death in 1995 was the Executive Director of the Institute for the Study of American Cultures, spent many years studying the cultural history of the Yuchi. He concluded that they were the legendary Shawano, the 'Eagle-Serpent People', who provided a secular and religious leadership to many of the Amerindian tribes of the southern states. Mahan also produced compelling evidence to show that the Yuchi were the direct descendants of the enigmatic mound-building culture that inhabited Florida and later occupied the Mississippi Valley.[8] As we have seen previously, there appears to be a direct relationship between the mound-builders of Cuba and both the St Johns river people of Florida and the Mississippi Valley culture.

In June 1957 Mahan was granted an audience with the Yuchi's hereditary chief, Samuel W. Brown Jnr, so that he might be allowed to prepare a written account of the tribe's sacred history. According to Mahan in his fascinating book *The Secret – America in World History before Columbus*, the chief spoke of the tribe's origins in the following manner:

> The Yuchis have a persistent legend that their original homeland was an island somewhere to the east. Their chief recorded a more concise statement of this legend for me asserting that the Bahama Islands are remnants of the legendary island which was destroyed ages ago in an enormous natural catastrophe.[9]

Chief Brown alluded further to this catastrophe, stating that the land was 'destroyed by fires and clouds of different colors which came from the west and the north'.[10] According to Mahan the great island then sank beneath the sea and 'only a few survivors managed to reach "the cape", as they called it, which Brown identified with Florida. He asserted without any doubt that this island was in the area of the Bahamas; he mentioned the island of Andros specifically.'[11]

Andros is the largest island in the Bahamas group, and we shall review its mysteries in due course. However, what Chief Brown related to Joseph Mahan is quite remarkable, for it appears that the Yuchi tribe's earliest ancestors were displaced forcibly from an island landmass which was drowned during an almighty cataclysm.

The most obvious identity of the island landmass spoken of by Chief Brown is the Great Bahama Bank, of which Andros is the largest surviving remnant. Is it possible that this enormous submarine platform, which takes the shape of an inverted horseshoe and is the size of England, Scotland and Wales combined, was truly drowned in the manner described?

Once again there are inconsistencies in the story. As already stated, *tsunami* waves of the sort described in the Yuchi account do not permanently drown landmasses. Moreover, marine geologists consider that the Great Bahama Bank submerged very gradually between *c.* 8000 and 3000 BC.[12] Clearly, the Yuchi were not referring to this event, but to one that engulfed large areas of the Bahamas in an instant of time. Can this be right, or are they fusing together more than one event?

Attempting to understand what Chief Brown might have meant when he said that the catastrophe which engulfed their former homeland took the form of 'fires and clouds of different colors which came from the west and the north' is even more difficult to determine. One explanation is to suppose that these effects were caused by atmospheric debris being thrown high into the sky by a severe disturbance at ground level. It is known, for instance, that volcanic eruptions can expel so much debris that it can cause atmospheric disturbances and strange colorations of the sky for many days, if not weeks, after the initial event.

So is this what occurred – the Great Bahama Bank was overcome by the effects of a volcanic eruption that completely devastated the former landmass? Unfortunately not, for there are no volcanoes whatsoever in the Bahamas. The closest examples are to be found in the Greater and Lesser Antilles, and these would never have caused the type of destruction suggested by the Yuchi.

In spite of its contradictions, there is a vividness to the Yuchi story that reaches far beyond the idea that their tribal flood myth is simply an idealised view of how their earliest ancestors emerged from the mythical world. If the Yuchi really have preserved a racial memory of an event that devastated the Bahamas thousands of years ago, we would have to explore the possibility that, prior to its final submergence, the Great Bahama Bank had been occupied. We will also have to consider the possibility that the Yuchi, as the Eagle-Serpent People, and the former inhabitants of this sunken landmass, might just turn out to be linked with Plato's Atlantean race.

Such thoughts go completely against everything that archaeologists tell us about the prehistory of the Bahamas. In their view, the first peoples to occupy this archipelago were the Lucayans, a branch of the Caribbean Taino, who migrated to the region via the Greater Antilles sometime around AD 600–700.[13] We shall see, however, that the archaeologists are entirely wrong in this respect.

Entering the Seven Caves

After spending time at Pinar del Río, my travelling companion and I returned to Havana and caught the flight out to the Isle of Youth. The date was Thursday 2 September 1998. As earlier described in this book, we landed at Nueva Gerona airport and finally hired a four-wheel-drive vehicle for the day. Yet having realised only once we were on the island that the Punta del Este caves were located in a military zone, and that a special permit was required to pass an army checkpoint, we secured the services of local archaeologist Johnny Rodriguez and a driver from the hire firm. Neither of them spoke much English, although their assistance proved invaluable in helping us to obtain permission to pass through the hazardous swampland towards the south-east corner of the island.

A flight of steps beyond a more or less derelict telecommunications station took us down to the level of the sandy swampland, home to sand crabs, crocodiles, vultures, mosquitoes and the occasional Cuban sandhill crane. Being careful to avoid some poisonous shrubs for which we had no antidote, the four of us made our way towards Cueva # 1, which is located on slightly raised ground within a low cliff face engulfed by trees. Modern debris was scattered about outside the cave entrance, although a metal plaque on the right-hand side confirmed we had reached our final destination. After months of careful planning, with some trepidation I set foot in what might well have been the original Seven Caves.

CHAPTER XX

SNAKE OF FIRE

THE LONG WAIT WAS WORTH it. What lay in front of me in the depths of Punta del Este's Cueva # 1 was something quite special. The entrance is perhaps seven metres in width and three metres in height, and inside is a central chamber around twelve to fifteen metres deep. Positioned around its walls are a series of separate bays of different shapes and sizes, and a long corridor off to one side. It possessed roughly seven bays or compartments, perhaps reflecting the septuple symbolism of Chicomoztoc, the Seven Caves.

The corridor, or chamber, on the right-hand side was around ten metres in length and of undoubted human manufacture. Johnny Rodriguez, the Cuban archaeologist, pointed out that here the skeletons of Guayabo Blanco women had been found. Each one, over 2,000 years old, was laid out in a foetal position and covered in red ochre.

From this knowledge alone, it seemed clear that the Guayabo Blanco venerated this cave site as a womb-like structure. If this was true, it made sense of why Chicomoztoc was seen as the place of emergence of the present human race.

The Transit of Venus

Strewn across the cavern's dusty floor were fragments of conch shell left behind by the last Taino to occupy, or use, the grotto. Overhead were two circular skylights, like the 'zenith tubes' found at Olmec sites to mark the arrival of the sun at the time of the equinoxes. Beneath the one closest to the entrance was a circular concrete dais, where, according to Johnny, a stone platform would have been set in the ground. The rear skylight was difficult to approach, since it was now directly above a mound of earth displaced during excavations. Yet its apparent function was interesting indeed. According to those scholars who had studied these skylights, it marked the 584-day cycle of the planet Venus. How this might have been achieved was not made clear.

Should the skylight really mark the transit of the planet Venus, then this was extremely important. Quetzalcoatl was seen as the Morning Star, while his twin, Xolotl, was viewed as the Evening Star, names given to the dual aspects of Venus.

Had we truly found the original site of the Seven Caves? Did this riddle, preserved by the Aztecs, relate in some way to the manner in which Cueva # 1 was able to catch the planetary influence of Venus, which, together with the seven stars of the Pleiades, determined the 52-year calendar cycle marking the birthday of Quetzalcoatl? If this was correct, might there also be a connection between the seven-fold symbolism of the Seven Caves and the seven stars of the Pleiades? Remember, aside from being known as Ah-Canule, 'People of the Serpent', those who established high culture in Mexico and the Yucatán were known as Ah-Tzai, 'People of the Rattlesnake'.[1]

As a constellation, the rattlesnake was composed of a series of stars that emanated from the Pleiades which formed its seven-fold rattle. If we recall, too, that Quetzalcoatl's own serpentine body was that of the rattlesnake, and that the entire cult of the Chanes, or 'serpents', appears to have revolved around a species of rattlesnake known as the *Crotalus durissus durissus*,[2] then this deadly snake begins to play a hitherto unknown role in the gradually unfolding story.

Orbit of the Sun

I have saved until last the description of the dozens of mesmerising petroglyphs that adorn the walls and ceiling not only of Cueva # 1's central chamber but also of the side corridor where the female burials were unearthed by archaeologists. They are composed of many series of concentric rings, geometric forms, and other strange devices either in charcoal-black, ochre-red or two-tone black and red. Many series overlap with others, while some are grouped together inside further concentric shapes like dumbbells.

One point that struck me almost immediately was that Cueva # 1 contained neither stickmen nor animals of the type which indicated the handiwork of Taino artists. Even though the Taino had unquestionably occupied the cave, it would seem as if they considered it too sacred to be defaced, as was done in the decorated caves on the Cuban mainland.

In the side corridor was a cross formed out of gradually unwinding concentric rings which made me recall the labyrinth designs found among the Hopi art of the Four Corners region in the United

States. On a straight edge nearby were a series of linear strokes of various sizes painted in lines. In my opinion they bore a resemblance to the Celtic script known as ogham, which in its unvowelled form has been detected at various Amerindian cave sites in the southern United States.

Of all the petroglyphs, the most stunning is a huge target-like design composed of somewhere in the region of between 50 and 55 concentric rings, alternating in black and red. I cannot be more specific in the ring count since one side appears to have more circles than the other. Superimposed on this incredible image are another nine series of concentric rings, as well as a double arrow that begins in the centre of the image and reaches out beyond the largest ring, which is approximately a metre in diameter. Other series of concentric rings surround the overall design, and it is difficult not to view the whole thing as a representation of the orbit of planets, with the main two-tone target representing the sun.

Some confirmation of this fact was offered by Johnny, who said that, on the equinoxes, a beam of sunlight penetrates the cave through the forward skylight and slowly crosses from the centre of the target to its edge via the arrow-like image. His description of this remarkable solar event reminded me of the 'sun daggers' that illuminate geometric designs at cave sites in the south-west United States. For instance, in a cave at Holly Canyon, near Hovenweep Castle in the south-east corner of Utah, a shaft of light enters on the summer solstice and proceeds to pierce a carving of three concentric rings, which are said by the local Pueblo Amerindians to represent the sun.[3] At another site, an outcrop of rock close to the entrance of Chaco Canyon, New Mexico, named Fajada Butte, a 'dagger of light' enters between a gap in three stacked slabs of stone and penetrates a large spiral pattern on various dates of the year. On the summer solstice it pierces the centre of the target-like design. On the midwinter solstice two 'daggers of light' are cast on the spiral, one either side of its outer rim, while on the equinoxes a dagger passes through the right-hand edge of the image.[4] According to the Navaho, these features were created long ago by the people known as the Anasazi, the 'old ones'.[5]

What relationship this solar art might have to the geometric designs in Punta del Este's Cueva # 1 is unclear. All that can be said with any certainty is that the Anasazi reached the peak of their power during the twelfth and thirteenth centuries AD, and that their ruling elite are thought to have come originally from Mexico. They may thus have been related to the Toltec, who were also at the height of their power during this same period of time.

All of these solar events seem uncannily representative of how the present human race emerged from the Seven Caves only after the sun had shot an arrow of sunlight into its darkened interior. Did the entry of the 'sun dagger' into Cueva # 1 signify some kind of penetration of an earthly womb and the subsequent rebirth of life? Could those who created this clear religious symbolism in Cueva # 1 have carried it to Central America?

Signs of Serpents

That there was a relationship between the petroglyphs found in Cueva # 1 and celestial bodies, such as the sun, the moon and the planets, did not seem in doubt. Indeed, these celestial images appeared to determine certain fundamental religious concepts obviously held by those who most anciently revered this cave site. These would seem to have included the symbolic regeneration and re-emergence of the human race from the womb of the earth following its penetration by a dagger, or arrow, of sunlight. The sexual union of sky father and earth mother is a universal symbol.

All this was deduced from just a few minutes listening to Johnny and examining the petroglyphs of Cueva # 1. To me, however, the great target-like design suggested something else – the idea of ripples caused as raindrops fall on to water.

I ventured into the side corridor where the female burials were found and had another look at the various designs that adorned its ceiling. One drew my attention more than any other. It was composed of a series of concentric rings adjoined to a strange S-shaped tail enclosed by even more concentric rings. For some reason it bore a resemblance to a comet in the sky, leading me to rethink the imagery in the main chamber. What if the water ripples suggested by the concentric rings were not being made by raindrops? What if they were really something else hitting water, like stones falling from the sky? What if this cave imagery was recalling some kind of oceanic impact, or series of impacts, caused either by an asteroid or a comet?

These were bizarre thoughts, but I felt I should ask Johnny whether anyone had ever considered that the geometric designs in Cueva # 1 represented comets. He quickly affirmed that this was indeed the case.

I thought further on the matter and recalled that comets have also been discerned in rock carvings found at various Neolithic sites in Britain. Catastrophe scientists Victor Clube and Bill Napier, in their book *The Cosmic Serpent*, published in 1982, examined examples of comet-like 'cup and ring' markings at megalithic sites. Among them were carvings on a large flat slab at Ardmarnoch in western Scotland, which show 'serpent-like lines with haloes'. In their opinion: 'It is possible therefore that the Ardmarnoch array shows a family of comets moving through a star field'.[6]

A further example of a comet-like object, composed of concentric rings and a series of lines that emerge from a central design, is depicted on a rock taken from a site called Traprain Law. It is currently housed in the National Museum of Antiquities of Scotland in Edinburgh. To Clube and Napier it bore 'the appearance of a long curved comet tail and a huge halo surrounding a comet head that was probably as bright as the full moon'.[7] I was simply stunned by the similarity between the Traprain Law carving and the cave's main target design, right down to the fact that both examples have arrow-like devices emerging from their centre.

That comets were anciently seen as fiery serpents in the skies might also be of interest here, for I already knew that in the mythology of the Maya the rattlesnake had a celestial counterpart that sprang from the seven stars of the Pleiades. Since the rattlesnake is not indigenous to the Greater Antilles, the importance implied by Cueva # 1's seven-fold symbolism and snake-like imagery lay not in the creature itself but in the apparent association between comets and the constellation of the Pleiades.

Evidence of Impacts

For the moment, I could offer little more on the subject. Yet in the wake of my all too brief visit to Punta del Este's Cueva # 1, the feeling that at some time in prehistory the Bahamas and Caribbean had been devastated by a comet impact would not leave me. It made complete sense of the various legends told by the indigenous peoples of the Caribbean, as well as the story related by Chief Brown of the Yuchi tribe, who believed that his earliest ancestors had migrated to Florida from a former Bahaman landmass. Moreover, I became convinced that Cueva # 1 was like some kind of ancient shrine preserving both the memory of this event and the re-emergence of humanity once order had been restored in the outside world.

When I returned to England I checked again for any evidence of an impact that might have devastated the western Atlantic seaboard in prehistoric times. What we do know is that the asteroid, or meteor, now thought to have been responsible for the extinction of the dinosaurs at the end of the Cretaceous period, some 65 million years ago, probably created the huge impact crater discovered in 1991 on the edge of the Yucatán Peninsula. It has a diameter of 160 kilometres and, due to the rising sea-level, part of its rim now lies beneath the Gulf of Mexico. Clearly the so-called KT (Kretaceous-Tertiary) boundary event has nothing whatsoever to do with any lingering folk memories of comet impacts in the Caribbean. However, the fact that the world's most famous asteroid impact occurred in precisely the region under scrutiny was promising, to say the least.

In addition to the proposed KT boundary event crater, there is also other evidence of impacts in the Caribbean. A number of so-called bediasites – particles of molten rock debris ejected into the atmosphere at the point of impact – have been found on some of the islands.[8] What kind of event might have been involved remains uncertain, although scientists see these objects (also known as tektites) as residue of an impact that created debris stretching from the Indian Ocean across the Pacific to the Caribbean.[9]

The volume of debris material thrust into the upper atmosphere during an impact event would remain at high altitudes for weeks, if not months or even years, causing the sun to become obscured and other strange atmospheric effects to take place – something scientists refer to as a 'nuclear winter'. This might go some way to explain the 'fires and clouds of different colors' which Chief Brown said destroyed the Bahaman landmass.[10] We must also not forget that the Quiché-Maya and Cakchiquel tribes of Guatemala spoke of their departure from the ancient homeland during the perpetual darkness that prevailed before the first dawn. The Quiché additionally recorded that rain fell perpetually, and when the sun finally appeared its fierce heat dried the land which had become 'soggy' and 'muddy'.[11] A form of lethal acid rain will accompany a nuclear winter caused by an oceanic impact event which would obviously vaporise large quantities of seawater.

An oceanic impact would also help explain why the indigenous peoples of the Caribbean, from Hispaniola to the Lesser Antilles, appear to have preserved the memory of a sudden inundation of the islands. A comet or asteroid impacting with the ocean would create successive tidal waves many hundreds, if not thousands, of metres high. These would completely devastate island landmasses and low-lying coastal regions. Yet could I find any evidence of such an event? Had anybody ever proposed such a theory? I searched long and hard and finally came across a scientific paper written in 1954 that seemed to echo exactly these sentiments.

Extraterrestrial Chunks

The article in question, published in an issue of the *International Anthropological and Linguistic Review*, was written by Dr Alan H. Kelso de Montigny, a brilliant anthropologist of Dutch extraction, who lived for many years on Cuba before migrating to the American mainland. Entitled 'Did a Gigantic Meteorite, i.e. an Asteroid, fall into the Caribbean, and thus create the Lesser Antilles about

6,000 years ago?',[12] it begins by reviewing earlier material that the author had presented in the same journal regarding the origin and nature of lunar craters.[13] It goes on to propose that 'as the earth is much larger and heavier than its satellite, the gravitational pull of the earth is also several times as great as that of the moon, i.e. the earth must have attracted at least ten times as many gigantic meteorites and asteroids as its satellite'.[14]

Kelso de Montigny further pointed out that, aside from the constant bombardment of smaller 'extraterrestrial chunks of matter', the earth must have suffered at regular intervals from impacts caused by countless larger 'projectiles', or 'gigantic chunks'.[15] Consequently, every several thousand years or so, an asteroid causes 'immense cataclysm, floods, [as well as] a glacial epoch, and a wholesale extermination of humans and animals'.[16]

Kelso de Montigny felt he had detected evidence that just such an event had occurred in the Caribbean 'in 4000 or 3000 BC'.[17] Moreover, he tantalisingly alluded to the fact that he had found:

> . . . some confirmation of this thesis in numerous Indian traditions that said that many centuries ago 'a moon' fell out of the sky onto the earth, looking – during its passage through the sky – like A FIERY SNAKE (the fiery tail of the burning asteroid), that there were terrible earthquakes (the impact of the asteroid), that the day turned into a permanent night (the dust, smoke and water vapor produced by the impact), that there was a gigantic flood and a formidable rain that lasted many, many days (the seawater, displaced, as well as evaporated by the impact of the asteroid), and that the only people that were saved were those that succeeded in reaching mountain peaks and finding shelter there in caves.[18]

The reader can well imagine my feelings when I first read these words on my return from Cuba. Everything I had conceived of having occurred in the Caribbean many thousands of years ago was here presented in one paragraph, written by an astute anthropologist who had himself lived in Cuba!

Here then was the reason behind the expression 'the ole moon broke', used in the folk account preserved among the islanders of Tobago in the Lesser Antilles. By the 'ole moon' they meant the nucleus of some kind of extraterrestrial object that fell, according to Kelso de Montigny, into the ocean, causing mass destruction on a scale expressed in the various myths and legends preserved by the indigenous peoples of the Caribbean.

Unfortunately, Kelso de Montigny failed to provide details of the primary sources consulted during the preparation of his paper. For instance, there was no indication whether or not the reference to the 'moon' falling might relate to the folk account preserved on

Tobago. Regardless of this, he did go on to state:

> When the present writer travelled, many years ago, in Venezuela, he made the acquaintance of an Indian medicine man from the western part of that country, who spoke some Spanish. He stated that his father had taught him that ages and ages ago, a gigantic snake of fire had passed through the sky, and that then the world had almost come to an end, because there came an interminable night with a terrible flood and fearful rains. That nearly all the people had been drowned, except a few that could escape into the mountains.[19]

The 'medicine man' would appear to have preserved a memory, passed on from generation to generation across many thousands of years, of what can only be described as an impact that caused mass destruction in what appears to have been the Caribbean. The description of the incoming object as a 'gigantic snake of fire' could not be more pertinent to the seven-fold symbolism and cave art of Punta del Este's Cueva # 1.

Faced with so much circumstantial evidence from oral traditions existing in so many parts of the Caribbean, Mesoamerica and South America, it seems difficult to deny that an impact of immense proportions might have occurred in the vicinity of the Caribbean during some past epoch. However, such stories were simply not enough. What I needed was hard scientific evidence to substantiate these bold claims.

Meteoric Remains

In an attempt to back up his own hypothesis, Kelso de Montigny proposed that although marine geologists consider that the break-up of the islands of the Lesser Antilles took place between 10,000 and 20,000 years ago, this event must have occurred in more recent times. He cited as evidence the fact that on several of the islands is a species of poisonous snake called fer-de-lance (*Bothrops atrox* or *Lachesis lanceolatus*) which is also found in Central America.[20] Since this species is unlikely to have been introduced to the islands by human hands, he believed that this supported his contention that 'a solid stretch of land', a kind of land-bridge stretching between the South American mainland and the uppermost islands of the Lesser Antilles, existed until *c.* 4000–3000 BC. He pointed out that if it had been broken up any earlier, then the fer-de-lance snakes would have evolved so differently that their common ancestry would have been lost completely.[21]

The only other support presented by Kelso de Montigny for an impact in the Caribbean was the simple fact that the curve formed by the Lesser Antilles chain is highly suggestive of an impact crater.

He also pointed out that the waters at the centre of this circle (or ellipse) are the deepest in the southern Caribbean.[22] He recommended that this region of the sea 'should be investigated for meteoric remains under the mud of the sea bottom'.[23] He concluded the article by predicting that: 'If such remains of the impact of a gigantic chunk of extraterranous matter were still found, and that giant catastrophe thus proven to the hilt, we would immediately have an explanation for the last ice age of America and Europe.'[24]

Dr Alan H. Kelso de Montigny is no longer with us as he died in 1972. So having tracked down his son, Alan R. Kelso de Montigny, an artist who lives in Miami, I asked him to tell me more about his father's work. He informed me that the article which had appeared in the *International Anthropological and Linguistic Review* was the only one he published on the subject. However, I was intrigued to discover that right until his death, Kelso de Montigny believed that the asteroid he proposed had devastated the Caribbean was also responsible for the destruction of Plato's Atlantis.[25]

As tempting as it might be to accept the idea of an impact in the Caribbean somewhere around *c.* 4000–3000 BC, there is actually very little evidence to support such a contention. Having read various scientific papers on marine geology, sediment levels, climate changes and sea-level rises in the Bahamas and Caribbean over the past 15,000 years, I could find no significant evidence that any dramatic changes had taken place in the western hemisphere at this time.

This was quite obviously a major blow, since I knew that this was the earliest possible time period for any migrations from the Greater Antilles to the Central American mainland. To make matters worse, there is no other evidence whatsoever to confirm the theory put forward by Dr Kelso de Montigny that until *c.* 4000–3000 BC the Lesser Antilles had been a land-bridge linking the South American mainland with the northern end of the present island group. Thus the species of fer-de-lance snake found on various islands of the archipelago either retained their unique characteristics for tens of thousands of years following the separation of the islands, or the earliest inhabitants really did introduce them (although this last solution is extremely unlikely).

In addition to these facts, there is currently no supporting evidence to suggest that the rim of the Lesser Antilles was formed by an asteroid impact in the location proposed by Kelso de Montigny. No debris has ever been found and, to my knowledge, no independent scientist has ever come up with a similar theory regarding the deepest chasms of the Caribbean Sea. This is not to say that he was wrong, only that at the present time I have been unable to substantiate these claims.

The Secret of Atlantis

Not a little disappointed by these findings, and personally still believing that an impact might indeed have occurred in the time-frame suggested, I looked again for hard evidence of an impact in the vicinity of the Bahamas and Caribbean. In the meantime, I read for the first time a work on Atlantis which, I must confess, had lain undisturbed on a bookshelf throughout the entire preparation of this book. Entitled *The Secret of Atlantis*, its author was Otto Heinrich Muck, one of the most enigmatic figures ever to enter the field of Atlantology. Born in Germany, he was the inventor of the U-boat snorkel and before his death in 1965 held no fewer than 200 patents under his name. Yet more significantly, in the Second World War he had been a member of the infamous Rocket Research Team at Peenemünde, where the V-1 and V-2 rockets were developed, tried and tested.

In a manner similar to many other authors before him, Otto Muck's book reviewed the evidence for Plato's Atlantic island before going on to propose that it had been a huge landmass which once sat astride the Mid-Atlantic Ridge. What caught my attention, however, was not his placement of Atlantis but the means by which he conceived of its disappearance. His conclusions are best summed up by historical writer Peter Tompkins in his introduction to *The Secret of Atlantis*:

> . . . at 8 p.m. on June 5, 8498 BC, the accused, named Asteroid A, did wildly go off its course, break into pieces, plunge into the Atlantic's Bermuda Triangle, and engender a holocaust worse than 30,000 hydrogen bombs, dragging with it, like some Lucifer, an entire island civilisation and the better part of mankind on the planet.[26]

Such a grand explanation might at first reading seem ludicrous, and an exact date and time for the event scholarly suicide. Yet intrigued by Tompkins' words, I read on and was utterly astonished by what I read, for it would appear that this German ex-rocket scientist may well have stumbled on the mechanism behind the destruction of Atlantis.

CHAPTER XXI

COSMIC PINBALL

WHAT THE ALLIES FOUND WHEN they overran the Peenemünde research establishment at the end of the Second World War was a world away from the science laboratories of Britain and the United States. Indeed, its highly talented Rocket Research Team was considered so important that some 120 of its top scientists, including Wernher von Braun, agreed to join America's own rocket programme as part of Operation Paperclip.

Yet what we also know is that the highly advanced work of the research team at Peenemünde was influenced by bizarre scientific views promoted in Nazi Germany during the 1920s and 1930s. They included the opinions of Austrian mechanical engineer and inventor Hans Hoerbiger, who in 1913 published a book entitled *Glazialkosmogonie,* which expounded his so-called 'Cosmic Ice', or 'World Ice' theory.[1] This proposed that the current moon was originally a planet orbiting the sun which was captured by the earth's gravitational field around 12,500 years ago. Prior to this age, another moon, described as the 'Tertiary satellite', had occupied the same position. Yet over tens of thousands of years its orbit had brought it closer and closer to the earth until finally it had broken up, causing catastrophic devastation right across the planet. Before the Tertiary epoch of earth's geological history (which began after the KT boundary event of 65 million years ago and ended around 500,000 years ago), even earlier moons had, according to Hoerbiger, been captured and then destroyed in a similar manner, a pointer therefore towards the ultimate fate of our present moon.

Since Hoerbiger had concluded that moons are covered in ice, the destruction of the Tertiary satellite would have sent enormous chunks of ice on a collision course with the earth. Their disintegration on impact would have caused catastrophic earthquakes, volcanic eruptions, fiery rains and periods of darkness.

Quite naturally, Hoerbiger, and his English prodigy, the writer

H. S. Bellamy, saw the Cosmic Ice theory as explaining the universal myths regarding the destruction of previous world ages. In his book *Moons, Myths and Man*, Bellamy cited folk myths preserved by the Botocudos and Tupi tribes of western Brazil which, like those found on the Caribbean island of Tobago, spoke of the old moon falling to earth.[2] He felt that these stories helped support Hoerbiger's views concerning the destruction of the Tertiary satellite. Bellamy also cited many examples of legends concerning fiery serpents as explaining the comet-like appearance of the present moon on its capture by the earth's gravitational field. More important, Bellamy believed that this same monumental event had created the universal flood responsible for the destruction of Atlantis.[3]

Hoerbiger's Cosmic Ice theory has now been disproved. We know that the moon's surface is not covered with ice. Furthermore, the rock samples brought back from the moon by the Apollo landing missions make it clear that our lunar satellite could not possibly have been 'caught' by the earth's gravitational pull just 12,500 years ago. Yet since Germany's Nazi party readily embraced the Cosmic Ice theory and its implications for the world, scientific research into catastrophe theories, cosmic impacts and the destruction of former civilisations was eagerly encouraged.

It was out of this distorted vision of prehistory that, shortly after the end of the Second World War, Otto Muck emerged to make his own literary contribution to the problem of Atlantis. Picking up on the work of Dr Alan H. Kelso de Montigny, he began to explore hydrographic charts of the ocean floor and noticed two large holes, elliptical in shape and orientated north-west to south-east. They occupied an area of 'about 77,000 square miles (200,000 sq. km)' and lay in deep water, east of Florida and north of the Caribbean island of Puerto Rico.[4] As Muck pointed out: 'It must have been an indescribably powerful force that drove these deep holes in the sima floor of the Atlantic basin . . . In the age of the atom bomb one is tempted to think of it in terms of a colossal submarine nuclear explosion.'[5]

To him the holes represented not 'enormous sinkholes', as marine geologists might have supposed, but 'the unhealed scars left by two deep wounds inflicted on the Earth's crust by the impact of a celestial body of considerable size'.[6] Moreover, their north-west orientation implied that the fragments of the object had been on this trajectory when they struck the ocean.[7]

The Carolina Bays

The approach of such a celestial body would, in Muck's words, have 'grazed the remaining land in the northwest', i.e. the south-east United States.[8] 'In searching for evidence on the strip of land that has remained, we would expect to find a field of craters, preserved through the thousands of years that have passed since the catastrophe.'[9] He therefore switched his attentions to the American Coastal Plain and chanced upon something of immense importance to his argument.

In 1930 Myrtle Beach Estates, timber merchants of Horry County, South Carolina, conducted an aerial survey of the company's pine resources in order to facilitate the sale of its timber. For this purpose, it engaged the services of Fairchild Aerial Survey, who photographed some 800 square kilometres of land in the Myrtle Beach area. On development of the films, Edwin H. Corlett, one of Fairchild's engineers, noticed something highly unusual about the landscape under scrutiny. It was quite literally pockmarked with hundreds of elliptical depressions, some so large that they dwarfed surrounding agricultural fields. There were elongated dry 'bays', a local term used to denote depressions, as well as huge egg-shaped lakes and ponds, some superimposed on others.

Corlett was perplexed by the mystery, and so brought the photographs to the attention of Frank A. Melton, a geology professor at the University of Oklahoma. Spreading out the photomosaic, Corlett let him ponder over the possible cause of these bays before sharing his own feelings on the matter. In his view, they were meteoritic scars caused by the impact of literally thousands of what he took to be 'comets'. Melton was suitably impressed, and with Dr William Schriever, a professor of physics at Oklahoma, he conducted a further aerial survey of the strange features before initiating on-site investigations of the elliptical bays around Myrtle Beach. The two men singled out some 43 examples for study and prepared a detailed report, presented at the 1932 annual conference of the Geological Society of America. It was finally published the following year in the *Journal of Geology* under the title 'The Carolina "Bays" – Are They Meteorite Scars?'[10]

Melton and Shriever concluded that there were at least 3,000 of these shallow, perfectly formed depressions, almost all of them orientated north-west. In their estimates they covered an area of around 160,000 square kilometres and could be found in three separate states: Georgia, North Carolina and South Carolina.[11] At the south-eastern end of many of those examined was a pronounced sandy rim, often up to two metres in height.[12] This was indicative of the low trajectory of the incoming meteorites which must have appeared in quick succession, accounting for the overlapping of bays.[13] In their final opinion, the bays represented an immense crater field produced by a whole 'swarm' of objects which had approached from the north-west and struck the American south-east between '50,000 to a million years ago'.[14]

These were bold statements for their time. However, even Melton and Schriever underestimated the full potential of the so-called

24. The Temple of Kukulcan at Chichén Itzá in the Yucatán. This great cult centre of the Yucatec Maya was said to have been founded by Kukulcan, the Feathered Serpent, who arrived 'from the east' in the company of '20 illustrious leaders', each one bearded and dressed in 'long, flowing clothes'.

25. Photograph of a stone-frieze from an unknown site in the Yucatán, taken by Maya scholar Teobert Maler (1842–1917) and formerly in the possession of American author Robert B. Stacy-Judd. Does it show a Noah-like flood hero departing Tulan, the mythical homeland of the Maya, amid the cataclysms recalled in the *Chilam Balam of Chumayel*?

26. The heads of plumed serpents on the Temple of Quetzalcoatl at Teotihuacán. Note the carvings of seashells identified by Mesoamerican scholar George C. Vaillant as specifically Caribbean in origin. Do they indicate the direction of the Feathered Serpent's original homeland?

27. Chicomoztoc, the Seven Caves of the Mexica, from the *Historia Tolteca-Chichimeca* codex. From here emerged the first human beings at the beginning of the current world age, but where was it located and could it be found today?

28. Stone pillars uncovered in 1966 by archaeologists at a 4,000-year-old occupational site in Guanahacabibes, located in Cuba's western province of Pinar del Río. Who constructed this monument of a type so familiar to the Bronze Age cultures of Eurasia?

29. Cueva #1, the most important of the 'seven caves' at Punta del Este on the Isle of Youth, south of the Cuban mainland. Its walls are adorned with dozens of petroglyphs many thousands of years old. Do they tell of catastrophic events that devastated the western Atlantic seaboard around 10,500 years ago?

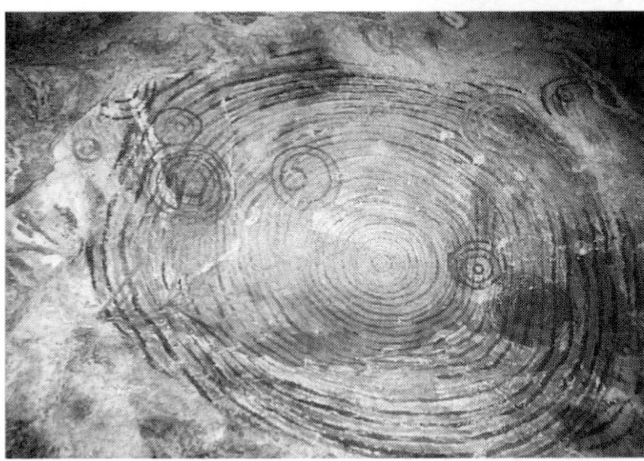

30 & 31. Two examples of the prehistoric cave art found inside Punta del Este's Cueva #1 on the Isle of Youth. The first picture, left, shows the main 'target' design pierced by an arrow or dagger-like symbol, which is traced by the sun at the time of the equinoxes. The second example, right, shows a serpent or comet-like feature, highlighting the clear celestial nature of the many designs found in the cave.

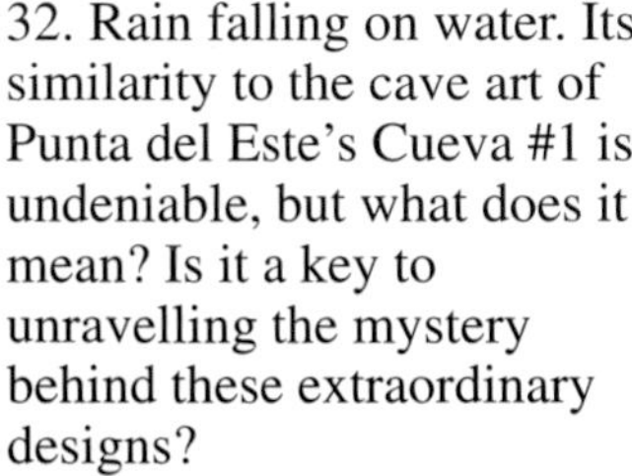

32. Rain falling on water. Its similarity to the cave art of Punta del Este's Cueva #1 is undeniable, but what does it mean? Is it a key to unravelling the mystery behind these extraordinary designs?

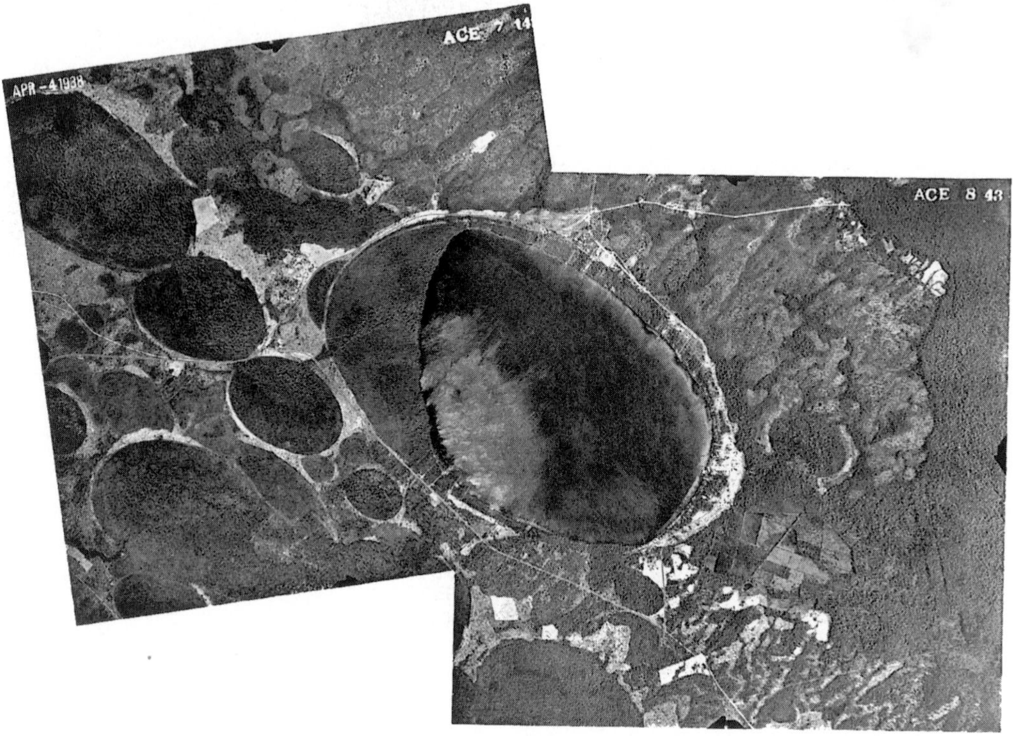

33 & 34. Two examples of Carolina Bays – top, White Lake Bay in Bladen County, North Carolina, and, below, more bays at Myrtle Beach, South Carolina. Countless thousands of these elliptical scars cover large parts of Georgia, Virginia and the Carolinas. What kind of impact might have been responsible for their construction around 10,500 years ago?

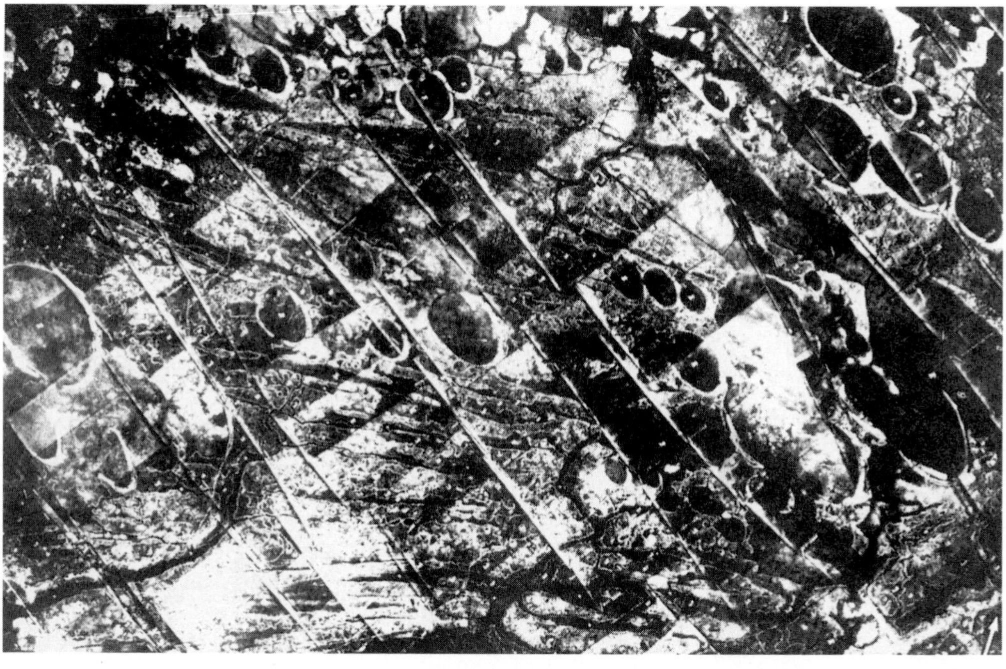

35. The 'temple' site first located north of Andros Island in the Bahamas by pilots Robert Brush and Trigg Adams during the summer of 1968. Do these stone foundations constitute evidence of a prehistoric Bahaman culture or are they simply the low walls of a modern sponge pen built in the 1930s?

36. A huge 100-metre triple-circle of loose stones first noticed off the south-west coast of Andros Island by pilot Robert Brush in the late 1960s. Whether or not this site is natural or artificial may never be determined as it has now been lost beneath the shifting sands.

37 & 38. Two examples of masonry discovered either on or close to the Bimini Road. Left, a black granite slab removed from the sea-bottom by dive shop owner Bill Keefe in 1995 and, right, Dr David Zink examines a tongue and groove stone found during his Poseidia expedition in 1975. Are all such stones simply discarded ships' ballast or do they constitute hard evidence of an antediluvian Bahaman culture?

39. (Above and opposite top) Photomosaic of part of the Bimini 'Road' site, west of Paradise Point, North Bimini, made in 1969 by underwater surveyor Dimitri Rebikoff. Geologists dismiss this curious feature as an outcrop of offshore beachrock but Atlantean researchers continue to cite evidence for its artificial construction, so what is the true answer?

40. Explorer and marine archaeologist J. Manson Valentine. Before his death in 1994 he highlighted no fewer than 60 sites of possible archaeological interest located on the submerged Great Bahama Bank.

41. Just one of the curious underwater features investigated by J. Manson Valentine and his team. Here we see a series of hexagonal cells located in shallow waters close to Moselle Reef, north of Bimini. Are such sites of artificial construction?

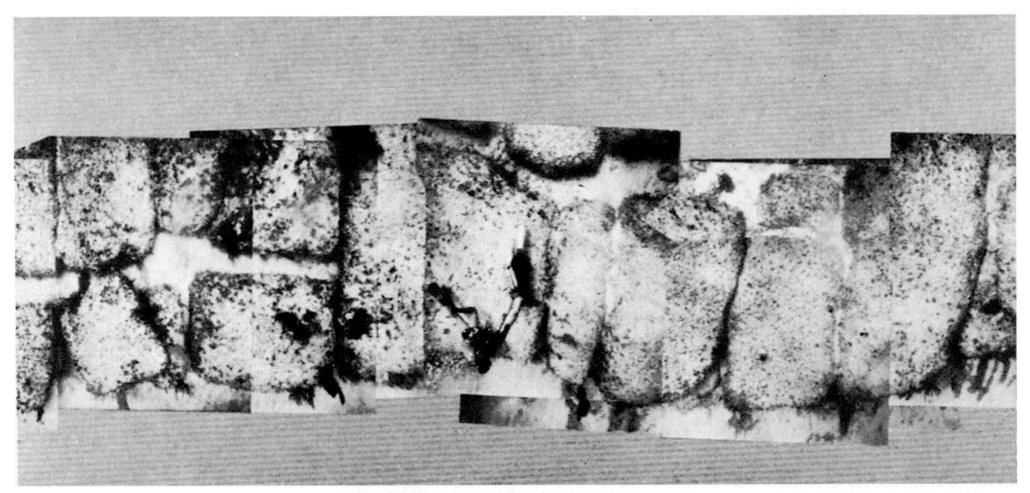

42. One of the many cut, dressed and drilled stones lying in shallow waters close to Moselle Reef, north of Bimini. Their presence has frequently led to unsubstantiated claims that Atlantean temples await discovery in the shallow waters of the Bahamas.

43. Decorated underwater cave found off the east coast of Andros Island by diver Herb Sawinski in 1963. The rise in sea-level that followed the cessation of the last Ice Age would suggest that this prehistoric art could be many thousands of years old.

44. The Palace at the ancient Maya centre of Palenque. In the eighteenth century Friar Ramon de Ordoñez y Aguilar associated this site with the City of the Serpents, founded by Votan, the 'son of the serpent', who came from a land in the east named Valum Chivim. Is it possible to identify Votan's original homeland?

45. Enormous elongated skull found in the Yucatán. Since this practice was exclusive to the Chane, or 'Serpent', priesthood of the Maya, do skulls like this, and others like it, imply that these walking Serpents represented an ancestral line in which gigantism was present?

46. One of the curious viper-faced statues with elongated heads produced by the Ubaid culture of ancient Iraq, c. 3500 BC, and now thought to represent members of the ruling elite. Was the memory of their presence in Mexico preserved in the stories of civilising Serpents and Feathered Serpents, such as Votan and Quetzalcoatl?

47. Maya ancestor god from a wall frieze at Palenque. Although this figure is identified today as cigar-smoking God L, nineteenth-century Italian scholar Dr Paul Cabrera believed him to be Votan the Feathered Serpent of the Tzendales.

'Carolina Bays', as they quickly became known. For it is now known that there are an estimated *half a million* such depressions,[15] in at least six states. Aside from Georgia, North and South Carolinas, they are also to be found in other bordering states such as Maryland, Virginia and Florida.[16] Their frequency is astonishing. One area of Bladen County, 8 kilometres by 6.4 kilometres, has a 67 per cent covering of bays.[17] Other areas of the Carolinas have as much as 50 per cent bay cover.[18] No fewer than 140,000 of these are of moderate to large size, with lengths of more than 152.4 metres.[19] One of the biggest depressions is Big Swamp Bay in central South Carolina, which is 6 kilometres from one end to the other.[20] Other examples found nearby are small by comparison, measuring between 91 and 122 metres in length.[21] By contrast, there is even evidence of bays over 11 kilometres long.[22]

Many of the depressions are elongated in shape, while others, usually much smaller in size, are almost circular.[23] Yet there is a definite pattern to their appearance, orientation and arrangement, which varies in accordance with their placement.[24]

Impact Craters?

In the wake of Melton and Schriever's announcements regarding the origins of the Carolina bays, alternative theories as to their cause came thick and fast. They included vulcanism, glaciation, artesian springs, fish spawning grounds, buffalo wallows, wind erosion and dust devils.[25] Despite these bold attempts to explain away the depressions in terrestrial terms, other academics immediately stepped forward to support Melton and Schriever's meteorite 'swarm' hypothesis.[26] By far the greatest threat to this idea came from Douglas W. Johnson, a geologist with the University of Columbia, who from 1934 onwards argued that the bays were formed through the actions of wind on artesian wells.[27]

Yet it was always going to be the most sensational explanation that would capture the imagination of the media and public alike. In 1933 Edna Muldrow, a writer for the popular magazine *Harper's Monthly*, used Melton and Schriever's published paper as the basis for a seven-page article on the likelihood of a 'comet' striking the earth – one of the first occasions that this topic was highlighted in such a public manner.[28] She attempted to conjure the image of a 'bad half hour when the whole heavens burst into one blinding flame', causing mass destruction across the United States.[29]

Aerial Detonation

Quite obviously, the orthodox scientific community did not greet the promotion of 'crackpot' ideas of this type too kindly. Charles

Darwin's theories of evolution, based on the notion of the survival of the fittest, saw fauna, including the human species, as having developed over many millions of years. In the minds of the neo-Darwinists of the time, catastrophe theories were nothing more than a popular myth.

The 1950s, however, saw a shift away from the scientific belief in a gradual transition of world ages, most probably because humanity had now seen the effects of atomic bombs, and so realised just how easy it is to raze cities and destroy countless human lives. With this change in outlook came even more ambitious theories concerning the origins and nature of the Carolina bays. In February 1952 William F. Prouty, a geologist at the University of North Carolina, proposed that the bays were created by powerful air-shock waves produced by the impact of incoming meteors towards the *end* of the Pleistocene epoch of geological history, *c.* 9000 BC.[30] In an attempt to prove his case, he had conducted a series of experiments whereby he shot bullets into a layer of powder at a low angle from a distance of nine metres. The air-shock waves created elliptical craters more or less identical to those of the Carolina bays.[31] He also pointed out that on-site surveys of a large percentage of the bays demonstrated that they possessed magnetic anomalies which hinted strongly at the meteoric origin of the depressions.[32]

To some degree, Prouty's 'Revised Meteorite Theory' for bay construction drew inspiration from the scientific community's new knowledge of an incident that had shaken an inaccessible part of central Siberia, in the upper basin of the river Podkamennaja Tunguska (60 degrees north, 101 degrees east) on 30 June 1908.[33] According to one witness account:

> About eight o'clock in the morning, I had been sitting on the porch with my face to the north, and at this moment in the northwest direction appeared a kind of fire which produced such a heat that I could not stand it . . . And this overheated miracle I guess had a size of at least a mile [1.6 kilometres]. But the fire did not last long, I had only time to lift up my eyes and it disappeared. Then it became dark, and then followed an explosion which threw me down from the porch about six feet [1.8 metres] or more . . . but I heard a sound as if all houses would tremble and move away. Many windows were broken, a large strip of ground was torn away, and at the warehouse the iron bolt was broken.[34]

When finally a team led by Russian scientist Professor Leonid A. Kulik reached the site in 1927, it found that a massive area of forest 24–32 kilometres in diameter had been scorched bare and laid flat in an enormous radical fan-like effect. At the blast's epicentre, where they expected to find an impact crater, Kulik and his team found only an area of denuded trees that still stood upright, suggesting that the celestial body had detonated aerially. Despite returning to the site three years running, Kulik was unable to find any conclusive evidence to show that the devastation was caused by a meteorite.[35]

Mercifully, the area around the point of impact had been completely devoid of human habitation, so there were no human casualties as a result of the aerial blast. Yet had this celestial visitor rendezvoused with the earth just four hours later, it would have decimated St Petersburg, levelling the city and wiping out its entire population.

If the Carolina bays were created by the disintegration of a single celestial body, as their parallel alignment seemed to indicate, then the event in question had been of unthinkable proportions. From the sheer number of depressions, it must have equalled something like 100,000 Tunguska-style aerial detonations, all occurring either synchronously or in direct succession. Some evidence of the effects of just one of these detonations came to light on a farm at Camden, South Carolina, close to some of the bays. During the construction of a drainage ditch, excavators exposed, at a depth of 4.3 metres, a mass of prostrate trees. They all bore the same alignment and looked as if they had been subject to a 'massive blowdown', indicating that the trunks had been uprooted during an almighty cataclysm that bore distinct similarities to the aftermath of the 1908 Tunguska event.[36]

Further Depressions

More intriguingly, huge elliptical depressions, or lakes, of a type very similar to those labelled as Carolina bays exist close to Point Barrow, in the north-west United States. They are found in the permafrost, the frozen subsoil of the polar regions, and range in size from 14 kilometres by 5 kilometres to 1.6 kilometres by 800 metres.[37] They cover an area of around 72,000 square kilometres, and number in their thousands, with an average trend in orientation of 12 degrees west of north.[38] In common with the Carolina bays, the troughs of Point Barrow are always shallow. Moreover, some overlap each other, showing that they were not created simultaneously, but in succession.

In addition to the elongated depressions near Point Barrow, other similar examples exist at Harrison Bay, Alaska, as well as on the Old Crow Plain in the Yukon area of Canada.[39] They are also found in the Beni region of north-east Bolivia distributed over a region spanning 72,000 square kilometres.[40] Once again the depressions in all these cases are elongated, shallow and regularly have axis orientations west of north.[41]

Since no suitable terrestrial solution exists to explain these elliptical depressions in the western hemisphere, there is every likelihood that they were produced by shock waves from aerial detonations caused by a disintegrating extraterrestrial object. But what sort of object, and exactly *how* were they formed, and when?

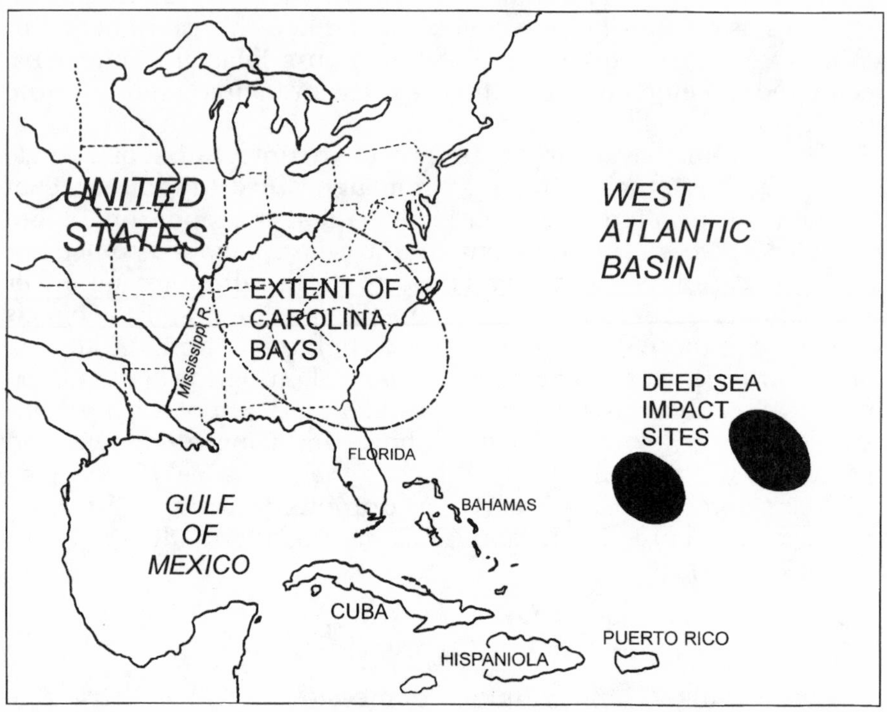

The United States and western Atlantic seaboard showing the extent of the Carolina bays (after W. F. Prouty) and the suggested impact site of much larger fragments of a celestial object (after Otto Muck). Did this cometary event around 10,500 years ago result in the submergence of large parts of the Bahamas and Caribbean?

Asteroid A

Otto Muck dismissed the notion that meteorites could have been responsible for creating the Carolina bays. They would have made circular depressions, like the famous Meteor, or Devil's, Crater of Arizona. He likewise dismissed the notion that the depressions could have been produced by a comet head, since it 'is much too small and too deficient in mass. Its explosion might have caused an impressive display of celestial fireworks in the marginal zone of the nitrogen envelope, but these illuminations high up in the atmosphere would have had no consequences on Earth.'[42]

In an attempt to understand fully the nature of the celestial body involved with the Carolina bays event, Muck used the statistics from an estimated 10,000 depressions to make various theoretical calculations. Assuming that an average trough had a diameter of 500 metres, he worked out that the 10,000 fragments involved would have possessed a mass volume of 500 cubic kilometres.[43] Using these figures, and assuming that the specific gravity of their mass was around 2 tonnes per cubic kilometre, 'then the weight of the solid core of the exploded celestial body' would have been 'in excess of 10^{12} tonnes' each.[44] If the presupposed nickel-iron core of the object had equalled this weight, he estimated that the total mass of the object had originally been in the region of 600–700 cubic kilometres, 'which corresponds to a sphere about 10 kilometres in diameter'.[45] In view of these calculations, Muck concluded that the 'Carolina Meteorite', as he referred to it initially, must have had 'an energy density' at the point of impact 5 million times greater than the Tunguska object of 1908.[46] If this was the case, then he felt it could better be described as an asteroid, or a minor planetoid, and so named it 'Asteroid A'.[47]

Asteroids are huge rocky bodies that generally orbit the sun between Mars and Jupiter, and are probably the remains of a planet or at least the constituents of a planet that never came to be. Yet not all asteroids are to be found in the belt between these two planets. Occasionally collisions send large fragments careering off into other parts of the solar system. Some end up on courses that cross the earth's orbit, making them potential 'global killers'. It may well have been one of these stray asteroids that hit Arizona, creating Meteor Crater, or, indeed, that caused the KT boundary event that wiped out the dinosaurs 65 million years ago.

Clues from Tunguska

Since the 1950s, when Otto Muck's book was mostly researched, opinion has swayed away from the Carolina bays being created by either a meteorite swarm or a disintegrating asteroid. No meteoric fragments have been found in connection with the depressions, and no suspected large meteorite, or asteroid, impact site in any other part of the world is known to have left up to half a million elliptical depressions over an enormously large area.[48] Furthermore, other telltale evidence that is usually present at impact sites is noticeably absent from the Carolina bays. For instance, they do not contain what scientists term 'shatter cones' or high-pressure changes in quartz grains.[49] Moreover, there are no noticeable differences between the mineralogy of sediment cores taken from the bays and samples extracted from beyond the rim.[50]

Obviously, these findings have suggested that the cause of the craters is terrestrial in origin. Yet at the same time new evidence has emerged concerning the cause of the 1908 Tunguska event. When Russian scientist Leonid Kulik and his team reached the site of the aerial blast in 1927, they found no evidence of meteoric fragments. What they did find, however, was that the whole area had been pockmarked by a series of 'shallow, funnel-shaped depressions of variable width but not more than four or five metres in depth'.[51]

What could have caused these depressions if it was not either a meteorite or an asteroid? All sorts of rumours abounded. A fragment from a supernova, a mass of antimatter and even an exploding UFO have all been proposed to explain the Tunguska explosion. None, however, makes any scientific sense. So what is the real answer?

In 1961 another scientific team managed to reach the remote site of the Tunguska event, and this time it did retrieve what seemed to be physical evidence of the assumed impact event. Tiny spheroids were found mixed among soil samples taken from the epicentre, which, after careful analysis, were found to be grains of non-icy 'dirt' *from a comet nucleus*.[52]

If this was indeed the case, it meant that the aerial detonation which caused the Tunguska explosion, and left in its wake a series of shallow impressions, was in fact a small, but highly volatile, comet nucleus.[53] Since the countless shallow depressions found in various regions of the American continent compared favourably with the shape and depth of the much smaller Tunguska depressions, geologists now feel that the Carolina bays might also be the result of aerial detonations produced by a disintegrating comet nucleus.[54]

Dirty Snowballs

Astronomers generally believe that comet nuclei consist of an icy core mixed with dust, the so-called 'dirty snowball' theory first proposed by Fred L. Whipple of Harvard University during the 1950s. In size they can be as much as several kilometres in diameter or as small as a house. Indeed, it was very probably a comet of this smaller size that caused the 1908 Tunguska event.[55]

Many comets belong to our solar system. They have long elliptical orbits that take them far out beyond Pluto, the most distant planet, before they arc around to begin their return journey towards the inner solar system. Some of these comets have orbits of just a few years. Comet Encke, for example, comes around every 3.3 years. Others have orbits that take them so far out into deep space that they can be tens of thousands of years in duration.

Still others come out of nowhere and cross through our solar system. Many do so without being disturbed, while a few are affected either by the gravitational pull of the sun, or by one or more of the planets, usually the largest, Jupiter, hit in July 1994 by 21 fragments of Comet Shoemaker-Levy 9. When this occurs, a comet can be catapulted on to a new course, which will send it careering towards any planet, including the earth. This game of cosmic pinball is most likely to occur after a comet has swung around the sun during its perihelion (i.e. the closest point it comes to the solar orb) and is in retrograde, in other words it is on its way back out of the inner solar system. Should it cross the earth's orbit at such a time, it would enter its atmosphere both at a very acute angle and at an extremely high velocity. Such a trajectory is completely in keeping with what is known about the Tunguska comet, which struck at eight o'clock in the morning and was seen by eyewitnesses on a low south-easterly trajectory before its final detonation.

If these same data are applied to the Carolina bays mystery, their characteristic appearance, arrangement, orientation and relationship start to make sense. Could it be possible that we have evidence here of a high-velocity, low-altitude comet nucleus that entered the earth's atmosphere on a retrograde course somewhere over the Asian continent before heading south-eastwards towards the American continent? If this was correct, did its core fragment into countless pieces as the earth's gravitational field drew it gradually downwards? Did its disintegration over the United States cause massive aerial detonations and air-shock waves that produced elongated craters beneath its more or less horizontal flight-path?

Quite clearly, the axis of orientation of the Carolina bays would align with the proposed trajectory of each incoming comet fragment. So long as these individual aerial detonations continued to take place, a shallow depression would form. Such an effect helps to explain not only the estimated 500,000 bays located in the south-east United States but also why they have pronounced rims at the south-eastern ends.[56]

As the proposed comet nucleus continued to disintegrate, large fragments would break away and veer off at a tangent, separating even further as they careered closer and closer towards the earth. The air-shock waves would produce elliptical craters, aligned not with the trajectory of the nucleus but with the course of the smaller fragments that had departed from the main core. This therefore accounts for the slightly different orientation of bays in separate regions, as well as the overlapping of depressions and just plausibly the elongated lakes in other parts of the American continent. All this would appear to have been caused by the fragmentation of a single comet nucleus that quickly dissolved into millions of pieces, like some kind of unimaginable millennial firework. This then is currently the most likely explanation for the presence of the Carolina bays.[57]

An example of the modern understanding of the mechanism behind the formation of the Carolina bays is provided by Henry

Savage Jnr in his definitive work *The Mysterious Carolina Bays*, published by the University of South Carolina Press in 1982. After summarising the available evidence associated with the bays, he proposed that:

> . . . these half million shallow craters represent the visible scars of but a small fraction of the meteors that fell to earth long ago when a comet smashed into the atmosphere and exploded over the American Southeast. Countless thousands of its meteorites must have plunged into the sea beyond, leaving no trace; while other thousands fell into the flood plains of rivers and streams that soon erased their scars. Millions must have smashed into the less friable, more resistant surface soils and rocks of the hills and mountains of the western Carolinas, Georgia and Virginia, eastern Tennessee and Kentucky, to be generally volatized in the terrific heat of impact, leaving only surface scars, soon eroded from the hills and mountains that generally characterize those regions.[58]

Despite Savage's suggestion that thousands of comet fragments (he calls them 'meteorites') 'must have plunged into the sea beyond', to my knowledge no geologist or astronomer has ever embraced Otto Muck's claims regarding the origins of the two deep elliptical holes in the West Atlantic Basin. This surprises me, for their shape and north-west orientation hint clearly at an association with the Carolina bays event.

It might be argued that if comets are simply masses of icy dirt, then once the nucleus has vaporised there would be no fragments left to plunge into the Atlantic Ocean. However, NASA scientists are no longer willing to accept that comets are simply 'dirty snowballs'. There is good reason to suggest that they do contain solid cores which, once the icy nucleus has burned away, resemble what can only be described as typical asteroids.[59] Indeed, there is now growing evidence to suggest that some asteroids are really 'comets in disguise'.[60] Should this be the case, there is no reason why the comet nucleus that seems to have created the Carolina bays did not contain a solid core. If it did, then we must ask ourselves whether two of its fragments created the deep holes identified by Muck in the West Atlantic Basin.

Even if the Carolina bays comet was not responsible for these elliptical trenches, from Savage's own words it is clear that thousands of fragments would have plummeted into the Atlantic Ocean, causing untold devastation.

Ravishing of the Great Serpent

Although much of the data contained in this chapter was unavailable to Muck when he wrote *The Secret of Atlantis*, the German rocket scientist felt he had discovered the mechanism behind the disappearance of Atlantis. Indeed, he was quite amazed that there had been 'no mention of Atlantis' in connection with the extra-terrestrial event surrounding the formation of the Carolina bays.[61]

Yet Muck also knew that earlier authors had already used worldwide catastrophe myths to help confirm the reality of Plato's Atlantis account. Perhaps the first person to do this was Ignatius Donnelly, American author of *Atlantis: The Antediluvian World*, originally published in 1882. Just four years later a sequel appeared under the title *Ragnarok: The Age of Fire and Gravel*. Although it did not match the success of the first book, its extraordinary contents, inspired by the extensive archive research Donnelly had already conducted in connection with Atlantis, were explosive in their implications. The book demonstrated that a fiery comet had shattered the relative calm of the Pleistocene epoch of geology history, bringing on an intense conflagration and flood.[62]

As we have seen, H. S. Bellamy used Hans Hoerbiger's Cosmic Ice theory to demonstrate that Plato's Atlantic island had been drowned in the aftermath that surrounded the capture of the earth's present moon. Yet it was Colonel Alexander Braghine, in his thought-provoking book *The Shadow of Atlantis*, first published in 1940, who cited, quite convincingly, various myths and legends from across the Americas in an attempt to prove that Atlantis was destroyed by an extraterrestrial object remembered in terms of a fiery serpent.[63]

In this fascinating work, Braghine devoted a whole chapter to the *Chilam Balam of Chumayel*, which we have already encountered in connection with the coming of 'the First People', or Ah-Canule, 'People of the Serpent'. Yet this ancient text – written in the Latin alphabet and accredited to J. J. Hoil, a Maya scribe who lived in the second half of the eighteenth century – also speaks of the events that supposedly preceded the departure of the People of the Serpent from their original homeland.[64] For instance, Book v states:

> . . . when the Earth began to waken. Nobody knew what was to come . . .
>
> And the Thirteen Gods were seized by the Nine Gods. And a fiery rain fell, and ashes fell, and rocks and trees fell down. And He butted trees and rocks against each other.
>
> And the Thirteen Gods were seized and their heads were cut off, and their faces were slapped, and they were spat out, and weights were placed upon their shoulders.
>
> And their Great Serpent was ravished from the heavens, together with the rattles of its tail and also with their quetzal feathers . . .
>
> And then their skin and pieces of their bones fell here upon the Earth. And then their heart hid itself, because the Thirteen Gods did

> not wish to leave their heart and their seed. And the arrows struck orphans, aged ones, widowers and widows, who lived, not having strength for life.
>
> And they were buried on the sandy shores, in sea-waves. And then, in one watery blow, came the waters. And, when the Great Serpent was ravished, the sky fell down and the dry land sank. Then Four Gods, the Four Bacab, destroyed everything . . .
>
> And the Great Mother Seiba arose amidst recollections of the destruction of the Earth. She rose straight up and elevated her head, begging for herself the eternal foliage. And by her branches and by her roots she called her Lord.[65]

Everything about these words appeared to speak of a terrible cataclysm that accompanied some kind of awesome aerial spectacle surrounding the 'Thirteen Gods' of the Maya and Ahau Can, the Great, Lordly Serpent. References to 'their skin and pieces of their bones' falling 'upon the Earth', mentioned in the same breath as a fall of ashes, the crashing down of 'rocks and trees', as well as the collapse of the sky and an inundation, hint clearly at an event like that which caused the formation of the Carolina bays.

This was also the conclusion drawn by Otto Muck with respect to the *Chumayel* account, for he stated:

> . . . it is very detailed and originates in a country not far from the coast that was struck by the Carolina Meteorite . . . It is difficult to think of any other image that could so vividly and accurately describe this event, the nature of which was almost beyond the power of words to portray.[66]

What Otto Muck seemed unaware of is that the *Chilam Balam of Chumayel* describes events which occurred *before* the People of the Serpent left their original homeland. As I have shown in these pages, the creation myths of the Mesoamerican tribes point clearly towards Cuba being the source of these ancient memories. There also exist various stories which speak of the forerunners of the Yucatec Maya arriving on the peninsula following a great deluge.[67] Furthermore, we know that the cataclysms recounted so vividly by the indigenous peoples and Afro-Caribbean communities of the Antilles speak of the break-up of a former landmass through disaster and flood, followed by the sudden emergence of individual islands. The *Chilam Balam of Chumayel*'s reference to 'sea-waves' covering the 'sandy shores' in 'one watery blow' seems remarkably like the description of a super-*tsunami* of the sort that would have unquestionably accompanied such a catastrophic event.

As we will also recall, the Yuchi tribe of Oklahoma spoke of the destruction of their Bahaman homeland 'by fires and clouds of different colors which came from the west and the north', causing it to sink beneath the sea.[68] The directions from which these 'fires and clouds of different colors' are said to have come are so close to the south-easterly trajectory of the Carolina bays comet that a connection between the two events seems highly probable indeed.

Had the Yuchi, the Maya, the Quiché, the Cakchiquel, the islanders of the Antilles, the Venezuelan 'medicine man' encountered by Kelso de Montigny, and the native peoples of Brazil all been describing the very same sequence of events that devastated the western hemisphere thousands of years before recorded history? How many more ancient myths and legends from tribal cultures all over the Americas were abstract accounts of these same terrifying events?

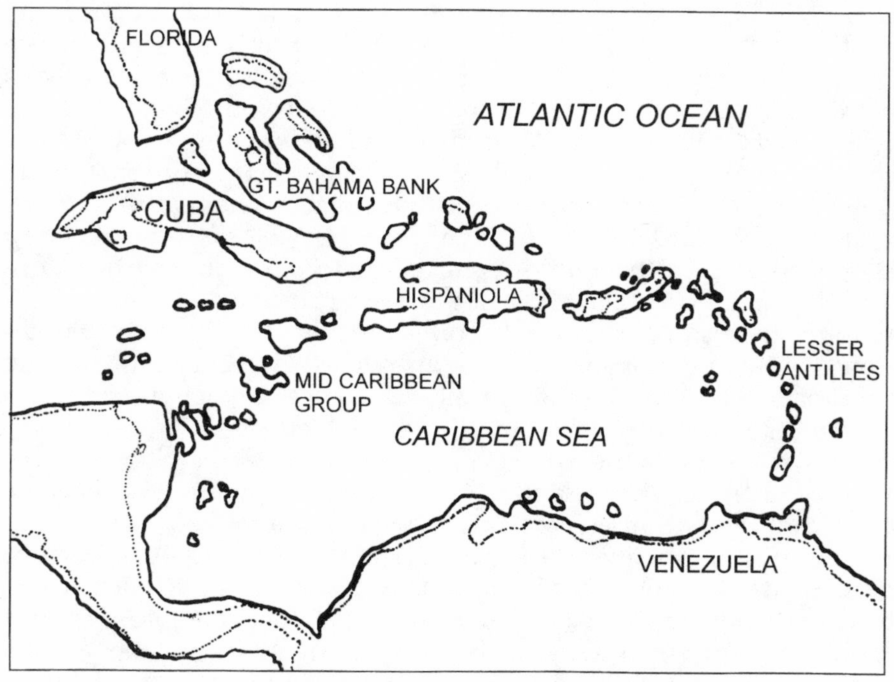

Map showing the extent of the Bahamas and Caribbean prior to the Carolina bays event *c.* 8600–8500 BC. The Great Bahama Bank represented a huge low-lying landmass that equalled the size of England, Scotland and Wales.

The Destruction of Atlantis

It is worth recalling at this juncture the words of Plato regarding the destruction of Atlantis, for they now become much more pertinent to the matters under discussion:

> . . . there was a time of inordinate earthquakes and floods; there came

> one terrible day and night, in which all your men of war were swallowed bodily by the earth, and the island of Atlantis also sank beneath the sea and vanished.[69]

If the two deep sea holes in the West Atlantic Basin *are* impact craters connected with the proposed Carolina bays event, I feel we may conclude that whatever caused them would have made quite a mess of any low-lying island landmasses located in the North Atlantic Ocean! The Bahamas lay just 1,000 kilometres west of the impact site, while Cuba and Hispaniola were situated at a similar distance to the south-west. Puerto Rico, on the other hand, would have been just 700 kilometres south of the epicentre, and is therefore likely to have suffered the full effects of the devastation.

If the Great Bahama Bank, the Little Bahama Bank and the various other low-lying regions of the Caribbean were above sea-level when the core fragments of the proposed Carolina bays comet hit the surface of the ocean, there is no doubt that the resulting *tsunamis* would have drowned them completely. At the same time almighty earthquakes, caused when the core fragments penetrated the ocean floor, would have shaken the entire western Atlantic seaboard, creating even further *tsunamis* and pushing Bahaman and Caribbean flora and fauna to the point of extinction.

If the Greater Antilles did once form part of the Atlantean island empire, then Plato's words become much more poignant. Somehow, he would appear to have preserved a recollection of the aftermath surrounding the proposed comet impact in the West Atlantic Basin at the end of the Pleistocene epoch.

Otto Muck made the same connection, although he placed Atlantis elsewhere in the Atlantic Ocean. In his opinion, the oceanic impact of the two huge core fragments of 'Asteroid A' would have triggered submarine volcanic explosions all along the weak fracture lines of the tectonic plates marked by the north–south-orientated Mid-Atlantic Ridge. Within just 24 hours, 'one terrible day and night', the plates would have split apart, allowing the earth's magma to come into contact with the waters of the ocean. The resulting explosion would have blown the island landmass sky-high. Any part of it that remained would have sunk down into the cracks and hollows that had opened up in the ocean floor.

As Muck triumphantly concluded: 'The previous day, that bed had been a large island with high mountains and splendid buildings. Today Atlantis lies some 2 miles (3 km) lower, in the center of the depression . . . a submarine landmass, a mysterious broadening of the Atlantic Ridge, which is no longer so mysterious now that its origin has become clear. All that remains visible of Atlantis is nine small islands rising above the sea, displaying their bare slopes to those who pass in ships. The Azores.'[70]

As I have demonstrated elsewhere, there is no convincing evidence to suppose that an Atlantean landmass ever existed on the Mid-Atlantic Ridge, meaning that the Azores are not the surviving tips of the lost continent's highest mountains. Muck chose to believe in a utopian Atlantis of modern conception, and thus its destruction had to be one of such totality that it would explain why no trace of its former civilisation could be traced today. The view that the Bahaman and Caribbean archipelagos were the real components of Plato's Atlantean island empire, with Cuba as its crowning jewel, allows us to conceive of a more realistic vision of what Plato seems to describe in his Atlantis narrative. Although low-lying landmasses or regions would have been drowned temporarily in the aftermath of the Carolina bays event, islands as a whole would have stayed very much the same as they were before the *tsunamis* had struck.

End of an Era

The Carolina bays event does more than simply provide us with a possible mechanism behind the destruction of Atlantis. Among those who have realised its greater significance is Emilio Spedicato. In his all-important paper on Apollo objects he proposes that both the end of Atlantis and the termination of the glacial age were the product of a single oceanic impact:

> We conjecture that the location was in the North Atlantic, somewhere east of the Carolinas . . . The evidence from the Atlantis story . . . points to a great *tsunami* and a flood originating from the Atlantic area. We also remark . . . that elliptical flat depressions (the Carolina bays), filled with water, with major axis pointing south-eastwards to the Atlantic, characterize in number of thousands the Carolina coast (extending also from New Jersey to Florida). The time of their formation is not certain, but can well be the end of the last glaciation.[71]

Is this possible? Is it conceivable that there is a relationship between these two quite separate events in the history of our planet? Was the last Ice Age brought to a close by the same comet impact that destroyed Atlantis?

What we do know is that at the termination of the glacial age immense ice sheets, which had engulfed a large part of North America and Europe for a period of anything between 25,000 and 50,000 years, vanished in a matter of 2,000 years. Furthermore, during this same time-frame there are powerful indications that dramatic events were occurring across the American continent. For instance, in the glacial 'muck' pits of Alaska, Frank C. Hibben, the Professor of Archaeology at the University of New Mexico, discovered overwhelming evidence to show that tens of thousands of animals had suddenly met with the most hideous of deaths. In his book *The Lost Americans*, published in 1946, he states:

> In the dark gray frozen stuff is preserved, quite commonly, fragments of ligaments, skin, hair, and even flesh . . . The evidences of violence there are as obvious as in the horror camps of Germany. Such piles of bodies of animals or men simply do not occur by any ordinary natural means.[72] . . . Mammoth and bison alike were torn and twisted as though by a cosmic hand in Godly rage. In one place, we can find the foreleg and shoulder of a mammoth with portions of the flesh and the toenails and the hair still clinging to the blackened bones. Close by is the neck and skull of a bison with the vertebrae clinging together with tendons and ligaments and the chitinous covering of the horns intact . . . The animals were simply torn apart and scattered over the landscape like things of straw and string, even though some of them weighed several tons. Mixed with the piles of bones are trees, also twisted and torn and piled in tangled groups; and the whole is covered with fine sifting muck, then frozen solid.[73]

Such horrific scenes can only have been caused by violent upheavals of an unprecedented nature, a theory supported by layers of black ash found in both Alaska and Siberia and corresponding to the end of the Pleistocene epoch, *c.* 9000–8500 BC.[74] In Hibben's estimates over 40 million animals perished on the American continent alone. Whole species, including the giant beaver, mammoth, mastodon, sabre-toothed tiger, the giant sloth, Alaskan lion, American camel and horse and many more became extinct almost overnight.[75] At the same time, the giant ground sloth, *Megaelocsus*, and other Pleistocene megafauna, disappeared completely from the Greater and Lesser Antilles. Since these islands were supposed to have been devoid of human life until *c.* 6000 BC, it indicates strongly that these animals coud not have been simply hunted to extinction as some palaeontologists have supposed. Were they too destroyed in the cataclysm?

We must listen when Hibben tells us: 'The Pleistocene period ended in death. This is no ordinary extinction of a vague geological period which fizzled to an uncertain end. This death was catastrophic and all-inclusive . . . The large animals that had given the name to the period became extinct. Their death marked the end of an era. But how did they die? What caused the extinction of forty million animals?'[76]

Could the Carolina bays comet really have been responsible for the termination of the glacial age? Did it cause the mass devastation of animal life described so graphically by Professor Hibben in the 1940s? More pertinently, had it been instrumental in creating the dramatic ending to Plato's Atlantis?

CHAPTER XXII

END OF THE ICE AGE

ONCE UPON A TIME THE sun, whose name was Ta-vi, roamed the earth at will. He would also spend long periods inside a cave, during which time the world would become dark and cold. On one such occasion his brother, the hare-god Ta-wats, waited so long that he fell asleep by his campfire. When the wayward sun finally re-emerged, he brushed so close by Ta-wats that his shoulder was scorched. Realising the anger this would arouse in his brother, the sun fled back into the cave.

For many years the hare-god sought out Ta-vi, and after several adventures he finally came to the edge of the world. As he stood waiting, the sun emerged from his cave. Seizing the opportunity to avenge himself, Ta-wats raised his bow and shot an arrow at his brother's brilliant face. Yet the fierce heat scorched and then consumed the arrow. The hare-god fired another arrow, and then another, but always the heat burned them up. Only one arrow now remained, and this was a magical arrow that never missed its mark. So Ta-wats brought the barb to his eye and, after baptising it with a tear, let the arrow find its target. It struck his brother 'full in the face, and the sun was shivered into a thousand fragments, which fell to the earth and caused a general conflagration'.[1]

Ta-wats decided that he must get away from the destruction he had caused, and so fled quickly as the flames consumed first his feet, then his legs, then his body and hands, and finally his arms. Only his head now remained, and this tumbled over and over, crossing burning mountains and rolling through fire-engulfed valleys until eventually, swollen with heat, his eyes burst and tears gushed forth which then covered the earth and quenched the flames.

Ta-vi the sun-god had been conquered and, for the part he played in causing the world to be consumed by fire, the council of gods sentenced him to encircle the sky for ever, thus creating day and night, until the end of time.[2]

★ ★ ★

This is the tale that was once told by the Ute tribe of the American south-west to explain why the sun crosses the sky each day. Yet this curious account also appears to contain elements that go far beyond merely explaining the sun's daily course. It seems to preserve vital information about an intense conflagration and deluge that the Ute believed had befallen the primordial world.

Is it possible to see in the wandering sun named Ta-vi a bright incoming comet that disintegrated into a 'thousand fragments, which fell to earth', causing fierce infernos? Was the sun's disappearance inside a cave the recollection of a dark nuclear winter brought on by such a catastrophe? Was the flood caused by the tears which issued forth from Ta-wat's eye sockets an abstract memory of the *tsunamis* that inundated low-lying regions when the comet's fragmentary core plunged into the ocean?

I would not be the first writer to draw attention to the significance of this powerful Amerindian folk tale. Ignatius Donnelly included it in his compelling work *Ragnarok: The Age of Fire and Gravel*, first published in 1886. 'Here we have the succession of arrows, or comets', he asserted. 'And here, again, we have the conflagration, the fragments of something falling on the earth, the long absence of the sun, the great rains and the cold.'[3]

Donnelly knew he was on to something of immense importance. The folk tales he collected from all over the American continent, and beyond, spoke clearly of a cometary impact of incredible magnitude, linked in some inextricable way with the catastrophic events that accompanied the cessation of the glacial age. Yet in 1886 he had no scientific proof to back up what he believed had occurred during this dramatic period in the earth's long history. The Tunguska event was still another 22 years away, and it would be three-quarters of a century before the full implications of the Carolina bays would be realised.

A Fiery Chariot

One might doubt the ability of indigenous peoples to be able to preserve the memory of catastrophic events that occurred so long ago. It is, however, worth pointing out that the Amerindians of Arizona recall how once their ancestors watched as a fiery chariot fell on Coon Mountain. At the exact spot they say it happened is the famous Meteor, or Devil's, Crater, formed perhaps 20,000 years ago.[4] It is 1 kilometre across, some 200 metres deep and is thought to have been made by a meteorite just 100 metres in diameter.[5]

If the Ute really have provided us with an abstract account of the cosmic visitor that wrought havoc across the American continent around the end of the glacial age, is it possible that the indigenous peoples of the Bahamas and Caribbean also preserved a memory of this same awesome event? Might this explain Plato's statements concerning the supposed destruction of Atlantis?

As we saw in the last chapter, influential scientists such as Emilio Spedicato are willing to consider that, in his Atlantis account, Plato had been alluding to events surrounding the termination of the glacial age. This is very promising indeed. Yet to access the picture fully, we must determine what happened at the end of the last Ice Age and decide whether or not the glaciation was terminated by the aftermath of an oceanic impact. Before we can do this it will be necessary to establish the exact age of the Carolina bays to verify once and for all their part in this enigmatic story.

Searching for Sediment

In the 1950s a scientific survey team, funded by Duke University, collected a large number of sediment cores from Carolina bays as much as 160 kilometres apart. These showed that at the base of some of the depressions there was a layer of blue-grey clay, blown into the bays after a sudden deforestation and desiccation of the region.[6] This proved to be the key to dating the bays, for the bottom sediment directly beneath this clay layer revealed pollen spectra relating specifically to the tundra forests that had dominated North America until the end of the glacial age, *c.* 9000–8500 BC. Yet in contrast, the sediment layer immediately above the blue clay produced carbon-14 dates in the region of *c.* 8000 BC, hundreds of years after the ice sheets had finally receded.[7]

Were these dates correct? Did they really spell out the age in which the Carolina bays comet struck the American south-east?

Over the years, the age of the Carolina bays has been hotly debated. Melton and Schriever were of the opinion that they had formed between '50,000 and a million years ago'.[8] Yet there are strong indications that the bay formation process occurred at a much later date, for as William F. Prouty pointed out in 1952, some 'clearly cut beach ridges developed on late Pleistocene terraces'.[9]

Carbon-14 dating of the bays has varied considerably. One survey conducted by the University of South Carolina in the 1970s provided dates between *c.* 70,000 years and 6,000 years BP (before present),[10] while another set of tests showed dates that ranged between 18,460 and 8,355 BP.[11] Henry Savage noted that five individual test samples examined by the university produced an average date in the region of '10,500 years ago' which, as he pointed out, 'is well within the range of origins of tribal legends'.[12] This date accords very well with the sequence dating of the bays deduced by Duke University in the 1950s, as well as with the observations of geologists such as William F. Prouty, who concluded that the bays 'cannot be older than late Pleistocene if formed by meteorites'.[13]

From this information we can see that within just a few hundred years of the bays' formation, the Ice Age was over. This meant that whatever caused them must have struck during this same time-frame. Yet could we find further evidence to link the proposed Carolina bays comet strike with the termination of the glacial age and the mass destruction of the Pleistocene animals right across the American continent? Even though a slow thaw had been occurring for as much as 7,000 years before the suggested date of the cometary impact, *something* brought the Ice Age to an abrupt close, and it certainly wasn't a gradual change in the weather.

Abrupt Changes

In 1960 a scientific paper by Wallace S. Broecker and his colleagues Maurice Ewing and Bruce C. Heezen, of Lamont Geological Observatory at Columbia University, Palisades, New York, appeared in the *American Journal of Science*. Entitled 'Evidence for an Abrupt Change in Climate close to 11,000 years ago', it advanced the theory that 'a number of geographically isolated systems' suggested 'that the warming of world-wide climate which occurred at the close of Wisconsin glacial times was extremely abrupt'.[14]

By examining sediment cores taken from various deep-sea locations, Broecker and his team were able to demonstrate that around *c.* 9000 BC the surface water temperature of the Atlantic Ocean increased by between six and ten degrees centigrade,[15] enough to alter its entire ecosystem. More significantly, it was found that the bottom waters of the Cariaco Trench in the Caribbean Sea, off Venezuela, suddenly stagnated, showing that an abrupt change in water circulation had taken place coincident to the warming of the ocean.[16] Additionally, the silt deposits washing into the Gulf of Mexico from the Mississippi Valley abruptly halted and were retained in the valleys and deltas, as the waters from the glacier-bound Great Lakes switched directions and began draining through previously frozen northern outlets.[17] With extreme rapidity, the water levels of these lakes shrank from maximum volume, down to the much lower level they occupy today.[18]

Among the data drawn on by Broecker and his team to make their findings was the work conducted in 1957 by Cesare Emiliani of the Department of Geology at the University of Miami. He found that deep-sea cores displayed clear evidence of an abrupt temperature rise around *c.* 9000 BC, the date given for the other changes set out by Broecker et al.[19] However, since other cores examined by Emiliani had not shown the same rapid transition, he decided that the anomalous cores lacked vital sediment layers covering a period of several thousand years of ecological history, and so dismissed them as unreliable.[20] Yet Broecker and his colleagues disputed Emiliani's interpretation of the results. They could find no reason to suppose that key sediment layers could have been lost in the manner suggested. As a consequence, they reinstated Emiliani's controversial findings as crucial evidence of a major shift in oceanic temperatures around 11,000 years ago.[21]

Although Broecker et al seemed keen to promote a date of *c.* 9000 BC for the rapid transition from glacial to post-glacial ages, there are indications that this event did not occur until a slightly later period. At least three lake sites in the Great Basin region revealed carbon-14 dates around 8000 BC for a maximum water level shortly *before* they experienced a sudden desiccation after the withdrawal of the ice sheets.[22] In addition to this, marine shells from the St Lawrence Valley, which provided evidence of an invasion of seawater coincident to a rapid ice retreat, frequently produced dates *post* 9000 BC.[23]

Broecker and his colleagues accepted the presence of these much lower dates and suggested that the whole matter was complicated by the fact that there had been an estimated 200-year resurgence of glacial conditions, known as the Valders re-advance, around the mid-ninth millennium BC. They therefore acknowledged that their own findings might in fact relate to the recession of the ice fields after this time, bringing the dates of their suggested 'major fluctuation in climate' and 'the sharp change in oceanic conditions' down to well below *c.* 9000 BC.[24]

The Evidence of Pollen Spectra

Further evidence that dramatic changes accompanied the transition from glacial to post-glacial ages came from the work of Herbert E. Wright Jnr, of the School of Earth Sciences at the University of Minnesota, Minneapolis,[25] and J. Gordon Ogden III of the Department of Botany and Bacteriology at the Ohio Wesleyan University, Delaware.[26] Both examined the pollen spectra range from sediment cores taken from various lake sites in the Great Lakes area and found that they provided clear evidence of an abrupt shift in flora at the end of glaciation. The spruce forests that had thrived in the cold harsh climate for many thousands of years were supplanted swiftly, first by pine and then by mixed hardwood forests, such as birch and oak. Deciduous trees, as we know, only thrive in a warmer climate.

The significance of these findings is the acceleration at which this transition took place. In an article for the journal *Quaternary Paleoecology* in 1967, Ogden pointed out that some pollen spectra samples showed a 50 per cent replacement from spruce to pine occurring in just 10 centimetres of sediment.[27] In one sample taken from a site named Glacial Lake Aitkin in Minnesota, the transition from 55 per cent to 18 per cent spruce pollen occurred in only 7.6

centimetres of sediment, representing a deposition corresponding to just 170 years.[28] The problem here is that conventional geologists and palaeoecologists consider that the transition from glacial to post-glacial ages occurred over several *thousand* years, not just a few hundred years.

These findings so baffled Ogden that he was led to comment: 'The only mechanism sufficient to produce a change of the kind described here would therefore appear to be a rapid and dramatic change in temperature and/or precipitation approximately 10,000 years ago.'[29]

What kind of climatic 'event' might have been responsible for this 'rapid and dramatic change in temperature' in the American Midwest, sometime around *c.* 8000 BC? Had it been a consequence of the proposed cometary impact that devastated the western hemisphere during this same epoch?

The knowledge that some 65 million years ago the Cretaceous period had been abruptly brought to a close by just such an impact has softened the most stubborn of minds concerning such a possibility. Broecker himself, in an article written for *Scientific American* in 1983, now accepted that asteroid or comet impacts might be responsible for the instigation and termination of glacial ages.[30]

This is indeed what Emilio Spedicato has suggested as the mechanism behind the revolution in climate and ocean temperature experienced during this period. In his words:

> The paroxystic effects associated with an oceanic impact are expected to last only a few days (the *tsunami*) or a few weeks (the 'universal deluge' following magmatic emission). It is unlikely that all the ice cover can be eliminated in such a short period, and in fact this is not what is observed from geological evidence. It is however possible that the albedo factor be modified so profoundly for the Earth to revert, in a few additional centuries, to the climatic conditions of non-glacial times. This agrees with the geological records.[31]

These are powerful statements, although Spedicato goes on to date this event, using a recent geological survey of the Atlantic Ocean, to *c.* 9450 BC (+/−80 years) – a date determined from dendrochronology (tree-ring calibration – see below) in association with ice core samples and carbon-14 dating techniques.[32] However, the findings of Broecker, Emiliani, Wright and Ogden, as well as the dating of the Carolina bays and further evidence presented below, all suggest that these events happened as much as 1,000 years later. If this was the case, we can safely say that the initial drowning of the Bahamas and Caribbean must also have occurred during this same time-frame.

As we have seen, *tsunamis* produced by an oceanic impact would not have submerged entire island landmasses. After a succession of tidal waves that might have lasted for many hours, if not days or even weeks, the ocean waters would have receded to leave the landscape hardly altered.

What I propose therefore is that within a matter of 200 to 300 years after the *tsunamis* had devastated these island groups, abrupt climate changes brought on by the aftermath of the Carolina bays comet impact finally brought the Ice Age to a close. With the sudden emergence of a warmer climate, the ice-sheets receded, causing a progressive outpouring of ice meltwater into the Gulf of Mexico and the western Atlantic seaboard. A similar situation would have occurred in northern Europe, which also saw the termination of its own glacial age during this same period.

Inevitably, the rapid increase in meltwater reaching the Gulf of Mexico, and the oceans as a whole, would have raised the sea-level, drowning not only low-lying coastal regions but also whole island landmasses in the Bahamas and Caribbean. So having initially been inundated by *tsunamis*, they were then submerged for a second time. Studies in sediment build-up at the edge of submerged landmasses in the Bahamas have provided a date of *c.* 10,000–8000 BC for Cay Sal Bank, north of Cuba,[33] and *c.* 8120 BC for the basal sediment of the Great Bahama Bank.[34] If these figures are right, we can say that the inundation process began sometime towards the end of the ninth millennium BC. Depending on the height above sea-level of the different landmasses, this process would have continued to submerge low-lying regions at a gradually declining pace until the waters finally stabilised in *c.* 3000 BC.

The Emiliani Controversy

There is, however, one final piece of scientific evidence to link the termination of the glacial age and the inundation of the low-lying regions of the Bahamas and Caribbean with, quite literally, the drowning of Atlantis. We have already read how in 1957 Cesare Emiliani noted that certain deep-sea sediment cores displayed clear evidence of sharp temperature rises in *c.* 9000 BC.[35] Yet since Emiliani was unwilling to accept that the transition from glacial to post-glacial ages had occurred in just a few hundred years, he dismissed these test samples as unreliable.

Obviously Emiliani had a change of heart between 1957 and 1975, for it was in this year that the prestigious journal *Science* published an important paper by a team of geochemists and marine scientists led by Emiliani.[36] It set out to show that analysis of core samples from the De Soto Canyon area of the Gulf of Mexico could now 'identify an episode of rapid ice melting and sea-level rise at about 9600 years BC'.[37] This had been determined by the dramatic increase in sedimentation that had resulted from the outpouring of ice meltwater leaving the Mississippi river. In itself, this was further confirmation of the scenario presented within these pages. More incredible, however, were Emiliani et al's views on the implications of these findings. For in their opinion:

> We submit that this event, in spite of its great antiquity in cultural terms, could be an explanation for the deluge stories common to many Eurasian, Australasian, and American traditions. Plato . . . set the date of the flood at 9,000 years before Solon, equal to 9600 years BC or 11,600 years BP: this date coincides, within all limits of error, with the age of both the highest concentration of ice meltwater in the Gulf of Mexico and the Valders readvance.[38]

This was strong stuff from the scholarly world, especially one headed by a scientist of Emiliani's calibre. Along with his colleagues at the University of Miami he had managed to propose a solution explaining the destruction of Atlantis in a manner that no other academic had ever dared before. During the mid-1970s, when Emiliani et al's paper appeared, historians saw Atlantis as a memory of the volcanic eruption that had destroyed Thera and devastated the Minoan civilisation of Crete. To the international media these findings, sensibly reported in *Science*, were like manna from heaven. They seized on Emiliani and his associates' conclusions and rather prematurely announced that scientists had at last confirmed the reality of Atlantis.

Not unnaturally, the academic community reeled, and so readied themselves for a concerted attack on this American scientist who dared to suggest that Atlantis had existed, not just in the Atlantic Ocean, but also in the time-frame given by Plato. To spearhead the assault, the critics called on no less an authority than Herbert E. Wright Jnr. He had ably demonstrated how sediment cores extracted from lake sites in the American Midwest showed that the transition from glacial spruce forests to post-glacial hardwoods had been 'abrupt', implying 'a marked shift in ecological conditions' in *c.* 8500–8000 BC.[39]

Wright's Attack

It was in an important article written for the authoritative work *Atlantis: Fact or Fiction?*, edited by Edwin S. Ramage and published by the Indiana University Press in 1978, that Wright chose to deliver his attack on Emiliani and his associates.[40] After reviewing the manner in which Atlantologists distort scientific evidence to fit their own ideals, Wright went on to question Emiliani et al's belief that the ice meltwater surging into the Gulf of Mexico from the Mississippi river occurred during the Valders re-advance. Wright pointed out that surges of meltwater are caused not by snow 'accumulation and wastage, but rather an abrupt change in the physical factors controlling ice flow'.[41] This, of course, is correct. However, all Emiliani and his colleagues had suggested was that these events occurred as a *result* of the ice re-advance, not necessarily during it. It was the article's wording that had been at fault, not its findings.[42]

Wright went on to query the effects an increase in the sea-level of the sort implied by Emiliani et al might have had on low-lying regions. In Wright's opinion, if it had occurred in a matter of a few brief years, coastal areas would have been affected only slightly. Such an outpouring of meltwater would hardly have drowned whole islands![43] Yet what Emiliani and his associates actually said was that, according to their calculations, there would have been an 'accelerated rise in sea level, of the order of decimeters per year'.[44] As anyone can work out, over a 200-year period an increase of this order would have caused, as they say, 'widespread flooding of low-lying areas, many of which were inhabited by man'.[45]

Also questioned was Emiliani's date of 9600 BC for the high point of the surge of ice meltwater reaching the Gulf of Mexico. In Wright's opinion the Valders re-advance took place as early as 11,000 BC,[46] completely invalidating the suggested 9600 BC date. Yet dating evidence from various disciplines would tend to show that the abrupt transition from glacial to post-glacial ages, which occurred in association with the Valders re-advance, took place around 10,500 years ago. So neither Emiliani nor Wright would appear to have been correct in this respect.

Not helping their case was Emiliani et al's presumption that the greatest surge of ice meltwater occurred exactly halfway 'between 12,200 and 11,000 years ago, that is, about 11,600 years ago', i.e. 9600 BC.[47] Not only did these dates ignore a more varied range of figures determined by carbon-14 testing (for instance, one key sample produced a date of 10,865 (+/−145) years), but there is no way of knowing exactly when the maximum output of meltwater took place. It could have happened anywhere within the suggested 1,200-year period.

As a consequence of these findings, Wright concluded that by citing a date of 9600 BC Emiliani and his colleagues had encouraged a spurious link between the events surrounding the Valders re-advance and the flood alluded to by Plato in his Atlantis dialogues.[48]

'In view of the numerous difficulties in relating glacial events to short-term global sea-level changes,' Wright concluded, 'Atlantists will have to look elsewhere for their catastrophes',[49] i.e. in the Aegean Sea. For in his words, 'the scientific documentation of the magnitude and chronology of the explosion and collapse of

Santorini . . . establishes this locale as a leading contender for Atlantis',[50] bringing us back full circle to the academic view of the Atlantis myth.

By removing the significance of the chosen date and dismissing the idea of a sudden influx of meltwater into the Gulf of Mexico, Wright felt he had demolished any scientific grounds for placing Atlantis in the Atlantic Ocean. This was regrettable, for it really does seem as if Emiliani and his associates at the University of Miami recognised the true mechanism behind the rapid drowning of low-lying regions of the Bahamas and Caribbean, the very heartland of the Atlantean island empire. Yet all the indications are that the events described by Emiliani et al in their *Science* article, along with the Carolina bays comet impact, occurred a full 1,000 years after 9600 BC, the traditionally held date for the destruction of Atlantis.

The Tollmann's Flood

Despite this clear conclusion, drawn from an examination of primary scientific sources, a date of 9600 BC in connection with a global catastrophe event during this time-frame has surfaced again in the work of Edith Kristan-Tollmann and Alexander Tollmann of Vienna University's Geological Institute. By combining together evidence from various disciplines (including the global distribution of tektites and a study of world-wide myths and legends), they have proposed that a comet approached the earth from the south-east and fragmented into seven pieces which fell subsequently into the oceans causing mass destruction on all continents.[51] One piece is believed to have landed in the North Atlantic, while another is considered to have fallen into 'the Central Atlantic south of the Azores'.[52] More than this, they have concluded that these cometary impacts resulted in universal floods, including the Great Flood of the Bible.[53]

Initially, the Tollmanns concluded that this unimaginable event occurred at '3 am [Central European Time] on 23 September 9,545 years ago [i.e. 7545 BC]', based on carbon-14 evidence, ice core samples and dendrochronology.[54] Since their theories were first published in 1992, they have also recognised an earlier event around the date '9600 BC'.[55] Since one of the main catastrophe myths cited by the Tollmanns as evidence of an impact in the Central Atlantic is Plato's story of Atlantis, it seems clear that they have embraced this new date to coincide with the supposed destruction of the Atlantic island, which they propose was located in the vicinity of the Azores. Indeed, it is their conclusion that: 'As far as we are concerned, Atlantis fell victim to one of the comet impacts.'[56] Taking a leaf out of Otto Muck's book, they go on to say: 'This may have been directly on Atlantis itself, but an impact in the vicinity would probably have sufficed to disrupt the relatively thin crust of the seabed at this point.'[57]

As there is no reason to assume from the evidence presented above that a cometary impact occurred in the Atlantic Ocean in '9600 BC', or that it fell in the vicinity of the Azores, I will treat the Tollmanns' promotion of this date with some caution. Moreover, as we shall see in Chapter Twenty-six, there is good reason to suppose that the seven-fold symbolism attached to catastrophe myths does not necessarily relate to the fragmentation of any incoming comet, but to the direction from which it came. In spite of this, we cannot ignore the fact that as respected geologists the Tollmanns have also recognised the overwhelming evidence for an assumed cometary impact, or, indeed, series of impacts, which caused a global catastrophe of incredible proportions around the end of the last Ice Age.

Zero Day One

To many Atlantologists, suggesting that Atlantis might have been drowned in a slightly later period to the one implied by Plato flies in the face of the facts. In the *Critias* it states that the Atlantic island was submerged 9,000 years before the dialogue in which the subject of Atlantis was debated by Socrates, Timaeus, Critias and Hermocrates.[58] Since this fictitious meeting is set in the year 421 BC, it provides a hypothetical date of 9421 BC for the 'earthquakes and floods' that supposedly destroyed Atlantis in 'one terrible day and night'. Yet as we saw in Chapter Three, this date appears only in the *Critias,* the second of the Atlantis dialogues, and is almost certainly the product of an error on Plato's part. Earlier, in the *Timaeus,* the war with Athens and the destruction of Atlantis is said to have taken place only after the foundation of Egyptian civilisation. Since the old priest of Sais tells us that the sacred records of the temple were already 8,000 years old by the time of Solon's visit to Egypt in *c.* 570 BC, this means that Atlantis must have been submerged *after c.* 8570 BC.

Otto Muck also realised the greater significance of this lower date in his book *The Secret of Atlantis.* By using a rather unorthodox interpretation of the Maya long-count calendar – suggested by the work of Professor H. Ludendorff of the Astrophysical Observatory at Potsdam, Germany – Muck concluded that the asteroid he saw as having destroyed Atlantis struck the Atlantic Ocean on Zero Day One. This date, he said, corresponded with 5 June 8498 BC in the Gregorian calendar.[59]

No other scholar of the Maya calendar has been able to verify these calculations, and most authorities are of the opinion that the long-count system was backtracked to start on a date corresponding with 13 August 3114 BC.[60]

I feel it would be ridiculous to ascribe any single date to the catastrophic events that appear to have twice drowned large parts of the Bahamas and Caribbean. Yet the clear indications from the various dates, provided by those who have recognised signs of an abrupt termination of the glacial age, suggest that the Carolina bays comet impact occurred in the region of *c.* 8600–8500 BC. Should this prove to be correct, it would mean that the subsequent drowning of the low-lying islands and coastal regions of the Bahamas and Caribbean began after the Valders ice re-advance, and so a time-frame of *c.* 8300–8000 BC seems appropriate here. Of course, we can never be certain about dates this long ago, as they are derived from the results of carbon-14 tests on organic materials extracted, for the most part, from sediment cores.

Since the 1980s there has been a tendency among archaeologists to use dendrochronology to re-calibrate carbon-14-produced dates, which are themselves only accurate within a +/−range of perhaps 400 years with organic materials over 10,000 years old. This controversial process, derived using carbon-14-dated tree-ring sequences, increases existing dates of 10,000 years by around another 1,200 years. Until such times when it is convincingly shown that dendrochronology is accurate, meaningful and free of academic bias I will stay with more conventional dating techniques.

These problems aside, a time-frame of *c.* 8600–8000 BC for *all* the dramatic events described in these pages is, I believe, a fair assessment of the evidence at hand. Indeed, the fact that Plato implies that Atlantis submerged after *c.* 8570 BC confirms, once again, that the *Timaeus* is more historically reliable than its companion, the *Critias*. We might be excused for thinking that Plato was privy to some kind of ancient lore, perhaps derived from Mesoamerican sources, which preserved across millennia the precise time period for the catastrophic events recorded in the *Timaeus*. Could it be possible that Otto Muck was correct in defining Zero Day One of the Maya calendar as the exact date for the Carolina bays comet event? Did it really occur on 5 June 8498 BC?

King-Lists and Chronologies

Unfortunately, the true answer is likely to be much more tangential. It is extremely unlikely that Plato derived his Atlantean chronology from any ancient Mesoamerican source, for this data would have had first to be assimilated into either Phoenician or Carthaginian tradition before it finally reached the ancient world. This seems an unlikely route for such specific chronological information to be transmitted across the Atlantic Ocean for the benefit of Plato. As outlined in Chapter One, it seems certain that his dates were provided by pharaonic king-lists such as the Royal Canon of Turin.

If correct, it is significant that ancient Egyptian texts speak of the age of the gods being brought to a close by dramatic events that bear a striking similarity to American catastrophe myths featuring fire, flood and periods of darkness.

The building texts carved on the walls of the Ptolemaic temple of Edfu in southern Egypt, for example, state that during *sep tepi*, the First Occasion, the so-called first period of creation was brought to a close by an enemy serpent known as the Great Leaping One.[61] It is said to have returned the world to darkness and raised a flood that submerged the so-called Island of the Egg at Wetjeset-Neter, the name given to the 'homeland' of the first divine inhabitants. Mass devastation followed, bringing decay to the land, and once the waters had finally receded, the occupants of the island habitation were called '*ddw*-ghosts', implying that they were killed in the devastation.[62] We are told that life returned to Wetjeset-Neter and a second period of creation commenced. It was at this point that divine beings known as *netjeru* and *Shebtiu* appeared for the first time.[63] It was these mysterious individuals that went on to lay the foundations of Egyptian civilisation.[64]

There is every reason to link the symbol of the Great Leaping One, which brings darkness, destruction, flood and decay, with the aftermath of a catastrophic comet impact. We must also not forget the Middle Kingdom text known as the Tale of the Shipwrecked Sailor, reviewed in Chapter Nine. It contains the story of an Egyptian sailor who recalls how he was shipwrecked after his vessel encountered waves eight cubits (3.6 to 4.4 metres) high during a voyage to the king's mines, located in a foreign land. All the crew except for him are killed, and after being cast on to the 'island of the *ka*', he meets a huge bearded serpent 30 cubits (13.5 to 16.5 metres) long. It addresses the sailor, telling him that it is the surviving member of a family of 75 serpents who lived on the island before a 'star fell, and they [the serpents] went up in flames through it'.[65]

Although the island in question probably lay off the east coast of Africa, the manner in which its serpentine inhabitants were engulfed in flames by a falling 'star' suggests, once again, that it is an abstract memory of either a comet or meteorite impact. Like the myths and legends of the Americas, these stories feature celestial snakes, falling stars, conflagrations, periods of darkness, a universal flood and the destruction of an earlier world race.

From the evidence available it seems unlikely that the ancient Egyptians were recalling the events surrounding the Carolina bays comet. This aside, we cannot discount the possibility that, as the Tollmanns have concluded, separate fragments of the same comet did not devastate other areas of the globe. Indeed, only recently it has been realised that a 'charcoal-rich layer' has been detected by geologists at the boundary between the Pleistocene and the current Holocene age in several countries including the Netherlands, France, Germany, Belgium, Britain, White Russia, India, South Africa, Australia and, more significantly, Egypt. Known as the Usselo horizon, after the site of its initial discovery in the Netherlands, this knowledge could now provide the impetus for scientists to begin looking for further evidence of this conflagration event in other parts of the world.[66]

Even though it would be foolish to make too much of Plato's chronology in his Atlantis dialogues, in citing 8,000 years between the foundation of Egyptian civilisation and Solon's visit to Egypt he coincidentally chose the exact time-frame of the Carolina bays comet impact of *c.* 8600–8500 BC.

This then is why Plato got it right when he cited a date post *c.* 8570 BC for the destruction of Atlantis. Having stolen Egypt's mythical chronology to bolster his case for the antiquity of the Athenian race, he went on to connect the core Atlantis legend with the same distant epoch, probably without realising the accuracy of the Egyptian records. What this implies is truly astonishing, for it would appear that Plato ascribed Atlantis the correct date for its supposed destruction *simply by default*.

So having already established that Plato described the island of Cuba when he wrote about his Atlantic island, we now find that he pinpointed accurately the time-frame in which the Bahamas and Caribbean had been drowned by proposed *tsunamis*, prior to their low-lying island landmasses and coastal regions being lost for ever. However he managed to achieve this great feat, there is no doubt that Plato created a masterpiece of historical fiction.

Yet we still have one major dilemma to resolve.

If the myths and legends surrounding the inundation of the Bahamas and Caribbean derive originally from *eyewitness* accounts, it would mean that these archipelagos must have been occupied at the time. Yet such a conclusion goes against everything that the archaeologists tell us about the earliest inhabitants of the islands. In their opinion the first Palaeo-Amerindian peoples to reach the Greater Antilles arrived in only *c.* 6000–5000 BC. As far as they are concerned, there is no archaeological evidence to even hint at a prior occupation of the islands.

This is a matter crucial to our debate, for if the archaeologists are correct, then there was *never an Atlantean race*, just a series of uninhabited island landmasses that played no active role in the Atlantis story, despite the catastrophe myths told by their *later* inhabitants. As we shall see next, outside the constraints of archaeological opinion, there is compelling evidence to show that the sunken regions of the Bahamas and Caribbean still hold important clues concerning the historical reality of lost Atlantis.

PART FIVE
EMERGENCE

CHAPTER XXIII

SUNKEN SECRETS

IT WAS THE SUMMER OF 1993 and the hurricane season was not yet upon the sun-drenched Bahamian island. Daily, huge motor cruisers, going between Florida and the more popular resorts in the archipelago, drew into Bimini's busy marina. Many came specifically to follow in the footsteps of the island's most famous resident, the American writer Ernest Hemingway. He lived here periodically between 1931 and 1937, spending much of his time big-game fishing. Bimini's main nightspot, The Compleat Angler, is a shrine to the island's celebrated hero, its walls adorned with black and white pictures of the 'old man of the sea' standing proud next to strung-up marlin or sailfish.

Yet behind the lazy façade of fishing exploits, rum punches and laid-back islanders, something else stirred on the island. From her base on North Bimini (there are in fact two adjacent islands – North and South Island), Bahaman historian Donnie Fields readied herself for another day of field exploration along its slim coastline. She is a key member of a dedicted team of volunteers, headed by Californian anthropologist William 'Bill' Donato and united under the banner 'Project Alta', who come to the island each year in search of indisputable proof that Bimini was a surviving fragment of lost Atlantis.

Prehistoric Footprints

Donnie – who through her frequent visits to the island has become almost a guardian of Bimini's lost heritage – decided to examine a remote area of beach for evidence of ancient occupation. Having cut her way through thick, inhospitable undergrowth, she stepped down on to the hot sand and saw before her something of immense value to our understanding of Bahaman prehistory.

On exposed mud-rock, leading right to the water's edge, were human footprints. Investigating further, she uncovered no fewer than 24 individual impressions belonging to three separate individuals, probably a family unit consisting of a father, mother and child.[1]

The direction of the footprints was quite clear. They led directly out into the channel that lay between the two small islands. It meant that those who had walked this path before the mud hardened did so when the sea-level was much lower and the islands still formed part of a single landmass.

Realising the immense significance of her discovery, Donnie made casts of several of the footprints and submitted them for scientific analysis. Those who saw them proposed that the shape and depth of one of the sets implied that they belonged to a person 1.63 metres in height.[2] Furthermore, it was considered that 'the casts also evidence the toes in relation to a high arch often associated with Cro-Magnon humans and some Amerindian peoples'.[3]

Donnie showed photographs of the casts to marine geologist Dr John Gifford of the University of Miami, who had previously contested evidence that the Great Bahama Bank had been occupied before its final submergence (see below). Yet he had no hesitation in accepting the footprints as genuine and proposed that they were perhaps 7,000 years old.[4] Such an admission was truly astonishing. That an academic of Dr Gifford's calibre should have conceded that the footprints were this old meant that they were probably much older still.

In making such an assessment, Dr Gifford had gone completely against conventional archaeological opinion concerning the prehistory of the Bahamas. This contends that the archipelago was unoccupied before the Lucayan Amerindians arrived in AD 600–700. Furthermore, as we have already established, the Great Bahama Bank, on which the Bimini islands are situated, disappeared for the most part between 6000 and 3000 BC, even though this inundation process probably began as early as 8000 BC.[5] Gifford's proposed date for the age of the footprints was based purely on his understanding of Caribbean archaeology, which asserts that the earliest inhabitants arrived in the Greater Antilles sometime around 6000–5000 BC. It is therefore possible that the footprints were those of individuals who occupied the Great Bahama Bank *before* the sea began to submerge the landmass about 10,000 years ago.

So who were these unknown individuals, walking across an open mud-flat in the northern part of the Bahaman landmass thousands of years before the Lucayans reached the islands? Were they ancestors of the Yuchi tribe of Oklahoma, who believed they inhabited the former Bahaman landmass before it was torn apart 'by fires and clouds of different colors', causing it to sink beneath the waves?[6] Were they the ancestors of Mesoamerican peoples, such as the Quiché-Maya and the Cakchiquel, who left their mythical homeland in the east during a period of darkness? Were they related to the People of the Serpent, who arrived on the mainland by boat out of the east, after the Great Serpent had fallen to earth, causing devastation and floods?

These were tantalising possibilities, although in isolation the prehistoric footprints discovered by Donnie Fields in 1993 were simply not enough. More hard evidence would be needed if Project Alta was going to demonstrate that the Great Bahama Bank had formerly been occupied by a prehistoric race connected with Plato's Atlantis. Yet their quest is by no means a new one. Indeed, the very reason why the team visits Bimini so regularly is a fascinating, though highly unusual, story that cannot be ignored.

The Sleeping Prophet

It begins in September 1926, when Bimini's lazy world was rudely interrupted by one of the Bahamas' fiercest foes – the tropical hurricane. It wreaked havoc across the island, tearing down trees, razing homes and destroying commercial property. Victims included the Bimini Bay Road and Gun Club, as well as Hotel Bimini, both owned by an American millionaire who had invested heavily in the island.

Shortly before the disaster struck, this unnamed millionaire had been introduced to a very remarkable man from Hopkinsville, Kentucky, who ran a rather unorthodox medical practice in Virginia Beach, Virginia. It was said that he could prescribe treatments for ailments and problems simply by falling into a trance-like sleep and pronouncing the solution – the reason why he had become known to his friends as the 'sleeping prophet'.

This gifted individual, whose name was Edgar Cayce (1877–1945), had demonstrated already the potential of his strange psychic talents. He had helped to restore the sight of one of the millionaire's business associates, who suffered blindness following an automobile accident. Suitably impressed, the millionaire and his business circle had offered Cayce the finance he required to build a hospital at Virginia Beach. This they would provide in exchange for psychic information relating to potential mineral deposits and oilfields in the states of Kentucky and Florida.[7] The collaboration worked well, and eventually Cayce was asked to switch his attentions to Bimini in the hope that he might be able to detect untapped sources of oil and gold, and to substantiate local rumours and stories concerning the presence on the island of Spanish treasure.

Cayce's first psychic session in connection with Bimini took place in his office at Virginia Beach just a month before the hurricane struck. It confirmed that the island did indeed contain 'gold, bullion, silver, and . . . plateware'.[8] More pertinently, he spoke of Bimini as being 'the highest portion left above the waves of once a great continent'.[9]

In the wake of the hurricane, the millionaire needed desperately to re-create his offshore empire. So Cayce was asked to accompany him and his business associates to Bimini for a three-day visit. He accepted, and the journey finally took place in February 1927. On his arrival in Bimini (incidentally, the only time he was to visit the island), Cayce was taken out to one of the sites he had earlier pinpointed in his psychic 'readings'. Here he lay down and promptly provided four further channelled messages. These confirmed that they were indeed at the correct spot. Yet after the party failed to find anything of significance, Cayce came under increasing pressure to explain what was going on.

In response, the 'sleeping prophet' produced even more readings. These suggested that no treasure would be found, 'not because of the information being incorrect', but because it came from 'a universal and infinite source' which had been channelled through a 'carnal or material plane', in other words Cayce and his business associates.[10] 'Hence we know sin lies at the door, and in that information as has been given respecting same, that *the house must be set in order* [author's emphasis]' before anything at all could be found,[11] the moral of the story being that his psychic abilities could not be exploited in such an apparently selfish manner.

The psychic's unconscious mind now offered the Bimini businessmen other, more spiritually sound enterprises that would enable them to profit from the island's natural resources. These included the construction of a resort city, the reclamation of submerged land and the utilisation of wave power to create a hydroelectric plant as an unlimited source of free energy.[12] None of these proposals was ever realised.

The Slime of Ages

Cayce did not take part in any further psychic questing on Bimini. Yet having become interested in the island's unknown past, his channellings began to focus on its role as the remnant of a sunken continent. Over a period of 17 years, from 1927 until 1944, the lost world of Atlantis became a familiar theme in Cayce's psychic dialogues (although his first readings on the subject were given as early as 1924).[13] In all he made over 800 references to the lost continent,[14] which his unconscious mind saw in terms of an enormous ocean-bound landmass that stretched from the Bahamas and Caribbean across to the West Coast of Africa.

On a number of occasions during his later life, Cayce alluded to Bimini in connection with Atlantis' central island, which in his 'readings' he referred to under the name of Poseidia. On 19 December 1933, for example, while speaking of three locations where the 'records' pertaining to the arts and sciences of the Atlantean civilisation were hidden prior to its destruction, he revealed that one of them would be found:

> . . . in the sunken portion of Atlantis, or Poseidia, where a portion of the temples may yet be discovered, under the slime of ages of sea water – near what is known as Bimini, off the coast of Florida.[15]

Whether or not the person to whom the 'reading' was being directed was familiar with Cayce's earlier business interests in Bimini is questionable. What does seem clear, however, is that his extraordinary talents, in respect of both his diagnosis of medical ailments and his vision of the world's early history, provided him with a huge following towards the end of his life. It led eventually to the formation of the Edgar Cayce Foundation, a worldwide organisation dedicated to the preservation and final confirmation of Cayce's psychic 'readings', which included predicted world changes in the lead-up to the new millennium (very few of which have been fulfilled).

Prophecies of Poseidia

It was in 1940 that Edgar Cayce delivered what is arguably his most important prophecy on Atlantis' imminent re-emergence. Although Bimini is not referred to directly in this all-important 'reading', Cayce claimed that 'Poseidia [i.e. the sunken lands off the islands of the Bahamas and Caribbean] will be among the first portions of Atlantis to rise again. Expect it,' he said, 'in sixty-eight and sixty-nine; not so far away!'[16]

It was this profound statement that was to initiate a number of well-coordinated research expeditions to the Bahamas in the years that followed. Invariably, these would be organised by members of the Association for Research and Enlightenment (ARE), the research division of the Edgar Cayce Foundation, often under the leadership of Edgar Cayce's son, Hugh Lynn Cayce.[17]

With the approach of 1968 – the much-anticipated first year of discovery – the ARE stepped up its surveillance of the waters around Bimini. More expeditions were mounted and flyovers made. From 1965 through to 1968, the organisation's interests in the Bahamas were handled by geologist William Hutton who, for some reason, liked to refer to himself in official ARE publications simply as 'The Geologist'.[18] Intriguingly enough, nothing that might help confirm the presence of a former Atlantean civilisation was discovered on any of these expeditions, dampening hopes that Cayce's prediction concerning the re-emergence of a 'portion' of Poseidia would be fulfilled during the allotted time-frame of 'sixty-eight and sixty-nine'.

The Temple Site

It was at this point that fate stepped in and took a hand in affairs. On a regular flight between Miami and Nassau during the summer of 1968, Captain Robert Brush and his co-pilot Trigg Adams found themselves north of Andros, the largest island in the archipelago. As they made visual contact with the tiny islet known as Pine Cay, the two men noticed a well-defined rectangular structure in the waters below. It was identified as the foundations of a building, the eastern end of which had been sectioned off about a quarter of the way along its length by an interior wall.[19]

In all their previous flights over these sun-kissed isles, the two pilots – both of whom were members of the ARE[20] – had never seen anything like this before. Captain Brush in particular realised that they had discovered something of possible archaeological significance.

On their return to Miami, Brush and Adams excitedly related news of the discovery to two friends, both of whom were also followers of Edgar Cayce. They were J. Manson Valentine, a zoologist and research associate of Honolulu's Bishop Museum, as well as the Honorary Curator of the Museum of Science at Miami, and Dimitri Rebikoff, a noted French oceanographer and underwater surveyor. So impressed were they by what Brush and Adams had to say that plans were made immediately to hire a boat and dive on to the site, which they succeeded in doing during the second half of August 1968.

Valentine and Rebikoff determined that the underwater feature was approximately 34 by 20 metres and orientated perfectly east–west. It was defined by a thick layer of dark sea-grass, beneath which they said were perfectly laid limestone blocks about a metre in thickness.[21]

Satisfied that the ruin was indeed the remnant of a lost civilisation, Valentine and Rebikoff made the decision to join forces with Brush and Adams to form the Marine Archaeology Research Society (MARS) in order to search for further evidence of anomalous underwater features.[22] More pertinently, Valentine and Rebikoff agreed, somewhat prematurely, to promote the Andros site as firm evidence of Atlantis' re-emergence during the all-important year of 1968.

In a press release dispatched from Miami on 23 August 1968, Valentine boldly announced that 'an ancient temple' had been located in the Bahaman waters.[23] Its 'walls are sloping. I dug into the sand and managed to feel about another three feet [one metre] down. It is obviously much deeper, but we will not know how much until we excavate. The material is a kind of masonry and it is definitely man-made.'[24] He ended the statement by saying that he hoped the 'temple' might be 'part of Atlantis, the ancient lost continent, which, legend has it, vanished beneath the sea after a mighty cataclysm centuries ago'.[25]

Not everyone shared Valentine and Rebikoff's view that the Andros 'temple' site constituted proof of Atlantis' re-emergence. In the late 1970s, Dr David Zink, professor of English at the US Air Force Academy in Colorado, investigated the structure with a diving team as part of his annual 'Project Poseidia' expeditions on Bimini.[26] They found it to be constructed not, as was first imagined, of enormous limestone blocks, but of piles of loose rock. Indeed, Zink stated in his book *The Stones of Atlantis*, originally published in 1978, that a reporter named John Keasler of the *Miami News* interviewed an Andros islander named Reuben Russell, who claimed to have helped build the structure as a sponge pen for a Nassau gentleman sometime in the 1930s.[27]

Despite these revelations, Dr Zink remained unconvinced of the 'temple' site's modern construction. He pointed out that its great distance from the shoreline seemed to argue against its use as a sponge pen. Furthermore, the fact that it was located in just one metre of water would have made if difficult for local fishing boats to approach the structure.[28] Moreover, there is no hard evidence to suppose that the statement made by Reuben Russell even related to the same structure as the one found by Brush and Adams.

Anthropologist R. Cedric Leonard in his book *Quest for Atlantis*, published in 1979, makes some interesting observations about the site, which he visited with a party of friends on 3 June 1970. According to him:

> The local inhabitants, for at least the last three generations, believed this ruin to be the remains of a pen for storing conch shells and sponges: there are many such pens scattered about the area, but none of them are built of stone. Such pens are built of wood, much smaller, of light construction, and in deeper water so that boats may easily pass over. Moreover, they are not laid out in perfectly straight lines having 90° corners.[29]

The jury is still out as to the true identity of the Andros 'temple' site. Yet the publicity that inevitably surrounded its discovery swiftly drew others to begin their own search for sites of archaeological interest, particularly in the shallows off Andros. At little more than a metre or so in depth, its waters are ideal for aerial surveillance, and very quickly new underwater features were coming to light.

It was Robert Brush who discovered what is arguably one of the most enigmatic structures to be noted in the waters off Andros. On a flight a little west of its southern coastline, he spotted what appeared to be a huge dark ring around 300 metres in diameter and a metre or so in width. Within it were two further concentric circles of approximately the same thickness. This inexplicable feature lay in just half a metre of water and only 20 metres out from the shoreline. On-site investigations revealed that the largely fragmentary rings were defined by a 'three-tiered' layer of stone covered by a mass of sea-grass.[30]

During the late 1970s, film footage of this new Andros site was included in an unbroadcast television documentary entitled 'A Special Report: Atlantis in the Bahamas', put together by producers Douglas Kenyon and Thomas Miller and director Cecilia Gonzalez. The footage taken from the air seems to confirm its artificial construction, although nobody can be sure, for the site has now been lost beneath the shifting sands. Furthermore, other similar rings, marked out by sea-grass and of approximately the same size, were discerned from the air off the coast of Andros by myself in June 1998, begging the question of exactly what these sites might actually represent.

Diving Tales

During the early 1970s, the search for Atlantis in the Bahamas drew the attention of various internationally renowned authors, whose popular books have featured this subject (often with little concern for notes and references or primary sources of information). Among the most prolific writers in this field were Charles Berlitz, Brad Steiger and Alan Landsburg, the last of whom focused on Andros in his own quest to find evidence of a lost civilisation. With an enthusiasm that matched, and possibly even outshone, his contemporaries, Landsburg obtained interviews with local divers who claimed to have found no fewer than *fourteen* artificial structures in its coastal waters.[31]

His quite staggering findings are outlined in a book, co-written with his wife Sally and published in 1974, entitled *In Search of Ancient Mysteries*. Apparently, these structures, once again in just a metre of so of water, were said to possess walls of 'big blocks of beautifully square-cut [lime]stone, tightly fitted together', and up to 1.3 metres thick.[32] Some of the sites were fairly close together, while others were as much as eight kilometres apart.[33] The largest known structure was allegedly 81 metres long, 27 metres wide and divided into 3 separate rooms or compartments.[34]

An 'underwater explorer' interviewed by Alan Landsburg insisted that, on digging close to the base of one of the structures, he had come across 'buried pottery and ceramic figures'.[35] Apparently, the figurines were tested using the process known as thermoluminescence which can determine the age of ceramics. The results provided a date of manufacture in the region of 5000–3000 BC.[36] Unfortunately, the Landsburgs failed to record the current whereabouts of these important artefacts.

If such claims are to be taken seriously, then it would seem that the shallow waters off Andros contain striking features that give the impression of being of artificial manufacture. Yet because not one of these sites has ever been properly investigated, we can take the matter no further. It is an enigma that cries out for further attention.

The Road to Nowhere

On 2 September 1968, just days after the ill-conceived press release concerning the discovery of the Andros 'temple', Valentine and his diving colleagues were taken out to a location some 800 metres beyond Paradise Point on Bimini's North Island. Here a local guide named Bonefish Sam showed them an underwater structure that has become known to the world as the Bimini Road.

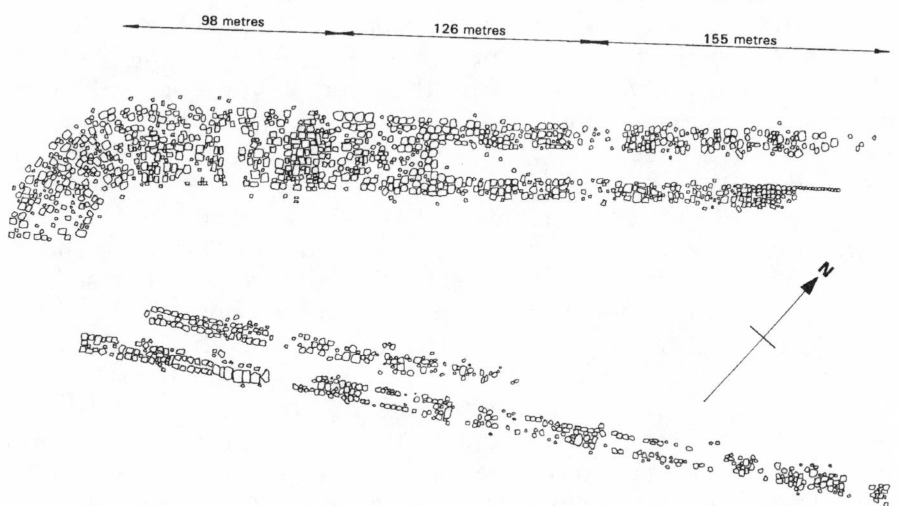

Ground plan of the stone causeway known as the Bimini Road, located close to the Bahaman island of North Bimini (after David Zink). Is this feature simply a formation of local beachrock or does it represent the work of human hands?

This enigmatic feature, over 638 metres in length, is made up of a double row of enormous regular-shaped blocks that are almost totally immersed in the sand. Some are as much as four metres square across their smooth, pillow-like upper surfaces. Extending beyond this section of the Road is a mosaic of much smaller rectangular stones, many up to two metres square, that curve gracefully to make a ninety-degree turn in the direction of the nearby beach. Their placement gives the whole structure the appearance of a letter J. After this point, the causeway continues in a fragmentary form for another 110 metres before it peters out and becomes lost beneath the shifting sands. Although the Road appears at first to run parallel with the local coastline, it is in fact 14 degrees askew (the structure itself has a south-westerly axis).

The thickness of the blocks in the parallel row vary, although for the most part they have a depth of between 60 and 90 centimetres.[37] Some blocks are placed on top of others, but the majority rest on the bedrock. Generally, stones are parted by gaps of between 10 and 15 centimetres, although some are as much as 67 to 78 centimetres distance from each other.[38]

Having become convinced that the Road structure was of artificial construction, Valentine announced the discovery in the summer 1969 issue of *Muse News*, the journal of the Miami Museum of Science.[39] Like his press release of the previous summer concerning the Andros 'temple' site, this news piece prompted a fierce reaction, particularly from marine geologists such as Dr John Gifford, who was at the time a geology student preparing for his Master's thesis at the University of Miami. Under the sponsorship of the National Geographic Society, Gifford, in the company of several well-qualified colleagues, including Dr John E. Hall, the Associate Professor of Archaeology at Miami, investigated the Road site in December 1969.[40]

Unanimously they concluded that the structure was simply 'Pleistocene beach rock', a well-known feature on Bahaman shorelines. This is formed over a long period of time, often several thousand years, by the accumulation on the sea bottom of aquatic debris, most commonly crushed seashells, or 'shell-hash'. The mixture cements together to form a coarse-grained limestone which, through the destructive actions of storms, marine life and wave erosion, often cracks and fractures to produce individual blocks placed in such a manner as to resemble an artificial causeway.

Further condemnation of the Road structure came from Wyman Harrison, a geologist with Environmental Research Associates Inc. Along with two colleagues, Dr R. J. Byrne and M. P. Lynch, he investigated the site in 1971. In an important article published subsequently in the magazine *Nature*, Harrison outlined his own reasons for concluding that the feature was indeed beachrock.[41] Despite such criticisms, supporters of the Road structure have attempted to highlight geological anomalies that in their opinion are indicative of its artificial construction.[42]

In June 1998 I was able to view the Bimini Road in the company of Donnie Fields, Bill Donato and other members of the Project Alta team. An hour or so was simply not enough for me to make a reliable assessment of what I saw that day in the shallow waters off Paradise Point. The pillow-like surfaces of the stones were unquestionably caused by water erosion when the stone blocks lay at low-tide mark thousands of years ago. Moreover, their regular shape seemed overly accentuated by the sand and sea-grass that fills the gaps between each stone. Sadly, I saw nothing which might prove that the geologists had got it wrong. Yet the possible archaeological significance of the Road site cannot be decided simply on its own merit, for there is clear evidence of human activity in its vicinity over a prolonged period of time.

Ancient Artefacts or Ship's Ballast?

A number of curious stone artefacts have been found in the shallow waters off Paradise Point. One of the first of these was a cut and dressed piece of masonry picked up in 1975 by Dr David Zink close to the Road's fragmentary southern arm, known to Bimini researchers as Rebikoff's Pier.[43] Originally the stone would have been 32 centimetres square across its upper surface, with a thickness of just 8 centimetres, although a large chunk is now missing from one corner. It appears to be made from a conglomerate containing a mixture of chert and limestone not native to the Bahamas.[44] On two of its edges are clearly defined tongues that run along their entire length, while on a third edge is a long straight groove that would fit either of its 'male' counterparts nicely.[45]

Its origin, or how it came to be here, remains obscure.

Many more examples of worked stones have been located in the proximity of the Road. They include several pieces of granite and marble, neither rock being indigenous to the region.[46] A large chunk of marble, weighing between 90 and 135 kilogrammes, was found, for instance, in 1975 close to the Road by Gary Varney, a dowser and member of Zink's Poseidia diving team. On examination it was considered to resemble a stylised feline head, although this interpretation is open to question.[47]

One of the most baffling finds to be made in the vicinity of the Road was retrieved from its southern arm in June 1995 by local diver Bill Keefe, the owner, with his wife Nowdla, of the Bimini Undersea Adventures Shop. It is an intriguing example of cut and dressed masonry, measuring 56 by 47 centimetres across its upper surface with a thickness of just 11 centimetres. It weighs 25 kilogrammes and has smooth edges that seem to have been eroded by the actions of the sea.

After Nowdla had cleansed off its encrustation, this clearly worked stone was found to be made from black 'fine grained granite' of a type quarried only in Vermont, New Hampshire, Washington State and Italy.[48] More important, it possessed a 'sophisticated joining feature' in the form of a deep triangular groove, or notch, cut into the edge of one of its surfaces.[49] Few would argue that the Keefe Stone is definitely not the product of a culture known to have occupied the Bahamas. Moreover, no one can deny that it is a dressed stone which shows clear evidence of tool marks and long-term erosion. Yet exactly how old is it? Is it really a building block belonging to some hitherto unknown culture, or is it simply discarded ship's ballast?

For long journeys empty trading vessels would be weighed with quarry stones, either placed loose in the hold or bolted to the hull. When the ship reached port the ballast would be removed and left on a quayside. Here it would remain until required by a vessel that had been emptied of its cargo and needed to be stabilised for its return journey. If a ship laden with ballast was wrecked, as frequently occurred in the treacherous shallows of the Bahamas, its masonry would be disgorged across the ocean floor. In time, tropical hurricanes and tidal movement would scatter these pieces far and wide, leading any underwater explorer who came across them to conclude that they had discovered the remnants of a lost world.

If, as local tradition asserts, the Road structure was once considered a hazard to local shipping, it is conceivable that trading vessels were occasionally wrecked here, thus explaining the various loose pieces of masonry found in its vicinity. On the other hand, the uniqueness of some of these finds, such as the tongue and groove stone found by Dr Zink and the black stone retrieved by Bill Keefe, does suggest that there could be other, more intriguing explanations for their presence in these waters.

When visiting Bimini in 1998, I found the Keefe Stone lying in a shed filled with diving tanks and weight belts. It is just about manageable, and so Bill Donato and I carried it on to the quayside for closer inspection. Since Nowdla had removed almost all of its encrustation, it was difficult to estimate how long it might have lain in the water before discovery. The shallow, triangular groove was certainly interesting, but what drew my attention most was its sheer blackness. It was not a form of granite I recognised, and in my opinion it more resembled hornblende schist. All I can conclude is that it seems unlikely that this stone began its life as discarded masonry destined for the cargo hold of a colonial vessel.

Several other artefacts of purported human manufacture have also turned up on the seabed close to the Road. They include a number of large hexagonal slabs around a metre in diameter yet only a few centimetres deep,[50] as well as much larger stones identified as fallen monoliths. The first of these was discovered during one of Dr Zink's Poseidia expeditions in the 1970s. A second example was found by Bill Donato on Rebikoff's Pier during the early 1970s.[51] It tapers towards one end and may well have stood erect, like the monoliths so familiar to the prehistoric world.[52] A third example was found north of the Road by Donnie Fields. Nearby was a ring of large stones with a diameter of around three metres.

Are these really evidence of a lost civilisation, or are they simply the product of yearning desires of those who need desperately to confirm the validity of Edgar Cayce's spiritual prophecies? Perhaps the former solution is correct, although before anyone is going to take these claims seriously more detailed reports, drawings and photographs of discoveries will need to be submitted and acknowledged by scientific institutions.

The Mystery of Moselle Shoal

Over the years there have been repeated claims of ruined Atlantean temples that await discovery off the coast of Bimini. Even though these reports have always proved groundless, the most frequently mentioned location in connection with them is Moselle Shoal, a north–south-aligned reef located some five kilometres north of Bimini. Its entire length is strewn with shipwrecks and discarded ship's ballast, including cut, dressed and drilled granite and marble blocks often regarded as evidence of lost civilisations.

There is, however, more than simply scattered masonry in the waters around Moselle Shoal. On a surveillance flight south of the reef during the mid-1970s, J. Manson Valentine, in the company of long-time friend and colleague Jim Richardson, identified a cluster of possible archaeological features in between five and nine metres of water. They included 'an area criss-crossed by an intricate grid-work of straight and curved lines',[53] as well as 'an extremely complex, underwater system of squares, rectangles and divided circles'. In the same vicinity was a cluster of 'cell-like units, the whole forming an artefact fully a hundred yards [i.e. 91.5 metres] long, shaped roughly like a foot of many toes'. This, he calculated, 'pointed at Bimini's northern cape'.[54]

Jacques Mayol, the famous world-record-holding freestyle diver, investigated the site on behalf of Valentine. He took a series of quite remarkable photographs, which on development showed the precise regularity of these cell-like structures. According to Valentine, they were 'delineated by straight, dark lines as uniform as the rulings on a tennis court'.[55] Hexagonal markings and depressions in the sand were also identified, where the 'cells', which averaged around four metres across, appeared to be most numerous.[56]

The whole complex apparently conveyed to Valentine and his colleagues a mathematical symmetry which led them to conclude that 'this astonishing artefact was the work of highly sophisticated men, probably at some time in the remote past'.[57] Judging by the resulting photographs, the team did indeed discover a site of potential archaeological interest constructed by a culture of graceful sophistication.

Whether or not these strange sub-surface features related to the Bimini Road, its supposed fallen monoliths, the retrieved pieces of masonry or the various underwater features off Andros is now impossible to determine. Time and time again, anomalies identified in the shallow waters of the Great Bahama Bank are all too easily dismissed as the delusions of gullible believers in the mysteries of Atlantis.

This is a sad situation. What seems inescapable, however, is the part that has been played by Edgar Cayce. Whether or not his predictions concerning the re-emergence of Atlantis are real or imaginary is now irrelevant, for over the past 60 years they have gained so much attention that they have now taken on a life of their own.

As fate would have it, strange underwater structures were indeed found in the waters off Andros and Bimini during the summer of 1968, the first of the two designated years of discovery according to Cayce's crucial 1940 reading. Even though these enigmatic features were brought to the public's attention by existing members of the Edgar Cayce Foundation, this whole sequence of events shows the sheer power of prediction, whatever the historical validity of the structures involved.

Edgar Cayce became embroiled in the greater mysteries of Bimini following his participation in a bizarre psychic quest to find buried treasure on the island. The exact story behind this misadventure may never be known. Did his channelled 'readings' allude to Atlantis simply to impress the businessmen who promised him financial help for his proposed hospital in Virginia Beach? Could they have learned of local legends suggesting that Bimini was once part of a sunken landmass?

Interestingly enough, tantalising evidence does exist to suggest that an age-old tradition regarding the break-up of the Great Bahama Bank was preserved on Bimini until fairly recently. On Sunday 17 June 1990 the *Miami Herald* ran a feature covering the island's proposed associations with lost Atlantis. After reviewing the case for the Bimini Road and highlighting the meditational activities of Edgar Cayce's latter-day followers, the article went on to quote one of Bimini's elderly fishing guides, a colourful figure named 'Bonefish' Ben Francis. On being questioned as to whether he believed the island to have once formed part of lost Atlantis, he had apparently responded: 'I heard stories from the old people when I was a little boy that the [Bahaman] islands were once all one mass.'[58]

Since Ben Francis must have been well past the age of retirement when he was interviewed by the *Miami Herald*, he would seem to have been recalling childhood memories from the 1920s or 1930s, the time-frame in which Edgar Cayce announced for the first time that Bimini was a remaining 'portion' of lost Atlantis.

Is it possible that Cayce's pronouncements concerning Atlantis' imminent re-emergence influenced local lore, or could it be that the businessmen who financed Cayce's trip to Bimini were blatantly aware of a tradition among the islanders which spoke of the Bahamas as once being 'all one mass'? Did they then look towards Kentucky's 'sleeping prophet' for confirmation of these stories, which might have been construed as evidence that Bimini was a surviving fragment of lost Atlantis? If this was so, then in some strange way they would appear to have got it right.

So far, Andros, Bimini and Moselle Shoal have offered up sunken secrets. Yet this was just the beginning. As the 1970s got under way, those who sought to locate the 'mother lode' or nerve centre of the Bahamas' antediluvian world were about to be rewarded.

CHAPTER XXIV

OUT OF THE BLUE

FOLLOWING HIS SLIGHTLY PREMATURE ANNOUNCEMENT suggesting that an Atlantean 'temple' had been located off Andros Island in August 1968, J. Manson Valentine adopted a more scientific approach to his archaeological exploration of the Bahamas. Along with close friend Jim Richardson, he familiarised himself with all the natural and artificial features one might expect to find in Bahaman waters and began to make a series of important aerial surveys over every part of the former landmass. Where possible, the diver Jacques Mayol would trail behind in a motor cruiser listening for instructions from the circling light aircraft. It was a combination that would repeatedly pay dividends.

Valentine and Richardson initially concentrated their efforts on the 50-kilometre stretch between Beach Keys and South Riding Rocks, on the northern edge of the Great Bahama Bank.[1] Here they were able to make out several 'straight divisions' in outline, as well as 'a right angle and triangle', none of which had any obvious explanation.[2] One and a half kilometres further south, just north of the island of Orange Key, they were able to trace 'an assemblage of abutting rectangles on a grand scale, dimly but positively delineated'.[3]

Another anomalous feature located close to Bimini's North Island was 'a strangely formed "arrow" marked out in the sea-grass' with a north-west axis, 'its shaft attached to a U-shaped base, causing the whole design to resemble a gigantic spur'.[4] On closer inspection it was found to be 33 metres long and constructed of huge stone blocks. A similar structure of almost identical design, although much larger in size, was identified by Valentine and Richardson on the banks of Joulter's Key, some 48 kilometres to the east.[5]

More peculiar was a site located 100 kilometres east-south-east of Bimini. It consisted of two 'very conspicuous' parallel tracks that ran for 'nearly seven miles [11 kilometres]' in the direction of an islet named Russell Light House.[6] These linear features converged on an enormous star-shaped enclosure, completely devoid of vegetation, focused on 'three polygonal holes'.[7] Valentine's colleague, Jacques Mayol, dived on to the site and found that the main hole was stopped up by a loose pile of gigantic stones.[8]

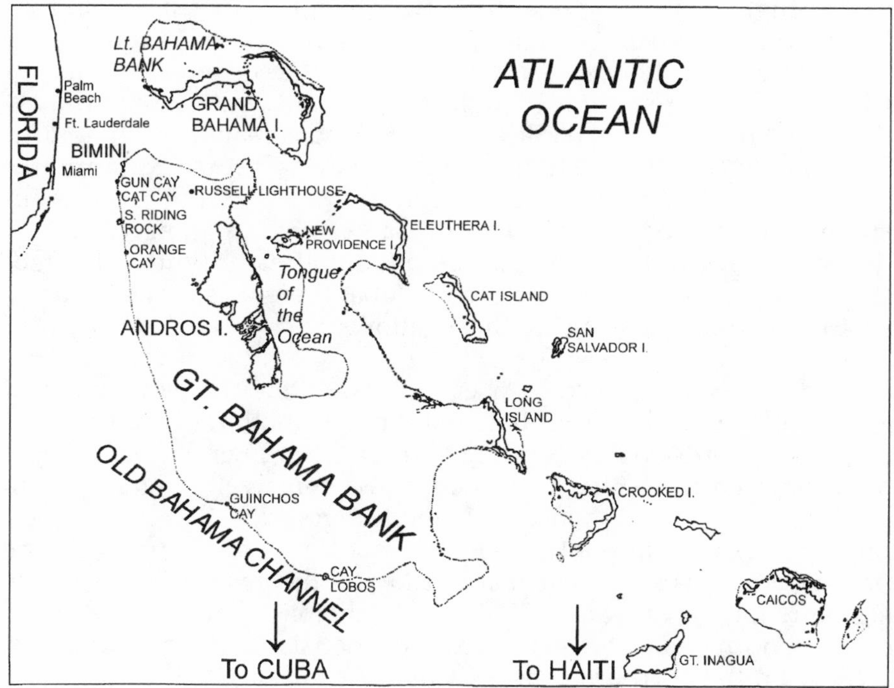

Extent of the Great Bahama Bank and other submerged land platforms of the Bahamas, highlighting sites mentioned in this work.

In Search of the Mother Lode

The true purpose of Valentine's surveillance of the Bahamas was to discover the heart and soul of what he took to be Edgar Cayce's Poseidia. It was with such thoughts in mind that he and Jim Richardson made a highly important flight along the leeward (western) edge of the Great Bahama Bank on 29 September 1972.

This low-level journey by light aircraft took them south to a point where the great sea-shelf drops sharply down to the Old Bahama Channel, a deep waterway which forms the division between the former Bahaman landmass and Cuba, situated to the south. Turning to a south-easterly heading, they remained at a height of 700 metres and followed the edge of the shallow bank until they could see below them the tiny island of Cay Guinchos.

In the shallows, Valentine and Richardson could make out 'the most striking assemblage of biserial lines yet seen . . . the total effect being not unlike that produced by terracing since the avenues are more or less parallel'.[9] Clearly enthralled by what they were observing, Valentine speculated that 'perhaps this rich site will turn out to be some sort of ancient, ceremonial center'.[10]

The flight continued south-eastwards for between 55 and 65 kilometres until Valentine and Richardson reached another tiny islet named Cay Lobos, also on the very edge of the Old Bahama Channel. Having spotted its lighthouse below, the two men knew they were now within 20 kilometres of Cuba, a realisation that must have unnerved them slightly. Since Fidel Castro's Communist regime forbade any American aircraft from entering Cuban air-space, they were now risking life and limb in their efforts to discover underwater features. Yet, having already flouted US federal laws by venturing this close to Cuba, there was no going back, so they continued to scan the shallows for further evidence of ancient occupation.

What they witnessed next was what Valentine felt he would find in this section of the Great Bahama Bank, something he referred to as the 'mother lode', the shining gem of the sunken landmass. For, according to him, the two men now perceived 'algal growth patterns of such obviously planned regularity that it is quite apparent they could not have been created by random proliferation of the flora'.[11] These linear features lay on the absolute edge of the sea-cliff, facing out across the Old Bahama Channel towards a corresponding shallow reef in front of the island of Cayo Romano, located on the northern coast of Cuba.[12]

Continuing along the line of the sea-cliff, Valentine and Richardson noticed even more distinctive features. He described them as 'an enormous, patterned field of dark algae enclosing a pale trapezoid at one end . . . margined by a dense border . . . undulating on the "land" side but absolutely straight along the drop-off on the outside'.[13] There seemed every likelihood that what they could see were walls. Further away, they could make out 'many shadowy, rectangular forms and more straight lines'.[14]

As they neared Diamond Point, close to the south-west corner of the Great Bahama Bank, the two men now identified a whole series of 'straight lines' intersecting 'at right, obtuse and acute angles'.[15] It was a view that later prompted Valentine to picture the setting as 'an architect's plan for an exceedingly complex urban development'.[16] Indeed, Valentine imagined that he and Jim Richardson might even have been 'gazing at the remnants of an antediluvian city'.[17] For some while the two men circled over what was conceived to be the 'mother lode', taking photographs and calculating coordinates.

There are no easy explanations for such well-defined underwater features. Having flown low over the Bahamas in search of potential archaeological anomalies, I can confirm that, after just a few hours of flight-time, natural features become easily recognisable. For kilometre after kilometre there may be nothing but shifting sands or vast areas of dark marine growth. Any linear or curvilinear feature, generally highlighted by sea-grass, instantly draws your attention and looks completely out of place in the midst of the sparkling blue waters.

The Cuban Connection

What exactly did Valentine and his co-pilot Jim Richardson discover on that eventful day in September 1972? What were these regular features etched out in the shallows of the former Bahaman landmass? Were they simply anomalies of nature, or did they represent the remnants of a veritable metropolis, once occupied by a race that thrived on the edge of the Great Bahama Bank? If this was indeed the case, its positioning, so close to the outlying islands on Cuba's northern coast, implied that the Bahaman 'mother lode' was some kind of staging post that linked these two similarly sized landmasses.

Interestingly enough, it was Valentine himself who first proposed a prehistoric connection between the Great Bahama Bank and Cuba. In an article written in 1976 for *The Explorers' Club Journal* he pointed out that:

> . . . both coasts run a parallel course, strongly suggesting contact at one time, an assumption that is well borne out by the fact that there are many endemic faunal elements common to both Cuba and the Bahamas, animals whose presence in both regions cannot easily be explained by transportation, especially in view of the fact that they have never spread to the neighbouring mainland.[18]

Valentine correctly surmised that the relationship between the two landmasses was originally a geological one, in that previously they had been joined together like Siamese twins, back to back, before being split apart by rift faulting in some past geological age, perhaps as early as the Tertiary.[19]

More pertinently, it has long been considered that the shallow waters north of Cuba might hold important clues concerning the Great Bahama Bank's strange antediluvian world. As early as the 1950s light-aircraft pilots reported seeing what they described as underwater 'stonework' that was 'well within Cuban waters'.[20]

Similar sightings 'north of Cuba' of an alleged 'submerged building complex covering over ten acres' might even have convinced the Cuban government that a veritable city awaited discovery in its vigorously defended waters.[21] There are, for instance, unconfirmed reports that this 'building complex' was explored with the assistance of Soviet submarines.[22] As unlikely as this story might seem, it is a fact that following the publication of Russian academic Nikolai Zhirov's authoritative work *Atlantis – Atlantology: Basic Problems* in 1970, the Soviet Union embraced his findings and actively sought evidence for the existence of Atlantis in different parts of the Atlantic Ocean.[23]

Among those who felt they had glimpsed the remains of a lost citadel in Cuban waters was Leicester Hemingway, brother of the writer Ernest Hemingway. During a flight into the country, Leicester noticed, beyond its northern coast, 'an expanse of stone ruins, several acres in area and apparently white, as if they were marble'.[24] The exact location of these underwater features remains unclear. If it was not on the southern extremity of the Great Bahama Bank, it is likely to have been in the vicinity of one of the many islets and cays that mark the position of Cay Sal Bank. This is an enormous three-sided sea-shelf over 100 kilometres in length and width, situated approximately 70 kilometres north of Cuba.

The Case for Cay Sal

As mentioned in Chapter Twenty-two, Cay Sal Bank was drowned rapidly following the rise in sea-level which accompanied the termination of the glacial age, *c.* 8000–6000 BC. Yet here curious features of possible archaeological interest have been noted by professional diver Herb Sawinski, a former chairman of the Museum of Science and Archaeology at Fort Lauderdale, Florida, who spent many years exploring underwater caves and blue holes throughout the Bahamas. They include two further Bimini Road-like features, one off Anguilla Island and the other off the main island of Cay Sal; a pair of enormous cut and dressed blocks located inside a sea-cave known as the Quarry; as well as evidence, both here and in another cave at Raspberry Reef, of quarry marks.[25] Since these caverns have been underwater for several thousand years, the possibility that they might have been hewn out, or at least enhanced, by human hands is most baffling.

In June 1988 I was fortunate enough to be able to visit Cay Sal Bank with Project Alta, who, with funding from the Edgar Cayce Foundation, hired an ex-US Navy research vessel, the *Ocean Window*, for this express purpose. During a three-day trip out from our base in Bimini, we were able to inspect the stone causeway off Anguilla Island. The whole operation was conducted with almost military precision, with various divers being designated a specific area to investigate and photograph. I swam the entire length of the 'road' two or three times and can confirm that it does indeed resemble its counterpart off Bimini. Yet this example runs at a right angle out from the nearby coastline, in contradiction to the marine geologists' view that beachrock only forms parallel to the shore. All I can say is that whatever action was responsible for this structure was also responsible for the Bimini Road. The two features are so similar that a common origin is certain.

I was also assigned to examine various sea-caves off Anguilla Island. I found no evidence of prehistoric occupation, although one of the other divers found what he took to be a conch-shell firestone of probable Lucayan origin. On land, Bill Donato found evidence of more recent occupation in the form of a makeshift camp and other discarded rubbish. Quite clearly, the island had become a temporary haven for Cuban refugees fleeing Castro's Communist regime. Whether these individuals made it to Florida, or were rounded up by the Cuban authorities and taken back to the mainland, we shall never know.

The only point I can add is that Cay Sal Bank, and Anguilla Island in particular, has one of the most eerie atmospheres I have ever encountered on my travels. This rather subjective opinion was not helped by the fact that, while exploring the underwater shoreline in the company of another member of the team, I was pursued by a particularly ferocious barracuda over a metre long. For several minutes it pinned us against the razor-sharp reef, baring its teeth. It was an experience that I would not like to repeat in a hurry!

The Atlantean Race

By the end of 1974 J. Manson Valentine had compiled a dossier on some 30 sites of potential archaeological interest located in shallow waters on the Great Bahama Bank. At his untimely death (caused through complications following a spider bite) on 2 September 1994 – coincidentally, the twenty-sixth anniversary of the discovery of the Bimini Road – his dossier was bulging with files on no fewer than 60 sites, most of which warranted further investigation.[26]

Many of these features would perhaps turn out to be of natural origin – flights of fancy on the part of those who discovered them. Nevertheless, it would be foolhardy to dismiss all such claims in this manner. If it could be ascertained that just one of them was of artificial construction, it would open the way for serious debate on the possibility that a previously unknown culture occupied the Great Bahama Bank, prior to the aftermath of the Carolina bays comet impact *c.* 8600–8500 BC. Furthermore, it would imply that this veritable Atlantean race reached a level of sophistication comparable to that of the Neolithic peoples of the Near East, *c.* 9000–8000 BC. Low circular and linear walls or enclosures imply domestic functions, such as the containment of animals, the cultivation of domesticated plants or the foundations of buildings. On the other hand, some of the structures might have served more religious functions, similar to the stone buildings and monuments of Nevali Çori and Çayönü, Neolithic sites in eastern Turkey which date from *c.* 8400–7600 BC (see Chapter Twenty-five).

What we might also say is that the proposed archaeological anomalies on the Cay Sal Bank, as well as the widespread placement of unidentified features on the very edge of the Great Bahama Bank, hint strongly at ancient contact between this hypothetical race and nearby Cuba. Is it therefore simply coincidence that Cuba fits all the criteria for having been Plato's Atlantis? If a high culture of this order did once exist, then it must have extended across from Cuba to the former Bahaman landmass. As we shall see, tangible evidence of antediluvian contact between Cuba and the submerged regions of the Bahamas does exist.

Guardians of the Deep

At 170 kilometres in length, Andros is the largest of the Bahamas group. It is in fact composed of two main islands divided by a channel that cuts through the centre of the landmass. Unbelievably enough, with its pine-covered valleys and freshwater lakes, the topography of Andros more resembles a Swiss Alpine landscape than it dōes a tropical island. Its virtually inaccessible lakes also conceal entrances to blue holes that plunge downwards for depths of up to 135 metres before linking with a maze-like network of passageways and caverns that extend for kilometre after kilometre, and often exit far out to sea. Many contain stalagmites and stalactites, showing that at various points in their history, most probably during periods of glaciation, these caves were above the water line. Their true age is conjectural, although one estimate places a date of 40,000 to 50,000 years ago for their original formation by the actions of the sea.[27]

The wildlife that inhabits the blue holes and caverns of the Bahamas might as well be from another planet. Strange blind white fish, unique species of giant crustaceans and other rare molluscs survive in almost total darkness, away from the light of the sun. The Seminole Amerindians, who reached Andros from Florida in the nineteenth century, firmly believed that the blue holes were also home to an altogether more bizarre occupant – a sea-beast known as the lusca, described either as half-octopus, half-shark, or half-snake, half-squid.[28] With a tentacled head and bulbous body, it could grow to over 70 metres in length and was said to gorge on those unlucky enough to be sucked into the whirlpools, known as the 'breath of the lusca', which mark the entrance to blue holes. Disturbingly, this chthulhoid creature, like something out of an H. P. Lovecraft horror story, is no myth, either.

There are several well-attested cases of giant 'scuttles', Bahaman for octopus, attacking fishing boats off the coast of Andros.[29] More disturbingly, in 1896 a giant carcass of an unknown species of cephalopod was washed up on the beach of Anastasia Island, off Florida. One of its damaged tentacles was 10 metres in length.[30] Tests conducted in 1957 on samples taken from the 'Florida monster', as it became known, revealed that it was indeed an unknown species of octopus. During the 1970s or 1980s part of a badly decayed tentacle five metres long was washed up on a beach near Small Hope Bay Lodge on Andros. Tissue samples extracted from the remains produced similar results to that of the 'Florida monster'.[31]

It was these same blue holes off Andros that diver Herb Sawinski was exploring in 1963 when he entered a previously uncharted cavern beyond the island's eastern shoreline. Inside, his flashlight picked out something that seemed totally inconceivable. Despite the fact that the cave was flooded permanently with water, the walls bore several carved petroglyphs of geometric forms, concentric rings, and stickmen, similar to those executed by cave artists in other parts of the Bahamas and Caribbean.[32] Yet as we have seen, archaeologists consider that Andros was uninhabited prior to *c.* AD 600–700. So what was this decoration doing in a cave submerged beneath 7.5 metres of water? The petroglyphs in particular must have been done by a culture comparable with the Guayabo Blanco, who occupied Cuba between *c.* 5000 BC and AD 250. This therefore implied that the cave artists who painted these petroglyphs must have inhabited Andros before the waters rose up to reclaim the island's low-lying areas sometime around 5000–3000 BC.

Herb Sawinski kindly sent me a copy of the black and white photograph he took of the underwater petroglyphs. Although it is difficult to make out individual designs, it is clear that they do resemble the Guayabo Blanco cave art found on Cuba. More difficult to explain are the stickmen, for, as we have already noted, these are considered by archaeologists to date to a much later period, suggesting that they were executed by Lucayan artists. Yet this seems impossible, unless we take into account minor drops in sea-level which occurred between 2700–2000 BC and 1500–600 BC.

That the Lucayans utilised partially submerged caves for burials is not in doubt. Skeletal remains have been found in caverns off Andros in particular, while in the imaginatively named Stargate Blue Hole, divers found a virtually intact Lucayan canoe. However, these items could have been placed in easily accessible caves and blue holes by swimmers. It does not imply that the waters rose up to reclaim them after the burials had taken place.

If nothing else, such discoveries show how strongly the Lucayans, like the later Seminole Amerindians from Florida, revered the blue holes and caverns of Andros as otherworldly entrances guarded by sea-beasts, such as the tentacled lusca.

Rob Palmer's Underworld

More difficult to explain is the evidence of human activity found in the blue holes and caverns on Grand Bahama, an island at the northern end of the archipelago, which once formed part of the Great Bahama Bank's northerly placed neighbour, the Little Bahama Bank.

Rob Palmer was a British diver of great renown who, before his tragic death in 1997, enthusiastically explored the cave systems of the Bahamas. He also wrote a book on the subject entitled *The Blue Holes of the Bahamas*, published in 1985. Palmer is a prime example of someone who was not restrained by orthodox opinion. Had he known that archaeologists consider the Bahamas to have been uninhabited prior to *c.* AD 600–700, Palmer would not have told us: 'Man moved into the Bahamas *before* the seas ceased rising, barely 5,000 years ago [author's emphasis].'[33] This statement was made not by consulting archaeological books but through his own knowledge and experience of the region.

Among the many discoveries Palmer made during his dives in and around Grand Bahama was a 'communal grave mound' inside the so-called Skylight Room, a high-domed hall that forms part of the island's Lucayan Caverns. These consist of a whole series of winding passages and caves that extend for at least 10 kilometres beneath the island. The mound was in fact a large cone-like structure made up of loose boulders positioned in an enormous chamber, which Palmer believed had once contained an underground lake.[34] Indeed, he speculated that the mound, or stone cairn, may have been built so that it stood within its darkened waters,[35] like some kind of mound of first creation emerging from the primal chaos.

More significant is the fact that directly above the position of the mound was a circular skylight. Even though the roof of the cavern is permanently under water, the setting, according to Palmer, was spectacular: 'When the sun is overhead, a single shaft of light pierces the darkness, lancing down through the clear water to illuminate the top of the mound. The individuals buried here must have been great indeed to warrant such a monument. Who they were, we shall never know.'[36]

And indeed we won't, for when the location of the mound

became more widely known, less scrupulous cave-divers pulled it apart looking for souvenirs.[37] Mercifully, Rob Palmer and his colleagues managed to retrieve a few loose bones, including part of a human skull and a shinbone, which were sent to the Smithsonian Institution for examination. From the 'flatness' of the skull, it was concluded that it had belonged to a Lucayan Amerindian.[38]

I have a problem with this explanation, since it makes no sense of the evidence available. As with the decorated cave discovered off Andros by Herb Sawinski, the Skylight Room among the Lucayan Caverns on Grand Bahama must have been under water for at least 5,000 years, and possibly even longer. The 'communal burial mound' and overhead skylight can only have been constructed by an unknown culture that long antedated the arrival in the Bahamas of the Lucayan Amerindians. More significantly, there seems to be a direct relationship between the design of the Skylight Room and the many Cuban caverns that also have circular skylights. These, as we have seen, enabled shafts of sunlight to pick out specific petroglyphs or areas of the cave at the time of the equinoxes, like the zenith tubes of the Olmec civilisation. If this comparison is valid, it provides evidence of contact between those responsible for the decorated caves of Cuba and the unknown individuals buried in the communal grave mound inside the Skylight Room on Grand Bahama. Since the Cuban cave art – particularly that in Punta del Este's Cueva # 1 – could date to as early as *c.* 5000 BC, it suggests that the culture responsible for the communal grave mound and cave art of the Bahamas might also have thrived during this same age, and, conceivably, even earlier still.

Elsewhere on Grand Bahama another underwater cavern has produced evidence of early human occupation. At the eastern end of the island, by Sweetings Cay, is an underwater complex of passages and caves known as the Zodiac Caverns, each bearing the name of one of the 12 astrological signs. They are accessed via various entrances located *beneath* the island's lakes. It was deep inside the narrowing of one such entrance, which leads into Gemini, that in 1982 one of Rob Palmer's colleagues, Rob Parker, came across a 'scattered area of bones'.[39] At first it was assumed that they might have been washed into the cave entrance by an exceptionally high tide. However, this seemed improbable as the cave was 'well below water when man first arrived in the area'.[40] A second theory suggested the bones might be 'the remains of some animal from the far past of the cave', i.e. when it was still above sea-level.[41] Yet subsequent analysis of the remains have shown them to be human bones, with one piece being part of a cheekbone.[42] For them to have come to rest so deep inside an underwater cave strongly indicates that they date from a time-frame before the cave system's most recent inundation, which ended around 5,000 years ago.

Mel's Last Message – A Final Clue?

Donnie Fields' prehistoric footprints on Bimini prove that there *was* human occupation on the Great Bahama Bank prior to the submergence of its low-lying regions. More important, the evidence of a human presence in underwater caves on Andros and Grand Bahama, as well as the accumulation of linear and curvilinear features on the south-western edge of the former Bahaman landmass, all suggest that this antediluvian race was related directly to the earliest inhabitants of Cuba.

Is it possible that the prehistoric race of Cuba, as well as the displaced peoples of the former Bahaman landmasses, evolved into the mound-building cultures of Cuba, Florida and the Mississippi Valley? Were they also the ancestors of Mesoamerican peoples such as the Quiché, the Cakchiquels and the People of the Serpent of Maya tradition? Were their descendants the Yuchi tribe of Oklahoma, who as the legendary Shawano Eagle-serpent people were the ruling elite among the Amerindian mound-builders? Was this antediluvian culture the true Atlanteans, the real inhabitants of Plato's ill-fated Atlantic island?

I think the answer is yes. Whereas Cuba might have been Atlantis' shining jewel, the former Bahaman and Caribbean landmasses, especially the Great Bahama Bank and Cuba's Bay of Batabanó, can be seen as Plato's sunken kingdom, while the archipelagos as a whole constitute Atlantis' island empire.

There seems every indication that the shallows of the Great Bahama Bank, as well as the other submerged regions of the Bahamas and Caribbean, hold important clues regarding the genesis of American civilisation. More than this, they may well provide us with proof positive of an organised island culture that achieved a settled, Neolithic lifestyle before its expansion was rudely curtailed in the aftermath of the proposed Carolina bays comet impact of *c.* 8600–8500 BC.

Those who were not drowned in the earthquakes and *tsunamis* that would have accompanied this event were displaced initially on to the American mainland, preserving the memory of the fiery snake, or 'ole moon', that had fallen to earth, causing mass devastation and floods. Later migrations to and from the Antilles, the 'homeland', helped confuse the lingering myths and legends concerning this catastrophe that had occurred in some past epoch of humankind. Eventually these stories were conveyed to transatlantic voyagers, who carried them back to the ancient world. Finally, they came to the attention of a Greek poet and philosopher named

Plato, who went on to create the story of Atlantis. In the opinion of the author, no other scenario fits the evidence.

This is not to say that we now have proof that Plato's magnificent Atlantean city never existed. It may yet lurk beneath the 'slime of ages' that covers the edge of the Great Bahama Bank, where J. Manson Valentine and Jim Richardson detected their 'mother lode' in September 1972. Alternatively, it could await discovery within the murky waters of Cuba's Bay of Batabanó, which may well have been the role model for Plato's Atlantean plain. On the other hand, the city of Atlantis might appear out of the blue in an altogether different part of the Caribbean.

In 1998 I learned that world-renowned treasure salvor Mel Fisher was confident that he had at last located the city of Atlantis. He would not reveal where it had been found, and made it clear to close friends that he would only ever divulge his findings when the government of the country in question was on better terms with the United States.

Mel Fisher was the celebrated discoverer, following a 20-year search that ended in 1985, of the Spanish treasure galleon *Nuestra Señora de Atocha,* which sank off the Florida Keys after hitting storms on a journey from Havana to Spain in September 1622. This man was arguably one of the greatest treasure hunters ever, and so learning that he believed he had now found Atlantis was not to be taken lightly.

Through the cooperation of his daughter Taffi, I was able to speak with Mel by telephone on several occasions during the second half of 1998. He confirmed the rumours about his discovery of Atlantis, and told me that the underwater site in question had been detected initially through satellite imagery and later verified by sonar scans. He was sure that what he had found matched *exactly* Plato's description of the Atlantean city. In a later conversation Mel let slip certain facts which led me to conclude that the site in question consisted of a whole series of submerged structures located in the Caribbean Sea, not that far from Cuban waters.

Exactly what Mel Fisher had discovered may now never be known, because it is possible that he took the secret with him to the grave, for sadly he died, at the age of 76, on 19 December 1998. We must therefore keep on searching in the hope that one day the world will have the final answers to history's greatest enigma.

There is, however, one final twist to this tale . . . one that involves the Feathered Serpents and their great interest in the seven stars of the Pleiades.

CHAPTER XXV

THE ODYSSEY OF VOTAN

IN 1691 NUÑEZ DE LA Vega, Bishop of Chiapas, a Mexican province bordered by Yucatán, Tabasco and Guatemala, may have held the ultimate key to unlocking the final secrets of Atlantis. Yet, sadly, he burned it. I speak of a codex written most probably in the local Tzendal language, which recorded the odyssey of a culture hero named Votan – 'the first man that God sent to divide up' the lands of America and bring civilisation to the native peoples.[1]

Fortunately, before the Spanish bishop destroyed the priceless codex, he copied sections of it, and these were shown to Friar Ramon de Ordoñez y Aguilar, canon of the cathedral town of Ciudad-Réal in Chiapas. He enters the picture after having set out in 1773 in search of an abandoned city of stone, which local people asserted was close to the village of Santo Domingo del Palenque at the base of the steep Tumbalá Mountains. On his arrival at the site, Ordoñez had been amazed to find an entire stone complex overgrown with a canopy of hostile undergrowth. Yet so taken had he been by what he saw at Palenque, that on his return to Ciudad-Réal, the Spanish friar wrote a memoir of the events surrounding the discovery of this lost city entitled *Descripcion de la ciudad palencana* (*Description of the City of Palenque*). More significantly, he went on to write a somewhat fantastic account of the history of Palenque entitled *Historia de la creacion del cielo y de la tierra* (*A History of the Creation of Heaven and Earth*), outlining his view that this sacred city had been built by the aforementioned Votan.

The Odyssey of Votan

Votan's self-penned odyssey would seem to have been a quite extraordinary, and totally unique, piece of work which set out to prove that he was descended from Imos, who was of the line of

'Chan' or 'Serpent'.[2] Who Imos was is not clear, although he is known to have presided, like Votan, over one of the 20 days in the Tzendal and Guatemalan calendars.[3] Accordingly, the latter's 'image represented him as a bird above and a serpent below', making him a feathered serpent *par excellence*.[4] According to both Nuñez de la Vega and Ordoñez y Aguilar,[5] Votan claimed to have come from Valum-Chivim, the 'land of Chivim',[6] and that he belonged to the race of Chanes, or 'Serpents', giving him 'his origin from Chivim'.[7] More curiously, Votan asserted that he was a 'Son of the Serpent'.[8]

On his way to America Votan was said to have stayed for a while at a place called Valum-Votan, which Ordoñez identified with Cuba.[9] Indeed, he spoke of Votan leaving Havana bound for Palenque. From Cuba his 'large boats' reached the Yucatán and then made their way along the Gulf coast until they came upon the islands that form a barrier between the Lagoon de Terminos and the open sea.[10] Here the flotilla of ships is said to have disturbed a flock of wildfowl, causing them to launch into the air and disperse in every direction.[11] Having entered the great lake, Votan and his people followed the course of the nearby Usumacinta river south-west towards what is today Guatemala. Some 80 kilometres upstream, Votan and his fellow leaders entered the Usumacinta Valley and there founded Na-chan, the 'city of serpents', which Ordoñez identified with Palenque.[12] Archaeologically speaking, such an assumption makes little sense, for today this famous Maya city is considered to have been built as late as AD 600 by a local king named Pacal. Either Votan founded another city altogether, or Palenque marks the site of a much earlier settlement.

Curiously, Ordoñez recorded that because the foreigners arrived in large boats and wore 'long, flowing clothes' the local Tzendal tribe gave them the name Tzequiles, that is 'men in women's petticoats'.[13] Yet it would seem that the local population came to treat the strangers as brothers, and in return Votan enlightened and instructed them on the basics of government, and divided up the lands into provinces.[14] He thus became their first legislator, instituting the holy laws of his own land.[15] The Tzendal submitted to his rule, and offered up their daughters with whom Votan and his leaders entered into 'alliance'.[16]

Four times Votan travelled back to Valum-Chivim, which Ordoñez clearly believed to be the kingdom of Israel.[17] On these journeys he would go first to Valum-Votan before making for somewhere referred to as the 'Dwelling Place of the Thirteen Snakes'.[18] On one return journey to Valum-Chivim he is said to have witnessed 'the house of God' being built,[19] an allusion to the foundation of King Solomon's Temple. On another occasion he visited the ruins of an ancient edifice with 'a very large wall', a reference to the remains of the Tower of Babel,[20] struck down by God after mankind attempted to reach the heavens. More curiously, on a second visit to the 'house of God' Votan 'was made to traverse an underground passage which ended at the root of the heavens'. Moreover, that this 'passage was nothing less than a snake hole, where he entered because he was a Son of Serpents'.[21]

On his return to Palenque, Votan found that there was now insurrection among the indigenous population. The Tzequiles whom he had left in charge had usurped his authority and carved out their own territory.[22] Yet to his credit, Votan is said to have used diplomacy to settle the disputes. As a consequence, he established four kingdoms and allowed his compatriots to rule one of them from the city of Tulhá, built close to the modern town of Ococino on the other side of the Tumbalá Mountains.[23] A curious Tzendal legend prevails to the effect that an underground passage links Palenque with the ruins of Tulhá. Ordoñez recorded that Votan constructed this mythical tunnel 'in memory of that where, during his travels, in his quality of Son of the Serpent, [he passed through] in order to reach the root of heaven'.[24]

Heart of the People

These are the basic details of Votan's odyssey as recorded by Ordoñez y Aguilar. We must be very careful about some of the detail, since it is clear that he introduced fanciful biblical elements in the belief that Votan was Canaanite in origin. However, Nuñez de la Vega also recorded his own account of Votan's exploits in his *Constituciones Diocesianos del Opispado de Chiappa* (*Constitutions for Diocese Opispado of Chiapas*), published in 1702. He told of how Votan went to a place named Huehuetlan, located close to the Pacific coast in the modern province of Soconusco. Here he introduced the animal known as the tapir and placed 'a considerable treasure' in a 'gloomy house' which 'he built in a breath'.[25] A 'woman and some Tlapianes [guardians]' were commissioned to watch over it.[26] This treasure is said to have 'consisted of some large urns made from baked earth and a room containing antique figures of esteemed ancestors who were noted in the calendar, made from chalchihuitl [a hard green stone], with other superstitious figures'.[27]

Nuñez de la Vega recorded that he went to Huehuetlan in order to learn the whereabouts of this 'gloomy house'. On its discovery, he ordered the current guardians to deliver up what had lain undisturbed in this dark vault for countless generations. What he records happened next is one of those terrible moments of history that just makes you want to hang your head in despair, for he tells us that: 'Everything was publicly burnt in Huehuetlan when we made our pastoral visit to this province in 1691.' Yet we are told 'the Indians still revere this Votan, and in some towns they see him as the Heart of the People'.[28]

Map of Central America showing the distribution of tribal cultures featured in this work.

Seafaring Serpents

That Votan was a genuine character in Tzendal history does not seem in doubt, as he was clearly venerated by the local population. Aside from featuring as one of the 20 names in the Tzendal and Guatemalan calendars, his name also appears, again with Imos, in local calendars from the provinces of Chiapas, Soconusco and Oaxaca.[29] Furthermore, Tzendal history preserves the memory of a whole dynasty of Votanide princes who ruled from the City of the Serpents.[30] They include Votan's direct successor Canam-Lum, the

'Snake of the Earth',[31] Been or Ben, a conquering prince, commemorated on a stela in the town of Comitan, located on the border between Chiapas and Guatemala,[32] and Chinax, a great warrior, who was said to have died in flames.[33]

Most intriguing of all is that at Huehuetlan Votan was said to have established a secret society. In this aspect he was known among the Tzendal as 'Seigneur of the Holy Drum',[34] since the ceremonies involved a hollow wooden drum called a 'tunkul'. This was used during a sacred dance known as the 'Zayi', or tapir, the reason perhaps why this animal was seen as sacred to Votan.[35] A form of this secret society, known as the Sh'Tol Brothers, continued in the Yucatán through to the twentieth century. Edward H. Thompson in his book *People of the Serpent* describes coming across one of its lodges after hearing the sound of the tunkul. He was allowed to witness the ceremony in progress and later joined the brotherhood, in time becoming one of its Tatiches, or Elders.[36] He was even granted permission to take the tunkul back with him to the United States, where it was presented to the Peabody Museum at Harvard University.[37]

Votan is an enigma to Mesoamerican scholars, and most tend to ignore his legendary story. What is more, he was not simply a localised form of Itzamna, the great civiliser of the Yucatec Maya, even though both of them were considered to have founded the city of Mayapan. Neither was he a memory of Quetzalcoatl or Kukulcan, the Feathered Serpent so intimately connected with the emergence of the Nahua and Maya tribes. They seem to represent a quite separate wave of influence that finally usurped the power of the Votanides.

Yet the common thread to all the early civilisers of Mesoamerica is always their connection with birds and snakes. Like Itzamna, Votan claimed to belong to the priestly line of Chanes, or 'Serpents',[38] establishing 'his origin from Chivim'.[39]

What did all this mean – establishing 'his origin from Chivim'? Only by retracing Votan's odyssey back to its starting point will we be able to determine any real answers.

Cuban Staging Post?

Votan is said to have begun the final stage of his odyssey from Valum-Votan, the 'land of Votan', identified by Ordoñez as Cuba, and in particular Havana.[40] As we have already noted, in 1857 Brasseur de Bourbourg asserted that: 'Modern travellers assure that they have seen sculpted rocks and ruined buildings around Havana indicating the presence of ancient civilised populations on this Island.'[41] I have argued that Cuba was most probably the ancient homeland of the ruling elite and earliest ancestors of the various Mesoamerican tribal cultures. It can also be identified as Antilia, the Island of the Seven Cities, one of the Hesperides and, most important of all, the flagship of the Atlantean island empire. So to find that Votan might also have established some kind of settlement or colony on Cuba before moving on to the American mainland did not surprise me. Unfortunately, we have no idea how Ordoñez might have come to this conclusion, although it is just possible that it was knowledge preserved among the Tzendales or Yucatec Maya.

Yet Ordoñez's account of Votan's odyssey reveals that Cuba was in fact merely a staging post for the foreigners, and that he and his companions had come from much further afield, plausibly from the other side of the Atlantic. We are informed, for instance, that after leaving Valum-Votan on voyages back to his homeland he would first pass the 'Dwelling Place of the Thirteen Snakes'.[42] From here he would continue on to Valum-Chivim, identified by Ordoñez with the kingdom of Israel in the reign of King Solomon, *c.* 970 BC.[43]

Assuming that Votan did indeed arrive in Cuba and Mexico from some distant land in the east, where might we locate the 'Dwelling Place of the Thirteen Snakes'? Some writers have assumed it to be the 13 islands of the Canary Isles.[44] Although it is possible that Votan might have made transatlantic crossings via the Canary Isles, the name evokes a vision not of 13 islands, but of a single location inhabited by 13 'Snakes', connected perhaps with Votan's own serpentine ancestry. Moreover, there are in fact seven principal islands in the Canaries group and of these only six were known to ancient geographers (see Chapter Five).

In Search of Valum-Chivim

Our only clue as to the whereabouts of Votan's original homeland is the name by which it was known – Valum-Chivim, the 'land of Chivim'. Since Votan also claimed 'his origin from Chivim', it would appear to be either an ancestral line or a race of people. Brasseur de Bourbourg tried unsuccessfully to find a root for this name in one of the Mesoamerican languages.[45] Ordoñez on the other hand felt that Chivim denoted the pre-Israelite peoples known as the Hivites.[46] They occupied northern Canaan and Jordan and are often confused with the Hittites, an Anatolian people that occupied parts of Canaan.[47] The Hivites are thought to have been connected with another Canaanite race known as the Horites,[48] who may well have been the Hurrites. They inhabited Canaan in the fifteenth and fourteenth centuries BC, at a time when Egypt referred to this land as Hurru.[49]

It is possible that Ordoñez might have been correct in assuming that Votan was a Hivite. However, there exists no corroborating evidence which might help substantiate his claim in this respect.

Taking another approach, Constance Irwin in *Fair Gods and Stone*

Faces argued that Chivim derived from the Semitic root *Chna,* a Greek name for Canaan, land of the Phoenicians.[50] She also pointed out that the word Chivim bears a striking similarity to Chittim, or Kittim, the name given in the Book of Genesis to the descendants of Javan, the offspring of Japheth,[51] a son of Noah.[52]

Mediterranean scholars feel that the biblical 'Chittim' might in fact refer to a Phoenician colony established on Cyprus named Kition.[53] This may have been so. However, we also know that the name Chittim originally referred to Phoenicians in general, and that eventually it became a term used to denote any Phoenician colony which thrived as a sea power after the fall of Tyre and Sidon in the early sixth century BC.[54]

Is it possible that Votan and his companions, with their long, flowing clothes, were really Phoenicians? Certainly, there should be no problem in proposing such a theory, especially as so much circumstantial evidence exists in support of the view that Iberic Phoenicians and Carthaginians visited the Americas during the first millennium BC. However, this solution lacks any real cohesion.

First, the Phoenicians and Carthaginians were seafarers, traders and entrepreneurs, not great civilisers. Instead of building empires they concentrated their efforts on extending trade routes and ports of contact. Their process of dumb commerce recorded by Herodotus is typical of the way in which they were concerned only with exchanging merchandise, and not effecting the greater destiny of alien cultures and civilisations with whom they came into contact. Secondly, and perhaps more pertinent to the debate, neither the Phoenicians nor the Carthaginians were big on the serpent.

The most important symbols in the religion of the Phoenicians were the bull, sacred to the gods El and Ba'al; the cow, sacred to the goddess Ba'alat, Lady of Byblos; and the lion or sphinx, sacred to the god Ruti.[55] Only the fertility goddess Astarte was linked with the symbol of the snake, and she was most probably cognate with the Hebrew Eve (see below). For the Carthaginians it was the ram, sacred to Ba'al-Hammon.[56] The only other animal with a special importance to their nation was the horse. Not only was it the emblem for the city of Carthage, but the prows of vessels were carved in the shape of a horse's head as a symbol of good fortune on sea journeys.

Sons of Serpents

If we are looking for a people in the eastern Mediterranean who venerated, worshipped and even reviled the serpent then we need look no further than the Jews. They saw the snake as a symbol of both wisdom and retribution through its association with Moses the Lawgiver. More significantly, it became the personification of sin and evil through its role in the story of Adam and Eve in the

Garden of Eden. In this capacity it was seen as an anthropomorphic being cursed to slither for ever 'upon thy belly' after beguiling Eve into committing the first sin.[57]

Although the Hebrew for snake, or serpent, is *nahash*, the roots of the name 'Eve' – the Hebrew *chevvah*, Arabic *hawwa* – are inextricably linked with various interrelated words meaning 'life' or 'snake'. For instance, her name translates as 'mother of all living',[58] while in Arabic *hayyat* means both 'life' and 'serpent'.[59] Lastly, we are informed by Clement of Alexandria (*d.* AD 213), a prominent Greek father, that 'according to the strict interpretation of the Hebrew term, the name Hevia, aspirated, signifies a *female serpent*'.[60]

Eve was thus seen as 'a female serpent', and as a 'mother of all living' things. Additionally, in Jewish folklore she was considered through her 'daughters' to be the ancestor or progenitor of the Nephilim,[61] an ancient race of the Bible who were also known as the *gibborim*, 'strong ones'. More significantly, they bore the name *awwin*, which is generally taken to mean 'serpents',[62] although it is more correctly rendered descendants, or sons, of the serpent.

I find it therefore beyond coincidence that in the Semitic language of the Hebrews the word Chivim also means descendants, or sons, of the serpent, or serpents. The *ch* of Chivim is merely a 'hard' letter *h* leaving us with the word *hivim*. The suffix, *m*, written *im*, denotes plurality and is usually applied to a specific group or tribe, as in the biblical Anakim – the descendants or 'sons' of Anak (see below). Thus *hivim* can be read as the 'descendants', or 'sons' of *hiv*, as in *hevia*, 'female serpent' (in Hebrew *i* and *e* are interchangeable as vowels), in other words Eve. Chivim is therefore identical to *awwim*, an alternative name borne by the Nephilim.

Are we then suggesting that Votan was a Nephilim, and that he came originally from the land of the Nephilim? Just who were the Nephilim, and what role might they have played in the appearance of the wisdom-bringing Feathered Serpents of Mesoamerican tradition?

Men of Renown

The Hebrew name *nephilim* means 'those who have fallen', or the 'fallen ones'. They appear in Chapter Six of the Book of Genesis, where it says: 'The Nephilim were in the earth in those days, and also after that, when the sons of God [*bene ha-elohim*] came in unto the daughters of men, and they bare children to them: the same were the mighty men (*gibborim*) which were of old, the men of renown.'[63]

In Jewish apocryphal and pseudepigraphal works such as the Book of Enoch and the Book of Giants – both written in the second and first centuries BC although derived from an earlier text known to scholars as the Book of Noah – the Nephilim were the offspring of a race known as the *eyrim*, or *irin*, 'those who watch'. In the

Septuagint, the Greek version of the Old Testament, this Hebrew name is rendered *grigori*, or 'watchers', who are also identified as the Sons of God, the *bene ha-elohim*. The Watchers are described as 'serpents', making their offspring 'sons' of the serpents. For example, the Book of Enoch speaks at one point of a Nephilim as 'the son of the serpent named Tabâ'et'.[64]

The Nephilim's connection with Eve is also explained, for the Book of Enoch asserts that the 'serpent' which 'led astray Eve' in the Garden of Eden was Gâdreêl, one of the Watchers.[65] Yet in effect this legend is merely an abstract example of the way in which the Watchers are said to have taken wives from among 'the daughters of men', who bore unto them children known as Nephilim.

It was through this female alliance that the Watchers, like Votan and his compatriots, are said to have revealed to humanity the secret arts of civilisation. The Book of Enoch tells us that their leader, Azazel, 'taught men to make swords, and knives, and shields, and breastplates, and made known to them the metals [of the earth] and the art of working them'. Azazel also instructed men on how to make 'bracelets' and 'ornaments', and showed them the use of 'antimony', a white brittle metal employed in medicine.[66] To women Azazel taught the art of 'beautifying' the eyelids, and the use of 'all kinds of costly stones' and 'colouring tinctures'.[67]

One is reminded here of the words spoken to Quetzalcoatl by the gods of Anahuac. Having failed to prevent him leaving for Tlapallan, they say: 'Go, then, happily, but leave us the secret of your art, the secret of founding in silver, of working in precious stones and woods, of painting, and of feather-working, and other matters.'[68]

The Watchers revealed to humanity other scientific matters as well. They included 'astrology', 'the knowledge of the clouds', the 'signs of the earth', even geodesy, geography and the 'signs' or passage of celestial bodies such as the sun and moon. Another of their leaders, Shemyaza, is accredited with having taught 'enchantments, and root-cuttings',[69] a reference to the occult practices shunned by orthodox Jews. One of their number, Pênêmûe, taught 'the bitter and the sweet', a reference to the use of herbs and spices in foods, while instructing men on the use of 'ink and paper', implying that, like Itzamna in the Yucatán, the Watchers introduced the earliest forms of writing.[70] More disturbing is Kâsdejâ, who is said to have shown 'the children of men all the wicked smitings of spirits and demons, and the smitings of the embryo in the womb, that it may pass away'.[71] In other words he taught women how to abort unborn foetuses.

Cradle of Civilisation

Although Hebrew textual accounts of the Watchers imply that they were supernatural or even angelic in origin, it can be shown that they were a quite human race that occupied the biblical land of Eden.[72] Although this might at first seem absurd, it is a fact that Eden was once a geographical region of the Near East. In the Book of Ezekiel, for instance, Eden is listed alongside 'Haran [Harran in northern Syria] and Canneh' and 'Assur [Assyria] and Chilmad' as one of the 'traffickers of Sheba'.[73] The author says that this far-off land dealt in exotic spices, gold, precious stones, 'choice wares' and 'chests of rich apparel'.[74]

Elsewhere I have demonstrated that the land of Eden corresponds with the politically sensitive country of the Kurds, located between the north Syrian coast of the Mediterranean and Lake Van. This huge inland sea, 96 kilometres in length and 56 kilometres in width, forms the border between Turkey and the former Soviet republic of Armenia. Legend asserts that beneath its watery depths lies the Garden of Eden, drowned at the time of the Great Flood.[75] In Kurdistan, Muslims, Jews and Christians all believe that Noah's Ark came to rest not on Mount Ararat, which they assert is a late invention, but on Al Judi, or Cudi Dag, a mountain located 104 kilometres south-east of Van.[76] I cite these legends in order to show how in Jewish religious tradition both the place of emergence of the human race, i.e. the Garden of Eden, and its point of re-emergence after the Great Flood were situated in far-off Kurdistan, where the earliest Semitic peoples almost certainly developed as early as the fourth or third millennium BC. It was only at the time of Abraham, *c.* 2000 BC, that the Jewish tribes departed Harran bound for the land of Canaan.

There is every reason to believe that, like the Feathered Serpents of Mesoamerican tradition, the Watchers were a ruling elite responsible for the development and organisation of the earliest Neolithic communities in the Near East – the traditional Cradle of Civilisation. As early as *c.* 8400–7600 BC, the Neolithic peoples at sites such as Nevali Çori and Çayönü in eastern Turkey constructed extraordinary megalithic complexes with carved standing stones, perfectly finished terrazzo floors and sculptured art.[77] More significantly, the very first advances in agriculture, metalworking, smelting, painted pottery, writing, alcoholic beverages, monetary tokens and jewellery manufacture all took place in this one small region of the globe between the tenth and sixth millennia BC.[78]

Even though the Book of Enoch tells us that the Watchers' descendants, the Nephilim, were destroyed in a conflagration and flood, it is clear that some of them must have survived, for in the Book of Numbers it states:

> And there we saw the Nephilim, the sons of Anak, which come of the Nephilim: and we were in our own sight as grasshoppers, and so we were in their sight.[79]

Elsewhere in the Book of Numbers the sons of Anak, or Anakim, are described as 'men of great stature' who inhabit Canaan.[80] Hebron, or Kirjath-arba, described as the 'chief city of the Anakim', is said to have been built by a Nephilim named Arba, 'the greatest man among the Anakim'.[81] Here they were finally attacked and defeated by Caleb and the forces of Joshua, the successor of Moses the Lawgiver, in *c.* 1250–1200 BC.[82]

Visage like a Viper

The great stature of the Watchers, Nephilim and Anakim is emphasised again and again.[83] Moreover, in the Book of Enoch, as well as in other 'Enochian' texts found among the corpus of Jewish literature known as the Dead Sea Scrolls, the Watchers are described more specifically. They are said to have been taller than any man,[84] or as tall as 'trees';[85] their long curly hair was 'white as wool';[86] their skin was 'whiter than snow',[87] or 'like white men',[88] and yet as 'red as a blooming of a rose',[89] while their eyes were said to glow like 'burning lamps'[90] and their faces bore a shining countenance 'like the sun'.[91] More important, their serpentine nature is also elaborated on.

In a fragmentary text found among the Dead Sea Scrolls known as the Book of Amram, there is an account of a dream-vision in which two Watchers appear to Amram, the father of Moses. '[One] of them,' the text informs us, 'was terr[i]fying in his appearance, [like a s]erpent, [his] c[loa]k many-coloured yet very dark . . . [And I looked again], and . . . in his appearance, his visage like a viper.'[92]

Elsewhere I have argued that the allusion to the Watcher possessing a 'visage like a viper', and having an appearance '[like a s]erpent', relates most probably to elongated facial features.[93] This alone would have made these individuals stand out among the more round-faced peoples that inhabited the Near East during this age. This is perhaps the most obvious explanation as to why the Nephilim were said to have borne many of the physical traits of their serpent fathers, and so became known as *awwim*, 'sons of serpents'.

Men with Feather Coats

More pertinent to our knowledge of the civilisers and wisdom-bringers of Mesoamerican tradition is the fact that, like Votan, the Watchers were linked strongly with bird imagery. The fragmentary account in the Book of Amram speaks of one of the Watchers as dressed in a 'c[loa]k many-coloured yet very dark'. In a text known as the Book of the Secrets of Enoch, written in Greek from a Hebrew original during the first century AD, there is a very similar account of a visitation of two Watchers, this time to the antediluvian patriarch Enoch. Here, when it talks about their attire, we are told: 'Their dress had the appearance of feathers: . . . [purple].'[94] Although it goes on to state that their wings were 'brighter than gold', theological scholars accept that such fantastic elements were added to existing texts by early Christian scribes.[95] Before this time the account would not have included any reference to wings.

The Nephilim, too, are connected with bird symbolism. For instance, in the Book of Giants the two sons of Shemyaza, one of the leaders of the Watchers, are said to have been associated 'not [with] the . . . eagle, but his wings',[96] while in the same breath the two brothers are described as 'in their nest'.[97] Statements such as these, and others like them, led Hebrew scholar J. T. Milik to conclude that the Nephilim of the Book of Giants 'could have been bird-men'.[98] That Votan's 'image represented him as a bird above and a serpent below' seems to link him firmly with the appearance of both the Watchers and their descendants the Nephilim.

The dark, irridescent nature of the feather coats worn by the Watchers would tend to suggest that they represented the plumage of a carrion bird, such as the vulture, which was seen as the ultimate symbol of death and rebirth among the formative Neolithic communities in the Near East. Early Neolithic art featuring the serpent and vulture together has been uncovered in the cult building at Nevali Çori dated to *c.* 8400–7600 BC, demonstrating that these were the preferred motifs of the ruling elite from very earliest times.[99]

The use of totemic forms, such as serpents and birds, has always been the domain of the shamans, the spirit walkers of tribal communities. In many early cultures the human soul was thought to take the form of a bird to make its flight from this world to the next, which is why it is often depicted as such in prehistoric art. Shamanic practices still continue today among various native peoples in many parts of the world.

Some idea of the shamanistic nature of Quetzalcoatl is gleaned from his association with the rattlesnake and quetzal bird. He was said to have been 'a species of snake, having a bunch of feathers on his head in the form of a plume; [and] at a given time, the snake would change itself into one of the green feathered birds which are found in a great number in the regions around Xicalanco'.[100] This clear transformation from snake to bird alludes to the altered states of consciousness achieved by shamans in order to attain astral flight. The Watchers and Nephilim of the Near East would have used the vulture and quite possibly other carrion or raptorial birds under very similar circumstances. Obviously, the beautiful quetzal bird would appear to have been the more natural choice as a totemic form for shamans in Mesoamerica.

Nephilim in the Americas

If Votan, along with his companions, really did originate in the ancient world, was it possible that he was a Nephilim, an *awwim*, one of the sons of the serpent in ancient Hebrew tradition? Could the other Feathered Serpents of Mesoamerican tradition also be of this same lost race? Was the priestly line of Chanes, or 'Serpents', as well as royal dynasties such as the Itzaes and Cocomes (*cocom* is the plural of the Nahuatl word *coatl*, 'snake') also descended from the Nephilim?

There is a clue to this last question in our knowledge of the Maya cult of the rattlesnake. The Maya historian José Diaz Bolio told British author Adrian Gilbert that the Chanes, or 'Serpents', insisted that the heads of newborn babies born into their community were deformed at birth using boards and wrappings to enable the child to become eligible for the priesthood when he came of age.[101] This was achieved in order to create an effect known as a polcan – a long serpentine head in memory of Ahau Can, 'the Great, Lordly Serpent'. Since the Chanes saw themselves as descendants of either Itzamna, the Serpent of the East, or Votan, the Son of the Serpent, is it possible that they, too, possessed extended facial features?

From the extraordinary appearance of enormous elongated skulls found at various sites in the Yucatán, particularly Merida, there is certainly a case for showing the presence among the peninsula's earliest inhabitants of individuals with oversized craniums, even without deformation.[102] Since this practice appears to have been exclusive to the Chane priesthood, it really does imply that these walking Serpents represented an ancestral line in which gigantism had been present.

Curiously enough, Toltec myth speaks clearly of a race of giants known as the Quinamés, Quinametin or Quinametl who ruled the country in its earliest days.[103] Yet having abandoned themselves to 'vices and luxury', the giants were finally vanquished by the Olmec, who thereafter dominated the region.[104]

Amazingly enough, head deformation of exactly the same kind was practised among the ruling elite of the Halaf and Ubaid peoples who occupied the Kurdish highlands and Fertile Plateau of Iraq from the sixth to the fourth millennia BC.[105] There seems every reason to believe that in doing so they were attempting to re-create the serpentine features of the Watchers. This seems to have been in order that they could claim lineal descendancy from these individuals who they saw as serpent-like in appearance.[106]

A further link between the Watchers and Nephilim of the ancient world and the People of the Serpent who entered Mexico is Edward H. Thompson's assertion that, like their Near Eastern counterparts, those who arrived at Tamoanchan by boat from the east were tall, fair-haired, light-skinned individuals.[107] Do we have here the recollection of a journey made to the New World by Nephilim from the eastern Mediterranean? Were the stories of the Quinames, the giants of Toltec myth, a memory of the Nephilim's presence in ancient Mexico? Remember, too, that the islanders of Tobago spoke of the Caribbean islands being inhabited originally by 'very, very big men',[108] while the 20 leaders who arrived out of the east with Kukulcan were said to have been 'dressed in long, flowing clothes and had big beards'.[109]

In Old Testament tradition there is much textual evidence to suggest that the Anakim, the last of the Nephilim, came up against Joshua as he attempted to take Canaan on behalf of the tribes of Israel.[110] Moreover, there is some evidence in the writings of Sumer and Akkad to indicate that the accounts of great battles being fought between mythical kings and demons dressed as bird-men might well preserve the distorted memory of actual conflicts against Nephilim-led tribes.[111] More significantly, these same accounts suggest that after their defeat the Nephilim disappeared from the pages of history.

Was it possible that certain Nephilim ended their days in the Americas? Was there any evidence from the ancient world to suggest that they were capable of making Atlantic sea-voyages? If this was so, what knowledge might they have gained concerning Cuba's role as a surviving remnant of lost Atlantis?

CHAPTER XXVI

RATTLING OF THE PLEIADES

WE HAVE ALREADY ENCOUNTERED THE work of Sanchoniathon of Berytus (Beirut), the earliest known Phoenician historian, who lived *c.* 1100 BC. His *Theology of the Phoenicians,* preserved in the writings of a first-century historian named Philo of Byblos, provides a fascinating account of the origins of the Phoenician race, whom he asserts inherited their maritime capability from a dynasty of gods that founded the city of Byblos.[1] These mythical individuals introduced civilised society, possessed 'light and other more complete ships',[2] and gave birth to many sons and daughters who bore the names of later Phoenician city-states and countries throughout the eastern Mediterranean. Their leader was Cronus (Saturn), the son of Coelus or Ouranus, the father of the six Titans and their six female counterparts, the Titanides. Sanchoniathon tells us that Coelus ruled Coele-Syria, a country that stretched from the Levant coast of the Lebanon to the eastern extremes of Syria.

Cronus, if we dare to presume he was ever human, is remembered for the power struggle he fought and lost against his son Zeus, the leader of the gods of Olympus. Some sources say that he was banished to Italy, where he civilised 'the barbarous manners of the people' and introduced agriculture.[3] Cronus' reign here was so peaceful and virtuous that it was remembered as the Golden Age. As an emblem, Cronus is shown holding a scythe 'with a serpent which bites its own tail, which is an emblem of time and of the revolution of the year'.[4]

In the wars against Zeus and the gods of Olympus, Sanchoniathon states that Cronus' 'auxiliaries' or 'allies' were the 'Eloeim',[5] a misspelling of Elohim, or the *bene ha-elohim,* the name given in the Old Testament to the Watchers and Nephilim.[6] If we might accept that Cronus' struggles with his son Zeus recall real events in the history of humankind, could it imply that the maritime gods of Byblos were allies of the Watchers and Nephilim?

In Greek myth the Nephilim are equated directly with the Titans, and Gigantes,[7] or 'Giants', who waged war on the gods of Olympus and, like Cronus, were said to have been the offspring of Coelus and Terra. For example, in the Greek Septuagint and in the King James Bible, the term Nephilim is substituted with the words Gigantes, or Giants. With this in mind, it is interesting to note that the Titans are supposed to have sided with Cronus against their father Coelus, the same role played by the 'Eloeim'. According to the various ancient writers,[8] a war also broke out between Cronus and his brother Titan, born to Coelus and Terra. Lactantius (AD 250–325), for instance, records that with the help of his brothers, Titan was able to imprison Cronus and hold him safe until Zeus was old enough to rule by himself.[9]

Westwards, in Hell

Family feuds between the titanic offspring of Coelus perhaps led to the final defeat of the Titans by Zeus and the other gods of Olympus. As punishment, they were banished to Tartarus, a mythical region of hell said to have been enclosed by a brazen wall and enshrouded perpetually by a cloud of darkness. The Gigantes, too, were linked with this terrible place, for they are cited by the first-century Roman writer Caius Julius Hyginus (*fl. c.* 40 BC) as having been the 'sons of Tartarus and Terra (i.e. the earth)'.[10] Although Tartarus has always been considered a purely mythical location, there is good reason to suggest that it was in fact synonymous with the prehistoric Iberian city-port of Tartessos (Tarshish of the Bible).

The evidence is this: Gyges, or Gyes, is said to have been a son of Coelus and Terra, and thus Cronus' own brother. He was also seen as both a Gigante and a Titan (demonstrating how originally their legends were interchangeable),[11] and so was a key figure in the wars fought against Zeus. Most curious of all, Gyges is said to have had 50 heads and 100 arms, which leads me to conclude that he is very probably the generic memory of a whole group of individuals.

Classical writers such as Ovid (43 BC–AD 18) wrote that, as punishment for the part he played in the wars against the gods of Olympus, Gyges was banished to the prison of Tartarus.[12] Yet an account of this same story preserved by a Chaldean writer named Thallus states that instead of being banished to Tartarus, Gyges was 'smitten, and fled to Tartessus'.[13] If this is a genuine rendition of the same story then it tells us that Tartarus was simply another name for Tartessos.

The prehistoric sea-port of Tartessos was situated on an island-like delta at the mouth of the Guadalquivir River, although no trace of its former existence remains today. What we do know is that it attained a high state of civilisation and traded extensively with Atlantic and Mediterranean ports. We also know that Tartessos had very ancient maritime origins. As we have seen, Elena M. Whishaw, in her *Atlantis in Andalucia*, describes the discovery of a complex of Neolithic 'galleried dolmens . . . temples, fortresses, hydraulic systems, and port and harbour works' at Niebla, near the site of ancient Tartessos.[14] It led her to conclude that an advanced maritime culture had occupied the Iberian peninsula as early as the 'Copper Age', *c.* 2500 BC. She also proposed that those responsible for this prehistoric sea-port made long-distance Atlantic journeys and were perhaps part of a trading colony belonging to the Atlantean island empire described by Plato.[15]

Is it possible that these various mythical accounts from Greece and Phoenicia imply that, after their defeat at the hands of Zeus and the gods of Olympus, the remaining Titans or Gigantes, i.e. the last of the Nephilim, were banished to Spain? Were they responsible for creating the sea-ports of Niebla and Tartessos, if indeed they were originally separate places? Did they achieve this with the aid of the god-like Byblos culture, which Sanchoniathon implies possessed 'light and more complete ships'? We certainly know that the Byblos culture had established trading links with Egypt and Crete as early as *c.* 3000 BC, and so why suppose that they did not reach Spain in the same epoch? More important, did Tartessos act as a springboard for the exploration of new territories outside the influence of those who had cast them into this prison on the edge of the known world?

There is yet further evidence which adds weight to the idea that the banished Titans may have ended their days in Tartessos. The Turdetans, the ancient race that inhabited the Iberian province of Baetia, of which Tartessos was the principal city and port, claimed to be of the same race as the Pelasgians, the earliest inhabitants of Greece.[16] Like the Nephilim, they were said to have been 'men of extraordinary stature . . . [and] that they were called Titans because they claimed to have been descended from the god Tis or Teut [the Phoenician god Taautus?]'.[17] This clearly shows that the founders of Tartessos believed themselves to be descendants of the Titans, through their link with the giant-like Pelasgians of ancient Greece.

In separate traditions the Titans were said to have been defeated by the gods of Olympus 'near the Straits of Hercules', demonstrating once again their association with south-west Spain.[18] However, it is important to point out that other claimants for the site of their celebrated defeat include 'Thrace, Italy and the south of Gaul'.[19]

Although there is no direct evidence for the presence of Nephilim in Spain, it is a fact that, even today, certain colloquial folk events in parts of the country feature men dressed entirely in feather coats. For instance, at a fiesta held at Piornal in the Cáceres province of central Spain, a bird-man, complete with pointed headdress and beak, becomes the subject of abuse as it goes through the streets beating a drum.[20] The presence of such bird-men is considered an intrusion to local lifestyle and thus a concerted attempt is made to drive them out of town. Where such ideas originate is beyond comprehension, although there has to be a chance that it is a racial memory of individuals who once walked among them dressed in exactly this manner.

The Confinement of Cronus

As we have seen from the biographer Plutarch's *The Face of the Moon*, for the part he played in the wars against his son Zeus, Cronus was banished out beyond the Pillars of Hercules, which once bore his name and not that of the Greek hero-god.[21] This knowledge is revealed during a discourse between Plutarch's grandfather Lamprias and a Carthaginian named Sextius Sulla on the nature of the moon and the soul. Sulla states that Ogygia, Homer's island, is five days' sail westwards of the British Isles.[22] Moreover, we learn also that beyond this even are three islands in the direction of the 'summer sunset', and that on one of these: 'Cronus is confined by Zeus, and the antique (Briareus), holding watch and ward over those islands and the sea . . . The great mainland ['continent'], by which the great ocean is encircled, while not so far from the other islands, is about five thousand stades from Ogygia, the voyage being made by oar.'[23]

As detailed in Chapter Seven, there is every reason to conclude that these three 'other' islands spoken of by Plutarch are synonymous with the three islands of 'immense extent' which Marcellus connected with the sunken Atlantean landmass. Furthermore, there is good reason to conclude that they are the three main islands of the Greater Antilles – Cuba, Hispaniola and Puerto Rico – reached, according to the account, via Britain and the Northwest Passage.

If these conclusions are correct, does it imply that Cronus, whoever or whatever he represents, eventually reached the Greater Antilles? Can we see in this supposed mythical account an echo of real events that might have occurred thousands of years before the advent of recorded history? If so, it hints at a line of transmission from the Mediterranean coast of Syria and Lebanon to the Greater Antilles, perhaps via the Spanish sea-port of Tartessos. More than this, it provides us with a working hypothesis that permits us to assume that some of the Nephilim, as Titans, banished to Tartessos, departed Iberia bound for the Americas.

There is a wealth of material which compares Bronze Age stone monuments of Western Europe, in particular those of the Iberian peninsula, with various examples attributed to either Amerindians or early colonial 'druids' in New England.[24] These include fine examples of dolmens, chambered barrows, stone circles and cairns of a type which closely resemble their European counterparts of *c.* 2500–1350 BC. Is it possible that Bronze, or indeed 'Copper', Age seafarers from the Iberian peninsula reached New England and other parts of the American continent during this early epoch?

On the Isle of Lewis in the Scottish Outer Hebrides, there is a curious legend told about those who built the famous stone circle at Callanish. It states that long ago a priest-king adorned in a robe of feathers, taken from the sun-bird, came to the island with a fleet of ships containing black men, and together they erected the famous Celtic cross-shaped monument.[25] Callanish is a quite extraordinary site that dates back to the early Bronze Age, *c.* 2800–2200 BC, possibly even earlier. Even if these individuals were not responsible for the construction of the stone circle, could this persisting legend recall the memory of feather-clad Nephilim arriving on the island in the company of black Africans, perhaps Lixitae from North Africa? Were they making a stopover before continuing their voyage towards the Northwest Passage?

Is it possible that the 'Dwelling Place of the Thirteen Snakes' encountered by Votan on his voyages to and from America was either the Iberian peninsula or one of the larger offshore islands of Britain? On some of these the number and arrangement of megalithic monuments often reflects a 12- or 13-fold division of land, focused around a central axis stone, or monument.[26] Even the main circle at Callanish is made up of 13 tall standing stones.

Cronus as Votan

Is the story of Cronus' banishment to the Island of Cronus tied in with Votan's arrival in Valum-Votan, the 'land of Votan', which Ordoñez identified as Cuba? Were the two simply abstract memories of transatlantic journeys made by Nephilim, working in concert with the Byblos culture, who went on to become the ruling elite of indigenous tribes both in Cuba and on the mainland? Should this surmise prove correct, when might these events have occurred?

The Phoenician sea-port of Gades in south-west Spain was founded *c.* 1100 BC, although Tartessos was probably established as a city-port much earlier. The power struggles between the Nephilim and the armies of Sumer and Akkad suggest a time-frame somewhere in the region of the last quarter of the third millennium BC, while the confrontations between the Anakim and the armies of Joshua took place *c.* 1250–1200 BC. After due consideration of the facts, a time-frame of 2200–1250 BC might be considered for the banishment of the Nephilim to Iberia and their subsequent journey to the Americas. If this was so, it could mean that the later Iberic Phoenicians of Gades inherited the knowledge of sea routes to America from their precursors, the Byblos culture and their assumed allies, the Nephilim. Whether they might have utilised the Northwest Passage or the North Equatorial Current via the Canary Isles is open to debate. Yet their destination would appear to have been the same – the Greater Antilles, Cuba in particular, and the fertile regions that lay beyond the Gulf coast of Mexico.

The Feathered Serpents

On his final journey to the American mainland, Votan would appear to have set out from Cuba. As this was obviously the name given to the island only after Votan's stay, it suggests that he established some kind of settlement here.

Since the most likely timescale for the proposed departure of the Nephilim from Iberia is *c.* 2200–1200 BC, can we conceive of their arrival in Cuba during this same period? These dates tie in very well with the emergence of Cuba's mound-building culture, which included the erection of stone and earthen monuments like those so familiar to Neolithic and Bronze Age cultures across Europe. Might we suggest that the Nephilim united the indigenous peoples, the Guayabo Blanco, and engaged their culture in a building programme to create an organised society with religious and administrative centres? Could this have been the prototype for what was to come on the American mainland? Did stage two of their development programme result eventually in the rise of major civilisations such as the Olmec, the Maya, the Toltecs and, finally, the Aztec Empire?

Perhaps the viper-faced Nephilim learned that the indigenous peoples of Cuba preserved a belief concerning an almighty cataclysm that had devastated the islands long ago. The visitors could have learned that a memory of these events was contained in the island's sacred caverns, which were also seen as places of emergence for the present human race. The most important of these grottoes was the decorated seven-fold cave located on the offshore island known today as the Isle of Youth. This one was special because it lay in the middle of the fertile plain submerged during the flood which accompanied the destruction.

Did the Nephilim visit this 'snake's hole' and take from it the bones of those considered to have drowned during the cataclysm? Did they also take other artefacts, such as the Giron-Gagal power stone, said to have been given to the Cakchiquel by the Feathered Serpent named Nacxit before their departure from Civán-Tulán?

Accompanied by representatives of the different clans or tribes from the island, we can conceive of Votan and his Nephilim cohorts journeying on to the Yucatec coast. Did they make landfall on the main island that borders the Lagoon de Terminos, where the Olmec and Xicalanca were said to have also first set foot on Mexican soil? Perhaps others of their race made their landfall at Tamoanchan, the Place Where the Serpent People Landed, at the mouth of the Panuco river, or even in Florida or on the Gulf coast of North America. Was it from such locations that the Feathered Serpents, the sons of the Watchers, began their mission to civilise and rule this rich and fertile world so far away from their own? In time their descendants would continue the association with the serpent, becoming the Chane, or Serpent, priesthood in Mesoamerica and, just possibly, the Shawano Eagle-serpent people who ruled the mound-building cultures of North America.

Was it because of Cuba's former significance as a staging post into the Gulf of Mexico during the Early Bronze Age that some knowledge of its topography and indigenous mythology reached Tartessos in Spain? Had it been Turdetan descendants of the Titans, or Nephilim, who passed on knowledge of Cuba's maritime importance to the later Iberic Phoenicians and Carthaginians, who occupied Tartessos after *c.* 1100 BC? Is this why English archaeologist Elena Whishaw became convinced that the 'Copper Age' sea-port of Niebla was part of a trading colony belonging to the Atlantean empire described by Plato in the *Timaeus* and *Critias*? If so, it strengthens still further Cuba's claim to be the jewel in the crown of Plato's Atlantis.

The Day of the Dead

That Ahau-Can, the Great, Lordly Serpent of the Yucatec Maya, was personified as the rattlesnake had other connotations as well. The *Chilam Balam of Chumayel* spoke of an almighty cataclysm during which the 'Great Serpent' was 'ravished from the heavens, together with the rattles of its tail', so that its 'skin and pieces' of its 'bones fell here upon the Earth'.[27] Since we know that in Maya astronomy the seven stars of the Pleiades were viewed as its seven-fold rattle, does this imply that the celestial serpent responsible for the destruction that brought to a close the previous world age originated from the direction of the Pleiades? This is certainly a conclusion that has been drawn by some catastrophe theorists.[28] Could it be that so no one would ever forget the direction from which the fiery serpent had emerged, the stars that marked its position became the rattles of the snake that warns its potential victim of an imminent strike?

Other cultures of the western hemisphere would also seem to have preserved a memory of how the fiery serpent that brought destruction in previous world ages was intimately connected with the Pleiades constellation. For example, the Caliña Carib tribe of the Surinam (formerly Dutch Guiana) on the north-east coast of South America believe in a supreme being called Amana, a virgin mother and water-goddess who has 'no navel' and is 'a beautiful woman whose body ends in a serpent. She is the essence of time, has borne all things . . . and exercises her power from the Pleiades. She is also called a serpent spirit and a sun serpent . . . She renews herself continually, by sloughing her skin like a snake.'[29] Amana gave birth to twin brothers, Tamusi and Yolokan Tamulu, the first born at dawn, the other at dusk, making us recall the similar roles played by Quetzalcoatl and Xolotl.

Of the two, Tamusi became the principal god of the Caliña Caribs, and like his mother he ruled from the Pleiades. His adversaries, the fiends, were signified by a celestial serpent 'which has already several times devoured the Pleiades and thus brought the world to an end. Each time Tamusi created the world anew, and he will do so once again.'[30] According to one Guianan Carib tribe this destruction took the form of 'a great fire and a deluge' sent by the god Purá,[31] and we have already seen how the Antilian Caribs saw these cataclysms as having split apart a former island landmass.

It seems that those who inhabited the land of Anahuac came to fear the arrival of another fiery snake that would once again emerge from the Pleiades and destroy the world. So much so that at the beginning of November each year, when the Pleiades rose in the evening for the first time, the Aztec priests would appease the great snake with human sacrifice when at midnight it reached its zenith.[32] This gruesome ceremony was implemented so that they would never forget that on this day in some past epoch 'the world had been previously destroyed', since 'they dreaded lest a similar catastrophe would, at the end of a cycle, annihilate the human race'.[33]

This, I believe, was the knowledge preserved in the seven-fold design of Chicomoztoc, the Seven Caves, and reaffirmed on the American mainland by Votan and the other Feathered Serpents. This is why so much seven-fold symbolism is connected with universal catastrophe myths, and not because the incoming comet broke into seven pieces as has been proposed by the Tollmanns. If this is true, then some knowledge of the fiery serpent that once destroyed the world should already have been known to the Nephilim. Age-old Hebrew folklore asserts that the Great Flood was caused after 'the upper waters rushed through the space left when God removed two stars out of the constellation Pleiades'.[34] More extraordinary still is the fact that the Jews believed this event had occurred on a date corresponding in the Gregorian calendar with 17 November.[35] Nineteenth-century mythologist

R. G. Haliburton, who made a special study of the Pleiades in myths and legends worldwide, found it beyond coincidence that separate races on two different continents honoured the catastrophe that brought about the Great Flood in the very same calendar month. He therefore proposed a common origin for this belief in a global catastrophe connected quite specifically with the constellation of the Pleiades.[36]

Plato himself, in the preamble leading up to his account of the destruction of Atlantis as given in the *Timaeus*, states: 'There have been, and will be hereafter, many and diverse destructions of mankind, the greatest by fire and water.'[37] He goes on to say that the primary cause of such conflagrations and floods 'is a deviation of the bodies that revolve in heaven round the earth',[38] an allusion to the passage of comets, such as Phaeton, the 'child of the sun', that 'once harnessed his father's chariot but could not guide it on his father's course and so burnt up everything on the face of the earth'.[39] Whether or not he realised it himself, Plato was alluding to the Carolina bays comet that may well have brought to a close the glacial age and, in 'one terrible day and night', devastated Atlantis with 'earthquakes and floods'.

Our maritime journey is over. It has been a long and arduous one. Yet having passed through the gateway towards Atlantis we can see now that the voyage of discovery is an ancient one. Indeed it has shown us the reality of Plato's Atlantic island. Yet it does far more than this, for our new understanding of his tale reveals unexpected dangers and perils that the world might one day face again.

When Plato wrote about the tragedy of Atlantis, he was trying to warn his own and future generations of their precarious existence. If this is so, then the Hollywood scriptwriters of apocalyptic action films have been trying to do much the same thing – using a fictional situation based on reality to warn us that one day it could happen for real. The big difference here is that the superhero is able to save the world, giving us hope that when a global killer does finally threaten the earth we will have the means and know-how to prevent it from wreaking its destruction. Today we still search for that capability. Yet what seems blatantly clear is that if it had not been for Plato's Atlantis account, and the understanding of catastrophe myths it has taught us, we might still have been in the dark when the lights go out for ever. Let us hope that we ourselves never live to hear the rattling of the Pleiades.

APPENDIX I

THE COLOUR PURPLE

We accredit the Phoenicians as being the pioneers of the trade in purple dye and know that knowledge of its extraction from the murex shellfish died out long before the Spanish reached the New World. The presence in 1440 of 'purple hats and purple trains' in the court of Byzantium is its last known mention in the ancient world.[1] After this time the processes involved were all but forgotten in Europe (although it has been speculated that Scottish and Norse fishermen used a species of North Sea shellfish to dye linen between the sixteenth and eighteenth centuries).[2]

Then in 1648 an English Dominican named Thomas Cage reported that the natives of Nivoya, on the Pacific coast of Costa Rica, extracted purple dye from shellfish by rubbing them together.[3] Apparently, Cage 'regarded this Indian product as comparable to the purple of the Ancients'.[4] Like the Mediterranean world, the cost of the purple textiles produced by this process was extremely high, with Cage recording that in the equivalent of English money a yard of purple cost around £8.[5]

A century later two Spanish scientists, the brothers George and Antonio de Ulloa, alongside a Frenchman named Condamine, were surveying St Elena, near Guyaquil, on the Pacific coast of Ecuador, when they, too, noticed the native peoples extracting a purple dye from shellfish. According to the Ulloas it was used for ribbons, lace, 'and for fancy sewing and embroidery. All such goods are highly prized, owing to the rare and beautiful colour.'[6]

America's surviving trade in purple dye extraction went relatively unnoticed until it was properly recorded for the first time by the nineteenth-century German zoologist Professor Ernst von Martens in his 1874 book *Purpura und Perlen* (*Purple and Pearls*). He found that the juice of the purpura shellfish was being used to dye textiles in the district of Tehuantepec, close to the Pacific coast of southern Mexico, a practice that had been recorded a century beforehand by the explorers Edward and Cecily Seler.[7] He also found that purple skirts and purple-striped shawls were being made by the Huave Indians who lived to the south-west of Tehuantepec. Von Martens was later able to examine fragments of pre-Columbian textiles in the Berlin Museum of Ethnology. He found that those produced by the Huave Indians were exactly the same shade as the items on display, including a robe from Peru.[8] In addition to this, he found that purple dyes were still being used by the native peoples of Costa Rica.[9]

Von Martens determined that the type of shellfish used to produce the purple dyes in Mexico and Costa Rica was not from the murex family. It was in fact a species of purpura, native to the Pacific coast of Central America, known as *Purpura haemastoma*, which, curiously enough, had also been important to the purple dye industry of the eastern Mediterranean.[10] He therefore concluded that the extraction of dyes from shellfish in the Americas was extremely old and had not been introduced to the New World after the time of the Conquest.[11]

It was, however, American ethnologist Zelia Nuttall who first realised the full significance of von Martens' findings. In an important article published in 1909 she acknowledged his early work in this field and drew direct comparisons between the lost purple industry of the Mediterranean and that present among the native peoples of Mexico. She also visited the native Tehuantepec Indians and found that cotton strands used in the dyeing process were first sent to Huamelula, a small town on the Pacific coast. Here fishermen in small vessels would row up and down the coast during the month of March looking for shellfish. On being found, they were removed from the wet rocks and blown on, an act that would make them discharge their dye. A strand of cotton would then be dabbed into the resulting milky substance of as many shellfish as it would take to saturate it, a time-consuming process that ensured a very high price for both purple textiles and finished garments.[12]

Obviously this method of dye-extraction was ecologically sound, as it did not harm the shellfish. After use, they would either be replaced on the rocks or dropped in a large bowl of water so that they could be removed again and used to produce a second, though much weaker, discharge. In the Mediterranean the processes of extraction were somewhat different. Shellfish would be collected in their thousands and then boiled to release the milky substance (which turned green and then purple on exposure to sunlight), something that was unavoidable as it was much more difficult to make the murex shellfish discharge its dye. Ancient writers noted that this method of extraction produced a foul smell, which was also noticed by Zelia Nuttall on purple skirts she examined at

Tehuantepec. Mrs Nuttall concluded that the survival of purple dyeing in Mexico stemmed originally from 'the ancient European tradition', which we know originated with the Phoenicians of the Levant.[13]

Quite clearly, the presence of purple dye processes in Costa Rica, Mexico and Ecuador, as well as in Peru, could well constitute positive proof of transoceanic contact with ancient seafarers from the eastern Mediterranean. Indeed, this is exactly what some open-minded scholars have concluded. In 1937 Wolfgang Born, a specialist in shellfish dyes, wrote that: 'It is impossible that so many similarities should be accidental; a common source of the two civilizations must therefore be assumed, and there is no doubt that the purple-industry of Central America is derived from that of the Mediterranean people.'[14] Furthermore, Thomas Crawford Johnston, in his book *Did the Phoenicians Discover America?*, published in 1913, wrote: 'There is probably no stronger evidence of the presence of the Phoenician in the New World than can be drawn from the use of dyes [especially purpura].'[15]

Phoenician manufacturers guarded closely the processes involved with the extraction of purple dye from the murex shellfish. It is unlikely, therefore, that similar processes developed independently in other parts of the world, due to the very specialised nature of the methods involved. It is more reasonable to assume that existent manufacturers of purple dye exchanged their skills with foreign cultures, knowing that they would never encounter their own trading rivals.

Supporters of transpacific contact with the American continent will propose that the presence of purple dye manufacturing processes in ancient Japan is evidence that it was introduced to the Americas from Southeast Asia.[16] On the other hand, it is equally feasible that if some form of transpacific, cross-cultural contact was occurring at this time, the extraction of purple dye from shellfish could have been introduced to traders from Southeast Asia by native Amerindians, who had themselves gained this knowledge from Phoenicians and Carthaginians. This is surely a far more reasonable solution, and one that also fits the available facts.

APPENDIX II

COTTON MATTERS

WHEN CHRISTOPHER COLUMBUS AND HIS crewmen first reached Cuba in October 1492, they found that the islanders cultivated not just maize – the first time this cereal had ever been seen, handled and eaten by Europeans – but also tobacco and, more important, cotton. From it the Amerindians would weave nets and beds, as well as undergarments for women. In one house alone, '12,500 pounds' of woven cotton was found stored. In fact, it was present in such great quantities that huge basketfuls were exchanged with Spanish crewmen for simple items such as leather thongs.[1]

When during the first half of the sixteenth century the Spaniards pushed forwards into Mexico and Peru they also found cotton being grown and woven. This was considered a curious discovery, for in the Old World cotton had also been cultivated, spun and made into cloth using very similar processes for thousands of years. Archaeologists later determined that the earliest appearance of cotton in the Americas was during the third millennium BC, primarily among the Huaca Prieta culture of northern Peru.[2]

The presence of cotton in the New World prior to the time of the Conquest was an enigma that perplexed Sir Joseph Burtt Hutchinson, a distinguished botanical scientist, and his two colleagues, R. A. Silow and S. G. Stephens. Could it be possible that there might be some relationship between the cultivated cotton of the ancient world and the domesticated species present in the Americas? Research began into the genetic relationship between the various species of cotton, and very quickly this work produced some remarkable results. The three scientists found that both wild and domestic cotton present in the Old World has 13 *large* chromosomes, while a wild species found growing naturally in certain parts of the Americas has 13 *small* chromosomes. Yet the cotton samples taken from textile fragments removed from grave sites belonging to the Huaca Prieta peoples of northern Peru were found to possess 26 chromosomes – 13 large ones and 13 small ones.[3] The same results were achieved from samples of domesticated cotton from other parts of the Americas, and also from certain Polynesian islands in the Pacific (unquestionably introduced through trade with the Americas). The implications of these findings are enormous, for they tell us that the variety of cotton cultivated in the New World from very earliest times is a hybrid form derived from an Old World species crossed with species native only to the American continent.[4]

The scientists were at a loss to determine exactly how these quite separate strains of the cotton plant could have been cross-fertilised in this manner. Perhaps it had been introduced via early human migrations across the Bering Strait land-bridge that once linked together the continents of Asia and America.[5] Yet this theory is simply not tenable, for the land-bridge submerged following the rise in the sea-level at the end of the last Ice Age thousands of years before the domestication of cotton in the New World.

Like so much found on the isolated American continent, cotton from the ancient world can only have been introduced to the Americas through transoceanic contact, either via the Indus Valley, China and the Pacific or across the Atlantic. Exactly which route it might have taken is still a matter of personal opinion among diffusionists. However, it is worth noting that in Peru the spindle whorls and looms used in the weaving process, along with the high-quality loincloths and cloaks made from spun cotton, were all found to have striking similarities to their equivalents in the ancient Mediterranean world.[6] It is therefore conceivable that the cotton industry was introduced to the Americas by traders from the Mediterranean.

Since we know that at the time of the Conquest cotton was found growing only in Peru, Mexico and the West Indies, what possible relationship might there have been between these three quite separate regions of the New World? I have argued for a three-way trading cartel existing between the Chavín of Peru, the Olmec of Mexico and the Phoenicians (and later the Carthaginians). Did this trade exchange also extend to the West Indies? Remember both maize and tobacco were present in the West Indies at the time of the Conquest, suggesting perhaps that they, too, had been introduced from the mainland. Were the islands of the West Indies ports of call for Atlantic voyagers, perhaps on their way to or from the Gulf coast of Mexico? Might it have been through contact with this proposed trading cartel that the Phoenicians and Carthaginians gained confirmation of the cataclysms that the indigenous Amerindians believed had broken up the great landmass and created the individual island groups?

POSTSCRIPT

GATEWAY TO *ATLANTIS* IS ONE of the new genre of scholarly works that are now challenging our accepted views of the past. If, through reading this book, it has inspired you to begin your own investigations into the mysteries of Atlantis, transoceanic contact in ancient times or the Watchers of the Book of Enoch, or if it simply makes you question our current understanding of history, then it has achieved its aim.

If you wish to take these matters further, may I suggest you review the selected book list and bibliography. Almost all the titles are available through the library Interloan service. Ask your local librarian for details.

Should you feel that you can add to our understanding of the subjects under discussion in this book, and/or you wish to be kept informed of future publications, conferences, tour expeditions, or simply new developments in the field of ancient history, write to Andrew Collins at PO Box 189, Leigh-on-Sea, Essex SS9 1NF. Also why not visit Eden – the Andrew Collins website at www.andrewcollins.net for exclusive articles, new material and further insights into *Gateway to Atlantis* and other related topics.

RECOMMENDED BOOK LIST

Allan, D. S., and J. D. Delair, *When the Earth Nearly Died,* 1995
Babcock, William H., *Legendary Islands of the Atlantic,* 1922
Braghine, Col. A., *The Shadow of Atlantis,* 1940
Camp, L. Sprague de, *Lost Continents,* 1954
Collins, Andrew, *From the Ashes of Angels,* 1996
Collins, Andrew, *Gods of Eden,* 1998
Donnelly, Ignatius, *Ragnarok: The Age of Fire and Gravel,* 1886
Fell, Barry, *America BC,* 1976
Irwin, Constance, *Fair Gods and Stone Faces,* 1963
Ramage, Edwin S., *Atlantis: Fact or Fiction?,* 1978
Savage, H., Jnr, *The Mysterious Carolina Bays,* 1982
Spence, Lewis, *Atlantis in America,* 1925
Stacy-Judd, Robert B., *Atlantis – Mother of Empires,* 1939
Tompkins, Peter, *Mysteries of the Mexican Pyramids,* 1976
Van Sertima, Ivan, *They Came Before Columbus,* 1976
Whishaw, E. M., *Atlantis in Andalucia,* 1929

For full details see the Bibliography

NOTES AND REFERENCES

Notes: cf.= carried from; fn.= footnote; npn.= no page number; pl.= plate.

Introduction

1 Lawton and Ogilvie-Herald, p. 4.

One: The Old Priest Speaks

1 The chronology and reigns of all Egyptian kings are taken from Gardiner, *Egypt of the Pharaohs*.

2 Herodotus, *History*, 2. 177. For a further discussion on Solon's visit to Egypt, see Freeman, *The Work and Life of Solon*, pp. 155–7, 179–85; Forsyth, *Atlantis: The Making of Myth*, pp. 37–40.

3 Plato, *Timaeus*, 22b. The English translation of the *Timaeus* used in the text is that of F. M. Cornford from his definitive work entitled *Plato's Cosmology*. This was chosen for its concise English and standard referencing system.

4 Ibid.

5 Ibid., 22c.

6 Ibid., 22e.

7 Ibid., 23b.

8 Ibid., 23b–23c.

9 Plutarch, *Lives*, 'Solon', p. 69.

10 Plato, *Timaeus*, 23c.

11 Ibid., 23e–24a.

12 Ibid., 24e.

13 Ibid.`

14 Ibid.

15 Ibid.

16 Camp, *Lost Continents: The Atlantis Theme in History, Science, and Literature*, p. 28.

17 See, for example, Allen, *Atlantis: The Andes Solution*, pp. 9–10, 15; Zapp and Erikson, *Atlantis in America: Navigators of the Ancient World*, pp. 142–3.

18 Plato, *Timaeus*, 24e.

19 Pseudo-Aristotle, *De Mundo*, 3, 392b.

20 Camp, p. 293.

21 Pseudo-Aristotle, 3, 392b.

22 Ibid.

23 Aelian, *Historical Miscellany*, III, xviii.

24 Ibid.

25 Ibid.

26 Ibid.

27 Ibid.

28 Ibid.

29 Ibid.

30 Strabo, *Geography* I, iv, 6.

31 Ibid.

32 Plato, *Timaeus*, 24e.

33 Ibid., 25a.

34 Ibid.

35 Ibid., 25a–25b.

36 Ibid., 23e.

37 Ibid.

38 Plato, *The Laws*, 656E–657A.

39 Gardiner, *The Royal Canon of Turin*, pl. 1, c. 2, ll. 1–9. Many thanks to Dr Bill Manley and David Rohl for examining the original Egyptian text and translating these figures on my behalf.

40 Ibid. The characters here are damaged, so the exact figure is unclear.

41 Manetho, a priest of the city of Heliopolis who lived in the third century BC, spoke of a period of 36,525 years before the ascent of Menes, the first dynastic king (Manetho, *De Myst.*, 8, c. 1 in Cory, *Ancient Fragments*, p. 95 fn.), while the Greek historian named Herodotus (484–408 BC) observed in his Canon of the Kings that 11,340 years had elapsed since the rule of the first pharaoh (Herodotus, 'Canon of the Kings of Egypt', in Cory, p. 171).

42 Ammianus Marcellinus, *The Roman History of Ammianus Marcellinus*, 22, xvi, 21.

43 Ibid., 22, xvi, 22.

44 Plato, *Timaeus*, 24d.

45 Ibid., 25b.

46 Ibid., 25c.

47 Ibid., 25b–25c.

48 Ibid., 25c–25d.

Two: Egyptian Heritage

1 Plutarch, *Lives*, 'Solon', p. 69.

2 Ibid., p. 72.

3 Ibid., pp. 69–70.

4 Herodotus, *History*, 2.169–171, 175.

5 Ibid., 2.177.

6 Plutarch, *Isis and Osiris*, 354d–e.

7 Ammianus Marcellinus, *The Roman History of Ammianus Marcellinus*, 22, xvi, 22.

8 See, for example, Gamboa, *History of the Incas*, p. 25. He, however, makes different calculations based on events in the Bible and his own knowledge of the life of Solon.

9 Griffiths, 'Atlantis and Egypt', in Griffiths, *Atlantis and Egypt with other Selected Essays*, pp. 11–12, after the work of Max Pieper.

10 For a full account of the dating of the Thera eruption, see Phillips, *Act of God*, pp. 227–32.

11 Ibid., p. 214.

12 Ibid., p. 217.

13 Ibid., pp. 217–18, 220–22.

14 Griffiths, p. 12, after the work of Max Pieper; Galanopoulos and Bacon, *Atlantis: The truth behind the legend*, p. 96.

15 See, for example, Luce, *The End of Atlantis: New Light on an Old Legend;* Galanopoulos and Bacon; and Mavor, *Voyage to Atlantis.*

16 Galanopoulos and Bacon, pp. 38, 170.

17 Ibid., pp. 132–4.

18 Griffiths, p. 20.

19 Plato, *Timaeus*, 24e.

20 Bramwell, *Lost Atlantis*, p. 137.

21 Galanopoulos and Bacon, pp. 96–7.

22 Zangger, *The Flood from Heaven: Deciphering the Atlantis Legend*, p. 109; Servius, *In Vergilii Aeneidos librvm sextvm commentarivs*, XI, 262, in *Servii Grammatici qvi fervntvr*, vol. 2.

23 Zangger, for a full account of the author's view that Troy was Atlantis.

24 Fears, 'The Historical Perspective', in Ramage, *Atlantis: Fact or Fiction?*, p. 131.

25 Plato, *Timaeus*, 25d.

26 Ashe, *Land to the West: St Brendan's Voyage to America*, p. 135.

27 Pseudo-Scylax, *Periplus*, 112, English translation from Nordenskiöld, *Periplus: An Essay on the Early History of Charts and Sailing-Directions*, p. 8.

28 Ibid.

29 Aristotle, *Meteorologica* II, i, 354a.

30 Avienus, *Ora Maritima*, ll. 114–132. Translation from the Latin original by Ann Deagon. See also ll. 405–415: 'For the most part, beyond extends a shallow road-stead, so that it barely conceals the underlying sands. Frequent seaweed projects above the shoals, and here the tide is impeded by the

swamp. A power of sea monsters swims through the whole sea, and a great terror of wild creatures inhabits the narrows. Long ago Himilco the Carthaginian reported that he himself had seen and proved these things upon the ocean. We have set down for you at great length these things derived from the deepest annals of the Carthaginians.'

31 *The New Encyclopedia Britannica*, Vol. 10, s.v. 'Sargasso Sea', p. 452.

32 Columbus, *The Life of the Admiral Christopher Columbus by his Son Ferdinand*, p. 69.

33 Ibid., pp. 69–70.

34 Ibid.

35 Babcock, *Legendary Islands of the Atlantic: A Study in Medieval Geography*, p. 29.

36 Columbus, p. 70.

37 Craton, *A History of the Bahamas*, pp. 43–4.

38 Hosea, 'Atlantis: A Statement of the "Atlantic" Theory Respecting Aboriginal Civilisation', *The Cincinnati Quarterly Journal of Science*, Vol. II, no. 3, July 1875, p. 198.

39 *The New Encyclopedia Britannica*, Vol. 10, s.v. 'Sargasso Sea', p. 452.

40 Honorius of Autun, in Ashe, *Land to the West: St Brendan's Voyage to America*, p. 139.

41 Plato, 25d.

42 Ashe, pp. 170–72.

43 Ibid., p. 172.

44 Kurlansky, *Cod: A Biography of the Fish that Changed the World*, p. 29.

45 There are countless instances of Roman coins being found in New England, and one of the most compelling cases concerns the alleged discovery of Roman relics on a beach at Plum Island, Massachusetts. Two young men, Al Locke and Sheldon Lane, were out metal-detecting after a particularly violent storm when they came across a large piece of waterlogged wood, which they presumed had been dislodged from the sea bottom. Unexpectedly, it gave a positive reading. On inspection the men found that a partially worn bronze coin, the size of a silver dollar (a British tenpence piece), was embedded in the wood. They found that the wood also contained two ship spikes some 15 centimetres long and cast from bronze. Later it was determined that the coin was a Roman Setterii, bearing the head of the emperor Severus Alexander, murdered in AD 235 (Cahill, *New England's Ancient Mysteries*, p. 14). The discovery attracted local publicity, and subsequently it transpired that a local coin dealer named Peter Pratt had also found a bronze Roman Setterii of the third century while metal-detecting in the same area of Plum Island (ibid.).

In addition to Roman coins, a number of terracotta amphorae, either of Iberian or Carthaginian origin, have been found at various locations in New England. For instance, two intact examples were pulled out of the waters of Castine Bay, Maine, by scuba-diver Norwood Bakeman. At first he was unsure of the significance of the discovery, although on being examined by American epigrapher and prehistorian Jim Whittall, they were formally identified as 'Spanish olive jars' (ibid., p. 15). He found that they showed 'wear from constant chafing, caused by the rolling of the vessel on long journeys at sea while the jars were secured by lines to the deck or in the hold' (ibid., p. 15). More Iberian amphorae were dredged up from a depth of 36 metres by the nets of a fishing vessel out of Newburyport in 1991 (ibid., p. 15). Other examples have also been found at Boston, Massachusetts, and Jonesboro, Maine (ibid.).

Evidence of an Iberic Phoenician and Carthaginian presence in Massachusetts has come with the discovery of coins, oil lamps and sword blades of various dates (see Chapter Ten).

In addition to the discovery of various out-of-place artefacts, there exists a whole range of inscribed stones that are considered to be evidence of pre-Columbian contact with North America. One such stone was found as early as 1658 being used as a stepping stone into an Indian church on a reservation at Bourne, near Cape Cod, Massachusetts (ibid., pp. 9–10; Reader's Digest, *The World's Last Mysteries*, p. 55). In size it is 1.5 metres in length and 4.5 metres wide, while its underside bears a curious inscription. For hundreds of years no one could interpret it, but then it came to the notice of Barry Fell. He determined that its strange characters were Iberian, a language developed by the Phoenician colonists of south-west Spain. After carefully translating the stone's short inscription, he concluded that the message read: 'A proclamation of annexation. Do not deface. By this Hanno takes possession' (Fell, *America BC: Ancient Settlers in the New World*, pp. 95, 160–61).

Academics were not entirely convinced by Fell's findings, since it was assumed that the Hanno in question was the Carthaginian general and navigator who attempted to circumnavigate Africa with a fleet of 60 ships and 30,000 men around 425 BC (see Chapter Five). Yet there is no reason to make this conclusion. The inscription does not say which Hanno was responsible for its carving. Furthermore, we know that Hanno was a common name in Carthage, for at least two others are recorded – both Carthaginian commanders who lived in the second half of the third century BC.

Many other inscribed stones have been unearthed across the United States. There are simply too many to list individually, but some are incontestable and imply that foreign visitors from various different cultures travelled to the Americas and left their mark in a number of different ways. See McGlone et al, *Ancient American Inscriptions: Plow Marks or History?*

46 See Koudriavtsev, *Atlantis: Ice Age Civilisation*.

47 See, for example, Ashe, p. 139.

48 Zhirov, *Atlantis – Atlantology: Basic Problems*, pp. 179–85.

49 O'Brien & O'Brien, *The Shining Ones*, pp. 438–41.

50 Ibid., pp. 436–8.

51 Ibid., p. 439.

52 Ibid.

53 Ibid., p. 441.

54 Ibid.

55 Ibid.

56 Personal conversations with Edmund Marriage, nephew of Christian and Barbara Joy O'Brien, in May 1998.

57 Babcock, p. 78, cf. A. S. Brown, *Guide to Madeira and the Canary Islands (with notes on the Azores)*, 5th edn., London, 1898, p. 148.

Three: The Atlanticus

1 Camp, *Lost Continents: The Atlantis Theme in History, Science, and Literature*, p. 210; Chambers, *The History and Motives of Literary Forgeries*, p. 11.

2 Chambers, p. 11.

3 Ashe, *Atlantis: Lost Lands, Ancient Wisdom*, p. 26.

4 Proclus, *The Commentaries of Proclus on the Timaeus of Plato, etc.*, Vol. 1, p. 168.

5 Proclus, Vol. 1, p. 169.

6 Plato, *Critias*, 108e. The English translation of the *Critias* employed in this book is that of A. E. Taylor from his *Plato: Timaeus and Critias.*

7 Ibid.

8 Ibid., 108e–109a.

9 Ibid., 112e.

10 Ibid., 113a–113b.

11 Ibid., 113b.

12 Ibid.

13 Ibid., 113c.

14 Ibid.

15 Ibid., 113d.

16 Ibid., 113e.

17 Ibid.

18 Ibid.

19 Ibid., 114a.

20 Ibid.

21 Ibid.

22 Lemprière, *A Classical Dictionary*, s.v. 'Neptunus', pp. 391–2.

23 Ibid.

24 Plato, *Critias*, 114b.

25 Ibid.

26 Lemprière, s.v. 'Gades', pp. 243–4.

27 See Schulten, *Tartessos, ein Beitrag zur altesten Geschichte des Westerns.*

28 Plato, *Critias*, 114c.

29 Plato, *Timaeus*, 25a.

30 Ibid., 24e.

31 Plato, *Critias*, 114d–114e.

32 Ibid., 114e.

33 Ibid., 116c.

34 Ibid., 114e.

35 Zhirov, *Atlantis – Atlantology: Basic Problems*, pp. 46–7.

36 Plato, *Critias*, 114e.

37 Donato, *A Re-examination of the Atlantis Theory*, p. 46, after K. O. Emery in *Oceanus* magazine, Hansen, p. 399.

38 Newby, *Warrior Pharaohs*, p. 77.

39 Reeves and Wilkinson, *The Complete Valley of the Kings*, p. 77.

40 Plato, *Critias*, 115a–115b.

41 Vaughan and Geissler, *The New Oxford Book of Food Plants*, p. 22; Corner, *The Natural History of Palms*, pp. 290–91.

42 Heyerdahl, *Early Man and the Ocean*, pp. 218–19.

43 Ibid., after the work of H. P. Guppy.

44 Ibid., p. 219.

45 Kelly and Dachille, *Target: Earth – The Role of Large Meteors in Earth Science*, p. 253.

46 Plato, *Critias*, 115b–115c.

47 Ibid., 115d–116a.

48 Ibid., 116c.

49 Ibid.

50 Ibid.

51 Ibid., 116e.

52 Ibid., 117a.

53 Ibid., 117b.

54 Ibid., 117b–117c.

55 Ibid., 117c–117d.

56 Ibid., 118d–118e.

57 Ibid., 117e.

Four: The View Over Atlantis

1 Plato, *Critias*, 117e–118a. The English translation of the *Critias* quoted in this book gives the measurements in furlongs, whereas the original Greek text provides them in stadia. To confirm the original measurements I consulted the edition of the *Critias* translated into English by Henry Davis in 1849.

2 Ibid., 118a.

3 Ibid., 118b.

4 Ibid., 118c–118d.

5 Ibid., 119c.

6 Ibid., 119d.

7 Ibid., 119e.

8 Ibid., 120a.

9 Ibid., 120b.

10 Ibid.

11 Thucydides, *The History of the Peloponnesian War*, 1, 4.

12 Camp, *Lost Continents: The Atlantis Theme in History, Science, and Literature*, pp. 187–8.

13 See, for example, Mavor, *Voyage to Atlantis*, pl. 23b.

14 Lemprière, *A Classical Dictionary*, s.v. 'Neptunus', pp. 391–2.

15 Camp, p. 188.

16 Ibid.

17 Plato, *Critias*, 121b–121c.

18 Babcock, *Legendary Islands of the Atlantic: A Study in Medieval Geography*, p. 3.

19 Forsyth, *Atlantis: The Making of Myth*, pp. 172–3.

20 Ibid., p. 172.

21 Ibid., pp. 175–6.

22 Ibid., pp. 169–76.

23 Camp, pp. 188–9.

24 Ibid., p. 231.

25 Herodotus, *History*, 1.98.

26 Plato, *Critias*, 118a–118b.

27 Ibid.

28 Ibid., 113d.

29 Ibid., 117e.

30 Plato, *Critias*, 108e–109a, in Donnelly, *Atlantis: The Antediluvian World*, pp. 11–12.

Five: Isles of the Blest

1 Strabo, *The Geography*, II, iii, 6.

2 See, for example, Proclus, *The Commentaries of Proclus on the Timaeus of Plato, etc.*, Vol. 1, p. 64. The author records views and opinions for and against Atlantis as debated during the third century AD by the philosophers of the Platonic Academy at Alexandria.

3 Zhirov, *Atlantis – Atlantology: Basic Problems*, p. 60.

4 This figure is probably derived from the *Pinakes*, the catalogue compiled by librarian Callimachus of Cyrene (*c.* 310/305–240 BC). See Green, *Alexander to Actium: The Hellenistic Age*, pp. 88 n. 46, 666–7.

5 Harden, 'The Phoenicians on the West Coast of Africa', *Antiquity*, XXII, 1948, p. 142.

6 Ibid. Our earliest manuscript version of Hanno's journey, the Codex Heidelbergensis 398, dates only to the tenth century AD.

7 Hanno, III, after Harden, *The Phoenicians*, p. 174, cf. C. Muller, *Geographi Graeci Minores*, 3 vols., Paris, 1855–61.

8 Ibid., IV.

9 Harden, 'The Phoenicians on the West Coast of Africa', *Antiquity*, XXII, 1948, p. 142.

10 Hanno, VI.

11 Harden, *The Phoenicians*, p. 176.

12 Hanno, VII.

13 Ibid.

14 Ibid., VIII.

15 Ibid.

16 Ibid., IX.

17 Ibid., XIII.

18 Ibid., XIII–XVII.

19 Ibid., XVIII.

20 Harden, *The Phoenicians*, p. 177.

21 Harden, 'The Phoenicians on the West Coast of Africa', *Antiquity*, XXII, 1948, pp. 145–6.

22 Ibid., pp. 141–50.

23 Harden, *The Phoenicians*, p. 176.

24 Ibid.

25 Hanno, VIII.

26 Harden, 'The Phoenicians on the West Coast of Africa', *Antiquity*, XXII, 1948, p. 144.

27 Pseudo-Scylax, *Periplus*, 112. English translation quoted in Nordenskiöld, *Periplus: An Essay on the Early History of Charts and Sailing-Directions*, p. 8.

28 Ibid.

29 Ibid.

30 Pseudo-Aristotle, *On Marvellous Things Heard*, 84, cf. Camp, *Lost Civilisations: The Atlantis Theme in History, Science, and Literature*, p. 294.

31 Ibid.

32 Ibid.

33 Ibid.

34 Pliny, *Natural History*, VI, xxxvi, 203.

35 Gordon, *Before Columbus*, p. 39.

36 Harden, *The Phoenicians*, p. 63.

37 Pseudo-Aristotle, 136.

38 Ibid.

39 Ibid.

40 Diodorus Siculus, *Library*, III, 53.

41 Ibid.

42 Ibid.

43 Ibid., III, 54.

44 Ibid.

45 Ibid.

46 Herodotus, *History*, 4.184.

47 Ibid.

48 Diodorus Siculus, III, 54.

49 Ibid.

50 Ibid.

51 Ibid., III, 55.

52 Ibid.

53 Ibid.

54 Ibid.

55 Ibid., III, 56.

56 Ibid., III, 54.

57 Ibid., III, 60.

58 Ibid.

59 Ibid.

60 Hellanicus of Lesbos, *Atlantis*, in James, *The Sunken Kingdom*, p. 289.

61 Lemprière, *A Classical Dictionary*, s.v. 'Pleiades', pp. 484–5.

62 Keyser, 'From Myth to Map: The Blessed Isles in the First Century BC', *The Ancient World*, Vol. 24, pt. 2, 1993, p. 152.

63 Keyser, p. 149.

64 Hellanicus of Lesbos.

65 Pliny, *Natural History*, IV, xii, 58.

66 Keyser, p. 162.

67 Diodorus Siculus, V, 19.

68 Ibid.

69 Ibid.

70 Ibid.

71 Pseudo-Aristotle, 84.

72 Diodorus Siculus, V, 20.

73 Ibid.

74 Ibid.

75 Harden, *The Phoenicians*, p. 178.

76 The discovery of two Atlantic islands in the manner described by Plutarch in his 'Life of Sertorius' is a theme that earlier appears in a relatively unknown work by Sallust, a Latin historian of the first century BC. See Keyser, p. 157.

77 Plutarch, 'Life of Sertorius', pp. 399–400.

78 Ibid., p. 400.

79 Ibid.

80 Ibid.

81 Ibid., pp. 399–400.

82 Harden, 'The Phoenicians on the West Coast of Africa', *Antiquity*, XXII, 1948, p. 141 n. 3, after an account by a Swede named Podolyn in 1778, who took possession of the coins in Madrid. Podolyn's story is quoted in full in R. Hennig, *Terrae Incognitae* (Leiden, 1936).

83 Lemprière, s.v. 'Elysium', pp. 219–20.

84 Ibid.

85 Ibid.

86 Thomson, *History of Ancient Geography*, p. 41, p. 41 n. 1, after Dornseiff in *L'Ant. Classique*, 1937, p. 239.

87 Gordon, p. 39.

Six: Forty Days' Sail

1 Pliny, *Natural History*, II, xcii, 205.

2 Ibid., IV, xxii, 119. For a translation of the name Cassiterides see Wilson, *Lost Lyonesse: Evidence, Records and Traditions of England's Atlantis*, p. 16.

3 Pliny, IV, xxii, 119.

4 Lemprière, *A Classical Dictionary*, s.v. 'Fortunatae insulae', p. 241.

5 Pliny, VI, xxxvi, 199.

6 Ibid., VI, xxxvi, 199–201.

7 Keyser, 'From Myth to Map: The Blessed Isles in the First Century BC', *The Ancient World*, Vol. 24, pt. 2, 1993, map on p. 168.

8 Galvão, *The Discoveries of the World from their first originall unto the yeere of our Lord 1555*, pp. 11, 26.

9 Babcock, *Legendary Islands of the Atlantic: A Study in Medieval Geography*, p. 1.

10 Cortesão, *The Nautical Chart of 1424 and the Early Discovery and Cartographical Representation of America*, p. 48.

11 Ibid., p. 97.

12 Ibid., p. 48 n. 1.

13 Lemprière, s.v. 'Hesperia', p. 273.

14 Ibid., s.v. 'Hesperus', p. 274.

15 Hesiod, *Theogony*, vv. 214–16, 518.

16 Apollodorus, *The Library*, II, v. 11.

17 Honorius of Autun, in Ashe, *Land to the West: St Brendan's Voyage to America*, p. 139.

18 Ashe, p. 137.

19 Columbus, *The Life of the Admiral Christopher Columbus by his Son Ferdinand*, p. 57.

20 Pliny, VI, xxxvi, 201.

21 Galvão, p. 4.

22 Pliny, VI, xxxvi, 201. English trans. Ann Deagon.

23 Pliny, VI, xxxvi, 200.

24 Columbus, p. 68.

25 Ibid., pp. 120, 126.

26 Lemprière, s.v. 'Solinus C. Julius', p. 574.

27 Official case document dated 31 December 1536, in Nash, *America: The True History of its Discovery*, pp. 159–60.

28 Solinus, *Polyhistor: De Memoralibus Mundi*, Fvi(r).

Seven: Clues to Catastrophe

1 Ashe, *Atlantis: Lost lands, Ancient Wisdom*, p. 16.

2 Proclus, *The Commentaries of Proclus on the Timaeus of Plato, etc.*, Vol. 1, p. 64.

3 Ibid.

4 Ibid., Vol. 1, p. 86.

5 Ibid., Vol. 1, p. 64.

6 James, *The Sunken Kingdom*, pp. 172–3.

7 Proclus, Vol. 1, p. 64.

8 Ibid.

9 Taylor, 'Introduction', in Proclus, cf. Plato, *Timaeus*, 37–40. See also Cornford, *Plato's Cosmology*, pp. 75–93, 120–34.

10 Ibid.

11 Bramwell, *Lost Atlantis*, p. 64; Camp, *Lost Continents: The Atlantis Theme in History, Science, and Literature*, p. 18.

12 Proclus, Vol. 1, p. 148.

13 Ibid., Vol. 1. pp. 80–81.

14 Diodorus Siculus, *Library*, II, 47, 2.

15 Ibid., II, 47, 3.

16 Proclus, Vol. 1, p. 148.

17 Homer, *Odyssey*, vii, 24.

18 Plutarch, *The Face of the Moon*, 26. 941a–941c. I have chosen to use the Loeb translation and have included in brackets alternative renditions for the two key words. Other English translations vary considerably, changing the emphasis or meaning of this passage.

19 Keyser, 'From Myth to Map: The Blessed Isles in the First Century BC', *The Ancient World*, Vol. 24, pt. 2, 1993, p. 163.

20 Ashe, *Land to the West: St Brendan's Voyage to America*, pp. 180–81.

21 Plutarch, *The Face of the Moon*, 26, 941a.

22 Ibid., 26, 941a. fn. a.

23 Ibid., 26, 941b.

24 Ibid., 26, 941b fn. cf. Charax, Frag. 16 in *Frag. Hist. Graec.* iii, p. 640; Aelian, *Var. Hist.*, v. 3; Aristotle, frag. 678.

25 Irwin, *Fair Gods and Stone Faces*, p. 241.

26 Ashe, *Land to the West: St Brendan's Voyage to America*, p. 191.

27 Ibid.

28 These titles were Ashe, *The Quest for America*, pp. 42–5, a book that also featured contributions from major writers such as Thor Heyerdahl and J. V. Luce, and *Atlantis: Lost lands, Ancient Wisdom*, pp. 26–7, published as part of Thames and Hudson's Art and Enlightenment series in 1992.

29 Gaffarel, *Histoire de la découverte de l'Amérique*, Vol. 1. p. 18.

30 Ibid., p. 19.

31 Frazer, *Folk-lore in the Old Testament*, Vol. 1, p. 281.

32 Cruxent and Rouse, 'Early man in the West Indies', *Scientific American*, Vol. 221, 1969, p. 71.

33 Ibid.

34 Hine and Steinmetz, 'Cay Sal Bank, Bahamas – A Partially Drowned Carbonate Platform', *Marine Geology*, Vol. 59, 1984, p. 157; Wilber, Milliman and Halley, 'Accumulation of bank-top sediment on the western slope of Great Bahama Bank: Rapid progradation of a carbonate megabank', *Geology*, Vol. 18, October 1900, p. 973.

35 Hine and Steinmetz, p. 157.

36 Ibid.

37 Ibid.; Wilber, Milliman and Halley, p. 973.

38 Clarke, *Examination of the Legend of Atlantis in Reference to Protohistoric Communication with America*, p. 29.

39 Plato, *Timaeus*, 25a, in Clarke, p. 24.

40 Clarke, p. 24.

41 Spedicato, 'Apollo Objects, Atlantis and other Tales: A Catastrophical

Scenario for Discontinuities in Human History'.

42 Ashe, *Atlantis: Lost lands, Ancient Wisdom*, p. 27.

43 Proclus, Vol. 1, p. 151.

44 Aelian, *Historical Miscellany*, III, xviii.

Eight: Dealing in Drugs

1 James and Thorpe, *Ancient Inventions*, p. 350.

2 Balabanova, Parsche and Pirsig, 'First Identification of Drugs in Egyptian Mummies', *Naturwissenschaften*, 79, 1992, p. 358.

3 'Mystery of the Cocaine Mummies', Equinox, Channel 4, 1996.

4 Balabanova, Parsche and Pirsig, p. 358.

5 Galvão, *The Discoveries of the World from the first originall unto the yeere of our Lord 1555*, p. 87: 'Also there groweth in these fields, notwithstanding the great heate of the land, good maiz, and potatos, and an herbe which they name *Coca*, which they carrie continually in their mouthes . . . which also (they say) satisfieth both hunger and thirst.'

6 James and Thorpe, p. 340.

7 Jacobs, 'Toke Like an Egyptian', *Fortean Times*, FT117, December 1998, p. 36.

8 Ibid.; Balabanova, Parsche and Pirsig, p. 358; Unknown, 'Research Verifies Use of Hashish, Cocaine, Nicotine in Prehistoric Cultures', *Sociology of Drugs*, March 1993.

9 Jacobs, p. 36.

10 'Mystery of the Cocaine Mummies', Equinox, Channel 4, 1996.

11 Ibid.; 'Research Verifies Use of Hashish, Cocaine, Nicótine in Prehistoric Cultures', *Sociology of Drugs*, March 1993.

12 'Research Verifies Use of Hashish, Cocaine, Nicotine in Prehistoric Cultures', *Sociology of Drugs*, March 1993.

13 'Mystery of the Cocaine Mummies', Equinox, Channel 4, 1996, after the work of Rosalie David, Manchester Museum.

14 Ibid.

15 Przeworski, 'Notes d'Archéologie Syrienne et Hittite', *Syria*, 11, 1930, p. 133–45.

16 Ibid., p. 142.

17 Ibid., p. 140.

18 Ibid., p. 136.

19 Ibid., pp. 134–5.

20 Ibid.

21 Ibid., p. 137.

22 Ibid., p. 137 n. 2.

23 Ibid., p. 133.

24 Ibid., p. 140.

25 Ibid.

26 Gordon, *Before Columbus*, p. 142.

27 Ibid., p. 142 n. 127.

28 Ibid., p. 142.

29 Ibid.

30 Przeworski, pp. 138–9.

31 James and Thorpe, p. 349.

32 Ibid., p. 348.

33 Van Sertima, *They Came Before Columbus*, pp. 213–22.

34 Ibid., p. 215.

35 Ibid.

36 Ibid., p. 214.

37 Ibid., p. 216.

38 Ibid.

39 Ibid., pp. 216–17.

40 Ibid., p. 213.

41 Ibid.

42 Ibid.

43 Ibid., p. 214, after G. Binger, *Du Niger au Golfe de Guinée*, Paris, 1892, Vol. 2, p. 364. Also Weiner, Leo, *Africa and the Discovery of America*, Innes & Sons, Philadelphia, 1922, Vol. 2, p. 91.

44 Ibid., p. 216.

45 Sceptics of the cocaine mummies theory have pointed out that a species of Erythroxylon, the genus of the coca plant, is found on the island of Mauritius in the Indian Ocean, suggesting that coca chewing might once have been practised in the Old World. Yet when European sailors reached there in the sixteenth century, it was found to be uninhabited and no evidence of any former human occupation has so far been determined. Until we find evidence to suggest that the cocaine present in Egyptian mummies derives from a source other than the species indigenous to the Americas, where coca chewing was common practice, we must assume this to be the most obvious source of the drug.

46 See last Note.

47 Van Sertima, pp. 9, 12.

48 Ibid., p. 10.

49 Jaime Ferrer, letter to Christopher Columbus, dated 5 August 1495, in Thacher, *Christopher Columbus: His Life, His Work, His Remains*, Vol. 2, pp. 368–9.

50 Ibid., Vol. 2, p. 369.

Nine: Olmecs and Elephants

1 O'Connor, 'The Earliest Royal Boat Graves, *Egyptian Archaeology*, 6, 1995, pp. 3–7.

2 Ibid.

3 Herodotus, *History*, 4.43.

4 Ibid.

5 Ibid.

6 Harden, 'The Phoenicians on the West Coast of Africa', *Antiquity*, XXII, 1948, p. 146.

7 See Lichtheim, *Ancient Egyptian Literature, Vol. 1: The Old and Middle Kingdoms*, 'The Tale of the Shipwrecked Sailor', pp. 211–15 ll. 1–185.

8 Ibid., l. 25.

9 Ibid., l. 29.

10 Kaster, *Wings of the Falcon*, in Gordon, *Before Columbus*, p. 58.

11 Lichtheim, l. 98.

12 Ibid., l. 130.

13 Ibid., ll. 148–54.

14 Gordon, p. 63.

15 Houlihan, *The Animal World of the Pharaohs*, p. 199.

16 Smith, *Elephants and Ethnologists*, pp. 22–3, pl. 2 opp. p. 20; pl. 4 opp. p. 23.

17 Soustelle, *The Olmecs: The Oldest Civilisation in Mexico*, p. 44.

18 Ibid., p. 21.

19 Ibid., pp. 9–10, 15.

20 Stirling, 'Discovering the New World's Oldest Dated Work of Man', *National Geographic Magazine*, Vol. 76, August 1939, pp. 183–218.

21 Irwin, *Fair Gods and Stone Faces*, pp. 141, 157.

22 Ibid.

23 Soustelle, p. 9.

24 Gordon, *Before Columbus*, pp. 21–5.

25 Jairazbhoy, *Ancient Egyptians and Chinese in America*, p. 20.

26 Ibid.

27 Drucker, Heizer and Squier, 'Radiocarbon dates from La Venta, Tabasco', *Science*, Vol. 126, 12 July 1957, pp. 72–3.

28 Soustelle, pp. 47, 49.

29 Jairazbhoy, pp. 12–13.

30 Ibid., p. 16.

31 Van Sertima, *They Came Before Columbus*, pp. 146–7.

32 Jairazbhoy, p. 16. See also Soustelle, p. 5.

33 Gilmore and McElroy, *Across Before Columbus?*, p. 299.

34 Ibid., p. 300.

35 Ibid.

36 McGlone et al, *Ancient American Inscriptions: Plow Marks or History?*, pp. 21, 24.

37 Campbell and Abadie, *The Mystic Image*, Vol. 2, pp. 145–7.

38 Fritze, *Legend and Lore of the Americas before 1492*, s.v. 'Jumon/Valdivia Trans-Pacific Contacts (3000 BC)', pp. 141–2. See also Pearson, 'Migration from Japan to Ecuador: the Japanese Evidence', *American Anthropology*, Vol. 70, 1968, pp. 85–6.

39 See Meggers, 'Jomon–Valdivia Similarities: Convergence or Contact?', in Gilmore and McElroy, *Across Before Columbus?*, pp. 11–19.

40 Guthrie, 'Human Lymphocite Antigens: Apparent Afro-Asiatic, South Asian

& European HLAs in Indigenous American Populations', unpublished draft, February 1998.

41 See, for example, Irwin, pp. 68, 70–71, regarding the reliefs known as the 'dancers' at Monte Alban.

42 See, for example, Gordon, pp. 21–35; Irwin, pp. 175–88.

43 Vaillant, 'A Bearded Mystery', *Natural History*, Vol. 31, May–June 1931, pp. 243–52.

44 Ibid., p. 250.

45 Stirling, 'Great Stone Faces of the Mexican Jungle', *National Geographic Magazine*, Vol. 78, no. 3, September 1940, pp. 326–7. See also Irwin, p. 144.

46 Irwin, pp. 146–54.

47 Ibid., p. 153.

48 Ibid., pp. 151, 156.

49 Ibid., pp. 156–7.

Ten: The Murex Merchants

1 Wright, *Biblical Archaeology*, p. 187.

2 Ward, 'Ancient Lebanon', in *Cultural Resources in Lebanon*, p. 18.

3 Ibid., pp. 18–19.

4 Sanchoniathon, in Cory, *Ancient Fragments*, p. 9.

5 Ibid., pp. 7, 14.

6 Bunbury, *A History of Ancient Geography*, p. 14 n. 9.

7 Herodotus, *History*, 4. 196.

8 Ibid., 4. 42.

9 Ibid.

10 Pliny, *Natural History*, VI, xxxvi, 199–201.

11 Babcock, *Legendary Islands of the Atlantic: A Study in Medieval Geography*, p. 1.

12 Harden, *The Phoenicians*, p. 176.

13 Bunbury, p. 86.

14 Strabo, *Geography*, III, v, 11.

15 Gordon, *Before Columbus*, p. 125.

16 Ibid., pp. 124–5.

17 Harden, *The Phoenicians*, p. 104.

18 Gordon, p. 125.

19 Ibid.

20 Ibid.

21 Personal communication from Gordon to Sorenson dated September 1995. See Sorenson and Raish, *Pre-Columbian Contact with the Americas across the Oceans: An Annotated Bibliography*, Vol. 1, entry G-165, pp. 375–6.

22 2 Sam. 5:11; 1 Chr. 14:1. All Bible references and quotations from Authorised and Revised edition of 1611, Oxford University Press, 1905.

23 1 Kings 5:1, 9:10; 2 Chr. 2:3.

24 Picard and Picard, *The Life and Death of Carthage*, p. 287.

25 Cahill, *New England's Ancient Mysteries*, p. 8.
26 Ibid.
27 Ibid.
28 Ibid., p. 9.
29 Ibid.
30 Ibid.

Eleven: Shipwrecks and Sailors

1 Marx, *The Search for Sunken Treasure*, p. 33.
2 Ibid.
3 Ibid.
4 Ibid.
5 Ibid., p. 34.
6 Ibid.
7 Fell, *America* BC, revised 1989 edition, p. 320.
8 Marx, pp. 34–5.
9 Ibid.
10 Fingerhut, *Explorers of Pre-Columbian America: The Diffusionist Inventionist Controversy*, p. 20.
11 Ibid.
12 Ibid.
13 Marx, p. 34.
14 Eccott, 'Comalcalco: Maya innovation or Old World Intervention?', *Ancient American*, Vol. 3, no. 24, July–August 1998, p. 9; Steede, 'Comalcalco: An Early Classic Maya Site', in Gilmore and McElroy, *Across Before Columbus?*, pp. 35–6.
15 Steede, 'Mexico's pyramidal Comalcalco – a thousand years older than suspected', *Ancient American*, Vol. 4, no. 26, January–February 1999, p. 16.
16 Ibid.
17 Fell, 'Alphabetic Libyan Mason's Marks on Mochica Adobe Bricks', *ESOP*, Vol. 20, 1991, pp. 224–30.
18 McGlone et al, *Ancient American Inscriptions*, pp. 313–14.
19 Ibid.
20 Eccott, 'Comalcalco – The "Roman mason marks": A closer look', unpublished paper, 1999.
21 Steede, 'Mexico's pyramidal Comalcalco – a thousand years older than suspected', *Ancient American*, Vol. 4, no. 26, January–February 1999, p. 16.
22 Eccott, 'Comalcalco: A Case for Early Pre-Columbian Contact and Influence', *Chronology and Catastrophism Review*, Vol. 1, 1999, pp. 21–9; 'Comalcalco – The "Roman mason marks": A closer look', unpublished paper, 1999.
23 Eccott, 'Comalcalco: A Case for Early Pre-Columbian Contact and Influences', *Chronology and Catastrophism Review*, Vol. 1, 1999, pp. 21–9.
24 Prescott, *History of the Conquest of Mexico*, Vol. 1, p. 228; Steede, 'Comalcalco: An Early Classic Maya Site', in Gilmore and McElroy, p. 35.

25 Eccott, 'Before Columbus (the Calixtlahuaca Roman head)', *Quest for Knowledge*, Vol. 1, no. 5, Autumn 1997, pp. 18–19; Heine-Geldern, 'Ein Römischer Fund aus dem Vorkolumbischen Mexiko', *Anzeiger der Osterreichischen Akademie der Wissenschaften*, no. 16, 1961, pp. 117–19.

26 Irwin, *Fair Gods and Stone Faces*, p. 258.

27 Fell, *America* BC, revised 1989 edition, p. 318; Sorenson and Raish, *Pre-Columbian Contact with the Americas across the Oceans: An Annotated Bibliography*, Vol. xx, entry M-143, p. 106.

28 Ibid.

Twelve: Atlantic Voyagers

1 Miller and Taube, *The Gods and Symbols of Ancient Mexico and the Maya*, s.v. 'tobacco', p. 169.

2 Ibid.

3 Ibid., s.v. 'Schellhas gods', pp. 146–7.

4 For Iberic-Celt dating in America see Fell and Whittall, 'Proposed Correlation of North American and European Culture Sequences', 1976, in Fell, *America* BC, rear inside board.

5 Whishaw, *Atlantis in Andalucia*, pp. 44, 46, 71, 76, 173.

6 Ibid., pp. 6, 71.

7 Ibid., pp. 6, 33, 76.

8 Strabo, *Geography*, III, i, 6.

9 Whishaw, p. 150.

10 James and Thorpe, *Ancient Inventions*, p. 340.

11 Ibid., pp. 340–41.

12 Personal communication with Dr Colin McKeown of the British Museum in February 1999.

13 Irwin, *Fair Gods and Stone Faces*, p. 286, after the work of Philip Drucker and Robert Wauchope.

14 Ibid., after Robert Wauchope.

15 Ibid., p. 286.

16 Bankes, *Peru before Pizarro*, p. 138.

17 Ibid.

18 Burger, *Chavín and the Origins of Andean Civilisation*, p. 16.

19 Ibid., p. 70.

20 Ibid., p. 181.

21 Ibid., p. 165.

22 Ibid., p. 129.

23 Ibid., p. 168.

24 Ibid., p. 180.

25 Ibid., p. 129.

26 Ibid.

27 Ibid., p. 117.

28 Ibid.

29 Irwin, p. 287.

30 Mortimer, Peru: *History of Coca – The Divine Plant of the Incas*, p. 228.

31 'Prospective Jeunesse asbl – Histoire de la Coca', 1998, @ www.prospective-jeunesse.be/drogues/coca/histoire.htm.

32 Plato, *Critias*, 114b.

33 Ibid.

34 Pliny, *Natural History*, IV, xxii, 120.

35 Odelain and Séguineau, *Dictionary of Proper Names and Places in the Bible*, s.v. 'Geder', p. 134, cf. Jos. 12:13.

36 Ibid., s.v. 'Gedor', cf. Hb. 1–2.

37 Bérard, 'L'Atlantide de Platon', *Annales de Géographie*, Vol. 38, no. 213, 15 May 1929, pp. 193–205. See also Forsyth, *Atlantis: The Making of Myth*, p. 100.

38 Pseudo-Scylax, 112, English translation from Nordenskiöld, *Periplus: An Essay on the Early History of Charts and Sailing-Directions*, p. 8.

39 Diodorus Siculus, *Library*, III, 54.

40 Bramwell, *Lost Atlantis*, p. 110, after the work of Felix Berlioux.

Thirteen: The Return to Paradise

1 Columbus, *The Life of the Admiral Christopher Columbus by his Son Ferdinand*, pp. 46–7.

2 Cortesão, *The Nautical Chart of 1424 and the Early Discovery and Cartographical Representation of America*, p. 59, after Jean Nicholas Buache (1741–1825). The original word 'Antillia' in Buache's legend has been substituted with the preferred 'Atulliae' proposed by Kretchner in 1897.

3 Ibid., pp. 59–60, after Dr Heinrich Wuttke, who in 1870 proposed that the key word was in fact A(r)cules; Crone, 'The Origin of the name Antillia', *The Geographical Journal*, March 1938, pp. 260–62; Crone, 'The Pizigano Chart and the "Pillars of Hercules" ', *The Geographical Journal*, April–June 1947, pp. 278–9.

4 Cortesão, p. 60; Crone, 'The Pizigano Chart and the "Pillars of Hercules" ', *The Geographical Journal*, April–June 1947, pp. 278–9.

5 Cortesão, p. 59, after K. Kretchner, *Die Entdeckung Amerikas*, 1892, pp. 195–7.

6 Babcock, *Legendary Islands of the Atlantic: A Study in Medieval Geography*, p. 70.

7 Ibid.

8 Ibid., p. 169, cf. Humboldt, *Examen Critique*.

9 Cortesão, p. 109.

10 Ibid., p. 85.

11 Ibid., p. 78.

12 Benincasa map, 1482, in Ravenstein, *Martin Behaim: His Life and His Globe*, map 2.

13 Cortesão, p. 67.

14 Ibid., p. 74.

15 Ibid., p. 68, table III: 'The Antilia Group of Islands in Fifteenth Century Cartography'.
16 Bradford, *Christopher Columbus*, pp. 45–6.
17 Babcock, pp. 70, 151.
18 Ravenstein, *Martin Behaim: His Life and His Globe*, p. 46.
19 Cortesão, p. 94.
20 Babcock, p. 146.
21 Ibid.
22 Ibid., p. 145.
23 Whishaw, *Atlantis in Andalucia*, p. 91, cf. Fray Angel Ortega, *Historia de la Rabida.*
24 Ibid.
25 Ibid., pp. 92–3.
26 Ibid., p. 93, cf. Fray Angel Ortega, *Historia de la Rabida.*
27 Babcock, p. 145.
28 Ravenstein, p. 77.
29 Cortesão, p. 70.
30 Galvão, *The Discoveries of the World from their first originall unto the yeere of our Lord 1555*, p. 26.
31 Ibid.
32 Ibid.
33 Bradford, p. 71.
34 Deacon, *Madoc and the Discovery of America*, pp. 7–8.
35 Columbus, p. 50.
36 Pseudo-Aristotle, *On Marvellous Things Heard*, 84.
37 Columbus, p. 50.
38 Ibid., pp. 50–51.
39 Cortesão, p. 70.
40 Babcock, p. 78; Johnson, *Phantom Islands of the Atlantic*, p. 112.
41 Johnson, p. 112.
42 Ravenstein, p. 46.
43 Cortesão, pp. 2–3.
44 Ibid., p. 110.
45 Babcock, pp. 153–5, 162.
46 Camp, *Lost Continents: The Atlantis Theme in History, Science, and Literature*, pp. 21–2.
47 Hapgood, *Maps of the Ancient Sea Kings*, p. 61.
48 Ibid., pp. 61–2.
49 Bradford, pp. 125–6; Columbus, p. 82.
50 Bradford, p. 126.
51 Ibid., p. 129.
52 Ibid., p. 131; Columbus, p. 86.
53 Strode, *The Pageant of Cuba*, p. 43.

54 Ibid., p. 45.

55 Ibid., p. 48.

56 Ibid., pp. 43, 48.

57 Ibid., p. 49.

58 Strode, p. 54.

59 Babcock, p. 75.

60 Ibid., p. 74.

61 vonHagen, *The Golden Man: the Quest for El Dorado*, pp. 55, 125.

62 Wilson, *The World Atlas of Treasure*, p. 163.

63 vonHagen, p. 90.

64 For a full account of the expedition, see Raleigh, *The Discoverie of Guiana.*

65 vonHagen, pp. 82–90.

66 Cortesão, p. 88.

67 Babcock, p. 69.

68 Ibid.

69 Cortesão, p. 106.

Fourteen: The Exalted One

1 Thacher, *Christopher Columbus: His Life, His Work, His Remains*, Vol. 1, p. 295.

2 Cortesão, *The Nautical Chart of 1424 and the Early Discovery and Cartographical Representation of America*, p. 94.

3 Ibid., p. 73.

4 Columbus, *The Life of the Admiral Christopher Columbus by his Son Ferdinand*, p. 51.

5 Ibid., p. 57.

6 Williams, *Madoc: The Making of a Myth*, pp. 39–40, cf. Dr John Dee, *Great Volume of Famous and Rich Discoveries*, 1577.

7 Nordenskiöld, *Periplus: An Essay on the Early History of Charts and Sailing-Directions*, p. 54.

8 Ibid.

9 Cortesão, p. 81.

10 Ibid., p. 73.

11 Thacher, Vol. 1, p. 290.

12 Castle, *The Proceedings Against the Templars in France and England for Heresy, etc.* AD *1307–11, taken from the Official Documents of the Period*, p. 15.

13 Ibid.

14 Ibid., p. 37.

15 Burman, *Supremely Abominable Crimes: The Trial of the Knights Templar*, p. 816.

16 Berry, *Encyclopaedia Heraldica*, s.v. 'Knighthood', Vol. 1, npn.

17 Ibid. Also personal communication with Robert Bryden, an expert on the Knights Templar, March 1999.

18 See, for example, Gardner, *Bloodline of the Holy Grail*, p. 400.

19 Columbus, pp. 39–40.

20 Ravenstein, *Martin Behaim: His Life and His Globe*, pp. 29–30.

21 Ibid., p. 30.

22 See ibid., pp. 30–31, for a full appraisal of Martin Behaim's conferred knighthood. Ravenstein points out that Behaim could not have belonged to the Order since he is never shown in portraits bearing its red cross insignia. He further points out that shortly after Behaim's supposed investiture, he married his second wife. Since knights were only permitted to marry after a constitution was passed to this effect in 1495, it proves that Behaim could not have been a member at that time.

23 Ibid., p. 29.

24 Ibid.

25 Babcock, *Legendary Islands of the Atlantic: A Study in Medieval Geography*, p. 7; Moore, *The Penguin Encyclopedia of Places*, s.v. 'Azores', pp. 68–9.

26 Babcock, p. 168.

27 Ashe, p. 138; Cortesão, p. 40.

28 Babcock, p. 7.

29 Cortesão, p. 40.

30 Babcock, p. 7.

31 Cortesão, p. 48.

32 Babcock, p. 146.

33 Ibid., p. 47.

34 Ibid., p. 147.

35 Nordenskiöld, p. 15.

36 Babcock, p. 148.

37 Ibid., p. 149.

38 Odelain and Séguineau, *Dictionary of Proper Names and Places in the Bible*, s.v. 'Attalia', pp. 46–7.

39 Hosea, 'Atlantis: A Statement of the "Atlantic" Theory Respecting Aboriginal Civilisation', *The Cincinnati Quarterly Journal of Science*, Vol. II, no. 3, July 1875, p. 199.

40 Ibid., pp. 199–200.

41 Personal communication with Clifford Wright, the Professor of South Asian Studies at the School of Oriental and African Studies, London, in April 1999.

42 Ibid.

43 Herodotus, *History*, 5. 58.

44 Odelain and Séguineau, s.v. 'Athaliah', p. 46. Confirmed by Jo Ann Hackett, the Professor of Biblical Hebrew at Harvard University, Ma., March 1999.

45 Personal communication with Jo Ann Hackett, the Professor of Biblical Hebrew at Harvard University, Ma., March 1999.

46 Harris, *A Grammar of Phoenician Language*, s.v. 'atla', p. 136.

47 Personal communication with Jo Ann Hackett, the Professor of Biblical Hebrew at Harvard University, Ma., March 1999.

48 *Cassell Pocket English Dictionary*, s.v. 'elevated', p. 261.

49 Ibid., s.v. 'elevate', p. 261.

50 Lemprière, *A Classical Dictionary*, s.v. 'Atlas', p. 92.

51 Homer, *Odyssey*, I, 52–4.
52 Hesiod, *Theogony*, l. 517–19.
53 Galvão, *The Discoveries of the World from their first originall unto the yeere of our Lord 1555*, p. 5.
54 Bunbury, *A History of Ancient Geography*, pp. 74, 86.
55 Ibid., p. 7.
56 Re. the linguistic root of Elysium see Thomson, *History of Ancient Geography*, p. 41, p. 41 n. 1, after Dornseiff in *L'Ant. Classique*, 1937, p. 239.
57 Homer, *Iliad*, XIV, 201.
58 Nordenskiöld, p. 161.
59 Hosea, p. 200.
60 Ibid., pp. 200–201, cf. Brasseur de Bourbourg.

Fifteen: Fair Gods From Afar

1 Galvão, *The Discoveries of the World from their first originall unto the yeere of our Lord 1555*, p. 51.
2 Prescott, *History of the Conquest of Mexico*, i, p. 188.
3 Davies, *The Aztecs*, p. 254, cf. Bernal Díaz, *Chronicles*, p. 142.
4 Sahagún, *General History of the Things of New Spain*, bk. 12, p. 44.
5 Davies, p. 255, cf. Díaz, *Chronicles*, p. 142.
6 Sahagún, bk. 12, p. 44.
7 Pagden, ed., *Letters from Mexico by Hernando Cortés* (1519), pp. 85–6; Carrasco, *Quetzalcoatl and the Irony of Empire: Myths and Prophecies in the Aztec Tradition*, pp. 201–2.
8 Cortés, *The Conquest of Mexico*, pp. 96–9.
9 See, for example, Miller and Taube, *The Gods and Symbols of Ancient Mexico and the Maya*, s.v. 'Quetzalcoatl', pp. 141–2; Mackenzie, *Myths of Pre-Columbian America*, p. 260.
10 Brasseur de Bourbourg, *Histoire des nations civilisées du Mexique et de l'Amérique-centrale, etc.*, Vol. 1, p. 151.
11 Prescott, i, p. 52.
12 Davies, p. 258.
13 See, for example, Quetzalcoatl atop a pyramid in the Codex Telleriano-Remensis, sixteenth century, Aztec, in Miller and Taube, s.v. 'Quetzalcoatl', pp. 141–2; Spence, *The Myths of Mexico and Peru*, p. 80.
14 Spence, *The Myths of Mexico and Peru*, p. 81; Carrasco, *Quetzalcoatl and the Irony of Empire: Myths and Prophecies in the Aztec Tradition*, pp. 56–8.
15 See, for example, Pohl, *Prince Henry Sinclair: His Expedition to the New World in 1398*.
16 Sinclair, *The Sword and the Grail*, p. 134.
17 See, for example, ibid., p. 134, for a reference to a species of aloe cactus found carved in Rosslyn Chapel; ibid., pl. opp. p. 150, for reference to 'Indian (American) corn' in same; and personal conversations with historian Niven Sinclair and the author's own observations of the Dance of Death imagery in the chapel.

18 Brasseur de Bourbourg, Vol. 1, p. 109, cf. Sahagún, *Hist. de las cosas de N. España*, bk. x, cap. 29.
19 Prescott, i, p. 62.
20 Spence, p. 65.
21 Ibid.
22 Ibid., p. 79; Prescott, i, p. 52.
23 Spence, p. 65.
24 Burland and Forman, *Feathered Serpent and Smoking Mirror*, pp. 115–16; Miller and Taube, s.v. 'Quetzalcoatl', p. 142.
25 All accounts of omens taken from Prescott, i, pp. 258–9.
26 Ibid., i, p. 259.
27 Ibid., i, pp. 259–60 n. 11.
28 Burland and Forman, p. 110.
29 Prescott, i, p. 344, cf. *History de Tlascala.*
30 See Carrasco, pp. 200–204.
31 Prescott, i, p. 292, cf. Bernal Díaz.
32 Ibid., i, p. 261.
33 Ibid., i, p. 533.

Sixteen: People of the Serpent

1 Miller and Taube, *The Gods and Symbols of Ancient Mexico and the Maya*, s.v. 'creation accounts', pp. 68–71.
2 Brasseur de Bourbourg, *Histoire des nations civilisées du Mexique et de l'Amérique-centrale, etc.*, Vol. 1, p. 110, cf. Ixtlilxóchitl, *Sumaria Relacion, etc. – Hist. des Chichiméques*, bk. 1, cap. 1.
3 Ibid., Vol. 1, p. 111, cf. Ixtlilxóchitl, *Sumaria Relacion, etc. – Hist. des Chichiméques*, bk. 1, cap. 1.
4 Irwin, *Fair Gods and Stone Faces*, p. 62.
5 Miller and Taube, s.v. 'Quetzalcoatl', pp. 141–2.
6 Mackenzie, *Myths of Pre-Columbian America*, p. 257.
7 Tedlock, *Popol Vuh: The Mayan Book of the Dawn of Life*, p. 21.
8 Ibid., p. 145.
9 Ibid., s.v. 'Sovereign Plumed Serpent', p. 356.
10 Ibid., p. 192.
11 Ibid., p. 149, s.v. 'Serpents *Kumatz*', p. 355.
12 Thompson, *People of the Serpent*, p. 79.
13 Stacy-Judd, *Atlantis – Mother of Empires*, pp. 101, 285–6, after Daniel G. Brinton.
14 Brasseur de Bourbourg, Vol. 1, p. 77.
15 Ibid., pp. 77–9.
16 Stacy-Judd, pp. 285–6.
17 Brasseur de Bourbourg, Vol. 1, p. 77.
18 Ibid., Vol. 1, p. 79, cf. Lizana, *Hist. de Nuesta Señora de Izamal*, pt. I, cap. 4.

19 Ibid., Vol. 1, p. 80.

20 Stacy-Judd, pp. 286–8.

21 Brasseur de Bourbourg, Vol. 1, p. 110, cf. Las Casas, *Hist. Apolog. De las Indias-Occid.*, bk. III, cap. 123.

22 Ibid.

23 Gilbert and Cotterell, *The Mayan Prophecies*, p. 118.

24 Ibid., p. 122.

25 Love, *The Paris Codex: Handbook for a Maya Priest*, p. 95.

26 Ibid.

27 Thompson, pp. 21, 77.

28 Ibid., p. 77.

29 Ibid.

30 Ibid., p. 78.

31 Ibid., pp. 78–9.

32 Ibid.

33 Brasseur de Bourbourg, Vol. 1, p. 108, cf. Sahagún, *Hist. de las cosas de N. España*, Intro.

34 Ibid.

35 Spence, *Myths of Mexico and Peru*, p. 233.

36 Miller and Taube, s.v. 'Aztlan', p. 42.

37 Spence, p. 11.

38 Durán, *Historia de las Indias de Nueva España e Islas de Tierra Firme* in Markman and Markman, *The Flayed God*, p. 415.

39 Davies, *The Aztec Empire: The Toltec Resurgence*, p. 17.

40 Ibid.

41 Davies, *The Aztecs*, p. 6.

42 Ibid.

43 Davies, *The Aztec Empire: The Toltec Resurgence*, p. 17; Van Zantwijk, *The Aztec Arrangement: The Social History of Pre-Spanish Mexico*, p. 54.

44 Davies, *The Aztecs*, p. 7.

45 Toor, *A Treasury of Mexican Folkways*, p. 457. Many thanks to my colleague Richard Ward for coming across this valuable reference.

46 Ibid.

47 Prescott, *History of the Conquest of Mexico*, i, pp. 10–11 fn.

48 Brotherston, *Painted Books from Mexico*, p. 48.

49 Prescott, i, p. 10.

50 Ibid., i, p. 10 fn.

51 Mackenzie, *Myths of Pre-Columbian America*, p. 87, cf. Brasseur de Bourbourg.

52 Tedlock, p. 148.

53 Davies, *The Aztecs*, pp. 8–9, cf. Diego Durán, ii, p. 26.

54 Tedlock, p. 152.

55 Ibid., p. 158.

56 Ibid., p. 159.

57 Ibid., pp. 161–2.

58 Ibid., p. 160.

59 Ibid., p. 179.

60 Ibid.

61 Ibid., p. 296.

62 Ibid., pp. 149–52.

63 'Title of the Lords of Totonicapán', in *The Annals of the Cakchiquels/The Title of the Lords of Totonicapán*, p. 170.

64 'The Annals of the Cakchiquels' in Merezhkovsky, *The Secret of the West*, p. 127.

65 'The Annals of the Cakchiquels', in *The Annals of the Cakchiquels/The Title of the Lords of Totonicapán*, p. 43.

66 'Title of the Lords of Totonicapán', in ibid., p. 170.

67 Ibid.

68 'The Annals of the Cakchiquels' in ibid., p. 64, p. 64 fn. 84. Nacxit is an abbreviation of the name Topiltzin Acxit Quetzalcoatl mentioned in both Quiché and Cakchiquel documents. He is also mentioned in the Books of Chilam Balam texts under the name Nacxit-Xuchit.

69 'Title of the Lords of Totonicapán', in ibid., p. 170.

70 The Giron-Gagal is probably the same artefact as the Chay, or Obsidian Stone, 'created by the wondrous Xibalbay' and given to the Cakchiquels. See 'The Annals of the Cakchiquels', in ibid., p. 45, p. 45 fn. 9. Rock crystal was used extensively by Carib shamans for cures and by the Maya to fashion votive objects such as goblets and crystal skulls. See Zerries, 'Primitive South America and the West Indies', in Krickeberg, Müller, Trimborn and Zerries, *Pre-Columbian American Religions*, p. 248, for an account of the Makiritare Carib use of rock crystal. See Mitchell-Hedges, 'Atlantis Was No Myth but the Cradle Of American Races, Declares Hedges', *New York American*, 10 March 1935, for the discovery of the so-called 'skull of doom' found at the Maya centre of Lubaantun in British Honduras, modern Belize.

71 'Title of the Lords of Totonicapán', in ibid., pp. 180, 182.

72 'Title of the Lords of Totonicapán', in ibid., p. 184.

73 'The Annals of the Cakchiquels', in ibid., p. 48.

74 Tedlock, p. 158.

75 Ibid., p. 301.

76 'The Annals of the Cakchiquels' in *The Annals of the Cakchiquels/The Title of the Lords of Totonicapán*, p. 55.

77 Cruxent and Rouse, 'Early man in the West Indies', *Scientific American*, Vol. 221, 1969, p. 71.

78 Irwin, p. 53.

79 Ibid.

80 Brasseur de Bourbourg, Vol. 1, pp. 151, 155.

81 Miller and Taube, s.v. 'Chicomoztoc', p. 60.

82 Miller and Taube, s.v. 'mountains', pp. 119–21.

83 Stacy-Judd, pp. 296–7.

84 Brasseur de Bourbourg, Vol. 1, p. 68; cf. Lizana, *History of de Nuestra Señora de Izamal*, pt. I, cap. 3.

85 Ibid., Vol. 1, p. 108, cf. Ixtlilxóchitl, *Sumaria Relacion*, etc., Las Casas, *Hist. Apolog. de las Indias-Occid.*, MS. De la Biblioth. Royale de Madrid, bk. I, cap. 54.

86 Fallon, *Guide to Cuba*, p. 231.

87 Ibid.

88 Ibid.

Seventeen: The Old, Old Red Land

1 Steward, *Handbook of South American Indians, vol. IV: The Circum-Caribbean Tribes*, pp. 23–4.

2 Cruxent and Rouse, 'Early man in the West Indies', *Scientific American*, Vol. 221, 1969, p. 72.

3 Keegan, *Bahaman Archaeology*, pp. 13, 28–9.

4 Irwin, *Fair Gods and Stone Faces*, p. 98.

5 Brasseur de Bourbourg, *Histoire des nations civilisées du Mexique et de l'Amérique-centrale, etc.*, Vol. 1, p. 68.

6 Brinton, 'The Archaeology of Cuba', *American Anthropologist*, Vol. 10, 1898, in *Archaeological Tracts 1895–8*, pp. 231–4.

7 Ibid., p. 232.

8 Ibid.

9 Hill, *Cuba and Puerto Rico with the Other Islands of the West Indies*, p. 249.

10 Brinton, p. 232.

11 For the earliest dates for the Mississippi Valley mound-building culture, see Kennedy, *Hidden Cities*, pp. 12, 279–80.

12 Brinton, p. 232.

13 Ibid., p. 233.

14 Ibid.

15 Ibid.

16 Harlow, 'Hard Rock: A mineralogist explores the origins of Mesoamerican Jade', unpublished paper, Department of Mineral Sciences at the American Museum of Natural History, New York.

17 Riverend, *Brief History of Cuba*, p. 18.

18 Ibid.

19 Ibid.

20 Tabío and Rey, *Prehistoria de Cuba*, p. 230.

21 Cruxent and Rouse, p. 77.

22 Ibid.

23 Ibid., pp. 77–8.

24 Moure and de la Calle, *Arqueologia Aborigen de Cuba*, p. 78.

25 Ibid.

26 Ibid.

27 Jimenez, *Cuevas y pictografias*, p. 69.

28 Hadingham, *Early Man and the Cosmos*, p. 177.

29 Miller and Taube, *The Gods and Symbols of Ancient Mexico and the Maya*, p. 28; s.v. 'caves', p. 56.

30 Crampsey, *Puerto Rico*, p. 29.

31 Ibid.

32 Ibid.

33 Miller and Taube, s.v. 'directions', pp. 77–8.

34 Braghine, *The Shadow of Atlantis*, p. 253.

35 Hill, p. 77.

36 Ibid.

37 Personal communication with Dr A. J. Reedman, head of the British Geological Survey International, the overseas division of the British Geological Survey, in May 1999.

38 Information supplied by the North Prairie Wildlife Center/US Geological Survey in June 1999.

39 Ibid.

40 Morison, *Christopher Columbus, Mariner*, p. 119.

41 Ibid.

42 Ibid.

43 Strode, *The Pageant of Cuba*, p. 36.

44 Ibid.

45 Fallon, *Guide to Cuba*, p. 223. It must be pointed out that due to a confusion in Columbus' diary for this period it is unclear whether or not his vessel had laid anchor off the Isle of Youth or in the Bay of Batabanó, off mainland Cuba, when this incident occurred. However, the pine forests, cranes and local tradition all suggest that this incident did indeed occur on the Isle of Youth.

46 Durán, *Historia de las Indias de Nueva España e Islas de Tierra Firme*, in Markman and Markman, *The Flayed God: The Mythology of Mesoamerica*, p. 415.

47 *Annals of the Cakchiquels*, in Merezhkovsky, *The Secret of the West*, p. 127.

48 Ibid.

49 Brasseur de Bourbourg, in Mackenzie, *Myths of Pre-Columbian America*, p. 87.

Eighteen: Hispaniola versus Cuba

1 Clarke, *Examination of the Legend of Atlantis in Reference to Protohistoric Communication with America*, p. 24.

2 Spedicato, 'Apollo Objects, Atlantis and other Tales: A Catastrophical Scenario for Discontinuities in Human History'. The first revised edition was published in *Journal of New England Antiquities Research Association (NEARA)*, Vol. 26, 1991, pp. 1–14, and also *Kadath*, Vol. 84, 1995, pp. 29–55. All references taken from the fifth section entitled 'An Interpretation of the Platonic Story of Atlantis' of the revised edition.

3 Ibid.

4 Ibid.

5 Ibid.

6 Ibid.

7 Ibid.

8 Ibid.

9 Based on the view that between *c.* 14,000 BC and *c.* 2000 BC the sea-level rose by as much as 105 metres. Unfortunately, very few marine geologists agree on the rate or amount the sea-level rose following the termination of the last glacial age. See, for instance, Hine and Steinmetz, 'Cay Sal Bank, Bahamas – A Partially Drowned Carbonate Platform', *Marine Geology*, Vol. 59, 1984, p. 157, regarding rises in the Bahamas and Caribbean. More important, there is good reason to suggest that the rate of rise was infinitely greater somewhere between *c.* 10,200 and 9000 BC. See Emiliani, 'Paleoclimatological Analysis of Late Quaternary Cores from the Northeastern Gulf of Mexico', *Science*, Vol. 189, 26 September 1975, pp. 1,083–8.

10 Plato, *Critias*, 113c.

11 Keegan, *Bahaman Archaeology*, p. 88.

12 Ibid., p. 89.

13 Ibid.

14 Ibid.

15 Ibid., p. 10.

16 Joyce, *Central American and West Indian Mythology*, p. 181.

17 Hill, *Cuba and Puerto Rico with the Other Islands of the West Indies*, pp. 12, 52.

18 Plato, 118a.

19 Moure and de la Calle, *Arqueologia Aborigen de Cuba*, p. 16.

20 Ibid., p. 107.

21 Ibid., p. 106.

22 Mellaart, *Çatal Hüyük – A Neolithic Town in Anatolia*, p. 170.

23 Plato, 119e.

24 Hill, p. 108.

Nineteen: The Ole Moon Broke

1 Tabío and Rey, *Prehistoria de Cuba*, p. 51.

2 Gaffarel, *Histoire de la découverte de l'Amérique*, Vol. 1, p. 18.

3 Ibid., Vol. 1, p. 19.

4 Frazer, *Folk-lore in the Old Testament*, Vol. 1, p. 281.

5 Peter Martyr d'Anghiera, *Decades of the New World or West Indies*, 1511, in Craton, *A History of the Bahamas*, p. 16.

6 Wilkins, *Secret Cities of Old South America: Atlantis Unveiled*, p. 112.

7 Thompson, *People of the Serpent*, p. 77.

8 Mahan, *The Secret – America in World History before Columbus*, p. 5. I would like to thank Bill Donato for drawing my attention to this important work.

9 Ibid.

10 Ibid., p. 30.

11 Ibid.

12 See, for example, Hine and Steinmetz, 'Cay Sal Bank, Bahamas – A Partially Drowned Carbonate Platform', *Marine Geology*, Vol. 59, 1984, p. 157.

13 Keegan, *Bahaman Archaeology*, pp. 13, 28–9.

Twenty: Snake of Fire

1 Thompson, *People of the Serpent*, p. 79.

2 Gilbert and Cotterell, *The Mayan Prophecies*, p. 118.

3 Hadingham, *Early Man and the Cosmos*, p. 156.

4 Ibid., pp. 154–5.

5 Ibid., pp. 145–7.

6 Clube and Napier, *The Cosmic Serpent*, p. 263.

7 Ibid., p. 263.

8 Ibid., p. 108.

9 Ibid.

10 Mahan, *The Secret – America in World History before Columbus*, p. 30.

11 Tedlock, *Popol Vuh: The Mayan Book of the Dawn of Life*, pp. 161–2.

12 Kelso de Montigny, 'Did a Gigantic Meteorite, i.e. an Asteroid, fall into the Caribbean, and thus create the Lesser Antilles about 6000 years ago?', *International Anthropological and Linguistic Review*, Vol. 1, no. 4, 1954, pp. 229–38.

13 Kelso de Montigny, 'Redating the Past', *International Anthropological and Linguistic Review*, Vol. 1, no. 2–3, 1954, pp. 185–7.

14 Kelso de Montigny, 'Did a Gigantic Meteorite, i.e. an Asteroid, fall into the Caribbean, and thus create the Lesser Antilles about 6000 years ago?', *International Anthropological and Linguistic Review*, Vol. 1, no. 4, 1954, p. 229.

15 Ibid., p. 230.

16 Ibid., p. 233.

17 Ibid.

18 Ibid., pp. 233–4.

19 Ibid., p. 234.

20 Ibid., p. 235.

21 Ibid., pp. 235–7.

22 Ibid., p. 237.

23 Ibid.

24 Ibid.

25 Personal communication with Alan R. Kelso de Montigny in December 1998 and June 1999.

26 Tompkins, in Muck, *The Secret of Atlantis*, p. viii.

Twenty-one: Cosmic Pinball

1 Goodrick-Clarke, *The Occult Roots of Nazism*, p. 174; Sklar, *Gods and Beasts: The Nazis and the Occult*, p. 74.

2 Bellamy, *Moons, Myths and Man: A Reinterpretation*, pp. 61–2.

3 Ibid., p. 266.

4 Muck, *The Secret of Atlantis*, pp. 152–3.

5 Ibid., p. 153.

6 Ibid.

7 Ibid., p. 152.

8 Ibid., p. 154.

9 Ibid.

10 Melton and Shriever, 'The Carolina "Bays" – Are They Meteorite Scars?', *Journal of Geology*, Vol. 41, 1933, pp. 52–66. See also Melton, 'The Origin of the Carolina "Bays" ', *Discovery*, June 1934, pp. 151–4.

11 Melton and Schriever, p. 59.

12 Ibid., pp. 55–6.

13 Ibid., p. 55.

14 Muldrow, 'The Comet that Struck the Carolinas', *Harper's Monthly Magazine*, no. 168, 1933, p. 87.

15 Prouty, 'Carolina Bays and their Origin', *Bulletin of the Geological Society of America*, Vol. 63, February 1952, pp. 167–222.

16 Ibid., p. 178.

17 Ibid., p. 179.

18 Ibid.

19 Ibid.

20 Savage, *The Mysterious Carolina Bays*, p. 7.

21 Ibid.

22 Prouty, p. 214.

23 Ibid., p. 174.

24 Savage, p. 7.

25 Ibid., pp. 27–8.

26 Nininger, 'When the Sky Rains Stone and Iron', *Literary Digest*, Vol. 117, 17 March 1934, pp. 16, 29; Wylie, 'On the Formation of Meteorite Craters', *Popular Astronomy*, Vol. 41, 1933, pp. 211–14.

27 Johnson, 'Supposed Meteorite Scars of South Carolina, *Science*, Vol. 79, 1934, p. 461.

28 Muldrow, pp. 83–9.

29 Ibid., p. 88.

30 Prouty, pp. 167–224. See also McCampbell, 'Meteorites and the "Carolina Bays" ', *Popular Astronomy*, Vol. 53, 1944, pp. 388–92, for a review of the air shockwave theory.

31 Prouty, p. 221.

32 Ibid., pp. 174, 222.

33 Olivier, 'The Great Siberian Meteorite: An Account of the Most Remarkable Astronomical Event of the Twentieth Century, from Official Records', *Scientific American*, July 1928, pp. 42–4.

34 Ibid., p. 43.

35 See Kobres, R., 'The Path of a Comet and Phaeton's Ride', *The World and I*, Vol. 10, February 95, pp. 394–405.

36 Savage, p. 96.

37 Carson and Hussey, 'The Oriented Lakes of Arctic Alaska', *Journal of Geology*, Vol. 70, 1962, pp. 417–39.

38 Kelly, 'The Origin of the Carolina Bays and the Oriented Lakes of Alaska', *Popular Astronomy*, Vol. 59, 1951, p. 204.

39 Plafker, 'Oriented Lakes and Lineaments in Northern Bolivia', *Bulletin of the Geological Society of America*, Vol. 75, 1964, pp. 503–22. See pp. 513–17.

40 Ibid., pp. 503, 509.

41 Ibid., pp. 516–17.

42 Muck, p. 157.

43 Ibid., p. 164.

44 Ibid.

45 Ibid.

46 Ibid., p. 184.

47 Ibid., p. 167.

48 Eyton and Parkhurst.

49 Ibid.

50 Ibid.

51 Ibid. According to Kulik he found 'innumerable "shell-holes" or craters which vary in diameter from one to perhaps 50 yards in diameter, scattered all over the central area. Their edges are mostly steep, the bottoms flat and swampy, and sometimes with traces of a central elevation.' See Olivier, 'The Great Siberian Meteorite: An Account of the Most Remarkable Astronomical Event of the Twentieth Century, from Official Records', *Scientific American*, July 1928, p. 43.

52 Ibid.

53 Ibid.

54 Ibid.

55 Levy, *Comets: Creators and Destroyers*, p. 156.

56 Eyton and Parkhurst.

57 Ibid.

58 Savage, p. 23.

59 Hancock, Bauval and Grigsby, pp. 254–6, particularly after the work of Sir Fred Hoyle.

60 Ibid., p. 255.

61 Muck, p. 156.

62 See Donnelly, *Ragnarok: The Age of Fire and Gravel*.

63 Braghine, *The Shadow of Atlantis*, pp. 256–7.

64 Ibid., p. 250.

65 Ibid., pp. 252–3.

66 Muck, pp. 169–70.

67 One post-Conquest account of the arrival of the People of the Serpent was recorded by the fanatical Catholic Diego de Landa, Bishop of the Yucatán.

Between 1549 and 1563 he worked in the province attempting to stamp out the native beliefs of the Maya, a crusade which apparently included the public burning of whole piles of sacred texts in the ancient town of Mani. However, after he was seriously criticised for his treatment of the Indians, de Landa had a change of heart and in 1566 penned a valuable work on Maya history and religion entitled *Relación de las Cosas de Yucatán*. In this he states: 'Some of the old people of Yucatán say they heard from their ancestors that this land was occupied by a race of people who came from the east and whom God had delivered by opening twelve paths through the sea.' (See Landa, *Relación de las Cosas de Yucatán*, in Tompkins, *Mysteries of the Mexican Pyramids*, p. 348.) In a Maya document entitled *The History of Zodzil* it affirms that the earliest inhabitants of the Yucatán arrived after the sea-level rose, for it states: 'the most ancient people who came to populate this land [i.e. the Yucatán] were those who populated Chichen-Itza . . . and [they] were the first after the flood'. (*The History of Zodzil*, trans. Juan Darreygosa, in *Unedited Documents Relating to the Discovery and Conquest and Organization of the Ancient Spanish Possessions Beyond the Seas*, in Stacy-Judd, *Atlantis: Mother of Empires*, p. 102.)

68 Mahan, *The Secret – America in World History before Columbus*, p. 30.

69 Plato, *Timaeus*, 25c–25d.

70 Muck, p. 188.

71 Spedicato, 'Apollo Objects, Atlantis and other Tales: A Catastrophical Scenario for Discontinuities in Human History'.

72 Hibben, *The Lost Americans*, p. 170. For a full account of the Pleistocene fauna found in the Alaskan muck see pp. 91–8. For the reference to the suspected age of the glacial destruction in Alaska being 'ten thousand years ago', see p. 91.

73 Ibid., pp. 177–8.

74 Ibid., p. 177.

75 Ibid., pp. 91, 97, 168.

76 Ibid., p. 168.

Twenty-two: End of the Ice Age

1 Powell, 'Mythologic Philosophy', *Popular Science Monthly*, October 1879, p. 799.

2 Ibid.

3 Donnelly, Tagnarok: *The Age of Fire and Gravel*, p. 179.

4 Spedicato, 'Apollo Objects, Atlantis and other Tales: A Catastrophical Scenario for Discontinuities in Human History'.

5 Ibid.

6 Ingram, Robinson and Odum, 'Clay Mineralogy of some Carolina Bay Sediments', *Southeastern Geology*, Vol. 1, 1959, pp. 1–10.

7 Ibid.

8 Muldrow, 'The Comet that Struck the Carolinas', *Harpers' Monthly Magazine*, no. 168, 1933, p. 87.

9 Prouty, 'Carolina Bays and their Origin', *Bulletin of the Geological Society of America*, Vol. 63, February 1952, p. 192.

10 Savage, *The Mysterious Carolina Bays*, pp. 78–9, cf. Kaczorowski.

11 Ibid., p. 95, cf. Kaczorowski.

12 Ibid.

13 Prouty, p. 209.

14 Broecker, Ewing and Heezen, 'Evidence for an Abrupt Change in Climate close to 11,000 years ago', *American Journal of Science*, Vol. 258, June 1960, pp. 429–48. See p. 429.

15 Ibid., p. 435.

16 Ibid.

17 Ibid., pp. 438–40.

18 Ibid., pp. 437–8.

19 Ibid., p. 434 n. 1.

20 Ibid., p. 434 n. 2.

21 Ibid., pp. 434–5 nn. 2 and 3.

22 Ibid., p. 437.

23 Ibid., p. 440.

24 Ibid., p. 441. 'It is entirely possible that the sharp change in oceanic conditions correlates with the post Younger Dryas rather than the pre Younger Dryas warm period . . .' The European ice re-advance known as the Younger Dryas occurred between approximately 8500 and 8300 BC. It coincided with the Valders re-advance in North America.

25 Wright, Patten and Winter, 'Two Pollen Diagrams from Southeastern Minnesota: Problems in the Regional Late-Glacial and Postglacial Vegetational History', *Geological Society of America Bulletin*, Vol. 74, 1963, pp. 1,371–95 + plates.

26 Ogden, 'Radiocarbon and Pollen Evidence for a Sudden Change in Climate in the Great Lakes Region approximately 10,000 years ago', *Quaternary Paleoecology*, 1967, pp. 117–27.

27 Ibid., p. 121.

28 Ibid., pp. 121, 123–4.

29 Ibid., p. 124.

30 Broecker, 'The Ocean', *Scientific American*, no. 249, 1983, p. 146.

31 Spedicato.

32 Spedicato, after the work of S. Björck et al, 'Synchronized Terrestrial-Atmospheric Deglacial Records Around the North Atlantic', *Science*, no. 274, 1996, pp. 1,155–60.

33 Hine and Steinmetz, 'Cay Sal Bank, Bahamas – A Partially Drowned Carbonate Platform', *Marine Geology*, Vol. 59, 1984, pp. 135, 157.

34 Wilber, Milliman and Halley, 'Accumulation of bank-top sediment on the western slope of Great Bahama Bank: Rapid progradation of a carbonate megabank', *Geology*, Vol. 18, October 1980, p. 973.

35 Broecker, Ewing and Heezen, p. 434 n. 1.

36 Emiliani, 'Paleoclimatological Analysis of Late Quaternary Cores from the Northeastern Gulf of Mexico', *Science*, 26 September 1975, Vol. 189, pp. 1,083–8.

37 Ibid., p. 1,083.

38 Ibid., p. 1,086.

39 Wright, Patten and Winter, p. 1,386. Carbon-14 testing of the core samples examined by Wright demonstrated that this rapid alteration in the flora had taken place between *c.* 8500 and 8000 BC. For example, at two of the lakes, Kirchner Marsh and Lake Carlson, carbon-14 tests revealed a date of 10,230 +/−110 BP, while at Weber Lake tests provided an average date of 10,365 BP for the sudden rise in mixed hardwoods.

40 Wright, 'Glacial Fluctuations, Sea-level Changes, and Catastrophic Floods', in Ramage, *Atlantis: Fact or Fiction?*, pp. 161–74.

41 Ibid., p. 168.

42 Emiliani, p. 1,087: 'This age coincides with that of the Valders readvance; because this readvance was accompanied by a rapid rise in sea level, it was apparently a surge, which brought ice to lower latitudes and caused rapid melting.'

43 Wright, p. 169.

44 Emiliani, p. 1,086.

45 Ibid.

46 Wright, p. 169.

47 Emiliani, p. 1,086.

48 Wright, pp. 169, 173.

49 Ibid., p. 174.

50 Ibid., p. 162.

51 See Tollmann and Tollmann, 'The Flood came at 3 o'clock in the morning . . .', *Austria Today*, Vol. 4, 1992, pp. 40–47; Kristan-Tollmann and Tollmann, 'Der Sintflut-Impakt: The Flood impact', *Mitt. Österr. Geol. Ges.*, Vol. 84 (1991), June 1992, pp. 1–63.

52 The other five locations are given as 'to the south-east of Australia (probably in the Tasman Sea), in the South China Sea, the west-central Indian Ocean . . . the Pacific Ocean off the Central American coast, and probably in the South Pacific just to the west of Tierra del Fuego at the southern tip of South America'. See Tollmann and Tollmann, 'The Flood came at 3 o'clock in the morning . . .', *Austria Today*, Vol. 4, 1992, p. 40.

53 Ibid., p. 42.

54 Ibid., p. 44.

55 'Comet that Launched Noah's Ark', *The Times*, London, 22 April 1996.

56 Tollmann and Tollmann, p. 45.

57 Ibid.

58 Plato, *Critias*, 108e.

59 Muck, *The Secret of Atlantis*, p. 248.

60 Coe, *Breaking the Maya Code*, p. 275.

61 Reymond, *The Origins of the Egyptian Temple*, pp. 35, 113. For a full appraisal of the Edfu Building Texts see Collins, *Gods of Eden*, pp. 173–80.

62 Reymond, pp. 108, 118.

63 Ibid., p. 119; Jelinkova, 'The Shebtiw in the temple of Edfu', *ZAS*, no. 87, 1962, p. 41, cf. E. VI, 51.

64 Reymond, pp. 28–9, 142–3, 208.

65 Lichtheim, *Ancient Egyptian Literature, Vol. 1: The Old and Middle Kingdoms*, 'The Tale of the Shipwrecked Sailor', pp. 211–15, l. 130.

66 Kloosterman, 'The Usselo Horizon, a Worldwide Charcoal-rich Layer of Alleröd Age', unpublished paper, 1999.

Twenty-three: Sunken Secrets

1 Joseph, 'Project Alta: Search and Discovery in the Bahamas,' *Ancient American*, Vol. 3, no. 23, April/May 1998, p. 2.

2 Ibid.

3 Ibid.

4 Ibid.

5 Wilber, Milliman and Halley, 'Accumulation of bank-top sediment on the western slope of Great Bahama Bank: Rapid progradation of a carbonate megabank', *Geology*, Vol. 18, October 1980, p. 973.

6 Mahan, *The Secret – America in World History before Columbus*, p. 30.

7 Hutton, *Coming Earth Changes – the Latest Evidence*, pp. 168–9.

8 Edgar Cayce reading, 996–1, 14 August 1926, cf. ibid., p. 170.

9 Ibid.

10 Edgar Cayce reading, 996–8, 7 February 1927, cf. ibid., p. 171.

11 Ibid.

12 Edgar Cayce reading, 996–12, 2 March 1927, cf. ibid., p. 173.

13 Cayce, Hugh Lynn, Introduction, in Cayce, *Edgar Cayce on Atlantis*, p. 12.

14 Cayce, Edgar, *Atlantis – The Edgar Cayce Readings*, Vol. 22, p. 1.

15 Edgar Cayce reading, 440–5, 19 December 1933, in Hutton, p. 183.

16 Edgar Cayce reading, 958–3, 28 June 1940, in ibid., p. 174.

17 Cayce, Schwartzer and Richards, *Mysteries of Atlantis Revisited*, pp. 156–7.

18 Hutton, pp. 176–7.

19 Berlitz, *Mysteries from Forgotten Worlds: Rediscovering Lost Civilisations*, p. 92; Berlitz, *The Mystery of Atlantis*, 2 plates, between pp. 96–7; Zink, *The Stones of Atlantis*, pp. 9–10; Valentine, 'Underwater Archaeology in the Bahamas,' *The Explorers' Club Journal*, December 1976, p. 180.

20 Zink, p. 9.

21 Donato, *A Re-examination of the Atlantis Theory*, pp. 128–9.

22 Cayce, Schwartzer and Richards, *Mysteries of Atlantis Revisited*, p. 159.

23 Quotes from a teletype based on statements originally made by J. Manson Valentine and received by Robert Cummings, a Canadian broadcaster, as quoted in Steiger, *Atlantis Rising*, p. 147.

24 Ibid.

25 Ibid.

26 See Zink.

27 Ibid., p. 21.

28 Donato, *A Re-examination of the Atlantis Theory*, pp. 129–30.

29 Leonard, *Quest for Atlantis*, pp. 48–9.

30 Valentine, 'Underwater Archaeology in the Bahamas', *The Explorers' Club Journal*, December 1976, p. 180.

31 Landsburg and Landsburg, *In Search of Ancient Mysteries*, p. 71.

32 Ibid., p. 72.

33 Ibid., p. 73.

34 Ibid.

35 Ibid.

36 Ibid., p. 74.

37 Harrison, 'Atlantis Undiscovered – Bimini, Bahamas', *Nature*, Vol. 230, 2 April 1971, p. 287.

38 Zink, p. 47; Steele, 'Bimini revealed', in Hitching, *The Mysterious World – An Atlas of the Unexplained*, p. 142.

39 Valentine, J. Manson, 'Archaeological Enigmas of Florida and the Western Bahamas', *Muse News*, June 1969.

40 Gifford, 'The Bimini "cyclopean" complex', *International Journal of Nautical Archaeology and Underwater Exploration*, Vol. 2, 1973, p. 189.

41 See, for example, Harrison, 'Atlantis Undiscovered – Bimini, Bahamas', *Nature*, Vol. 230, 2 April 1971, pp. 287–9. His arguments against the Road's artificial manufacture can be summarised as follows:

(a) the formation is composed of 'coarse-grained limestone lying on a stratum of denser limestone of finer grain'. The stone blocks are therefore still *in situ*, and so could *not* have been removed from elsewhere;
(b) an 'examination of the opposing faces of the lifted and unmoved pieces indicates an exact correspondence of bedding planes and surface morphology', implying that the characteristic features present in one block are more or less identical to those directly facing it, once again proving that they remain *in situ*;
(c) 'at no place are blocks found to rest on a similar set beneath', showing that they have not been stacked in courses which would, of course, have added weight to the idea that the Road was of artificial construction;
(d) the formation is composed of 'shell-hash cemented by a blocky calcite' of a type common to the area and formed when the land was still sub-aerial, that is above sea-level.

See also Shinn, 'Atlantis: Bimini Hoax', *Sea Frontiers*, Vol. 24, no. 3, May–June 1978, pp. 130–42, for further arguments against the Road's artificial construction.

42 The points in favour of the Road's artificial construction can be summarised as follows:

(a) Harrison's conclusion that the formation was composed only of beach-rock left *in situ* should be questioned in the knowledge that the Road stones are in fact made of three different types of rock (personal communication with Bill Donato, June 1998). These include bioclastic limestone, oolitic limestone and the much harder substance called micrite (personal communication with Bill Donato, April 1998; Valentine, 'Underwater Archaeology in the Bahamas', *The Explorers' Club Journal*, December 1976, p. 176). Even though these rock types *are* indigenous to the area, they could never have formed together, side by side, suggesting that at least some of the blocks originated at different locations and were removed to their present site in antiquity;

(b) the geologist's claim that the characteristic features present in one block are more or less identical in pattern to those directly facing it is based on just a few samples taken from rocks using hand tools alone (personal communication with Bill Donato, April 1998). Although it is openly accepted that some of the blocks were obviously 'neighbours' when *in situ*, the presence of rock types from other strata completely disproves this theory. Furthermore, John Parks, a geologist who accompanied David Zink's Poseidia expeditions during the 1970s, examined rock samples from several different stones, some of them neighbours, and found that their composition varied from stone to stone. For example, 'one sample was dominated by aragonite crystals, another by sparry calcite. This implied that adjacent stones were formed in different chemical environments' (see Zink, *The Stones of Atlantis – New and Revised*, p. 58);

(c) Harrison's claim that at no place were blocks found to rest on similar blocks is also questionable. Although double or multiple layering is indeed rare, on the Road's southern leg – the so-called 'long arm' of the J – many stones in the middle of the 90-degree curve are more than one course in height (see Zink, *The Stones of Atlantis – New and Revised*, p. 58). Furthermore, some have flat stones – occasionally with sharply defined angles, others of a different composition – wedged beneath them. More important, several examples *have small stone legs beneath their corners* (see Cayce, Schwartzer and Richards, *Mysteries of Atlantis Revisited*, p. 163; Donato, 'Bimini and the Atlantis Controversy', *The Ancient American*, Vol. 1, p. 3, November/December 1993, p. 9; Valentine, 'Underwater Archaeology in the Bahamas', *The Explorers' Club Journal*, December 1976, p. 177).

43 Zink, p. 60.

44 Ibid., p. 62.

45 Ibid., p. 60; Steele, in Hitching, *The Mysterious World – An Atlas of the Unexplained*, p. 143; Donato, *A Re-examination of the Atlantis Theory*, p. 135.

46 Donato, 'Bimini and the Atlantis Controversy', *The Ancient American*, Vol. 1, no. 3, November/December 1993, p. 9.

47 Zink, pp. 62–3.

48 Joseph, 'Project Alta: Search and Discovery in the Bahamas', *The Ancient American*, Vol. 3, no. 23, April/May 1998, p. 7. See also Donato, 'Project Alta: Parts 2 & 3, and the Television Productions', *The Atlantis Organisation Journal*, no. 14, November 1995, p. 3.

49 Donato, 'What you did not see (or hear) on Arthur C. Clarke's Mysterious Universe', *The Ancient American*, no. 14, 1996, p. 6.

50 Donato, 'Bimini and the Atlantis Controversy', *The Ancient American*, Vol. 1, no. 3, November/December 1993, p. 9.

51 Donato, 'The Architecture of Atlantis: A General Survey', *The Atlantis Organisation Journal*, no. 15, December 1996, p. 29.

52 Ibid.

53 Valentine, 'Underwater Archaeology in the Bahamas', *The Explorers' Club Journal*, December 1976, p. 182.

54 Ibid., p. 183.

55 Ibid.

56 Ibid.

57 Ibid.

58 *Miami Herald*, 17 June 1990, p. 41.

Twenty-four: Out of the Blue

1 Valentine, 'Underwater Archaeology in the Bahamas', *The Explorers' Club Journal*, December 1976, p. 178.

2 Ibid.

3 Ibid.

4 Ibid., pp. 179–80.

5 Ibid., p. 180.

6 Ibid., p. 182.

7 Ibid.

8 Ibid.

9 Ibid., p. 181.

10 Ibid.

11 Ibid., p. 182.

12 Ibid.

13 Ibid.

14 Ibid.

15 Ibid.

16 Ibid.

17 Ibid.

18 Ibid., p. 181.

19 Hill, *Cuba and Puerto Rico with the Other Islands of the West Indies*, pp. 381–3.

20 Berlitz, *Atlantis – The Lost Continent Revealed*, p. 81.

21 Berlitz, *The Mystery of Atlantis*, p. 178.

22 Ibid.

23 See, for example, Collins, 'Soviet oceanographers stir up Atlantis myth', *Strange Phenomena*, Vol. 1, no. 1, 1979, pp. 36–7, for a review of the discoveries made in 1979 by the Soviet survey ship *Vitias*, under the directorship of Dr Andrei Aksenov, Deputy Director of the Soviet Academy's Institute of Oceanography.

24 Berlitz, *Atlantis – The Lost Continent Revealed*, p. 81.

25 In a letter from Herb Sawinski to Bill Donato, dated 21 May 1998, the following anomalies are described:

(a) an underwater causeway of large pillow-like stones, similar to the Bimini Road, runs in a south-easterly direction from a position some 20 metres out from the largest of the Anguilla Isles, located in the south-east corner of the Cay Sal Bank. The blocks are regularly four metres square and must weigh as much as several tonnes apiece. They run for a distance of around 100 metres towards a smaller cay before disappearing beneath the sand. Significantly, the causeway is orientated at 90 degrees to the nearby coast, invalidating the idea, asserted by marine geologists, that formations of beachrock only ever run parallel to the shoreline. According to Sawinski, caves close to the Anguilla Road have also produced various inexplicable artefacts including conch-shell firestones, pottery shards and bones of unknown origin;

(b) a similar stone causeway located off the main island of Cay Sal is, according to Sawinski, 'not as distinctive as those off Bimini and Anguilla'. Once again, it is at an angle of 90 degrees to the nearby shoreline and runs for only a short distance before making a right-angle turn. It then continues for a distance of approximately one and half kilometres before coming to an abrupt halt in front of a sheer drop off to a depth of 480 metres. Another breakaway wall-like structure departs from the main feature and continues in a south-south-easterly direction towards a small cay. Under the guidance of Sawinski, this particular structure was investigated in the early 1980s by Charles Berlitz and his wife Lin. Photographs of the site were subsequently featured in Berlitz's best-selling book *Atlantis – The Lost Continent Revealed*, first published in 1984;

(c) at a cay referred to by Sawinski as 'The Quarry' are several underwater caves, one of which contains 'two large cut stones about 5 × 5 × 8 [feet, i.e. 1.5 × 1.5 × 2.4 metres], one lying on top of the other'. Apparently, the walls of the cave are remarkably 'smooth and straight', implying that it started its life as a quarry. Sawinski also points out that 'you'll know you're in the right area, when you find a large, ancient anchor lying across the blocks';

(d) a cave located at what Sawinski refers to as 'Raspberry Reef' has interior walls that he concludes are 'hewn and sculptured', suggesting that it began life as a quarry.

26 Personal communication with Vanda Osman and Bill Donato, December 1997, based on earlier conversations with J. Manson Valentine's widow, Anna.

27 Palmer, *The Blue Holes of the Bahamas*, pp. 78, 141.

28 Bright, *There are Giants in the Sea*, p. 137; Palmer, p. 73.

29 E-mail communication dated 8 December 1998 from Rose Blanchard, who worked at the Forfar Field Station on Andros from 1975 to 1979; Bright, p. 137.

30 Bright, pp. 131, 133, after Professor Addison Verrill.

31 E-mail communication dated 8 December 1998 from Rose Blanchard, who worked at the Forfar Field Station on Andros from 1975 to 1979.

32 Personal communication with Herb Sawinski, various occasions, 1998 and 1999. Also e-mail communication from Sawinski dated 2 February 1999.

33 Palmer, p. 20.

34 Ibid.

35 Ibid.

36 Ibid.

37 Ibid., p. 87.

38 Ibid.

39 Ibid., p. 90.

40 Ibid.

41 Ibid.

42 Ibid.

Twenty-five: The Odyssey of Votan

1 Brasseur de Bourbourg, *Histoire des nations civilisées du Mexique et de l'Amérique-centrale, etc.*, Vol. 1, p. 42, cf. Nuñez de la Vega, *Constituciones dioeces., etc.*

2 Ibid., Vol. 1, p. 71, cf. Ordoñez, *Hist. del cielo y de la tierra, etc.* All references carried from Ordoñez are from this work unless otherwise stated.

3 Ibid., Vol. 1, p. 71 n. 2.

4 Hastings, *Encyclopaedia of Religion and Ethics*, Vol. 11, p. 402. See also Müller, *Geschichte der Amerikanischen Urreligionen*, pp. 486–91.

5 Brasseur de Bourbourg, Vol. 1, pp. 71–2, cf. Nuñez de la Vega and Ordoñez.

6 Ibid., Vol. 1, p. 71, cf. Ordoñez.

7 Ibid.

8 Ibid., Vol. 1, p. 73, cf. Ordoñez, MS fragments.

9 Ibid., Vol. 1, p. 68, cf. Ordoñez.

10 Ibid.

11 Ibid., Vol. 1, p. 69, cf. Ordoñez.

12 Ibid., Vol. 1, p. 69 n. 4.

13 Ibid., Vol. 1, p. 70, cf. Ordoñez.

14 Ibid., Vol. 1, pp. 70, 78, cf. Ordoñez.

15 Ibid., Vol. 1, pp. 70–71, cf. Ordoñez.

16 Ibid., Vol. 1, p. 70, cf. Ordoñez.

17 Ibid., Vol. 1, p. 71, cf. Ordoñez.

18 Ibid.

19 Ibid., Vol. 1, pp. 71–2, cf. Ordoñez.

20 Ibid., Vol. 1, p. 72, cf. Nuñez de la Vega and Ordoñez.

21 Ibid., Vol. 1, p. 72, cf. Ordoñez.

22 Ibid.

23 Ibid., Vol. 1, p. 73, cf. Ordoñez.

24 Ibid., Vol. 1, p. 73, cf. Ordoñez, MS fragments.

25 Ibid., Vol. 1, p. 73, cf. Nuñez de la Vega.

26 Ibid., Vol. 1, pp. 73–4 n. 5.

27 Ibid.

28 Ibid.

29 Ibid., Vol. 1, pp. 94–5.

30 Ibid., Vol. 1, pp. 95–6.

31 Ibid., Vol. 1, p. 96.

32 Ibid.

33 Ibid., Vol. 1, p. 97.

34 Ibid., Vol. 1, p. 80, cf. Nuñez de la Vega.

35 Ibid., Vol. 1, p. 81.

36 Thompson, *People of the Serpent*, pp. 42–6.

37 Ibid., p. 47.

38 Brasseur de Bourbourg, Vol. 1, p. 71, cf. Ordoñez.

39 Ibid., Vol. 1, p. 72, cf. Ordoñez; p. 73, cf. Ordoñez, MS fragments.

40 Ibid., Vol. 1, p. 68, cf. Ordoñez.

41 Ibid., Vol. 1, p. 68.

42 Ibid., Vol. 1, p. 71, Nuñez de la Vega and Ordoñez.

43 Ibid.
44 Irwin, *Fair Gods and Stone Faces*, p. 98; Tompkins, p. 78.
45 Brasseur de Bourbourg, Vol. 1, p. 71.
46 Ibid.
47 Gen. 34:2, Jos. 9:7; 11:19.
48 Gen. 14:6.
49 Ordelain and Séguineau, *Dictionary of Proper Names and Places in the Bible*, s.v. 'Horites', p. 164.
50 Irwin, p. 100.
51 Gen. 10:4.
52 Gen. 10:1.
53 Easton, s.v. 'Chittim', pp. 141–2; Harden, *The Phoenicians*, pp. 58–9.
54 Easton, s.v. 'Chittim', pp. 141–2.
55 Graves, *New Larrouse Encyclopaedia of Mythology*, pp. 73–5.
56 Ibid., p. 84.
57 See Gen. 3: 14–15.
58 Staniland Wake, *Serpent-Worship and Other Essays, etc.*, pp. 15, 125.
59 Ibid., p. 15.
60 Clement of Alexandria, Vol. I, p. 27 in *Ante-Niocene Christian Library*, Vol. iv.
61 Graves and Patai, *Hebrew Myths – the Book of Genesis*, p. 100.
62 Ibid., p. 106.
63 Gen. 6:4.
64 1En. 69:12. All references for 1En. from Charles, *The Book of Enoch or 1 Enoch.*
65 1En. 69:6.
66 1En. 8:1.
67 1En. 8:2.
68 Spence, *The Myths of Mexico and Peru*, p. 65.
69 1En. 8:3.
70 1En. 69:8–9.
71 1En. 69:12.
72 2En. 8:1–6. All references for 2En. from Morfill and Charles, *The Book of the Secrets of Enoch.*
73 Ez. 27:23.
74 Ez. 27:24.
75 Massey, *The Natural Genesis*, Vol. 2, p. 231.
76 See Collins, *From the Ashes of Angels*, pp. 161–3, 238–9, for arguments on Al Judi being the Place of Descent in the story of Noah's Ark.
77 See Collins, *Gods of Eden*, pp. 234–44.
78 See Collins, *From the Ashes of Angels*, pp. 242–5, and Collins, *Gods of Eden*, pp. 220–26.
79 Num. 13:33.
80 Num. 13:32.
81 Jos. 14:14–15; Graves and Patai, pp. 106–7.

82 Jos. 15:13–14.

83 For the height of the Watchers see 2En. 1:4; for the Nephilim see 1En. 7:2; for the Anakim see Num. 13:32.

84 2En. 1:4.

85 Milik, *The Books of Enoch – Aramaic Fragments of Qumrân Cave 4*, p. 306; Henning, 'The Book of the Giants', *Bulletin of the School of Oriental and African Studies*, Vol. 11, pt. 1, p. 66; see also 'The Midrash of Semhazai and 'Aza'el' quoted in Milik, p. 327.

86 1En. 106:2.

87 2En. 1:5.

88 1En. 87:2.

89 1En. 106:2.

90 2En. 1:5.

91 1En. 106:2; 2En. 1:5.

92 Eisenman and Wise, 'Testament of Amram', 4Q543, *The Dead Sea Scrolls Uncovered*, p. 156.

93 Collins, *From the Ashes of Angels*, p. 49.

94 2En. 1:4–5; Morfill and Charles, p. 2 n. 6.

95 Collins, *From the Ashes of Angels*, pp. 49–51.

96 Henning, p. 61.

97 Ibid.

98 Milik, p. 306. See also Collins, *From the Ashes of Angels*, p. 391.

99 Hauptmann, 'Ein Kultgebäude in Nevali Çori', *Between the Rivers and over the Mountains: Archaeologica Anatolica et Mesopotamica*, pp. 55, 66; Meyers, *Oxford Encyclopaedia of Archaeology in the Near East*, s.v. 'Nevali Çori', Vol. 4, p. 133; Collins, *Gods of Eden*, p. 239.

100 Brasseur de Bourbourg, Vol. 1, p. 111, cf. Las Casas, *Hist. Apolog. de las Indias-Occid.*, bk. III, cap. 123.

101 Gilbert and Cotterell, *The Mayan Prophecies*, p. 122–3.

102 Janku, 'Skulls from Ica, Peru, and Merida', Mexico', unpublished paper, 1996, available @ *www.paradigm-sys.com/ae/lib/archeo/skulls.html*.

103 Brasseur de Bourbourg, Vol. 1, p. 153, p. 153 n. 3, cf. Codex Chimalpopoca, *Hist. Chron.*

104 Ibid.

105 Molleson and Campbell, 'Deformed Skulls at Tell Arpachiyah: The Social Context', in Campbell and Green, eds., *The Archaeology of Death in the Ancient Near East*, Oxbow Monograph No. 51, 1995, pp. 45–55.

106 Collins, *Gods of Eden*, pp. 259–65.

107 Thompson, p. 77.

108 Wilkins, *Secret Cities of Old South America: Atlantis Unveiled*, p. 112.

109 Brasseur de Bourbourg, Vol. 1, p. 110.

110 Jos. 14:12.

111 See Collins, *From the Ashes of Angels*, pp. 231–3, for a full account of the connections between the Nephilim and the demonic 'men with the bodies of birds' that the Babylonian tablet known as the 'Legend of Creation from Cutha [Kutha]' says engaged the earliest kings of Sumer and Akkad.

Twenty-six: Rattling of the Pleiades

1 Sanchoniathon, in Cory, *Ancient Fragments*, p. 9.
2 Ibid., p. 9.
3 Lemprière, *A Classical Dictionary*, s.v. 'Saturnus', pp. 545–6.
4 Ibid.
5 Sanchoniathon, in Cory, p. 9.
6 See Collins, *From the Ashes of Angels*, for a full account of the relationship between the Watchers, Nephilim and Elohim.
7 See, for instance, the works of Berossus, Eupolemus and Alexander Polyhistor, as well as 'The Sibylline Oracles', all as quoted in Cory.
8 See, for instance, Berossus and Alexander Polyhistor, as well as 'The Sibylline Oracles', all as quoted in Cory.
9 Lemprière, s.v. 'Titan', p. 620.
10 Lemprière, s.v. 'Gigantes', p. 249.
11 Ibid.; Eupolemus, in Cory, p. 53.
12 Lemprière, s.v. 'Gyges', p. 256; Ovid, *Tristia*, 4, vii, 18.
13 Thallus, in Cory, p. 53.
14 Whishaw, *Atlantis in Andalucia*, p. 173.
15 See Whishaw, *Atlantis in Andalucia*.
16 Pardo, *The World of Ancient Spain*, p. 30.
17 Ibid.
18 Ibid., p. 32.
19 Ibid., p. 33.
20 Rodero, *España Oculta: Public Celebrations in Spain, 1974–1989*, pl. 57.
21 Plutarch, *The Face of the Moon*, 26, 941b fn., cf. Charax, Frag. 16, *Frag. Hist. Graec.*, iii, p. 640.
22 Ibid., 26. 940–14.
23 Ibid., 941a–941b.
24 See, for example, Cahill, *New England's Ancient Mysteries*, and Fell, *America BC: Ancient Settlers in the New World*.
25 Scrutton, *Secrets of Lost Atland*, p. 61.
26 See Michell, *At the Centre of the World: Polar Symbolism Discovered in Celtic, Norse and Other Ritualized Landscapes*, and Michell and Rhone, *Twelve Tribe Nations and the Science of Enchanting the Landscape*.
27 Braghine, *The Shadow of Atlantis*, pp. 252–3.
28 See, for example, Allan and Delair, *When the Earth Nearly Died*, p. 317.
29 Zerries, 'Primitive South America and the West Indies', in Krickeberg, Müller, Trimborn and Zerries, *Pre-Columbian American Religions*, p. 246.
30 Ibid.
31 Ibid., p. 243.
32 Haliburton, *The History of Man derived from a companion of the customs and superstitions of Nations: The Festivals of the Dead*, p. 17.
33 Ibid., p. 13.
34 Ginzberg, *The Legends of the Jews*, i, 162.

35 Haliburton, p. 13 fn.
36 Ibid., pp. 13–14.
37 Plato, *Timaeus*, 22b–22c.
38 Ibid., 22d.
39 Ibid., 22c.

Appendix I: The Colour Purple

1 Born, 'The Use of Purple among the Indians of Central America', *Ciba Review*, Vol. 4, 1937, p. 126.
2 Ibid.
3 Ibid., Vol. 4, p. 125.
4 Ibid.
5 Ibid.
6 Ibid.
7 Ibid., Vol. 4, p. 124.
8 Ibid.
9 Ibid.
10 Ibid., Vol. 4, p. 126.
11 Ibid.
12 Ibid., Vol. 4, pp. 124–5.
13 Ibid. The article by Zelia Nuttall is entitled 'A Curious Survival in Mexico of the Use of the Purpura Shell-Fish for Dyeing', 1909.
14 Ibid., Vol. 4, p. 127.
15 Johnston, *Did the Phoenicians discover America?*, p. 211.
16 Jett, 'Dyestuffs and Possible Early Contacts Between Southwestern Asia and Nuclear America', in Gilmore and McElroy, p. 145.

Appendix II: Cotton Matters

1 Columbus, *The Life of the Admiral Christopher Columbus by his Son Ferdinand*, p. 86.
2 Irwin, *Fair Gods and Stone Faces* pp. 278–9.
3 Irwin, p. 280; Heyerdahl, *Early Man and the Ocean*, p. 82; Hutchinson, Silow and Stephens, *The Evolution of Gossypium and the Differentiation of the Cultivated Cottons.*
4 Irwin, p. 280.
5 Ibid.
6 Heyerdahl, p. 83.

BIBLIOGRAPHY

Notes: If two dates are shown, the first given is the original year of publication and the second is the edition consulted by the author.

Abbreviations: npp. = no place of publication; nd. = no date; OUP = Oxford University Press, Oxford; ESOP = Epigraphic Society Occasional Publications/Papers; *ZAS* = *Zeitschrift für Agyptische Sprache*, Leipzig.

Aelian, *Historical Miscellany*, ed. and English trans. N. G. Wilson, Harvard University Press, Cambridge, Mass., and London, 1997

Allan, D. S., and J. B. Delair, *When the Earth Nearly Died*, Gateway Books, Bath, 1995

Allen, Jim M., *Atlantis: The Andes Solution*, The Windrush Press, Moreton-in-Marsh, Gloucestershire, 1998

Ammianus Marcellinus, *The Roman History of Ammianus Marcellinus*, trans. C. D. Yonge, Henry G. Bohn, London, 1862

'The Annals of the Cakchiquels', trans. Adrián Recinos and Delia Goetz, see *The Annals of the Cakchiquels/The Title of the Lords of Totonicapán*

The Annals of the Cakchiquels/The Title of the Lords of Totonicapán, University of Oklahoma Press, Norman, Oklahoma, 1953

Apollodorus, *The Library*, trans. Sir James George Frazer, 2 vols: Vol. 1, Wm. Heinemann, London, and G. P. Putnam's Sons, New York, 1921

Aristotle, *Meteorologica*, English trans. H. D. P. Lee, Wm. Heinemann, London, Harvard University Press, Cambridge, Mass., 1962

Pseudo-Aristotle, *De Mundo*, trans. E. S. Forster, see Ross, *The Works of Aristotle*

Pseudo-Aristotle, *On Marvellous Things Heard*, Hett translation, in Camp, p. 294

Ashe, Geoffrey, *Atlantis: Lost lands, Ancient Wisdom*, Thames and Hudson, London, 1992

Ashe, Geoffrey, *Land to the West: St Brendan's Voyage to America*, Collins, London, 1962

Ashe, Geoffrey, Thor Heyerdahl, Helge Ingstad, J. V. Luce, Betty J. Meggers and Brigitta L. Wallace, *The Quest for America*, Pall Mall Press, London, 1971

Avieni, *Ora Maritime (Periplus Massiliensis saec. VI. A. C.)*, ed. Adolf Schulten, Apud Librarium/A. Bosch, Barcinone and Apud Weidmannos, Berolini, 1922

Avienus, Rufus Festus, see Avieni

Babcock, William H., *Legendary Islands of the Atlantic: A Study in Medieval Geography*, American Geographical Society, New York, 1922

Balabanova, Svetlana, Franz Parsche and Wolfgang Pirsig, 'First Identification of Drugs in Egyptian Mummies', *Naturwissenschaften*, 79, 1992, p. 358

Banks, Revd J., *The Works of Hesiod, Callimachus and Theognis, etc.*, Geo. Bell and Sons, London, 1909

Bankes, George, *Peru before Pizarro*, Phaidon, Oxford, 1977

Bellamy, H. S., *Moons, Myths and Man: A Reinterpretation*, 1936, Faber & Faber, London, 1949

Bérard, Victor, 'L'Atlantide de Platon', *Annales de Géographie*, Vol. 38, no. 213, 15 May 1929, pp. 193–205

Berlitz, Charles, *Atlantis – The Lost Continent Revealed*, Macmillan, London and Basingstoke, Hants., 1984

Berlitz, Charles, *Mysteries from Forgotten Worlds – Rediscovered Lost Civilisations*, Souvenir Press, London, 1972

Berlitz, Charles, *The Mystery of Atlantis*, 1969, Panther, Frogmore, St Albans, Herts., 1977

Berry, William, *Encyclopaedia Heraldica*, 3 vols, Sherwood, Gilbert and Piper, London, 1837

The Holy Bible, 1611, Revised, OUP, 1905

Björck, Svante, Bernd Kromer, Sigfus Johnsen, Ole Bennike, Dan Hammarlund, Geoffrey Lemdahl, Göran Possnert, Tine Lander Rasmussen, Barbara Wohlfarth, Claus Uffe Hammer, Marco Spurk, 'Synchronized Terrestrial-Atmospheric Deglacial Records Around the North Atlantic', *Science*, Vol. 274, 15 November 1996, pp. 1,155–60

Born, Wolfgang, 'The Use of Purple among the Indians of Central America', *Ciba Review*, Vol. 4, 1937, pp. 124–7

Bradford, Ernle, *Christopher Columbus*, Michael Joseph, London, 1973

Braghine, Col. A., *The Shadow of Atlantis*, 1940, Adventures Unlimited Press, Kempton, Ill., 1997

Bramwell, James, *Lost Atlantis*, Cobden-Sanderson, London, 1937

Brasseur de Bourbourg, l'Abbé, *Histoire des nations civilisées du*

Mexique et de l'Amérique-centrale, durant les siècles antérieurs à Christophe Colomb, Libraire de la Société de Géographie, Paris, Vol. 1, 1857

Bright, Michael, *There are Giants in the Sea*, Robson Books/Guild Publishing, London, 1989

Brinton, Daniel G., 'The Archaeology of Cuba', *American Anthropologist*, Vol. 10, 1898, in *Archaeological Tracts 1895–8*, Judd and Detweiler, Washington DC, pp. 231–4

Brinton, Daniel G., *The Myths of the New World: A Treatise on the Symbolism and Mythology of the Red Race of America*, Leypoldt & Holt, New York, 1868

Broecker, Wallace S., 'The Ocean', *Scientific American*, no. 249, 1983, pp. 146–60

Broecker, Wallace S., Maurice Ewing and Bruce C. Heezen, 'Evidence for an Abrupt Change in Climate close to 11,000 years ago', *American Journal of Science*, Vol. 258, June 1960, pp. 429–48

Brotherston, G., *Painted Books from Mexico*, British Museum Press, London, 1995

Bunbury, Edward Herbert, *A History of Ancient Geography*, 2 vols, 2nd edn., 1883, Dover, New York, 1959

Burger, Richard L., *Chavín and the Origin of Andean Civilisation*, 1992, Thames and Hudson, London, 1995

Burland, Cottie, and Werner Forman, *Feathered Serpent and Smoking Mirror*, Orbis Publishing, London, 1975

Burman, Edward, *Supremely Abominable Crimes: The Trial of the Knights Templar*, Allison & Busby, London, 1994

Bury, the Rev. R. G., *Plato: Timaeus, Critias, Cleitophon, Menexenus, Epistles*, Loeb/Wm. Heinemann, London, G. P. Putnam, New York, 1929

Cahill, Robert Ellis, *New England's Ancient Mysteries*, Old Saltbox Publishing House, Salem, Mass., 1993

Camp, L. Sprague de, *Lost Continents: The Atlantis Theme in History, Science, and Literature*, 1954, Dover Publications, New York, 1970

Campbell, Joseph, and M. J. Abadie, *The Mythic Image*, 2 vols, Princeton University Press, Princeton, NJ, 1974

Carrasco, David, *Quetzalcoatl and the Irony of Empire: Myths and Prophecies in the Aztec Tradition*, 1982, University of Chicago Press, Chicago and London, 1984

Carson, Charles E., and Keith M. Hussey, 'The Oriented Lakes of Arctic Alaska', *Journal of Geology*, Vol. 70, 1962, pp. 417–39

Cassell Pocket English Dictionary, 1891, Cassell, London, 1995

Castle, Brother E. J., *The Proceedings Against the Templars in France and England for Heresy, etc.* AD *1307–11, taken from the Official Documents of the Period*, privately published (and in the possession of Templar expert Robert Bryden of Edinburgh), *c.* 1900

Cayce, Edgar, *Atlantis – The Edgar Cayce Readings*, Vol. 22, ARE, Virginia Beach, Va., 1987

Cayce, Edgar Evans, *Edgar Cayce on Atlantis*, ed., Hugh Lynn Cayce, 1968, Howard Baker, London, 1969

Cayce, Edgar Evans, Gail Cayce Schwartzer and Douglas G. Richards, *Mysteries of Atlantis Revisited*, Harper & Row, San Francisco, 1988

Chambers, Edmund Kerchever, *The History and Motives of Literary Forgeries*, 1891, Folcroft Library, npp., 1975

Charles, R. H., *The Book of Enoch or 1 Enoch*, OUP, 1912

Clarke, Hyde, *Examination of the Legend of Atlantis in Reference to Protohistoric Communication with America*, June 1885, Longmans, Green & Co., London, 1886

Clement of Alexandria, Vol. 1 in *Ante-Nicene Christian Library: Translations of the Writings of the Fathers down to AD 325*, Vol. 4, T. and T. Clark, Edinburgh, 1867

Clube, Victor, and Bill Napier, *The Cosmic Serpent*, Faber & Faber, London, 1982

Coe, Michael D., *Breaking the Maya Code*, Thames and Hudson, London, 1992

Collins, Andrew, *From the Ashes of Angels: The Forbidden Legacy of a Fallen Race*, Michael Joseph, London, 1996

Collins, Andrew, *Gods of Eden: Egypt's Lost Legacy and the Genesis of Civilisation*, Headline, London, 1998

Collins, Andrew, 'Soviet oceanographers stir up Atlantis myth', *Strange Phenomena*, Vol. 1, no. 1, 1979, pp. 36–7

Columbus, Ferdinand, *The Life of the Admiral Christopher Columbus by his Son Ferdinand*, trans. & anno. Benjamin Keen, The Folio Society, London, 1960

'Comet that Launched Noah's Ark', *The Times*, London, 22 April 1996

Corner, E. J. H., *The Natural History of Palms*, Weidenfeld & Nicolson, London, 1966

Cornford, Francis Macdonald, *Plato's Cosmology; The Timaeus of Plato translated with a running commentary*, Kegan Paul, Trench, Trubner, New York; Harcourt, Brace, London, 1937

Cortés, F., *The Conquest of Mexico*, J. Newbury, London, 1760

Cortesão, Armando, *The Nautical Chart of 1424 and the Early Discovery and Cartographical Representation of America: A Study of the History of Early Navigation and Cartography*, University of Coimbra, Coimbra, Portugal, 1954

Cory, Isaac Preston, *Ancient Fragments etc.*, 1832, Wizards Bookshelf, Minneapolis, Minn., 1975

Crampsey, Robert A., *Puerto Rico*, David & Charles, Newton Abbot, Devon, 1973

Craton, Michael, *A History of the Bahamas*, 1962, Collins, London, 1968

Crone, G. R., 'The Origin of the name Antillia', *The Geographical Journal*, March 1938, pp. 260–6

Crone, G. R., 'The Pizigano Chart and the "Pillars of Hercules" ', *The Geographical Journal*, April–June 1947, pp. 278–9

Cruxent, José M., and Irving Rouse, 'Early man in the West Indies', *Scientific American*, Vol. 221, 1969, pp. 42–52

Davies, Nigel, *The Aztecs*, 1973, Abacus, London, 1977

Davies, Nigel, *The Aztec Empire: The Toltec Resurgence*, University of Oklahoma Press, Norman, Oklahoma, 1987

Davis, Henry, *The Works of Plato*, Vol. 2: 'The Republic', 'Timaeus' and 'Critias', Henry G. Bohn, London, 1849

Deacon, Richard, *Madoc and the Discovery of America*, Fredk. Muller, London, 1967

Diodorus Siculus, *Library*, trans. C. H. Oldfather, 10 vols, Wm. Heinemann, London, Harvard University Press, Cambridge, Mass., 1935

Donato, William M., 'The Architecture of Atlantis: A General Survey', *The Atlantis Organisation Journal*, no. 15, December 1996, pp. 28–31

Donato, William M., *A Re-examination of the Atlantis Theory*, privately produced Master's thesis, California State Univ., Fullerton, Calif., 1979

Donato, William M., 'Bimini and the Atlantis Controversy', *The Ancient American*, Vol. 1, no. 3, November/December 1993, pp. 4–13

Donato, William M., 'Project Alta: Parts 2 & 3, and the Television Productions', *The Atlantis Organisation Journal*, no. 14, November 1995, pp. 1–7

Donato, William M., 'What You Did Not See (or Hear) on Arthur C. Clarke's Mysterious Universe', *The Ancient American*, no. 14, 1996, pp. 4–7

Donnelly, Ignatius, *Atlantis: The Antediluvian World*, 1882, Harper, New York, London, 1902

Donnelly, Ignatius, *Ragnarok: The Age of Fire and Gravel*, 1886, Sampson Low, Marston, Searle and Rivington, London, 1888

Drucker, Philip, Robert F. Heizer and Robert J. Squier, 'Radiocarbon dates from La Venta, Tabasco', *Science*, Vol. 126, 12 July 1957, pp. 72–3

Durán, Diego, *Historia de las Indias de Nueva España e Islas de Tierra Firme*, trans. Doris Heyden, in Markman and Markman

Easton, M. G., *The Illustrated Bible Dictionary*, 1894, Bracken Books, London, 1989

Eccott, David, 'Before Columbus (the Calixtlahuaca Roman head)', *Quest for Knowledge*, Vol. 1, no. 5, Autumn 1997, pp. 18–19

Eccott, David, 'Comalcalco: A Case for Early Pre-Columbian Contact and Influence', *Chronology and Catastrophism Review*, Vol. 1, 1999, pp. 21–9

Eccott, David, 'Comalcalco: Maya innovation or Old World Intervention?', *The Ancient American*, Vol. 3, no. 24, July–August 1998, pp. 8–16

Eccott, David, 'Comalcalco – The "Roman mason marks": A closer look', unpublished paper, 1999

Eisenman, Robert H., and Michael Wise, *The Dead Sea Scrolls Uncovered*, Element, Shaftesbury, Dorset, 1992

Emiliani, Cesare, 'Paleoclimatological Analysis of Late Quaternary Cores from the Northeastern Gulf of Mexico', *Science*, 26 September 1975, Vol. 189, pp. 1,083–8

Eyton, J. Ronald, and Judith I. Parkhurst, 'A Re-evaluation of the Extraterrestrial Origin of the Carolina Bays', Department of Geography Paper No. 9, University of Illinois, Urbana Champaign, Ill., April 1975

Fallon, Stephen, *Guide to Cuba*, 1995, Bradt, Chalfont St Peter, Bucks.; The Globe Pequot Press, Old Saybrook, Conn., 1996

Fears, J. Rufus, 'Atlantis and the Minoan Thalassocracy: A Study in Modern Mythopoeism', in Ramage, pp. 103–36

Fell, Barry, 'Alphabetic Libyan Mason's Marks on Mochica Adobe Bricks', *ESOP*, Vol. 20, 1991, pp. 224–30

Fell, Barry, *America BC: Ancient Settlers in the New World*, 1976, Quadrangle/The New York Times Book Co., New York, 1977; revised ed., Pocket Books, New York, 1989

Fingerhut, Eugene R., *Explorers of Pre-Columbian America: The Diffusionist Inventionist Controversy*, California State University, Los Angeles/Regina Books, Claremont, Calif., 1994

Flem-ath, Rand, and Rose Flem-ath, *When the Sky Fell: In Search of Atlantis*, Weidenfeld and Nicolson, London, 1995

Forsyth, Phyllis Young, *Atlantis: The Making of Myth*, McGill-Queen's University Press, Montreal, Croom Helm, London, 1980

Frazer, James George, *Folk-lore in the Old Testament*, 3 vols, Macmillan, London, 1919

Freeman, Kathleen, *The Work and Life of Solon*, Univ. of Wales Press, London, 1926

Fritze, Ronald H., *Legend and Lore of the Americas before 1492*, 1988, ABC-CLIO, Santa Barbara, Calif., Denver, Colo., Oxford, 1993

Gaffarel, Paul, *Histoire de la découverte de l'Amérique depuis les origines jusqu'à la mort de Christophe Colomb*, 2 vols, Société Bourguignonne de Geographie et d'Histoire, Paris, 1892

Galanopoulos, A. G., and E. Bacon, *Atlantis: The truth behind the legend*, Nelson, London, 1969

Galvão, Antonio, *The Discoveries of the World from their first originall unto the yeere of our Lord 1555*, see Raleigh

Gamboa, Pedro Sarmiento de, *History of the Incas*, and Captain Baltasar de Ocampo, *The Execution of the Inca Tupac Amaru*, trans. Sir Clements Markham, Hakluyt Society, 1907

Gardiner, Alan H., *Egypt of the Pharaohs*, 1961, OUP, 1964

Gardiner, Alan H., *The Royal Canon of Turin*, 1959, OUP, 1987

Gardner, Laurence, *Bloodline of the Grail*, Element Books, London, 1996

Gifford, John A., 'The Bimini "cyclopean" complex', *International Journal of Nautical Archaeology and Underwater Exploration*, Vol. 2, 1973, p. 189

Gilbert, Adrian, and Maurice Cotterell, *The Mayan Prophecies*, Element Books, Shaftesbury, Dorset, 1995

Gilmore, Donald Y., and Linda S. McElroy, *Across Before Columbus? Evidence for Transoceanic Contact with the Americas prior to 1492*, NEARA Publications, Edgecomb, Maine, 1998

Ginzberg, L., *The Legends of the Jews*, Vol. 1, The Jewish Publication Society of America, Philadelphia, Pa., 1909

Goodrick-Clarke, Nicholas, *The Occult Roots of Nazism*, 1985, I.B. Tauris, London/New York, 1992

Gordon, Cyrus H., *Before Columbus: Links between the Old World and Ancient America*, 1971, Turnstone Press, London, 1972

Graves, Robert, ed., *New Larousse Encyclopaedia of Mythology*, 1959, Hamlyn, London, 1983

Graves, Robert, and Raphael Patai, *Hebrew Myths – the Book of Genesis*, Cassell, London, 1964

Green, Peter, *Alexander to Actium: The Hellenistic Age*, Thames and Hudson, London, 1993

Griffiths, J. Gwyn, 'Atlantis and Egypt', in Griffiths, *Atlantis and Egypt with other Selected Essays*, pp. 3–30

Griffiths, J. Gwyn, *Atlantis and Egypt with other Selected Essays*, University of Wales Press, Cardiff, 1991

Guthrie, James L., 'Human Lymphocite Antigens: Apparent Afro-Asiatic, South Asian & European HLAs in Indigenous American Populations', unpublished draft, February 1998

Hadingham, Evan, *Early Man and the Cosmos*, Wm. Heinemann, London, 1983

Haliburton, R. G., *The History of Man derived from a companion of the customs and superstitions of Nations: The Festivals of the Dead*, T. Chamberlain, Halifax, Nova Scotia, 1863

Hancock, Graham, Robert Bauval and John Grigsby, *The Mars Mystery*, Michael Joseph, London, 1998

Hapgood, Charles, *Maps of the Ancient Sea Kings*, 1966, Turnstone Books, London, 1979

Harden, Donald, *The Phoenicians*, Thames and Hudson, London, 1962

Harden, Donald, 'The Phoenicians on the West Coast of Africa', *Antiquity*, XXII, 1948, pp. 141–50

Harlow, George, 'Hard Rock: A mineralogist explores the origins of Mesoamerican Jade', unpublished paper, Department of Mineral Sciences at the American Museum of Natural History, New York, nd., *c.* 1998

Harris, Zellig, *A Grammar of Phoenician Language*, American Oriental Society, New Haven, Conn., 1936

Harrison, W., 'Atlantis Undiscovered – Bimini, Bahamas', *Nature*, Vol. 230, 2 April 1971, pp. 287–9

Hastings, James, ed., *Encyclopaedia of Religion and Ethics*, 13 vols, 1915, T. & T. Clark, Edinburgh, 1930

Hauptmann, Harald, 'Ein Kultgebäude in Nevali Çori', *Between the Rivers and over the Mountains: Archaeologica Anatolica et Mesopotamica*, Alba Palmeiri Dedicata, ed. Marcella Frangipane et al, Rome, 1993, pp. 37–69

Heine-Geldern, Robert, 'Ein Römischer Fund aus dem Vorkolumbischen Mexiko', *Anzeiger der Osterreichischen Akademie der Wissenschaften*, no. 16, 1961, pp. 117–19

Henning, W. B., 'The Book of the Giants', *Bulletin of the School of Oriental and African Studies*, Vol. 11, pt. 1, 1943, pp. 52–74

Herodotus, *The History of Herodotus*, 1910, 2 vols, J. M. Dent, London; E. P. Dutton, New York, 1940

Hesiod, *Theogony*, see Banks

Heyerdahl, Thor, *Early Man and the Ocean*, Geo. Allen & Unwin, London, 1978

Hibben, Frank C., *The Lost Americans*, Thomas Y. Crowell, New York, NY, 1946

Hill, Robert T., *Cuba and Puerto Rico with the Other Islands of the West Indies*, T. Fisher Unwin, London, 1898

Hine, Albert C., and John C. Steinmetz, 'Cay Sal Bank, Bahamas – A Partially Drowned Carbonate Platform', *Marine Geology*, Vol. 59, 1984, pp. 135–64

Hitching, Francis, *The Mysterious World – An Atlas of the Unexplained*, 1978, Holt, Rinehart & Winston, New York, 1979

Homer, *The Iliad*, English trans. A. T. Murray, 2 vols, 1925, Harvard University Press, Cambridge, Mass.; Wm. Heinemann, London, 1967

Homer, *The Odyssey*, English trans. A. T. Murray, 2 vols, 1919, Harvard University Press, Cambridge, Mass.; Wm. Heinemann, London, 1984

Hosea, L. M., 'Atlantis: A Statement of the "Atlantic" Theory Respecting Aboriginal Civilisation', *The Cincinnati Quarterly Journal of Science*, Vol. II, no. 3, July 1875, pp. 193–211

Houlihan, Patrick F., *The Animal World of the Pharaohs,* Thames and Hudson, London, 1996

Hutchinson, J. B., R. A. Silow and S. G. Stephens, *The Evolution of Gossypium and the Differentiation of the Cultivated Cottons,* Geoffrey Cumberlege/OUP, London, New York and Toronto, 1947

Hutton, William, *Coming Earth Changes – the Latest Evidence,* 1996, ARE Press, Virginia Beach, Va., 1997

Ingram, Roy L., Maryanne Robinson and Howard T. Odum, 'Clay Mineralogy of some Carolina Bay Sediments', *Southeastern Geology,* Vol. 1, 1959, pp. 1–10

Irwin, Constance, *Fair Gods and Stone Faces: Ancient Seafarers and the New World's Most Intriguing Riddle,* 1963, W. H. Allen, London, 1964

Jacobs, William, 'Toke Like an Egyptian', *Fortean Times,* FT117, December 1998, pp. 34–8

Jairazbhoy, R. A., *Ancient Egyptians and Chinese in America,* Geo. Prior Associated Publishers, London, 1974

James, Peter, *The Sunken Kingdom: The Atlantis Mystery Solved,* 1995, Pimlico, London, 1996

James, Peter, and Nick Thorpe, *Ancient Inventions,* 1994, Michael O'Mara Books, London, 1996

Janku, Lumir G., 'Skulls from Ica, Peru, and Merida, Mexico', unpublished paper, 1996, @ www.paradigm-sys.com/ae/lib/archeo/skulls.html

Jelinkova, E. A. E., 'The Shebtiw in the temple of Edfu', *ZAS,* no. 87, 1962, pp. 41–54

Jett, Stephen C., 'Dyestuffs and Possible Early Contacts Between Southwestern Asia and Nuclear America', in Gilmore and McElroy, pp. 141–9

Jimenez, A. Nuñez, *Cuevas y pictografias,* Estudios Espeleologicos y Arquelogicos, Havana, Cuba, 1964

Johnson, Donald S., *Phantom Islands of the Atlantic,* 1994, Souvenir Press, London, 1997

Johnson, Douglas W., 'Supposed Meteorite Scars of South Carolina', *Science,* Vol. 79, 1934, p. 461

Johnston, Thomas Crawford, *Did the Phoenicians discover America?'* James Nisbet, London, 1913

Joseph, Frank, 'Project Alta: Search and Discovery in the Bahamas', *The Ancient American,* Vol. 3, no. 23, April/May 1998, pp. 2–7

Joyce, Thomas A., *Central American and West Indian Archaeology,* Philip Lee Warner, London, 1916

Keegan, William F., *Bahaman Archaeology: Life in the Bahamas and Turks and Caicos before Columbus,* Media Publishing, Nassau, Bahamas, 1997

Kelly, Allan O., 'The Origin of the Carolina Bays and the Oriented

Lakes of Alaska', *Popular Astronomy*, Vol. 59, 1951, pp. 199–205

Kelly, Allan O., and Frank Dachille, *Target: Earth – The Role of Large Meteors in Earth Science*, Target: Earth, Carlsbad, Calif., 1953

Kelso de Montigny, Alan H., 'Did a Gigantic Meteorite, i.e. an Asteroid, fall into the Caribbean, and thus create the Lesser Antilles about 6000 years ago?', *International Anthropological and Linguistic Review*, Vol. 1, no. 4, E. J. Brill, Leiden, Holland, 1954, pp. 229–38

Kelso de Montigny, Alan H., 'Redating the Past', *International Anthropological and Linguistic Review*, Vol. 1, no. 2–3, E. J. Brill, Leiden, Holland, 1954, pp. 185–7

Kennedy, Roger G., *Hidden Cities – The Discovery and Loss of Ancient North American Civilisation*, Penguin, London and New York, 1994

Keyser, Paul T., 'From Myth to Map: The Blessed Isles in the First Century BC', *The Ancient World*, Vol. 24, pt. 2, 1993, pp. 149–68

Kloosterman, Johan B., 'The Usselo Horizon, a Worldwide Charcoal-rich Layer of Alleröd Age', unpublished paper, 1999

Kobres, R., 'The Path of a Comet and Phaeton's Ride', *The World and I*, Vol. 10, February 1995, pp. 394–405

Koudriavtsev, Viatscheslav, *Atlantis: Ice Age Civilisation*, Institute of Metahistory, Moscow, 1997

Krickeberg, W., W. Müller, H. Trimborn and O. Zerries, *Pre-Columbian American Religions*, Weidenfeld & Nicolson, London, 1968

Kristan-Tollmann, Edith, and Alexander Tollmann, 'Der Sintflut-Impakt: The Flood impact', *Mitt. Österr. Geol. Ges.*, Vol. 84 (1991), June 1992, 1–63

Kurlansky, Mark, *Cod: A Biography of the Fish that Changed the World*, 1997, Jonathan Cape, London, 1998

Landsburg, Alan, and Sally Landsburg, *In Search of Ancient Mysteries*, Corgi, London, 1974

Las Casas, Bartolomé, *History of the Indies*, trans. Andrée Collard, Torchbook/Harper & Row, New York and London, 1971

Lawton, Ian, and Chris Ogilvie-Herald, *Giza: The Truth*, Virgin, London, 1999

Lemprière, J., *A Classical Dictionary*, Routledge, London, 1919

Leonard, R. Cedric, *Quest for Atlantis*, Manor Books, New York 1979

Levy, David H., *Comets: Creators and Destroyers*, Touchstone/Simon & Schuster, New York, 1998

Lichtheim, Miriam, *Ancient Egyptian Literature: Vol. 1: The Old and Middle Kingdoms*, 1973, University of California Press, Berkeley, Los Angeles, Calif., London, 1975

Love, Bruce, *The Paris Codex: Handbook for a Maya Priest*, University of Texas Press, Austin, Texas, 1994

Luce, J. V., *The End of Atlantis: New Light on an Old Legend*, 1969,

Thames and Hudson/Book Club Associates, 1973
McCampbell, John, 'Meteorites and the "Carolina Bays"', *Popular Astronomy*, Vol. 53, 1944, pp. 338–92
McGlone, William R., Phillip M. Leonard, James L. Guthrie, Rollin W. Gillespie, James P. Whittall Jr, *Ancient American Inscriptions: Plow Marks or History?*, Early Sites Research Society, Sutton, Mass., 1993
Mackenzie, Donald A., *Myths of Pre-Columbian America*, Gresham, London, nd., *c.* 1924
Mahan, Joseph B., *The Secret – America in World History before Columbus*, privately published, Columbus, Georgia, 1983
Markman, Roberta H., and Peter T. Markman, *The Flayed God: The Mesoamerican Mythological Tradition*, Harper, San Francisco, Calif., 1992
Marx, Robert F., *The Search for Sunken Treasure*, Key Porter Books, Toronto, 1996
Massey, Gerald, *The Natural Genesis*, 2 vols, Williams and Norgate, London, 1883
Mavor, James W., *Voyage to Atlantis*, Souvenir Press, London, 1969
Meggers, Betty J., 'Jomon–Valdivia Similarities: Convergence or Contact?', in Gilmore and McElroy, pp. 11–19
Mellaart, James, *Çatal Hüyük – A Neolithic Town in Anatolia*, Thames and Hudson, London, 1967
Melton, F. A., 'The Origin of the Carolina "Bays", *Discovery*, June 1934, pp. 151–4
Melton, F. A., and W. Schriever, 'The Carolina "Bays" – Are They Meteorite Scars?', *Journal of Geology*, Vol. 41, 1933, pp. 52–66
Merezhkovsky, Dimitri, *The Secret of the West*, 1933, Jonathan Cape, London, 1936
Meyers, Eric M., *Oxford Encyclopaedia of Archaeology in the Near East*, OUP, 1997
Michell, John, *At the Centre of the World: Polar Symbolism Discovered in Celtic, Norse and Other Ritualized Landscapes*, Thames and Hudson, London, 1994
Michell, John, and Christine Rhone, *Twelve Tribe Nations and the Science of Enchanting the Landscape*, Thames and Hudson, London, 1991
Milik, J. T., *The Books of Enoch – Aramaic Fragments of Qumrân Cave 4*, OUP, 1976
Miller, Mary, and Karl Taube, *The Gods and Symbols of Ancient Mexico and the Maya*, 1993, Thames and Hudson, London, 1997
Mitchell-Hedges, F. A., 'Atlantis Was No Myth but the Cradle Of American Races, Declares Hedges', *New York American*, 10 March 1935
Molleson, Theya, and Stuart Campbell, 'Deformed Skulls at Tell

Arpachiyah: The Social Context', in S. Campbell and A. Green, eds., *The Archaeology of Death in the Ancient Near East*, Oxbow Monograph No. 51, 995, pp. 45–55

Moore, W. G., *The Penguin Encyclopedia of Places*, 1971, Penguin, Harmondsworth, Middx., 1978

Morfill, W. R., trans. and ed. and intro. R. H. Charles, *The Book of the Secrets of Enoch*, Clarendon Press, Oxford/OUP, 1896

Morison, Samuel Eliot, *Christopher Columbus, Mariner*, 1942, Meridian/Penguin, London, 1983

Moure, Ramón Dacal, and Manuel Rivero de la Calle, *Arqueologia Aborigen de Cuba*, Gente Nueva, Havana, Cuba, 1986

Muck, Otto, *The Secret of Atlantis*, 1976, Collins, London, 1978

Muldrow, Edna, 'The Comet that Struck the Carolinas', *Harpers' Monthly Magazine*, pt. 168, 1933, pp. 83–9

Müller, J. G., *Geschichte der Amerikanischen Urreligionen*, Schweighauferischen Berlagsbuchhandlung, Basel, Switzerland, 1855

Nash, William Giles, *America: The True History of its Discovery*, Grant Richards, London, 1926

The New Encyclopedia Britannica, Vol. 10, University of Chicago, Chicago, Ill., 1993

Newby, P. H., *Warrior Pharaohs: The Rise and Fall of the Egyptian Empire*, Faber & Faber, London, 1980

Nininger, H. H., 'When the Sky Rains Stone and Iron', *Literary Digest*, Vol. 117, 17 March 1934, pp. 16, 29

Nordenskiöld, A. E., *Periplus: An Essay on the Early History of Charts and Sailing-Directions*, 1897, Burt Franklin, New York, nd.

O'Brien, Christian, and Barbara Joy O'Brien, *The Shining Ones*, Dianthus Publishing, Kemble, Cirencester, Glos., 1997

O'Connor, David, 'The Earliest Royal Boat Graves', *Egyptian Archaeology*, 6, 1995, pp. 3–7

Odelain, O., and R. Séguineau, *Dictionary of Proper Names and Places in the Bible*, 1966, Robert Hale, London, 1991

Ogden III, J. Gordon, 'Radiocarbon and Pollen Evidence for a Sudden Change in Climate in the Great Lakes Region approximately 10,000 years ago', *Quaternary Paleoecology*, 1967, pp. 117–27

Olivier, Chas. P., 'The Great Siberian Meteorite: An Account of the Most Remarkable Astronomical Event of the Twentieth Century, from Official Records', *Scientific American*, July 1928, pp. 42–4

Ovid, *Tristia and Ex Ponto*, trans. Arthur Leslie Wheeler, 1924, Wm. Heinemann, London, Harvard University Press, Cambridge, Mass., 1965

Pagden, A., ed., *Letters from Mexico by Hernando Cortés* (1519), Yale University Press, New Haven, Conn., and London, 1986

Palmer, Robert, *The Blue Holes of the Bahamas*, Jonathan Cape, London, 1985

Pearson, Richard, 'Migration from Japan to Ecuador: the Japanese Evidence', *American Anthropology*, Vol. 70, 1968, pp. 85–6

Phillips, Graham, *Act of God: Moses, Tutankhamun and the Myth of Atlantis*, Sidgwick & Jackson, London, 1998

Picard, Gilbert Charles, and Colette Picard, *The Life and Death of Carthage*, Sidgwick & Jackson, London, 1968

Plafker, George, 'Oriented Lakes and Lineaments in Northern Bolivia', *Bulletin of the Geological Society of America*, Vol. 75, 1964, pp. 503–22

Plato, *Critias*, see A. E. Taylor

Plato, *The Laws*, trans. Trevor J. Saunders, 1970, Penguin, Harmondsworth, Middx., 1984

Plato, *Timaeus*, see 1) Cornford, 2) Davis

Pliny, *Natural History*, English trans. H. Rackham, 10 vols: Vol. 1, 1938, Harvard University Press, Cambridge, Mass., Wm. Heinemann, London, 1979; Vol. 2, 1942, Harvard University Press, Cambridge, Mass., and London, 1989

Plutarch, *The Face of the Moon*, see Plutarch, *Plutarch's Moralia*

Plutarch, *Isis and Osiris*, see Plutarch, *Plutarch's Moralia*

Plutarch, *Lives*, trans. John and William Landhorne, William Tegg, London, 1865

Plutarch, *Plutarch's Moralia*, 'The Face of the Moon', trans. H. Cherniss and W. C. Helmbold, Wm. Heinemann, London, 1957

Pohl, Frederick J., *Prince Henry Sinclair: His Expedition to the New World in 1398*, David-Poynter, London, 1974

Popol Vuh, see Tedlock

Prado, A., *The World of Ancient Spain*, Minerva, Genéve, 1976

Prescott, William H., *History of the Conquest of Mexico, etc.*, 2 vols, Geo. Routledge and Sons, London, new and revised edition, 1843

Proclus, *The Commentaries of Proclus on the Timaeus of Plato, etc.*, trans. Thomas Taylor, 2 vols, privately printed, London, 1820

'Prospective Jeunesse asbl – Histoire de la Coca', 1998, @ www.prospective-jeunesse.be/drogues/coca/histoire.htm

Prouty, W. F., 'Carolina Bays and their Origin', *Bulletin of the Geological Society of America*, Vol. 63, February 1952, pp. 167–222

Przeworski, Stefan, 'Notes d'Archéologie Syrienne et Hittite', *Syria* 11, 1930, pp. 133–45

Raleigh, Sir Walter, *The Discoverie of Guiana*, 1596, and Galvão, Antonio, *The Discoveries of the World from their first originall unto the yeere of our Lord 1555*, 1601, Bibliotheca Americana/The World Publishing Company, Cleveland, Ohio, 1966

Ramage, Edwin, S., *Atlantis: Fact or Fiction?*, Indiana University Press, Bloomington, Ind., London, 1978

Ravenstein, E. G., *Martin Behaim: His Life and His Globe*, Geo. Philip, London, 1908

Reader's Digest, *The World's Last Mysteries*, Reader's Digest Association, London, New York, Montreal, Sydney, Cape Town, 1977

Reeves, Nicholas, and Richard H. Wilkinson, *The Complete Valley of the Kings*, Thames and Hudson, London, 1996

Reymond, E. A. E., *The Mythical Origin of the Egyptian Temple*, Manchester University Press, 1969

Riverend, Julio le, *Brief History of Cuba*, Instituto Cubano del Libro, Havana, Cuba, 1997

Rodero, Christina García, *España Oculta: Public Celebrations in Spain, 1974–1989*, Smithsonian Institution Press, Washington DC, 1995

Ross, W. D., *The Works of Aristotle*, Vol. III, 1931, OUP, 1963

Roux, Georges, *Ancient Iraq*, 1966, Penguin, London, 1980

Sahagún, Fray Bernardino de, *General History of the Things of New Spain (Florentine Codex) Book 12 – The Conquest of Mexico, c.* 1570, trans. and eds. A. J. O. Anderson and C. E. Dibble, The School of American Research and the University of Utah, Santa Fe, Mexico, 1975

Sanchoniathon, *The Theology of the Phoenicians*, see Cory

Savage Jnr, H., *The Mysterious Carolina Bays*, University of South Carolina, Columbia, South Carolina, 1982

Schulten, Adolf, *Tartessos, ein Beitrag zur altesten Geschichte des Westerns*, L. Friederichsen, Hamburg, 1922

Scrutton, Robert, *Secrets of Lost Atland*, 1978, Sphere Books, London, 1979

Servius, *Servii Grammatici qvi fervntvr in Vergilii Aeneidos*, trans. Georgivs Thilo, 2 vols, Aedibvs B. G. Tevbneri, Lipsiae, 1878

Shinn, E. A., 'Atlantis: Bimini Hoax', *Sea Frontiers*, Vol. 24, no. 3, May–June 1978, pp. 130–42

Sinclair, Andrew, *The Sword and the Grail*, 1992, Century, London, Sydney, Auckland, Johannesburg, 1993

Sklar, Dusty, *Gods and Beasts: The Nazis and the Occult*, Thomas Y. Crowell, New York, 1977

Smith, G. Elliot, *Elephants and Ethnologists*, Kegan Paul, Trench, Trubner, London; E. P. Dutton, New York, 1924

Solinus, Caius Julius, *Polyhistor: De Memoralibus Mundi*, Venice, 1498

Sorenson, John L. and Martin H. Raish, *Pre-Columbian Contact with the Americas across the Oceans: An Annotated Bibliography*, 2 vols, 1990/1996

Soustelle, Jacques, *The Olmecs: The Oldest Civilisation in Mexico*, 1979, University of Oklahoma Press, Norman, Oklahoma, 1985

Spedicato, Emilio, 'Apollo Objects, Atlantis and other Tales: A Catastrophical Scenario for Discontinuities in Human History'.

The first revised edition was published in *Journal of New England Antiquities Research Association (NEARA)*, Vol. 26, 1991, pp. 1–14, and also *Kadath*, Vol. 84, 1995, pp. 29–55

Spence, Lewis, *Atlantis in America*, Ernest Benn, London, 1925

Spence, Lewis, *The Myths of Mexico and Peru*, 1913, Geo. G. Harrap, London, 1920

Stacy-Judd, Robert B., *Atlantis – Mother of Empires*, 1939, De Vorss & Co., Santa Monica, Calif., 1973

Staniland Wake, C., *Serpent-Worship and Other Essays with a Chapter on Totemism*, 1888, The Banton Press, Largs, Scotland, 1990

Steede, Neil, 'Comalcalco: An Early Classic Maya Site', in Gilmore and McElroy, pp. 35–40

Steede, Neil, 'Mexico's pyramidal Comalcalco – a thousand years older than suspected', *The Ancient American*, Vol. 4, no. 26, January–February 1999, p. 16

Steele, John, 'Bimini revealed', in Hitching, *The Mysterious World – An Atlas of the Unexplained*, pp. 141–3

Steiger, Brad, *Atlantis Rising*, 1973, Sphere, London, 1977

Steward, J. H., ed., *Handbook of South American Indians, Vol. IV: The Circum-Caribbean Tribes*, Cooper Square Publishers, New York, 1963

Stirling, Matthew W., 'Discovering the New World's Oldest Dated Work of Man', *National Geographic Magazine*, Vol. 76, August 1939, pp. 183–218

Stirling, Matthew W., 'Great Stone Faces of the Mexican Jungle', *National Geographic Magazine*, Vol. 78, no. 3, September 1940, pp. 309–34

Strabo, *The Geography of Strabo*, English trans. Horace Leonard Jones, 8 vols: Vol. I, 1917, Vol. II, 1923, Wm. Heinemann, London, Harvard University Press, Cambridge, Mass., Vol. I, 1949, Vol. II, 1988

Strode, Hudson, *The Pageant of Cuba*, Jarrolds, London, 1935

Tabío, Ernesto E., and Estrella Rey, *Prehistoria de Cuba*, Historia, Editorial de Ciencias Sociales, Havana, Cuba, 1985

Taylor, A. E., *Plato: Timaeus and Critias*, Methuen, London, 1929

Tedlock, Dennis, trans., *Popol Vuh: The Mayan Book of the Dawn of Life*, 1985, Touchstone/Simon & Schuster, New York, 1996

Thacher, John Boyd, *Christopher Columbus: His Life, His Work, His Remains*, 3 vols, 1903, AMS Press/Kraus Reprint Corp, New York, 1967

Thomson, J. Oliver, *History of Ancient Geography*, Cambridge University Press, 1948

Thompson, Edward Herbert, *People of the Serpent: Life and Adventure Among the Maya*, G. P. Putnam's Sons, London, 1932

Thucydides, *The History of the Peloponnesian War*, trans. Richard

Crawley, 1910, J. M. Dent, London, 1957
'Title of the Lords of Totonicapán', trans. Dionisio José Chonay, see *The Annals of the Cakchiquels/The Title of the Lords of Totonicapán*
Tollmann, Edith and Alexander Tollmann, 'The Flood came at 3 o'clock in the morning . . .', *Austria Today*, Vol. 4, 1992, pp. 40–47
Tompkins, Peter, *Mysteries of the Mexican Pyramids*, 1976, Thames and Hudson, London, 1987
Toor, Francis, *A Treasury of Mexican Folkways*, Crown, New York, 1947
Unknown, 'Research Verifies Use of Hashish, Cocaine, Nicotine in Prehistoric Cultures', *Sociology of Drugs*, March 1993
Vaillant, George C., 'A Bearded Mystery', *Natural History*, Vol. 31, May–June 1931, pp. 243–52
Valentine, J. Manson, 'Archaeological Enigmas of Florida and the Western Bahamas', *Muse News*, Miami Museum of Science, June 1969
Valentine, J. Manson, 'Underwater Archaeology in the Bahamas', *The Explorers' Club Journal*, December 1976, pp. 176–83
Van Sertima, Ivan, *They Came Before Columbus*, Random House, New York, 1976
Van Zantwijk, R., *The Aztec Arrangement: The Social History of Pre-Spanish Mexico*, University of Oklahoma Press, Norman, Oklahoma, 1984
Vaughan, J., and C. A. Geissler, *The New Oxford Book of Food Plants*, OUP, 1997
vonHagen, Victor W., *The Golden Man: the Quest for El Dorado*, Saxon House/BCA, Farnborough, Hants, 1974
Ward, William A., 'Ancient Lebanon', in *Cultural Resources in Lebanon*, Beirut College for Women, Beirut, 1969
Whishaw, E. M., *Atlantis in Andalucia: A Study of Folk Memory*, Rider, London, 1929
Wilber, R. Jude, John D. Milliman and Robert B. Halley, 'Accumulation of bank-top sediment on the western slope of Great Bahama Bank: Rapid progradation of a carbonate megabank', *Geology*, Vol. 18, October 1990, pp. 970–74
Wilkins, Harold T., *Secret Cities of Old South America: Atlantis Unveiled*, 1950, Rider, London, 1952
Williams, Gwyn A., *Madoc: The Making of a Myth*, Eyre Methuen, Fakenham, Norfolk, 1979
Wilson, Beckles, *Lost Lyonesse: Evidence, Records and Traditions of England's Atlantis*, 1902, AdCo Associates, London, 1986
Wilson, Derek, *The World Atlas of Treasure*, Pan Books/BCA, London, 1981
Wright, G. Ernest, *Biblical Archaeology*, Westminster Press, Philadelphia, Pa., Gerald Duckworth, London, 1957

Wright Jnr, H. E., Harvey L. Patten and Thomas C. Winter, 'Two Pollen Diagrams from Southeastern Minnesota: Problems in the Regional Late-Glacial and Postglacial Vegetational History', *Geological Society of America Bulletin*, Vol. 74, 1963, pp. 1,371–95 + plates

Wright Jnr, Herbert E., 'Glacial Fluctuations, Sea-level Changes, and Catastrophic Floods', in Ramage, pp. 161–74

Wylie, C. C., 'On the Formation of Meteorite Craters', *Popular Astronomy*, Vol. 41, 1933, pp. 211–14

Zangger, Eberhard, *The Flood from Heaven: Deciphering the Atlantis Legend*, Sidgwick & Jackson/Book Club Associates, London, 1992

Zapp, Ivar, and George Erikson, *Atlantis in America: Navigators of the Ancient World*, Adventures Unlimited Press, Kempton, Ill., 1998

Zerries, Otto, 'Primitive South America and the West Indies' in Krickeberg, Müller, Trimborn and Zerries, *Pre-Columbian American Religions*

Zhirov, N. F., *Atlantis – Atlantology: Basic Problems*, Progress Publishers, Moscow, 1970

Zink, David, *The Stones of Atlantis*, Prentice-Hall, Scarborough, Ontario, 1978

TV Documentaries

'A Special Report: Atlantis in the Bahamas', produced by Douglas Kenyon and Thomas Miller, directed by Cecila Gonzalez, unbroadcast, *c.* late 1970s

'Mystery of the Cocaine Mummies', Equinox, Channel 4, 1996

INDEX

Page numbers in *italics* refer to illustrations in the text.

INDEX

Azores
Pillars of Hercules
Straits of Gibralter
Sargasso Sea
ostracon
Nereids

p60-62 descrip to Atlantis

Greek Historian: Diodorus Siculus

Plinius Secondus

Plato
• Timaeus
• Critias

LOVE

Emotion, Myth and Metaphor

ROBERT C. SOLOMON

LOVE

Emotion, Myth and Metaphor

DISCARD
L.C.C.C. LIBRARY

Anchor Press/Doubleday • Garden City, New York
1981

The Anchor Press edition is the first publication of
LOVE Emotion, Myth and Metaphor

Anchor Press edition: 1981

Library of Congress Cataloging in Publication Data
Solomon, Robert C.
Love.
Includes index.
1. Love. I. Title.
BD436.S63 128'.4
ISBN 0-385-14118-1 AACR2

Library of Congress Catalog Card Number 81-43045
Copyright © 1981 by ROBERT C. SOLOMON
All Rights Reserved
Printed in the United States of America

First Edition

CONTENTS

for Kristine

Do you know what it is like to be a self-centered not unhappy man who leads a tolerable finite life, works, eats, drinks . . . sleeps, then one fine days discovers that the great starry heavens have opened to him and that his heart is bursting with it. It? She. Her. Woman. Not a category, not a sex, not one of two sexes, a human female creature, but an infinity. . . . What else is infinity but a woman become meat and drink to you, life and your heart's own music, the air you breathe? Just to be near her is to live and have your soul's own self. Just to open your mouth on the skin of her back. What joy just to wake up with her beside you in the morning. I didn't know there was such happiness.

WALKER PERCY, *Lancelot,* p. 129

PREFACE

"FALLING IN" LOVE

Locate I
love you *some-*
where in
teeth and
eyes . . .

Words
say everything,

I
love you
again,

then what
is emptiness for. . . .

ROBERT CREELEY, *The Language*

We'd known each other for years; and for months, we were—what?—"seeing each other" (to choose but one of so many silly euphemisms for playful but by no means impersonal sex). We reveled in our bodies, cooked and talked two or three times a week, enjoying ourselves immensely, but within careful bounds, surrounded by other "relationships" (another euphemism), cautiously sharing problems as well as pleasures, exorcising an occasional demon and delighting each other with occasional displays of affection, never saying too much, or revealing too much, or crossing those unspoken boundaries of intimacy and independence.

Then, we "fell in" love. What happened?

There was no "fall," first of all. Why do we get so transfixed with that Alice-in-Wonderland Heideggerian metaphor, and not just that one but a maze of others, obscuring everything; what is a "deep" relationship, for example? And why is love "losing" yourself? Is "falling for" someone really "falling for"—that is, getting *duped?* Where do we get that imagery of tripping, tumbling, and other inadvertent means of getting *in*-volved, *im*-mersed and *sub*-merged in love, "taking the plunge" when it really gets serious? If anything, the appropriate image would seem to be openness rather than "depth," flying rather than "falling." One "makes" love (still another euphemism, this one with some significance), but our entire romantic mythology makes it seem as if it "happens," as if it is something someone "suffers" (enjoying it as well), as if it's entirely "natural," a "need" and something all but unavoidable.

In our case, it was clear. Love was a *decision,* a mutual decision—fully conscious, conscientious, deliberate. In particular, it was the decision to say a word.

It is often said, particularly by psychiatrists, that love is a *need.* (Why are so many books on love written by psychiatrists?) But our sense of need *followed,* rather than preceded, our decision to love. Before that moment there was no need, no sense of urgency, nothing missed when we were not together. In fact we later confessed that we were each wholly agreeable, not resigned but almost indifferent, to the likelihood of our not seeing each other again. Our decision was in part a decision *that* we would "need" one another, and to create that need we rearranged our world, seeing ourselves in terms of each other. But "need" is too static a term, a sense of *deficit* in the satisfactions of life. In that sense, we surely didn't need love at all. This was a luxury, not a necessity, not one of the requirements of human nature but a passion most *un*-natural, however "natural" it is (wrongly) supposed to be.

Nothing had changed. We had long been comfortable together, seemingly satisfied with our thrice weekly intimacy rituals, showing none of those unwelcome signs of boredom or encroaching indifference, no sense of need or nagging anxiety; and yet we can pinpoint the moment when we *decided* to love. I remember rehearsing five possible consequences and conversations, weighing the not inconsiderable risks and then *leaping*, not falling, into that vast indeterminacy. It was anything but a "commitment," that overused, much-abused, quasi-marital legalistic existential pretension that is supposed to be definitive of love but in fact only substitutes for *lack* of passion. What I said was "I-love-you"—not a description or confession of feelings already felt but the *creation* of an emotion, a work of conceptual art, the shared fabrication of an experience.

So, I believe, do we construct our grandest—and our pettiest—passions, from words, concepts and judgments. Not from nothing, of course. She was there, and so was I. The time was evidently "ripe" for both of us. We already had our own brief history, our excitement, our fantasies. And, of course, our desires. Who knows what else? (In a brilliant but ephemeral film a few years ago, Claude Lelouch used three hours and three generations to set up, at the last moment of his story, a young man and woman meeting "by accident" on a plane, "love at first sight," with the whole of history behind them.) But whatever else may have been there, the love itself was a decision, a choice, a leap. There was nothing "right" about it. We did it. That's all. I said the word, and after a moment's surprise ("I never thought I'd hear that from you"), she said it too. (How would I have responded if she had said it first? I'm not so sure.)

It is often said that love is a feeling. And, indeed, we were weeping, choking, shaking, bordering on incontinence—much like the symptoms of our annual flu. But none of this was the cause of our emotion, much less its essential nature. At most, it was an uncomfortable distraction, a mere effect, not cause but consequence. How could anyone confuse *that* with love, regardless of the circumstances?

Once we had decided, there was nothing more to be said or wondered about whether it was "real." Decisions are like that. They make themselves true. Sometimes they even feel as if they "happen" to you. But they never do.

It was then that everything changed. The way we looked at each other—constantly, searchingly, obsessively. Now we did indeed feel a "need" to be together, to imagine a future (at least dinner), as if to confirm and reconfirm our decision of the night before. There was that sense that "making love" was no longer physical but *meta*-physical, whatever that means. Something *profound* seemed to be happening. Words like "forever" began to creep into our thinking, but luckily not into our speech. Should they be taken seriously? Even as we feared a disaster at every moment?

What could "forever" mean in a moment of passion? (A high school girl friend once pleaded, "Tell me you love me forever, if only tonight.") Why does a moment of emotion have to be justified, as if its "truth" consisted only in its duration? Why is "true" love supposed to be eternal? Or could the whole of Western metaphysics be but the slippery slope toward God and marriage, nailing the moment onto the cross of eternity?

We wanted a word, a name that would clarify everything. But "love," once said, could no longer provide it. First it had opened a door, but now a thousand repetitions brought us no further; they were assurances, but they failed to clarify, they failed to express, they failed to *do* anything any more. Why? Because the emotion itself was that grand sense of indeterminacy, a burst of freedom. Two lifetimes of proud resolutions and fears forgotten. (Was it really only last month that I said I'd never do this again?) We were inventing a universe, as if for the first time. The great poet Goethe was simply wrong when he said "only the first love is true." (Every love is first love, and "the best," "the most," etc.) And if names seemed wholly inadequate, if love seemed "mysterious" and "indescribable" (amor-fuss?), that was only because love was first this sense of being *open*, creative. Nothing fixed and finished existed yet to be named or finally described.

So we turned to poetry and metaphor, clumsily trying to express in our painfully limited language—no, to give shape to—this new half-invented world, as if some image—any image —or even a sound, might make it comprehensible. And so, "love." A cheap linguistic trick, rendering common an experience we knew to be unique. But without the word, would there have been the emotion? Then why was it that, in our uniqueness, we found ourselves mouthing the words of a hundred popular songs? Once I even caught myself thinking, "You light up my life"—surely one of the more mawkish musical hits of the seventies. So much for both uniqueness and imagined profundity.

Love is "letting go," we hear, even a loss of control. But "letting" is an *act*, something done deliberately, rather than simply *losing* control. In fact we were in total control, with all the complexities of our mutual uncertainty. We enjoyed a new and passionate recklessness, making new rules only to break them. We shut ourselves off from the world, arrogant, terrified. Our terror was not fear—fear of falling, fear of "being hurt," fear of being foolish—so much as anxiety—*angst* to the professionals. Fear is being afraid of what will happen to you; anxiety is uncertainty about what you will *do*. True anxiety is not the merely neurotic and pathetic paralysis discussed by psychiatrists; it is rather a quite ordinary—yet extraordinary—sense of power, an awareness of risk, a kind of enthusiastic fatalism. It was not an unpleasant feeling—even exhilarating—the beginning, or at least the possibility, of a whole new world. *Amor fati*, the philosopher Nietzsche called it—love of fate, living on the edge, in the heights, being vulnerable, "open," excited. Our love was an adventure, a risk, the emotional equivalent of exploring—a rebellion, against the banal authorities of reasonableness and sensibility, against the stale dictates of propriety and tired rules and duties—all of those little lists and obligations that made up our lives. All these small vanities—being on time, afraid of being missed at the meeting, keeping the respect of those one despises—became but little jokes, along with words like "responsible," "sensible" and "respectable." We floated free from the world with our affection and our foolishness, not oblivious to but only amused by how others came to view us—suspiciously, of course. We risked our friends and our careers—we, two so careful people—redefining our world as it suited us at the moment, and only on our own frivolous terms. We were exiles and outcasts, in our own little world, making guerrilla excursions, when it suited us, into a hostile but harmless public world.

("The one thing your friends will never forgive you," writes Camus in *The Fall*, "is your happiness.")

As in all revolutions, we were driven to excesses by the sheer indeterminacy of our newly declared freedom, by the breakdown of normal restraint and formal courtesies. Nowhere was this more evident than in the very substance of our wholly unreasonable and utterly obsessive *lust*. Now it is often said, with no small amount of self-righteous piety by those who neither love nor lust, that love and lust are two different worlds, the first sacred and "spiritual," the second "profane." Ever since the twelfth century the ideal of love without lust has even had a special name, "platonic love," for which Plato should not wholly be blamed. Desire is degraded and an emasculated concept of love is elevated to the status of a religion, with endless litanies on cardinal sins, lust, greed, gluttony and the virtues of impotence. But if there was one thing that was utterly obvious to us, it was the *sanctity* of sex. Sex as a ritual. Sex as expression. Sex as creative desire, not a need, not "satisfaction." The more we had, the more we wanted, the more dissatisfied we became, the less sex was "sex" and the less we even knew *what* we wanted. What once seemed obvious now became a bewildering question: what do we want when we "want" someone?

We seemed insatiable, always wanted more; not sex itself but certainly something *through* sex. How silly it seemed, thinking of Freud's view that love is but sublimated lust; how could that even make sense, when we were making love all day? Sex and love, in love, are as inseparable as a word and its meaning. But what, in this case, was the meaning?

Strangely enough, Plato (my primary antagonist in this book) caught this in his *Symposium* (but, significantly, through the voice of Aristophanes, not Socrates):

> The intense yearning which lovers have toward each other does not appear to be the desire for sexual intercourse, but for something else which the soul of each desires and cannot tell, and of which he/she has only a dark and doubtful presentiment.
>
> *Symposium*, Jowett trans., p. 192

It is this continuing sense of something more to come, this "dark and doubtful presentiment," that introduces the metaphysical element of love. Love is philosophy, a certain view of the world, not merely a "feeling." The ominous word "metaphysical," however, does *not* mean that love is a cosmic process, the union of the Eternal genitalia or any of the other erotic allegories that love theorists prefer to discuss instead of love itself.

Love, Plato warns, is never satisfied. But satisfaction isn't the point, since what defines the emotion is not the quest for satisfaction, not even for "happiness," but its very opposite, this continuing reckless frenzied sense of dissatisfaction, which expressed itself so clearly in our sexual excesses, excitement as its goal, not contentment. It was the desire that we desired, not its satisfaction, the emotion and not its reasonable resolution. If I wrote in my diary, "I've never been happier," that was a superfluous surprise, a fringe benefit, for, as Aristotle rightly argued, you can never *aim* for happiness. And as for those who would reduce the whole of metaphysics to the mere search for pleasure, it must be said that we never even noticed how much we were enjoying ourselves—perhaps the true test of pleasure. Satisfaction, happiness and pleasure—those are the results of small desires, desires too easily answered, desires devoid of passion. We would have none of that. All we wanted—at least for a while—was love.

AUTHOR'S NOTE

I have tried to write a book appropriate to its subject:
too often serious
overly playful, in compensation
irresponsible
repetitious
not always consistent
contentious, but (I hope)
entertaining.

Its virtues—and vices too—I owe to my friends, who have given me ideas, encouragement, solace, delusions and, not least, love. I owe a special debt of gratitude to my editor, Loretta Barrett, particularly for her patience, to my agent, Molly Friedrich, for her encouragement and support, to Shelby Hearon for her prompting and friendship, and, of course, much more than gratitude to Kristine Hanson, to whom the book is dedicated.

INTRODUCTION

Romantic Love

I heard of a man and woman recently who had fallen in love. "Hopelessly in love" was the woman's antique phrase for it. I hadn't realized people still did that sort of thing jointly. Nowadays the fashion is to fall in love with yourself, and falling in love with a second party seems to be generally regarded as bad form.

RUSSELL BAKER, *New York Times Magazine,* March 1978

Adults dismiss it as adolescent. Adolescents are embarrassed by it and deride it as childish. Children are bored by it. Therapists try to cure it. "True" men regard it as feminine. Feminists attack it as oppressive. Radicals demean it as frivolity. Frivolous people see it as absurdly serious. Christians call it "profane." Libertines mock it as "pious." Biological realists accept it as "Nature's way of telling us what to do." Social realists tolerate it as Western society's slippery slope to marriage. Businessmen sell it. Consumers voraciously buy it. (Master Charge and Visa are now accepted.) Cynics sneer at it, a nasty gloss over timid sexual lust. Puritans are appalled by it, a timid gloss over nasty sexual lust. Self-styled romantics, of course, think it's "divine," but they make such fools of themselves that they only confirm what everyone else suspected all along—that romantic love is like a disease, perhaps "incurable."

It is appropriate to horny Victorians, Shakespearean tragedies, afternoon soap operas and adolescents.

It is acceptable—briefly—in middle-aged men and recent divorcees, frowned upon but tolerated in people over forty-three.

For some, love is a game, often ending in marriage (which is emphatically *not* a game) or in "heartbreak," which is a metaphor.

In any case, love is a passion. But what is a passion but a passing obsession, not to be taken seriously except as a "passage," or a joke, or a literary device, or perhaps an experience we all *ought* to go through? (A bit of moralizing is sure to take the wind out of its sails.)

It is romantic love that one "falls into," that resembles a kind of terror, or an illness, marked by fever, loss of appetite, shaky knees, nervous twittering and a certain looseness in the brain and bowels. It is romantic love that, as the Spanish philosopher Ortega y Gasset describes it, "is a state of mental misery which has a restricting, impoverishing and paralyzing effect upon the development of consciousness." And yet we not only enjoy this but we consider it the richest experience of all. (Isn't this odd?) It is romantic love for which men and women wreck careers and abandon families and obligations, which provides plots for soaps and operas, which Plato called a kind of madness and which so infuriated St. Paul, which inspired Shakespeare if not also Dante and led to the downfall of Antony, Juliet, Romeo, Samson, Emma Bovary and King Kong.

We are obsessed by it, this passion. We are *the* romantic society, for whom all of our successes sometimes seem but distractions, inessential periods of happiness, during our search for our "one true love." We do indeed have a *moral* view of this passion. To accuse someone of being "incapable of love" is an indictment, as if he or she is less than wholly human. Not to have ever been in love is a matter of grave concern, as if one has not yet really lived, or as if one might have some probably fatal flaw in his or her moral character. Christian love has long been said to be the highest *duty* of humanity, even a gift from God. Psychiatrists refer to our "tragic incapacity to love," the "disintegration" and the "banalization" of love, leaving no doubt about their own role as the new high priests of a still unearthly and inaccessible God.

> They had always known, they say, that they could only be cured by love, and before the treatment began they had expected that through this relation they would at last be granted what life had hitherto withheld from them.
>
> FREUD, *Introductory Lectures,* p. 441

There is no topic that has inspired more garbled and wishful thinking than love, or more garbage to be written about it. ("Garbage is garbage," said the logician Burton Dreben of Harvard, "but the history of garbage is scholarship.") We are treated to our daily dose of off-the-cuff witticisms, such as "Love means never having to say you're sorry," and a monthly best seller with the message that love, though rare, is the answer to all of our problems. "All you need is love," sang the Beatles fifteen years ago. "Only love is real" is the recurrent cosmological theme and, in a slightly more Newtonian vein, "Love makes the world go round." This unqualified cosmic praise has been repeated by some of the greatest minds in history in their weaker moments. Benjamin Disraeli, for example, a hardheaded realist in his politics if not in his affairs with women, declared, "Love is the principle of existence and its only end." Konrad Lorenz, the great biologist for whom evolution became something of a religion, called love "the most wonderful product of ten million years of evolution." Several philosophers, Jesus and Hegel among them, have believed that society could and should be ruled through love alone, and Mozart, in his *Magic Flute,* musically tried to make it happen, "happily ever after" of course. From the Bible comes the simplest piety, "God is love" (I John 4:8), but Gertrude Stein, as usual, wins the prize for succinctness. "Love IS," she insists, and who can disagree with her?

Whether they are as oratorical and edifying as Rollo May or

as mellow and dramatic as Erich Segal, these are more than harmless valentines, thoughtless praises for a grand and beautiful passion. They reflect a *dangerous* view of love, and everything we say about it, think about it, write about it, wish about it and especially *do* about it betrays our confusion. We are taught that love is everything, the key to happiness, that love is "the answer," the way to God, the keystone of human nature, that everyone not only can but ought to love, and that those who do not are less than wholly human. In the midst of our passion we say, "I'll always love you," but we don't. And so, of course, we are disappointed—not in love but in ourselves. These seemingly harmless valentines are sadistic, manipulative epigrams on the death of a feeling. They announce ideals and set up expectations which no experience can possibly match. They make us feel impoverished with the experiences that we do have. They demand sacrifices that no one in his or her right mind would ever make. They turn an emotion into a religion, and when it can't bear its own solemnity, it is made to look foolish, adolescent, irresponsible or childish by contrast. It is then said to be "not the real thing." We have killed love, by bloating our expectations with cosmic praise, by obscuring love and turning it into a weapon. And just in case we have our doubts, we are told that love is "ineffable," beyond the realm of explanation and, most assuredly, beyond suspicion.

Now you might say, "No one really believes all this stuff. In our enthusiasm, we—shall we say—stretch the truth a bit." But why such unbridled enthusiasm, which so often turns to embarrassment? And what we say—even in love—is a good indication of what we believe—or hope. Everywhere we turn, we learn, from Plato to St. Paul, from comic books to the *Cosmo* quiz-of-the-month, that love is the most important ingredient in human life, that we cannot do without it, and in any case we would not want to. And not surprisingly we find ourselves believing it.

> Perhaps they were right putting love into books. . . . Perhaps it could not live anywhere else.
>
> WILLIAM FAULKNER, *Light in August*

Against this backdrop of bloated love, this bladder filled with hot air and piety, it is easy to understand the bitter disillusionment of the cynic.

If love is so obviously not what it has so long and so loudly been said to be—the answer to everything, the key to being "human" as well as happy—then, the cynic concludes too quickly, love must be an illusion, a bad joke or a conspiracy. First Marx and Freud, then Marxists and feminists, started to suspect the sinister effects of this bloated and pious view of love. Freud once suggested that romance was nothing but lust, "plus the ordeal of civility." Marx and Engels hypothesized that romantic love was a rationalization of (lifelong) prostitution, and an entire generation of feminists have rightly complained that they find themselves caught between feeling that love is inescapable and all-important and the realization that it is political manipulation and degrading. The miracle of love becomes a myth, and the religion becomes but an extravagant façade for lust, an opiate more powerful than religion precisely because it is entirely personal; we must always blame its failures on ourselves.

The two sides of the schizoid view play against each other, piety against cynicism, and the result is our curious confusion about love. We snicker at love as children, only to be told that it is the most important thing in life. We praise love to the heavens as adults, worry endlessly about finding it, keeping it, losing it, not being able to feel it, getting trapped by it and getting over it, only to make ourselves miserable, disappointed and ultimately cynical. Our confusion is promoted by our pop psychotherapists, who play off an ethereal ideal in order to make what we actually feel seem pathetic—or worse—by comparison. Thus Erich Fromm, for example, defends his quasi-religious "art of loving" to the millions by contrasting this with the "neurotic" love he holds in such contempt, the same emotion that most of us experience with such satisfaction. The idea that love is a need gets coupled with the idea that we moderns ("modern man") have made it impossible; thus Rollo May, for instance: "Where love was once considered the answer, it now is the problem." "*What* problem?" we should ask, and leave open the possibility that Dr. May may be himself the problem, with his cosmic view of *eros* and his persistent accusations that we are failing to live up to *his* ethereal ideal of love.

One asks a simple question, "What is it to fall in love?" or "Why is love so important to us?" and in return what we get are murky allegories and the mythological heroes of ancient Greece and Rome, biological studies of the mating habits of insects, fish, birds and monkeys, "how to" and "how not to" books about almost everything, surveys, interviews and confessions, bad poetry and volumes of vacuity the only point of which seems to be to impress us with the author's own sensitivity. We get greeting-card platitudes, and voyeuristic anthropology (1001 ways the savages and the French make love and the curious things they believe about it) and, of course, psychiatric diagnoses and advice, often bemoaning the perennial "tragedy of modern man's inability to love." Everything but an answer.

So why another book on love? I haven't discovered that love prevents, or causes, cancer, hemorrhoids or heart disease. I see no need once again to repeat the same tired and inevitably inaccurate Greek allegories, or intimate along with so many religious leaders and psychiatrists in recent years, that I know what true love is and you do not—much to your disadvantage, of course.

What I want to contend in this book, although it is hard to say it with quite the piety or flamboyance of those who praise love along with the Lord or condemn it as a capitalist conspiracy, is this: love is an emotion, just an ordinary, non-cosmic, luxurious but not essential emotion. It is not divine, much less eternal, it is not a part of human nature or the key to the gates of happiness or any kind of "answer" (to questions mostly unasked and unknown). It is an emotion long surrounded by myths and metaphors, motivated by false hopes and the desire for a guarantee that, somehow, a miserable life can be turned into happiness at a single stroke, that love once found will last, even "forever," that one will be loved, "no matter what." These are illusions, and much of what has been said about love is nothing but illusion, in Freud's sense—a kind of wishful thinking, even when it parades as poetry—or psychiatry. But it does not follow that love itself is an illusion, as many Marxists, feminists and Freudians (not Freud) have insisted. And my purpose in this book is precisely to separate the passion from the illusions, to explode the myth without in any way demeaning or denying the importance of the emotion. Indeed, it is the importance of this emotion that itself has to be explained, but in so doing one makes clear its limitations as well.

The reader has a right to know what to expect in the following pages, to be on guard and ready with objections in mind, because there is nothing more infuriating—to me anyway—than those grand tomes on the magnificence of love, whose titles promise some great revelation but, 462 pages later, not a single theme has emerged. So what I want to argue, in blunt and clumsy summary, is this:

• Much of what we believe about love is a confusion of myths and metaphors, some quaint, some innocent, some amusing, some vulgar, some nuts-and-bolts and matter-of-fact, and some insidious. The most insidious myth begins with Plato, who defended a view of love in his dialogue *Symposium* which de-emphasized sex and turned *eros* to the service of impersonal knowledge. It is Plato who begins the march of love toward divinity and away from simple personal relationships, who takes love out of the realm of ordinary emotions and friendship and pretends that it is something spectacular, our psychic introduction to an ideal world, beyond mere emotion, which is eternal. It is a myth picked up and fostered by Christianity, by St. Paul in particular, who so vehemently condemns love that is "profane" (that is, what we know as love) and praises love divine, sacred love, indeed so sacred that he tells us over and over again that it is a love of which we are not even capable. And the myth is picked up again in different guise in the twelfth century, during which a group of poets called "troubadours" wandered around France "devoting" themselves to singing mediocre love songs to women—usually married—who rarely gave them the favors they so desired. And it was this longing, the *languor,* the protracted but intentional sexual frustration that came to be identified by scholars as the origins of "romantic" love as such. And in Italy, about the same time, Plato's heritage was fully recognized by a number of monks who canonized "Platonic love," ideal love without sexual expression or desire, which is, ultimately, aimed only at God and therefore lasts, happily, forever.

Now there may well be some poetic pleasure in protracted sexual self-denial, and I do not doubt that there is that peculiar religious experience that Freud called "oceanic," which one might call "love." (Why not?) But none of this has anything to do with romantic love, nor is it in any way necessarily opposed to it, an alternative to it, or (as in Plato) an improvement upon it. Romantic love, unlike the love of God and the languor that comes of frustration, is essentially sexual, secular, personal and always tentative, tenuous, never certain. Love is not inhuman, or superhuman, or in any way impossible, but then too, there are no metaphysical guarantees.

• Love is an emotion, nothing else. But emotions are not—traditional linguistic usage and certain current popular songs aside—"feelings." Our emotions are neither primitive nor "natural," but rather intelligent constructions, structured by concepts and judgments that we learn in a particular culture, through which we give our experience some shape and meaning. And it is not only love that gives meaning to life but all emotions—hatred, anger and envy too. But if emotions are primarily judgments, ways of shaping the world, then one might say that we do not "fall in" love at all. Quite to the contrary, the fall is rather a creation, which we have been taught to make by a thousand movies, stories and novels; its most essential ingredient—too often hidden in the language of "spontaneity" and "chance"—is personal *choice*. This in turn raises the question, "Why?" Why choose love at all? And why choose to love this particular person? (All the more urgent a question when the choice continues to be disastrous.) Love does not prick us from behind (we've had enough of the metaphor of Cupid's arrows). We choose it, and if we often choose badly or desperately, that does not prove that love is irrational. People are irrational.

• If emotions are learned and purposeful ways of structuring our experience, it follows that what emotions one has or can have depend in part upon the particular culture one belongs to. Having a certain emotion is restricted to those who share certain concepts, or speak a certain language, and make certain kinds of judgments about themselves and the world. A great many writers on the topic of love assume, without argument, that the features they recognize in themselves and their friends (or patients) are, to borrow a phrase from Rollo May, "universal human characteristics." But love is not the keystone of "human nature" (if there is any such thing, which I would deny). The English sailors under Captain Cook may have had a grand time in Tahiti—followed by the fictional characters on His Majesty's good ship *Bounty*—but they found no romantic love there, except what they brought with them (along with syphilis). Anthropologists who have spent years with certain Eskimo communities may or may not have seen the proverbial nose rubbings, but they did not find romantic love. In fact the number of societies that would recognize or would have recognized romantic love at all, at least as anything more than Western foolishness, is extremely small throughout history. (The number is no doubt exploding now, with the invasion of American television even onto the islands of Micronesia and the systematic destruction of traditional community bonds.) Romantic love is a cultural artifact, something along the lines of cooked carrots and kosher butchers. There is nothing "natural" about it. (Sex, of course, is quite "natural," but even this is extremely misleading: what sex *means* is not natural and, in particular, sex as an "expression" of love is a highly specific—and peculiar—cultural invention.)

• What kind of society makes romantic love possible? (This is not yet to ask what kind of society makes this emotion desirable, much less an obsession which is said to "make the world go round.") My answer, briefly, is that it is a society which places extraordinary emphasis on the concept of individuality and individual self-identity, a society which distinguishes more or less plainly between public positions and personal roles, a society which places a premium on individual idealization, fantasy and fiction, and, perhaps most importantly, a society that grants a high degree of mobility and flexibility in relationships in general, places personal choice at the core of mating and marriage rituals and the idea of what we call "intimacy" (again, not a global concept) at the very center of interpersonal relationships. But if this is what is necessary to make romantic love *possible,* what more is needed to make it seem like a need, a *necessity?* What kind of society would make this one emotion, among a hundred other emotions no less moving, no less complex, no less "human," so enormously important, so urgent, so crucial to one's very conception of oneself and "who I am"? It is a society in which independence and mobility are celebrated even at the cost of massive loneliness and the systematic destruction of almost all seemingly "natural" bonds. Family ties, community bonds, ethnic identity and tribal membership have all been sacrificed to "making it" and "finding oneself." It is a society in which the family is a nest to be kicked *out* of, and "home town" is the place where you are *from.* In such a society, where long-term bonds no longer serve as a source of constant familiarity and intimacy, an emotion whose primary purpose is the rapid formation of interpersonal ties and intimacy serves an all-important purpose. Romantic love provides a transient sense of "belonging" in a society that is self-consciously in perpetual disarray. And what could serve as a better medium for this emotion than sex? It is as universal as any human attribute, as intrinsically enjoyable as any other human activity and readily available as a bond of intimacy, personal tastes and choice aside. It is sudden "spontaneous" intimacy—in our culture symbolized and synthesized by sex—that forms the structural core of romantic love.

• Even so, love is not everything, and not for everybody. Love is a luxury, not a need. It is not the only emotion to play this role, even in our society. We have not yet done away with friendship and family, colleagues at work and the boys in the band, shared oppression and the company of misery. Romantic love is just one option among many. Even within a couple in love, there are a hundred other emotional bonds of no less significance, if considerably less melodrama: shopping together at the same old Safeway and putting together the rent, trying to be on time and deciding between Werner Herzog and *The Muppet Movie.* And if these admittedly unromantic connections do not find their way into our epic love sagas, that may not be so much because they are irrelevant as because our conception of the exclusive importance of love is so exaggerated and our conception of the alternatives so impoverished. Romantic love is not for everyone, and there may be good reasons for rejecting it. The intimacy of love may violate a person's sense of individuality and solitude—and it should not be concluded that he or she "is afraid of intimacy" any more than an aversion to brussels sprouts should be automatically considered akin to anorexia. And, on the other side, the privacy and exclusivity of romantic love may well offend a person's sense of the larger community or interfere with friendship and tribal camaraderie. It is said that lovers love the world, but a more accurate description would be that love systematically reduces a couple's concern to "their own little world." For good reason, all the world does not love a lover.

• I have said that intimacy is the core of romantic love, but it is not all that obvious what intimacy is. Let me begin by saying what it is *not:* intimacy has nothing to do with telling your lover your "innermost secrets"; and yet, in almost all of the scientific literature that exists on the subject, such "disclosure" is the definition of intimacy. What I shall argue here, though it is impossible to summarize in a paragraph, is that intimacy—and love—consist in *shared identity,* a redefinition of self which no amount of sex or fun or time together will add up to. Most of the final parts of the book, in fact, are dedicated to working out this somewhat paradoxical notion—how two people in a society with an extraordinary sense of individuality and individual identity mutually fantasize, verbalize and act their way into a relationship that can no longer be understood as a mere conjunction of the two but only as a complex one.

• But even this would be too simple. (It always is.) Television preachers often tell us that the couple (heterosexual and married, of course) form a "union" (pronounced "*yewn*-yon"), but this is only half true. If romantic love presupposes a strong sense of individuality and individual identity, but also requires a sense of shared identity, it is not hard to see that the dynamics of romantic love are inevitably going to be *tension,* the assertion of individuality coupled with the mutual sense of identity. Early in a relationship the exhilaration of the newly created sense of unity may be overwhelming; later on the sense of unity or worse, "being stuck with one another," may manifest itself in that all too familiar scenario of two people, who claim without a twitch of doubt that they love each other, devoting every comment and gesture to the annoyance or embarrassment of one another, as if to prove to themselves and all who see them that they are, after all, two distinct people, locked in what appears to be lifelong mortal combat. But in between the exhilarating initiation period and the hopefully avoidable epoch of *kvetch* and humiliation is a sequence of moves that a philosopher will recognize as a *dialectic*, the constant interplay of words and roles through which two (or more) people define themselves and each other *both* as individuals and as a shared identity. A sense of shared identity alone, without a dialectic, is not romantic love, whatever else it might be. But neither is mere companionship, a partnership, in effect, the same as romantic love. And when a couple of friends of yours, fighting it out all the time, inevitably end up in bed for a bout of (what they describe as) "incredible" love-making, they might in fact be a better example of romance than all the unrequited Romeos and tragic Juliets and hopeful, junior psychology students who populate the literature on the subject. But are two people fighting still in love? Of course. The tune might be in the key of B♭ but a dissonant A is still part of the melody.

• One point which will lie at the basis of virtually everything I say in this book deserves explicit mention, if only occasional discussions as such. Romantic love need have nothing to do with *gender*. There is romantic love between men and men and between women and women in no sense different from the more usual paradigm case (which it was not for the ancient Greeks) between man and woman. The precise significance of the male and female genitalia is of at most incidental interest to love as such, but this is not to deny that a *particular* relationship might well be defined in terms of male and female sexuality or—what is entirely different—masculine and feminine roles. (One need not be female to be feminine, or a man to be masculine, and one need be neither to be in love.) But this point is more than a bow to liberalism, for if romantic love were anything like what some people have thought it is—a distinctive set of gender roles—then one could not define the emotion at all without distinguishing explicitly male and female, and co-ordinately masculine and feminine roles, much to the detriment of the female. If that were true, love might well turn out to be indefensible.

• What I have just said about the gender of people in love also applies to the *concept* of love. It is being said with some frequency today that our concept of romantic love—and even the whole system of our concepts of science, knowledge, philosophy and culture—is a purely male fabrication, foisted upon females who accept it under duress or pretend to accept it to satisfy the foolish male ego. There are indeed aspects of our conception of love roles that lend themselves to this charge, particularly the idea that a woman's love requires "submissiveness" and the like. But it is hard to know what to make of the claim that men and women's *concepts* of love are so different that they are mutually unrecognizable. For the most part, we share our concepts as we share our language and culture: *Wuthering Heights* and even *The Second Sex* and *The Women's Room* are part of *our* literature. There is no such thing as a "woman's novel" any more than there is such a thing as "a man's magazine." If men and women think about love differently, it is essentially one and the same concept of love about which they disagree. If not, what is it that they disagree about?

There may be—I cannot deny it—some unchecked male bias in my theory. If so, that is a flaw in it. But the concept I am trying to understand is not itself biased, whatever inequities and asymmetries have been promoted in its name and continue to color our judgments about it. It may be that we have different expectations and hopes, sometimes contradictory fears and demands. But the current insistence that "men are incapable of love" or, conversely, that (romantic) love is only a male invention, clarifies nothing and leads to no understanding of any kind. Indeed its effect as well as its intention is precisely the opposite, to fortify mutual misunderstanding and declare, once and for all, that nothing better will ever take its place.

• Love is not a "commitment," has nothing to do with commitment, indeed is the very antithesis of commitment, as that term is used so much today. Love is an emotion; a commitment is a promise (whether to oneself or someone else) to do something—or continue to do something—*whatever* one's feelings. If you're in love, you don't need to make a commitment; if you need a commitment, it has nothing to do with love.

• One last point of no small importance: along with the idea that one would like to be loved "forever" often goes the desire to be loved "no matter what." Sometimes this is an excuse for discourtesy and slovenliness; after all, it does tend to be a bother to keep up the appearances which made one seem so lovable in the first place, to maintain conversation at such an exalted level ("When was the last time we talked about the importance of Proust for the existentialists?"), and just to be so concerned, to listen so carefully, to watch so closely, to behave so respectfully. "No matter what" has a way of sneaking out of the bottom drawer, like an old pair of comfortable pajamas, as if, now that we've "hooked" ourselves a lover, he or she is bound to love us whatever we do. Indeed, some people call this the "test" of love. In modern humanist parlance, this is expressed as the love of the "total person," in all of his or her "uniqueness and individuality" (the phrase is from psychologist Victor Frankyl). Against this, I want to argue that the idea of the unqualified, unspecified, open-ended and totally tolerant love of "the individual human being" is just another part of the love myth, derived, perhaps, from the Christian concept of the "soul"—that essential spiritual pit that lies at the core of each of us, beneath our clothes and our manners and our bodies and our genitals and our intelligence and accomplishments. But this is motivated, as usual, by our childish desire for a guarantee, as if hard-earned love, once "won," will not be so easily lost. But love always has its "reasons." Every love has its built-in limitations, and the question then, both in the abstract and in every particular relationship, becomes, "What are these reasons, and these limits?" Is money a legitimate reason for loving someone? (If not, why not?) Personality? Sexual performance? A chance to get ahead? The fact that he/she loves me? Her legs? His arms? But in no case the "total person." This adds an additional kink to the traditional mythological picture of love: if one loves a person "for reasons," what about someone else, someone new, who satisfies those same reasons, perhaps even more so, and in any case adds a bit of novelty? Are lovers replaceable? Is love exclusive? Indeed, perhaps romantic love not only fails to last "forever" but has the faults of its own collapse already built right into its structure.

My aim in this book is to attempt what might be called a philosophical reconstruction of our conception of romantic love. It is, on the one hand, a rather harsh and sometimes belligerent attack on the nonsense that has been perpetrated—often with the most benign of intentions—in praise of this much-praised emotion, but it is also an attempt to describe the experience of love and its place in our lives from the point of view of an enthusiast. It is an attempt to take account of the sense within the nonsense and look once again at the very tangible facts of our collective experience, not least our literature and late night conversations, separating out the wishful thinking from the nature of the experience itself. It is looking at some of the seemingly "obvious" features of love with an eye to peering beneath the surface and seeking out the not so obvious and trying to make sense of what most of us would agree to be at one and the same time the most seemingly simple and tortuously complex emotion in the Western world.

At the end of *Annie Hall*, Woody Allen tells us a bad joke: a man complains that his brother imagines that he's a chicken. "Why don't you take him to a psychiatrist?" asks a well-meaning friend. "Because we need the eggs" is the answer. "Relationships are like that," Allen explains—they are necessary illusions. What I want to do here, philosophically, is to distinguish the chicken from the eggs.

PART I:
Emotion, Myth and Metaphor

IN THE BEGINNING, THE WORD 1

There are many people who would never have been in love, had they never heard love spoken of.

La Rochefoucauld, *Maxim* 136

What is love?

Or should we rather begin by asking, What is "love"? for it is an open question—or should be—whether we are ultimately concerned more with a word than a feeling. We use one and the same word to refer to so many different sensibilities; we love our country as well as our friends, one loves chocolate cheesecake as well as the sun and a day on the beach. And even limiting ourselves to the love between two people, there is the love of a mother, the love of a brother, the love one feels for an old teacher, the love of a friend, the love of a hero as well as the love of a lover. And even love between lovers seems so varied and in many cases unique that it is only with some hesitancy and in haste that we cover them with the same word. Thus Albert Camus, in his *Myth of Sisyphus*, writes, "We call love what binds us to certain creatures only by reference to a collective way of seeing for which books and legends are responsible. But of love I know only that mixture of desire, affection and intelligence that binds me to this or that creature. That compound is not the same for another person. I do not have the right to cover all these experiences with the same name" (p. 55).

Consider, by way of contrast, the wealth of meticulous and

fine distinctions we make in describing our feelings of hostility: hatred, loathing, scorn, anger, revulsion, resentment, envy, abhorrence, malice, aversion, vexation, irritation, annoyance, disgust, spite and contempt, or worse, "beneath" contempt. And yet we sort out our positive affections for the most part between the two limp categories, "liking" and "loving." We distinguish our friends from mere acquaintances and make a ready distinction between lovers and friends whom we love "but not that way." Still, one and the same word serves to describe our enthusiasm for apple strudel, respect for a distant father, the anguish of an uncertain romantic affair and nostalgic affection for an old pair of slippers. One begins to wonder if "love" means anything more than "warm affection," occasionally, enthusiasm.

The vagueness of this word and its expansive domain have been pointed out by virtually every writer on love or "love," but what is remarkable is how rarely this has raised an eyebrow, much less inspired some serious re-evaluation of our favorite word, if not also our favorite emotion. If it is true, as our linguists tell us, that a language tends to make distinctions in proportion to the importance of the subject matter (thus the Eskimos and their fifty-one words for "snow"), then the poverty of our language of love, compared to the exquisite richness of our language of hostility, should make us suspicious indeed. The French, by contrast again, have a dozen categories where we have but one. Thus one wonders whether it is only a word, a grab-bag category for feelings not important enough to deserve their own special name. Or perhaps one wonders why a word that works so hard for us ought still to remain so obscure, unless it is hiding something, serving some function not readily admitted, perhaps giving the appearance of a concrete and specific feeling when in fact there are a multitude of feelings, including even those of envy, hostility and jealousy, mutual bitterness and protracted annoyance, sanctified by a word, "love."

"Love" is a *political* word. It does not just name an emotion; it is itself emotive. It is not so much a "sign" that refers as a sigh that applauds, a sound that transforms; it does not describe so much as congratulate. To be in love, writes Rollo May of the Victorians, was to be one of the elect, with a sense of salvation and a right to be self-righteous (*Love and Will*, pp. 13–14). But it is the right to use the word, rather than the discovery of any particular emotion, that bestows this confidence. Everyone knows at least one unhappy couple who, despite the fact that they have spent every day for the past ten years bickering and suffering mutual self-abasement, consider themselves the very model of love. Every word and gesture signals contempt; some of them, according to Dr. John L. Schimel of New York University, cannot remember a time when either of them has ever said anything complimentary or positive. They wrangle from breakfast until bedtime, and they insist that they "love" one another. Grant them that word, acknowledge that they do indeed love one another, and all will be well. Deny them the word, and you have crushed them, accused them of a meaningless and mean-spirited life. But this is the power of "love," not love. As Romeo says, "Call me but love, and I'll be new baptized."

The word "love" is so full of praise and self-congratulation that just to use it is already a sign of character; to use it to describe one's own feelings—no matter how complex or confused those feelings might actually be—is to display one's enthusiasm, to grant oneself an exalted status in the world of emotions, to prove oneself a "loving person," as Erich Fromm would say, regardless of whom or what one loves, or how. Twenty-five hundred years ago Plato had the first speaker in his classic *Symposium* praise love or *eros* by arguing its successful effects in battle, and St. Paul and his successors half a millennium later saw quite clearly how effective a weapon love could be. Or rather, "love" (as *agape*), the Word, for it was not by loving their enemies that the early Christians succeeded in opposing them. They battered down their defenses with the Word. For who could fight against "love"? It was the Word that became invincible, irrefutable, like the word "freedom," with which it shares many similarities. Both mean so much that they might well be thought to mean nothing. In fact both are words so hallowed that no one could possibly be against them. "Even the Nazis said they were for freedom," writes philosopher Frithjof Bergmann. And who would not also be "for" love?

Given the varieties of affection that can count as love, and the variety of "objects" that can be loved, it is easy to understand how it is that, even restricting themselves to love between peers and excluding motherly love and the like, those who write about love end up talking about very different phenomena, choosing very different paradigms and arguing very different political positions as well. A happily married couple quite understandably take themselves as an example and look with compassion or contempt on those who are too "unsettled" or "immature" to enjoy the same. Wise old Socrates praised wisdom itself as the only "true" love, and the novelist Stendhal, in justification of his amorous but often troubled adventures in Italy, celebrated love only as passionate, desperate yearning. Psychoanalysts naturally tend to emphasize motherly love, feminists often choose to point out those cases in which love is primarily overidealization and disillusion, and writers with an aesthetic bent (including Plato) often tend to take love to be intense admiration. The Spanish philosopher Ortega y Gasset, for example, calls love "gravitation toward a beautiful object." But then, is there any significant difference between loving a lover and loving a sports car or a painting? Or, for that matter, wouldn't a little boy passing a pastry shop come to count as the consummate lover? The examples are most revealing.

If we push past the ordinary toward the gruesome, it becomes even more obvious how elastic and political the word can become. A man murders his lover "because of love." A couple radiate mutual loathing but stay together—"where else would we go?" They insist that they "love" each other. A woman sacrifices her career for her husband and calls it "love." We then start to wonder, what could *not* be called "love," at least by way of *an excuse?* Thus deprived of determinate content, we can easily understand why some recent critics, in conjunction with Camus, have insisted that "love" is *just* a word and nothing more.

> There are so many sorts of love that one does not know where to seek a definition of it.
>
> VOLTAIRE

Of course the word "love," given a suitable context, does have a meaning. A woman asks a man if he loves her, and it will not do, for even so odd a character as Meursault in Camus's *The Stranger*, to say, "The question doesn't mean anything." We know what it means, and we know its importance. The problem is how to be clear about the meaning and also capture the importance, since clarity in such matters often succeeds only at the expense of significance.

In order to both clarify and glorify love, the bookkeepers of the love-chat industry have developed two complementary and by now well-established methods to minimize confusion and avoid the unwanted conclusion that love is something quite ordinary. First, they have learned to routinely separate different "kinds" of love. Thus motherly and brotherly love are distinguished from romantic love and friendship. My love of New York cheesecake is safely insulated from the tragic love of Romeo and Juliet, and our wild weekend in the Bahamas is distinguished from the calm comfortable "conjugal" love of an old married couple. And all of these, in turn, are to be sharply (and usually unflatteringly) distinguished from those more abstract "kinds" of love, the love of humanity, the love of God, love *as* God, sometimes called "Platonic." This would be unobjectionable if the various "kinds" of love were not so immediately confused with one another, set to war against one another to see which of them is most "true," reduced one to another as if romantic love were "nothing but" sublimated Oedipal motherly love, for example, or conjugal love, ultimately, nothing but the love and grace of God. What begins as an attempt at clarification soon becomes a muddy battlefield, much more confused than before.

The second bookkeeping gambit is often linked to the first, but its efforts lie in the direction of turning what might otherwise be a prosaic routine into a task that requires enormous learning and sensitivity. It consists, quite simply, of obscuring the word "love" further by translating it into Greek.

> "I am not very well versed in Greek," said the giant.
> "Nor I either," replied the philosophical mite.
> "Why then do you quote Aristotle in Greek?" resumed the Sirian.
> "Because," answered the other, "it is but reasonable we should quote what we do not comprehend in a language we do not understand."
>
> VOLTAIRE, *Micromegas*

To see how this technique works, we might turn to one of the recent classics of the genre, Rollo May's much-read treatise on *Love and Will*. He begins his discussion by flatly listing, as if in a dictionary or a Burpee seed catalogue, "four kinds of love in Western tradition." They are: sex, *eros*, *philia* and *agape*. Sex is the only word not translated back into the Greek (it comes from the Latin *secare*, to divide), but to call sex a "kind of love" is already highly suspicious, particularly since May defines the central dilemma of his book as "the separation of sex and love." *Eros*, as May defines it, is "the drive to procreate or create—the urge, as the Greeks put it, toward higher forms of being and relationship." *Philia* is friendship, "brotherly love." And *agape* "is devoted to the welfare of the other, the prototype of which is the love of God for man."

Now the first thing to say about this is that the terms are *archaic;* their etymology is confused even in ancient Greek and they can mean almost anything a scholar wants them to mean. *Eros,* for instance, is a term with an extremely varied and unsettled history (which becomes so obvious in the arguments in Plato's *Symposium*) and, in any case, it was invented by an all-male warrior society for whom relationships with women were considered "vulgar" and for whom pederasty was the accepted practice and a good time was knocking the genitals off Athenian statues and Persians. *Agape,* on the other hand, is a later concept, promoted particularly by St. Paul and the early Christians (sometimes in the Latin, as *caritas*). It is not, as May suggests, a complement, "blended in various proportions" with *eros,* but rather an explicit verbal rejection of *eros* and "pagan" love, that is, sexual, sensual, personal love. *Agape* tends to be abstract, impersonal and distinctly unromantic. It is sometimes called "the love of humanity," often identified with the love of God, or the love that is appropriate to God. Much of the history of Western love, written primarily by theological scholars and German philologists, has consisted in the mock battle between these two Greek words, complete with shifting definitions which, in any case, would not be recognizable to the Greeks who used them in the first place. Needless to say, the battle usually gets resolved in favor of the "higher" love, *agape,* much to the detriment of *eros.* But all of this has nothing to do with love, or "love"; it is rather a technique to indulge in scholarship and avoid looking at any actual experience or emotion. Indeed, rather than clarify the issues, this scholarly piddling is itself another political move, a way of making an ordinary emotion sound impressively profound—and of making us sound pathetic by comparison.

The second thing to say about *eros* and *agape,* and *philia* too, is that love in the West doesn't come so neatly packaged. Indeed, one should ask very critically, for example, why *eros* and *philia* should be so distinguished, since many Greek writers (Aristotle, for example) used them more or less interchangeably, and since—to return to ordinary English—it is a very real question why we are so adamant about distinguishing friendship from romantic love, that is, apart from the initially obvious fact that the latter is intrinsically sexual and the former is not. But why should this be the case? Perhaps we place an excessive emphasis on sexual relationships? Or maybe we have an emasculated notion of friendship. Anyway, why distinguish sex from *eros* unless, perhaps, one means by "sex" mere physical intercourse and by *eros*—as we find in *Love and Will*—everything Good, True, Spiritual, Inspiring, Creative, Healthy, Courageous and Beautiful. There have been attempts to make the distinction between *eros* and *agape* more compatible; Paul Tillich (May's teacher), for example, defined them as "possessiveness" and "giving" respectively, but are these in any sense "kinds of love"? And to make this classic-minded list of four even far less palatable, one need only point out that "motherly love," the "kind" of love that would seem most obvious to Dr. May, who is a Freudian of sorts, does not even appear on the list. That would be news to Oedipus, and also to Erich Fromm, also a Freudian and keen on reducing love to variations of motherly love. Indeed, one need not be a gung-ho Freudian to appreciate the tenuousness of the distinction between motherly and romantic love, at least in some fairly familiar relationships.

One could pursue the "kinds of love" game probably endlessly. (Is the love of an old uncle the same as the love of a young grandfather? Is the love of a lover on Sunday afternoon the same as the love of the same lover on a dreary Monday morning?) But the point is that if we are going to learn anything about love at all the way *not* to begin is by reinforcing the rigid distinctions between different "kinds" of love. Consider, for example, the distinction between romantic love and friendship (*philia,* as in "Philia-delphia"). Of course there is friendship that stops short of sex, and friendship that stops short of love, but could it be that our notion of friendship is a particularly limp version of what in some societies and often in our own is a particularly powerful bond of affection, difficult to distinguish and often in competition with romantic love? Perhaps the fact that we sometimes choose as "lovers" (that is, sexual partners) people who could never be our friends shows much more about the significance of sex (or lack of it) than it does about the distinction between love and friendship. Indeed, it could be argued that our word "friend," just as much as the word "love," has become cheapened almost to the point of worthlessness. We at least verbally count as "friends" people who more accurately are mere acquaintances, or less. And the idea of living with a friend is usually considered at most a temporary convenience while waiting for something better (namely love) to come along.

It is worth mentioning, without becoming scholarly about it, the classic discussion of friendship to be found in Aristotle's *Nicomachean Ethics,* written in the fourth century B.C. "No one would choose to live without friends," he begins, but what we should add immediately is that the Greeks did not separate sex, love and friendship as we do, and Aristotle's description might serve us as a preliminary entry into romantic love as well. After insisting on the all-importance of friendship-love, Aristotle distinguishes three "objects of love," and three corresponding "kinds" of friendship—love of the useful, the pleasant and the good (VIII.2). He eliminates the love of "lifeless objects" because they cannot give us "mutual love," and then distinguishes:

(1) Friends who are useful. People who can get us what we want. There need be no reciprocal concern for the good of the other, except in so far as this is required for what one wants. A

friend who loans money or grants access to power, for example, would be an example of this kind of "friendship." (Aristotle hesitates to use the word.) But the problem with thus "using" one another is that the friendship depends wholly on the changing circumstances and "when the motive is done away . . . the friendship is dissolved." There is no friendship except in need, indeed.

(2) Friends who are pleasant. Companions, drinking partners and, one presumes, casual sex partners. A tennis partner should not be described as someone we "use" to play tennis, nor a dinner companion described as someone we "use" as company for dinner. Mutual enjoyment is essential, and such friendships also tend to begin and end abruptly: "This is why young people tend to fall in and out of love so quickly, changing even within a single day." But, unlike utility friendship, friends for pleasure at least enjoy one another, enjoy being together and can with some truth be said to be "friends"—but not ideal friends.

(3) "Perfect friendship." "The friendship of men who are good and alike in virtue," who not only wish each other well and enjoy one another but are a source of mutual inspiration and virtue. This is the friendship celebrated by the speakers at Plato's *Symposium*, a kind of love that Aristotle says "should be infrequent, for such men are rare." Such friendship requires "time and familiarity," as well as a sense which I will call "shared identity," not just the friendship of convenience or pleasure, but something of a "unity," which poets and philosophers have often struggled to describe. But at least it means this—that there is a sense of shared self, a common good, over and above just "good for me and good for you too."

Now it is clear that we use the word "lover" with the same lack of discrimination that Aristotle complains about regarding friendship, to apply to people who are just "using one another," for sex or social status or security, for a place to call

"home" or a way to keep from being bored on Saturday afternoons. People who enjoy sex together and, perhaps, an occasional movie, drink and dinner are too easily called "lovers," and one claims to be "in love" on the basis of merely a mood, sometimes with candles and flowers, not to mention the moon. But what we should say about love and friendship—leaving the degree of sexuality an open question—is that they are essentially the same, that friendship worthy of the name should have all the characteristics we normally reserve for love, and that "lovers" worthy of the name must be friends as well.

With Aristotle as our guide, we can specify with considerable caution what distinguishes romantic love. First, we should say, as he did not, that romantic love is essentially *sexual*, a form of enthusiasm which is not to be understood as "just sex," and sexuality is not to be understood as heterosexual intercourse. Indeed, there may be (and have often been) overwhelming reasons why romantic love cannot or should not be "consummated," or even acknowledged as such, and this in turn raises the socially horrifying question whether some other "kinds" of love—the love of a mother and her child, the love between a nun and a priest, the roughhouse love between two brothers—might not be considered romantic (but "repressed") as well. It does not follow, of course, that a steamy sexual relationship—even as part of an established couple or marriage—is romantic love. Sex and love are still not the same, even when they cannot be distinguished. Second, romantic love is *reciprocal* love, or what Aristotle calls "mutual"—but again this has to be qualified. So-called "unrequited" love is still romantic love, for actual reciprocity, like sexual fulfillment, is not as such essential to the emotion. It is the desire for reciprocity that is necessary; thus one can romantically love another person, but not a piece of pie or a sports car.[1] Third, let's say in a

[1] A recent *Playboy* poll listed "the most important features in an ideal lover." [To]p honors went to "someone to be totally open and honest with." Next was [so]meone to feel comfortable with" and then "someone who accepts you as you

preliminary way that romantic love is love for a particular person. Thus we can eliminate the in fact fascinating discussion about the status of my love for my dog as well as the various difficulties involved in a *ménage à trois*. Let's leave it an open question whether one can love more than one particular person at a time, as well as what it means, more precisely, to love a particular person. And fourth, I want to restrict romantic love to Aristotle's third "kind": shared identity rather than mutual pleasure or mere utility. Love is more than companionship. ("If you can't be with the one you love, love the one you're with.") I have already said that I want to leave open all questions of gender, and in what follows I want to make no distinction whatever between hetero- and homosexual romantic love. In fact I want to argue that there is an "equality" requirement that eliminates much of what is (falsely) considered to be one of the most objectionable features of romantic love, namely the idea that males must dominate females, "be the boss"—however more politely or with whatever dubious biological analogues this might be formulated. The equality requirement probably eliminates motherly love from consideration, since there is at least one clear sense in which the love of mother for child and the love of infant for mother are wholly unequal, and it eliminates the love of God, needless to say, which is not, even for the German romantics, romantic love. It also eliminates *agape* as well as Erich Fromm's celebrated notion of "being a loving person," since the love of humanity, however passionate, is neither sexual (presumably), nor reciprocal (perhaps unfortunately), nor personal. Indeed, what is called "Platonic" love is so different from romantic love that it surel

are." And, of course, "physically attractive," suspiciously only fourth. W noteworthy is that my cat fulfills all four criteria; my old bedroom slir only the last of them. The notion of reciprocity—which is not th "someone to be open and honest with" much less "feeling comfor does not enter into the survey at all.

should *not* be called by the same name, much less confused or compared favorably with it.

To say that romantic love is sexual, reciprocal, personal and shared is not to say very much, but even while drawing our boundaries so broadly we can say, without any hesitation, that we are clearly referring to an emotion which is quite specific, which can be described matter-of-factly and without self-congratulation (as Aristotle did *in opposition to* his pious teacher Plato). It is quite obviously a real and tangible passion in our emotional repertoire, not just a myth or an "illusion." "Love" is not just a word, then, but it has been obscured considerably by a variety of images, models and metaphors which are not essentially part of its structure. Granting that we do sometimes have mutual, passionate, sexual (but more than sexual) feelings about another person, the question is, *what more* do we add to this simple set of ingredients to cook up that rich, muddy and sometimes indigestible emotional stew that we call, with considerable confusion, *romantic love?*

2 MODELS AND METAPHORS: "THE GAME OF LOVE"

Let me say—why not?—that yellow is the color of love.
GILBERT SORRENTINO, *Splendide Hotel,* p. 59

We look at love, as we look at life, through a series of metaphors, each with its own language, its own implications, connotations and biases.

For example, if someone says that love is a game, we already know much of what is to follow: relationships will tend to be short-lived. Sincerity will be a strategy for winning and so will flattery and perhaps lying. ("All's fair . . .") The person "played with" is taken seriously only as an opponent, a challenge, valued in particular for his or her tactics and retorts, but quickly dispensable as soon as someone has "won" or "lost." "Playing hard to get" is an optional strategy, and being "easy" is not immoral or foolish so much as playing badly, or not at all.

On the other hand, if someone sees love as "God's gift to humanity," we should expect utter solemnity, mixed with a sense of gratitude, seriousness and self-righteousness that is wholly lacking in the "love is a game" metaphor. Relationships here will tend to be long-lasting, if not "forever," fraught with duties and obligations dictated by a "gift" which, in the usual interpretations, has both divine and secular strings attached.

The "game" metaphor is, perhaps, too frivolous to take seriously. The "gift of God" metaphor, on the other hand, is much too serious to dismiss frivolously. We will discuss it, and the damage it has done, at length in several later chapters. In this chapter what I would like to do is display the variety and richness of the metaphors through which we tend to talk about, and experience, love. Not surprisingly, these love metaphors reflect our interests elsewhere in life—business, health, communications, art, politics and law as well as fun and games and religion. But these are not mere "figures of speech"; they are the self-imposed structures that determine the way we experience love itself. (For this reason, we should express some pretty strong reservations about some of them.)

Tit for Tat: Love as a Fair Exchange

One of the most common love metaphors, now particularly popular in social psychology, is the *economic* metaphor. The idea is that love is an exchange, a sexual partnership, a trade-off of interests and concerns and, particularly, of *approval.* "I make you feel good about yourself and in return you make me feel good about myself." Of course exchange rates vary—some people need more than others—and there is a law of diminishing returns; that is, the same person's approval tends to become less and less valuable as it becomes more familiar. (This law of diminishing returns, which we experience as the gradual fading of romantic love, has been explored by the psychologist Eliot Arenson of the University of California at Santa Cruz. His theory has been aptly named by his students "Arenson's Law of Marital Infidelity.") In some relationships the balance of payments may indeed seem extremely one-sided but the assumption is, in the words of the Harvard sociologist Homans, that both parties must believe they are getting something out of it or they simply wouldn't stay around.

Now this economic model has much to offer, not least the fact that it gives a fairly precise account of the concrete motivation for love, which is left out of more pious accounts that insist that love is simply good in itself and needs no motives. But the problem is that it too easily degenerates into a most unflattering model of mutual buying and selling, which in turn raises the specter that love may indeed be, as some cynics have been saying ever since Marx (Karl) and Engels, a form of covert prostitution, though not necessarily—or even usually—for money. "I will sleep with you and think well of you or at least give you the benefit of the doubt if only you'll tell me good things about myself and pretend to approve of me."

It may be true that we do often evaluate our relationships in this way, in terms of mutual advantage and our own sense of fairness. The question, "What am I getting out of this, anyway?" always makes sense, even if certain traditional views of love and commitment try to pretend that such selfishness is the very antithesis of love. But the traditional views have a point to make too, which is, simply, that such tit-for-tat thinking inevitably undermines a relationship based on love, *not* because love is essentially "selfless" but because the bargain table is not the place to understand mutual affection. Love is not the exchange of affection, any more than sex is merely the exchange of pleasure. What is left out of these accounts is the "we" of love, which is quite different from mere "I and thou." This is not to say that fairness cannot be an issue in love, nor is it true that "all's fair" in love. But while the economic exchange model explains rather clearly some of the motives for love, it tends to ignore the *experience* of love almost altogether, which is that such comparisons and evaluations seem at the time beside the point and come to mind only when love is already breaking down. It is the suspicion, not the fact, that "I'm putting more into this than you are" that signals the end of many relationships, despite the fact that, as business goes, they may have been "a good arrangement."

The Job of Loving: The Work Model

A very different model is the *work* model of love. The Protestant ethic is very much at home in romance. (Rollo May calls love the Calvinist's proof of emotional salvation.) And so we find many people who talk about "working out a relationship," "working at it," "working for it" and so on. The fun may once have been there, of course, but now the real *job* begins, tacking together and patching up, like fixing up an old house and refusing to move out until the roof caves in. This is, needless to say, a particularly self-righteous model, if for no other reason than that it begins on the defensive and requires considerable motivation just to move on. Personal desires, the other person's as well as one's own, may be placed behind "the relationship," which is conceived of as the primary *project*. Love, according to the work model, gets evaluated above all on its industriousness, its seriousness, its success in the face of the most difficult obstacles. Devotees of the work model not infrequently choose the most inept or inappropriate partners, rather like buying a run-down shack—for the challenge. They will look with disdain at people who are merely happy together (something like buying a house from a tract builder). They will look with admiration and awe at a couple who have survived a dozen years of fights and emotional disfigurements because "they made it work."

A Madness Most Discrete: The (Melo) Dramatic Model

In contrast to the work model, we can turn with a sense of recreation to the *dramatic* model of love, love as theater, love as melodrama. This differs from the game model in that one's roles are taken *very* seriously, and the notions of winners and losers, strategy and tactics are replaced by notions of performance, catharsis, tragedy and theatricality. Roles are all important—keeping within roles, developing them, enriching them. The dramatic model also tends to play to an audience, real (whenever possible) or imagined (when necessary). Fights and reconciliations alike will often be performed in public, and an evening at home alone may often seem pointless. Some dramatic lovers are prima donnas, referring every line or part back to themselves, but one can be just as theatrical by being visibly selfless, or martyred, or mad. Lunt and Fontanne or Bogart and Bacall might well be models, and lovers will strain without amusement to perfect for the appropriate occasion someone else's drawl, insult, posture or sigh. Unfortunately the dramatic model too easily tends to confuse interpersonal problems with theatrical flaws, to praise and abuse itself in those mincing terms that are, appropriately, the vocabulary of the theater critic. (Clive Barnes as Cupid?) The worst that one could say of such love, therefore, is that it's "boring" or "predictable."

"Relationships": Banality as Metaphor

Blandness can be just as significant as profundity and excitement, and a metaphor may be intentionally noncommittal as well as precise. Thus we find the word "thing" substituted as a grammatical stand-in for virtually everything from sexual organs (a young virgin gingerly refers to her first lover's "thing") to jobs, hang-ups and hobbies (as in "doing your own thing"). Where love is concerned, the most banal of our metaphors, so pervasive and so banal that it hardly seems like a metaphor, is the word "relating," or "relationship" itself. There's not much to say about it, except to ponder in amazement the fact that we have not yet, in this age of "heavy relationships," come up with anything better. There is a sense, of course, in which any two people (or two things) stand in any number of relationships to one another (being taller than, heavier than, smarter than, more than fifteen feet away from . . . etc.). The word "relations" was once, only a few years ago, a polite and slightly clinical word for sex (still used, as most stilted archaisms tend to be, in law). People "relate" to each other as they "relate a story," perhaps on the idea that what couples do most together is to tell each other the events of the day, a less than exciting conception of love, to be sure. But metaphors can be chosen for their vacuousness just as for their imaginative imagery, and the fact that this metaphor dominates our thinking so much (albeit in the guise of a *meaningful* relationship) points once again to the poverty of not only our vocabulary but our thinking and feeling as well. Anyone who's still looking for a "meaningful relationship" in the 1980s may have a lot to learn about love, or not really care about it at all.

Love and Electronics: The Communication Metaphor

A powerful metaphor with disastrous consequences that was popular a few years ago was a "communication" metaphor, often used in conjunction with a "relating" metaphor, for obvious reasons. Both were involved with the then hip language of media and information theory: "getting through" to each other and "we just can't communicate any more" gave "relationships" the unfortunate appearance of shipwrecked survivors trying to keep in touch over a slightly damaged shortwave radio. The information processing jargon ("input," "feedback," "tuning in" and "turning off") was typically loaded with electronic gadget imagery, and good relationships appropriately were described in terms of their "good vibrations." But, like all metaphors, this one revealed much more than it distorted, namely, an image of isolated transmitters looking for someone to get their messages. It was precisely this milieu that gave birth to Rollo May's *Love and Will,* and his concern that we had rendered love between us impossible. Love was thought to be mainly a matter of self-expression, largely but not exclusively verbal expression. Talk became enormously important to love; problems were talked over, talked through and talked out. The essential moment was the "heavy conversation" and, appropriately, talk about love often took the place of love itself. Confession and "openness" (telling all) became the linchpins of love, even when the messages were largely hostility and resentment. Psychotherapist George Bach wrote a number of successful books, including *The Intimate Enemy* (with Peter Wyden), which made quite clear the fact that it was expression of feelings, not the feelings themselves, that made for a successful relationship. On the communication model, sex too was described as a mode of communication, but more often sex was not so much communicating as the desire to be communicated with. Sex became, in McLuhanesque jargon, a "cool" medium. And, like most modern media, the model put its emphasis on the medium itself (encounter groups, etc.) but there was precious little stress on the *content* of the programming. Not surprisingly, love became an obscure ideal, like television advertisements full of promise of something fabulous yet to come, hinted at but never spoken of as such. In fact the ultimate message was the idea of the medium itself.

The Ontology of Loneliness: Love and Aloneness

In our extremely individualistic society we have come to see isolation and loneliness as akin to "the human condition," instead of as by-products of a certain kind of social arrangement, which puts mobility and the formation of new interpersonal bonds at a premium. This individualistic metaphor, which I call "the ontology of loneliness," is stated succinctly, for example, by Rollo May: "Every person, experiencing as he [sic] does his own solitariness and aloneness, longs for union with another" (*Love and Will*, p. 144). Similarly, Erich Fromm preoccupies himself with "our need to escape the prison of our aloneness," and the radical feminist Shulamith Firestone complains about the same need "to escape from the isolation of our own solitude." Love, then, is a refuge from an otherwise intolerable existence. Our "natural" state is aloneness; our escape from this state, hopefully, is love. "Love," writes the poet Rilke, "is two solitudes reaching out to greet each other."

This is a viewpoint that has been argued by many philosophers under the name of "solipsism" ("the only sure thing is one's own existence") and has been developed by the vulgar philosopher Ayn Rand into an argument for selfishness: "Each of us is born into the world alone, and therefore each of us is justified in pursuing our own selfish interests." But the premise is false and the inference is insidious. Not even Macduff (who was not, strictly speaking, "of woman born") came into the world by himself. And not only in infancy but in adulthood we find ourselves essentially linked to other people, to a language that we call our own, to a culture and, at least legally, to a country as well. We do not have to find or "reach out" to others; they are, in a sense, already *in us*. Alone in the woods of British Columbia, I find myself still thinking of friends, describing what I see as if they were there—and in their language. The idea of the isolated self is an American invention—reinforced perhaps by the artificially isolated circumstances of the psychiatrist's office and our fantasies about gunfighters and mountain men, but this is not true of most of us. And this means that love is not a refuge or an escape either. Our conception of ourselves is always a social self (even if it is an antisocial or rebellious self).

Our language of love often reflects this idea of natural isolation, for example in the "communication" metaphor in which isolated selves try desperately to "get through" to one another. But this is an unnecessarily tragic picture of life and love, and its result is to make love itself seem like something of a cure for a disease, rather than a positive experience which already *presupposes* a rather full social life. Indeed, it is revealing that, quite the contrary of social isolation, romantic love is usually experienced only *within* a rather extensive social nexus. "Sure, I have lots of friends and I like my colleagues at work but, still, I'm lonely and I want to fall in love." But that has nothing to do with loneliness. It rather reflects the tremendous importance we accord to romantic love in our lives, not as a cure for aloneness, but as a positive experience in its own right, which we have, curiously, turned into a need.

"Made for Each Other": The Metaphysical Model

Standing opposed to the "ontology of loneliness" is an ancient view which takes our *unity,* not our mutual isolation, as the "natural" state of humanity. The classic statement of this view, brilliant in its poetic simplicity, is Aristophanes' speech in the *Symposium,* in which he describes our "natural" state as double creatures, cleft in two by Zeus for our hubris, struggling to be reunited through love. Our own image of two people "being made for each other" is also an example of the metaphysical model, together with the idea that marriages are "made in heaven" and the idea that someone else can be your "better half." The metaphysical model is based not on the idea that love is a refuge from isolated individualism but, quite the opposite, on the idea that love is the realization of bonds that are already formed, even before one meets one's "other half."

The ontology of loneliness treats individuals as atoms, bouncing around the universe alone looking for other atoms, occasionally forming more or less stable molecules. But if we were to pursue the same chemical metaphor into the metaphysical model, it would more nearly resemble what physicists today call "field theory." A magnetic field, for instance, retains all of its electromagnetic properties whether or not there is any material there to make them manifest. So too, an individual is already a network of human relationships and expectations, and these exist whether or not one finds another individual whose radiated forces and properties are complementary. The old expression about love being a matter of "chemical attraction" (from Goethe to Gilbert and Sullivan[1]) is, scientifically, a century out of date; "attraction" is no longer a question of one atom affecting another but the product of two electromagnetic fields, each of which exists prior to and independently of any particular atoms within its range. So too we radiate charm, sexiness, inhibition, intelligence and even repulsiveness, and find a lover who fits in. The problem with this viewpoint, however, is that it leaves no room for the *development* of relationships but rather makes it seem as if, if the love is there at all, it has to be there, and be there in full, from the very beginning.

Love and Disease: The Medical Metaphor

"Love's a malady without a cure," wrote Dryden, and today, our favorite metaphor, from social criticism to social relationships, has become the disease metaphor, images of health and decay, the medicalization of all things human, from the stock market to sex and love. Not surprisingly, a large proportion of our books about love and sex are written by psychiatrists and other doctors. (They used to be written by priests and theologians.) Our society is described in terms of "narcissism" (a clinical term), as an "age of anxiety," and as "decadent" (the negative side of the biological process.) For Rollo May and Erich Fromm, lack of love is the dominant disease of our times. For others, *Love and Addiction* author Stan-

[1] Hey diddle diddle with your middle-
class kisses.
It's a chemical reaction, that's all. (Gilbert and Sullivan)

ton Peele, for instance, love is itself a kind of disease, an "addiction," waiting to be cured. Some feminists have seized on the disease metaphor (a disease invented by and carried by men): Ti-Grace Atkinson (in *Amazon Odyssey*) calls love "a pathological condition," and Erica Jong (in *Fear of Flying*) calls it "the search for self-annihilation." But whether love is the disease or love is the cure, what is obvious is that this model turns us all into *patients,* and one might well ask—the professional interests of the A.M.A. aside—whether that is the arena within which we want to talk about love.

The Art in Loving: The Aesthetic Model

Perhaps the oldest view of love, the pivot of Plato's *Symposium,* is an *aesthetic* model: love as the admiration and the contemplation of *beauty.* The emphasis here is on neither relating nor communicating (in fact, unrequited love and even voyeurism are perfectly in order). On this model, it is not particularly expected that the lover will actually *do* much of anything except, perhaps, to get within view of the beloved at every possible opportunity, as one might stand before the fireplace and admire one's favorite painting over the mantel. It is this model that has dominated many of our theories about love, though not, luckily, our actual practices. It is this model that best fits the moaning troubadours in twelfth-century France, composing poetry about the inaccessible beauty of the maiden up there on the tower balcony, visible but untouchable. It is this model that feminists rightly complain about when they accuse men of "putting them up on a pedestal," a charge that too often confuses the idealization that accompanies it with the impersonal distancing that goes along with the pedestal. The objection is not to the fact that it is a pedestal so much as the fact that it is usually a very *tall* pedestal, so that any real contact is pretty much out of the question and the fear of falling is considerable. Or else it is a very *small* pedestal, "and like any small place," writes Gloria Steinem, "a prison."

Love and Commitment: The Contract Model

An old view of love, which dominated much of the eighteenth and nineteenth centuries, was a *contract* model, a specific instance of a more general "social contract" theory that was then believed by most people to be the (implicit) basis of society itself. Contracts in love were exemplified, of course, by the quite explicit and wholly legal contract of marriage, but even then, and especially now, the idea of implicit contracts was taken for granted too. (*Cosmopolitan* magazine last year reran one of its most popular pieces, about "secret" contracts in love, two hundred years too late to be in vogue.) What is crucial to this metaphor, however, is the fact that *emotion* plays very little part in it. One accepts an obligation to obey the terms of the contract (implicit or explicit) whether or not (though hopefully whether) one wants to. The current term for this ever popular emasculation of emotion is *commitment*. In fact there seems to be an almost general agreement among most of the people I talk to that "commitment" is what constitutes love. (The contrast is almost always sexual promiscuity or purely "casual" affairs.) But commitment is precisely what love is *not* (though of course one can and often does make commitments on the basis of the fact that he or she loves someone). A commitment is an obligation sustained *whether or not one has the emotion that originally motivated it*. And the sense of obligation isn't "love."

Freudian Fallacies: The Biological Metaphor

The idea that science itself can be but a metaphor strikes us as odd, but much of what we believe about love, it seems, is based on wholly unliteral biological metaphors. For example, we believe that love is "natural," even an "instinct," and this is supported by a hundred fascinating but ultimately irrelevant arguments about "the facts of life": the fact that some spiders eat their mates, that some birds mate for life, that some sea gulls are lesbians, that some fish can't mate unless the male is clearly superior, that chimpanzees like to gang bang and gorillas have weenies the size of a breakfast sausage, that bats tend to do it upside down and porcupines do it "carefully." But romantic love is by no means "natural"; it is not an instinct but a very particular and peculiar attitude toward sex and pair-bonding that has been carefully cultivated by a small number of modern aristocratic and middle-class societies. Even sex, which would seem to be "natural" if anything is, is no more mere biology than taking the holy wafer at high mass is just eating. It too is defined by our metaphors and the symbolic significance we give to it. It is not a "need," though we have certainly made it into one. Sex is not an instinct, except in that utterly minimal sense that bears virtually no resemblance at all to the extremely sophisticated and emotion-filled set of rituals that we call—with some good reason—"making love." And where sex and love come together is not in the realm of nature either, but in the realm of expression, specific to a culture which specifies its meaning.

There is one particular version of the biological metaphor, however, which has enjoyed such spectacular scientific airplay, ever since Freud at least, that we tend to take it as the literal truth instead of, again, as a metaphor. It is the idea that love begins in—or just out of—the womb, and that our prototype of love—if not our one "true" love—is our own mother.

This would suggest indeed that love is, if not an instinct, common to all human beings. But the argument turns on a number of obvious fallacies, starting from the premise that, because of the extraordinarily slow development of human infants, all of us, from our very birth (and perhaps before), need love. But . . .

(1) This isn't romantic love, in any case, and romantic love is in no way reducible to mere dependency. In fact, despite its "baby" imagery, romantic love presupposes just what infancy lacks: a sense of selfhood and a high degree of mobility and independence. Moreover, the view expresses an obvious male bias and leaves the romantic desires of women something of a mystery (for Freud in particular).

(2) To need love is not to need *to* love. Some people need desperately to be loved but have no inclination whatever to love in return.

(3) Babies need care and comfort, not necessarily love. In fact regular tender care is far more desirable than adoring but erratic attention. Romantic love, of course, thrives on the latter, gets too easily bored with the first.

(4) In few societies is the care of a particular mother expected by either the infant or society, and the idea that one has special affection for one person exclusively is an anthropologically peculiar notion which in fact is disintegrating in our society too. In most societies, increasingly in our own, an infant is cared for by any number of different people, male as well as female, and the idea of a single utterly dominant dependency figure—which so obsessed Freud—is a peculiarity of the Victorian Viennese middle-class ethic, not a universal human characteristic.

(5) It is most implausible that any adult emotion is simply reducible to an infantile need. To identify a radical politi-

cian's moral indignation with infantile rage would be offensive as well as simply wrong; to think of sexual jealousy as merely an adult extension of a child's possessiveness is not only to misunderstand jealousy but to misunderstand children as well. And even in those relatively few cases in which the so-called "Oedipal complex" reigns supreme, it is a mistake to reduce all subsequent affections to a mere repetition of family dynamics. Some psychologists, Gordon Allport for example, have come to refer to this rejection of Freudian reductionism as "the autonomy of motives." No matter how revealing the origins of one's affections, it is their development and differences that define them. We think it noteworthy when a man dates a woman who resembles his mother, not when he does not. The Oedipal complex is desperately looking for an occasional instance as if to confirm it.

We sometimes plague ourselves with the idea that we are "hung up" on Oedipal images. In high school I worried about the fact that the girls I "dated" bore a sometimes striking resemblance to my mother. (They were usually short, bright, creative and Caucasian.) I had read enough Freud for this to worry me. Many years later a psychotherapist convinced me, or I "discovered," that, indeed, I was looking for a woman who was more like my father, which confused me considerably, needless to say, but worried me too. But this limited number of alternatives, always clouded by the threat of "neurosis," turns out to be nonsense, or worse—it is the Freudian doctrine of original sin, a new source of unnecessary guilt and just as much a myth as the original Original Sin. In fact our models and prototypes of love include not only our parents but brothers, sisters, teachers in junior high school, first dates, first loves, graduating-class heroes and heroines, hundreds of movie stars and magazine pictures as well as a dozen considerations and pressures that have nothing to do with prototypes at all. Indeed, even Freud insists that it is not a person's *actual* parent who forms the romantic prototype but rather a phantom, constructed from memory, which may bear little resemblance to any actual person. But if this is so, perhaps one's imagined mother is in fact a variation on one's first girl friend, or a revised version of Myrna Loy. Why do we take the most complex and at times exquisite emotion in most of our lives, and try to reduce it to the first and the simplest?

Or, if the Oedipal theory is right, why didn't Romulus, raised by a she-wolf, rape his dog, instead of the Sabine women? Mere motherhood is not everything, even in ancient mythology.

"The Flame in My Heart": The Emotion Metaphor

Love is an emotion. But the way we talk about emotions is itself so pervaded by metaphors that one begins to wonder whether there is anything there to actually talk about. We talk about ourselves as if we were Mr. Coffee machines, bubbling over, occasionally overflowing, getting too hot to handle, and bursting from too much pressure. We subscribe in metaphor if not in medicine to the medieval theory that the seat of the emotions is in the heart, and in love it is the heart that pounds, beats, breaks and is bound and occasionally butchered. We describe love in terms of heat, fire, flame—all of which are expressive and poetic but, it is sometimes hard to remember, metaphors all the same. But is love really that sense that one is going to burst? The warm flush that pours through one's body when *he* or *she* walks into the room: is that love? And if so, why do we set so much store by it? It is for this reason, no doubt, that the age-old wisdom about love has made it out to be more than a mere emotion—a gift from God, a visitation from the gods, the wound of Cupid's arrow, the cure for a disease or a disease itself, the economics of interpersonal relations or even "the answer" to all life's problems. But then again, maybe we underestimate our emotions.

What is love? It seems to be almost everything except, perhaps, "never having to say you're sorry." Love is a series of metaphors, which we glorify selectively, picking one out and calling it "true" love, which itself is another metaphor.

Not all metaphors are created equal. Some are profound, some are banal, some increase our self-confidence, others make us feel slimy, defensive or sick. There is no "true" love, for there is no singly true metaphor, but this does not mean that one should not choose carefully. For choosing one's metaphor is, in fact, choosing one's love life as well.

3 WHAT I FEEL IN MY HEART

Luv dub luv dub[1]

[1] Actually I don't feel anything in my heart, since it has no efferent sensory nerves. What I really feel in my chest is the dull thud made by the tricuspid and mitral valves snapping shut just prior to contraction, then the slight change of pressure through the thin skin that covers some of my superficial veins—some considerable time *after* the actual "beat" of the heart. But while I'm so scrupulously paying attention to my pulse, am I indeed paying attention to my love? Or am I rather distracting myself from it? And if I add to the rhythmic contractions of my heart the fact that I'm also slightly short of breath, that my throat feels cramped, my bowels are uncertain and my knees feel queasy, is *that* love? And in the pages that follow, is *that* what you are going to keep accusing me of "leaving out"? Mere *symptoms?*

LOVE IS AN EMOTION 4

Love, music, passion, intrigue, heroism,—these are things that make life worth while.

Love is not a biological drive, not a "need," not a gift from God (much less *is* it God). It is neither natural nor necessary nor necessarily healthy, helpful or human. Neither is it "divine," and it is certainly no "mystery," unless, of course, we refuse even to look at it. Love is an emotion, nothing else.

We have a general view of emotions, however, which explains not only our resistance to thinking, talking and theorizing about love—pretending that it is a mystery and both demeaning and idolizing it at the same time—but also our confused and sometimes tragic attitudes toward emotions in general. One symptom, among many, is the way we criticize emotions in men and belittle them in women. ("Oh, women are so emotional!" he screeched.) Emotions are thought to be inferior, opposed to our "higher" faculties of reasoning, rationalizing and calculating the weekly budget. ("Be reasonable" often means "Don't be emotional.") Emotions, accordingly, are thought to be intrinsically "irrational." ("Don't be emotional" means "Don't cause any trouble.") We are counseled in the "control" of our emotions, as if they were beasts in a fragile cage; we are praised for being "cool" and chastised for "letting ourselves go." We are warned against the dangers of pride, envy and anger, which are catalogued as three of the seven "deadly sins." And in the whole history of Western thought the emotions have been treated as the "lower" parts of the human soul, what we share and inherit from the animals, while it is reason that makes us human, even "a spark of the divine."[1] No wonder, then, that love also finds itself in a problematic conceptual situation, and small surprise that its proponents so often defend it by denying what it really is, an emotion, and turning it into something else.

> "Falling in love" is an inferior state of mind, a form of imbecility.
>
> ORTEGA Y GASSET, *On Love*

In a book called *The Passions*, a few years ago, I attacked what I called "the myth of the passions," the core of which is this systematic degradation of emotion in favor of the "higher" faculties of reason throughout our culture. But the degradation of emotions is based in turn on a view of emotions which makes it difficult to take them seriously. Quite simply, we have been taught to view our emotions as primitive forces, intrusions in our otherwise orderly, rational lives. We are taught, virtually as a matter of language, that emotions are "feelings," that is, general sensations, the most prominent features of which are a certain sense of innervation, visceral disturbances, including a queasy stomach and a sometimes embarrassing looseness in the bowels and bladder, frequent flushing, blushing, a certain shakiness in the knees, intense irritability and other familiar and generalizable quasi-physiological reactions that we associate with almost every strong emotion, from fear and anger to "falling in love."

Because emotions are so closely associated with these physical feelings and diagnosable on such an obvious physiological basis (the pumping of adrenalin, for example), it is quite reasonably believed that there is little to be said about them and

[1] Goethe, *Faust*. Aristotle, *Ethics*.

even less to *do* about them, except, perhaps, avoid situations that incite them or take tranquillizers to control them. And because emotions are so clearly bodily (as opposed to cerebral), it is assumed that they are "instinctual," biologically determined, unlearned and therefore uneducable. Our ways of talking about them show quite clearly that we see our emotions as *happening to us*, and so we "fall in love," as one would into a swamp; we are "plagued" by remorse, as if by Alaskan mosquitoes, "struck" by jealousy, as if by an Oldsmobile, "crushed" by shame, like a bug beneath a boot, "paralyzed" by fear, as if by a stroke, and distracted by guilt, as if by a trombone in the kitchen. We are "heartbroken," "smitten," "carried away," "transported" and "overwhelmed" by emotions. And our vocabulary of romantic love sounds like a surgeon's or a butcher's: hearts cleft in two, bruised as well as broken, pounding now and then, grown cold, bursting, aching, torn and tender. Emotions, as Freud stated so graphically, are part of the *Id* ("it"), which is opposed to and perennially endangers the tenuous rationality of the poor, noble Ego ("I"). Emotions, for him and most psychotherapists, are typically destructive, dangerous, disruptive. And romantic love, as an emotion, is surely no exception. Luckily, however, it tends not to last (except in neurotic "romantics"), and so it can safely be replaced by far safer brands of feelings, nominally "love" too—habitual conjugal love, which is or can be devoid of the violent passions of uncertain romance, and emasculated Platonic love, in which contemplation and quiet faith make love far more like reason and philosophy (which is also a "love of") than passion.

Consider, for a moment, the way we talk about anger, as one representative emotion. We "bottle up" our anger and "let off steam." Our emotion is "pent up" and when we are ready "to blow up," we finally "vent our rage." We "dam up aggression" and "blow our tops." We "feel something bubbling up inside of us," as if "ready to burst," then we "explode." The image is *hydraulic,* the human psyche as a boiler system, filled with volatile gas or superheated steam, sometimes contained, always explosive. The metaphors tell us a lot about how we see ourselves, and it is not just the poets who invent them. The most sophisticated psychological theorists, Freud and William James, for example, employ the same images. Freud's terminology of "cathexis" (filling) and "catharsis" (discharge), "repression" (keeping the lid on), "sublimation" (letting it out through a safer viaduct) and "vicissitudes" (alternative viaducts) are all based on the same metaphorical image. And even those many psychologists who openly reject Freud's theories of the mind sometimes fall back to the hydraulic model when discussing emotion. In a debate in the magazine *Psychology Today,* for example, the hot dispute was between those who would "bottle up anger" and the "ventilationists" who encouraged its free release, both of course in the name of mental health. Even "Rational-Emotive therapy," which makes at least some valiant attempt to overcome the traditional hydraulic view by stressing the patient's own responsibility for his or her emotions, ultimately falls back on the hydraulic model of emotions, emotions as "inside" us, beyond our direct control (what we control are our beliefs), still irrational, disruptive and, in excess, unhealthy.

The physiology of the hydraulic model is often medieval, the image of the various "humours" circulating through the body. Though we long ago gave up the physiology, we still hang onto the imagery, and talk without hesitation of "my blood boiling" and "so much bile" or "spleen" or "gall." (Should we resist the temptation to mention "hot under the choler"?) Even the law excuses the most abominable actions if they are carried out "in hot blood." Occasionally the image becomes more centrifugal instead of hydraulic, as in "flying off the handle," but the mechanical model is still in effect, and it is still Isaac Newton who provides our basic emotional models. Even in the ancients, who were less mechanistically inclined, we find the same kind of picture of anger as an affliction, a kind of madness, an attack by the "Furies." And in the beginnings of modern philosophy too, for example, in Descartes and Malebranche, emotions are identified as "animal spirits," flowing through our bodies and, typically, causing trouble.

This is not to say, of course, that we can never enjoy these disturbances. Depending on the cause, these various physiological disruptions can even be interpreted, as they were long ago, as a kind of divine "possession," such as the rapture of St. Agatha and, slightly less divine, the common discomforts of an adolescent in love. But here is where our ambivalence becomes transparent; in so far as these experiences are deemed profound or significant, they are no longer treated as mere emotions. Religious thinkers have always been hesitant to place very much confidence in passive emotional trauma, just as most societies have, quite wisely, known better than to base the essential structures of marriage and the family on so fleeting and flimsy a foundation as mere "feeling." Love is an instance of the animal in us, not to be dismissed, perhaps, but not to be taken too seriously either. Romantic love, we still read in *Cosmopolitan,* is "a matter of chemistry," an image that has its support even in the writings of the greatest of poets, in Shakespeare, for instance, and in Goethe, whose novel *Elective Affinities* (a chemical term of his times) has been prime reading in Europe for almost two centuries. While anger is usually viewed as a hot gas, however, love is often compared to fire itself, "the flame of love" (the lover as "flame" too), fanning and dying embers, and "a fire in the blood." Bad physiology, perhaps, but impressive and telling metaphors, taking us in for centuries.

We are "passive" regarding our passions; that is the bottom line of these traditional models. Our emotions happen to us, intrude in our lives, and so they are relegated to the fringes and interstices of experience: love affairs while on vacation, an occasional bout of anger, a healthy "outlet" at the right time, but something to be "gotten over" nevertheless. Love is no different in this regard, and it is to save this savored emotion from the degradation due most of our passions (such as those that make the "deadly sins" list) that love is transformed into something else—something impersonal, selfless, abstract and emasculated—"Platonic" love of God or beauty, or that sexless love called *agape* that good people everywhere are supposed to have for everyone, especially the poor, the grotesque and the damned. Romantic love, however, still so tied to the flesh and to passion, still so "out of control" and filled with involuntary (if enjoyable) suffering, is to be tolerated only in small and insignificant amounts. Like a child with a new surfboard, we are permitted to ride the waves of our passions with the understanding that, inevitably, we will come crashing back down on the cold sands of reality. (If God had meant us to soar with our emotions, we read in such philosophers as Aristotle and Kant, he would not have made us so *reasonable*.)

Not only do we say that we "fall in" love, but love "strikes us," often unawares, "from behind," if it does not "slap us in the face." We are wounded by Cupid's arrows—a telling metaphor of love's passivity. Love *poisons* us, drives us "insane." But the theme I want to pursue with love is precisely the opposite. Love is not passive and not something we "suffer." (The very word "passion" literally means "suffering," as in "the passion of Christ.") The passiveness of the passions is indeed a "myth," as I argued a few years ago, but it is not a myth born merely of ignorance. Like most of our false beliefs about ourselves, this one serves a self-interested purpose. How often have you heard someone say (or have you said yourself), "I couldn't help it, I was so . . ."—where the ellipsis names an emotion? "I couldn't control myself, I was in love," or "It wasn't entirely his fault; he lost his temper." The myth of the passions provides us with an *excuse*, a way of denying responsibility (or at least full responsibility) for doing what in fact we want to do *most*. By seeing ourselves as victims, we can remain happily oblivious to those passions which are indeed the main motives in life. But they do not merely happen to us. We *do* our passions. We *are* them. And we have now reached the point where our excuse has turned on us, and it demeans us more than it saves us. We have come to see our emotions in an almost wholly negative light, so that we (ironically) get angry at ourselves for being angry, get embarrassed because we find ourselves embarrassed, become guilty, according to the latest theories, just because we find ourselves feeling guilty. And romantic love is still viewed with suspicion, as being merely "in love with love"; for men, it becomes an excuse to be demanding, foolish, childish; for women, it becomes idealized submissiveness, which, not surprisingly, is encouraged by men.

We do not "fall" into love or, if we do, it is after a lifetime of conscientious activities, not the least of which are our fantasies and constant conversations, ten thousand movies and books, the cultural junk from which we build an emotional nest, ready from the age of twelve to lie or be laid down in it with someone whose fantasies complement our own. And we do not fall "in" love either, for love, like all emotions (even the "withdrawal" emotions) is a reaching *out*, the projection of a structure, a meaning, a way of personally relating to the world. Love is one among the many ways we subjectively organize our experience, see ourselves in certain roles (e.g., the lover) and establish our sense of other people (e.g., as lover too). But to understand love this way, not as something that invades, not as a sometimes enjoyable physiological dysfunction, not as an instinct (nor as necessary and certainly not "natural"), requires an entirely new view of what the emotions, in general, are like. "We are often most ignorant of that which is closest to us," says Nietzsche, and this is certainly true of emotions. And first, we will have to get rid of that almost obvious belief that emotions, in short, are "feelings," for that is where the myth of the passions, the myth of passivity, begins.

"FEELINGS" 5

. . . emotions correspond with processes of discharge, the final expression of which is perceived as feeling.

FREUD

It sounds trivial to say that emotions are feelings, so it would no doubt sound absurd to say that they were *not* feelings. But there are many kinds of "feelings," from Einstein's very sophisticated feeling (intuition) that "gravitation might be explained by way of particle theory" to the not so intricate feeling of cold water running down my thigh. If the sentence "Emotions are feelings" is supposed to mean something like the latter, as William James and sometimes Freud once argued, then emotions are assuredly *not* feelings. It is true that romantic love sometimes includes weeping eyes, a choking throat, loss of appetite, weakness in the limbs, loose bowels and a general sense of excitement that can only tangentially be considered sexual, but it would be absurd to say, as James did, that this set of flulike symptoms *is* the love. Is that the basis of Western romanticism, for which Romeo and Tristan died and kings and queens have yielded thrones? Of course, we might well be suspicious of a lover who never cries, whose physiology remains imperturbable even in crisis and for whom making love is as moving as making breakfast. But feelings are the consequences of love, its physical symptoms at most, and if romantic love is unimaginable without a certain amount of physical discomfort (though even this is highly overrated) this is *due* to the excitement of love, not the other way around. In fact one might say that love is not so much physical as metaphysical discomfort, a revolution in the perspectives through which we see the world.

But surely this leaves something out. At no time do I *feel* love so intensely as those times when I am indeed physiologically distraught, literally choked with emotion. Sometimes, conscientiously, we mutually induce that exquisite sense of sexual desperation, whose purpose is not purely the pleasure of its "release" (as Freud once argued) but the intensification of emotion, building to a never completed crescendo (though the sex, of course, may be completed), which is typically called the "expression" (literally, "pressing out") of love. But again it is not the feeling that *is* the love; rather the feeling *augments* the emotion. (The musical terms are wholly appropriate here; think of the difference between caressing to a Gregorian chant and bouncing away to the Rolling Stones. Can one feel passionate to Muzak or gently touch to punk rock?) Emotions may be supported by (but do not require) the bodily sensations created with or by them, like the musical accompaniment in a Puccini aria, providing a richness and intensity they might not have on their own. But the sensations alone, the "feelings" in this specific sense, are not themselves the emotions.

Where do we get the idea that sensations—"feelings" of a bodily nature—are the essence of emotion? I think the answer comes from a certain limited set of examples—a faulty paradigm of emotions, in which physiological disruptions play an inordinate role. The most common example is this one, taken from William James's still influential essay "What Is an Emotion?" (1884): I'm walking through the woods when from behind a tree appears a gigantic brown bear, and I feel—quite "naturally"—*fear*. What is this fear? It is a visceral disturbance caused by my perception of the bear. It is not just the visceral disturbance, of course, any more than the cause of my emotion is just the bear; it is the *appearance* of the bear, my *perception* of it. The fear itself is my perception of those visceral disturbances in body which in turn cause my "impulse to vigorous action," in this case, an overwhelming urge to run. It all happens so fast, of course, it is difficult to tell what happens first. "Common sense," James tells us, believes that the perception causes the emotion which causes the bodily changes; he says that it is the other way around, that the perception of the bodily changes is the emotion. (Thus, "A woman is sad because she weeps; she does not weep because she is sad.") But this much seems undeniable—that one cannot even imagine fear in such an instance without including an overwhelming physiological feeling in one's image. And from this it is all too easy, whether we agree with James or rather with "common sense," to conclude that the emotion *is* the feeling.

But emotions are not just feelings. It has long been argued by a great many authors in psychology, philosophy and physiology that James's account of emotions as physiological feelings is simply inadequate to account for even the grossest differences between emotions, such as fear and hatred, or love and embarrassment. James's account of the *experience* of the emotion is disastrously incomplete; only part of what we feel, and by far the least significant part, consists of physical symptoms such as flushing, excitement and so on. But we must go further than this and attack not just the details of the "feeling" theory but its very foundations. What James has chosen as an example immediately loads the case toward the feeling view, since in panic it is indeed difficult not to recognize the paralytic flush of adrenalin pumping through one's arteries as the most prominent symptom of the emotion. But to choose this case, or one like it, which is by its very nature based upon an urgent situation and an emergency "gut" reaction, is to choose a paradigm which will guarantee our misunderstanding of an emotion like love. In the case of fear, one does indeed have these feelings, *as well as* the emotion, but one can imagine another kind of fear that, because of its duration, could not possibly be identical with the continuous outpouring of adrenalin, for example, the fear of an employee that he will be fired from his job, for the three months following his boss's announcement that thirty per cent of the staff will soon be let go. The employee may, indeed, have specific moments of panic, but he need not in order to be afraid. His fear is rather the *structure* of his experience, from the time he gets up in the morning until his second martini at night. It is not a sudden intrusion, which so many authors continue to confuse with the essence of emotion itself.

When we turn to love, it is obvious that the emergency paradigm is almost wholly beside the point, except, perhaps, for that first fateful meeting or awkward first date, the evening when one person works up the courage to say "I love you" or an occasional moment by the firelight flushed with wine as well as adrenalin. On these occasions love may indeed involve palpitations for a moment or two, but to confuse these with the emotion itself is to misunderstand the emotion entirely. Indeed, even in panic (which has its place in romantic love too) the emotion is not just a feeling but a complex structure of our experience which the simple "feeling" theory refuses to recognize.

If an emotion isn't a feeling, what is it?

In *The Passions,* I argued at length that emotions must be understood as a much more sophisticated and far more important aspect of our lives than mere feelings, disruptions or even, as in the James-and-the-bear case above, biological survival mechanisms. Quite the opposite of these unlearned, bodily responses, emotions are *activities,* like complex thoughts and fantasies (which were also once believed to be *given* to us, for example, by the gods). We *do* them, and we *learn,* from our culture and our friends, from movies, books and, originally, from our parents, *how* to do them. We talk about emotions as "natural," "instinctual," "primitive," but in fact they are cultural, learned and highly educated ways of projecting ourselves into, not just reacting to, our world.

Love, in particular, is a way of living in the world that we *construct* for ourselves. This is not to say that each of us invents love for him or herself, of course; we imitate our parents, perhaps, and on successive nights Bogart, Belmondo or Bacall, Deneuve or Woody Allen, clumsily appropriating lines and roles that we have learned, the structures of this emotional world. Occasionally we do invent our own lines, ad-lib the role so to speak, but only with great difficulty and only *within* the scenario that we have been learning all of our lives. (When we speak "from the heart" we are most likely, in fact, to repeat the most common banalities, the most current platitudes, or the last thing we happened to read.) *Love is this scenario,* like a stage setting, in which we act out a role—whether well or ill defined. It is a scenario *constituted* by us—to use now the proper philosophical term—literally "set up" (as a *constitution* "sets up" a government) according to an elaborate but rarely explicit set of judgments and rules we have been taught by our culture. Having an emotion thus becomes *the playing of a role* —for example, in anger—the wronged, in resentment—the martyr, in envy—the deprived, in sadness—the bereaved, and in love—the lover. Thus William James rightly suggests that "a woman is sad because she weeps," but not because of her physiology. And Lewis Carroll, in *Alice in Wonderland,* summarizes our theory precisely in his couplet, "'I'll be judge, I'll be jury,' said cunning old Fury." Our emotions are not feelings of which we are the victims; they are rather more like theatrical performances, in which we are both the leading actor and the director. But then again, we did not write the play, which has been handed down to us by the whole of our culture.

Theorists have often wondered about the peculiar connection between emotions and their expressions. Charles Darwin, a hundred years ago, argued the thesis that these expressions are "natural," and that our tendency to gnash our teeth when angry, for example, is a vestigial remnant of our once less inhibited urge to *bite* the person who has offended us. Amusing, but what is left out is the incredible finesse and creativity which we add to these evolutionary remnants, if indeed there are any. Edgar Rice Burroughs imagines a people who laugh when unhappy, cry when delighted. This may not be so strange as he thought, but his point is precisely that our expressions are neither necessary nor "natural," but strictly contingent and conventional ("Whenever you feel this, act this way"). But what he leaves out in turn is precisely what Darwin recognized: the functional—if vestigial—connection between emotion and expression. Each of these views is partially correct. There is indeed a connection between an emotion and its expression, but this is not at all some curious linkage between an "inner" feeling and an "external" expression. An emotion is not something "inside of us" that seeks an "outside" expression ("ex-pression" = literally a *forcing out*). An emotion is already "outside"—if this spatial metaphor makes any sense at all—as a projection into the world, the setting of a scenario, the playing of a culturally defined role. It is also, of course, a matter of consciousness—the way we *look* at things—but no emotion is merely this; it is always, in James's phrase, "a tendency to vigorous action" as well, if indeed it is an emotion at all. But "vigorous" is perhaps too energetic a term, for the gentle caress of a lover, for instance, or for the bitter withdrawal of simmering resentment, which, after all, is a form of emotional action too.

Every emotion is a system of judgments, about ourselves and our place in the world (which most often means our relations with other people), through which we cast ourselves a scenario, act out and fantasize a world in which we occupy roles of considerable significance. (Indeed, the function of many emotions, I will argue, is precisely this sense of increased self-importance.) These judgments, scenarios and roles are learned, transmitted by our culture, our language and, more immediately, our family, friends, books and movies. This is not to deny that there might be easily specifiable "natural" or instinctual or infantile prototypes of these emotional phenomena, but it is to say that, whatever these prototypes, love like a lover's first clumsy gestures is wholly taught, refined, interpreted and encouraged by a particular society. In virtually no case (except, perhaps, for pure panic) are these roles, judgments and gestures simply "natural"; and to understand romantic love is not at all to understand anything about human nature, but rather to understand something about a certain sort of society, in which blood relations and family ties play an extraordinarily diminished role and mobility, individuality and chance encounters hold a remarkably dominant position in the determination of "who we are." Indeed, every emotion—love in particular—is a primary mode of judging and acting out precisely who we are. Emotion, expression and self-identity are learned as one, first as parody, only later as "natural" (that is, effortless and accomplished). Lovers are made, not born (but so are martyrs, revolutionaries, saints and magistrates). To love is to play the lover. Thus André Gide rightly argued that pretending to love is already to be in love, and wondering whether one loves is already to love a little less.

Because emotions are composed of judgments which are learned within a particular culture (or subculture), there is no reason to expect that all human beings will share the same emotions. Of course, probably everyone, Davy Crockett excepted, will feel fear when confronting a large bear in the woods, but in virtually all other cases, I want to resist the phrase "human emotion," since this phrase too easily slips into the *a priori* assumption that there is, in fact, some universal set of emotions, "human nature," which anyone must have to be human.[1] Regarding romantic love, in particular, it is important continuously to remind ourselves how rare this emotion really is, and how it appears *only* in those societies in which individ-

[1] See my *History and Human Nature* (Harcourt Brace Jovanovich, 1979).

uality is extremely important. And even within such societies, it is worth noting, the roles and rituals and expressions of love are largely dictated by an extremely precise and even explicit set of rules—in Victorian England, for example, as described in Jane Austen's novels. Only Americans presume that they are completely "on their own" when it comes to *making* love, because we have a *choice* of so many roles and expressions. But we too have our restrictions and rituals, though not, in our case, to "control" our emotions so much as to give them some shape, to narrow down a frightening list of possibilities to something more manageable. The process we curiously call "dating" and what we too glibly criticize as "playing games," perhaps even sex itself, are all part of our quasi-institutionalized romantic rituals. A couple never goes to bed alone: they are joined, in a sense, by the whole of their culture and society. And what they "feel," in fact, is their participation in a set of well-established and highly esteemed roles, as "lovers," which have come down to us through generations of stories, novels, movies and communal experience.

The key to romantic love, as an emotion, is the concept of *choice*. Love may sometimes be "spontaneous," but more often than not we talk or think our way into love, and in every case the whole weight of our Western romantic tradition goads us on. But to have an emotion, to be in love, is to enter into a certain kind of world, voluntarily, if sometimes erratically, whimsically or "irrationally." Love is something *done* rather than suffered, not just a feeling but an *art*, as Erich Fromm rightly argued. What seems to be passive and "spontaneous" may be a matter of bad memory. And in a society in which so often love is a relationship between *strangers*, the element of choice—whether fully conscious or not—is inescapable. The fact that we form almost instant and utterly intimate relations with people we have never met before, preferring their company to the continued companionship of our own family and friends, strikes much of the world as a form of lunacy, to say the least. Indeed, what distinguishes romantic love from many other emotions, including other forms of love (motherly, brotherly, etc.), is precisely this emphasis on freedom of choice. Not only do we in some sense choose our emotion (which is true of virtually all emotions) but in love the choice itself—often combined with the contingencies of chance—is its most striking characteristic.

We often talk in terms of the "magic" or the "chemistry" of love, particularly in "love at first sight," when there seem to be no actual *grounds* for affection, only that immediate and most striking "feeling." It is this lack of grounds that leads the radical Freudian sociologist Philip Slater to suggest that "love at first sight," because it obviously can't be based on anything in the present, must be based in the past, in other words, in the Oedipal conflict. This is too quick a conclusion. Indeed, even in a "feeling" view of emotions this is highly implausible: there are other people in one's past in addition to Mom—first loves, grade school teachers, a friend of the family, a dozen movie stars and the girl next door. The tantalizing phenomenon of "love at first sight" is indeed explained in terms of the fact that the person we meet just so obviously fits—or at least seems to fit—the roles we ourselves have been fantasizing for years, but this does not necessarily mean the Oedipal mommy-me-daddy scenario. Nor need it be a single fantasy.

A role is established; it need only be filled. We even say, "I feel as though I've known you for years," and in a sense one has. Fantasy, we all know, plays an enormous role in romantic love but not, as even Webster's Dictionary suggests, as a source of unreality and self-deception. There need be nothing *false* about fantasy. Fantasy is imaginative judgment, projection, expectation, the kind of fantasy that goes into the *direction* of a play, not a distraction from it. It is fantasy that guides the reality of love, even if it *also* leaves lots of room for self-deception. And it is fantasy, not mystery, that provides the "magic" of love.

This "magic" is shared by all emotions. Jean-Paul Sartre, in a small book on emotions published in 1938, called the emotions "magical transformations of the world." And indeed they are. Every emotion has this ability to transform our world, "from the inside," to alter through fantasy the way we experience, and so the way we live in, the world. Love, in particular, may be a sudden but by no means unanticipated transformation of the way we see another person, a change that, at least initially, requires no change at all—or even acknowledgment—on his or her part. And it is a change that can be maintained indefinitely, by continuing "magic." An emotion, like God's creation of the universe, is a continuous process, not a "*state*," and the shimmering "magic" of love in particular requires constant attention, like a spell which must be cast continuously, even if it seems—when we do it well—that indeed it has been cast *on us* instead.

We can now state our strategy with some precision: to say that love is an emotion is to enable us to look at it with a more matter-of-fact eye than those who praise it uncritically, but without falling into cynical reductionism either. Love is nothing more than an emotion, but nothing less either. Many of the virtues we so readily attribute to love are in fact common to most emotions, for example, love's celebrated "magic" and its famous "yearning." Sartre shows how sadness, for example, has exactly these properties too, how the sad person never seems sad enough, and how one *chooses* one's sadness as a way of defining a world. Indeed, the idea that love changes our whole world around is itself a general property of emotions. "A depressed man lives in a depressed world," wrote the depressed philosopher Ludwig Wittgenstein. And so indeed every emotion is a world, a world defined by that emotion and its judgments. Anger is obsessed with questions of blame and vengeance. Envy is defined by its sense of inequity. Sadness is voluntarily trapped in the past, while hope is fixated on the future. All emotions are obsessive. All emotions are self-concerned (which is not to say "selfish" or "self-indulgent," though they may be this as well). All emotions seem as if they are unique, and it is just as common to feel that one has never been so angry as it is to believe that one has "never been in love before—at least, not like this." It is not just love that gives life meaning, but emotions in general, and it is not just love—if it is love at all—that "makes the world go round."

But most importantly, rendering love as an emotion and emotions as systems of judgments evaporates the "mystery" that supposedly surrounds love. Indeed, the mystery instead becomes *why* we single out love for special treatment, praising it and distinguishing it from all other emotions, even turning it alone into a metaphysical principle—as if a mere emotion could not possibly deserve such an important place in our lives. But placing love back among its sibling affections also points to the peculiarity of the extreme expectations and demands we apply to just this emotion, for example, the idea that "true" love should last "forever," or for a significant period of time. Imagine saying, "You couldn't have been so angry; you only wanted to kill her for two and a half weeks." Our black and white attitudes toward love ("She loves me, she loves me not") become at least curious in this perspective, and our demand for *total* love becomes absolutely terrifying, because it is so obviously impossible. Our exclusivist view of love—"You can only love one person (at a time)"—is at least thrown into serious question by comparison with other emotions, since exclusivity is clearly not required in order to be "truly" angry at someone, or envious. And the idea that love is a "mystery" is itself partially clarified as we look at the general view of emotions that has been with us virtually since ancient times, for if even such mundane passions as shame and anger have been treated as if they were temporary possessions by devils or furies, why not love too? But neither Cupid nor the sting of his arrows is any longer part of our mythology. Love is not a feeling of which we are the victims but a world of which we are (collectively) the authors. Romantic love is an emotion created and cultivated by a certain kind of society, to serve certain kinds of functions and expectations. Thus the question turns from psychology to sociology: what kind of society? And why romantic love?

ON THE (ALLEGED) ORIGINS OF ROMANTIC LOVE 6

The cultivation of passionate love began in Europe as a reaction to Christianity (and in particular to its doctrine of marriage) by people whose spirit, whether naturally or by inheritance, was still pagan. . . .

But this would be mere theory and highly disputable were it not that we are in a position to trace the historical ways and means to the rebirth of Eros. We have already settled on a date. The earliest passionate lovers whose story has reached us are Abélard and Héloïse, who met for the first time in 1118! And it is in the middle of this same century that love was first recognized and encouraged as a passion worth cultivating. Passionate love was then given a name which has since become familiar. It was called cortezia, *or courtly love.*

DENIS DE ROUGEMONT,
Love in the Western World

It is practically a platitude, in scholarly circles, that romantic love began to flower (what other image could be appropriate?) in the twelfth century, mainly in France (where else?) and in particular with a self-styled *avant-garde* kind of popular poet, the *troubadour*. The troubadours did not just fornicate—or not; they *longed* for their women, who, as often as not, were wholly inaccessible, usually married to somebody else and rarely if ever forthcoming with the sexual favors so desperately desired. And when they did grant their "favors," they took a long, long time about it, even prolonging the ritual so far as nights lying naked together without a hope of physical fulfillment. The fact seemed to be, as for adolescents now (and not only adolescents), that the moment of physical fulfillment was also the end of the poetry and—if it deserved the title at all—the "affair." As one French proverb properly put it, the object of desire is not its satisfaction but its prolongation.

Now, on the one hand, this picture of the troubadours as paragons and pathetic romantics has its virtues. The discipline of *devotion*—formerly appropriate only to the Lord and lords—now becomes favored for a "maiden," usually a young woman, and on the basis of her beauty alone, above all else. Today, we find this emphasis on beauty to be dubious, if not offensive, but at the time, it was something of a discovery. For those of us who have grown up confronted with *Playboy* and movie starlets, the very idea of finding a woman primarily beautiful, instead of *useful*, would seem to be a step backward. But, indeed, it was a first step in treating women as other than property. Of course, there were occasional beauties in history—Helen of Troy, for example—but the Greek conception of beauty was concentrated mainly on the male, and when women were so celebrated it was almost always because they were goddesses. (The idea that Helen's *face* launched the thousand ships was coined by Marlowe in the sixteenth century: what then concerned the Greeks was rather that Paris had stolen Menelaus' property, a good enough excuse to sack the gold of Troy.)

Along with the troubadours emerged a very different kind of character—the chivalric knight, for whom devotion was also a virtue but chastity not such a necessity—Lancelot and Guinevere, for example. It is with the adoration of the troubadours and the chivalric ideal of the knight devoted to his lady that the idea of a woman as the "object" of love becomes of general significance, and not only "fair maidens" (i.e., white, wealthy and virginal) but married women as well. (Conveniently, a large number of husbands were off in the Holy Land for the Crusades, through much of the century, though this in fact provided the necessity of chivalry as well as its opportunity.) It is the *forbidden* nature of love that makes it "romantic."

What is most striking about the chivalric ideal, from a historical point of view, is its freedom, bordering on chaos. After a thousand gunfighter and samurai movies, we may well take for granted the idea of the armed free agent, "the knight-errant," roaming the country and devoting himself to whatever tasks he chooses, or to whatever maiden or mistress. But perhaps the key to understanding that whole century is the fact that such figures were quite novel, signifying a breakdown in traditional allegiances, leaving loyalty as well as love open to negotiation and individual choice. And indeed, I shall argue, it is this concept of individual choice, the intelligibility of devoting oneself to an unknown stranger, or someone else's wife, that marks the social-psychological precondition of what we call romantic love.

The new role for women, as objects of love, and the new freedom to choose, together marked the preconditions for love. But the love of the troubadours is almost always argued to introduce a third essential ingredient, whose role in our conception of romantic love is not all that clear. This is the idea of the lovers' *pathos*, desperation, the impossible love, doomed from the start. (Romeo and Juliet, for instance.) One might argue that the romantic sense of *yearning* (or *languor*) appears even in Plato's *Symposium* (in Aristophanes' speech), but the important difference is that Aristophanes' "yearning" continues *through* sexual intercourse. Though not satisfied, the lover is not thereby "doomed," while the "yearning" of the troubadours is based upon non-consummation, deliberate sexual frustration, even fatal desperation, thus leading to the still influential falsehood that the passion of romantic love is derived from if not wholly based upon frustrated sexuality. And this is true not only of male adolescents and the Viennese hysterics who visited young Dr. Freud's medical offices in the 1890s.

One aspect of this pathetic and intentionally desperate love mythology that was particularly striking and flattering (whatever is made of it now) was the tendency for the troubadours to keep their ladies *at a distance*, to "put them on a pedestal," an image that makes good literal sense when the lady in question was looking down from her tower. The woman became idealized, excessively so, given the twin confusions of distance and sexual frustration, to such an extent that the fantasy and the poetry could bear little if any resemblance to the woman herself. In fact, *not* knowing the lady, carnally or otherwise, was wholly intentional, since one of the persistent themes of the troubadours' poetry is the *happy* fact of that unhappy distance and ignorance, for it is that which makes passion possible. Presumably—though we do not know—this frustration and ignorance were mutual, and true of the woman as well. Romantic love was not, therefore, between married—even happily married—couples, but necessarily relegated to the realm of the forbidden, the illicit, the unattainable. Thus Denis de Rougemont rightly calls the practice of "courtly love" *anti-marriage* and "pagan." The Camelot story in its modern guise is only half right; Lancelot and Guinevere were indeed lovers, but not, in this exalted sense, Guinevere and Arthur. And so too, our romantic legends abound with the tragedies of Romeo and Juliet, Tristan and Isolde, and all those other couples, down to the West Side version by Leonard Bernstein, who long and perish for a love that is by its very circumstances impossible to fulfill.

What is most interesting about this picture, however, is what is left out of it. First, accepting it at face value as *a*—if not *the*—paradigm of romantic love, it is worth taking a careful look at the very unromantic nuts-and-bolts alterations in twelfth-century society in general, for romantic love, as we have already argued several times, can be seen to be the emotional product of a certain kind of society, a society whose origins can be traced to just this time in Western history. But what is also worth pursuing is the idea that the troubadours and their chivalric heroes do *not* in fact represent romantic love at its origins. One must ask, for example, to what extent the Greeks and Romans manifested the characteristics of romantic love, in their everyday behavior as well as in Sappho's poetry and Plato's *Symposium*, a millennium and a half before the troubadours. And, more to the point, we ought to be very critical of the idea, so central to the troubadours, at least, that romantic love is primarily a relationship (if that's the word) at a *distance*. Indeed, would we rather not say that *intimacy* is its essence? Perhaps the scholars' favorite example of romantic love is not that at all, but rather a curious perversion of interpersonal desire—not inappropriate to professors—from whose influence we are still suffering today.

Throughout this book, one of my main aims will be to stress the connection between romantic love and self-identity. Romantic love, in a certain type of society, is the search for and creation of personal identity, through not only one's thoughts and actions (too long the sole focus of philosophical attention, from Socrates to Sartre) but, primarily, through and with other people. We are, excessively, such a society, and in the absence of or in addition to the dozens of other definitive relations in which we take part, romantic love seems to be our obsessively singular source of personal worth, not only for women but, perhaps even more so, for men. But if this is so, then we should expect to find romantic love arise in precisely those epochs and cultures when self-identity is in question, when traditional roles and relationships fail to tell a person "who I am." In other words, we should expect to find the origins—or at least the intensification—of romantic love in the rise of the individual in the "West." And so, I want to argue, we do.

One of the scholarly platitudes of the past few centuries is that the concept of the individual, along with humanism and the "dignity of man" in general, came into existence only recently, namely, in the Renaissance, in the fourteenth and fifteenth centuries. Jacob Burckhardt, who wrote the still definitive text on that period a hundred years ago, argued in particular that the rise of the individual, the "discovery of man," the new sense of *humanitas* and human dignity, the dissolution of feudal society and the beginnings of international commerce on a grand scale, all led to a breakdown of traditional conceptions of identity and social roles, and made not only possible but necessary the new emphasis on individual character. But it is now agreed that this process in fact began several centuries earlier, in the late eleventh and the twelfth century, not so much as a reaction against the medieval church as *within* it. (The picture of the Renaissance as a reaction against the past rather than a development from it was invented by the Renaissance itself, and has continued to be the favorite stereotype of humanists ever since.) The crucial aspect of this change, from our point of view, was the attention given to—one might with some justification even say, the "discovery" of—*feelings*, or what were then called "affections." And feelings, as I have argued elsewhere,[1] are essential to our conception of ourselves as individual persons. So one might say that the twelfth century, more or less, was the epoch of the discovery and exploration of *personal character*.[2]

[1] *The Passions* (Doubleday, 1976).

[2] In his classic *De Amore*, for example, Andreas Capellanus suggests three ways for a young man to "win a virtuous woman"—a fine physique, courageous behavior and a good set of lines (i.e., "elegance of speech"). It is this last which *De Amore* is designed to teach (the medieval version of "50 Great Opening Lines and How to Woo a Woman"). But what is important about this list is that social position and wealth have virtually nothing to do with it, plus the fact that the idea of "winning" a woman by force of character is one of the most striking innovations of the period.

Needless to say, I do not mean that no one had "character," that there were no personal characteristics, that people didn't have feelings or that there were no eccentrics—village idiots and the like—before A.D. 1100. But these aspects of a person were considered entirely inessential, even negligible, and self-identity in virtually no sense turned on them. Even St. Augustine, who is usually credited as the foremost psychologist of the whole medieval epoch, spoke hardly at all of "affections," usually of "impulses." His *Confessions* were only circumstantially "personal" and in fact represented him*self* only as a representative of humanity in general. And from Augustine until Anselm, seven centuries later, the general idea was that individuals (a word which to them was strictly a logical category, meaning "not divisible") were but instances of the universal species, "mankind." A person was individual (in-divisible) in so far as each had a *soul,* and individuals could be distinguished by their various social and household[3] *roles,* obligations and loyalties. But character played little part in an individual's identity or distinguishing characteristics. Even *faith,* that singular emotion which has always played such an enormous importance in the Christian conception of individual worth, did not become centrally important as a distinction of *personal* character until, again, the twelfth century, when Peter Abelard, in particular, argued what was then still heresy—that personal feelings such as faith were of paramount importance in a person's relationship to God.

But as important as this new emphasis on feelings—what some have called a "spiritual psychology," others a "clinical theology"—was the renewed emphasis on interpersonal relations, that is, not merely social relations determined by household status and given obligations, but interpersonal feelings,

[3] Strictly speaking, it is the household—an economic unit—and not what we call "the family" that is at issue here. Indeed, what we call "the family" and think of as "most natural" was not invented until the seventeenth century.

in particular, feelings of friendship. Colin Morris, for example, in his *Discovery of the Individual: 1050–1200* (Harper & Row, 1973), argues at length that the new "cult of friendship" created an entirely new conception of Christianity, a conception of brotherhood, in which friends on earth became the surest guides to one's chances for salvation. And what distinguished friendship from virtually all other social relations was the fact that it was based on feelings, not obligations; in fact, social roles interfered with and even contradicted friendship, so that, not surprisingly, friendship blossomed best in that one institution where social roles of the usual variety were not to be found: the monastery. And it was in the twelfth century too, not only in the Renaissance, that there was a general turn back to the classics. For the "cult of friendship," the required text became Cicero's essay on friendship, which however "pagan" already included many of the attributes that would soon be incorporated into the new conception of romantic love —for example, the idea that "friendship is forever" and "divine" and that friendship consists mainly in a kind of "union" or "common mind" (*consensio*).

But as friendship was exalted as the "highest" of human virtues, there was no parallel exaltation of romantic love as such. Friendship was taken to be part of the whole Christian tradition (in retrospective interpretation, of course, for there is surprisingly little about it in the *New Testament*). Romantic love, on the other hand, seemed to be entirely new and, needless to say, shocking to traditional sensibilities. Friendship was a religious phenomenon; love remained "profane" and, consequently, clandestine, illicit, even revolutionary. Forbidden love was a dramatic exception (Abelard and Heloise, Tristan and Isolde, etc.), not the general rule. Morris comments, "What the church did for friendship, it signally failed to do for marriage." Sexual experience was deemed to have no religious value, even to the point that, according to one of the teachings of the contemporary Church, "Every ardent lover is an adulterer with

his own wife." And so romantic love, which has always been a combination of friendship and sexuality (for the Greeks too, one could argue), became a most uncomfortable concept in the twelfth century, as half of its nature was glorified, the other half condemned. No wonder, then, that the troubadours found themselves split between secular worship (literally, putting their lovers on pedestals) and prohibited sexual desires (pedestals, after all, are safely out of reach). And no wonder too that the emasculated concept of "Platonic love," which is the worshipfulness of romantic love stripped of desire, was invented and first promulgated about this same time by Marsilio Ficino in Italy.

The new emphasis on personal character had its most obvious manifestations in the new self-conceptions of both men and women. Nobles who had formerly been identified more or less completely by their household roles and allegiances found themselves literally "errant" in a society that was coming apart at its feudal seams. Where loyalty had once been a matter of given obligations, it now became a matter of voluntary oath. Where once allegiance had been a matter of social fact, it now became a matter of *devotion*. And warrior-nobles—"knights"—found themselves free agents—individuals, in other words, who could devote themselves and now their oaths as they saw fit. And why not, if they so desired, devote themselves to a lady, not because of political loyalty but out of sheer fascination? The ethics of chivalry, so conceived, became a matter of *distinguishing* oneself, not as a knight "of the realm" but the opposite, as a character, a courageous personality, worthy of love in return. And it is not at all insignificant that this conception of romantic love derived, in its very essence, from the feudal idea of *service*, that is, loyalty and devotion to a master. The master, in this case, was the lady herself, but the origins of romantic love, according to the chivalric tradition, cannot be separated from this conception. (Thus introducing some historical confusion into the male "I'm the boss" role.) The ideas

of self-sacrifice and "proving oneself," therefore, are as old as the notion of romantic love itself, and far more important, as far as origins go, than anything like *intimacy*—so central to our own conception, but virtually unknown (and unthinkable) to them.

Romantic love required a dramatic change in the self-conception of women as well. They too were freed ("liberated" would be the term some of my friends would prefer) from an identity that depended wholly on their social roles, that is, their blood and legal ties with men, as daughters, wives and mothers. It is in this period in Christian history that *looks* become of primary importance, that being beautiful now counts for possibly everything, not just as an attractive feature in a daughter or wife (which probably counted very little anyway) but as itself the mark of character, style, personality. Good grooming, as opposed to propriety, came to define the individual woman, and her worth, no longer dependent solely on her social worth, which in turn depended on the social roles and positions of her father, husband or children, now turned on her looks. The premium was placed on youth and beauty, and though some women even then may have condemned this emphasis as unjust, it at least formed a first breach with a society that, hitherto, had left little room for personal initiative or individual advancement. The prototype of the *Playboy* playmate, we might say, was already established eight hundred years ago, and it did not require, as some people have argued recently, Hugh Hefner's slick centerfolds to make youth, beauty and a certain practiced vacuity into a highly esteemed personal virtue. The problem is why we still find it so difficult to move *beyond* this without, like some Platonists, distaining beauty altogether—the opposite error.

But we can go still "deeper" into these "origins" and see that the new emphasis on individual worth and personal identity, and with it the renewed emphasis on personal-emotional

relations such as friendship and, with considerable confusion, romantic love, can be explained on the basis of still more general social phenomena, to which we have already referred by such large historical headings as "the breakdown of feudalism" and "the discovery of the individual." Colin Morris provides us with a persuasive picture of a century in the process not so much of "breakdown" as what we refer to in retrospect as "modernization," in particular, the development of commerce and, with it, of cities, and new kinds of loyalty, the centralization of some governments and the resultant "breakup" of others. Consequently, men (mainly) and women found their loyalties divided, their traditional roles in question, not just as individuals (that was the result, not the cause), but as social entities. With the growth of cities and the consequent increase in anonymity, we find the familiar paradox, that personal significance became more important as social significance came more into question. There were choices to be made where there had been none before. A knight could and had to *decide* to whom he would dedicate his talents. A lady had to *decide*, as she could not before, to whom she would bestow her affections. Sometimes she was even able to choose her husband. Merchants could choose their markets and their wares. People could choose their jobs (not a possibility, for example, in Plato's *Republic*). Men could choose their friends. And it is with all this emphasis on *choice* that the individual was "discovered," in fact *created*. (Existentialism in the twelfth century, one might say.) And as persons became more mobile, more malleable, more "free," personality became more of a crucial characteristic, personal feelings became more important, and personal relationships became increasingly all-important. The distinction between public roles and private lives became significant, perhaps for the first time, and love (and to a lesser but still significant extent, friendship) became relegated to the realm of the private. Indeed the separation of the social from the personal, and consequently the public from the private, is part of the very condition in which love is possible.

But is romantic love original to the twelfth century and the more or less poetic moanings of the troubadours? Or should we give more credit to the Greeks? At least some of the most important features of romantic love preceded the troubadours by fifteen centuries, not so much in Plato's *Symposium* (though the languor of love and the appreciation of beauty is to be found there too) but rather in the less effete works of the ancient love poets, the more secular and familiar praises of friendship in Aristotle's *Ethics* and the works of Ovid, Cicero and Sallust in particular. But perhaps more importantly, it is essential to argue against the scholarly tradition that much of the ideal "courtly" love of the troubadours is *not* to be taken as paradigmatic of the tradition they supposedly initiated, particularly the pathetic ideal of love-at-a-distance, such that sexual consummation was tantamount to the destruction, not the expression of love, and reciprocity with one's love was most often a fanciful dream. But we have seen that this perverted attitude is itself the product of a kind of confusion, caused by the diametrically opposed values placed on friendship and love at this time, so that romantic love, as a product of the two, was literally split apart by the twelfth-century emotional ethic. In this sense, the love of the troubadours was as much of an example of *what can go wrong* with romantic love as the dramatic model of its origins. And the Greeks, for whom friendship and sexual passion went, so to speak, hand in hand, become far better paradigms and ideals.

But then again, the lack of intimacy and importance of distance in early romantic love was not peculiar to the schizoid and troubled attitudes of the troubadours. For all of the modern lamenting about the "loss of intimacy in human relationships" (see Chapter 7), there really was very little intimacy, particularly in marriages, until quite recently. (Morris understates the case concerning the late medieval period: "For most, marriage was not an uplifting experience.") The knights who devoted themselves to their ladies were far more concerned with "service" than intimacy, and it is often said that knights and troubadours alike were far less in love with their ladies than they were with their own passions, a charge of "narcissism" which haunts romantic love to this day (e.g., in *The Golden Mirror of Narcissus in Courtly Love,* by the scholar Frederick Goldin, and, in Morris, "the birth of self through love," p. 118). It is true, in an extremely important sense, that both troubadours and knights were, as Morris proclaims, "not encountering others so much as extensively searching for self" (ibid., p. 118), but the charge rings false, not only for the twelfth century but for the twentieth as well.[4] Looking for a self *through* others is by no means tantamount to neglecting or "using" them, although the love-at-a-distance attitudes of chivalry and the courtly poets certainly lend credence to this interpretation. But that is all the more reason why we should, having taken due account of the twelfth-century phenomenon, reject the traditional treatment of it and pinpoint the origins of our own conception of romantic love neither there nor in the philosophical self-congratulation of Plato's Socrates but in the far more ordinary and less divine conception of mere friendship and fulfilled sexual desire, whether in the Greeks or in the forbidden affair between Lancelot and Guinevere, or, better yet, in our own peculiar needs in a society that is quite unlike either fourth-century B.C. Athens or the twelfth century A.D. in France.

> We must beware of the dangers of importing into the 12th century assumptions which are natural to us but would have been entirely foreign to them, for the characteristics of friendship and love, and the language in which they were expressed, differed a great deal from our own experience (Morris, p. 96).

[4] Christopher Lasch, *The Culture of Narcissism* (Norton, 1978).

7 THE MYTH OF PLATONIC LOVE: EROS BLOATED AND SEX DEMEANED

Oh Plato! Plato! you have paved the way,
With your confounded fantasies, to more
Immoral conduct by the fancied sway
Your system feigns o'er the controlless core
Of human hearts, than all the long array
Of poets and romancers:—You're a bore,
A charlatan, a coxcomb— . . .

BYRON, *Don Juan*, I, 116

Of all of the models of love, one in particular has been around long enough to proclaim absolute domain. Although it is not the same as romantic love—indeed, it often opposes itself to romantic love, as sacred to profane—it remains our richest source of metaphors, hopes and illusions. It is the view of love come down to us from Plato, as developed through Socrates' long-winded speech in the dialogue *Symposium*. It is, in a word, the model of love as an approach to the eternal and the divine, and thus itself divine. It is asexual, having "raised" itself above such "lower" desires as sex and companionship. It is love itself that forms its object, rather than the merely personal attraction of two merely mortal persons. Its goal is wisdom, one's lover becomes a means, and love becomes impersonal, eternity-minded, anti-sensual and wrapped in the metaphors of religion and metaphysics, instead of human relationships.

Plato's *Symposium* is too rarely read (even by students of philosophy), but few writers on love fail to mention and praise it as *the* classic text. Its ideas have filtered down indirectly through Christianity and St. Paul's conception of "Christian love" or *agape* to form what sometimes seems like a permanent bias in the writings of such love pundits as Rollo May, de-emphasizing sex and sensuosity and praising *eros* instead as a "cosmic" and even "daemonic" power. The upshot of all such views of love, whether interesting as metaphysical speculations or not, is that our ordinary emotion of romantic love seems pathetic by contrast, and the penumbra of Platonism encourages us, even forces us, to expect more of our emotion than any emotion could possibly hope to satisfy. Thus this chapter, in my mind crucial if controversial, is necessary to combat the damage, often promoted with the most benign intentions, of the ethereal views of love that still haunt us, twenty-five hundred years later. As well as, we shall see, the bitter cynicism that inevitably follows it.

Love among the Greeks was a perfectly secular, agreeable and tangible passion. No mysteries, no pieties, no cynicism. Plato begins his *Symposium*, for example, with the lament that no one has ever even bothered to sing love's praises; in retrospect, perhaps, that was just as well. And when Aristotle discusses the virtues of friendship, he makes it clear that love and friendship, together, are but one set of virtues among many, including having a good sense of humor, a sense of justice, an adequate income, honor and the ability to handle one's fair share of wine. (Plato makes a point of emphasizing Socrates' extraordinary ability to drink huge quantities as well as to abstain.) Although much has been made of Greek *eros* and the various distinctions derived from the Greek between different "kinds" of love, what is most remarkable is how unified these conceptions were and how integrated with a view of the "good life" (*eudaimonia*) in general. It is for this reason, perhaps, that scholars do not tend to think of romantic love as having a history in Greece. It is not, as it is for us, such a distinctly separate phenomenon, much less to be praised out of all proportion to everything else. Aristotle would have seen the idea that "all you need is love" as some kind of bad joke, and the ability of sexual love to bring about happiness, in isolation from family and friends and social position, would have been utterly incomprehensible to him. And sex, far from being fascinating, a source of continuous frustration and a topic for constant moralizing, was just, as we say, "a fact of life," not worth talking about, taken for granted in a fashion that we, perhaps, might find "promiscuous." This, however, is not at all true, for there was nothing indiscriminate about it. In fact, the *mores* (as opposed to the morals) of sexuality were rather well defined, just far more varied and far less moral than our rather simple-minded and one-dimensional concept of (heterosexual) human nature and "natural law."

Now it is not my point to praise the "natural" life of the pre-Platonic Greeks, an unhealthy exercise in scholarly voyeurism that has been extremely popular in Europe for the past several centuries. (Perhaps it is understandable as a reaction against seventeen hundred years of horror concerning most matters sensuous and "pagan." How many generations never even took a bath in their lives—because it was "pagan.") But it is strange that so many writers have assumed—to our obvious embarrassment—that the Greeks of the fifth century B.C. were so much better at lusty love than we are. Indeed, we have already pointed out that it is something of a cliché among scholars that the Greeks did not enjoy (or suffer) *romantic* love at all, though, as I have also suggested, this may be quite wrong. But the point to begin with, both in presenting Plato and in contrasting him with the mores of his own compatriots, is the enormous difference between us that is not to be measured in time and technology alone. Not least among these differences is the fact that they were not particularly interested in love between men and women.

Greek love was between men and men, with love and sex between men and women a distinctly "vulgar" activity that was strictly a practical concern—having children and keeping the *polis* populated. The love of women even had its own, distinctly inferior *eros*—a separate and "common" god—and was frequently called "lascivious." Paris, for instance, was despised precisely because he had such an unhealthy obsession for Helen, who may have been the romantic ideal for Faust, two millennia later, but for the Greeks was "just a woman." The idea that love was available to everyone would have struck even the democratic Greeks as absurd; it was restricted to male citizens, and mainly the aristocracy (as it would be again in the flowering of romantic love in France in the twelfth and eighteenth centuries). And even within the aristocracy the speakers in Plato's *Symposium* and Aristotle a few years later make it very clear that love is to be restricted to those rare men of virtue (of whom Socrates was the favorite philosophical example) and the most promising of the youths, the young men who would soon be "statesmen" (the highest vocation for anyone, unlike "politicians" in our own democracy). The idea that sex is an expression of love, we should point out, would also have been foreign to them, though the *with whom* (and in what position) of sex was of immense importance to them too. (In early Rome, Julius Caesar was sometimes the butt of sexual innuendoes not because he reputedly slept with everything that moved from the Forum to Britannia, but because he sometimes assumed the passive position, which was considered wholly inappropriate for a man of his rank.) And finally, again but most importantly, what we call "romantic" love, between an older man and a youth, part sexual and part educational, was not to be understood out of the context of everyday life as a whole. It was nothing "divine," nothing earth-shaking, nothing to write a book about.

And then, there is the *Symposium*, that towering classic that is not only the first but the paradigm of all future theories of love. The topic is unusual, as Plato's symposiasts tell us, and even the form of the dialogue is remarkably different from Plato's other works. But what is most important about it is that Plato's view of *eros*, as enunciated by Socrates, is so at odds with everything else we know about Greek culture of the time, so dramatically antithetical to the unpretentious secularity described by Aristotle, and so disastrous in terms of anticipating the bloating and corruption of *eros* to follow.

Now Plato's views and his importance, perhaps, and that of all historical figures, is a matter of fiction but, like all historical fictions, a convenience and, in any case, an already established precedent for all discussions of love. And what we find, or the scholars have found, in Plato, in his *Symposium* but even more in his lesser-known but more pious dialogue *Phaedrus*, is that love is not merely a secular passion between men but a "divine" relation to the Eternal, in which interpersonal feelings play at best a tangential role. Love may begin with the sensual appreciation of someone's beautiful body, but if it deserves the name "love" at all it must quickly be "elevated" to the love of Beauty itself, and thus the love of the Good and the True. And, ultimately, there is no question but that Plato thought that the only "true" lovers would be a band of (all male) philosophers, some young and beautiful as pupils, perhaps, but mainly old and wise enough to see through the merely sensuous and contemplate the Good, the True and the Beautiful together.

Now this is not the place to present a detailed analysis of the *Symposium*, and no doubt my bald description and blatant objections to it appear philistine without that context. One could argue that Plato's own view is not the same as the "Platonic" views of Socrates, or that Plato has been de-sexualized by so many Christian commentators, or that Plato isn't really concerned with "love" at all. But the story (in fact a retelling of a supposed after-dinner discussion at a somewhat drunken party) culminating in Socrates' speech can be summarized in the following way:

Several speakers precede Socrates, who is the last to speak; first is Phaedrus, who praises the practical virtues of love, then Pausanias, who goes on at length about the need to censure the more "vulgar" kind of love, including love between men and women. Aristophanes tells his delightful tale about "the original state of man" as a double creature, cleft in two by Zeus for *hubris* ("as one would split an apple") and ever since yearning to get together with the other half, and Agathon, a young and beautiful poet insists, not surprisingly, that love itself is young and beautiful and a poet. Socrates, old and anything but beautiful, begins his speech by refuting Agathon, thus setting the stage for his own view of *eros* in terms of wisdom, a virtue of age (he was seventy) rejecting the vanity of youth. *Eros,* he argues, too quickly and by way of some extremely dubious arguments, is ultimately aimed not at beautiful people but at Beauty itself, the eternal Idea rather than its merely mortal incarnations. And Beauty, he again argues much too quickly, is also the Good, and the True, and so in a few swift shifts of attention the subject moves from anything we—or Socrates' co-symposiasts—would recognize as "love," to straightforward philosophy, "the love of wisdom."

At this point the dialogue takes a rather remarkable turn: Socrates, who was parodied by Aristophanes and others as a windbag who would never shut up, pretends to yield the floor altogether and speaks instead, through what one might amusingly imagine to be a falsetto voice, as "Diotima," an old wise woman (who may or may not have actually existed). Through her voice, his argument then turns *eros* away from the secular and toward the divine, with the insistence that love is actually the search for immortality. The "vulgar" love between men and women, which has as its almost inevitable result children who will continue one's bloodline, is a "vulgar" and certainly "inferior" form of immortality, compared, for example, with the immortality of Homer—or, it is implied, of Socrates. And so the emphasis shifts further away from sexual relationships and toward the wise man's own search for immortality and wisdom, although Socrates, who had quite a reputation even at his age, insists that it is also his duty to educate the youths of Athens, the beautiful ones of course ("for in deformity he will beget nothing"), which was understood to include certain sexual "perks" as well. ("Alas, we have lost that ethereal sense of education," some of my colleagues cry.)

Then, the very heart of the argument, follows a passage known by scholars as "Diotima's ladder," a step-by-step progression from the "lowest" forms of love—namely, being enamored of beautiful bodies—to the "highest"—namely, philosophy. Having lusted after several beautiful bodies, so the argument goes, one should come to see that they are "essentially all the same." In the context of *Penthouse*, instead of a classic text, this would leave us aghast. But for Socrates, this leads us to the appreciation of beautiful souls instead, ultimately to Beauty as such, and Wisdom. We ordinary romantic folk, of course, are stuck on the lower rungs of the ladder, "clogged with the pollutions of mortality" in Plato's not very flattering words. The dialogue concludes, however, with a dramatically important scene in which Socrates shows himself indifferent to a somewhat heated competition for his favors between young Agathon and the warrior Alcibiades, who crashes the party late in the evening—drunk. The scene shows Socrates himself to be remarkably insensitive, perhaps Plato's way of casting his own doubts on the pretentiousness that has preceded. But in any case the dialogue ends with everyone but Socrates passing out. He goes home, takes a bath and starts his day "as usual," having changed the course of love in the West for another two and a half millennia.

The legacy of the *Symposium* is that ordinary love and friendship are "inferior" to a higher, impersonal love, as well as the more common Greek legacy that love between man and woman is "vulgar" (a legacy that we have not corrected; we have just prohibited the other kinds of relationships between men and men and women and women and rendered them even less legitimate). And to this we can add our distrust of beauty itself, which we consider "superficial" (only "skin deep"), and of intelligence, which we consider pretentious, and of wisdom, which we consider arrogance. And though these are no doubt to be attributed to our Christian and egalitarian heritage rather than to Socrates (who was an unabashed elitist), the etherealization of love to which they contribute is largely his invention. Love, simple sexual and romantic love, is demeaned, while something else, in part a "mystery" with inexplicable linkage to the "divine," is praised in its place.

In the third century A.D. the philosopher Plotinus furthered Plato's bloating of *eros* with a "tractate" of his own, in which he too insisted that the love of beauty itself is "higher" than mere sensual love, and that "universal love," which is no longer of the person but a cosmic principle, is still "higher" than that. Plotinus too treated *eros* as an independent spirit, a god, and thus considered the actual "mental state" only an instance of it, and "not to be confused with the Absolute Love, the Divine Being." In the twelfth century, Plato got his just deserts, when the Italian celibate Ficino coined the term "Platonic love" to refer to that peculiarly sexless and abstract emotion that may be directed *through* a person but ultimately only *to* God. In the *Symposium*, at least, we find an amusing if not always unambiguous mixture of raunchy sensuality and ethereal philosophizing, but in that love named after Plato the first is condemned and the latter becomes Christian theology.

As love is bloated to the level of a religious experience, we know full well what happens to sex; it is demeaned or condemned, even if, in the restricted circumstances of holy matrimony, it can be tolerated, in small amounts, if the pleasure is not excessive. (More than one early church authority condemned sexual pleasure even in marriage, as a sin as serious as adultery.) Love, which the Greeks accepted as an everyday matter, now became elevated to the "divine"; and sex, another everyday matter, was reduced to the "lower" desires, an animal need, a biological function. But if love was a matter of the purest of souls and sex was a bodily need, it is hard to see how the two would ever come together again. And this is true of not only Christian theologians but our best "humanists" too. Enlightenment humanism in the eighteenth century included the battle not only for reason and liberty but for sexual liberation as well; and yet love was still claimed to be a relation of "souls," which "have no sex." Bertrand Russell, no friend of Christian sexual morality to be sure, appeals to this abstract notion of love and a too vulgar notion of sex even when he attacks the Church and its moral restrictions. Rollo May treats sex as a mere Freudian "tension" but *eros* as cosmically wonderful, thus finding it all but impossible to carry out the aim of his book, which is "to reunite love (sex) and will." Humanist psychologist Abraham Maslow opposes sex to love as "lower" and "higher" needs in his hierarchy, and existentialist philosopher Peter Koestenbaum, in his *Existential Sexuality,* defines love as a relation of "two consciousnesses," with sexuality a matter of utter contingency, even if not a need.

We often talk today about love as a "commitment" and sex as "free," but this again creates an unmanageable and unnecessary tension between the two. Love becomes *serious* and sex fun. (Or, perhaps, solemn. Russell Baker: "Being solemn is easy. Being serious is hard. . . . Falling in love, getting married, having children, getting divorced and fighting over who gets the car and the Wedgwood are all serious. The new sexual freedom is solemn.") But again, the need to "elevate" love is a *moral* concern; to divorce sex and love is to make love more difficult than it needs to be, and sex much less than it is. And if love is a "commitment" and sex is "free," it is difficult to see what we are going to do with romantic love, which is both sex and love but neither committed nor free.

The Platonic tradition is carried on today not only by Christianity, in which we would expect an emphasis on the soul and the eternal instead of a celebration of physical beauty and sensuosity, but in other quarters, nominally at least opposed to that ethereal viewpoint. In particular, we can find it among the "humanists," of whom Rollo May, Abraham Maslow and Erich Fromm are, with regard to love, the best-known protagonists. *Humanism,* traditionally defined (since the twelfth century) as the respect for humanity, the primacy of people over gods, governments and nature, has become our most prominent religion. In retrospect, Socrates has been declared a humanist. In retrospect, the Church has embraced a partial humanism, and humanism has defined itself as the greatest enemy of the Christian Church, a false charge, considering the number of church doctrines it has taken along with it. And not least of these is the etherealization of love, the de-emphasis of sex, and the priestly status of those who "know" about love, namely, our psychiatrists.

In place of such words as "salvation" (which nonetheless pops up from time to time) we find the metaphors of health and "cure." In the place of the sermon is "understanding" and, most importantly, in place of the "soul" comes a new pretension, "the total human being." Now though these initially look like opposites, with regard to love they turn out to have the same function: to dismiss sex and sensuality and the limited ways in which we are attracted to and relate to each other in favor of an abstraction which is unobtainable, and perhaps unintelligible. And here we see the continuity between the old

Platonic ideal, the traditional Christian conception of love and contemporary humanism: in every case love is made out to be something mysterious and extremely difficult if not impossible, something much "more" than sensuous attachment to a particular person with whom one identifies and enjoys oneself. One sees it so clearly in Erich Fromm's classic *Art of Loving*, for instance, as he systematically brutalizes all of those forms of love of which he disapproves—too sexual, too dependent, too independent, too frivolous, too serious—as "pseudo-love," "pathological love" and simply not *love* at all. One finds it too in Rollo May's *Love and Will*, in which *eros* (continuously contrasted with mere sexuality) is praised as virtually everything Good, True and Beautiful, as "the spirit of life," "excitement," "the power which drives men towards God," which "takes wings from the human imagination and is forever transcending." *Eros* is power. *Eros* is self-realization, excellence, virtue, nobility, creativity and, finally, "beauty in the inward soul" which provides "higher levels of meaning." Thus Rollo May adopts Plato's ("Diotima's") hierarchy of desires quite explicitly, and one finds it too, with considerably more belligerence, in British poet David Holbrook's appropriately titled *Sex and Dehumanization* and in Victor Frankyl's *The Doctor and the Soul*. One finds it most recently, perhaps, in psychiatrist Samuel Peck's *A Road Less Traveled*. In every case, we are told, the doctor knows what is Bold, Beautiful and Profound—but we don't. Unless, of course, we read their books. The message is in the air, that love is something spectacular and marvelous, something that changes lives and lifts us "above" the world of the merely ordinary. And when the initial exhilaration of a new romance wears off or wearies, we are disappointed and confusedly come to believe that what is merely ordinary can't, therefore, be "the real thing."

The humanist's Christian heritage is nowhere more evident than in the propensity to declare that we are, regarding love, in the midst of a *crisis*. As if we have lost what we (that is, the ancient Greeks) once had, perhaps irretrievably. But any past will do, even the much-abused Victorians. They, at least, their sexual hangups aside, had love. In contrast to those often brutal times, however, we find Rollo May and Erich Fromm, for example, bemoaning "modern man's inability to love" and the "disintegration of love in our time." Here is Rollo May:

> The striking thing about love and will in our day is that, whereas in the past they were always held up to us as the *answer* to life's predicaments, they have now themselves become the *problem*. It is always true that love and will become more difficult in a transitional age; and ours is an era of radical transition. . . . The old myths and symbols by which we oriented ourselves are gone, anxiety is rampant; we cling to each other and try to persuade ourselves that what we feel is love. . . . Love has become a problem to itself.
>
> *Love and Will*, pp. 13–15

Of course, every age is a "transitional age," and it is far from clear that any society has believed more firmly that "love is the answer" than our own. In fact, it is doubtful that any society has believed that at all, even including our own, and the "old myths and symbols" are a problem not only because they are *not* "gone" but because we are urged to take them seriously in a way that they never were before. Even Christianity—or especially Christianity—knew how to separate divine but impossible ideals from reasonable human expectations.

Look at Erich Fromm's statement of the same crisis:

> No objective observer of our Western life can doubt that love—brotherly love, motherly love and erotic love—is a relatively rare phenomenon and its place is taken by a number of forms of pseudo-love which are in reality so many forms of the disintegration of love (p. 83).

Historically, one should ask, "compared with what?" With the mutual devotion of feudal brothers in medieval France, whose "love" consisted in waiting to poison each other for the family titles? To the hundreds of generations of mothers who had children because they couldn't help it or because the farm needed hands or simply because they were expected to? To the erotic love of the mythical South Seas—that perennial European sexual fantasy? The sense of crisis and loss of love perpetrated by these authors seems simply false. Indeed, one could argue without much difficulty—if such matters are measurable at all—that there is more love in the "modern" world than there ever has been in the past. Intimacy is, if anything, excessively celebrated in contemporary America. The significance of brotherhood and the joys of motherhood as well as the passions of romantic love have never been so alive. There is a problem only in that we expect even more; there is "disintegration" only in the mind of an observer, not objective at all, who holds up against our comparatively puny passions a heroic ideal that, ultimately, turns out to be impossible.

There is no "crisis" about love, and love is not a problem. (Nor is it the answer.) The melodramatic, myth-laden and medicinal picture of love we get from the humanists is, ultimately, a charge of fraud against us—you and me—in Dr. May's words, "as we try to convince ourselves that what we feel is love." The new priest has looked into our souls and found them empty. But as the Word is delivered now in the name of "science" instead of faith, and Rollo May tells us with authority, for instance, that the most important point in sex is the moment when the male enters the female, that the most enjoyable moment for the female is when *he* "abandons himself" in orgasm, and when he cruelly abuses women who desire "the vaunted orgasm, which should resemble a grand mal seizure" (p. 40), we start to see through the benign face of the therapist to the puritanical self-righteousness below. If there is a problem about love, it is not, as May argues, "the banalization of sex and love" but rather its *etherealization*. We have come to expect *too much* of love, and so have made ourselves vulnerable to these persistent attacks and the fear that we are—whether each of us or all of us together—"incapable of loving." When the fact might be that love is just one among a hundred other emotions, an ordinary emotion which is necessary neither for mental health nor for "self-actualization."

The myth of Platonic love is the self-degrading idea that "true" love is something extraordinary, something religious, spiritual and therefore "above" the merely sexual, much more than mere companionship and shared ideals and identities, much more than fleeting emotions and, indeed—if it's "true"—eternal. Today, perhaps, we tend to be less abstract and more practical; the "higher love" to which we aspire is "the meaningful relationship" rather than Plato's ideal Forms. But the accusation remains the same—why do we insist that love is significant only because it lasts, or because of what it leads "up" to? We say with regret, "It didn't work out," but why assume that we were "working" toward anything in the first place? Why assume that love and relationships are supposed to "go somewhere"? Why not accept love just as it is, an ordinary yet spectacular emotion which Plato, with his eyes on the heavens, never bothered to take the least bit seriously.

ENTER THE CYNIC 8

a net
work of connections coming down
to getting laid or not getting laid and by whom
SHARON THESEN, *Loose Woman Poem*

Against the backdrop of bloated Platonic love, cynicism professes a simple diagnosis: love is nothing but lust. Or nothing but an illusion, or a capitalist conspiracy, or a plot to maintain male superiority. Cynicism sees through the arrogant pretensions of Platonism and benign humanism, with a single "whack" knocks *eros* off its classical pedestal and reduces it to something wholly tangible. Sex, usually, or politics. But because its goal is reduction and clarification, rather than intentional obfuscation, cynicism has also succeeded in providing us with some of the best books on love. Embittered feminists, jaded Freudians, sneering Marxists (often some combination of the three) give us hardheaded theses with which we can agree or disagree, which can be tested in the court of our own experience, in place of the ethereal praise of the Platonists and humanists. But at the same time it is not unimportant to see the moral superiority (which Rollo May aptly calls "the new puritanism") that cynicism shares with Platonism. Whereas the latter keeps telling us, "You think you know what true love is, but you don't," the former seems to be telling us, "You think that there's such a thing as true love, but there isn't." In either case we are the ones who are fooled, so we read their books like dutiful children, waiting to be told what to do.

Sigmund Freud was by no means the first but he was the most systematic, most "scientific" and therefore respectable of a long line of cynical but romantic rationalists who saw through the cloud of hearts-and-flowers obscurantism to the primary candidate for the "dirty little secret"—sex. The troubadours, at least, were straightforward about it; romantic love, this momentous "yearning," was fueled by and made possible by the sexual inaccessibility of the (preferably married) "love object." But Freud's contemporary Victorians, with their pathetic verses filled with self-deception, were another matter. They denied sex, and insisted that their frustration was love. And so Freud weaved his intricate but ultimately simple theories—that love is a confusion of frustration and narcissism, that love is inherently irrational, compulsive, childish. He argued that even brotherly and, of course, motherly love were inherently sexual, also a combination of self-love and self-denial—devoid of reason, freedom or self-control. Love is nothing but lust, plus "the ordeal of civility."

The secret was out. The flabby priest was at last defrocked to reveal—Fred the Flasher, in pious disguise. His holy trenchcoat nothing but overalls for frustration. Like the wizard from behind the curtains at Oz, love emerged pathetically, apologetically, all too ready to confess.

And so the cynic has turned to sex itself, with or without love, with his or her own self-righteousness. In *Playboy* magazine, one can still find monthly articles blistering with piety and indignation which document the whole of Western civilization—the Christian part at least—as one long exercise in cruel inhumanity, the denial of poor innocent *eros*. The cynic sees in St. Augustine only a pitiful celibate, his hands in his pockets while his eyes are on the heavens. The cynic snickers at the troubadours, scoffs at old Ficino with his concept of "Platonic love" and, of course, at the Victorians, who, history aside, have continued to be the source of our very unhistorical horror. But the question to be raised against all this is whether there is not indeed something to be said for the "sublimation" and *stylization* of sex, neither of which is the same as frustration. Could it be that the notion of "free sexual expression" presupposes some basic stupidity about the nature of sexuality? And could it be that it is indeed the "yearning"—which is not to say merely sexual longing—rather than the sexual satisfaction, which is the "end" of not only love but sex as well?

The benign face of cynicism can be found in the neo-Freudian view that romantic love, as a product of sexual inhibition and repression, is quickly becoming a thing of the past. In fact, given the theory that love is nothing but sublimated sex, it is not surprising that the pundits are already predicting the death of sex, as well as love, since availability and boredom, it is presumed, go hand in hand. Over ten years ago Marshall McLuhan suggested no less, and more recently *Time* magazine, as infallible mouthpiece of American sensibility, has already run its story, "Love Is Dying" (September 26, 1977). The *Time* article was based on the research of Professor Marian Kinget of Michigan State, herself the most benign of cynics, who concluded that "the very conditions of Romantic love have ceased to exist." These conditions are, of course, the impossibility of sexual fulfillment. "The sting of sex has been removed," she says, and with it "the agony and the ecstasy," and the "longing of romance." These were, we now know, nothing but frustration glorified. ("Take that, Erich Segal," quips *Time.*) If Dante had married Beatrice, we are told, there would have been no *Divine Comedy.* If Goethe had had his chance at Helen (of Troy), we surmise, what then would the world have done for a German *Faust?* If the Brontë sisters were happily in love, would we still have *Jane Eyre* and *Wuthering Heights?* All the longing that made up love, the "oceanic feeling" that Freud referred to with an unusual combination of respect and curiosity, the creative spirit that infused the Renaissance, the romantic poets and the Victorian novelists, must have been nothing but the pumping of blood through the groin via the mind, frustration rendered creative through unhappy genius or, in lesser mortals, made tolerable by the myth of romantic love. If horniness was indeed a virtue, then suffering was the sign of one's sensitivity and humanity. Thus Kinget admits that the end of love will have a "stunting effect on creativity," but this should be balanced by the utilitarian virtue that marriages will now be founded on a more rational basis. Fewer Leonardos but a lower divorce rate by way of compensation.

Beneath this benign position, which culminates in happy households of wisely chosen mates, all the ingredients are available to the more malicious cynic who would like to turn this simple mistaken reduction into an all-out attack on contemporary American life. Suppose that our grandest passion is nothing but impotent self-deception—and perhaps too all our emotions? Suppose that love as such is an illusion artificially created by "civilization," for whatever reasons. Suppose that rare romantic love is in fact nothing but a rarefied distortion of readily available sex. Suppose that love is a form of capitalist prostitution and a form of conspiracy. One finds such a "critique," for example, in the philosophy of Herbert Marcuse. But the point is made most succinctly by Philip Slater, who summarizes the view as well as anyone in his *Pursuit of Loneliness:*

> Romantic love is one scarcity mechanism that deserves special comment. Indeed its *only* [my italics] function and meaning is to transmute that which is plentiful into that which is in short supply. . . . Although romantic love always verges on the ridiculous (we would find it comic if a man died of starvation because he could not obtain any brussels sprouts) Western peoples generally and Ameri-

> cans in particular have shown an impressive tendency to take it seriously (ibid).

and

> By the time an American boy or girl reaches maturity, he or she has so much symbolic baggage attached to the sexual impulse that the mere mutual stimulation of two human bodies seems almost meaningless. . . . The setting and interpretation of a sexual act comes to hold more excitement than the act itself (pp. 85–86).

Sex itself is simple; love is a complex illusion. But sex is not at all so simple, and certainly not "meaningless"; against Slater, it is essential that we insist that the meaning of sex is indeed the "interpretation" of its "symbolic" significance. But notice that Slater is opposing May in an interesting way; for him, sex itself is intrinsically meaningful, love is not. In fact, unlike the "natural" pleasures of sex and affection (Slater is careful not to equate sex with just intercourse and orgasm [p. 85]), love is an artificially inflated *commodity*, and it is this economic model that defines his analysis of love: "Why is love made into an artificially scarce commodity . . . pleasures that could be obtained at any time?" (p. 86). But even Freud knew at least that these "pleasures" could *not* be obtained at any time, and not just because of the inhibitions of a "deprived feeling" society (where Slater lays the blame). It is not just in a capitalist society that love must be *earned*, and even mother love (according to most Freudians, including Slater, May and Fromm) is an affection which, perhaps after the first few weeks or months, can be lost or won, though the expectation of motherly affection, to be sure, is easily taken for granted. (Erich Fromm, for example, betrays one common fallacy about parenthood by insisting that mother love is unconditional, father love conditional.) Romantic love, in particular, is not reducible to sex plus economics, for love is not a cause so much as a response to the breakdown of the more "natural" social ties whose loss Slater bemoans: "We make things scarce in order to increase their value, which in turn makes people work harder for them" (p. 86) and "The idea of placing restrictions on sexuality was a stunning cultural invention, more important than the acquisition of fire. In it man found a source of energy which was limitless and unflagging . . ." (p. 84).

It is a classic Freudian motif, the fuels of repressed libido firing up the organism and motivating virtually everything. And by making sex seem so readily available (he assumes that sexual scarcity was a human "invention"; was it?) he easily makes our constant pursuit of it look ludicrous, asking contemptuously, "How did man happen to transform himself into a donkey, pursuing the inaccessible carrot?"

The source of this self-contempt begins with a metaphor, posing as a model, masquerading as hard-headed analysis. It is the economic model, which Freud employed for more medical reasons (he saw the "psychic apparatus" as a quantitative energy system), that Slater and others use just to reduce something we find important to a mere game of supply and demand:

> We can think of this process as a kind of forced savings (indeed, emotional banking was probably the unconscious model for the monetary form). The more we build up an individual's erotic involvement in a restricted relationship the less he will seek pleasure in those forms that are readily available. He will consume little and produce much. Savings will increase, profits will be reinvested . . . (p. 87).

In other words, we tease and manipulate ourselves, a "ridiculous" enterprise made even more embarrassing by quick comparisons (donkeys and carrots, an obsession with brussels sprouts). But love is no commodity, *not* because it can't be quantified (see Chapter 9) but simply because its structure commands a very different interpretation, an interpretation in terms of significance and meaning, not merely exchange rates. This is not to say that love can't be bought and sold, nor even that it is not often a matter of exchange of some kind. But it is not the exchange and its commodity status that is primary or definitive. Perhaps a simple comparison with art and aesthetics will illustrate this point better. Of course art does enter into a "market," in which art works are commodities and value is determined by supply and demand; rarity increases demand and too easy obtainability lowers the price. But virtually no one, one would like to think, would say that the existence of an art work *as art* depends on its market value or its scarcity. Paintings by Vermeer may be particularly valuable because they are so few, but surely their value *as art* is irrelevant to their number. Balinese masks are or were, before their entrance into the international commodity market, easily accessible to every household, which made them no less significant. And the same must be said for sex and love: whether or not they are bought and sold. (We can agree that prostitution is a readily available metaphor for most of our interpersonal transactions—but why use it?) They are not primarily commodities but rather matters of intrinsic cultural significance, which is precisely what Slater the sociological cynic leaves out of account.

The commodity model introduces another consideration, brought out in Slater's comparison with "the man who loved brussels sprouts." Though surely amusing in a grim sort of way, the analogy makes too light of the fact that love (even sex) tends to be highly *selective* for us, not as a matter of cultural conspiracy (to make us work harder) and not simply as a matter of finickiness. Selection of mates is as "natural" as sexual desire itself, and if one thinks sex (much less love) is readily available in the state of nature (as Rousseau used to lustily imagine) one need only watch a small troop of baboons, for example, with one pathetic smallish male trying to sneak a quick entry into a female without being mauled by the alpha male, or a couple of caribou knocking their brains out to decide who gets a chance at the female. Our selection is not "natural," of course, in the sense that it is grossly influenced by our own cultural inventions: *Playboy* bunnies and Hollywood muscle men, witty talk show hosts and self-consciously neurotic "sex symbols." But it is one of the fantasies of the cynic that sex and love are "easily obtainable," so that (everyone else's) difficulty in obtaining them can then be a matter of ridicule. But the simple fact of the matter seems to be that the easy obtainability of even sex is a fantasy (thus Slater, like Freud, takes pains to insist that sexual satisfaction is not necessarily gained through sexual achievement). Sex need not be scarce but it is always selective.

Not even the most vulgar cynic would say, except as a matter of mere theory, that "everyone is just like any other," for this is to misunderstand not only the very essence of love but even sex as well. (One is *not* like any other.) Love is defined, as much as by any other factor, by its particularity. But to confuse this with a "scarcity mechanism," or to deny it in favor of some utopian vision of a world of anonymous (androgynous?) mutually replaceable creatures is not only a complete misunderstanding of love but a degrading depiction of human emotions. It is a form of cynicism that goes back to St. Paul: try to apply love—which by its very nature is highly selective—to everyone equally, and when this universal love turns out to be impossible, condemn *us* for being "incapable of love." The polar opposites of piousness and cynicism begin to look very similar indeed.

> "Love . . . Yuck! . . . it's one of those things they've erected . . . A bunch of nonsense . . . What's important is why they did it."
>
> MARILYN FRENCH, *The Women's Room*

The reduction of love to sex consists of a serious misunderstanding of both love and sex, but this is not the only source of cynicism. A much more powerful diagnosis is to be found in a certain set of feminist[1] arguments against romantic love, in essence, that romantic love is a *political* invention rather than a matter of economy, a question of power rather than the distribution of a commodity. Love, in short, is a male strategy for "keeping women in their place." It does this by assigning the female an emotional role, a role of submissiveness and dedicated passivity, which is then in turn justified by the tremendous importance of the emotion itself.

Until very recently the majority of writing about love and women was provided by men, who promised that love would make a woman happy, fulfilled and truly a *woman.* In fact men's enthusiasm about love tends to remain largely their own. (A recent study by the social psychologist Kephart revealed that sixty-five per cent of the men insisted they would not marry a person they did not love; seventy-two per cent of the women said they "weren't sure.") When psychiatrists talk about "the need to love," they inevitably end up defending—sometimes explicitly—a mode of behavior which is visibly disadvantageous for a woman, in which "femininity" or romantic attractiveness is in direct conflict with her career (unless her career itself happens to be romantic attractiveness). Thus love, so the argument goes, is a culturally created emotion, not a real need at all. It has been invented by men whose purpose is political superiority, as a way of keeping women isolated and at home, content (or feeling that they should be) with love alone, competitive with one another but out of the competition for social status and power, which is by default left to men alone.

Now, first of all, it is entirely correct to say that love is a culturally created emotion, not a natural need. Second, it cannot be denied that romantic love has indeed been used in precisely

[1] I do not want to give the impression that I think there is a single view of some single group called "the feminists." What concerns me here is a specific argument, which has many variations.

this mollifying way, to console women for their lack of power under the false guise of "what a woman needs to fulfill her." But the question concerning love as such is the question whether love itself is *nothing but* this political strategy, whether love is just a male conception, and whether the romantic roles which have been traditionally carved out for women are in fact essential to romantic love. Furthermore, even while one can agree that there is more than a small amount of flimflam in the intentional obfuscation of the everyday concept of love by male writers from Plato to Rollo May, it does not follow that love itself is an illusion, a "myth," a *man*-made concept which has been purposely obscured in order to hide the abuses it makes possible.

The problem appears most dramatically in a double bind which has been described by a great many women authors, from Virginia Woolf to Marilyn French. One has the intelligence and the political savvy to see through the myth of romantic love, but still carries the desperate feeling that one cannot live without it. Thus Val at the end of *The Women's Room* feels caught between a need she cannot deny and a cynicism she cannot reject. Doris Lessing, no friend of this passion either, catches her characters in the bind between needing love "and all that," on the one hand, and being destroyed by it. Ti-Grace Atkinson calls love "a pathological condition," and Shulamith Firestone, several years ago, argued most systematically that love is a male invention, based on the traditional division between the sexes but now an artificially enforced sense of *need* that no longer has any relationship to real biological needs at all. And yet, through all of her cynicism, she clings to love's ideal, wishfully.

Feminism, unlike cynicism in general, deserves a detailed answer to its charges; what we shall have to show is that the structures of love are not based on the power differences between male and female by way of dominance and submissiveness, and that, more generally, love has a set of defensible structures which are not mere "myth" or illusion. But this, of course, presupposes an over-all theory of love. Then, perhaps, we can show how it is that romantic love and feminism need not be antagonistic but, quite the contrary, mutually support and reinforce one another.

But for now, one point only ought to be made, which is why I want to at least introduce this feminist position under the rubric of "cynicism." The point is that a great many of the women who write about and find themselves in the double bind between needing love and despising love do exactly what their male cynical counterparts have done: accept what can indeed be called the "myth" and illusions of romantic love—derived from Platonism—as the "ideal" of love, and then bemoan the fact that what we actually experience as "love" falls so far short of that ideal. To the illusion comes the disillusionment. Thus one very recent feminist, Jill Tweedie, begins her diatribe against love:

> We die of love and die without it, our hearts beat for it and break for it. Love built the Taj Mahal, wrote the Song of Solomon and cooks a billion meals every day, across the world. Love is the only thing that matters, after all. . . . Or so they say. And in my opinion what they say, give or take an epigram or two, is rubbish. Take off the rose-colored glasses and what does a close examination of the facts reveal to the naked eye? That love, true love, is the rarest of all emotions and one that has been conspicuous by its absence ever since mankind dropped from the trees. . . .[2]

But perhaps one can reject the ideal as an illusion without thereby concluding either that we have failed to achieve it (if it is an illusion) or concluding that love itself is an illusion. Perhaps, indeed, that much more ordinary set of emotions that we

[2] *In the Name of Love* (Pantheon, 1979).

do, sometimes, feel for each other should be appreciated for what they are, and for no more, and as nothing less.

Looking back at the twentieth century, historians, if there are any, will no doubt be impressed by the invention of the airplane, nuclear weapons, the electric guitar and frozen foods; but the great revolution in our lives, wrought by simple technology, more significant even than pocket computers and excursion fares to the Orient, are the parasexual discoveries of the mid-century—effective birth control and penicillin. Already we children of the second half of the century take these utterly for granted and, with them, sex without terror, not "free love" but at least sex free from fear. Gone with a shot or a daily swallow is the biblical vengeance of unwanted pregnancy and venereal wrath. Gone too is "the fallen woman," the ruined life, the shotgun marriage, the Errol Flynn and Charlie Chaplin paternity suits. It is difficult for us to remember—or even imagine—what it once was like, to have sex so inescapably bound up with such threats and hazards, to feel so threatened and inhibited that any amount of sexual frustration was endurable given the risks and alternatives. And we might well understand how in such circumstances love could be confused with sexual frustration, or at least how difficult it might have been to tell them apart. Thus the desperate metaphysics of Platonism—in order to pry them apart. And thus the sneering revelations of cynicism, putting them together once again. But the cynic has been refuted by the times and, along with the cynic, the Platonist. For what is crystal clear is that the so-called "sexual revolution" and the new freedom of sex have not put an end to our sense of romance; on the contrary, they have made it possible, by purifying our motives, by eliminating fear and, as some of the feminists have aptly stated it, "by liberating us from our biology." Love has been freed, not left behind, and despite the predictable desperation of parents, preachers and Platonists, love can at last be seen and appreciated for what it is, distinguished quite clearly from mere lust: an ordinary emotion with a complex structure which plays an extraordinary role in our society. What we now have to do is to understand this emotion, without piety, without cynicism, without moralizing, without metaphors. And so, naturally, we turn to "objective" science for some unemotional understanding. What do the scientists tell us?

9 HOW DO I LOVE THEE? LET ME MEASURE SOMETHING (LOVE AND SOCIAL PSYCHOLOGISTS)

Like Leporello, learned men keep a list, but the point is what they lack; while Don Juan seduces girls and enjoys himself—Leporello notes down the time, the place and the description of the girl.

KIERKEGAARD, *Journals* (1834)

Within the last twenty years an academic industry has emerged, the measurement of love. Not surprisingly, it has attracted its detractors, including the Golden Fleece and research-minded William Proxmire, who lambasted the National Science Foundation, fuming, "No one can argue that falling in love is a science. . . . The impact of love . . . is a very subjective, nonquantifiable subject matter. Love is simply a mystery." The senator's lament is echoed by many people today, though without the power to withhold funding, on the grounds that love can't be studied "objectively," that love is "subjective," "ineffable" and a "mystery." That is, there is nothing that can be said about it.

Now that would be surprising if it were true, given the millions of words, many of them insightful, most of them at least relevant, that have been said about it. To say that love is "ineffable" or a "mystery" is a dangerous bit of nonsense. But this leaves open the question whether love can be studied "objectively" and what is meant by "science." Two researchers in particular, Elaine Walster (University of Wisconsin) and Ellen Berscheid (University of Minnesota), who have published extensively on the topic, rightly comment:

> It is odd that the notion that attraction, particularly such intense forms as romantic love, are simply "nonquantifiable" has lingered to the present day. It seems especially strange when we consider that each of us, every day and in a variety of ways, manages to quantify our attraction to others and measure their attraction for us.
>
> *Interpersonal Attraction,* p. 5

Of course, many of these "ways" are highly untrustworthy—for example, "I love you more than I've ever loved anyone." But the point is well taken. The problem is, what to measure? How does one measure an emotion? And here the layman's complaint begins to develop some teeth. Even if love is not a mystery and not immeasurable, it does not follow that what psychologists measure is love. And though we should applaud the attempt to deflate the bloated romanticism of the humanists with some hard-nosed research into what exactly *is* this thing called "love," we have to be very careful that, in trying to find something to measure "objectively," we don't measure something else instead, and miss the content of the emotion altogether.

There is nothing wrong with science or "objectivity" in the realm of emotions; in fact, some of the emotions themselves (for example, "the love of knowledge") are inseparable from the goals and structures of scientific, "objective" and even impersonal discipline. But there is more than room for suspicion when, in the name of this same impersonality, a researcher (who presumably has been in love) mentions not a word of her own experience but instead feels compelled by her discipline to lure a hundred unsuspecting freshmen and sophomores into a superficial setting in which their barely articulate verbal responses to a contrived and in any case shortsighted set of questions are to count as the "data." For instance, a popular professional ploy called "semantic differential" involves an enormously sophisticated statistical technique to measure what students think they mean by the words they frequently abuse; for example, ask them what they mean by "love." But wouldn't we be better served if the theorist—who takes some care in analysis and in any case has to stand by the results—simply tried to say what he or she means by these words? In what other context do we trust undergraduates—*en masse*—to do our research for us?

Meg Greenfield of the Washington *Post* and *Newsweek* recently assaulted "our statistical society." She wrote:

> My theory is that we are the most weighed, counted, measured and analyzed society in the history of civilization; that most of our political fights concern who gets to do the weighing and counting (Keeper of the Data is our Keeper of the Flame), and that as a consequence of this obsession we have begun to talk about ourselves as if we were someone else [*Newsweek*, September 10, 1979].

And, indeed, to analyze love, scientifically or poetically, on the sole basis of *other* people's experience should strike us as odd, to say the least. The problem, in other words, is not the use of science but a certain emasculation of science, an absurd set of restrictions on what can be considered, and considered seriously, and what cannot. Indeed, when the word "science" (*Wissenschaft*) came into common usage, only two centuries ago, it was an explicit appeal to the totality of one's own, carefully analyzed experience; the word "empirical," which today is used to eliminate the observer from the observed, originally meant precisely the appeal to what one did him/herself experience (in the work of philosopher John Locke, for example).

Two thousand years ago Ovid wrote his great observational treatise on love (*De Amore*), something in the style of sociologist Erving Goffman today, sitting on the sidelines, participating on occasion, taking notes. It is now increasingly apparent—in physics as well as psychology—that observer and participant are not separable roles, so the idea of a "participant observer" is no longer suspicious. But then, why not *begin* with the recognition of the psychologist's own familiarity with the subject? (It's bound to sneak in somewhere anyway.)

Ovid observed and participated and offered up what has endured as the classic seduction manual of Western literature, far closer to the nitty gritty of love than Plato's effete and sexless *Symposium*. He observed, for example, that an excellent way to woo a lady was to arouse her at the gladiatorial arena, since the emotion inspired by the various disembowelments and dismemberments below could easily be transformed into emotions of a very different type, a theory-laden bit of observation which has found its way into some of the most modern scientific theories of emotion, to be disemboweled shortly. But it is significant that Ovid has become a perennial starting point for today's social scientists interested in love, not so much for his observational hypothesis, but as an excuse to lament the fact that he was not a disciplined observer; for instance, he conducted no formal surveys (though no doubt he talked quite a bit with his friends). He set up no controlled experiments of his own, in which "controlled" may mean that the normal parameters and conditions of emotion are eliminated and replaced by a wholly artificial set of circumstances in which normal emotional response may be inappropriate.

Ovid was not a scientist.[1] We have no idea what measurement he used for "arousal," except for his own observation that

[1] Zick Rubin, for example, dismisses Ovid because "his recommendation was based on personal observation and experience—or, perhaps what we would call common sense—rather than any underlying scientific principle," *Liking and Loving* (Holt, Rinehart and Winston, 1973).

many if not most of the ladies so suitably aroused did indeed have sex with their arousers. (The modern university measure seems to be "accepting dates"—not quite the same.) But how many, what percentage, what is the likelihood of error in these observations? Could the same experiment have been repeated in Attica, where the gladiatorial events more often included wild animals? And what was the control group? Only those women who were seduced without the inspiration of the arena, and this was, even in Ovid's own experience, a most indefinite and ill-defined group, as were the conditions for their arousal. Ovid, in other words, "never transcended his own limited, personal experience."

A few years ago the social psychologist Robert Zajonc announced to his colleagues that "more than 90% of all social psychological research has been conducted during the last twenty years, and most of it during the last ten," thus dismissing Ovid and a thousand other Goffmans of all ages, simply out of hand.[2] Augustine's candid and sometimes pathetic descriptions of his own "impulses" obviously don't count, nor does Aristotle's remarkably insightful analysis of the social passions in his *Rhetoric* and *Ethics*. Shakespeare just didn't know how to quantify, nor did Elizabeth Browning, who suggested she count the ways, but then didn't. ("Factor analysis" is a relatively new invention.) What is now called social psychology, however, is among the *oldest* of the sciences (depending on how you measure). People have always been fascinated by people, and as a matter of necessity. One has to know at a glance whether the stranger outside your cave really just wants a bite of mastodon or has his eye on your dog or daughter. Mothers have long cultivated the art of sizing up a suitor by the way he stands, walks, looks. It was not just the art of seduction that inspired our ancestors to observe and manipulate the circumstances conducive to emotions of all kinds, but also the

[2] *Social Psychology* (Wadsworth, 1966), p. 3.

need to inspire fear in enemies, loyalty in the troops and faith in the congregation. Zick Rubin is right, perhaps, when he says his psychological colleagues have arrived "late in the party," when much of the work is already done. Indeed, as philosopher Frithjof Bergmann has argued, the problem with the social sciences is the fact that we already know *so much.* And that is all the more reason why a psychologist has to start from experience, not the pose of objectivity and personal indifference. Social psychology is nothing less than the sum total of the whole of our social experience—and the place to start looking for it (but not, by any means, the end of the search) is in our own so-called "personal" experience, which is nothing less in turn than the collective wisdom and foolishness of a generation or an entire culture. And it is here that we can understand how social psychologists do indeed contribute valuable insights and —even more important—new questions to our thinking and feelings about love. But it is a continuity with common sense, not a rejection or suspension of it, that makes this possible.

When an experiment is an extension of a real-life problem that already imposes itself upon us, results tend to be interesting, even fascinating, and hypotheses to explain them much in demand. Eliot Arenson (1969) begins to explain the diminution of love in terms of the increasingly predictable and so less supportive approval of a lover over the years, while the random approval of a complete stranger thereby takes on inordinate attractiveness ("Arenson's Law of Marital Infidelity"). But the findings and the theory wouldn't have much import if we weren't already concerned with the problem of love's fading and wondering how, if possible, to keep it alive. Experimental psychologists Jecker and Dandy (1969) have shown that benefactors come to love those on whom they have *bestowed* favors. (We usually assume that we love because we are bestowed upon.) Think of this next time you consider giving a dozen long-stemmed roses to your lover, not only in order to express your feelings but to intensify them. And this has implications too about the wisdom of turning down a gift, wrongly thinking that your humility will serve you well. Social psychologist Kephart (1961) provides us with a corrective to our romantic wanderlust: "Cherished notions about romantic love notwithstanding, it appears that when all is said and done, the 'one and only' may have a better than 50-50 chance of living within walking distance." This is the same theorist who more recently (1967) provided us with the survey asking students if they would marry someone they didn't love "if they had all the other qualities you desired"; few said yes, perhaps, but far more men than women said no, indicating the truth of what many of the feminists have argued—that romantic love is more a male than a female fantasy and men are more "romantic" than women. Social psychologist Heider (1958) has shown that people in love will believe almost anything to keep a relationship together ("to make the sentiment relationship harmonious with the unit relationship") and a large number of theorists have argued, with contradictory conclusions, the relationships between "falling in love" and self-esteem (Chapters 12, 23). The experiments are varied and sometimes ingenious, but the point to be made is that the above results are revealing only in so far as they continue and utilize our "pre-scientific" conceptions of love. On the other hand, ignoring or suspending those pre-scientific conceptions leads all too easily to results which do indeed earn the public abuse of the Proxmires of the world, such as: (1) people in love tend to think more highly of one another (Thurstone, 1928); (2) people in love tend to sit closer to one another (Byrne, Ervin and Lambreth, 1970); (3) people in love tend to do favors for one another (Bramel, 1969; "If we truly like someone, it pleases us to see him happy and it hurts us to see him suffer"); (4) people in love tend to make more eye contact than people who are not in love (Argyle, 1967; Rubin, 1970). Indeed, Zick Rubin has publicly bemoaned the unsympathetic treatment he has received from the press on his research on love (*Psychology Today,* January

1980). But the question he did not reply to—and the question that a critic from the outside can't help asking—is *why* an experiment measuring the amount of eye contact between lovers should even be necessary. Consider this:

We were sitting in a small Italian restaurant on Beach Street when it struck me what was wrong. Tonight, all evening in fact, you've been staring at your soup, watching your wine, looking askance at the table next to us. Even when you talk to me, your eyes are on the door, flitting to the waiter to your wine to my eyebrows, then down to the silverware. I even said to you, "I miss your eyes," and you glanced down painfully, gave a little smile, looked at me, and I knew it was over. You looked away; I cried, "Why won't you look at me?" You said, "I am," and there was nothing else to say.

There is nothing more to understand here, certainly no empirical question mark about its meaning. But here we hit the crux of the problem, which is not merely that such "findings" seek only to confirm the obvious, but rather that they take as an empirical question what is actually part of the essential structure of the phenomenon. The distinction between "empirical" and "essential" is not absolute, perhaps, but in any given domain of inquiry, the topic itself has its limits and its defining characteristics *within* which one asks more or less probing questions about its details. But to think of reciprocal attention and mutual looking as part of the detail of love, instead of its very essence, is to betray a preference for the empirical which looks suspiciously more like an antipathy to theory, an evasion of the hard work of science, which is not measurement but thinking.

One much-maligned symptom of the unnecessary isolation and anti-common-sense attitude of this self-consciously scientific discipline is its vocabulary. Is "companionate love" really "more precise" than "friendship"? Is "dyatic attraction" really less prone to misunderstanding than "How two people feel about each other"? Is "behavioral reinforcement" really easier to measure than "What are you getting out of this anyway"? Is the definition of "love" as "a state of intense absorption in another" any less metaphorical than a well-wrought line from Shakespeare's sonnets? Indeed, is this definition even plausible—as a characterization of what we ordinary folk mean by "love"? And if it is not intended to be that, but only a technical term for a measurable operation performed only by psychologists, why name it "love" at all? Again, the problem is a forced discontinuity with our personal experience and our way of talking about it.

There is, however, a powerful argument to the contrary. It is that our "common sense" conception of love is confused and that anything one says about love is just as likely to be correct as anything else. For example, we all know that "absence makes the heart grow fonder," but isn't "out of sight, out of mind" also true? So much for common sense, so the argument goes, and what we need is a carefully calculated experiment that will prove, once and for all, which of these common-sense platitudes is true and which is false. Indeed, some recent experiments throw fascinating light on this particular question, that is, that the first is true for men, the second more for women. But the place of experiment and the futility of common sense needs further argument, for the problem with these common-sense platitudes is rather that they are wrenched from context, namely, the context which picks out the appropriate guideline when we actually *use* these bits of ancient wisdom (deciding whether or not to accept a job away from home for a while, for example). But of course we can be wrong, and the experiment in question shows us one way we can be wrong. But what the attack on "the obvious" tends to prove is not the singular necessity of an experiment but the all-important role of *context* in developing any psychological knowledge. Psychology, like physics, begins not with a cosmic hypothesis but with a local and specific observation, a query, a question in context. But in psychology, unlike physics, that context is likely to be embarrassingly personal; to remove that personal context, rather than try to refine it, is not then to become "scientific" or "objective" but rather to give up the "data" (the given) with which any hypothesis must begin.

It is the question of context that raises the question I have not yet mentioned at all, namely, what kind of a view of emotions, what conception of love, do such theories tend to presuppose? Because they reject the legitimacy of personal experience, many experimenters thereby restrict themselves to "publicly observable (and measurable) phenomena." This includes physiological changes in the body, circumstantial stimuli, various bits of behavior (including first-person reports from other people) and, perhaps, a complex of biological, environmental, evolutionary and sociological variables.

The dominant model of the emotions in some psychological circles today was propounded by Stanley Schachter of Columbia University nearly twenty years ago. It is worth examining in some detail, because in it the necessity for a more personal and more experience-oriented ("phenomenological") theory of emotions becomes apparent. The theory begins with the often demonstrated defects of an illustrious theory developed simultaneously by William James in America and C. G. Lange in Denmark, just at the turn of the twentieth century. James and Lange argued that an emotion is a visceral reaction or, more accurately, our conscious perception of a visceral reaction. (See Chapter 5.) The problem was, this provided no mechanism whatever to distinguish between the various emotions, many of which have identical physiological components. Furthermore, it is possible to have the appropriate visceral reactions without having any emotion at all—immediately after being startled, for example, or when one has a fever or has been given a shot of adrenalin. So the question is, what makes a physiological reaction an emotion? And what determines what emotion it is?

It is here that Schachter, in a classic paper with Singer in 1962, advances his theory: an emotion has *two* components, both publicly observable (thus he discounts the "feelings" of his subjects in favor of their physiology) and both measurable. First is the physiological reaction itself, which can be measured by the amount of epinephrine or whatever else has been injected into the poor undergraduate subject. Second, as a solution to James's and Lange's deficiencies and as an answer to both of our questions above, there is the *"labeling"* of the emotion. In other words, what the subject *names* it.

Now this does indeed resolve James's deficiency, but only at the cost of an outrageous trivialization of the problem. Love is indeed distinguished from other emotions and mere physiological reactions by its correctly being called "love," but what, we have to ask, makes the label "correct"? Consider this: I am walking through the woods when a bear lumbers out from behind a rock: I see the bear, I have a rush of adrenalin. I have an emotion, presumably fear. The example is James's, and against him, one might ask, "How do you know that you were afraid of the bear? Perhaps you have just fallen in love?" James, to take care of this apparently absurd question, appeals to subsequent behavior, which does indeed make a difference but fits in quite badly with his theory. Schachter, on the other hand, solves the problem by insisting that the label one applies to one's emotion must be "appropriate" to the circumstances. Thus it is the circumstances, no longer what we would call the emotion, that provide the criterion for labeling. Thus we find ourselves in a theoretical dilemma: either our theory of emotions now becomes a semantic theory about the appropriateness of applying certain words in certain circumstances, *whatever I actually feel*, or else we fall back to the Jamesian physiological theory without any adequate way of distinguishing one emotion from another. But in either case what drops out is the emotion itself, the emotional experience. For whether or not the physiological reactions are similar to various emotions, our experience of different emotions is decidedly different. Moreover, as some of Schachter's disciples have repeatedly pointed out,[3] we are often prone to "inappropriately label" our emotions, especially love. But how can a label be "inappropriate" to the emotion if the emotion itself is not the criterion for its own identity? And, indeed, are not our emotions themselves often "inappropriate,"—love again in particular—out of context, out of character? Circumstances surely do not make the difference; it is flatly absurd to suggest that I can only love a person who is standing right in front of me (as a "stimulus") and to expand "circumstance" to include the whole of one's life loses all specificity. Indeed, I sometimes love most precisely when I am in wholly irrelevant circumstances, not at all aroused or otherwise physiologically excited, and indeed, not at all prone to—perhaps even resistant to—the labeling of my emotion as "love."

The various problems in Schachter's model which I have here only suggested can be reduced to the counterclaim that *neither* of the components in his "two-component theory of emotions" is either necessary or sufficient for emotion. The idea that not only romantic love but moral indignation, nagging jealousy, political resentment, religious devotion, morbid grief and Kierkegaardian dread are no more than adrenalin plus a word is so contrary to our emotional experience—so neglectful of our emotional experience—that one can only look for an explanation of its prominence within the parameters of social psychology itself. There is nothing in the "data" or even in Schachter's ingenious experiments that would suggest this emasculated view of emotions, *sans* experience. It is rather the requirement that a "scientific" view of emotions cannot begin

[3] For example, Elaine Walster and Ellen Berscheid, *Interpersonal Attraction* (Addison Wesley, 1969).

with—cannot even include—the description of emotional experience. And so it falsely concludes that the emotion is something else—the physiological cause and accompaniment of the emotion, plus its name in a particular society. Does that mean one could not have an emotion he or she could not name? Or that what we naïvely refer to as "the same emotion" in different linguistic groups (say, English- and French-speaking Québecois) are rather two emotions, perhaps as different as joy and jealousy, which indeed also differ—according to this theory—only according to their names? An emotion is neither a visceral reaction nor a name; it is an experience. And anything else, no matter what theoretical attractiveness it may yield, simply is not an emotion.

The romantic consequences of the Schachter theory have been spelled out laboriously by Elaine Walster and Ellen Berscheid. They have hypothesized, in a wide range of well-known essays and books, that the most widely praised of all of our emotions is nothing more than the label "love," applied (by whom, in what culture and context—and why?) to the physiological feelings of "sexual arousal, companionship and shared enjoyment."[4] The initial plausibility of the James-Schachter-type theories for fear and anger—where a visceral or "gut" reaction is typical of the emotional experience—is not in evidence here. What are the typical physiological feelings of companionship? Or shared enjoyment? Is sexual arousal *love*—if only one chooses to call it that? Indeed, that ploy has temporarily soothed the conscience of many a virgin, but the transparency of the ploy is exactly why we know to distinguish sexual arousal from the emotions which may—or may not—go along with it. Even passionate romantic love need not be characterized in terms of its enduring physiological symptoms, particularly when it goes on for months or years, and we will all

[4] Op. cit.

too readily admit that it is at least possible to love someone for quite some time and never be tempted to "label" it love. Yet indeed, constrained by the limited parameters of their theory, these authors argue this position to its absurd conclusion. Elaine Walster, for example:

> To love passionately a person must first be physically aroused, a condition manifested by palpitations of the heart, nervous tremor, flushing and accelerated breathing.
>
> Once he is so aroused, all that remains [!!] is for him [sic] to identify this complex of feelings as passionate love, and he will have experienced *authentic* love. [!!!] Even if the initial arousal is the result of an irrelevant experience that usually would produce anger, or even if it is induced in a laboratory by an injection of adrenalin, once the subject has met the person and identified the experience as love, it is love.[5]

"All that remains"!? "Authentic love"!? And "even if [the experience] is irrelevant"!? Has ever a theory produced counter-examples more fatal to itself? Indeed, in another article, Walster has argued that jealousy too is arousal *cum* label, and after some sensitive prefatory remarks proceeds with a similar conclusion—that we could eliminate jealousy if we could just get people to call it something else (sort of like eliminating crime in New York by repealing the criminal code).[6] It is as if the experience of jealousy—like the experience of love—does not count at all. I imagined a scene (The University of Verona, Psychology Department):

[5] From E. Berscheid and E. Walster, "Adrenalin Makes the Heart Grow Fonder," *Psychology Today* (1971, 5 (1) p. 47), though a virtually identical passage can be found in Walster's more professional essay "Passionate Love" in Murstein, ed. *Theories of Attraction and Love* (Springer, 1971). Expletives in brackets are my own.

[6] "Jealousy," in Gordon Clanton and Lynn G. Smith, *Jealousy* (Prentice-Hall, 1969).

ROMEO: But soft! What light through yonder doorway breaks? It is my social psychology 261b professor! O, it is my love! O, that she knew she were!
She speaks.

JULIET: Damn it.

ROMEO: O, speak again, bright angel, for thou art
As glorious to this afternoon
As a winged messenger of Heaven.

JULIET: Romeo? Romeo Montague? Wherefore art thou?

ROMEO: [*To himself*] Shall I hear more, or shall I speak at this?

JULIET: What manner of student art thou, bescreened in the dark of the hallway, so stumblest in on my office hour?

ROMEO: O, I love thee, Professor Capulet!

JULIET: How camest thou hither?

ROMEO: Down the hall, past the chairman's office, led by love, that first did prompt me to inquire.
He lent me counsel, and I lent him eyes.

JULIET: What is love? [*Sighs*]
Love is a smoke raised with the fume of sighs,
Being purged, a fire sparkling in the eyes,
Being vexed, a sea nourished with tears.
And what else?
But just a word, and nought else besides.

ROMEO: 'Tis true, I feel a fire, and my heart
poundeth in my bosom; I am sweating profusely
and I am nervous as a laboratory rat. But 'tis
the circumstances and the uncertainty.
Dost thou love me? I must know, or I'll frown and
be perverse, and most likely flunk thy course.

JULIET: What's in a name? That which we call love,
by any other name would be something else.
Without that label, Love, doff thy name,
For thou art not.

ROMEO: I know not how to tell thee what I feel,

Except by its name, 'tis true.

JULIET: But 'tis hardly appropriate, for thou knowest me not.

ROMEO: I've taken thine every course, and I've loved thee for three semesters.

JULIET: And thou hast been in such a state all the while? Thou must be exhausted.

ROMEO: My present anguish is my fear that thou mayest lower my grade, for surely I am none so wrought elsewhile.

JULIET: Perhaps then thou despiseth me; that would be more appropriate, but the same feeling as well.

ROMEO: Of course it's inappropriate, that's why I feel thus, but it's love. I beseech you, tell me, tell me.

JULIET: Dost thou love me? I know thou wilt say "Ay"
And I will take thee at thy word,
For that would be but a self-fulfilling prophecy,
Since thou art obviously aroused.

ROMEO: O wilt thou leave me so unsatisfied?

JULIET: What satisfaction canst thou have from me, this afternoon?

ROMEO: The exchange of thy love's faithful vow for mine.

JULIET: Indeed I am blushing.

ROMEO: Then call it love, before thou calmeth down.

JULIET: I have no joy in this contact,
It is too rash, too unadvised, too sudden
And inappropriate.
Next time, let's meet for dinner, with flowers and candles.

ROMEO: Swear by the blessed moon that thou will.

JULIET: Indeed, I feel a madness most indiscreet,
A choking gall and persevering sweet.
I'll not swear by the moon, so inconstant,
like my visceral disturbances,
Hark, I hear a noise within.

ROMEO: 'Tis thy belly churning, I heard it myself from here.

JULIET: But how do I know that it's thou, Romeo?

ROMEO: It matters not, by thine own theory. But label it "love," and all is well.

JULIET: Three little words, dear Romeo, and it will be a good night indeed.
If the bent of thy love be honorable,
Send me the words tomorrow.

ROMEO: I will not fail. 'Tis twenty year till then, but do bring some epinephrine to once again assure thy blush.

JULIET: Yet I could kill you with so much passion. But good day, good Romeo, parting while blushing is such sweet sorrow
That I shall say good day till it be morrow.

[*Exit*]

ROMEO: Hence will I to my chemistry professor's close cell,
His help to crave and my good fortune to tell.
And to keep myself aroused till tomorrow.

[*Exit*]

Tolstoy once said, what is undoubtedly untrue, that all happy families are the same, but every unhappy family is different. But when it came to understanding human relationships, whether the tragically unhappy marriage of Anna K. or the banal bliss of Pierre and Natasha, he knew that the studies he presented in such artful detail were both faithful to the experience of millions of readers too. No survey of separated couples in the Ukraine would ever add up to the essential insights of *Anna Karenina*, and no Pavlovian experiment with the undergraduates at Moscow U. could display the structures and complexities of love so well as the simple character of Natasha. The idea that a "controlled" experiment with 123 strangers is more revealing and more "objective" than the description of one's own experience is a view that has nothing to do with science or objectivity; it was by projecting the daily experience of gravity to the Heavens, not by ignoring it, that Isaac Newton succeeded, where centuries of science had failed, in seeing the continuity between the two. And when we study emotions—they are *our* emotions after all—what we are looking for are the common structures of experience which are to be found only through the thoughtful examination of our experience. For *that* is the emotion, not its physiological accompaniment, not what we happen to call it, and not the mere circumstances of its evocation. To quote Meg Greenfield once again, "It is a very insecure society that won't credit its own experience." Or, more scathingly, Margaret Atwood writes,

> I approach this love
> like a biologist
> putting on my rubber
> gloves and white lab coat.
>
> . . .
>
> You asked for love.
> I gave you only descriptions.
>
> MARGARET ATWOOD, *Power Politics*
> (New York: Harper & Row, 1973)

WHAT DO I WANT WHEN I WANT YOU? AN INTRODUCTION TO (TWO) METAPHYSICS 10

The intense yearning which each has towards the other does not appear to be the desire of intercourse, but of something else which the soul desires and cannot tell, and of which she has only a dark and doubtful presentiment.

Aristophanes in PLATO, *Symposium*

What do I want when I want you? There is a familiar adolescent, primarily male experience—no doubt some Freudians feel it too—which provides the most misleading answer to this seemingly simple question. The experience consists, first of all, in a ravenous desire, usually but not always explicitly sexual and obsessive, which is frustrated for one reason or another and whose result is a sense of urgency bordering on insanity. The troubadours did it to themselves; teenagers in the 1950s had it imposed upon them. (It may now be an experience whose frequency is on the wane.) Anyway, some horny Romeo exclaims his passion as nothing less than undying love, thus effectively overcoming the resistance of his rightly suspicious but much-flattered Juliet. She yields, perhaps because of her naïve belief that an emotion so intense could not possibly be other than what it seems to be.

We know the sad end of this little story. Perhaps immediately, in any case soon, our Romeo becomes indifferent, even cruel. Perhaps he is still possessive, but now out of pride rather than affection. He wonders what he was so excited about; she concludes that he never really wanted anything but "a good lay," as she puts it, with intentional crudity (and a bit of flattery for herself). The impression is often indelible on women, but seemingly even more so on some theorists about love. It is as if the "intense yearning" of love were nothing more than sexual desire, whipped to a frenzy, the love itself an illusion and the yearning wholly satisfied by sexual consummation. It is a shoddy view of love, and a pathetic one. Aristophanes, in any case, was not so easily fooled. He knew that the yearning of love was for something much more, and that the answer to the question, "What do I want when I want you?" was far from obvious.

Of course Aristophanes knew what many "Platonic" theorists later denied, that one does indeed want intercourse, but *also* something more. As soon as we try to characterize this "something more," however, we find ourselves too easily removed from concrete sexual desire and off into the abstract realm of metaphysics, for what one wants, as Aristophanes argued so dramatically, is nothing less than an ontological miracle, the eternal reunion with one's other "original" half, the re-creation of a "natural" whole. But it would be a mistake of profound proportions—though indeed it is the dominant tendency of the whole history of Western philosophy—to think that such "yearning," or desire in general, *must* be aiming at some such final and presumably eternal goal, some state of *Being* or an absolute "union." This was Plato's idea, and one finds it again in Plotinus and the medieval philosophers and in Spinoza and even in Freud and Jean-Paul Sartre. And if this seems so, we should not be surprised to hear that the ultimate love is the love of God (or the desire to *be* God), for where else would we find absolute identity, unity and eternity, if not with Him?

But the cost of this metaphysical vision is that the emotion itself, and the merely fleeting time one actually spends with a lover, is dismissed as insignificant, and love is said to be "true" only in so far as it *lasts*, indeed forever, as if duration, and not the passion itself, were the ultimate test.

But there is another answer to the question, "What do I want when I want you?" besides mere sex and the absolute. That answer is, "To want you." What I want when I want you is to want you—thus we are introduced to an entirely different metaphysics, in which states and eternity and even satisfaction are no more than illusions, and in which desire is not a temporary deficiency seeking to be fulfilled but is itself the end of life, its very essence, and of love too. Fulfillment is just another step to further desire.

In one of the few great books of philosophy to deal with the passions at length, David Hume distinguished, in his *Treatise on Human Nature,* between the *calm* and the *violent* passions. He thought these were *types* of emotions (for example, love was a violent passion, but the love of justice a calm passion)—whereas I would argue that virtually all emotions can take either form. Love, in particular, can be either calm or violent, and one of the most frequent debates in the history of the subject, between Aristophanes and Socrates, for example, is which of the two is more "true." A calm passion is no less a passion, however, and a violent passion, no matter how out of proportion, is not thereby "false." But we can see in Hume's distinction something more than a recognition of the various intensities and durabilities of the emotions; it is also the key to two very different visions of the cosmos, in which all talk of love inevitably participates. My purpose in this chapter is to make these clear, as well as to indicate my own metaphysical bias.

Ever since ancient times, before the first philosophers were crawling over the craggy peaks of Asia Minor, our dominant view of the world, the cosmos and ourselves, has been a wishful, *static* metaphysics, built upon the concept of *reality*, which boils down quickly to a series of tautologies, such as "Everything is what it is," and "Truth never perishes" (Seneca). However traumatically the world changes and our bodies and societies change, degenerating, finally dying, reality remains, eternally. In fact, reality was *defined* as that which does not change. Plato was the final step in a long line of thinkers who insisted that the *real* world was unchanging and eternal, a world of "Being," while changes, traumas and death were, ultimately, mere appearances. Before Plato, the philosopher Parmenides argued that reality was unknowable but nevertheless only reality, to state the obvious tautology, is real. After Plato, Christianity, imported from the Orient as much as derived from the Greeks, theologized this same metaphysics in an Eternal God and, by equating God and love, made love "real" too, but only by making it no longer a transient feeling but an eternal state. (Nietzsche: "Christianity is Platonism for the masses.")

The fear of growing old and ugly, losing one's fleeting beauty, even the fear of death, could be overcome by the knowledge that what was eternally beautiful, the invisible soul, would live forever. There was a political pay-off, too, since all souls, as opposed to minds and bodies, could be considered equal. The soul has no determinable characteristics; so too, this bloodless abstraction allowed the invention of the modern concept of "humanity," as if we were all, "deep down," metaphysically the same—whatever our culture, race or character. And so love too could be in all of us—as part of our "human nature"—whether or not we were willing to recognize that eternal verity in ourselves.

This soothing image of an unchanging reality came to define Western philosophy and religion. It continues into modern times. In chemistry, for example, the bases of nearly all theories up until this century were the various "conservation" laws, which say, in effect, that something—matter, energy, some basic particles—can be neither created nor destroyed. Something must be constant. The ancient assumption is that the "natural" state of things is equilibrium, "harmony." In Newtonian physics, an object tends to stay at rest unless pushed; it tends to move at a constant speed unless forced to slow down. It is a lazy universe. Even in Einstein, the *laws* are eternal, if nothing else is. And in high school biology we all learned the basic principle of *homeostasis*—namely, the tendency of organisms to stay in the "same state." If one is thirsty, one drinks some water; if hungry, one eats; if horny, one screws; if lonely, one loves. Freud picks up this image (he was, after all, a physician) and retains it throughout his career. He calls it his "constancy principle," and it says, in effect, that the "psychic apparatus," as he calls it, "divests itself of energy," tending to a state of rest. Excess energy, or *cathexis,* is experienced as pain, and release of energy, *catharsis,* is experienced as pleasure, and all the vicissitudes of psychoanalytic theory are descriptions of the "economics" of this apparatus, which ultimately wants to sleep. In 1927, Freud discovered the "death principle," in which the organism achieved its ultimate state of rest; this is a familiar feeling when one is very tired, perhaps, but a dubious foundation for a theory of human life.

We are afraid of death, afraid of aging, afraid of change, afraid of losing what we have. So we imagine a universe without change, an underlying state of *being,* devoid of life, perhaps, but also devoid of death and decay. Love, as an ideal, is the ultimate, eternal, harmonious state.

A recent and particularly impressive version of this cosmology has appeared in Gregory Bateson's *Mind and Nature* (Dutton, 1979), which, on the one hand, continues Bateson's well-known career as iconoclast eccentric regent at the University of California and on the other hand serves as a bridge between biology and moral philosophy. An idealist at heart, *the idea* holds center stage for him as it does for Plato. "Nature thinks," he insists, and the question is, How? The answer is cybernetics, a system of context-bound feedback and response systems, nature as fundamentally *conservative,* interrupted by aberrations and turbulence, striving to set itself back into balance again. Like most ecologists, Bateson puts all of his stress on this "balance," giving service to challenge and upheaval, but always putting his bets on the urge to a "steady state." Even evolution is a search for a steadier state.

We like to think in these terms—balance, states, security, evolution, growth, peace and predictability. We praise people for being "cool," for having an "even temperament," we encourage permanent relationships, predictable behavior, simple desires, calm passions and being "reasonable." Ideal love is love without ripples or squalls, life without dangers, love that endures as a steady state. Plato set the tone—the ideal life is the life of contemplation, a minimum of desires, peace of mind, "wisdom," Nirvana. Living beyond anxiety, vanity, wrinkles and trauma.

On this model, desire is a kind of disruption. Creativity is a danger, or an attempted solution to a self out of equilibrium. Emotions are superfluous, even if unavoidable, destructive interruptions of our otherwise "natural" and "rational" (orderly) state of being. Sex, like food, drink and sleep, is a *need,* a lack, an *excess* of libido, a *deficit* of love. (Sex *versus* ego, Freud thought: perhaps sex *as* ego—in either case, a need, a deficiency, a lack.) Satisfaction is a return to equilibrium, and all is well—that is, a state of well-*being*—until desire and emotion come again. (The passive imagery is essential.) Sex is transient tension, and romantic love, accordingly, gets classified with lust as a disruption, enjoyable, perhaps, leading to important things sometimes, but in itself wholly intolerable, a mere indulgence, "infatuation." We hate the thought that we will be wanted "only skin deep," so we pride ourselves on an invention, "deep inside," the *real* self, a soul, that won't wrinkle or wear out, eternally lovable. We shift the beauty that excites to something more secure, something abstract, and therefore indestructible.

Now we don't live this way, of course. Even those who sincerely believe in eternal souls and eternal love and an eternal God find themselves worrying about their fading beauty, fighting with their supposedly eternal partners, getting divorced and finding a new eternal partner, treating sex as something more than a transient need and life as more than mere vanity, despite the warnings of the eternal Church. But it is an image that we carry around with us, a tacit measurement that we use continuously. We might not believe that love is "forever," but we do say, of a glorious fling that lasted three months, "It didn't work out." What were we supposed to be working *for?* Why measure the success of a relationship by how long it lasts? (Consider, for example, someone who considered himself *really* angry only when he was angry for years.) We want a good thing to last, of course, but why build endurance into our conception of the emotion itself? Indeed, perhaps love thrives on change, occasionally even frenzy. It is revitalized, not merely punctuated, by insecurities and uncertainties. And even when love lasts a lifetime, is it ever the case that it is to be conceived as a *state*, rather than a continuous *consuming* of life and love itself?

Since and even before the ancient Greeks, too, there is a second metaphysical picture. It is most often mentioned in conjunction with the philosopher Heraclitus, a contemporary of Parmenides and also an influence on Plato. It was Heraclitus who supposedly said that you can't step in the same river twice, which led some of his critics to accuse him unfairly of bathing only once in his life. Heraclitus chose as his favorite element the vibrant dancing of fire, never at rest, consuming itself, disappearing altogether. For Heraclitus, permanence was the illusion, change or "flux" the reality. (He also believed in an underlying order, or *Logos,* but that is not particularly relevant here.) *States* are mere appearances, objects seem at rest only between moves. Security is a human delusion, and life is gluttony, power, *dissipation.* Even within the bounds of physics and chemistry, Nobel laureate Ilya Prigogine has developed a complex theory of "dissipative structures," organized complexes that emerge from chaos, temporary exceptions to entropy, structures that are based on change rather than steady states. It is an idea that has its most belligerent spokesman in the German philosopher Friedrich Nietzsche. Life is not a state but frenzy; desire is its substance, emotion and passion its meaning. Transient order emerges from chaos and consumes itself before coming to rest. "From desire I rush to satisfaction," writes the poet Goethe, "but from satisfaction I leap to desire." *Dis*satisfaction is the meaning of life; satisfaction is death. (Thus the absence of desire is quite rightly noted, by Buddhists and by Freud, to be ontologically akin to death.)

It is sometimes said that life is a process or progress, a metaphysical view that has been argued by Hegel and Whitehead, for example, in reaction against the more static Platonic model. Reality is history, says Hegel, in effect, but one look at history and we know that it is chaos, and any contemporary sophomore will tell you that every step in life is a step toward death and disintegration as well. The very idea of process, or progress, or "growth" (the modern favorite) presupposes an underlying pattern that is static, a direction, an order, and, not surprisingly, most "process philosophers" merge their theory with a theodicy, with God as the underlying and again eternal pattern (Hegel, Whitehead and Hartshorne, for example). Thus the image of eternity reappears, with the search for security, rationality and a guaranteed order. And when we talk about love in terms of a couple "growing" together, or an individual's "human potential," the same picture, of a pattern which is predictable and to be "worked out," is evident.

One of our favorite metaphors, when talking about love or at least new love, is Heraclitus' "flame" imagery. Love *burns.* Love *consumes.* Fire is heat and transience; it is never the same from moment to moment. And the "hot" passions of sex are not by any means a desire for mere release, nor mere satisfaction; they are frenzied *dis*satisfaction, not just the build-up of desire for catharsis but the urge to continue, the build-up of desire for its own sake, catharsis as a respite, not the end-state. Nothing, not even chaos, can last forever, but why do we insist on limiting such metaphors to only brief or troubled love? Why not love as such?

Between the specious moment, always disappearing, and eternity, which is incomprehensible, there is a more human kind of time, defined by *engagement,* by desire and its projection, time defined by enthusiasm rather than time measured by watching the clock. ("Do you realize we've been here for over five hours?") It is oblivious to time; and it is wholly absorbed *in* time. "A moment feels like eternity." But what does this mean except that those too static concepts of steady-state time have broken down, collapsed indifferently into their opposites, become utterly meaningless and irrelevant to us.

In life and in love, "eternity" is an empty word, a philosopher's fantasy, a daydream for the desperately dissatisfied. It is no part of experience but rather, in its lack of content, the desire for an end to experience, an end to passion, which is inescapably caught up in time. Love is not a state, but a set of erratic movements. True love is not "forever," but rather perpetually out of equilibrium, slightly off balance, oblivious to questions of eternity, however desperately it seeks to continue. It can last indefinitely, but not forever. It looks forward, but only to the concrete future, the next moment, the next time we're together, a trip in the future, perhaps even parenthood or old age together—but always in the form of the specific, never the abstractions of mere endurance. Love can be calm, of course, but it is every instant aware of its own contingency; it thrives on violence and change, even though it may not welcome them. It can be confident, but it is the confidence of a race-car driver, with that fateful sense of skilled but tentative control that feels itself skimming along the track as if over solid ice. It is that sense of movement, fraught with dangers, and here even Aristophanes transcends his own story, for he too sees that there is never a return to one's "original state"—which is only a fiction—but always the perpetual effort, the struggle, the "desperate yearning" that never ceases.

Can such love continue? That, of course, is the crucial question. But the point is not to confuse the desire that it will continue with the Platonic wish for eternity, and not to confuse the confidence that comes with continued love for the calm taken-for-granted security that comes with comfortable and accustomed indifference, which often goes under the same name. On the other hand, it is equally essential not to confuse the repetitive newness of several affairs for the rekindling of passion either, for if love is a *becoming*, however erratic and without direction, then it cannot be mere repetition and the uncertainty of random encounters.

I have an old and very dear friend. She leaps from one impossible love to another, each more desperate than the last. "I can't live this way," she complains every time, but she loves it. She's radiant. She works hard. She suffers. She walks with an arrogant confidence. She is—but certainly don't tell her so—happy. She is thriving, living. But in between, which seems like forever, she's bitter, cynical, lonely, *bored.* God forbid she should live "happily ever after." She would be miserable.

Now this second metaphysics isn't "real" either; it is hard to imagine what it would be like to live constantly "on the edge" without some fiber of security to hold us together. Today, both Romeo and Juliet probably have nine-to-five jobs and careers to pursue. Even the most "romantic" relationships have to face those thousands of small decisions—which restaurant, "your place or mine"—and all of those emergencies that emerge with time—the car won't start, a sudden bout of nausea, losing the contraceptives, a friend who calls in need in the middle of the night. Eventually, these do threaten love, which thrives not only on a reckless irresponsibility but also the absence of external distractions. But if *we* are responsible and involved in the world at large, it does not follow that our love is, and if *we* tend still to be caught up in the Platonic imagery of states and eternity, our love is not, for within that small world *a deux*, we know that it is the contingency of love, the fact that it has no guarantees, that defines what we want so much to continue.

What does it mean to be in love? Or, for that matter, to "fall in love"? "To be" seems to be a state, "to fall" appears to be suffering a movement, unexpected, out of control, even unwelcome. But if both of these images seem too simple and too extreme to capture the everyday vicissitudes of mutual affection, they nonetheless lie behind much of our thinking and our wishing, structuring our desires and forming our passions. It is for this reason that love inspires not only so much bad poetry, but bad metaphysics too, which nevertheless is necessary, as part of the emotion as well as its expression. Because what I want when I want you is a matter far from obvious, and what it is to love you, accordingly, is far from obvious too, no matter how simple it seems at times.

PART II:

Love: A Theory

WHAT LOVE IS: THE LOVEWORLD

All customs and traditions, all our way of life, everything to do with home and order, has crumbled into dust in the general upheaval and reorganization of society. The whole human way of life has been destroyed and ruined. All that's left is the naked human soul stripped to the last shred, for which nothing has changed because it was always cold and shivering and reaching out to its nearest neighbor, as cold and lonely as itself. You and I are like Adam and Eve, the first two people on earth who at the beginning of the world had nothing to cover themselves with—and now at the end of it we are just as naked and homeless.

Boris Pasternak, *Dr. Zhivago*

The question, What is love? is neither a request for a confession nor an excuse to start moralizing. It is not an invitation to amuse us with some *bon mot* ("Love is the key that opens up the doors of happiness") or to impress us with an author's sensitivity. And love is much more than a "feeling." When a novelist wants us to appreciate his character's emotions, he does not just describe sweaty palms and a moment of panic; he instead describes *a world*, the world as it is experienced—in anger, or in envy, or in love. Theorizing about emotion, too, is like describing an exotic world. It is a kind of conceptual anthropology—identifying a peculiar list of characters—heroes, villains, knaves or lovers—understanding a special set of rules and roles—rituals, fantasies, myths, slogans and fears. But these are not merely empirical observations on the fate of a feeling; none of this will make any sense to anyone who has not participated also. Love can be understood only "from the inside," as a language can be understood only by someone who speaks it, as a world can be known only by someone who has—even if vicariously—*lived* in it.

To analyze an emotion by looking at the world it defines allows us to cut through the inarticulateness of mere "feelings" and do away once and for all with the idea that emotions in general and love in particular are "ineffable" or beyond description. This might make some sense if describing an emotion were describing something "inside of us." It is not easy, for example, to describe how one feels when nauseous; even describing something so specific as a migraine headache falls back on clumsy metaphors ("as if my head's in a vise," "as if someone were driving a nail through my skull"). But once we see that every emotion defines a world for itself, we can then describe in some detail what that world involves, with its many variations, describe its dimensions and its dynamics. The world defined by love—or what we shall call the *loveworld*—is a world woven around a single relationship, with all else pushed to the periphery. To understand love is to understand the specifics of this relationship and the world woven around it.

Love has been so misunderstood both because so often it has been taken to be *other*-worldly rather than one world of emotion among others, and because it has sometimes been taken to be a "mere emotion"—just a feeling and not a world at all. Because of this, perhaps it would be best to illustrate the theory that every emotion is a world by beginning with a less problematic emotion, namely, *anger*. Anger too defines its world. It is a world in which one defines oneself in the role of "the offended" and defines someone else (or perhaps a group or an institution) as "the offender." The world of anger is very much a courtroom world, a world filled with blame and emotional litigation. It is a world in which everyone else tends to become a co-defendant, a friend of the court, a witness or at least part of the courtroom audience. (But when you're *very* angry, there are no innocent bystanders.) We have already once quoted Lewis Carroll from *Alice in Wonderland:* "'I'll be judge, I'll be jury,' said cunning old Fury." It is a world in which one does indeed define oneself as judge and jury, complete with a grim righteousness, with "justice"—one's own vengeance—as the only legitimate concern. It is a *magical* world, which can change a lackadaisical unfocused morning into a piercing, all-consuming day, an orgy of vindictive self-righteousness and excitement. At the slightest provocation it can change an awkward and defensive situation into an aggressive confrontation. To describe the world of anger is therefore to describe its fantasies, for example, the urge to kill, though rarely is this taken seriously or to its logical conclusion. It has its illusions too, for instance, the tendency to exaggerate the importance of some petty grievance to the level of cosmic injustice; in anger we sometimes talk as if "man's inhumanity to man" is perfectly manifested in some minor sleight at the office yesterday. It is a world with a certain fragility; a single laugh can explode the whole pretense of angry self-righteousness. And it is a world with a purpose—for when do we feel more self-righteous than in anger? Getting angry in an otherwise awkward situation may be a way of saving face or providing a quick ego boost; "having a bad temper" may be not so much a "character trait" as an emotional strategy, a way of *using* emotion as a means of controlling other people. To describe anger, in other words, is to describe the way the world is structured—and why—by a person who is angry.

The world of love—the loveworld—can be similarly described as a theatrical scenario, not as a courtroom but rather as "courtly," a romantic drama defined by its sense of elegance (badly interpreted as "spiritual"), in which we also take up a certain role—"the lover"—and cast another person into a complementary role—"the beloved." But where anger casts two antagonistic characters, romantic love sets up an ideal of unity, absolute complementarity and total mutual support and affection. It is the *rest* of the world that may be the antagonist. Boris Pasternak describes the loveworld beautifully—the world as Adam and Eve, naked, surrounded by chaos.

It is a world we know well, of course—the world of *Casablanca, Romeo and Juliet* and a thousand stories and novels. It is a world in which we narrow our vision and our cares to that single duality, all else becoming trifles, obstacles or interruptions. It is a magical world, in which an ordinary evening is transformed into the turning point of a lifetime, the metamorphosis of one's self into a curious kind of double being. It may seem like a sense of "discovery"; in fact it is a step in a long search, a process of creation. It has its fantasies and also its illusions: the fantasy of flying off together to some deserted island, the illusion that it will last forever. And as the music swells up and over, the sense of clichéd grandeur makes it quite clear what this emotion is all about—a "heightened" sense of one's own emotional significance, a fragile glorification of one's world by the contraction of everything to just one singsong glorious feeling which, at least for a moment, maybe indeed for a lifetime, dismisses the complex impersonality of the world and scorns it with a simple caress.

Like every emotional world, the loveworld has its essential rules and rituals, its basic structures and internal dynamics. Some of these rules and structures are so obvious that it is embarrassing to have to spell them out, for example, the fact that the loveworld (typically) includes two people, instead of only one (as in shame) or three (as in jealousy) or indeed an entire class of people (as in national mourning or revolutionary resentment). Or the fact that the loveworld involves extremely "positive" feelings about the person loved, perhaps even the uncritical evaluation that he or she is "the most wonderful person in the world." Or the fact that the loveworld is held together by the mutual desire to be together (to touch, be touched, to caress and make love) no less essentially than the world of Newton and Einstein is held together by the forces of electromagnetism and gravity. Such features are so obvious to us that we fail to think of them as the structures of love; we take them for granted and, when asked to talk about love, consider them not even worth mentioning. Having thus ignored the obvious, love becomes a mystery. But other seemingly equally "obvious" features of love may not be part of the structure of the loveworld at all—for example, the comforting equation between love and trust. Here, indeed, there is some room for "mystery" in love, not the emotion itself but its essential lack of predictability, the fascination with the unknown and the attraction that comes not with trust but with vulnerability, sometimes even suspicion and doubt. Similarly, we presume as in a cliché that romantic love presupposes respect ("How can you say that you love me when you don't even respect me?"). But it may be too that the nature of romantic love renders respect irrelevant, so that even when respect begins as a prerequisite for romantic attraction it gets booted out of the loveworld just as assuredly as a pair of fine leather shoes gets doffed as we get into bed. But each of these features has to be examined in turn, for the problem with talking about love is not that there is a mystery to be cleared up or that so much seems so obvious but rather that we take what we are told so uncritically, conflate the loveworld with everything that is good, true and desirable, confuse the structures of love with the conditions for security and happiness, assume without thinking that because suspicion is so painful trust must be essential to love, assume as a matter of wishful thinking that the same person who is in love with us must, if our lives are to be unified, respect us for what we do as well. So, at the risk of being extremely pedantic, I want to take these "obvious" and some not so obvious features of love and look at them one by one, here and in the chapters to follow, just to see what is, and what is not, the nature of the loveworld, its "object," its dimensions, its supposed "mystery" and "magic" and the ways it works for us. For those who want straightforward romantic praise, instead of somewhat tedious analytical prose, however, I am afraid the speculations that follow may seem excessive.

The "Object" of Love

Talking about the loveworld is not only a way to avoid the hopeless conception of love as a feeling; it is also a way of rejecting an insidious view of love—and emotions in general—which many philosophers have come to accept as "obvious," particularly in this century. The view simply stated, is that love is an attitude *toward* someone, a feeling directed *at* a person, instead of a shared world. The view is often disguised by a piece of professional jargon—an impressive word, "intentionality." It is said that emotions are "intentional," which is a way of saying that they are "about" something. What an emotion is "about" is called its "intentional object" or, simply, its "object." Thus shame is an emotion which is "about" oneself, while anger is "about" someone else. The language comes from the medieval scholastics, by way of an Austrian philosopher named Franz Brentano, one of whose students in Vienna was the young Sigmund Freud. Thus Freud talks all the time about the "object" of love, not without some discomfort, for though the conception fits his general theories perfectly, he nonetheless sensed correctly that some considerable conceptual damage was being done to the emotion thereby.

The idea—though not the terminology—of "intentionality" and "intentional objects" was introduced into British philosophy by the Scottish philosopher David Hume. He analyzed a number of emotions in terms of the "objects" with which they were "naturally associated," for example pride and humility, which both took as their "objects" oneself, and hatred and love, which both took as their objects another person. But we can already see what is going to be so wrong with this familiar type of analysis. First of all, all such talk about "objects" leaves out the crucial fact that, in love at least, it is the other as a "subject" that is essential. To be in love (even unrequited) is to be looked *at*, not just to look. Thus it is the eyes, not the body (nor the soul), that present the so-called "beloved," not as object but as subject, not first as beautiful or lovable but always as (potentially) lov*ing*. It's the eyes that have it, nothing else.

One supposedly looks "into" the lover's eyes; I never could. One no more looks into them than at them, for what one sees is always their looking back at you. The eyes, only the eyes, are the organs of love. I could imagine her as pure phantom, as tall or rotund, but not without those eyes, looking at me. Or not looking. Every lover, I would suppose, has beautiful eyes, for it is only the eyes that look back at you, that refuse to allow even the most beautiful lover to become a mere "object" of love, thus refuting with a glance some of the greatest philosophers in history.

Love is not just an attitude directed toward another person; it is an emotion which, at least hopefully, is *shared with* him or her. Sometimes it is said that the very word "object" is "dehumanizing," but this is probably too strong. (In treating Einstein as "the object of study" in physics class, for instance, are we thereby "dehumanizing" him?) But what is true is that such "object"-talk, in Freud in particular, too easily underscores our tendency to think of love as admiration, need or desire-at-a-distance, like the troubadours' pathetic versifying in the direction of their inaccessible ladies in the tower (or Stendhal swooning and bursting and hardly containing himself as his lovely Italian countess strolls into the ballroom). Sometimes, perhaps, and in some emotions, "object"-talk makes perfectly good sense; sadness at the loss of one's high school class ring, or the love of one's favorite first edition. But any account of love that begins with the idea of an "object" of love is probably going to miss the main point of the emotion, namely, that it is not an emotion "about" another person so much as, in our terms, a world we share.

This suggests in turn an even more serious problem in the "object" analysis of emotion, love in particular. When Hume picks out the "object" of love, he quite naturally chooses the person one is in love *with.* But this already leaves out half of the picture. An equally essential component of the loveworld is *oneself*. Love is not just an emotion directed toward another person—like Cupid looking for someone to shoot with his arrows. We are not in love *at,* but rather *with,* another person. I am not just the person who *has* the emotion; I am also part of it. The same is true of anger; when I am angry, I am not just the person with the emotion, I am also one of its crucial ingredients. Thus the talk about "intentionality" and the "object" of love leads us to look at only half of the emotional scenario, which will inevitably result in our hopelessly misunderstanding it.

The most obvious misunderstanding is this: the Christian view of love is not alone in teaching us that love is essentially *selfless*. Proponents of romantic love have argued that too. The idea is that love is thoroughly "about" another person, so that any degree of self-love is incompatible with, or at least a detraction from, "true," that is, selfless love. But this is not only not true; it is impossible. There is no emotion without self-involvement, and no love that is not also "about" oneself. The other side is just as confused, however; La Rochefoucauld, for example, insists that "all love is self-love." But to be self-involved is not yet to be selfish, nor does self-involvement in any way exclude a total concern for the other person as well. The practical consequence of this confusion, in turn, is the readiness with which we can be made to feel guilty at the slightest suggestion that our love is not "pure" but turns on "selfish" motives, and it renders unaskable what is in fact a most intelligible question—namely, "What am I getting out of this?"—to which the answer may well be, "Not enough to make it worth while." But then, love is not just what one "gets out of it" either.

Talking about love as a world with two people avoids these problems and misunderstandings. But there is one last set of complications which has been much discussed in the "object" way of talking which deserves special mention. The idea that the "object" of my love is another person suggests too easily that love is "about" a person *simpliciter*, the whole person, nothing but and nothing less than the whole person. This is simply untrue. I love *you*, indeed, but I love you only in so far as you fit into the loveworld. That may be for any number of reasons—because I think you're beautiful, because you love me too, because I admire you in your career, because we cook fine meals together. The list might well seem endless, but it never is. I might love you for just one reason, or I might love you for a hundred and fifty reasons. But those reasons (I might always discover more) circumscribe your place in the loveworld. The person I love is, consequently, not simply *you*, the whole person, but rather you circumscribed by that set of reasons. I might say, in a moment of enthusiasm, "I love everything about you," but that's just myopia, or poor editing. Sometimes I'm surprised. I find a new virtue, that I've never seen before. But sometimes I'm disappointed too. Sometimes I manufacture new and imagined virtues, as Stendhal suggests in his theory of "crystallization"—the "discovery" of ever new virtues in one's lover. But love is never unqualified acceptance of a lover, "no matter what," however much one would like to be loved, if not to love, without qualification. But this raises sticky questions about the vicissitudes of love, not least the nature of these reasons and the possibility that, if I love you "for reasons," might I not love someone else, just as much as or instead of you, for precisely those same reasons? Or is it possible that one might not know *whom* one loves, if it is true, for example, as every teenager soon learns, that one can love "on the rebound," transferring the frustrated love of one lover immediately onto another, who becomes something of a sparring partner to keep us in shape for the more important bout to come, holding a role in a loveworld in which he or she has no real place. The identity of the "beloved," in other words, is by no means so obvious as the "object of love"-talk would make it seem. It is even possible that the "beloved," as Plato argued in a more pious way, is nothing more than a set of ideal properties, indifferent indeed to the particular person who at any given instant happens to exemplify them.

To make matters even more complicated, we might point out that similar questions arise regarding one's own identity in the loveworld. I do not love "with all my heart and all my soul," but rather (if we want to talk about hearts and souls at all) only with half a heart—but not half-heartedly—and with a fraction of a soul. I love you in so far as I am a lover, but I am only rarely *just* a lover. No matter how much I'm in love, I do not live just in the loveworld. You may be the essence of the loveworld, but you don't fit into my career or, for that matter, into the world I enter when I watch Japanese movies. I love you when I feel romantic, perhaps too when I'm just relaxed, but when I'm frustrated about my work, or absorbed in a lawsuit, the self that is so involved is not the same self that loves you. It's not that *I* don't love you, or that I love you any less; it's just that the loveworld isn't my only world, or yours either, even if we agree that it is, for us, the best of our possible worlds. To say that love is a world of two people, therefore, is not at all to say something simple, much less "obvious."

The Dimensions of the Loveworld

If an emotion is a world or, in part, a way of "seeing" the world, then certain visual metaphors become particularly useful. I call them "scope" and "focus"[1] and the camera analogy is

[1] *The Passions,* Chapter 10.

particularly apt. Scope, quite simply, is the *size* of an emotional world. Some emotions, such as cosmic dread and depression, take in the whole of the universe; others, like petty anger and embarrassment, restrict their scope to a single event or incident. Focus, on the other hand, refers to what is attended to and clearly defined, what is rendered essential *within* that world. Even an emotion whose scope is cosmic—certain kinds of resentment, for example—may have an extremely narrow and sharp focus, sometimes seizing upon a single incident as a representation of the whole. Sometimes broad scope may combine with a virtual absence of focus, in joy, for instance. Albert Camus liked to dwell on the cosmic emotions; Jean-Paul Sartre loved the detail of the petty, the narrow, the obsessive. (But then, it was Camus who was wounded by small offenses, Sartre who took on the universe.)

Now love is often talked about as a cosmic emotion; lovers are said to love everything, and they sometimes stare at the stars. But though indeed lovers have their cosmic pretensions, and may at times demonstrate a particularly tolerant mood toward the "outside" world, the scope of love is in fact famously small, limited to a strictly private world of two people only. ("I only have eyes for you," for example.) In so far as the rest of the world is included, it is merely as a stage, perhaps as an audience to our impenetrable and even belligerent privacy. Sometimes the "outside world" simply serves as an enemy—the feud of the Montagues and the Capulets threatening the loveworld of their rebellious son and daughter—which makes love all the more "romantic," because forbidden. Thus it is rightly said that love is *a*moral, all but indifferent to the problems of the world and the larger issues of morality and community. And it is wrongly, even foolishly said that love is itself the spirit of community and even the glue that holds people together. Quite the contrary, romantic love has such small scope that it cannot even *see* the larger community (which is why political radicals are more often *against* it). So much for the "love should rule the world" of Mozart's *Magic Flute*, Plato's *Symposium* (Phaedrus' speech), St. Paul, and G. W. F. Hegel in his youthful works. In love, even three is a "crowd." Indeed, love thrives on rebellion and the rejection of community expectations and mores (Romeo and Juliet, Tristan and Isolde, Paris and Helen, Faust and Gretchen, Tom Jones and Sophie—just to name a few).

Only in a society with an enormously powerful ideology of the individual, in which the "alienation" of the individual from the larger society is not only tolerated but even encouraged and celebrated, can the phenomenon of romantic love be conceivable. Romantic love is not only distinct from, it is opposed to, *agape*, the "love of humanity," and one's "proper place" in society. It is, quite literally, "a little world of its own." The scope of the loveworld, in a word, is microscopic. It is a rejection of the world at large, and privacy is its domain. It is worth noting, with that in mind, that romantic love is just beginning to blossom in mainland China, not coincidentally among the same generation of former "red guards" who are also responsible for the sudden and sometimes alarming rise in "anti-social behavior" in the larger Chinese cities.[2]

The *focus* of love in the loveworld too tends to be extremely narrow, restricted not only to a single person but, as I have argued in a preliminary way, wholly concerned with certain aspects of a person—his or her beauty, or intelligence, or those activities we enjoy together, sex and conversation, presumably, foremost among them. The scope of love always includes the two of us, but the focus of love is indeed mainly concerned with the other person, "the beloved," and thus includes much of what the "intentionality" theorists have described in their talk about the "beloved" as an "object." For example, the "beloved" is always viewed from a certain perspective, defined by the emotion itself, in which virtues are exaggerated and faults

[2] Jay Mathews, reporting in the Washington *Post*, December, 1979.

are ignored or minimized. The intentionality theorists are also fond of pointing out that the "object" of one's love might not even exist (one can still be in love with a lover who has died, for example). Indeed, the actual person might be very different from the lover's conception (thus the many tales of the killer or prostitute who finds at least brief happiness in the eyes of an unknowing and unsuspecting lover), and indeed the alleged lover might be someone else altogether (thus Shakespeare's and Oscar Wilde's delight in mistaken identities). But the point to be pursued is that the focus of love is always something less than "the whole person" and, indeed, often includes features that are more fantasy than intimate knowledge, more wishful thinking than acute perception. But this does not mean, as it is sometimes said to mean, that love is essentially an illusion, any more than photographs, because they are able to distort and exaggerate, pick out and edit out, beautify the ordinary or dramatize the trivial, ought to be dismissed as illusory. Biased, yes; false, no. Focus is a part of seeing, which is not more true the less there is of it, or any less true because it can be so extreme.

Beyond the Mystery: On the Outside Looking In

My friend Christopher, who is a very fine poet, once pointed to a flower on the table in front of us. It was slowly opening up its petals before our slightly drunken eyes, and he called it a "mystery." I could not disagree with him. Not because I did not know about turgor and transpiration and absorption and all of the other hydraulic processes which we were forced to learn about in high school biology, but because to provide an explanation for the "mystery," in those poetic circumstances, would have been simply gauche.

What seems like a mystery may be only a refusal to listen to

—or the inappropriateness of—an explanation. What is said to be "magic" may only be an unwillingness to step outside the puzzle and see what is behind the curtain or up someone's sleeve. The wonder of the loveworld—without detracting from it—might well be accounted for by taking a step back, by looking in from the outside, and by seeing where this particular world fits in with all of the others.

Inside the loveworld, poetry reigns. Mawkish metaphors are perfectly appropriate, but explanations are not. In any particular case, it is easy enough to "explain" the attraction between two people—her resemblance to the woman who dumped him last year, his being just the opposite of the husband who gave her such a hard time. It is easy enough to explain what she gives to him, and he to her, but these explanations are simply out of place within the loveworld itself. Thus (as in all anthropological excursions) we find ourselves in a curious position: as outside observers of the rules and rituals, we are in a position to explain them, to understand why they should be as they are and not some other way. But as participants in the loveworld, we have to accept these rules and rituals as they are, without question and without explanation. There is no other way to understand, except by understanding that, on the inside, one systematically refuses to understand. Thus the "mystery."

The explanation of love, in general, the account of its importance in our culture, is easy enough—from the outside. We have already discussed it in some detail. Romantic love is an emotion that provides a powerful bond between two people, possibly strangers, on the basis of a single readily available shared and complementary set of attributes which we sometimes lump together with the simplistic name "sex." One can ask, from the outside, why we do not form our primary relationships on the basis of something else, something more indicative of our interests in life or our general living patterns, perhaps the people we work with or those who share the same dining habits, read the same books, or enjoy playing the same sports. Perhaps we could, and sometimes we do. But the fact is that sex has been chosen just because it is most commonly shared and at the same time most private. It varies only slightly from person to person, thus providing a universal vehicle for intimacy which can be (almost always) assumed to be ready and waiting from the outset in anyone whatsoever. From the inside, our meeting was "fate"; from the outside, it was mere chance or convenience, one possible encounter, perhaps out of thousands.

To say that sex is "natural" is to say, ultimately, just that everyone has it—or ought to. But this in turn can be explained when we understand the function of romantic love in the culture as a whole, as a means of very quickly establishing extremely strong interpersonal bonds among people who have left their more "natural" ties in family and the community they grew up in and gone off to "find themselves." In a strange city, a new job or a different university romantic love can provide for us what no other emotion can so well provide: instant intimacy, even where there is no one whom one has ever met before. It is thus, in a society that recognizes so few other interpersonal bonds as significant, that we give romantic love such exaggerated importance. Every emotion may provide some meaning to life, but it is romantic love that provides the specific meaning we need the most: the "meaningful relationship," that sense of belonging, in a world that has made belonging an achievement rather than a presupposition.

This is the explanation for the importance of romantic love, but inside the explanation is the "mystery" of the loveworld. Inside of love we narrow our view to the tiny world of the two of us, and instead of looking at the loveworld as part of the larger culture, indeed as one of its primary institutions, we pretend that we are in love *despite* its wishes, against its intentions, an act of rebellion instead of *the* all-American and favorite European ritual. But this too has its explanation; in a society that so prizes individuality and rebelliousness, it is extremely important that social institutions, including education, the press and teenage gangs, have the appearance—at least to themselves—of anti-establishment attitudes. And love, most of all, proves its role in the larger world it chooses to ignore by manifesting in a particularly belligerent if usually harmless manner its own sense of absolute autonomy and amoral social indifference.

It would be a mistake, however, to describe and explain the loveworld just as a deficit, a gap, a need to be filled in our larger social world. The loveworld is not just compensation for families lost and communities uprooted, the desperate search on a rather frivolous sensuous basis for replacements for intimacy that have become no longer possible. The emotion of the loveworld, first of all, is a far more powerful form of intimacy, for most of us, than the intimacies we left behind. It more than fills the gap and has virtues of its own. Participation in the loveworld provides us with a sense of self-esteem and grandeur, so obvious both in the emotion and in the music that sometimes accompanies it, which cannot be reduced to mere sexual intimacy, much less in lieu of a once playful relationship with a brother or a sister as children. Grandeur and self-esteem are motives in their own right, not mere "compensations." Finally, the seeming indeterminacy of the loveworld is itself wholly a part of the ideology of our culture in general. Romantic love is *freedom.* It is the freedom *from* determination by our families, from arranged marriages and fixed community roles, but it is also freedom *to* form our ties as we choose, for reasons that need be nobody's business but our own. What rules exist for love are there to be flaunted: the prince falls in love with the commoner, and he gives up the throne rather than give up his emotional autonomy. Free emotional choice reigns over pre-established social status. The Baptist boy from Texas falls in love with a Vietnamese girl, much to the horror of his parents, and the woman who has been groomed all her life to make a match in society turns around and falls in love with a cowboy.

It looks like caprice, emotional anarchy; but this is the rule of the loveworld. The lack of rules is itself the rule, or so it seems.

The hero and heroine of the loveworld make a choice and stick with it. At least for a while. The odder the choice and the greater the obstacles, the more heroic they are. Thus Romeo and Juliet. And Tristan, Lancelot, Isolde and Guinevere. It is the inappropriateness of their love, and their willingness to fight all odds because of it, that make them our romantic heroes. But to see the tragedy of these romantic heroes as the *ideal* of the loveworld is also to miss the point, for what makes them heroes is precisely the fact that their choices stretch the limits of the loveworld. They are heroes, ultimately, in the name of freedom. But the tragic *results* of their excessive freedom, their impossible demands and, consequently, the inevitable collapse of their increasingly desperate love, are not the ideal but rather the limit of the loveworld, its outer boundary. Even freedom has its limits.[3]

Love is not merely a need, and the loveworld is not just compensation for social deprivation. Romantic love provides us with our most powerful form of intimacy, a fact only partly explained by the gap in relationships encouraged by our society, which is not at all explained by the thrills of sex alone. Romantic love provides a sense of self-worth and an aura of grandeur that must be understood in its own terms, as an emotional strategy for enriching our world. Most of all, romantic love has to be understood as an emotion that thrives on *freedom*, as an emotion built around mobility and choice, as a lack of determinacy that we sometimes choose to ignore by pretending that love is primarily a matter of fate. But the power and grandeur of love and the loveworld lie precisely in the fact that, however "lucky" in love we might happen to be, it is our freedom and our ability to choose that make this emotion so enormously important to us.

[3] Thus feminist Uta West rightly writes, "Romeo and Juliet, Antony and Cleopatra,—what did they have to do with 'meaningful relationships'?"

Still looking in from the outside, however, this indeterminacy of love has one more consequence of some significance in understanding the "mystery." Most emotions, anger for instance, have a single scenario. One can describe the structures of anger pretty much all at once, and anger is fully anger even if it only lasts for an instant. Love, however, is more of a process than a single scenario; its progress is not merely a plot but rather a complex and conflict-ridden process called a "dialectic." This means that love takes some time. (This does not mean "forever.") Love is a development, a matter of mutual creation. What is created, however, is love. It is sometimes said, often by theorists who are not themselves either creative or in love, that love and creativity go hand in hand, supporting this dubious thesis with a dozen well-chosen anecdotes about painters and poets and their passions. But the truth of the matter seems rather to be that love, though indeed creative, spends most of its energies creating itself, whether or not it also inspires further energy for creating anything else. As creativity, however, love tends to be less predictable, as well as more complex in its vicissitudes, than most other emotions. And from the inside, indeed, this indeterminacy may well seem to be a "mystery."

What Love's About: Self

What love is about—the poles of the loveworld and the goal of its development—is the creation of self. But this does not mean that love is just about oneself, any more than love is just about another. For the self that is created through love is a *shared* self, a self that is conceived and developed together. It is not only the loveworld that is indeterminate but, as part and parcel of our largely indeterminate culture, our selves are always under-determined too. Jean-Paul Sartre states this as a paradox, that we are always more than we are. Our selves are formed in the cradle of the family, soon to be confused by the welter of different roles into which we are thrown with playmates, peers and even the most rudimentary social rituals and responsibilities. And all along we find ourselves redefining ourselves in terms of other people, people with whom we identify, those whom we admire, those we despise as well as all of those more or less anonymous faces and voices that surround us every day—smiling, abusing, criticizing, congratulating and cajoling. And in that confusion of roles and rituals which in our society (not all others) tends to be without an anchor, without an "essence" according to which we could say, once and for all, "I am x," we look for a context that is small enough, manageable enough, yet powerful enough, for us to define ourselves, our "real" selves—we think wishfully—and what could be smaller or more manageable than the tiniest possible interpersonal world, namely, a world of only two people. And so, in love, we define ourselves and define each other, building on but sometimes fighting against the multitude of identities that are already established, starting with but not always ending with the images, fantasies and roles which drew us together in the first place, made us seem so compatible, even "meant for each other." Romantic love is part of our search for selfhood, and the power of the emotion, our sense of tragedy when it fails as well as its overall importance in our culture, turns largely on the fact that it comes to provide what is most crucial to us—even more than survival and the so-called "necessities" of life—namely, our selves.

All emotions are self-involved. (In *The Passions,* I even define emotional judgments in terms of this self-involvement.) In love, what is so peculiar is that the self that is created in the development of the emotion is a shared self, an *ego à deux,* whereas in most emotions the self is set up in opposition to or in isolation from other people. In romantic love, as opposed to motherly or brotherly love, for example, the self is also created virtually anew, as if "from scratch," no matter how many influences may be behind it and no matter how thoroughly this might be explained by someone outside that tiny yet seemingly all-inclusive loveworld. To understand romantic love, therefore, is to understand this peculiar creation of a shared self, and to explain the importance of this one emotion in our world is to explain, most of all, its singular success in promoting our sense of ourselves and the meaningfulness not of a mere "relationship" but of life itself.

Most if not all emotions have as a motive the enhancement of self, or what I call *the maximization of self-esteem*. Thus in describing the world of anger, even in a brief paragraph at the beginning of this chapter, I commented that anger is a spectacularly *self-righteous* emotion. Through anger, we feel good about ourselves, morally superior, even in (especially in) circumstances which would otherwise feel extremely awkward. Someone insults me; I feel embarrassed; but with a single swoop of will I turn the tables, even if only in my own mind: I get angry, and my embarrassment turns to indignation; his insult becomes a crime and I am all judge and jury, ready to do him in. Thus a bad temper may well be a strategy for continuously manipulating other people and putting them on the defensive—a trick often learned in childhood temper tantrums. Anger is one of our favorite ways of making ourselves feel superior, providing ourselves with an air of potency, maximizing our self-esteem. And we do the same, in different ways and through different scenarios, in the different worlds of jealousy, resentment, scorn and envy, even—as Freud saw so clearly—in guilt and depression.

But of all the emotional strategies for self-enhancement, none succeeds so well as love. For one thing, the inevitable opposition in anger invites a counterattack of equal self-righteousness, and competitive emotions make it highly likely that one of us, at least, will lose. But in love two selves mutually reinforce one another, rather than compete with one another, and so the self-enhancement of love, insulated from the outside by indifference, mutually supported in a reciprocal way on the inside, tends to be an extremely powerful and relatively durable emotional strategy.

Love is grand; but built into the loveworld itself is this sense of grandeur. There are, from the inside, no petty passions. We construct the world around ourselves so that our passions seem to be "everything," at least for the moment. (The problem comes when we come to believe from the outside too that "love is everything" and "the answer to all of our troubles.") But love has a special sense of grandeur, in part because of the insulated mutual congratulation built into the loveworld. (After all, it is hard to celebrate by yourself.) But the sense of elegance and grandeur is also built into the very scenario of love—as self-righteousness is built into the world of anger. Much of this, of course, is sheer fantasy, but the fantasy of grandeur is just as essential to love as the sense of justice is to anger, and in no sense does that make these emotions "false." Fantasy must be carefully distinguished from illusions. Fantasies need not be false; illusions are. Fantasies, shall we say, are enthusiastic embellishments of the truth, exaggerations or celebrations but, in any case, not self-deceptions. And it is through fantasy—making comparisons with Bogart and Bacall, sunning in the tradition of the great lovers of history, treating ourselves to a rare evening at the Plaza and dining with an extravagance that we never have before, making love to Gregorian chants instead of the top-40 radio station or drinking together our first bottle of Dom Perignon (1955), punctuated by our own clumsy love talk (which sounds like pure poetry at the time)—that we create this sense of grandeur. It is not that the emotion itself is grand; the loveworld is grand. It is part of its structure, and to play the lover *is*, in part, to follow this long tradition. There is, even in a society without an energy crisis, no romantic loveworld without a few candles.

Love and Autonomy: The "Dialectic" of Togetherness

So what is love? It is, in a phrase, an emotion through which we create for ourselves a little world—the loveworld, in which we play the roles of lovers and, quite literally, create our selves as well. Thus love is not, as so many of the great poets and philosophers have taken it to be, any degree of admiration or worship, not appreciation or even desire for beauty, much less, as Erich Fromm was fond of arguing, an "orientation of character" whose "object" is a secondary consideration. Even so-called "unrequited" love is shared love and shared identity, if only from one side and thereby woefully incomplete. Of course, occasionally an imagined identity may be far preferable to the actuality, but even when this is the case unrequited love represents at most a hint toward a process and not the process as such. Unrequited love is still love, but love in the sense that a sprout from an acorn is already an oak, no more, however beautiful.

In love we transform ourselves and one another, but the key to this emotion is the understanding that the transformation of selves is not merely reciprocal, a swap of favors like "I'll cook you dinner if you'll wash the car." The self transformed in love is a shared self, and therefore by its very nature at odds with, even contradictory to, the individual autonomous selves that each of us had before. Sometimes our new shared self may be a transformation of a self that I (perhaps we) shared before. Possibly all love is to some extent the transposition of seemingly "natural" bonds which have somehow been abandoned or destroyed, and therefore the less than novel transformation of a self that has always been shared, in one way or another. But the bonds of love are always, to some extent, "unnatural," and our shared identity is always, in some way, uncomfortable. Aristophanes' delightful allegory about the double creatures cleft in two and seeking their other halves is charming but false. Love is never so neat and tidy, antigen and antibody forming the perfect fit. The Christian concept of a couple sanctified as a "union" before God is reassuring, as if one thereby receives some special guarantee, an outside bond of sorts, which will keep two otherwise aimless souls together. But the warranty doesn't apply. What is so special about romantic love, and what makes it so peculiar to our and similar societies, is the fact that it is entirely based on the idea of individuality and freedom, and this means, first of all, that the presupposition of love is a strong sense of individual identity and autonomy which exactly contradicts the ideal of "union" and "yearning to be one" that some of our literature has celebrated so one-sidedly. And, second, the freedom that is built into the loveworld includes not just the freedom to come together but the freedom to go as well. Thus love and the loveworld are always in a state of tension, always changing, dynamic, tenuous and explosive.

Love is a *dialectic,* which means that the bond of love is not just shared identity—which is an *impossible* goal—but the taut line of opposed desires between the ideal of an eternal merger of souls and our cultivated urge to prove ourselves as free and autonomous individuals. No matter how much we're *in* love, there is always a large and non-negligible part of ourselves which is not defined by the loveworld, nor do we want it to be. To understand love is to understand this tension, this dialectic between individuality and the shared ideal. To think that love is to be found only at the ends of the spectrum—in that first enthusiastic "discovery" of a shared togetherness or at the end of the road, after a lifetime together—is to miss the loveworld almost entirely, for it is neither an initial flush of feeling nor the retrospective congratulations of old age but a struggle for unity and identity. And it is this struggle—neither the ideal of togetherness nor the contrary demand for individual autonomy and identity—that defines the dynamics of that convulsive and tenuous world we call romantic love.

12 SELF, LOVE AND SELF-LOVE

"I wanted to go out with him into the world, to announce us as a unity. We love each other, we are together. Not for the sake of showing off, but out of, well, joy. I mean, it's as though you have a new identity; you're Mira and you're Mira and Ben. You want the world to recognize both. . . . But then of course you—well women, anyway—lose the other one, the private one. Men don't seem to, quite as much. I don't know why."

MARILYN FRENCH, *The Women's Room*, p. 471

"All love is self-love," wrote La Rochefoucauld.

Well, no, but love is essentially about oneself. What makes this familiar proverb unacceptable is the inevitable implication that love is *just* self-love, to the exclusion of the other person, the person purportedly loved. And this of course is nonsense. What makes love love is the *kind* of self that is loved, and that is a *shared self*, a self defined with, in and through a particular other person.

All emotions are about oneself, in the sense that they involve casting oneself into a role, in a specific emotional world. Sometimes that role may be secondary, or even infinitesimal, as in Iago's envy or Kierkegaard's humble but passionate religious faith, respectively. But whereas most emotions define the self in juxtaposition or opposition to other people (for example, the antagonism of anger, the hostility of resentment), love involves a mutual, as well as reciprocal, definition of selves. As I boost my image of you I boost my image of myself, through your eyes, and vice versa. In fact a somewhat Laingian if not overly "knotty" characterization of the dynamics of love, which might be found even in the dialectical vicissitudes of a first date, might look something like this: I feel good about myself because I'm with you. And part of the reason I feel good about myself because I'm with you is because you obviously feel good about me, in part because you feel good about yourself when you're with me. And that's no doubt in part because you see that I feel good about myself and good about you when I see that you feel good about yourself and good about me when I'm with you. And so on. But this should not be interpreted merely as mutual "feedback" of approval and admiration so much as the dialectical development of something quite different, the alteration of self through this process and the creation of a new conception of self in which the most crucial single determinant is the other person and his or her virtues and opinions, including those that I merely imagine or fantasize as well as those which he or she fantasizes and shares with me.

Even in this simple sketch, it should be clear why the process of love tends to be so explosive, makes us feel so vulnerable, and fills us with such joy and terror. Romantic love, even after a long and earnest search for love, involves nothing less than a change of self, and suddenly we find ourselves precariously dependent upon one another, exhilarated by our discovery but inevitably terrified as well. It is an inherently unstable situation, halfway between two identities, and we are no longer assured of either. We see what we would become, and we have our doubts. We look back at what we were, if only by way of contrast, and the differences overwhelm us, even if the only difference is the source of the identity itself.

The exhilaration of love is to be found in this sense of discovery and creation, and in love's tensions and insecurities too. Those who see love simply as a "union" misdescribe the emotion and lead us to expect a lifetime of calm satisfaction punctuated by joy and sometimes tragedy. In fact love is a struggle, albeit sometimes a delightful and always essential struggle, for mutual self-identity and a sense of independence at the same time. Lovers' battles are not gaps in love but part of its process, and indeed, love may be strongest between individuals who are themselves most vehemently individualistic and autonomous, in whom the struggle rages most violently. Conversely, love may be weakest in those who think they "need" it most, just because, so willing to "give themselves" to love, they may well have little self to give in the first place.

The idea that love is a shared self requires the rejection of a number of ideas that are far too impotent to characterize this often powerful emotion. For example, it is quite often said that love requires *compromise*, and of course living together or doing almost anything with another person does require compromises of all kinds. But in so far as one makes a compromise, one still holds one's self *in opposition* to another self, and this then is less than love. You can compromise with someone you love, but love itself isn't a compromise.

It is often said that to love is to give in to another person's needs, indeed, to make them more important than one's own. But to love is rather to take the other's desires and needs *as* one's own. This is much more than a merely grammatical point. It is a redefinition of the self itself, as a shared self, as a self in which my personal desires no longer command a distinctive voice. (Of course a shared self, like an individual self, might be inconsistent or schizoid.)

It is said that lovers want to be together, which is true, of course, but we should rather say that lovers want to *be* together, with that peculiar emphasis that has meaning only in metaphysical matters. For at least part of the answer to that strange question "What do you want when you want someone?" is "To become essential to that someone, to be everything for him," as Jean-Paul Sartre rightly puts it, indeed to *be* him, or her, a single unity without further thought of the possibility of separation or the conflict that could divide us. Even if, as we have argued, to be is only to *become,* and never in fact to *be* at all.

Shared Selves

This creation of a shared self is sometimes described in an overly mystical manner, as if common sense cannot fathom the synthesis of a single identity out of two atomistic and autonomous human beings. The assumption here is one of the metaphors we discussed in Chapter 2, which I called "the ontology of loneliness"—the idea that each of us is born into the world alone, an atom floating around in a hostile social universe, looking for companionship and protection. Given such a view of the self as an isolated monad, the concept of shared identity is indeed strange. But in fact there is nothing mystical about shared selfhood, self-identity conceived through identification with another person, or group, or institution. Being on a team with "team spirit," for example, is a sharing of one's self, at least for a few hours, perhaps for the season. One identifies with a dozen or so others *as* a member of such-and-such a team, in which the peculiarities of one's character are submerged or ignored altogether in favor of a group identity (as winners, losers, having a good defense or the worst coach in the league). Mutual recognition is the paradigm, but not necessary. (A "fan" of the team, for example, may, unbeknownst to the team, wholly identify with it.) But this simple example also underscores a very different point about shared selves—namely, that, although individual identity may become of minimal significance, this does not mean that individual differences are submerged. One's *position* on the team, for example, now becomes the most important single feature about oneself, which is, on the one hand, still an identification wholly in terms of the team, but nonetheless an identity that may be had by just one person.

In much the same way, in love one may come to identify oneself wholly in terms of the relationship, but it does not follow that individual roles and differences are submerged, or that opposing or conflicting roles might not be just as essential to the love as shared interests and agreed-upon opinions. Much of what women rightly fear as "loss of identity" in a relationship is not so much the fact that one does indeed take on a new identity as the fact that women, in particular, are often forced to *conform to* their male lovers. They are encouraged not to form a shared new identity but rather to become mere reflections, to accept roles that are strictly subservient, to accept as their own *his* old identity. But forming a shared identity is no more self-sacrifice than it is compromise or "giving in"; it is coming to accept a view of one's individual self as defined in and through the other person. This does not mean that one person becomes like the other, but rather that they define their differences—as well as their significant similarities—together.

Creating Your Self (Through Love)

> "I don't make the rules."
> "Sure you do, we all do."
> GARSON KANIN and RUTH GORDON,
> *Adam's Rib*

What we call "self" is a creation, the creation of a certain kind of culture and, ultimately, a concoction made up out of grammar. We refer to ourselves as a matter of syntactic necessity and come to suppose that we must be referring to some specific and concrete entity, our selves. Furthermore, we distinguish between our selves as we appear and our selves as we "really are," thus pushing the self below the surface into the depths, protecting it from too easy first impressions but also rendering it mysterious and inaccessible. Thus our entire psychological literature has grown up around the "depth" metaphor, the assumption that our "real selves" are down there below the surface: the immutable soul, the good intention, "depth of character" and, with a Freudian Jekyll and Hyde twist, the world of suppressed desires and wishes. A character like Jean-Jacques Rousseau could defend in his *Confessions* the goodness of his "inner soul" despite the fact that everything about him was mean-spirited, selfish and paranoid. Thus we too have the idea that our "real selves" are not necessarily, or even likely to be, what most people might believe us to be.

There are cultures with no conception of "self" in our sense at all. The German philosopher Hegel, in the early nineteenth century, insisted that the only real self is the One Self (which he called "Spirit") shared by all of us. In most cultures, what we call the self is a well-prescribed set of social roles and expectations, determined to a large extent from the circumstances of birth (boy or girl, first or second, where and when, social status, wealth, health) and fully determined by young adulthood—or what we call adolescence. In our culture, however, the most important single observation on selfhood in general—over and above our belief in a "real self" below the surface and hidden from public view—is the *indeterminacy* of self, the fact that not only is the self not fully determined by the time one is a young adult, when the question of self-identity is commonly most painful, but that it is *never* fully formed, always an open question and always open to change. Perhaps the most dramatic single example of that open-endedness is to be found in the standard Christian-Faustian story of the moment-before-death conversion, the salvation-transformation of self or "soul" even after a lifetime of sin and wrongdoing. But the idea of indeterminacy of self permeates our view of ourselves in a thousand less dramatic moments, in everything from our notion of "will power" to our conception of romantic love as the emotion "that will change your life." Without our belief in the indeterminacy of the self, there would be no such emotion as romantic love. But without our enthusiasm for romantic love, our conception of self would not be the same either.

What determines the self? This is one of the perennial disputes among philosophers and psychoanalysts, but certain ingredients are obvious: the simple facts about us (age, race, social status, skills, family) and the way we learn to think about ourselves. The two are often at odds, however, as the existentialists have pointed out so dramatically, since the way we think of ourselves in this society typically includes the denial, rejection or intention to overcome at least some of those seemingly "given" facts about our selves. I may be Jewish, but I hide that fact. I may be crippled, but I refuse to be treated any differently from anyone else. I may be a coward, but I intend to become a hero. We could argue about how effective such thinking and resolutions can be, but that is not our concern here. What is our concern, however, is the way in which romantic love fits so dramatically into this picture, for whether or not we can, as individuals, easily resolve to change our selves, it is clear that, with the support of a single other person, even against the whole of society and with all of the facts against us, such changes seem to be commonplace.

What is sometimes left out of the existentialist argument about the importance of self-determination—the determination of self even in the face of facts to the contrary—is a full appreciation of the extent to which our conceptions of self—and thus the self itself—are formed in and with other people, through interpersonal discourse and intercourse, in mutual roles and expectations. For Martin Heidegger, the German existentialist, for example, the self is originally formed through identification with the anonymous "they" of society in general, but his whole early philosophy is worked around the suggestion that this self is "inauthentic," and that the true or "authentic" self must be asserted by breaking away from this "they-self" and becoming truly "one's own." But what is missing in this pseudo-heroic picture of the individual against the whole mass of society is the importance of those small and specific interactions through which we define our selves which are not merely infusions of society (the "they") as a whole but very particular and very much voluntary interactions between friends, family and lovers, as well as colleagues and acquaintances. For our purposes here, we need not worry about the general determination of self by society (or what most of my eighteen-year-old students call "being conditioned" or "brainwashed") or about the extent to which change of self through self-manipulation ("pulling your own strings") is possible. But much of the determination of self—a process which is never completed—is to be located in our specific interpersonal relationships, not just what I think of myself but what *you* think of me, and what I think of the way you think of me, and what you think of the way I think of you, and so on.

Romantic love, as an emotion of shared self, must be understood in just these terms, as shared determination of self. And in a society that presents us daily with a dozen different determinations of self, many of them unflattering if not embarrassing, most of them beyond our control, romantic love becomes our way of choosing the self that we want, through mutual agreement with a single person who shares our most treasured self-images, which we can then define as "my real self," even against the consensus of all the facts and the opinions of all the world, as well as against our own uncertainties. ("If only I could get just one person to believe me, just one.")

Thus convicted felons and dastardly types can be defended by their wives or husbands or lovers with the plea, "If you only knew how he/she really is"—and we tend to believe them. And when we find it hard to believe that this so-called "real self" could be so different from all appearances, even then we are willing to give love the benefit of the doubt. "I don't know what she sees in him," is our skeptical way of acknowledging that the real self may be so hidden from view that no one but a lover has ever been able to see its virtues.

Roles

> Jackie refused to greet relatives on inauguration day, preferring the entire nation on TV rather than her family. To the nation, she was the first lady, to the Bouviers, just Jackie. To please both roles required an impossible shift of emotional gear.
>
> KITTY KELLEY, *Jackie Oh!*, p. 117

Being a lover—in other words, loving—is playing certain kinds of roles, not just for others but (primarily) for oneself. We sometimes think of the lover as a very narrowly defined, primarily male role, played by a special type of character (Don Juan or Flaubert's Rudolphe) and inimitable by virtually everyone else. But in fact playing the lover is not a single role but an extremely diverse set of *complementary* roles—that is, roles that one can never play by one's self but always with a partner (or several partners, though one doesn't have to be a Don Juan to be a "lover"). Playing the lover is a role that is open to virtually anyone (like being a coward, a "bastard" or a cheapskate). Anyone who is in love plays the lover, whether well or badly, and to understand what it is to love is largely to understand what it is to play this certain kind of role—or rather, certain kinds of complementary roles.

We sometimes think of roles as merely superficial, external impositions and impersonal slots that people fill despite themselves, in which the real self doesn't count at all. But though this may be true of bureaucrats (whose public role is defined by their impersonality and anonymity) it is not true of most roles—our roles as poets, bullies or saints, for example, or, most importantly, as lovers. We think of ourselves as *playing* a role, as if playing a game; but roles need not be frivolous or merely entertaining. They may be deadly serious. And roles need not be superficial; some of our roles define our selves, even our "real" selves. Sometimes we protest that we are "only playing a role." But just as often we may be playing the role of the person who is only playing a role, a role which in fact is central to self-determination and our self-image. This ploy is of no small importance in romantic love, where the dualism of selfhood allows easy shift of blame (as in any team effort in which individual efforts and errors are not easily discernible). But people choose their lovers as they choose themselves (since they choose the one through the other), and so one can choose a self even while complaining about it bitterly and blaming it on the other person, or on love itself. A person chooses to be a martyr and picks a lover who is certain to be oppressive, and then complains, self-righteously and full of self-pity, about the oppression. A person seeks an excuse to avoid responsibility, or to escape the tensions of a flagging career, or to flee the uncertainties of single life, and chooses a lover accordingly, then complains about it. In such cases one defines one's self both by playing the role and at the same time playing the role of just playing the role. But the self is not the face behind the various masks we wear; it is the wearing of the masks. And it is in love, we like to think, that the "real self" is to be defined. Thus some of our masks and roles—the ones we play in love—have been made into trump cards, the way we "really are," regardless of the strength or the suits of the others. To reject these roles as unreal is almost always to stop loving as well.

The roles that are played in love are distinguished by the fact that they are *personal* roles and essentially *private* (even in a melodramatic couple that enjoys playing out their affairs in public). Only in certain societies, however, are personal or private roles even possible, or, at least, distinguishable from public or social roles, and it is perhaps only in our peculiar culture that we insist on defining one's "real self" in terms of only personal and not public roles. Romantic love has utterly nothing to do with, and no concern for, social roles, a fact which is obvious in our literature, as princes fall in love with showgirls and empresses take as lovers their gardeners or mad monks from Siberia. Indeed, it is the separation of personal from public roles that makes romantic love even conceivable, and it is for this reason that the love among the ancient Greeks is sometimes denied to be romantic—since the distinction between the private self and the public self would have been incomprehensible to them—and it is for this reason too that the origins of romantic love are often located in the twelfth century in Europe, when this distinction first began to enter the social world.

Romantic love is strictly personal in that its roles are defined entirely in face-to-face confrontation, with a particular person (occasionally, persons). The fulfillment or failure of these romantic roles lies entirely within the domain and judgment of the persons involved, *and no one else*. Public or social roles, on the other hand, are entirely defined in their fulfillment or failure by "objective" standards, which means that what any particular individual thinks about them is of no relevance whatsoever. To fill the role of "the most powerful man in America" means to satisfy the entirely objective standards of power, no matter what delusions of importance one might have oneself and share with a small circle of friends. But to be "a wonderful lover," within the context of a particular sexual relationship, requires satisfying only one person, in addition to oneself, of course.

The question of satisfaction, however, has to do with fulfillment and failure, not with the definition of the roles themselves. Indeed, it would be hard to think of a role, or the general conditions for its fulfillment, which was not learned from society at large—from movies, stories and the examples of others. And of course it is possible at any time for public measurements to intrude and destroy what is a perfectly satisfactory set of personal roles, for example, when the sexologists repeatedly tell couples what they *ought* to do and enjoy, when psychiatrists in popular magazines portray a single standard of "true" love without any concern for personal differences, or when feminists impose the "objective" criterion of an "equal" relationship, which may make no concessions whatever to the personal feelings—whatever their origins—of the men and women who are so engaged. But the distinction between personal and public roles is, for us, all-important. Indeed we cannot imagine our lives or our conceptions of ourselves, much the phenomenon of romantic love, without it.

Personal Roles

The Danish philosopher Kierkegaard commented that it must always appear absurd to a third party, when two awkward lovers play the parts of love. But of course this is just the point; such personal roles as the role of the lover are not intended for anyone else. Indeed, the public role of the lover—the Valentino image, for instance—is quite rightly suspected of indicating the very opposite of love. A couple kissing and cooing or making love are playing a part only for themselves, and questions about how "well" they do it, from some outside point of view, are completely irrelevant. To love is to play the lovers, just for one another, not only in gestures of tenderness and sexual excitement, but in a thousand other roles and mutual activities as well, which together define the shared self that emerges in love.

A simple example of a personal role which has no obvious connection with sex or love but yet is one of love's common products is this: every couple I know includes one person who is "the sloppy one" and the other as "the neat one." In fact, they might both be terrible slobs, or terribly neat, by any reasonable "objective" standards. There may have been no difference in their habits whatsoever before they started living together, and in another relationship they may have had just the opposite roles. But somehow, early on, the difference is defined, the roles are cast, and each person plays into them, the sloppy person even taking some pride in sloppiness, the neat one taking pleasure in his or her remarkable toleration—or enjoying the continuous opportunity for criticism. And indeed one *is* sloppy, the other neat, and it does not matter at all what anyone outside of the relationship might think. What we call intimacy is built out of such seemingly unromantic, even conflicting roles.

Talking baby talk (which babies rarely do, and then in imitation of adults) is the playing of intimacy roles; so is doing what in public (or if overseen or heard) would be making a fool of oneself. The powerful executive goo-goos his or her lover, but quite the contrary of foolishness, the person who refuses to indulge in such play in private is more likely to be considered an emotional coward than a fool. The viability of such childish roles is often in contrast to the power one has in the public world; a successful man or woman might feel wholly free to regress to infancy in love, while a man or woman unsure of his or her status may be much more hesitant to play the same role. Couples fighting are as often as not playing roles, rather than trying to settle a point. Mindless conversations are badly understood as a pathetic exchange of information; they are role-playing too. The couples in which one person is responsible and the other not, in which one person is mechanically gifted, the other incompetent, the one socially adventurous, the other shy, may all be, like the sloppy-and-neat couple, playing roles, in which neither the real differences between them—or their similarities—make any difference.

It is a popular question among adolescents and some college professors: "Do we tend to fall in love with people like—or unlike—ourselves?" On the one side, we envision "Joe Fratrat" and "Mary Sorority," dressed like two beans in a pot in their matching red Izod shirts and Calvin Klein jeans; on the other,

Lady Chatterley and her lover, as opposite as one can imagine. But the question, like most simpleminded questions about love, fails to appreciate the complexity of the emotion in the too-familiar attempt to reduce it all to a simple one-dimensional model—in this case, the attraction and repulsion of likes and opposites. But love depends on both differences and similarities, mutually defined; love is itself the creation of similarities and differences, for that is how we define our selves. Indeed, to confuse the shared identity of love with mere similarity is a guaranteed way not to love at all.

"I had a date with my clone, but it didn't work out."

—*True Confessions* (May, 2081)

WHY DO I LOVE YOU? 13

KIP: *Mrs. Bonner, I love you. I love lots of girls and women and ladies and so on—but you're the only one I know why I love. And you know why?*

AMANDA: *What?*

KIP: *Because you live right across the hall. You are mighty attractive in every single way, Mrs. Bonner—but I would probably love anybody just so long as they lived across the hall. It's so convenient! Is there anything worse than that awful taking girls home and that long trip back alone?*

GARSON KANIN and RUTH GORDON, *Adam's Rib*

Why do I love you? What is it about you—your eyes, your hair, your smile? No, that can't be it. The fact that you make me happy? The way we have fun together? Sex together? Oh, I don't know—I just love you, that's all. I love *all* of you, nothing less.

But that's not true. Do you love all of me? The fact that I'm always five minutes late to everything? What about my athlete's foot? (After twenty-nine years, it certainly deserves to be considered a part of me.) You've always said that you'd leave in an instant if I were ever to strike you, and you'd certainly stop loving me too. It's not true that you love all of me, and it's not true that you love me "no matter what." Suppose I were to turn into a frog. Not a handsome prince turned into a frog, and not me temporarily a frog, but just a frog, and a frog forever. Would you still love me? Of course not. Granted you might give me a certain priority over the other frogs, at least for a while. And you might not eat frogs' legs again. But soon I'd be just one of the frogs to you, and there isn't much question about whether you'd still love me.

Now perhaps it's an accident of grammar, but the person you love is *me,* referred to by a simple pronoun, a single name. But this leaves entirely open the question of what or whom it is that you love. I love *you,* you know, but I don't love all of you either. Your jogging leaves me cold, and your addiction to okra repulses me. I don't love you "no matter what," much less "forever." I wouldn't love you if you turned into a frog. Indeed, I probably wouldn't love you if you got irreversibly fat. I don't love everything about you. In fact, most of the facts about you are a matter of indifference to me, not ways or reasons I love you at all. Of course, there is a sense in which I *accept* everything about you, including all the things that annoy me, the habits we fight about, the flaws I'd rather ignore, but that's a matter of ontological necessity, not love. It just happens that the things I don't like and don't care about are attached to the same person whom I do love and care about.

Does this mean that I don't love *you?* It does not. It only means that I love you—as you love me—*for reasons.* Some of these may never be stated as such. Some of them are "superficial." Some of them are sufficiently complex that it is unlikely we could ever state them. But nevertheless they are the reasons I love you, and the reasons you love me, and they define the conditions and the limits of our love.

Love and Beauty

> He kept telling her she had a "terrific body," one of several things she despised him for.
>
> TOM WOLFE, "The Independent Woman" (*Esquire* 1979)

One of the reasons I love you is that I think you are beautiful. It is not the only reason I love you, I hasten to add, but it is, I think, one of the most important. Does this mean that I would not be in love with you if you weren't so beautiful? Possibly. Perhaps probably. Of course I love you for many other reasons too. But then again, it would depend on just how much less beautiful you had become. (You couldn't turn into a frog, for example.) But my saying this jars our sensibilities. Love is not supposed to be conditional, and, in particular, it is not supposed to be conditional on such a temporary advantage as beauty. Why not?

Beauty, we are told, is only skin deep. It is "superficial," which is why it is not supposed to be a valid reason for loving someone. But of course it is a reason, and in the history of love almost everyone from Plato to the present has recognized the essential linkage between love and personal beauty, albeit often in the spiritualized version of "a beautiful soul." But the only picture we have of the human soul, wrote the philosopher Ludwig Wittgenstein, is the human body, and even Socrates argued, not without ulterior motives, that those who deserved the best education were also those who displayed the most beautiful bodies. (Not exactly the principle espoused by the National Education Association in this country.) Like it or not, we always end up coming back to the body, including, of course, the face. So what is the objection, to be found in Plato, then in St. Paul and so on in a hundred generations of "spiritual leaders," to beauty, albeit "superficial," as a reason for love—indeed, even as *the* reason for love?

The objection begins with a fear, first of all, among those who lack beauty and attractiveness that they will be less lovable and less loved. In the absence of other reasons, they are right. There has always been, and always will be, resentment of the beautiful, and the wishful ideal that love will see "deeper" than that. But the fear infects those who are unquestionably beautiful as well. "What will happen when I lose my beauty?" It is a reasonable question, and the answer, again in the absence of other, more durable reasons, is that one will no doubt lose one's love as well. But the objection to beauty as the reason for loving goes "deeper" than fear, indeed involves the "depth" metaphor itself which is so much a part of our psychology. Beautiful people do not want to be loved because they are beautiful. We have this sense that beauty is not a legitimate reason for love; it is too ephemeral, too "superficial." We imagine that beneath that obvious façade there must lie some deep reason for loving a person, namely, the soul, to which all of the trappings of beauty as well as intelligence, success, power and fame are mere vanities. Or, in more modern and less theological language, it is the "real" person, the "whole human being" that one comes to love, not for any single reason, much less a reason so impersonal and "superficial" as beauty.

The metaphysical move is simple, almost so quick as to be indiscernible, from the quite reasonable claim that one should not or cannot love a person simply for the reason that he or she is beautiful, to the metaphysically vacuous claims that one loves the inner soul or the total person. The idea that one loves a soul, "no matter what" the more superficial changes and blemishes, or loves "the total person," in which any particular reason is submerged in the whole, is the same familiar Platonic strategy of denying ourselves and pretending, instead, that in love, at least, we are safe from the ravages of time and the world. But it is not just beauty that is so dismissed as a reason for love; *all* reasons are rejected as irrelevant. It is not just the fear of losing that initial attractiveness which made one loved in the first place; it is an avoidance of being compared or evaluated in any way as if, in love, stupidity and lack of consideration, slovenliness and lazy self-indulgence all will be tolerated without question. We imagine love is eternal because we don't want to recognize that it is always conditional; we reject beauty as a reason for loving someone because beauty is so obviously but a temporary condition, and so a striking representative of all conditions. But the fact is, quite simply, I love you because you are beautiful—if for a thousand other reasons too—and to deny that or hide it under the metaphysical confusion of "a beautiful soul" is just not to understand what our love is all about. I love you for reasons, and though those reasons may change and new ones will no doubt emerge, those reasons set the conditions of love and its limits.

The objection to "reasons for" loving is in fact aimed against certain kinds of reasons, those that are, because most tangible, also the easiest to identify. The idea that a person might be loved "for money" horrifies us even more than love for beauty. The idea that a reason for loving someone might be mere convenience horrifies us even more than that. Loving someone for his or her intelligence seems not to be so despicable, but here perhaps we should object, "Why not?" Is intelligence any less superficial than beauty? Any more definitive of "the real person"? Are the public poses in the *New York Review of Books* any less calculated, any less obscene, than the poses in *Playboy?* What about loving a person for his sense of humor? Or her tough-minded way of asking questions? Or his skill at whipping up a batch of Chinese dumplings? Or her ability to fix the T.V. set? Why should these not be reasons for loving? They often are. But once one adds up the possibly large (but by no means infinite) number of such equally "superficial" reasons, need there be anything left over or left out for which we have to introduce the idea of the soul or "the total person"? Indeed, to insist upon either notion (the minimal self or the total self) is to obscure and ultimately to deny precisely what reasons one has for loving, and, as always, to make love itself—as well as love's demise—a "mystery."

Love for Reasons

Money can't buy love, but it improves your bargaining position.

LAURENCE J. PETER

What can count as a reason for loving someone? Could the fact that you were born on December 2 be a reason for loving you? Certainly those who write the astrology columns believe that it is. Could the fact that you are the third richest woman in America be a reason for loving you? Most people would say no, but they would probably point out too that it is a fact one should not let stand in one's way. Is your fame, your glamor, your success a reason for loving you? Well, at least it is obvious that these might well be reasons for being attracted to you in the first place, and it would be strange, to say the least, if they then were to drop out of the picture as if, once we are together, I love only your soul.

Loving a person for reasons, speaking phenomenologically, is to see that person from a certain perspective, within a certain kind of context. One might fall in love with a stranger in Rome whom one would not think of entertaining at home, and lovers who have lived together too long in the daily tedium of everyday rituals find that the passion they used to enjoy together is quickly rekindled as soon as they go on vacation or re-create the conditions of their original courtship. An exemplary if overly amusing case of a change in perspective is that of the male gynecologist who falls in love with one of his patients. There is an obvious sense in which he sees his lover in quite a different perspective from the way he saw his patient, although on rare occasions he may revert back to the former way. So too one rarely loves one's lover all the time; rather, love is an emotion which is more or less confined to certain situations, perhaps spilling over in expression or habit to a dozen other situations as well, but nevertheless quite distinct from them. While we're balancing the checkbook, one of us looks up and interrupts this compulsively practical activity by saying, "I love you." But balancing the checkbook together is not (usually) a reason for loving. Neither are living together, having children and making love necessarily reasons for loving, but needless to say they are usually very good if not overwhelming reasons for loving, and the fact that one loves, in its turn, may be a good reason for any of them.

It is hard (but not impossible) to imagine a circumstance in which a reason for loving a person would be the fact that he or she weighs exactly fifty kilograms, about the same as a very large sack of potatoes. (What would it mean to say, "I love the way you accelerate when you fall?") To describe a person as a biological organism, as a doctor does in diagnosis, is hardly a perspective in which love finds its reasons. ("I love the way the blood flows through your capillaries.") And this is true no matter what part of the body is being described, as long as it is mere biology. The way a penis or clitoris works might indeed be fascinating, and the fact that it works may indeed be a precondition if not a reason for some relationships. But it is hardly a standard example of a reason for love—which is not to deny that love has its biological preconditions.

Where the question of reasons becomes most difficult is that arena which is, on the one hand, typically public, social and even impersonal but nevertheless provides the most common reasons for one person's attraction to another. But attraction is not yet love, and reasons for attraction are not necessarily reasons for love. One might be initially attracted to a person because he or she is one of the great young violinists of the age. Or because he or she is particularly "attractive," that is, beautiful. Or because he or she is remarkably wealthy. When are they reasons for loving and when are they not?

Let us take the most difficult example—loving a person for his or her money. And to make it a more difficult, but purer case, let us even say that he or she is loved *just* for the money—

that is, if the money is lost, so for certain will be the love (allowing for a short period of courtesy of perhaps a week or so). But even this leaves open an essentially ambiguous set of alternatives. It is one thing to love *the money* (which means that, if one could take the money and run, one would do so). It is something else again to love the person because-of-the-money. Suppose a woman loves a man because-he-has-money. She has no desire for the money alone (perhaps she would not know what to do with it). She enjoys spending the money, but mainly *with him;* indeed, it is the one thing they like best doing together. We have postulated that she has no other reasons for loving him, but we should probably suppose, without rendering her a particularly disagreeable if not unbelievable character, that she finds him at least tolerable if not likable, perhaps even charming, attractive and pleasant to be with. But it is the money that draws them together, the money that keeps them together—the money that provides the network of shared activities and identity that constitutes their love. Is this possible? Can love be based on so "vulgar" a reason? Why not? The fact that he has money is no longer merely a matter of social impersonal fact but has been made very personal, now in the sense that it is the vehicle that they share, the way in which they value one another, the way in which they define themselves. And indeed, if this is not a love that we would bear ourselves, why do we insist on condemning it in others as a matter of moral principle, instead of personal taste?

We can add even more to the illustration by supposing that the man quite rightly sees himself as a person with no particularly lovable features; he is physically unattractive, intellectually clumsy, not particularly fun to be with except while shopping; he has no sense of humor to speak of and little of what can be called "style" except what money can buy. And so he identifies with his having money. It is not just the way she sees him; it is the way he sees himself, whether or not he would prefer to have other virtues as well. The fact is, he does not, and he knows it. And the reason he worked so hard for his money, he would be the first to admit, was in order to provide himself with a reason to be loved. And he did. And she loves him for precisely that reason. It is not for his soul, much less "the total person." It is not, the economy being as it is, "forever." But why should we say that it is not love, or that they have no reason for love? So long as those reasons are part of the person, defined in tandem with a lover who shares and mutually helps to define that identity, they are reasons for love. Just as much as, and not so different from, such respectable reasons as "being a good husband."

We play a dangerous game with such reasons. We depict the man or woman who is loved for money as the inevitable victim, as if to assure ourselves that love for us is something much better. We go out of our way to make our love deities as superficial, as one-dimensional and as unhappy as could possibly be believed, as if to assure us all that true love and happiness are best reserved for us modest folk, "for ourselves" and nothing less. Indeed, the conclusion of some of our myths—though rarely stated as such—is that true love is more likely to be found in the poorest and plainest, and for no "reasons" at all.

Suppose a male fetishist loves a woman because she has beautiful feet. (They met, of course, while he was working as a salesman in a shoe store.) Does he love her? That is, does he love *her?* Well, in this case, presumably, he does not have the option of running off with her feet. Nevertheless, we can make the distinction between his merely loving the feet and loving them because they are *her* feet, which means loving her. And this is true even if he *only* loves her for her feet. A truncated example of love, perhaps, but love all the same. If the example seems farfetched and a bit too perverse, I am sure the reader can with the same logic imagine several more standard parts of the body which serve as physical reasons for love. (Recent studies indicate that this is more true of men, who are "turned on" by particular parts of a woman, whereas women tend to be less physical in their reasons. This does not mean that women love "more" than men, however, but only that, as a flawed generalization, they love for different reasons.)

Why introduce a foot fetishist and a gold-digger in a discussion of love? My aim here is not to defend the equal validity of all reasons, much less to celebrate these curiously truncated, fetishistic and one-dimensional cases of love. What I do want to say is that love can still be love for whatever the reasons, and whether a reason is a *good* reason depends and ought to depend not so much on general moralizing as on shared interpersonal identities. If a person prides him- or herself on being beautiful, and perhaps nothing else, then that of course is a good reason for love; if a person truly believes that beauty is vanity and that self-identity lies in loftier characteristics, then his or her being beautiful is a very bad reason for love. Unfortunately, we are not usually so straightforward. A woman who is not particularly beautiful rejects beauty as a valid reason for love out of resentment and envy, but still wishes she were beautiful; someone falls in love with her because he thinks she is beautiful, and the result is, we all know, a confusion of identities. Intelligence is supposed to be a much better reason for loving someone, but again, whether this counts as a *good* reason or not will depend not only on whether it is true that the person is intelligent, but on how that intelligence fits into the overall scheme of shared self-identifications.

In unrequited love, however, one can love a person for any reason whatsoever, unrestrained by considerations of reciprocity and actually shared identities. Thus it is that unrequited love may well for a while provide fantasies and imagined satisfactions hard to find in the rough-and-tumble exchange of real relationships. But this is also to say that the less one feels constrained by the other person's self-identity and the freer one feels to indulge in his or her own reasons and remain indifferent to the lover, the less this deserves to be called love. No matter what the reasons. Because, ultimately, the reasons for love are of a very different kind—not facts about the person but aspects of the relationship itself.

The Reasons for Love

Beauty, fame, wealth, breasts, glamor, feet, even convenience can be reasons for love, as well as a hundred even more trivial and unremarkable advantages, comforts and petty virtues. Nevertheless, it is an exceptional instance of love which is no more than this, for not only are there a great many different reasons why most of us love, there are also different kinds of reasons. In addition to the above, there are also reasons that have more to do with a person's *personality*—the very word shows them to be pre-eminently personal. Indeed, even if one loves for beauty or wealth or whatever, it is difficult to imagine love that does not also have as its reasons a sense of humor, that certain playfulness, the hunger for affection, delight in giving, kindness, charm, a sense of honesty, generosity, toughness, meekness, a sense of strength, insecurity, self-sufficiency, childishness, zaniness, efficiency, brutality, hostility. All of these can be and often are (in different people and in various proportions) reasons for love. But the point to be made, again and again, is that almost all of these personality traits are not simply given but *defined within* the relationship. One person's humor is another's bad taste; what is playful in one relationship is teasing or hostile in another; what one man finds honest another considers indiscreet, and what one woman considers affection another finds weak and offensive. Thus the reasons for love that make up the complex network of most relationships are personal not just in the sense that they are part of one's "personality" but more importantly in that they are largely defined within the relationship itself. Indeed, some of the most important and compelling reasons for love may be aspects of character which are not generally considered part of a personality at all. A man who is universally considered to be brutal may find one woman who considers him, and makes him, gentle. A woman who is considered meek may find one man who thinks her, and makes her, aggressive.

But this set of reasons leads us to another set, even more important but even more difficult to articulate as reasons. They are the complex reciprocal roles and reflections on roles that we call *intimacy*. One might say that intimacy is itself a reason for love (if not also that intimacy *is* love, which is false) except that intimacy is rather a network of reasons and roles, shared attitudes and activities, ways of "fitting" together that, because they are entirely reciprocal and evident only when we're together, may escape our attention as reasons altogether. Indeed, reasons generally become apparent to us *as reasons* only when we back up a step or two and look at them from a distance. Thus, after several years together, I may in one sense forget how beautiful you are, which does not mean that I do not still *see* you *as* beautiful, or that your beauty isn't still a dominant reason for my loving you, but I have ceased to realize—what once was so obvious to me—that your beauty is a reason for my loving you. Lovers after a long time together may even become embarrassed by the very virtues that originally formed (perhaps still do) their reasons for loving—a woman is mortified by her husband's raucous sense of humor, a man is angered by his wife's assertiveness. And even something so seemingly tangible as money may, after a time, be forgotten as a reason and merely taken for granted. But in this most complex and important set of reasons, whose very nature is such that we can't take a step back and look at them, we can see why the most important reasons for love are those which are least rarely evident. And this in turn leads to the facile fallacy of supposing that, for want of anything else to say, what one loves is "the total person" or "something deep inside," when in fact these reasons, like all the others, are strictly superficial.

Intimate roles may be frivolous, so evident in baby babble and other infantile behavior that would be unthinkable in public. They are often sexual, thus leading to the common identification of intimacy and sex as such ("being intimate with" is a polite way of saying "having intercourse"). Intimate roles are by their very nature rare, if not exclusive; when intimate behavior is made public and common it may cease to be intimate and cease to be a reason for loving as well. A person who talks baby talk in public (a popular comedian, for example) loses that role as a vehicle for mutual intimacy, and sexual promiscuity, whatever else one might think about it, renders sex, too, unavailable for intimacy. (Thus prostitutes tend to reserve for their lovers at least one sexual activity which they refuse to their clients.) Beauty and wealth, we can now say, are usually not considered reasons for love because they are essentially public and therefore not matters of possible intimacy. But this goes too far, since, as I have argued, beauty and wealth can be *made* private and even exclusive—for example, in countries where women cover their bodies and faces in public; for couples who hide their wealth or have their special ways of enjoying it together. And despite our obsession with intimacy it is not true that intimacy provides the only reasons for loving (nor is intimacy necessarily loving; hatred can be intimate too).

Roles become reasons for loving when they participate in the formation of a shared self. Whether a particular activity contributes to shared selfhood and thus provides such a reason depends on the activity and on the relationship. For some couples, sexuality is a block to intimacy rather than its vehicle or expression; for some people, balancing the family checkbook might well be one of those intimate activities through which they define themselves. It is not always clear whether one loves because a role is shared or when a role is shared because one loves, but this seems to me to be not particularly important. Whether sex is "fabulous" because we are in love or whether fabulous sex is one of the reasons we are in love is not a worry worth worrying about. Indeed, to worry too much about the reasons one loves is itself an obstacle to love and, eventually, perhaps a reason for *not* loving. As André Gide once observed, "Even to wonder whether one loves is already to love a little less." That is not true, but the opposite may well be: we have so long been told that love is "without reasons" and even "beyond reason," that to specify reasons is already to love less, that we realize to our horror that our love has its limits, and then suspect, wrongly, tragically, that perhaps our love is not "true" at all. But why should love be love without limits, when we are limited ourselves?

14 "THE MOST WONDERFUL PERSON IN THE WORLD" (FANTASIES VERSUS ILLUSIONS)

I've always loved you, she said, and when you love someone, you love the whole person, just as he or she is, and not as you would like them to be.

TOLSTOY, *Anna Karenina*

Among the various reasons why we love someone, some are subtle, submerged, barely visible, perhaps unspeakable or shameful besides. But others are outrageous, extravagant, overwhelming; for nothing is more obvious about love than its enthusiasm. And enthusiasm tends to exaggerate, effuse superlatives, turning minor virtues into cosmic icons and ordinary charms into utterly unique and unimaginable blessings. Thus the person we first found attractive suddenly becomes fantastically beautiful, and the person we once thought was "nice" now becomes "the most wonderful person in the world." This is the process that Stendhal called "crystallization," the *creation* of sparkling "perfections" in our lover at every opportunity. Thus lovers discredit themselves, prove that love has an overactive imagination if it is not exactly "blind," which leads too easily to the cynical conclusion that love itself is an illusion, nothing but a peculiar form of madness which we continue to worship only for the flattering reason that, sometimes, we ourselves are the recipients of this extravagant praise.

Some reasons for loving someone seem to us to be bad reasons, and some reasons are quite unreasonable, or else simply false. A reason might be bad if, for example, it is a reason that offends the other person; a nun's beauty might still be a good reason to admire or appreciate her aesthetically, for instance, but not for loving her, since such a "reason" will not contribute (but more likely make impossible) the shared selfhood of love. A reason might be unreasonable if it includes expectations which a person cannot possibly—or in any event is highly unlikely to—fulfill. Loving a person for his or her "potential" usually carries this danger; so does loving someone because he or she "will make me happy for the rest of my life (even though I've been depressed for most of it so far)." A reason might simply be false: if I love you because you've told me that you're the illegitimate daughter of Jean-Paul Sartre, and I find out that that's not true, that's the end of my love—not because you have lied to me, but because my reason for loving you has disappeared. But besides these obvious ways in which reasons can go wrong, there are much more interesting exceptions to these ways, which turn out to be the very heart of love.

One of the reasons I love you is because I believe that you are the most beautiful woman in the world. As a matter of objective fact—if there can be such a thing—this is false, or at least provincial, since there are canons of beauty which you do not even approximate, much less perfectly fulfill. Does this make my reason a bad reason? Does it make my love for you, in part based on that reason, a mere illusion? Does the fact that I overlook your flat feet, or split ends, or chipped tooth, mean that love is a deception, or that I'm fooling myself? Does the very real possibility that someday I might look at you and no longer think you are beautiful mean that my love for you *now* is illusory? Could it be that I don't love *you* at all but simply some beautiful fantasy that I (unfairly) expect you to live up to?

The above questions, set as charges and accusations, have

been put forth in a powerfully convincing way by a number of recent women writers, most notably Marilyn French in *The Women's Room.* The entire novel, from our perspective, might be seen as a treatise on the illusions of love. In one of the most quoted scenes, the heroine Val goes on at length in mock awesome tones about the virility, charms and brilliance of a new lover, in great detail about the magnificence of his arms, his eyes, his wit, his sex. Then, "suddenly, one day, the unthinkable happens." He says something stupid, and then again; and then you see "he farts in bed, he's skinny, fat, flabby . . . and doesn't understand Henry James at all." The logic is simple, and devastating: love leads us to have all sorts of illusions and fantasies about our lovers which, inevitably, come crashing down in dis-illusion-ment and disappointment.

One answer to this set of accusations is to reply that one can also love a person *as is,* not as you would like him or her to be, not as you imagine him or her, not as ideal but just as "Joe" or "Sally," rather than Apollo or Aphrodite incarnate. But this flat and initially plausible if hardly exciting answer leaves out one of the most crucial ingredients of love—*fantasy.* It is simply false to say that we love—or can love—a person simply on the basis of "the facts." We select from those facts, and we idealize some of them. We share daydreams and hopes and plans, and without them love would be unimaginable. Fantasy, not music, is the food of love. Furthermore, this "realistic" response asks us to do the impossible in another sense; it requires us to be matter-of-fact in an emotion (like most emotions) whose whole essence is wrapped up in enthusiasm. It's as if we were told, "It's okay to have an emotion but don't get emotional about it." The idea of loving a person *as is* is a bit of wishful thinking, an attempt to reduce this most volatile of emotions to flat perceptions, without the chance of disappointment.

A different answer to the charge that love is an illusion is the pious answer—that whatever fantasies or illusions might provide the reasons for love, the fact that one loves, for whatever reasons, is all that counts. The idea, which we have already rejected, is that the reasons themselves don't really matter, that what one loves, if one "truly" loves at all, is the whole person, or the "soul." But reasons matter; the reasons define the nature and the limits of love. So if the reasons indeed are illusions, love will be an illusion too.

To love is to fantasize, to idealize, to see someone as "the most wonderful person in the world," perhaps the most beautiful, the most charming, and so on. This is not to say, however, that the lover is "all perfections," as Stendhal sometimes argues; the most wonderful person in the world might nonetheless have smelly feet, be incapable of carrying a tune and clumsy in certain social situations. Being in love does allow us to appreciate features of a person that might otherwise go unnoticed or unappreciated. Being in love also allows us to tolerate features that would otherwise be intolerable, and benignly ignore features that might otherwise be repulsive. And indeed one can still positively dislike features of a person one nonetheless loves, all of which is simply to say, in effect, that it is surely not true that lovers fail to recognize the faults in each other, that they are indiscriminately enthusiastic about everything. If anything, lovers are more critical, since, ultimately, it is one's *own* identity that is at stake. But this still leaves that core of reasons which are, indeed, unreasonably exaggerated and seem to be, undeniably, illusions. I might be realistic about your smelly feet, but I still think you're the most wonderful person in the world.

Fantasies (versus Illusions)

> But love—don't we all talk a great deal of nonsense about it? What does one mean? I believe I care for you more genuinely than nine men out of ten care for the woman they're in love with. It's only a story one makes up in one's mind about another person, and one knows all the time it

> isn't true. Of course one knows; why, one's always taking care not to destroy the illusion. One takes care not to see them too often, or to be alone with them for too long together. It's a pleasant illusion, but if you're thinking of the risks of marriage, it seems to me that the risk of marrying a person you're in love with is something colossal.
>
> VIRGINIA WOOLF, *Night and Day*

Love is not an illusion, but my argument against this now familiar charge does not deny that love sometimes involves illusions and does not at all deny the essential importance of fantasy in love. The argument turns instead on a distinction, often blurred over in this flurry of accusations, between fantasies and illusions, which are not the same. Not all fantasies involve falsehoods, and even among those that do, not all fantasies are explosive. Fantasies are indeed essential to love, but illusion and disillusionment are not.

The most common form of fantasy is simple daydreaming. I imagine our walking along the beach together. I relish the thought of making love to you this evening. I think of something amusing to say to you when you get home. I try to picture what we will do in Philadelphia this summer. But there is nothing illusory about the future, despite the fact that—certain metaphysical paradoxes aside—it does not exist, at least not yet. Sharing an identity (or, for that matter, simply having an identity) involves such daydreaming, planning and imagining, and whether or not dreams come true, indeed, whether or not they are even plausible, is not always important. Of course, if one's little plans and daydreams *always* end in nothing, not only love but one's whole attachment to reality might well be put in question. But even when a great many of our fantasies are unreal, it may be the fantasies themselves, especially when shared, that form the structure of our identity. Indeed, poets have argued that it is collective myths and fantasies—rather than anything "real"—that give whole cultures, as well as individuals, their identities. One can at least imagine a couple at home, Percy and Mary Shelley in their seaside retreat, perhaps, dreaming of a life together when in fact their life together is their dreaming. The truth of daydreams isn't important—only their shared significance. This sense of fantasy is quite distinct, obviously, from the pornographic daydreams that currently enrich our list of pseudo-scientific best sellers.

A second form of fantasy is *idealization*, the representation of one's lover as *ideal*, "perfect," the very embodiment of perfection. It is a mistake to think that idealization necessarily requires distortion, or exaggeration, or deluding oneself into thinking that something is what it is not. In fact, idealization is exactly the opposite, accepting something and celebrating it *for itself*, without distortion or even comparison. And yet idealization often looks like comparison, since it is typically expressed in comparative or superlative form: "the most wonderful," "the most beautiful" and "the best. . . ." But this is one of those times when the language of love—the expletives of enthusiasm—is not to be taken literally. Idealization is a *refusal* to compare. As a lover, I love your nose. Is it a "perfect" nose? "The best"? I haven't the faintest idea what that would mean. I might seek out a set of criteria or standards according to which your nose is indeed measurably perfect, but I would choose the criteria, needless to say, wholly on the condition that your nose fit exactly. Which is to say, the measurement, and the implicit comparison, are beside the point. And yet I say, as if to confuse myself, that it's the most beautiful nose in the world. That sounds like a comparison, but it is instead a way of *blocking* all comparison (as when we say, of a work of art, that it's "*in*valuable"). You ask, teasing but also quite serious, "But what about so-and-so the movie star's nose?" And I dismiss your question, with a bit of annoyance. You have missed the point, which is, "I love your nose."

Anyway, to get away from any suspicion of pronasal fetishism, let me make the point in a more abstract way: the idealizations of love are appreciations, not distortions or comparisons. In the nature of the case, there is nothing that can be false or erroneous about them, unless for instance one once too often admires a lover's coiffure and it turns out to be a wig, or extravagantly praises one's lover's poetic talent only to find out his verses have been plagiarisms. One can, of course, always change one's idealizations, now see as common what once seemed ideal, or now see as vulgar what once seemed generous or extravagant. Indeed, forcing real comparisons is an effective way of doing this. (One way of falling *out* of love is to compare one's [ex]lover in a systematically unflattering way—not only the faults but what one thought to be ideal as well.) But this is not at all a matter of *disillusionment*—the cracking of illusions. One has not deceived oneself or believed any falsehood. To see certain features as ideal is simply to be enthusiastic about them, whether as a reason for love or as a consequence. In love, we tend to idealize as much as possible. Out of love, we do not. But to infer from the fact that one later "sees through" one's former idealizations to the conclusion that the earlier idealizations (and perhaps the love too) were illusions is a self-defeating travesty of logic.

These are two kinds of fantasies that are clearly harmless, central to love, not prone to falsehood or illusions, and therefore not liable to disillusionment. But there are also fantasies which are by their very nature false and impossible, which nonetheless may play a crucial role in the shared experiences of love. Bored to tears at an office meeting, I imagine in magnificent detail the most physiologically unworkable and practically implausible sexual fantasy, which I'd like to try out right after this damned meeting is over. It's wonderful and later I tell you about it, you laugh, and add some twists and details I hadn't yet thought of myself. Indeed, the next day you are caught in an equally horrid office meeting and replicate a similar fantasy, and tell me about it, and this physically impossible fantasy life becomes part of our private world, a recurrent activity which allows both of us to feel extremely intimate even when we are very much separated. I can easily imagine, and I say to you, that I'd like to spend all day tomorrow making love to you a hundred times and, the exactitude of the number aside, this is a perfectly reasonable fantasy, provided, of course, I do not try to literally put it in action. I can fantasize about our life in the fourteenth century while we read *A Distant Mirror* together. I can fantasize you as Dido to my Aeneas, your Dulcinea to my Don Quixote, and the impossibility of my fantasies can hardly be viewed as illusions, much less as exemplary of the illusoriness of love. Even impossible fantasies can be distinguished from illusions and can provide a tangible structure for love.

Indeed, real-life, non-imaginary fantasies that are demonstrably false may not be illusory either. Consider this important example: two remarkably ugly people are sitting in front of you at the airport, billing and cooing and obviously very much in love. One's first feeling is akin to disgust, with a second feeling, akin to superiority, following rapidly on its heels. Then a third feeling, also quickly, of guilt and shame, that one should be so unsympathetic. But then there may well be a sense of empathetic delight, rendered up in some clumsy bromide such as "I guess there's someone in this world for everyone," or "There's no disputing a person's tastes." But now, what about the *truth* of their fantasy, which is (one hears them say) that they are both beautiful? In the name of The Truth, should one approach them and invite them to re-examine their partners a bit more objectively, so as not to be fooled into making such clearly erroneous claims? Or is it rather the case that "truth," as we self-righteously call it in such cases, is not of significance at all? Indeed, this is what we mean when we say that emotions are irreducibly *subjective*, not so much that they are false (though they may be) as that what other people think just doesn't matter. And it is in this all-important sense that—no matter what our media-hype single-type image of public beauty may be—*all* lovers are beautiful.[1]

Here, with the notion of subjectivity, we come to the heart of fantasy, which is not, as we preliminarily suggested, just a projection beyond reality but something more besides, a world *over and above* reality, a "sur-reality" which has its own rules and its own "truth" ("subjective truth," the Danish philosopher Kierkegaard called it). This is what distinguishes our fantasies from illusions, not just the negative fact that they are not dangerously false but the positive point that they are beyond objectivity and truth as well. They are simply a matter of the agreement of the participants, and immune to contradiction from anyone else. Two objectively ugly people may stay in love for years; two "gorgeous" movie stars may be repulsed by each other in weeks. This is not to say, of course, that what we believe and what we feel cannot be affected by others; no lover is immune, no matter how fanatic the love, to the constant reminders of friends and associates that his *femme fatale* is actually a less animated version of Miss Piggy, or that her Prince Charming has the personality of a veal chop. But more likely than not, the friends and associates will be sacrificed before the love will be, for it is not self-deception that leads us to protect our fantasies but the very real choice between public agreement and private enthusiasm, and in a society that provides too little public enthusiasm and too bland public fantasies, private fantasies limited perhaps only to the two of us, are bound to be preferable and to be protected even at considerable cost.

This notion of subjectivity, the more or less private creation of a mutually agreeable and irrefutable truth, lies at the basis of our concept of personal roles as well. In love we make our fantasies come true, not necessarily for the world at large, but at least with one other person, and sometimes that is sufficient.

[1] Assuming, that is, that beauty is relevant as a reason for love, in any particular relationship.

A timid man wants to feel dominating and so he finds a woman, who might well be a much stronger person than he is, objectively, who allows him to play that role with her. ("You're a real tiger," she purred, as she helped him into the bedroom.) To feel that one is a giving person, one need only find one person to give to. To feel frivolous (not merely ridiculous), one needs to find only one person to appreciate one's silliness. Sexual prowess can be proven with a single person—in fact, *preferably* with a single person, thus eliminating the possibility of comparison. Indeed, what often goes under the name of "looking for love" is more specifically a sought-after role looking for a partner, and/or a private audience.

The separation of the personal and the public is not, however, always so clear—even in our society (which is one of the few that so emphasizes this distinction). Many emotions include a sense of the public view (shame, for example), and even love, which systematically excludes the larger world, is subject to its opinions. The roles and fantasies according to which one chooses a lover are themselves determined in large part by the culture at large, and the plausibility of a relationship, one's probable success in maintaining the roles and fantasies of love, depends a lot more than we would like to think—in the initial arrogance of love—on the uninformed and even unsympathetic view of others. But even here it is essential to our analysis that this interference and influence be kept distinct from the structures of romantic love itself. A person may choose a lover, for example, for the sake of public approval, even applause. A man may fall in love with a woman because *everyone else* thinks she is beautiful, but—in addition to the gloomy prognosis such love deserves—there is also the question of whether the "everyone else" has in this case entered into the structure of the emotion as well. And the answer has to be no, not if it is love. Love must be solely a matter of the perceptions and fantasies of the lovers, and though the encouragement of others is surely not incompatible with love, indeed may even influence it mightily, it is never part of love, and this, perhaps, is the most dramatic single distinction between our own concept of romantic love and other emotions that might be called "love" in societies or contexts that do not have this rebellious subjective element—that our opinion (just the two of us) is all-important.

Illusions (versus Fantasies)

If all of this is defensible as fantasy, what then counts as illusion? Illusions are *falsifications* of reality. They are not mere daydreams or idealizations or playful images but unreal, unreasonable, self-deceptive and ultimately destructive expectations. To love someone who is quite ordinary and to fantasize extravagantly is not illusory, but to have expectations that will inevitably lead to disappointment and dis-illusion-ment is indeed illusion. The most common and familiarly tragic illusions in love have to do with reciprocity—believing that one is loved in return when in fact one is only getting kindness or courtesy, loving for unreasonable reasons or reasons one knows to be (but will not admit to be) fallacious. I play a role, and I assume you're playing too: in fact, you're only "humoring" me. Sometimes such illusions are wishful misperceptions; sometimes they are calculated appearances, for example, when one allows oneself "to be led on," even while knowing better. One can fantasize that one is loved when one knows one is not. I can imagine without illusion what it would be for my favorite actress or writer to love me. But when we come to believe what we fantasize or imagine, despite the fact that it is self-deceptive as well as destructive, that is illusion. And it is entirely different from fantasy—at least from most fantasies—for precisely that reason.

Many illusions, also common but less widely recognized, are not so much part of love as they are illusions *about* love. These are the illusions most vigorously and rightfully attacked in *The*

Women's Room and by other feminists: for example, expecting to be loved "no matter what," or expecting to keep on loving without effort, without doubts, without change. Indeed, lovers are often intolerant of the slightest shifts in the delicate structures that make up their love; forget about turning into a frog —one of my friends has threatened to divorce her husband if he simply shaves off his beard. The idea that love lasts "forever" is an illusion, even if it lasts. "This time will be different," uttered not as a resolution but as a simple expectation, is almost always an illusion, and the idea that love is "everything," that it alone will transform one's life, guarantee happiness and protect one from all disappointment, is an illusion.

Where illusions enter into the love itself, they may range from simple negligence to finally fatal misperceptions. But what makes illusions *illusions*, not mere mistakes and not fantasies, is an element of *will* involved in them. Illusions are, in Freud's sense, *wishful thinking*. A mistake may be a mere misperception or lack of information, not knowing any better. An illusion, on the other hand, is a *willful* misperception, a forced expectation, not "on top of" but despite the facts and what one knows. This is why illusions are so explosive; they involve not just a falsehood but a falsehood that one already knows to be false. Thus we *want* the security of being loved without qualification—though we know better—and so we convince ourselves through a thousand legends and poems that "true" love is indeed unqualified. Knowing our own fickleness and emotional variability, we wish we could guarantee our feelings, lock them into an ironclad warranty with the grace of God as their guarantor—and so we make ourselves believe that love is "forever." We are unhappy with our lives and wish that in a stroke they could be changed. Thus our schizoid attitudes to romantic love in general; it is not that romantic love itself is an illusion, but rather that, at one and the same time, we wish for everything and know full well that those wishes and expectations are foolish. Thus our piety and our cynicism, both at once. Thus our foolishness, and too much of our poetry and philosophy.

Many if not most of our illusions have a social background, based in the myth of romantic love and the stories we are told from childhood. It is indeed, as some feminists have charged, as if there were a cultural conspiracy to keep us indoctrinated, not just with harmless and edifying fairy tales but with dangerous and destructive deceptions, which we can see through but yet believe at the same time. We are told that love must be one sort of thing, and we inevitably find it to be something less, and we are disillusioned. But the illusions of love should not be confused with love itself. Because we deceive ourselves into expecting everything from love does not mean that love in fact gives us nothing. Because we wish the impossible does not mean that we have to deceive ourselves, and because love doesn't last forever does not mean that love itself is an illusion and not worthwhile while it lasts. Love does have its fantasies, and inevitably some of these may turn out to be illusions. But this is not to deny the difference between the two, much less to show that love itself is an illusion.

Does it really matter to anyone else if you *aren't* the most wonderful person in the world? In what sense does it even matter to me? To love is to share the loveworld together, and that is itself a fantasy, a fantasy in which it is, as far as we are concerned, "just the two of us." And that is why, ultimately, you are the most wonderful person in the world. Apart from me, you are the only other person in there.

"I'LL BE YOUR SLAVE" (IF ONLY YOU'LL GET UP ON THAT PEDESTAL) 15

A little less love, if you please, and a little more common decency.

KURT VONNEGUT, *Slapstick*

One of the clichés of love is the interconnection between love and respect. The fact that this often flies in the face of experience does not damage the cliché, of course, for, like all illusions about love, this one consists mainly of wishful thinking. It is not just an observation but a set of hopeful expectations—that in being loved we are guaranteed the respect that may evade us in everyday life. In fact, love is quite different from respect (which does *not* mean that you can love only someone you don't respect).

What is the connection between love and respect? How essential to love is a sense of equality (which is often confused with respect)? Women who have resigned themselves to a subservient lot in life (albeit as a "total" woman) expect by way of compensation their lovers and husbands to respect them and treat them as equals, because of love, but also as one of its preconditions. But there are still no small number of men who feel that love is *not* a matter of equality, though perhaps (also by way of compensation) still a matter of respect, and so the supposed equality of love often turns into a struggle for power and status, a question of "Who's boss?" in which mutual respect is famously absent. It is in love, but luckily not in war, that we have come to expect almost anything, as "fair."

The obvious fact of the matter, wishful thinking and egalitarian ideology aside, is that a great many love relationships are not either equal or symmetrical, and a great many love roles depend on a mutual sense of domination and submission, "S/M" relations (without leather and whips) in which one is the master and one the slave, in which power, status and responsibility, or the lack of them, provide the primary reasons for love. Is this love? And perhaps far more importantly, are these roles of superiority and inferiority to be equated, as many recent theorists have equated them, with male and female, masculine and feminine roles, whether allegedly "natural" or not?

Love and Equality

Virtually every emotion that is concerned with other people involves a set of judgments that have to do with *status.* In fact the objective of many emotions is to increase our status vis-à-vis other people, at least in our own eyes, to set ourselves up as superior or, in the image of the Orient and Erving Goffman, to "save face." ("The term *face* may be defined as the positive social value a person effectively claims for himself by the line others assume he has taken during a particular contact" [Goffman, "On Face-Work," *Interaction Ritual,* Doubleday, 1967, p. 5].) In the emotions pity and contempt, for example, I set myself up as markedly superior to another person. In worship, envy and resentment, on the other hand, I see myself as inferior, to God in the first case, to someone more powerful than I am in envy or resentment. (One can feel envious or resentful of inferiors only in so far as something about them is enviable or impertinent.) Anger is an emotion that requires more or less *equals,* even as it asserts a certain superiority by virtue of the emotion itself. To become angry with a child is not only to assert one's moral authority, it is also to treat the child as a responsible person. (As opposed, for example, to being merely annoyed with him, as one might be with a mosquito.) Thus a favorite strategy of servants and teenagers is to make a superior "lose his temper," so bringing him *down* to one's own level. Jealousy too involves a confrontation of more or less equals (thus distinguishing it from envy), and so does hatred (thus distinguishing that emotion from contempt and resentment). It is the black knight whom the white knight hates—not the trolls and ogres, whom he merely despises, or the dragon, which he fears.

But what about love? In *The Passions,* I came down rather flat-footed in the position that love demands equality. One might feel affection toward an inferior, or idolize a superior, but neither of these is love. To "care for" a person is not to love him, nor is it love when one admires, adores or worships. (What is it to think of adoration as an emotion appropriate for a woman toward a man, but think of a man treasuring or cherishing a woman?) One argument against any significant difference in status between lovers is that it creates a distance that seems incompatible with the intimacies of love. The troubadour's imagery of *devotion,* for example, re-creates the detachment of a lord and servant in a purely personal context (the woman in this case playing the lord) and this in turn makes difficult if not impossible a sense of shared identity. The other person becomes truly Other—"The Beloved" (which is one reason that term is so obnoxious). Slaves cannot be lovers of masters, nor masters of slaves. (Affection or adoration, yes; love, no.) For someone to be your slave may be a great convenience, even flattering, but slavery and devotion is not to be confused with love.

Loving someone who is superior, loving God for example, is always a kind of *hubris*—the Greek sin of supposing oneself God's equal. (This leaves open the question of whether it makes sense to believe that God loves us.) There is quite properly a sense in which we can be *offended* by the revelation that someone loves us, rather than simply amused or flattered or indifferent, if we think of that person as markedly inferior. Thus the gods did punish those mere mortals who sought to embrace them.

The other side of making oneself a slave is elevating one's loved one to some exalted status; "putting her on a pedestal" is the common expression when the loved one happens to be a woman. (When it is a man, he is adored or worshiped, but why *not* on a pedestal?) What is wrong with "being stuck on a pedestal"? Well, to begin with, as Gloria Steinem argues, "a pedestal, like any small place, is a prison." But it is the height of a pedestal, not its diameter, that is the objection against it. Height is distance, and distance is antithetical to love. And then there is the fear of falling. When a person is so idealized, he or she cannot help but be disappointing. This is a point made bitterly by feminists Shulamith Firestone and Marilyn French, but of course it is a problem equally shared by adored men. Simone de Beauvoir writes in one of her novels, "When a god falls, he does not become merely a man; he becomes a fraud." But, as we have already argued, idealization need not involve falsification, and thus not be inevitably disappointing. What is wrong with pedestals is the fact that they are indeed elevated, and thus at a distance, limiting reciprocity and mutual expression. This didn't bother the troubadours, whose ladies were already effectively on pedestals—in a high tower above the moat, according to the most common of our chivalric images—but then, I have argued that their devoted adoration should probably not count as full-blooded love either. The higher the pedestal, the less chance for mutual expression. Thus a woman rightly reacts, "When you idealize me so, I don't know how I can respond to you." Not because she is a prisoner (she can always jump), but because the distance itself makes response impossible, or inappropriate. Idolatry is sometimes an admirable and inspiring emotion, and being idolized can be both exhilarating and self-satisfying. But neither adoring nor being adored has anything to do with love. In fact (after the initial fascination at least) both may make love all but impossible.

There is a familiar objection to all of this, however, that must be put aside before we express reservations of our own. Some of our best-known romantic stories, "Cinderella," for example, are based on the premise that love involves lovers who are wholly unequal, a prince and a scullery maid, in this case. Or the countess falls in love with her chauffeur, fighting to defend her love in the face of the most socially embarrassing inequality. Aren't these clear counter-examples to the thesis that love is possible only between equals?

We have emphasized the notion of *personal* identity, in opposition to social roles and social identity, for precisely this reason. Indeed, what these examples show is precisely this opposition, for the inequalities are *social* inequalities, and the conflict—the source of the romantic elements of the story—is precisely the contradiction between these initial social inequalities and the personal equality that is required by love. ("Love does not find, but *creates* equals," writes Stendhal.) In the story of Cinderella, the prince not only marries the maid but raises her to the peerage, thus to live "happily ever after." King Edward VIII found it necessary to lower his social status to match that of the woman he loved, and Shulamith Firestone argues that this is the case for all men's love—"they fall in love to justify their descension to a lower caste." But the countess who cannot suitably elevate her chauffeur may well "lower herself" as well, and the adjustment of social status to match the personal requirements of love is not in itself a remark on the relative roles of men and women in love. The idea that, in our society, women more often move *up* to the social status of their lovers while men rarely agree to move *down*—if this is true—is certainly indicative of an asymmetry in *social* status, but not therefore in personal status as well. Indeed, it is part of our domestic mythology that it is the woman, in love, who is "on the pedestal" and women, in general, who are superior in all matters of emotion and personal relationships. Whether or not this is true, it shows quite clearly that personal status and social status are quite distinct for us.

And so we agree: *Love requires equals,* and where there are no equals, where one is the master and the other a slave, where one is adoring the other, who is high and far away—that is not love, whatever else it might be.

Romantic love is the great equalizer, as our grade B romantic novels are so fond of pointing out. It is sometimes said that sex serves this function. This is sometimes true but just as often not true at all. Taking off one's uniform may indeed bring a person "down to size," removing at least the most visible trappings of social status and power. ("He looks pretty good with his pockets on," according to an old Bogart line.) But sex can also be used as a vicious weapon for creating inequality, for degrading someone or making a person feel wholly inadequate. It is love, not sex, that creates equals, though sex *in love* is one of the primary structures of this equalization.

It is one of the dogmas of our pervasive egalitarianism that one loves another "just as a human being"; there is a crumb of truth in this wonderbread of modern humanism. The truth is that equality is essential to love, but to insist that one does not love a person for his or her social status does not entail the existence of some naked entity called "the human being," for a person stripped of social status nevertheless retains his or her character as a set of personal roles, and it is this character, these roles, that are engaged in love. Cinderella cannot love the prince *because he is a prince,* and neither can the prince—who has class identity problems—love Cinderella because she is a maid and a member of the proletariat. Love demands and if need be creates equals. The girl and boy next door may take this for granted, but nonetheless it is one of the structures of an emotion which otherwise has no right to the name "love."

Some equals, however, are more equal than others. An emotion may require more or less equals but yet include a significant difference in status. Anger, I suggested, is such an emotion; on the one hand, it requires equality, or it degenerates into scorn or contempt, or worse, thinking someone "beneath contempt." On the other hand, anger includes a rather dramatic sense of self-righteous superiority, with the other as a moral inferior—at least for the moment. And in love, one of the most common configurations of roles is the pairing of domination and submission, which at its extremes becomes sadism and masochism. Now it is all too easy to confuse this configuration with a master and slave relationship; Jean-Paul Sartre does exactly this when he interprets love relationships and their dialectic to the "master-slave" relationship discussed most famously by G. W. F. Hegel in his *Phenomenology of Spirit*. But the point to be made here is that domination and submission are not the same as master and slave roles, and in the context of love these roles must nonetheless be complementary relations between equals. And we should also say—again—that these roles need have nothing to do with male and female, masculine and feminine. Whatever the inequities of our social life, our personal roles seem far less one-sided. The domineering wife is at least as old and familiar an image as the overbearing husband. Equality here is a personal, not a social or sexual concern.

One way of putting this quite simply is to say that the masochist acts his or her role *voluntarily*, not out of fear of some greater punishment, in which case he or she would merely be a victim of kidnapping. And even the sadist is wholly concerned with the feelings and reactions of his masochistic partner, which is why he is a sadist in the first place. (The Marquis de Sade, who knew about such matters, argued that the whole purpose of sadism was to assure a sincere response from one's partner. Pleasure can be feigned, he argued, but not pain.) But leaving aside the extreme case of sadomasochism, emotional dominant and submissive roles play a part in almost all relationships at one time or another, though it is rarely the case that one person always plays the same role. In different contexts, the roles often switch—and sexual roles compose but one of the contexts within which these roles are played. The person who is typically the dominant conversationalist may well be the more passive sex partner, and the person who is physically more aggressive may well be the one who prefers to be hugged and stroked. In times of insecurity, one or the other may well find baby talk and what in public would be obnoxiously obsequious behavior the most comfortable role. Or else one may compensate for other inadequacies by being boldly assertive, even commandeering, with which the other may or may not comply. But the point to be made here is that domination and submission are not only intrinsic to love roles (and thus not to be condemned as such) but they also presuppose a mutually agreed-upon scenario between equals. Only equals can *act* inferior with one another and not be.

R-E-S-P-E-C-T

Love can be said with qualifications to be between equals. But what about *respect*, which is so often taken as a *sine qua non* of love and equality? "How can you love me if you don't even respect me?" But one can, and does. Respect, common wisdom aside, seems to have very little to do with love, although to be sure one would hardly want to be in love without it. Respect is an attitude that is distinctively impersonal, anonymous, the very antithesis of intimacy. When you are told by someone you love, "Well, I respect you very much . . ." you know that you've had it, and you expect a disappointing "but . . ." to follow.

It is most desirable if I love you that I also respect your professional ambitions, but it is a sad if long-standing fact that love in no way requires this, and sometimes contradicts it. And in so far as I respect your career, for example, my opinion is no different from anyone else's, however important it may be to you and to us. You may at some point insist that I respect you "as a human being," but respect, like equality, has meaning only when it has a specifiable content, and in so far as "being a human being" has content at all, it is minimal content, making you just one of the multitudes, not someone special, not someone with whom and through whom I define my identity. When you are in love with someone, respecting him or her as "a human being" is very little, requiring some "common decency" perhaps but wholly ignoring everything that makes this particular person—as opposed to just some stranger or other—very special. In much the same way so-called *self-respect*, difficult as it may sometimes be, makes utterly minimal demands on the self, whereas *self-love*, by way of contrast, requires seeing oneself as much more than minimal or merely equal—as superb or superior.

Respect is an emotion that, if not egalitarian, at least requires an open mind, a sense of distance if not indifference. Respect is never exclusive, as love often is; respect is never intimate, as love *always* is. Respect is not necessarily even personal, as love must be. In fact respect refers far more to social and public status than to personal status. That is why the question, "Will you still respect me in the morning?" is so philosophically significant; what it makes quite clear is the conflict between intimacy and neutral social respect. If respect were so like or part of love, as we often suppose, this question would not even make sense. Years ago, intimacy was rare, respect quite common. Curiously, we are now promiscuous with our intimacy, stingy with our respect. No wonder then that often we now prize the latter far more than the former—and wish that love would provide what our busy competitive world will not.

Holding you in my arms, the idea of "respecting you" is wholly foreign, not because I don't, but because it is only when I watch you at work, think of you at a distance, away from and distinct from me, that the question of "respect" arises. But this raises a specter of conflict, with respect and equality too, which has too rarely been viewed as a problem in love. If respecting a person means, in effect, letting him or her out of the loveworld, we can understand how an insecure relationship might well turn two lovers into antagonists, not mutually supportive but mutually threatening and wholly incompatible standpoints. The private world of love is threatened by the public world of respect. And the result, as many women have rightly complained, is the painful choice between love and success. But this is not an essential feature of love itself, as some feminists have complained; it is rather the somewhat pathetic feature of some men's insecurity and, consequently, some women's tragedy. (See Chapter 22.)

A similar conflict arises with regard to equality, which is more complex because equality, unlike respect, would seem to be part of love and the loveworld and therefore not opposed to it. And yet it is a familiar experience of the last several decades that fighting for equality *within* a relationship has a tendency to destroy love. Why? If love already presupposes equality, what could there be to fight for?

"Equality" is one of those political glow-words with very little determinate content, like "liberty." One gives it a content by giving it a context—for example, equal work time, equal pay, equal say in an issue, equal responsibility for some specific activity or equal power. And what counts as equality in a particular relationship may indeed be quite different from what counts as equality in another. The equality that is the precondition for love only consists in the demand that social differences do not matter, that both lovers are mutually willing to take up the various personal and private roles that make up intimacy. But as the notion of equality starts to become more "objective" and more concerned with social rather than personal status, as the private is measured by public criteria, the tacitly accepted roles within the relationship tend to be shattered. The quasi-political self-consciousness that replaces them undermines the intimacy of love. What was once a relationship now becomes a "partnership," which may well be more efficient, even a model of fairness and success in "having worked it out," but it isn't love. It is too dominated by foreign and critical observers, external measurements and publicly defined if nominally private roles.

The demands might all be completely reasonable. They may indeed force a relationship to conform to some more general and "objective" form of equity. But what follows too easily is the intrusion of external opinions and criteria which all but obliterate the delicate mutual understandings and adjustments of intimacy. And this is true of therapeutic advice regarding mutual communication (how much talk is "normal" or "healthy"), or the "correct" way to distribute the household chores, or the "normal" or "healthy" quantity and quality of sex a couple *ought* to enjoy. There are instances, of course, in which communication is so lacking, housework so inequitably distributed or sex so unsatisfying, that outside opinions are both welcome and necessary—but in these cases the intimacy that defines the relationship is probably already in shambles.

The division between the public and the personal, the concern for equality of the sexes in the public sphere (equal pay for equal work, equal access to jobs and careers, equal rights and responsibilities under the law), on the one hand, and the sense of equality that is the precondition for intimacy on the other, have been commonly confused by both feminist theorists and anti-feminists alike. Shulamith Firestone is just one of many theorists who have argued that romantic love and "the relegation of love to the personal" are part and parcel of the manipulative ploy to "keep women in their place" and to rationalize, even idealize, their class inferiority. But love is by its very nature personal, and if indeed it isolates women in romantic relationships it isolates men in exactly the same way. That is what we mean by a "personal" relationship. The mistake is to think that the *over*emphasis on the personal which is foisted upon women, to the exclusion of public roles and interests, is a feature of romantic love itself, and that the indefensible inequality in the public sphere necessarily has its counterpart in the personal sphere as well. But these are quite distinct, and to treat them together as a single problem may mean blurring the very different strategies that are required to deal with each of them.

Romantic love requires equality; it excludes what we usually call "respect." But within the equality of a relationship, dramatic variations in status are both possible and common. Indeed, to impose external standards of equality in a relationship may well be to destroy it. But so, too, to impose external criteria for roles of any kind may well mark an intrusion which undermines the very distinction between the personal and the public which love presupposes for its existence. Love is, first of all, a kind of personal freedom. And without that, neither love nor equality means much at all.

16 "WHY NOT GET ANOTHER GIRL?"

In her first passion woman loves her lover,
In all the others all she loves is love,
Which grows a habit she can ne'er get over,
And fits her loosely—like an easy glove,
As you may find, whene'er you like to prove her:
One man alone at first her heart can move;
She then prefers him in the plural number,
Not finding that the additions much encumber.

BYRON, *Don Juan*, III, 3

More than one anthropologist tells the story, though it may be apocryphal, of the Western visitor sitting around the communal fire in one of those societies we call "romantic" who know nothing of romantic love, telling one of our chivalric adventure stories. The brave knight whom he describes battles pirates, climbs glass mountains, slaughters ogres and slays dragons—all in order to rescue his maiden fair. After which the natives, amused and confused, ask simply, "Why didn't he just get another girl?"

It is a question that bores deep into our conception of romantic love, for if there is one feature that seems undeniable, it is the *particularity* of our lovers, and consequently their *irreplaceability*. It may not be true that "I'll never love anyone but you," and it may not even be true that I can love only one person (romantically) at any one time, but the fact that we love one particular person is essential to our conception of love, which is unimaginable without it. But why should this present a problem to us? Well, for one thing, because this seems not to be true of many other emotions: I can be angry indiscriminately with everyone who comes into my office, and that does not mean that I am not really angry. A person can be embarrassed constantly but is thereby no less embarrassed on any given occasion, and a person may be perpetually aggrieved at a large number of different losses without thereby being any less aggrieved at any one of them.

So why not love? It is worth noting, with anthropological fascination, how we are so suspicious about a person who loves several similar people in succession. Even if the sequence is quite limited—for example, a man or a woman who has three or four marriages over many years—we wonder whether he or she could really have loved them all. We have this sense that one can only *really* love once, and for every love after the first, we can wonder, "Do you really love me, or are you still in love with X?" Indeed, we have all had that experience which in high school we called "love on the rebound," when it was clearly obvious—to everyone else but us—that we were still in love with the last one, and our present lover was just a stand-in, a kind of compensation. Or if Freud is right, could it be that *all* of our lovers are "stand-ins," and we ourselves too? When the sequence involves a rapid turnover, the puddle-to-puddle romances of a Don Juan for example, our suspicions become the conviction that he could not possibly love *any* of them. But why? (We wouldn't doubt the claim that he really *hated* them all.) Thus Albert Camus suggests that what Don Juan really loves is the Platonic ideal, *Woman,* and he is poorly served by the many women he woos, who are merely imperfect instances of that ideal. Freud suggests that they all may be unsatisfactory sublimations for the primordial fantasy he has of his mother. But whether the sequence of lovers is extremely limited or extravagantly long, the idea that we can love only one particular person is thrown into question. And do we in fact love a particular person at all, or do we rather, as Freud

"WHY NOT GET ANOTHER GIRL?" 16

suggests, love a certain *type,* of which this person is an instance? This means, however, that he or she might be replaced by another instance of the same type, and we might be replaceable too.

This heretical query becomes urgent as soon as we see that love is *for reasons*. Indeed, the fear of replaceability is a powerful motive for the pious defense of love as the love of a "soul," of a "unique individual" rather than a person with properties who might be replaced by another person with similar properties. If indeed we love for reasons, and a lover loves beauty or money or fame, why not shift one's love to someone else who has more beauty or money or fame? The high school cheerleader falls in love every season with the new football quarterback, while the bass drummer in the band falls in love with the head majorette of every visiting team. A woman who married a man "because he would take care of me" leaves him for another man who will take better care of her, and a man who married the most sexually exciting woman he had ever known finally leaves her for someone new and more exciting (if only because she is new). These infidelities strike us as proof that one has not really loved at all, but why?

Now, granted that we do not generally go about exchanging lovers like sparkplugs, requiring only another of the same model and size, the reasons for this are not always obvious, which is why we feel compelled to invent reasons of a more than suspicious variety. For example, we claim that love can be "true" only in a single instance (for each of us) despite the fact that this has virtually no confirmation in our experience and is refuted every time we fall in love again. For example, it is said that love is particular because love is a "commitment," which is not true of love (see following chapter) and not yet an explanation in any case. (Why would one need to make a "commitment" unless the possibility of loving someone else is already recognized?) For example, it is insisted somewhat piously by the defenders of "true" love from Ann Landers to

Victor Frankyl that every person is different, and so every lover unique, and thus *as a matter of fact* irreplaceable. But the fact that no two people have the same fingerprints or dental work is never a reason for loving, and mere uniqueness—if it's true—is not the reason for our particularity. Even if the reason for loving is so central as "You're the most wonderful person in the world," the truth is that someone else, if loved, might be the most wonderful person in the world too. Indeed, it is not uncommon for men and women who have had many lovers to insist that they all, with several discreet exceptions, have been "the most wonderful people in the world."

In response to these fatuous explanations, not surprisingly, the cynics have come back with an explanation of their own. Could our insistence on exclusivity and irreplaceability in love possibly be a matter of simple insecurity? Could it be that most of us feel sufficiently lucky to find even one lover, and so we wish to close the doors to the possibility that he or she might find another? Could it be that the particularity and irreplaceability of lovers is just another illusion in the mythology of romantic love, making a matter of morality out of what in fact is a matter of personal weakness and insecurity? After all, ending a love affair is painful, and starting a new one is full of traumas and risks. Could it be, then, that our emphasis on "fidelity" in love is no more than a rationalization for being satisfied with what one has, and minimizing life's risks? The answer is no—but what are we to say instead?

Curiously, the problem of replaceability was raised explicitly by Plato in the *Symposium*. Plato's very proper commentators have preferred to focus on his complex doctrine of the soul and *eros*, of course, but there is a much more amusing argument that emerges from Socrates' weighty dialogue with the muse Diotima: a defense of promiscuity that might raise an objection even from Don Juan himself. What turns us on, according to the oldest Platonic lover, is the beauty of the other person.

But soon we see that this beauty is not unique to this one person, but common to others as well, and so it is the beauty itself we desire, not that particular person who exemplifies it. One is the same as another, and what one comes to realize is the naïveté of thinking that love is exclusive. Of course, ultimately, one comes to appreciate that it is not even beautiful bodies in general that one loves, but the Heavenly Form of Beauty itself. The desirability of particular persons drops out of the emotion, and one joins Socrates as a philosopher, a lover of beauty as such and, as Socrates so brutally demonstrates at the end of the dialogue, virtually indifferent to the feelings and beauty of his lovers. But the secular message is clear: particular people don't ultimately count; it is the Form that we love, Beauty itself.

A different form of the same argument permeates Sigmund Freud's theories. Let's not yet worry about whether the person whom we all *really* love is our mother or father and the person we seem to love is only a stand-in for the tabooed parent. Whether or not we agree with this popular "Oedipal" doctrine, it is clear that, on all of Freud's accounts, what one loves is not so much a person—the phrase "object of love" comes into modern parlance largely with him—as a cluster of properties and characteristics. These may or may not be "real." They may or may not succeed in satisfying the needs that require them. But the point is that the identity of the love "object" is seriously in question. Freud routinely talks of both love and sexual attraction in terms of "attachment," but what is clear about these attachments is that they are almost always (except for the originals) makeshift and undependable. The person one loves is a constellation of properties defined by one's own psychic needs and is therefore imminently replaceable, were it not for the severe restrictions imposed upon sexual exchanges by "civilization," that is, European middle-class morality and marriage.

Returning now to the orthodox "Oedipal" doctrine, if what one really wants is one's mother or father, then it is clear that getting what one wants is, for most of us, utterly impossible. But even this needs to be made more problematic, for Freud is quite clear about the fact that it is not one's actual mother or father that one wants, but rather some ideal fantasy, which may or may not be faithful to the way one's parent was once but is not now. It matters little whether the fantasy ever was "true," so long as it is indeed not true now. The point is that it is not even accurate to say that the person one really loves is his or her parent, for the parent, as much as or even more than the surrogates one auditions through life, is not the ideal that is required. Not only are lovers replaceable; they are all exchangeable like so many makeshift and ill-fitting parts to a fantasy that will never in fact be fulfilled. Even the parent at the back of the fantasy is nothing but a representative of an ontological ideal, like a "perfect gas" in a physics textbook, a mere approximation, and never real at all.

Philip Slater brings the Freudian position up to date, mixing it with a quasi-Marxist scarcity model of bourgeois society. He argues:

> Since romantic love thrives on the absence of prolonged contact with its object, one is forced to conclude that it is fundamentally unrelated to the character of the love object, but derives its meaning from prior experience. "Love at first sight" can only be transference, in the psychoanalytic sense, since there is nothing else on which it can be based. Romantic love, in other words, is Oedipal love. It looks backwards . . . it is fundamentally incestuous. . . .
>
> *Pursuit of Loneliness*, pp. 86–87

Of course it is wholly fallacious to leap from the fact that "love at first sight" cannot be based on merely present experiences with this brand-new, unknown person to the conclusion that it must be based on residual Oedipal love. Early friends and siblings, recent fantasies, past lovers, a collage of images from movies and magazines all contribute to the outline of an ideal lover which this new person just happens (or seems) to fulfill. (See Chapter 8.) But the point is still that the person one loves is indeed just a stand-in, and therefore replaceable by someone else having essentially the same (romantically relevant) features.

In response to this dangerous cynicism, we are assured that "marriages are made in heaven" (small compensation when we have to make them work here on earth). We assure each other that "we're perfect for one another"; but of course we are not. And even if we were, why think that no one else could be "perfect" too? But if you're dispensable to me, then it follows (even when I'm not in a rational mood) that I'm not indispensable to you either, and so we both accept the myth; better than facing that insecurity. One may even be so cynical as to suggest, as in an old Abbott and Costello routine, that it is better to fall in love with an ugly person. "Then you know you won't lose her," says Lou. "But what if you do?" asks Bud. "So who cares?" says Costello.

There is a term in law, which philosopher Ron de Sousa has interestingly introduced into philosophical discussions about love: *fungible*. (Try to ignore the mycological connotations.) Fungible goods are those which are exchangeable for others of the same kind. If the repair shop damages my radio beyond repair, it has legally discharged its obligations to me (would that it were always so simple) if I am given another radio, the same make, the same quality. Of course it doesn't have to be *exactly* the same, but I'd hardly get to court if I complained that the new one doesn't have the pencil scratches I'd accidentally scraped on the last one. Fungible goods satisfy certain conditions, and though people are not "goods," perhaps, we still might ask to what extent people—as lovers—are fungible in much the same sense.

To say that people are fungible is not to say that there are no differences between them, but only that, regarding this particular emotion in this particular circumstance, they are replaceable, satisfying all psychological conditions for the emotion. If I am sad because I've lost my watch, you can satisfy me and end my sadness by giving me another just like it—the watches are emotionally fungible. But what if that was the watch that my grandfather gave me? Then the new watch, even if exactly the same mechanically, etc., will not satisfy me, and it is not emotionally fungible. But here we see one good explanation for the irreplaceability of lovers, without metaphysical or moral embellishments. Lovers do not merely satisfy pre-existing needs and sentiments; they create (that is, we create) sentiments particular to the love, which are therefore difficult, if not impossible, to replace.

Suppose a man loves a woman for her money; he enjoys seeing her mainly because she has money though he also enjoys her sense of humor, her love-making, and the things they cook together (but none of these would be special *about her* if she didn't have the money). It is clearly predictable that he would be willing to leave her for someone else with money, although, because of the inconvenience, he may well require much more money, or something else besides, before he makes a move. We might despise such a man, but the point is that, given the rather limited reasons for his love, his lover is emotionally fungible in a rather obvious way. The same holds true of, let us say, a woman who loves a man for his magnificent body and love-making. We will readily expect that she will transfer her love to another man who has a more magnificent body and makes love better. But as the reasons for love become increasingly personal and not simply pre-existing aspects of a person but interpersonal creations of the relationship itself, we can see that this easy transferability becomes far more difficult. Time together cannot be transferred, nor can shared experiences and mutually defined roles, habits and expectations. For example, we build up a history together. ("We've been through so much together.") It is virtually impossible to find someone else with whom you also share that history. So powerful and obvious is this particular dimension of love that couples almost immediately start manufacturing a history, even before they have one. ("You were at the Segovia concert too! Well, maybe we even met there; where were you sitting?") Even when it is clearly too soon to forget we are already asking, "Do you remember the first time we . . . ?" and "How long has it been?" History is perhaps the best possible insurance against dispensability.

And yet we tend to make too much out of this. Obviously, if one thinks of having "invested" twenty years in a relationship, it is much harder (in terms of capital loss, perhaps) to leave. But even if histories aren't replaceable, that doesn't make them final or definitive. Our shared history may at most be *a* reason for my loving you, but it would be a peculiar case indeed in which that alone would suffice. What that history represents is more likely our identity together, and the quality of our present emotion depends then not on the history but on the nature of that identity *now*. *Having* loved someone is almost never a sufficient reason for loving them now.

The notion of time together, a shared history and identity, jointly created roles and a life together certainly explains why we do not easily transfer those relationships and emotions that are most valuable to us. Even if love is for reasons, a couple can compile and create so many good reasons that replaceability is all but out of the question, so long as we do not slip from that extreme improbability to the illusion of some metaphysical guarantees. But this does not yet answer our original question, which is—regarding the knight in love with his fair maiden, whom he has met only once and whose presence is signified only by the locket he wears attached to his armor—"Why not get another girl?" His own virtues of courage and perseverance must be set aside in considering this question, of course. (Mere obstinacy may inspire love, but it must not be confused with it.)

The question of replaceability has two facets, which must be kept separated. First there is the question of whether repetitive love can be genuine love, as repetitive anger is genuine anger and repetitive embarrassments are real embarrassments. Our answer here must be yes, that a person who loved a sequence of people for more or less the same reasons might nevertheless be in love every time, given a certain reasonable limit, of course; even an angry young man can be angry only so many times before we are willing to dismiss his anger across the board. So, too, Don Juan can have only so many lovers and still call it love. (Thus Byron's Juan, who has only a few, might genuinely be called a lover, but Mozart's Giovanni, with his "1003 in Spain alone," surely could not be.) But the second aspect of the replaceability question yields a very different answer: is romantic love as such a matter of fungibility? Can the knight indeed find himself another girl? The answer is, *of course* he can. Where there is not yet a "relationship," there are not yet those interpersonal bonds and reasons for particularity. Not only fair maidens, but knights and dragons, too, are a dime a dozen, and there are not yet intrinsic reasons why this one should be any more preferable than that one, why this love cannot be replaced without loss with another.

What we sometimes call the "depth" of love (too easily confused with its intensity) is in fact a measure of the ease or difficulty with which it can be transferred. Though "depth" need not depend wholly on time (some people can form a lifetime bond in only a few days), it does depend on the kinds of reasons for love and the likelihood of re-creating these reasons in another relationship. But there is nothing pathetic or insecure in this, as the cynic suggests, nor are there the specious metaphysical assurances demanded by the defender of "true love." Even in the most irreplaceable relationships, there are no guarantees, but it is a sign of how badly we want these that, when threatened, almost any argument for irreplaceability will do. ("But no one else will ever be able to rub your back the way I do.")

The lesson of "Why not get another girl?" is not, however, to remind us of our vulnerability, and certainly not to give another forum to the tiresome debate between the pious and the cynics. It reminds us, rather, of the fact that love is always a kind of achievement, a mutual building together, and it is this, nothing else, that keeps love alive. There may be any number of other forces keeping "the relationship" together, of course—the inconvenience of moving out, the embarrassment before one's friends and family, the legal liabilities that one would prefer to avoid—but in love there is but a single source of security, and that is the world we have built and are building together, and how good it is.

DECISIONS, DECISIONS (AND "COMMITMENT") 17

CHOICE. If you're looking for a simple truth to live by, there it is. CHOICE. To refuse to passively accept what we've been handed by nature or society, and to choose for ourselves. CHOICE. That's the difference between emptiness and substance, between life actually lived and a wimpy shadow cast on an institution wall.

TOM ROBBINS, "Meditations on a Camel Pack," *Esquire*, July 1980, p. 38

Love is a *decision*. A decision *to* love, and a decision about *whom* to love, and how, and when, and why. Romantic love is an emotion of *choice*. It may not feel like a decision; indeed our language and literature are filled with fine phrases and allegories in which love appears to be everything but a decision—a force, a disease, a gift of God, an imposition, a need, palpitations of the heart, the unwanted prick of Cupid's arrow. In fact everything about love is made to seem circumstantial, inexplicable, "spontaneous" and a matter of luck or misfortune. So in what conceivable sense can love be based on decisions and romantic love be a matter of choice?

If romantic love—and emotions in general—must be considered to be learned systems of roles and judgments, taught to us by our culture, then three different levels of decision, choice and responsibility can be demonstrated, three senses in which love must be seen as one's own "doing," no matter how chancy or spontaneous it might seem at the time. *First*, because they are systems of judgments, we are responsible for our emotions, which we "make" just as we "make judgments." As roles played, we are responsible for our choice of roles, as well as how well they are played. (The "art" in loving.) We rightly judge that our emotions are with or without justification or warrant. We get angry with or without provocation, with or without reason. We do or do not have a right to be jealous. And we love well or badly, wisely or foolishly, "deeply" or with one foot out the door and one eye open over our shoulder. Of course, to say that we choose our emotions is not to say that one can simply, by *fiat,* decide to fall in love or get angry. (There has to be someone with whom to fall in love or get angry, for example.) But that does not mean that we do not choose them, make essential decisions about them, or that we should not take full responsibility for them.

Second, there is an important sense in which a society as a whole "chooses" its emotional world, appropriate to the circumstances, usually, and only rarely as the explicit choice of any one person or group. It is a collective choice, perhaps never stated as such by anyone, but it is a choice nonetheless. Thus it can be argued that some much-studied Eskimo tribes have "chosen" their emotional life of resignation appropriate to the extreme discomforts and dangers of their environment. We often make such judgments about ethnic groups, though rarely in print, suspecting what we do not say: that cultures collectively choose their temperament just as surely as they do their cuisine. The chivalric age chose to invent romantic love as compensation for a society disintegrating, and the Victorians reaffirmed that choice, as Marx and Engels anticipated, because it served the purposes of the "nuclear" family, which in turn served the purposes of capitalism.

Of course as individuals we do not have this sense of collective decision making. Not only do we see our emotional world as a *fait accompli* but we do not see it as a decision at all, rather as a psychological "need." Thus psychiatrists slip happily from a discussion of infantile dependency and motherly affection to their fallacious conclusion that we all need (even "all we need") is love. Natural-love theorists trace it back to the birds and the bees, and philosophers propound on the nature of "human nature," projecting our culture's collective decisions onto "humanity" writ large. But the truth is that, in so far as romantic love is a need at all, it is a need which we have created—like catsup and sparkplugs. What we so easily attribute to the wisdom of Mother Nature might better be looked for at the movies.

One could argue, of course, that there is a genuine "need," that "man" is a social animal and needs other people, and here we have no choice. Perhaps. Even so, it is an entirely open question, after early infancy, whom one needs and how. Why not family? Why look for a stranger from outside the tribe? And as we read about the nature of exogamy and its economic and political explanations in everyone from Margaret Mead to the Marxists, the matter is clear. Whatever our primitive need for other people, or the sociobiological analogs of exogamy, the "needs" that make up romantic love are cultural inventions, the created structures of certain kinds of societies, a collective choice, not biological or psychological determinism. And what we have collectively chosen, because it is chosen, might always be reconsidered.

Third, regarding romantic love in particular, we *choose* our lovers. We often hide this fact under metaphysical disguises such as "we were made for each other" and "looking for Mr. Right," but no matter how predestined we now seem in retrospect, no matter how "lucky" it was that we both showed up in the same place the same time and no matter how "remarkable" that we both enjoy Mozart (after all, millions do), the simple fact is that we were complete strangers, from opposite ends of the country, with different religious backgrounds, entirely different upbringing and quite different expectations and demands. Both of us had histories of friends, lovers and would-be lovers from whom we could have chosen (and did). But we *chose* one another. I decided to love *you*. (In fact it was after I had chosen you that I decided to *love* you. Some people decide first to love and then go out into the world to find the *you* to love.) If we are so good together, that is in part because we have made that decision, and if we break up we will not be able to say, "We were wrong for each other," and leave it at that. We chose that too. Love is not predestination but a process, and some of the daily decisions that make up that process are divisive rather than unifying.

The enormous emphasis we place on choice in love is evident in two extreme examples. First, we are fascinated by forbidden love, love that breaks the rules and oversteps the bounds, that flies in the face of reason, convenience and even life itself. The same old examples keep appearing—Romeo and Juliet, Lancelot and Guinevere, Antony and Cleopatra, Rick and Ilsa in *Casablanca*. It is the fact that such love does not fit into any predictable social pattern, disrupts those patterns (even if love then forms a pattern itself), that displays what is too often called love's "irrationality" but is better understood as the extreme assertion of individual choice. Emma Bovary hated her husband, who was "right" for her but not her pick. But she loved her lovers, both of whom were disastrous—but her own choices.

The second example is our absolute horror of the idea of arranged marriages. The idea of forced intimacy, arranged by contract in advance by possibly wise and understanding parents or a professional matchmaker, based on similarities and complementarities of background, class, abilities, needs and temperaments, fills us with repulsion. An utterly rotten love affair, on the other hand, established on a basis of mutual misunderstanding and immaturity, founded on illusions and held together by mutual obstinacy, seems to us to be just the luck of love, the chances one takes—but at least it is freely chosen. My point is not to argue the preferability, much less the "sensibility," of the one over the other, but rather to show just how extreme is our preference for personal choice, even over the likelihood of happiness and security.

Choice usually refers to the realm of deliberate action, and it is distinguished from what happens to us, what we cannot control. But the vast region that lies between deliberate, intentional, overt action (e.g., attempting an assassination, signing a contract or doing the broad jump) and events of which we are clearly victims (being hit by a meteor or a lawsuit, having a gout attack) lies largely uncharted. Freedom and unfreedom are limits, abstractions. Even intentional action has its involuntary and mechanical components: the workings of the brain, the way one was toilet-trained, the immediate circumstances and the machinelike "action" of muscles and nerves, operating in mindless sequence though perhaps initiated by what older philosophers used to call "an act of will." And even our victimization is liable to blame: for luxurious living, for being too ambitious, or just for "being there" at the time. "There are no innocent victims," wrote Jean-Paul Sartre during World War II in France. His charge is extreme but, with regard to emotions and other "acts of mind," I would have to agree. Nevertheless, to say that our emotions are aspects of our freedom is not to say that they can simply be willed, *de nihilo,* from nothing, without restriction or limitation.

To say that love is a decision, therefore, does *not* mean that, with a snap of the fingers, one decides to love, as one might jump off a bridge (assuming, of course, that one is already on a bridge). Literature is full of such attempts, of course—the homosexual Daniel and pregnant Marcelle in Sartre's *Age of Reason,* for example—and they are inevitably failures. But this does not prove that one cannot decide to love, only that one cannot *simply* decide to love, regardless of the circumstances, one's already partially formed personality and emotions already established. There must be the person there who can serve as a plausible candidate for love—not likely between a woman-hating pederast and a much-pregnant woman. The circumstances have to be appropriate; one falls in love during a dinner more easily than during a funeral, but more easily then than during an Internal Revenue audit or an hour's wait at the dentist.

If much of love is fantasy, then one key to love is imagination. Imagination is a free act of mind, beyond question, but one can't simply imagine anything, at any time, conjure up an image as God could create an entire menagerie, with a simple act of will. One needs knowledge, time and the ability to will; it is hard to be properly indignant when you don't know what's going on. And it is hard to imagine, when you're in love, how this same so wonderful person could someday be a stranger again—or an enemy. The freedom we realize in imagination and emotions provides itself with its own limitations, its own barriers, beyond which it cannot or will not proceed. When I'm in love I forbid myself to imagine what I am told are your fatal flaws, and it is difficult if not impossible to make yourself love someone who already disgusts you. (Someone you hate, on the other hand, a good respectable enemy, is quite another matter.)

Our emotions are bounded by circumstance, by other emotions and by their own inherent limitations. But given a set of circumstances, and a psychological circumstance too, one can choose any number of different emotions. A relative dies; I can rationalize (a way of choosing) any number of different emotions—not only grief but anger, relief, indignation, renewed affection or even jealousy, or any combination of these. And given that I find myself in a "relationship," already filled with sexual excitement and mutual admiration, having gone on so long on a strictly day-to-day or week-to-week "casual" basis, it now becomes an urgent question (perhaps because I decide that it should be) whether I will continue to view all of this as a passing convenience, or make it into something "more," or make sudden demands which might, in effect, be tantamount to choosing that the relationship end immediately. I cannot make such a choice in a vacuum, without a "lover" in question to be loved; I cannot choose to love someone who bores me and I cannot choose to love when I am overburdened with other responsibilities. But, given some such relationship or a reasonably perceived possibility of one, I cannot help but choose, one way or another. Choosing to postpone the choice and continuing on a "casual" basis, of course, is a choice too and, under the usual circumstances, by no means the easiest of the alternatives to maintain over time.

A decision need not be deliberate, thought out or thought about; it need not even be conscious. It need not occur at a given moment; often it does, but often it only seems as if it occurred at a moment—midnight Sunday—when in fact it was in the process of formation for weeks or even months. The dominant model for decisions is the razor's edge—this way or that—which fits well enough when we are deciding where to go for dinner or whether or not to enlist in the army. But one also decides in a step-by-step way, like a Sunday afternoon drive in no particular direction which ends anyway at a favorite spot, after a series of insignificant choices of roads. Love may on occasion depend wholly on a "leap" (the active component of the "falling" metaphor); but more often it moves on a long series of decisions, one or two of which may well try to take the credit for all of them.

If love is a matter of choice, then how can we explain the fact that it so often seems like an obsession, not a matter of choice at all? Why is love so intractable and tenacious, even in (especially in) the most trying of circumstances, for example, when love has gone sour or is still unrequited? But obsessiveness and intractability are not marks of passivity. If I may use an economic metaphor (which has its admitted limitations in these romantic concerns) I would say that love, once chosen, involves an *investment* that is not easily withdrawn. All emotions, I have suggested, involve self-esteem and the reformation of self; love, in particular, is the formation of a shared identity, an identity tied up with, defined with, through and by this particular other person. To drop out of love is not therefore a casual decision, whose consequences are mere inconvenience or embarrassment. It is literally a part of one's self that is at stake. The intractability is not so much an inability to extricate oneself as an extreme *unwillingness* to do so, because the emotional cost is too great. Again, the difference between "cannot" and "will not" is not always clear, particularly in the realm of emotions. But as a historical corrective to the emphasis on passivity, at least, our own emphasis should be on the latter.

Good Decisions—and Bad

Like any other decision, love invites evaluation. Love is for reasons, and these reasons can be reviewed, as good or bad reasons, wise or foolish, rational or irrational. The language of "falling" in love tends to preclude such evaluation; one does not fall down well or badly, unless of course one is a clown or an acrobat. But we obviously love wisely or not so wisely. We choose our lovers well or badly. For right reasons and wrong.

This does not mean, however, that one can always or even usually construct a tally of reasons pro and con in order to decide, once and for all, whether to love or not to love, and whom. Reasons cannot always be quantified—much to the dismay of many utilitarians and other philosophical accountants—and therefore cannot be added up and weighed against one another. One can imagine sitting down to make a list, "counting the ways," in effect: "How do I love thee" on the left, "How I don't" on the right. And on the right (let's suppose it's a mean-spirited morning) one compiles a list of charges that would condemn a person in vagrancy court for life; on the left, one can only think to write, "Still, I want you." What is our verdict? To throw away the calculations, of course.

If emotions are judgments, it makes perfectly good sense to

evaluate them in terms of justification and reasonability, as we often do in everyday life. There may not be any ironclad decision procedure for us to pronounce final judgments *about* them (judgments about our judgments, in effect), but nevertheless there is something to say. It is often said that "love is irrational," and sometimes so it is. But it is essential to understand that emotions in general can be *ir*-rational only to the extent that they are also *rational*, in other words, based upon *reasons*. And it does not even make sense to say that the reasons for love are *always* bad reasons. Nor is it true, as our tally above might suggest, that we love *despite* our reasons. Reasons are reasons only in so far as they are the reasons one actually loves. Not just rationalizations. And though our reasons are often inarticulate and certainly unquantifiable, they are nevertheless our reasons, and often good reasons besides.

What would it be for a reason to be a bad reason? We have already explored several of these in previous chapters. A reason can simply be false. If I love you because we're sexually compatible or because we both love the Rolling Stones, my reasons are bad reasons if we aren't, or if you don't. A reason can be unreasonable, for example, if I've decided to love you because you've made one of those rash assurances that desperate lovers sometimes make, e.g., "I'll love you forever, no matter what." Two reasons can be contradictory, for example, if I love you because of your driving ambition and I love you because I love relaxing at home with you, day after day after day. Reasons can be trivial (although this must always be judged in the "eye of the beholder"). A reason might be true, reasonable and significant but not a real reason at all, in other words, just a rationalization. It sounds like a reason, indeed a good reason; but it is not *my* reason at all. (In her new novel, *Bleeding Heart*, Marilyn French describes a woman who feels compelled to continue to love her husband because he is "a good father." Indeed she even convinces herself, but in fact, in her own judgment, this is not a reason for loving him—though perhaps it is one for staying with him.)

Over and above these rather straightforward types of "bad" reasons is a category that concerns us far more in love but often escapes the theoreticians of love who underestimate the complexity of emotions. There is a criterion of worth which is more or less internal to our emotional worlds—the loveworld in particular—namely, the worth of the roles and consequently the self as constituted by that emotion. One might love a person for all of the "right" reasons but yet feel bored, suffocated, weak, unproductive, sexless or just plain guilty because of it. And one can love for all the "wrong" reasons and feel exhilarated, daring, adventurous and, in general, extremely good about oneself. Choice of the "wrong" lover can ruin your life, or at least several months of it, but in return for that disaster one might suffer grandly, feel nobly sorry for oneself, publish beautiful poetry, develop an exquisite sensitivity. On the other hand, the "right" relationship may be just that—two pieces of a puzzle that fit precisely, and that's the end of it. Nothing to build. No conflicts, nowhere to move. Nothing to complain about. These are extremes, but they pose a familiar dilemma—that what seems "irrational" in love depends on what you feel about yourself and what you want as a life: drama or stability, excitement or routine happiness. Stendhal enjoys condemning his characters to death as they fall in love, or otherwise minimizing contact between them and maximizing desperation. Tolstoy, on the other hand, portrays love and durable happiness hand in hand, despite his own unhappy marriage, which may be why Natasha and Prince Andrei are so much more persuasive than Natasha and Pierre, blissfully married.

Rationality, in love, is relative. Moralists beware, for the commandment to love has no set reasons. But this does not mean that love is beyond reason, or reasons. It does not mean that love is arbitrary, whimsical or "illogical," though it can on occasion be so. Love, like all emotions, has its "logic," its schemes and strategies, its reasons and fallacies. The problem, for each of us, is to see what these are.

Deciding What?

What do you decide when you decide to love someone? First, of course (though not always first in time), you decide on a person, a candidate, presumably someone palpably "lovable." This is true even if one is simply "in love with love," a clichéd idea (e.g., Byron, *Don Juan,* Canto III) which tends to hide our more significant obsession with the choice of lovers itself, no matter how unpredictable, whimsical or frequent. Indeed, the whimsical unpredictability of this choice (though not its frequency) is part of our paradigm of romantic love, and though it may in the final analysis be true that people are more likely than not to marry the boy or girl next door (or in the nearby vicinity) our romantic heroes and fantasies will continue to be the sudden stranger, the forbidden love, the unexpected. Of course one usually chooses to love from among a field of candidates already available, most often, perhaps, in a field of only one or two. But our obsession with love makes equally significant those who go out into the world with the loveworld already constructed, looking only for the first lovable person who will fit within its already tight-fitting roles.

Confining ourselves to the more usual instance, however, in which one decides to love a person one already knows and perhaps knows well, or chooses between two more or less "casual" lovers, what is it that one decides? What does *not* happen, as I want to argue at length in the following section, is that one "makes a commitment." What does happen is that one makes a decision within a context, open-ended for the future but based entirely in the present, that one will continue to foster the circumstances and the context in which love will flourish, in which shared interests can be developed and a shared identity is most likely to grow without external threats and avoidable uncertainties. Minimally, that means deciding to be together enough so that love is not mainly memory, so that bonds can be forged out of shared experiences, and differences can be defined and defused in repeated confrontations. It means sticking around when "the going gets rough," but not "no matter what." It means a selective deafness—not listening to alternatives, a kind of blindness, as the cliché declares, to facts and faults that might otherwise turn us away. It means making plans together. It means that one stops thinking in terms of self-interest as the criterion for making decisions. It means, paradoxically, ceasing to think in terms of self-esteem, even though the strategy of love itself is to maximize self-esteem. (The way to feel best about yourself is to stop trying to think about how you feel about yourself.) It means forgetting about one's "independence" as the ideal of self-identity. It means making an investment—by way of a telling confession or by intermingling our books and records on the shelves—such that it will be all the more difficult to back out later. But—and this is essential—it is not the difficulty of backing out in the future that is essential to the decision but rather the expression of confidence in the present. In this difference, so easily blurred in all talk of "commitment," lies the difference between positive decisions *to* love and negative and almost always self-destructive setups for future resentment and spite.

The decision to love, in other words, is a decision to foster a set of conditions conducive to love, encouraging but not requiring the formation of mutual interdependency and shared self-identity. It may include the exclusion of all other relationships (at least, other sexual relationships), but it need not. What it cannot do is allow other priorities to intervene, no matter how urgent, which conflict with the primacy of the new self-identity being formed. But because love is a continuous process, a sequence of constant decisions rather than a simple or single scenario, what one mainly chooses in choosing to love is not so much love itself as a set of circumstances conducive to love. What these are, of course, varies with the individual case. (For some people, deciding to live together is a way of fostering the conditons of love; for others, deciding not to live together may be the better way of fostering the conditions of love.)

"Commitment"

It is at this point that the common belief that love is a commitment ought to be confronted head on. Love is not, I want to argue, a commitment. It is the very antithesis of a commitment. The legal tit-for-tat quasi-"social contract" thinking of commitment talk fatally confuses doing something because one *wants* to do it and doing something because one *has* to do it, whether or not one wants to at the time. Immanuel Kant, the philosophical father of *duty* in general, conceived of the "moral worth" of an action strictly in terms of the extent to which we felt we *ought* to do it, regardless of our desires. In rejoinder, we might say that the *emotional worth* of an action is determined precisely by the degree to which we *want* to do it, regardless of our obligations. And that means that an act of love—and ultimately love itself—is the very opposite of a commitment of any kind.

Romantic love is founded on voluntary choice, even whim. We fall in love with a total stranger. A married man or woman. The son or daughter of the enemy. The Queen. A god. And the greater the danger, the greater often is the desire. But to evade or deny these dangers and uncertainties, and ultimately deny the desire itself, we seek out guarantees. We want the assurance we thought we had as children, the supposedly unconditional love of our mothers. (This is overrated too; very few mothers love their children "unconditionally," but that is another story.) The whole point of romantic love is that it is *not* based on such presumed assurances, but then we turn around and try to make love imperturbable, guaranteed if not by God, then at least by the sanctions of the state. Marriage, for many people, is not so much an expression of love as a request for guarantees, by way of sanctions, social approbation and the threat of legal harassment. And short of marriage, we invent the quasi-legal concept of "commitment," in order to set up a set of *moral* sanctions at least, thus turning love, which is a continuous stream of decisions, into a promise, an obligation, an act of prevention rather than a desire.[1]

In his *Discourse on the Origins of Inequality*, Jean-Jacques Rousseau formulated the distinction that now forms the heart of the *Cosmo* cosmology—that it is commitment that distinguishes casual sex from love. A commitment, of course, need not be made explicitly—and here is where the confusion begins. It may be understood as an inference from a declaration of love. It may be assumed—though rarely these days—just from the sexual relationship itself. But whether stated or inferred or simply assumed, a commitment is a kind of promise, a promise *to* someone to *do* something. But when does one make a promise without actually saying anything? To whom does one make this promise? And what, specifically, is it a promise to do?

A promise need not be stated as such, it is true. You ask me if I will take care of your children when you're away, and I nod. I have promised. Indeed, one gets into all kinds of obligations by tacit acceptance of a situation, not only with lovers but with strangers as well. Walking around a ladder, I am called to by a fellow at the top, asking me if I will hold it steady while he reaches for his cat. I grab the ladder, saying nothing; I have just assumed an obligation, and the fact that I change my mind in a moment makes not one bit of difference. Obligations and commitments are much clearer in such situations than in love, where intimacy and familiarity often allow us to neglect or ignore courtesies and responsibilities that we would owe to any stranger. But it is true that one makes commitments and accepts responsibility just by virtue of certain circumstances and relationships, and it would be most surprising if this were not true of love. (Thus love is not, in case you ever wondered, "never having to say you're sorry.")

[1] The boundaries between morality and legality are often smudged in our society, especially in the realm of sex, love and marriage. Thus it has become apparent in the courts that a moral commitment does have legal consequences similar to marriage. But marriage itself is more than a commitment, of course.

The problem is that, though a mutual commitment need not be actually stated as such, it must be mutually agreed upon, and explicit at least in that sense. Sometimes the agreement can be assumed without ever being mentioned; in an earlier generation, it could be assumed that two people in love would be sexually "faithful" to one another. Even so, it is clearly and unquestionably mutually understood. But to have the idea that being in love itself constitutes such a commitment, even if nothing is spoken or implied, is to move much too easily from the fact that not all commitments need be stated as such to the idea that there need not be an explicit agreement at all. And in so far as there are such agreements, tacit or stated as such, these are in no case the commitment *to love*. They are rather obligations understood and undertaken by the nature of the relationship, or by living together, or by mutual expectations that have been clearly assumed. Love itself is not a commitment, nor can it be committed.

I have said that love is a decision to foster a certain set of conditions conducive to love. But this decision is not a promise, and in particular it is not a promise to my lover. If I change my mind or find my emotional enthusiasm flagging, there has been no moral breach, no broken promise, no commitment unfulfilled. One might argue that I have made a commitment *to myself* but, although we often employ such expressions to express our resolutions, there is no such commitment. My commitment to you can be canceled, with your say-so; but changing my mind about a commitment to myself and giving my say-so to the change are one and the same act, which means that it makes no sense to talk about "commitment" to myself in the first place.

When I say "I love you," I am indeed setting up a set of expectations, implicit agreements and promises (see the following chapter). But what I have promised is to foster a set of conditions; I have not promised—I cannot promise—to love you in the future. I can be rightly accused of betraying your trust if I willfully make impossible those conditions (for example, by running off and marrying someone else), but not for ceasing to love you. I can promise you almost anything, except love.

The essence of romantic love is a decision, open-ended but by the same token perpetually insecure, open to reconsideration at every moment and, of course, open to rejection by one's lover at every moment too. One might reject romantic love—as too risky, as too insecure, as too unstable for a foundation of interpersonal relationships. In its place, one might well suggest a system of contracts, for five or ten years, complete with guarantees, promises and sanctions. But that is not romantic love. I can promise revenge: I can't promise to be angry. I can promise to stay with you, but not to love you.

To love is to protect a set of conditions, to take on responsibilities. But one accepts that set of conditions and those responsibilities because one *wants* to, not because one is *obliged* to. There may be obligations that require us to stay together in spite of love or the lack of it—but these are not to be confused with the conditions of love. There may be reasons for making a commitment—security, respectability, friends, to prove something, "for the sake of the kids"—but love itself is not one of these reasons, nor are commitments alone ever reasons for love.

Our society has gone litigation crazy, but the one area that is or ought to be immune from the ubiquitousness of the lawyers is love. It is the very nature of contracts that they are public and explicit, and that they are independent of our desires and emotions. But love *is* an emotion, and thus the very antithesis of a contract, even when it is made explicit. Would you really want me to say, "I promise I'll stay with you, no matter how I'll feel?" Could I promise, even if I wanted to, that I'll love you in three years, under circumstances wholly unknown and perhaps even unimaginable? Love is not only a decision, in other words, but a lifetime of decisions, and that is why it cannot also be "commitment."

"I-LOVE-YOU"[1] 18

I-love-you *has no usages: Like a child's word, it enters into no social constraint; it can be a sublime, solemn, trivial word, it can be an erotic, pornographic word. It is a socially irresponsible word.*

I-love-you *is without nuance. It suppresses explanations, adjustments, degrees, scruples . . . this word is always* true (*has no referent other than its utterance; it is a performative*).

Roland Barthes, *A Lover's Discourse*

"I love you."

What does that mean? Of course you know, but tell me.

A description of how I feel? Not at all.

An admission? A confession?

No, you don't understand, after all.

"I-love-you" is an action, not a word. It is not a short sentence. Of course it *looks* like a sentence, made up of words, but sentences can be transcribed and transformed. "I-love-you" is more like the word "this" or "here"; it makes sense only when spoken in a very particular context. In writing, in a letter, it has meaning only to you, and only while you can still imagine my speaking it. To anyone else, and after a while to you, it means nothing at all; like the word "here," just sitting on the page like an old coffee stain. Hardly a word at all.

"I-love-you" has no parts, no words to be rearranged or replaced. "You-I-love" is more than merely clumsy, like "Me Tarzan, you Jane." It is something like staking a claim. "John loves Sally," said by John to Sally, is absurd. "I-love-you" allows for no substitutions, no innovations. It stands outside

[1] With appreciation to the late Roland Barthes.

the language. It says nothing. If it is misunderstood, it cannot be explained. If unheard, it has not been uttered. And when it is heard, it no longer matters that you didn't mean to say it in the first place, that you "just blurted it out." You *did* it, and it cannot be undone.

"I-love-you" does not *express* my love. It need not already be there. Perhaps I didn't feel it until I said it, or just before. But then, in a sense, I didn't *say* anything at all.

One of the perennial misunderstandings about language is the idea that all sentences *say* something; words refer and phrases describe. But language also requests and cajoles, demands and refuses, plays, puns, disguises as well as reveals, creates as well as clarifies, *pro*vokes as well as *in*vokes, *per*forms as well as *in*forms. We *do* things with words, in words done by the late Oxford philosopher J. L. Austin. With words we make promises, christen ships, declare war and get married, none of which would be possible without them. Our sentences mean what we *do* as well as, or rather than, what we say. They bring things about as well as tell us what has already come about. And the meaning of "I-love-you" is to be found in what we *do* with it, not in what it tries to tell us.

If we so easily misunderstand language and persistently refuse to look at love, then of course we will miss completely the significance of the language of love, if, that is, it is a language. Or is it, as Barthes suggests, a *cry?* "I-love-you" mainly makes a demand. So when I say it you react—not "How curious that you feel that way" but rather "But what do you want me to do?" Its meaning is aimed at you, to move you. (A "perlocutionary act," Austin called it.)

I say, "I have a headache," and you say, "Poor Boobie." Perhaps you kiss my forehead, and I'm most grateful. But if you say, "Me too," I don't think, "What a coincidence"; I feel slighted. You've misunderstood me. Suppose I say, "I love you," and you kiss my forehead. I'm offended. That's not a reply but an evasion.

I say, "I love you," and I wait for a response. It can only be one phrase: "I love you too," nothing less, nothing more. Perhaps, "Me too," though it is ungrammatical and a serious confusion of pronouns, but it is also less than the proper formula. If you say, "*Je t'aime,*" you have not done it either; instead you are showing off.

I could be silent and just love you. And perhaps you'd know. I don't have to say, "I'm so angry with you," when I've been yelling at you for twenty minutes. I don't say, "I'm sad," when I'm crying. And yet I feel compelled to say, "I love you," even when it's obvious I do. "Nothing says I love you like 'I love you.'" But it is more than that too, more than something said.

The power of words, or at least certain words, sometimes is awesome. "I-love-you" is a magical phrase that ruins the evening. Or changes love into something more, even when it was love before. It is not an announcement, no R.S.V.P. No "if you please." It *demands* a reply; in fact, it *is* this demand. And a warning, and a threat. It is an embarrassment, first to me, but soon to you. It makes me vulnerable, but you are the one who is naked. I am watching your every move. Counting the fractions of a second. What will you do?

"I love you"; "what a terrible thing to say to someone." Terrible indeed.

"Tell me you love me."

"What are you expecting from me? You know I love you."

"Then say it."

"I don't want to say it."

(The evening's already lost, but I pursue.)

"If you love me, why not say it?"

"Oh. I don't know; it just changes everything."

"How can saying what is true change anything?"

But it does. "I-love-you" doesn't fit into our conversations. It interrupts them. Or ends them.

"I-love-you" is language reminding us of the unimportance of language, language that destroys language. It is language without alternatives, without subtlety, like a gunshot or the morning alarm. And then it's gone, not even a memory, and has to be done again.

But once said, it can never be said again. It can only be repeated, as a ritual, an assurance. Not to say it, when it's never been said, is no matter, a curiosity. But not to say it, once said, is a cause for alarm, perhaps panic. One commits oneself to the word, and to say it again. What else follows? Perhaps nothing.

Barthes says it is "released," but I say, *shot out,* like a weapon. Released like an arrow, perhaps. And if I make myself vulnerable in saying it, the real question is what it will do to you. I'm still watching you. Still counting the fractions of a second. What will you do?

I say, "I hate you," and you quite rightly ask "Why?" But I say, "I love you," and "Why?" is completely improper. A reasonable question, but a breach in the formula. You have turned the weapon back onto me, so of course I reply indignantly, "What do you mean? I love you, that's all." And I again await your reply. A second chance, but no more.

I say, "I love you," and you answer, "How much?" What are we negotiating? Perhaps you are saying, "Well then, prove it." And, having said the word, I am bound to. Nevertheless, your reply is insufferable. You're acting as if I actually *said* something which can now be qualified, quantified, argued for and against. But I didn't. I just said, "I love you." And that is, in terms of "How much?" to say nothing at all.

"I-love-you": a warning, an apology, an interruption, a plea for attention, an objection, an excuse, a justification, a reminder, a trap, a blessing, a disguise, a vacuum, a revelation, a way of saying nothing, a way of summarizing everything, an attack, a surrender, an opening, an end.

I say, "I love you," and I no longer remember the time I was with you when it was not said. And we will never be together again without it.

THE IMPORTANCE OF BEING HONEST 19

When my love swears that she is made of truth I do believe her, though I know she lies.

SHAKESPEARE, *Sonnet* 138

In 1976, Jimmy Carter provoked far more debate over his qualifications for the presidency with an interview for *Playboy* than he did with his various proposals concerning foreign policy. In essence, he *confessed:* "I have felt lust in my heart." Libertines chuckled that lust should be so limited; conservatives were horrified that the subject had been broached at all. But the point, of course, was *honesty*. Jimmy Carter, he and his aides assured us, would not lie to us, even about his private sins, small as they were. Honesty, it seems, has emerged as something like our ultimate value, the single most important mark of character. The Watergate follies have given renewed emphasis to this ancient virtue, but, where love is concerned, one would think it has never even been questioned.

My students, for example, display unembarrassed conformity in their agreement that people in love must be "totally honest" with one another. Trust, they say, is the essence of love, and a relationship without it—that is, without *complete* trust—"cannot be worth much." If this were so, however, no love would be "worth much" since total honesty and complete trust are impossible. To expect them as a matter of course, to demand them as the precondition of a relationship, is to adopt what may be today the most dangerous single doctrine of the myth of romantic love, the myth of "total openness," which is confused with trust and glorified under the banner of "honesty."

Now, of course I would not deny that love and trust stand in a particularly intimate connection with one another. James M. Cain, in *The Postman Always Rings Twice,* tells us that "when fear gets into love it just isn't love anymore; it's hate." This may be a good summary of the incompatibility of love and terror, love and *dis*trust. But the antithesis of distrust need not be trust, and the opposite of wholesale lying is not "total" honesty. Not telling is not necessarily deception, and deception is not always antithetical to love. Which raises the question of why truth and trust are so emphasized—I would say overemphasized—in most discussions about love. Why so much concession to what I call *the urge to tell,* as if in itself this were a virtue without which love cannot be? The truth of the matter seems rather to be that truth is a complex and negotiable issue and honesty is sometimes an obstacle rather than the essence of love.

To begin with, truth and honesty are never total, unqualified or absolute. At the extremes of human endurance, one can always discover a context in which a lie—albeit a "white" one—would be generally agreed to be justified, if, for example, a gangster threatens to kill both of us if I tell you where I've been tonight. But we need not go to the extremes to see that trust and honesty are not always virtues. A person who feels the urge to "tell all" will more likely be a bore than a saint, and we all know people who tell—under the guise of honesty and openness, of course—as a way of manipulating people, even as a way of destroying them. The urge to tell is not always motivated by virtue; it may also be a demand for attention, a way of trapping someone into a covenant that he or she would rather have avoided, a way of shifting the burden of guilt from oneself to another:

"I have a confession to make."

"Oh, you don't have to tell me if you don't want to."

"No, but I do. I feel I ought to tell you."

"Well, okay. [*Joking*] What monstrous crime have you committed?"

"I've been sleeping with so-and-so, your best friend."

"You what?!"

"Now don't get upset. That's why I'm telling you."

"How *could* you!"

"What are you getting so angry about?"

"You're telling me that you've been sleeping with my best friend, behind my back . . ."

"That's why I'm telling you now; I want to make a clean breast of it."

"But how could you? How could you?"

"You have no right to get so angry. You're making me feel guilty about it, and that's why I'm telling you, after all, so that I don't feel so guilty anymore. I'm just being honest; why can't you be understanding? This fight is all *your* fault, for being so unreasonable."

The urge to tell: it's more complicated than it looks. Lying, of course, need not involve the fabrication of actual falsehoods; it may sometimes be keeping silent or, as Camus writes (concerning his novel, *The Stranger*), "Lying is not only saying what is not true; it is also and especially saying more than is true and, as far as the heart is concerned, saying more than one feels."[1] And, we may suppose, saying *less* as well. As often as not, truth takes the form of confession, and it is the wisdom of Christianity, Freud too, to appreciate just how strong the urge to confess seems to be. Confession erases responsibility for sins. Not confessing multiplies them. And if it is easy to think of counter-examples to this simple two-part principle, it is just as important to realize how many of our "sins" are not

[1] Introduction to *The Stranger*, 1955 ed.

crimes at all but rather acts of an uncertain character, whose worth or blameworthiness depends wholly on absolution or approval, and it often doesn't matter much by whom.

In relationships, of course, it matters very much by whom, since it is indeed part of the essence of love that the opinion of one's lover counts far more than the opinion of anyone else, at least in matters that pertain to love. (If this sounds circular, of course it is.) Thus "telling all" is not an expression of love if the "all" doesn't pertain to the love. Recounting in tedious detail the events of the day may or may not become a part of love's daily ritual, but it has nothing to do with trust, honesty or openness. (In fact it may be evasion.) Not telling one's lover about one's past in certain circumstances may be awkward (the appearance of an old lover; the arrival of a letter from one's buddies in prison). Not telling one's spouse, for example, that you have been fired from your job may, to say the least, be a bit odd, though, according to some recent reports, this is a quite common reaction among professionals who have been "laid off" for the first time in their lives. But it is not a breach of love.

When is honesty relevant to love? Well, in romantic love, honesty about *sex* seems essential. One might not be dishonest when one fails to tell one's mother or brother about one's extramural sexploits, but, it will be argued, not telling one's lover would surely mark the ultimate breach of trust, and therefore a betrayal of the relationship itself. But something quite odd has happened in this regard; first, where sexual "fidelity" used to be considered an automatic presupposition of any "serious" relationship (in fact it tended to define such "serious" relationships), it no longer is. Most of my students make a firm distinction between relationships in which there has been some explicit agreement not to "see" other people and those in which there has not. The idea of an "implicit" or "tacit" agreement to that effect—usually nothing more than the fact that neither person has "seen" anyone else for a certain period of time—is not taken as morally binding. Once, sexual fidelity was considered one of the non-negotiable rules of romance, and sex with someone else was called "cheating." Now the rules are shifting, and many of my students even feel that other affairs are *desirable*, not only for their intrinsic pleasures, but as a way of testing the boundaries ("fetters," one student called them) of a relationship whose sexual parameters have not yet been settled. Telling, or not telling, is part of the test. Honesty, in other words, is now a negotiable tangent to love, not part of it.

Second, and consequent to this shift in presuppositions, is a most curious phenomenon concerning the importance of honesty. Sex itself is not considered so much a breach or betrayal of the relationship as the lying about it. "Well, at least you could have told me" is the most common phrase indicating this shift from the significance of sex to the importance of telling about it. In the wake of Watergate, the cover-up is considered far more deleterious to the relationship than the "crime" itself, whose status as a crime may even be in doubt.

With this shift in values (and I do not see it at all as a shift in the value of intimacy or "relationships" as such) the seeming abyss between casually thinking about sex with another person and actually having an affair closes up, and the problem of truth for Jimmy Carter and for *Tess of the D'Urbervilles* becomes essentially the same: to tell or not to tell? Tess had an affair and a baby; Carter only had thoughts. Tess lost a husband because she told: Carter almost lost an election. Why is honesty so important? And isn't *total* honesty, even on the most superficial analysis, absurd?

Consider this: when we're making love, and you bite my ear the way you do, I once flashed in my memory to a girl friend I had as a teenager, and the way we used to "make out" at the drive-in movies. This first association leads to another; we never actually "slept" together, which I've always regretted, and for a moment—just for a moment—I imagine, not wish, that you were she. Should I tell you?

The advantage of this example, over an actual affair, is that the likelihood of your "finding out" from someone else is indeed minimal. Too often the "tell or not to tell" dilemma is couched in the crude consequentialist terms of "what if she/he finds out?" thus missing the most interesting and important aspects of the problem. Sissela Bok, for example, in her book, *Lying,* sticks fairly close to this consequentialist account, which may be appropriate to lying in politics, perhaps, but is at most a secondary issue in personal relationships. Now if one takes telling the truth to be an absolute principle, at least in a love relationship, one will, whatever the consequences, tell. And just to make the dilemma clear, let's suppose that your lover is sufficiently sensitive that telling will, if not end the relationship altogether, put a serious crimp in it. If one holds an absolutist (or what philosophers sometimes call a "deontological") view about not lying, then the relationship be damned; the truth must out. But most of us would probably see this attitude as something akin to insanity. To tell the truth is not *always* a virtue.

In reaction to this absolutist position, however, too many theorists too easily shift to a wholesale consequentialist position: telling the truth is right or wrong depending on the consequences, namely, whether it will (in the long run) improve or endanger the relationship. Thus questions tend to focus on the likelihood of the other person finding out from someone else, or the discomforts and dangers of trying to hide the truth without inadvertently "blurting it out," the plausibility of the truth being accepted with good grace by the other, the pain of feeling guilty, the pain of a confrontation, and so on. These are, of course, relevant, and the decision to tell or not to tell is largely determined by them. But the urge to tell is more than this utilitarian calculation of feelings and consequences. It is also a question of motives and a shared identity.

I have already pointed out the ease with which telling can be turned into a kind of weapon, a "so now it's your problem" kind of strategy. Indeed, in the example we've chosen here, telling is so likely to be harmful that one can only suspect that malicious motives are indeed involved. What else would be? A desire to be cute? Sharing a bit of nostalgia? "Just being completely open with you"? Much more likely, "I just want you to remember that you aren't the only one that's excited me" or "Let me interrupt you in your moment of passion to shift the emphasis wholly to me." And if one does feel guilty about such thoughts (our linear model of the mind too easily makes us feel as if we can and should have "one thing only" on our minds at a time) it by no means follows that one ought to tell, even if (as may well be the case) telling will expiate one's guilt. With our new psychological frankness, we too often tend to think that telling is always justified, "letting out one's feelings"—in the name of honesty, of course. But it is not. Telling one's thoughts and feelings is not the trump card in our morality that we have recently tended to make it. And the idea that, whatever else one has done, one cannot be faulted for confessing is a dangerous and often vicious strategy that ought itself to be rejected as morally reprehensible. (One psychiatrist described his experience in a contemporary "let it all hang out" type of encounter group this way: "They were a lot of obnoxious people when they went in and they were just as obnoxious when they came out, except that they didn't feel guilty about it any more.") And lovers too find honesty a cure for guilt—in the name of righteousness, but often as a way of punishing one another.

The honesty dilemma has much to do with the mutual identity that is part of love. On the one hand, each of us wants—needs, demands—to be very special, uniquely special to the other person, and in today's ethics the other's thinking about someone else might be just as much (or more) of a threat to that sense of identity as his or her actually sleeping with someone. But on the other side there is the need for approval and acceptance of one's lover, and this includes—in the confessional mode—absolution for one's own transgressions, no matter how minor, which one fears might raise an obstacle to that shared identity. But to gain absolution means to threaten the other person's sense of uniqueness. And this is the dilemma. One tells in order to remove these obstacles in one's own thinking—in order to be absolved, to be told, "It's okay." But this makes the telling for the benefit of the teller—even when it is not malicious or manipulative. Concern for honesty as such is secondary, and one is concerned for the feelings of the other person only indirectly, in so far as he or she will be hurt by the confession, and in so far as the relationship itself might benefit from one's own renewed peace of mind. This is not to say that honesty is selfish. Nor is it to say that the urge to be honest itself is never a motive. But at least some of the time "honesty" is a virtuous way of referring to a verbal strategy whose main interest is always the comfort of one's own emotions, a means of resolving ambiguity, if not shifting the discomfort onto the other person, and then the enemy of love.

Honesty is a virtue, of course; what I am arguing against is the current idea that honesty is everything and excuses anything, even (especially) cruelty and irresponsible criticism ("I'm just telling you how I feel"). But honesty isn't everything. If what is at stake is sexual infidelity as such, it may be, as one of my (married) friends put it, that the only answer is "not to do it in the first place." Perhaps, but if the transgression is in the realm of a random thought rather than a premeditated deed, the problem of honesty arises with obstacles that can hardly be avoided, even if we're tempted to say that they are, in themselves, not very significant. The strict absolutist position would be that one still ought to tell, if there's anything to tell. The consequentialist would say that of course one should not tell, since no good could possibly come of it. But even the consequentialist seems to leave out something essential, namely the notion of shared identity itself, which is something more than mere "consequences."

The whole problem of trust can be viewed from the other side. This is one of those cases where the Golden Rule, "Do unto others as you would have them do unto you," makes considerable sense, not because it is a moral absolute, but rather because reciprocity is indeed the touchstone of love, whether or not it is so central to other human relationships as well. Instead of beginning with the question, "Should I tell or not?" therefore, let's see what happens when the question is phrased as, "Would I rather be told or not?" When the emphasis is on the telling, our attention tends to focus on such pragmatic questions as "Will he or she be hurt?" "How much?" and "What are the odds against being found out?" But when the emphasis is on being told, the focus tends to be less pragmatic and more concerned with the sensitivity of the relationship itself. The other person becomes less of an "other," to whom the truth is to be told or from whom it is to be hidden. And one sees oneself less as the victim of a possible deception and more as the consciousness through whom a relationship comes to have meaning.

Shakespeare clearly saw this difference. ("I believe . . . though/I know she lies.") Given the inevitability of lies, "white" or otherwise, the problem becomes not whether to tell but what to believe, and love, valuing itself more than some abstract value of honesty, is perfectly willing to forgo the evidence in return for an untrammeled sense of trust. But one does not love because one trusts; one trusts because one loves. And what one trusts is not *to* be told but its very opposite, *not* to be told, when the relationship is more important than the truth. (In *Casablanca*, Victor—who knows, asks Ilsa—who knows that he knows—"do you have anything to tell me?" She says "no." And there is no doubt that she is right.)

Suppose I ask, "Would *I* rather *be* told or not?" Our first tendency is to blurt out, "Of course," but this is perhaps misleading. I can't opt voluntarily for being lied to, if for no other reason than the logical oddity of my agreeing to accept something whose very nature presupposes my ignorance or lack of acceptance of it. And of course, if the dilemma is put in terms of "There's something you ought to know; do you want to know it?" the answer is rapidly forthcoming. But the reality of the circumstance seems more like the following: What I really prize—and what thus provides the criterion by which I form my preferences—is my love for you and yours for me. And what I know is this—that as "liberated" as I am and as much as I accept "intellectually" the likelihood of your at least desiring —if not consummating—sex with someone else from time to time, I know that I'd make more of it than I should, perhaps using it against you, in any case feeling unnecessarily hurt and neglected. And so I'd rather not know. It's not that ignorance is bliss, but rather that omniscience is a drag. Love can't stand distrust, so I *decide* to trust you—even if I don't. What I refuse to know might not hurt me.

To make things more complicated, however, I can't really *tell* you this preference of mine. "Do what you want, but I don't want to know" is itself an example of the manipulative use of telling one's feelings, and it puts pressure on the other person of a curious kind. It gives permission (and the very act of giving permission is a kind of power game, a way of staking out emotional territory). At the same time it forces the other person into an uncomfortable situation, of not being allowed to tell, which includes, therefore, an inability to declare one's innocence too. It's sort of like "Have you stopped beating your children?"—a question that indicts no matter what the answer. One is presumed guilty. So the preference not to know, and to ignore whatever evidence or rumors might lead one to know, is a decision that I can make but shouldn't tell you. And this, I might suspect, is the optimal strategy for you too. But we can't tell each other this, either, and for the same reason.

Immanuel Kant, who made lying one of the central examples of his absolutist "categorical imperative," advanced the following argument against lying in general: if everyone lied, no one would have any reason for believing anyone else, and communication as such would become impossible. Now whether or not the argument works on behalf of the general principle, it certainly makes sense in personal relationships. "If I suspect that you've lied to me even once," proceeds our paranoid romantic consciousness, "I will never be able to trust you again." It is in this sense that trust is essential to love, not in the positive sense that to love is to trust but in the negative sense that it is difficult to feel comfortable with someone whom you don't trust. But this doesn't make trust as such a part of love; at most it means that sufficient *dis*trust makes love difficult, and it is an open question whether distrust actually makes love impossible. The fact that we tend to see these two as mutually exclusive and exhaustive opposites only confounds our appreciation of the problem—and thus leads us to make absurd claims about the need for "total" honesty, as if there couldn't possibly be love without it. But if the criterion (as in Kant) is the ability to trust (and therefore love) at all, it must be said that the breach of trust may often be created by honesty rather than by lying; Kant's argument might just as easily be turned around as a way of showing that "total honesty" is morally impossible; if both of us were totally honest, there could not possibly be any relationship at all, if for no other reason than because we would continually bore or offend each other past the limits of endurance.

The upshot of this discussion is that honesty is overrated, which is not to deny, of course, that it still is a virtue—most of the time. Given the flexibility and uncertainty of contemporary ethics, it is surely desirable to be clear and honest about the boundaries of a relationship, making explicit when necessary certain limits and expectations beyond which the relationship is no longer viable. But within those limits and expectations, honesty and declarations of trust have become more of a strategy and a weapon than a virtue, less an expression of love than a technique of expiation that may itself be more of an obstacle to love than the sin for which one feels guilty in the first place. Love depends on shared identities and roles, many of which are better engaged in silence. To spell out the forms of our mutual engagement is often to trivialize them; to make them subject to a debate will sometimes destroy them.

We talk too much. (Too many books too.) Descriptions of love easily become accusations, and confessions are more damaging than what they're confessions of. Some questions can be "talked out," and explicit descriptions of what's going on can sometimes improve a relationship immensely, even in those areas where talk was formerly considered out of place, in sex particularly. But we have to reject the idea that the "heart-to-heart" talk is the essence of love, as well as the idea that honesty excuses everything and that "talking it out" will solve, instead of make worse, most romantic problems. We tend to think of what we *say* as somehow more definitive than what we do, ignore the most obvious gestures while waiting for something to be said. It is true that words tend to give a definite and explicit form to roles and to rules that were formerly vague and implicit. But to think that definition and explicitness are always virtues is to lose sight of what is most essential about love, that sense of shared identity and affection that precedes and may be trivialized by verbalization. Sex (and music, flowers and food) are better than words as the language of love. Romantic conversations, but not love itself, are so typically joyless. And "Platonic" love, if it is love at all, tends to be more pretentious than gratifying. (Socrates sent the flute girl away, which may be how he missed the point.)

In *The Passions*, I too joined the pious in declaring that love included "unqualified trust" (p. 338). But this emphasis on absolute trust and honesty tends to ignore the fact that trust is negotiable, like almost everything else in a relationship, and that trust may indeed be sacrificed to the passion itself, if need be. In fact distrust in moderation may serve the cause of passion more than honest revelation.

A few weeks ago you saw your old boy friend, and despite every assurance from you that there was no danger, I put myself into a holy twit. Why? Not because I didn't believe you or trust you, but because it was an opportunity for me to use a modicum of suspicion to inflame my passion for you, to remind myself how much I'm in love with you and how I'd hate to lose you. It was a way of making sure I didn't take you for granted, of not treating "trust" as one more virtuous euphemism for boredom. And here, even *dis*trust can function for the benefit of love. In fact, if a person never worries, never gets suspicious, never wonders, would we not wonder whether he or she is still in love, rather than merely comfortable?

It is probably true that we say, "I trust you completely," precisely when we don't, not as a lie, perhaps, but as a kind of wishful thinking, for example in those early moments of a relationship when one is desperately seeking an excuse to leap into an attitude whose structures will probably not be supportable for months to come. Sometimes "trust" is another way of announcing a decision to try.

And of course sometimes "I trust you" is a *warning*.

Sometimes *not* telling presents a special kind of problem; if I don't tell you (something that will hurt you) because I am protecting your feelings, does that mean that I am denying you "as an adult," paternalistically deciding *for you* what you ought to know and what not? If love is a relation of equals, this may indeed be a problem. And even if you *say*, "I can handle it," but I know pretty well that you can't, the problem is not resolved. If I don't tell, I'm not treating you as a fully self-sufficient autonomous adult; if I do tell, I've taken you at your word but hurt you and, consequently, us. What does the myth of "total honesty" say here? Do the consequences count for more than the way I feel about you? Is it so obvious, as my students seem to think, that if I can't be "totally honest, the relationship can't be worth much anyway"? Or could it be that honesty and trust are the *complications* of love, rather than its essence?

A recent acquaintance married a Japanese girl. He spoke no Japanese; she spoke no English. (With no third language between them.) And yet, as they acquired some mutual understanding, what became obvious was that their increased ability to explicitly express their emotions and state demands rendered the relationship not more intimate but less so. What Americans call explicitness she considered vulgarity and lack of style. A hint at most should be sufficient; anything more is a sign of gross insensitivity. What we call "making things clear" she considered a sign of disrespect ("Do you think I'm stupid?"); what we call "honesty" she called stupidity. It is an extreme example, but it separates, as we rarely do, the difference between love and contractual verbosity. Where love is concerned, honesty may be of very little importance. Which is not to say, however, that *dis*honesty has any place either. Sometimes, wisdom in love is just knowing when to shut up.

20 BEHIND CLOSED DOORS: LOVE, SEX AND INTIMACY

Dear Ann L:

My husband and I don't talk any more. I feel so far away from him. . . .

Dear ——: The results of a six-year study done by Dr. Ray L. Birdwhistell, an authority on non-verbal communication, should make you feel better.

In an effort to determine exactly how much conversation went on between married couples, Dr. Birdwhistell installed microphones and tape recorders in the homes and cars of selected pairs who had been married fifteen years or longer.

The results showed that couples who considered themselves happy spent 27½ minutes a week in conversation. The reason the figure was that HIGH, *Dr. Birdwhistell said, was because the couples selected for the study coincidentally went visiting a lot, and they had to give each other directions.*

Ann Landers
Washington *Post*, September 5, 1979

Love, sex and intimacy are so closely bound together that it is only with an effort that we can pry them apart. Love and sex, of course, are easily distinguished—perhaps too easily—whether or not it is also true that sex is better with love.[1] But when we add the ingredient of intimacy, it

1 Russell Vannoy, in *Sex Without Love* (Prometheus, 1979) argues that it is not.

is as if we've formed the perfect compound, sex providing the physical dimension of intimacy as the ultimate expression of love. But it is essential too that we distinguish between love and intimacy: unrequited love is love in which the issue of intimacy does not yet arise, and hatred can also be an extremely intimate emotion. Thus intimacy is not strictly necessary for love nor is it exclusive to love. Nevertheless it is hard for us to conceive of love without it.

What is intimacy? We think that we know but much of what has been said about it is, as I shall argue, dangerously confused. Too often intimacy is confused with vulnerability, sex alone or simply atmosphere. Sometimes intimacy is said to be an experience. Sometimes it is supposed to be a state of being, sometimes an activity or a kind of action. What I want to argue in this chapter is that it is essentially the experience of shared identity, the main metaphor for which is "closeness," for which sex provides the most readily available expression. "Feeling intimate" is sensing that breakdown of barriers and individual independence that is most commonly identified with intense sexual ecstasy and oblivion. "Being intimate" is a generalization of that experience, and sexual activity is but one among many actions and activities that contribute to that sense of "union." But intimacy, like love itself, has recently been shifted from the realm of sexuality, which has become all too common and routine, to the realm of the verbal, which has come to be the heart of intimacy, by way of "disclosure" and confession, "telling all" and perhaps being embarrassed by it. Therefore, though both sexual and verbal expressions are essential to romantic love, I want to spend most of this chapter emphasizing the first and de-emphasizing the second.

What is sex? An odd question, to be sure. If *anything* in the love-chat business is simply obvious and not worth defining, it is sexuality. But if love is not a mystery, perhaps sexuality ought to be more of one. Why should this physical activity—no matter how invigorating or pleasurable—be given such importance? On the basis of sexual attraction and sometimes little else, we fall in love, give a total stranger an extravagant place in our lives, shunt aside old friends, family and colleagues, and make commitments that may outlive our sexual enthusiasm. Why? We make no such fuss about our professional relationships, for example, whose significance is more a matter of convenience. We do not fall in love so readily with those with whom we share lifelong (non-sexual) interests—a favorite co-worker or tennis opponent. Why sex? And why is it so difficult, even in these "liberated" days of "casual" sex, to treat sex casually, like having lunch together—or just seeing a movie?

If one thinks of sex, as many do, as a merely pleasurable "natural" activity, the significance of sex will evade us, and the connection between sex and love will remain either a mystery or a curiosity. But if we conceive of sex as *expression*—and not the expression of love alone—then its importance becomes more evident. Romantic love, like most (but not all) emotions, involves an essentially *embodied* conception of self (which is why the concept of beauty, too, is so important to it). Romantic love is not an emotion that is possible between "two souls" or "pure consciousnesses." It is an emotion in which "the body is the meaning," according to the French philosopher Maurice Merleau-Ponty, and sex is "the projection of a person's manner of being into the world" (*Phenomenology of Perception*, p. 158). As intimacy lies right at the heart of love, sex as the expression of "closeness" is as essential to love as the desire for revenge is essential to anger, or covetousness is to envy. The urge to touch is the concrete expression of the more abstract desire to share the lover's self; the desire to hold and be held is the physical equivalent of the interlocking of two identities, distinct and different but now perfectly together. One might even say that sexual desire *is* love, by way of hyperbole, so long as one does not fallaciously conclude from that that all sexual desire is therefore love. The missing ingredient here is intimacy, for what determines the relationship between sex and romantic love is the desire, central to love but not necessarily to sex, to *be* together. For sex itself, now to complete our triangle, is not intimacy. Indeed, sex can be used precisely in order to deny or destroy intimacy. Even, sometimes, in love.

What Intimacy Is Not

Intimacy is not sex, and sex is not intimacy. It is true that one cannot be physically closer than in sex—unless one is a thoracic surgeon—but physical proximity is only sometimes an expression of intimacy. It is noteworthy that our euphemism, "to be intimate," is a polite way of saying "having sexual intercourse," but what this signifies is only that sex *sometimes* symbolizes intimacy—which no one would deny even in these promiscuous times. But one can have sex and not be intimate at all; in fact, sufficient attention to technique and sensations is a popular way of *avoiding* intimacy, as Rollo May and his colleagues are so fond of pointing out to us. Intimacy is possible without sex, of course, as in one of those often re-enacted Victorian garden parties we see on television, where two lovers exchange the most intimate glances as they properly trudge through the requisite rituals. Naked, touching and being touched, allowing oneself the unusually free expression of one's urges—it is hard to imagine any situation in which intimacy would be more at home. But sex alone neither guarantees nor is required by intimacy.

Intimacy is not mere endurance. Some couples seem to feel that they are "so close" just because they have managed to live together so long, put up with each other through so many problems, through sickness and poverty, mutual resentment and boredom. And one of them, no doubt, will be shocked and surprised when the other says, "I feel so far away from you." But intimacy, like "love," is a laudatory characteristic in our society, and so one ascribes it to oneself whenever it is remotely feasible. And having endured, one feels that one at least deserves that badge of credit. This has nothing to do with intimacy.

Intimacy is not familiarity. Feeling comfortable is not feeling intimate. One can feel comfortable alone, or with a bearskin rug, with friends, drinking partners and social workers. Feeling at home is not feeling intimate; one can enjoy that in a den before a warm fire, being greeted by the dog at the gate or the doorman at the portal. And what one *knows* about another person is not intimacy either, even if the knowledge is reciprocal. But here we enter a rather large topic and an enormous area of confusion.

Knowledge and intimacy are often thrown together, for instance in such phrases as "carnal knowledge," which may well be argued to be a confusion of epistemology, or sex, or both. The idea that *knowing* someone is either a prerequisite or equivalent to intimacy is so common that it seems like common sense. Having intercourse with someone is indeed a way of getting to *know* him or her and, at the same time, getting closer. An intimate conversation is often thought to be a revelation of secrets or a "heart-to-heart talk." Intimacy is, in particular, supposed to be the disclosure of those lesser-known, more embarrassing facts about you—your inability to hold onto friends or your incompetence with a checkbook. It is essential to intimacy that this knowledge *not* be common, for one cannot be intimate by quietly telling what everyone already knows. Thus intimacy becomes a private conversation, preferably with some sex (touching fingers and cheeks at the least), which includes the somewhat painful disclosure of embarrassing information about oneself. "I never told that to anyone before" is thus supposed to be a sure sign of intimacy and an indication of encroaching love.

Social psychologists, when they test hypotheses about intimacy, typically rely on what they can get people to *say* to one another. The results are then easily recorded and liable to only minimal misinterpretation. One set of experimenters, for exam-

ple, approached various passengers in an airport waiting lounge, initiated various conversations and then noted their responses.[2] When the initial remarks were impersonal and unrevealing, the replies tended to be very much the same. When the initial remarks were calculatedly personal and revealing, however, these total strangers would sometimes make the most intimate revelations, about their sex lives, their sense of success, their fears and insecurities. Now my point is not to report or comment on the truth or plausibility of the hypotheses being tested, but rather the presupposition of the test itself. That presupposition is that intimacy is a function of, or at least can be measured by, the kinds of information people exchange. Of course there is an obvious advantage in using such precisely recordable materials, but it is worth noting that no such precision is available in measuring, for instance, the tone of voice or the shifts in posture, much less the sense of distance and anonymity that lies behind these revelations. For, as we all know, it is often far easier to confess to a total stranger (airplane passengers are notorious) than friends, spouses and lovers. But perhaps this is precisely to say that exchange of information of this nature is not at all intimacy, but something we are often willing to do only when intimacy is *not* at issue.

One of several recent books on intimacy (there have been hundreds) expresses the psychological presupposition in its title: *Sharing Intimacy: What We Reveal to Others and Why*, by Valerian J. Derlega and Alan L. Chaikin (Prentice-Hall, 1975). The book is about intimacy, or what its authors call "self-disclosure." Their sociological presupposition is what they call "the lonely society." They presume an epistemology—as opposed to an ontology—of loneliness, the view that, even if we recognize our coexistence with other selves, we have enormous difficulties knowing anything about one another (Chapter 2). The problem seems to be our difficulty in "having someone to

[2] Zick Rubin, "Lovers and Other Strangers," *American Scientist*, Vol. 62, 1974.

talk to" and our response, accordingly, is to "share secrets." In fact "sharing secrets" becomes the essence of "self-disclosure," and most of the book is about the propriety, desirability and risks of sharing such secrets with strangers, friends, husbands and wives. It is what people *say* that is important, though to be sure there are other aspects of their behavior and other features of their situation which may be relevant as well. Sharing secrets lets us know that our problems are not unique. Sharing secrets is a way of "gaining feedback," "reducing uncertainty" and "putting our problems in perspective." Making friends and falling in love alike are based on "getting to know each other" and intimacy, as the sharing of secrets, is the key. In fact sex (particularly in the "inexpressive male") seems to have at most an instrumental role in intimacy, that is, something to talk *about* and a "medium of exchange for intimate information."

Intimacy is not knowledge, or familiarity, or comfort. Love and intimacy can always *use* knowledge, familiarity and comfort, of course; they may even be presupposed to a certain extent, but the nature of intimacy itself is to be found elsewhere. What we *know* in love, as well as what we say, is vastly overrated. Intimacy may include the exchange of secrets, but it need not. Indeed, one embarrassing implication of that theory is that two people who are sufficiently well known to each other and perhaps to the public at large (two "celebrities," for instance, or a psychiatrist and his or her patient) would have no room for intimacy; there would be nothing left to exchange. But the very opposite seems to be the case. It is their *privacy* that is intimate, not the exchange of information. And if the exchange of embarrassing information were the main ingredient in intimacy, it would follow that those of us with the most embarrassing information to exchange would be the most intimate, with a veritable wealth of love to go around. But indeed the truth seems to be very different. The exchange of embarrassing secrets may make me momentarily vulnerable but this is just as likely to *end* my sense of intimacy as to enrich it. Having shared my secret with you, blurting it out in a moment of carelessness, I now wish you would just disappear. And that, I would suggest, is hardly the mark of intimacy.

Perhaps it is true, as we have been reminded for so many years and in so many sermons, that "the flesh is weak" and "to err is human." But is love therefore to be confused with mutual confession and compassion? Is the basis of love embarrassment? The shameful do not make better lovers, whether or not they make better patients or confidants. Love is a sharing of strengths as well as weaknesses, and our conception of intimacy is too bound up with only the latter. There are, of course, emotions of mutual degradation, but love is not one of them. There is a sense in which intimacy involves knowledge, but knowledge and vulnerability are not themselves intimacy.

Sex as Language

Sex isn't something you've got to play with; sex is you. *It's the flow of your life, it's your moving self and you are due to be true to the nature of it. . . .*

D. H. LAWRENCE, *Collected Poetry*

Many of our most intimate moments are spent in silence. Silence, of course, can be awkward, but it can also be "pregnant," particularly in the midst of a longing gaze, when talk of almost any kind is a breach of intimacy. This is nowhere more obvious than in sexual desire, when talk tends to become mere chatter, a veil which at one dramatic instant is pulled away by silence. It is evident too in sex itself, looking and touching, and after, with that calm sense of closeness already achieved. It is sometimes said, by those who use sex as protection *against* intimacy (and as a masquerade for it), that sexuality involves turning the other person, and perhaps also oneself, into an "object." But in intimacy just the opposite is the case; the distance required by "objects" is broken down completely. We are two sensuous subjects, not pure consciousnesses, much less souls, but "embodied" lovers, feeling our bodies and each other's body and oblivious to the usual daily distinctions between what's yours and what's mine, what's body and what's mind.

Sex itself is not intimate, I have insisted, but it is nevertheless our primary vehicle for intimacy. This is not a natural necessity. Most animals do not experience anything like intimacy as they mate, and many people in many cultures would find our notion of intimacy foreign to themselves as well. Sex as such is underdetermined, in the sense that it can be made into a great many different types of activities—merely instrumental, a means to pregnancy or a release of tension, an assertion of privilege, a male "right" to his wife that is closed to all others—or it can be symbolic in a grander sense, as an expression of mythological proportions, "the flow of your life," according to Lawrence, or the enactment of the cosmic process, according to Rollo May. What sex is *not*, even in this most hedonistic of cultures, is mere *pleasure*. Sex is a *language*, in which we express our "deepest" feelings for one another. Love is by no means the only emotion so expressed, even between lovers. Sex is a non-verbal language, in which nothing is (verbally) explicit or need be actually *said*, but in which we therefore find it often easier to express what we will not say, and to find expressed what we will not easily hear.

Sex is our vehicle for intimacy, first of all, because it is an essentially *private* activity, in contrast with speech, which can be broadcast to millions all at once. And even sex in public (kissing and cooing in the park, for example) is almost belligerently exclusive, visible to others but shutting them out absolutely. It is the essence of intimacy that it be relatively rare, and sex provides this rarity, in part because of our insistence that it be a private activity, and in part because of the restrictions and taboos we impose upon it. But at the same time sex is the language of romantic love, in part because it is the common denominator of virtually all peoples in all cultures, and thus opens up the possibility of romantic choice to virtually everyone. This raises an innocent paradox: that love and intimacy employ sex as their primary language because it is both universal and rare, because everyone has it but every time it is considered unique and special.

To say that sex is a language, a (for the most part) silent, non-verbal language, is to allow ourselves to understand why sex is so important, not only in love, but in the expression of a great many other emotions besides. The standard "liberal" view of sex as pleasurable activity (the only restriction being that it be "between consenting adults"), makes it all but impossible to understand why this activity should be so important to us, so devastating when we fail or do without it, so exhilarating when it goes well and is obviously so much more than merely enjoyable. (Indeed, in the Freudian view of sex as pleasurable release or catharsis, it is not even obvious why we need to bother with other people, since we can "release" ourselves alone.) It is important if not obvious too that sex need not involve genital intercourse, but might indeed include any mutual bodily activities and expressions, including a languid look across the room and playing "footsies" under the dining-room table. But every move is a gesture filled with meaning. Sex as a language cannot be taken lightly, cannot be "casual," whatever our superficial moralizing might be. One cannot make a sexual gesture devoid of its meaning any more easily than one can say something in English, e.g., "It is cold," and not mean by it that it is cold.[3]

Because sex is a language it can be "spoken" well or badly, awkwardly or expertly, and the emotion expressed will get through better or worse depending on this. Technique im-

[3] But I can say, "It is cold," as a signal in a plot, for instance, and not mean that it is cold. So I can even have intercourse—e.g., in a Masters and Johnson experiment—and not, in this special case, mean anything by it either. The meaning is there perhaps, but I do not mean it.

proves articulation as well as pleasure, but too much emphasis on technique blocks expression altogether, like a memorized speech in a casual conversation. The very fact that two people kiss or have intercourse is itself immensely significant, of course, but every gesture and movement within that context is significant too. First of all, it signifies, in a very strong sense, *being* together, and it is not a mere matter of misunderstanding when one person says (afterward) to another, "I thought you agreed that this was just for fun." But sex is not just an expression of togetherness, a symbolic gesture of shared identity. It also involves the complex expression of many of those interpersonal privately defined roles which make up that shared identity, and it is here that the connection between love, sex and intimacy becomes most apparent. In silence.

Our most crucial roles together rarely have to be spelled out. And when they are, it may often be a shock or surprise. We sometimes trust not what's said but what's displayed, particularly where affection is concerned. But we also feel a lover's hesitation, a hint of avoidance, as well as vulnerability or dependency, long before these are ever expressed in words, even before we are conscious of it. Some roles defy intimacy: treating the other person as a confessor or acting like a confessor oneself can do this. Causing pain in sex can, but need not always, have this effect. Other roles are easy vehicles for intimacy—simple play, baby talk, touching or allowing oneself to be touched slowly, gently. But no gesture automatically initiates a role; it all depends on the context and the intention. Play can be avoidance; baby talk can be just silliness. A slow soft touch may be simply a step in a back rub as well as an excuse to "open up" completely. But then, a good Russian idiom, enunciated on the streets of Los Angeles, may not have a meaning either.

Sex is the vehicle for love and intimacy only in so far as it is mutually understood and accepted. The most loving touch is still an act of aggression when it is unwanted, unexpected, totally unsolicited. On the other hand, a brutal lunge or a painful pinch can be fully an expression of love, so long as it is a matter of mutual desire and expression. Sex consists of shared symbols as well as symbols of shared identity. Sadism itself is almost never an expression of love, but sadism with a masochist may well be. Indeed, the most common complementary roles in love and in sex are those of domination and submission, often alternating with an emphasis on an underlying sense of equality, all as a matter of gesture and almost never actually stated. Sexual "positions," which the guidebooks prefer to treat as a mere matter of "variety," are indeed gestures of great importance. "Who's on top" has much to say about the relationship itself, and some of the most crucial roles in love are expressed in just this way. The "dominant" position is also a symbol of dominance; so is "submission." Switching roles frequently is a way of emphasizing equality. Some couples find only one position comfortable, making rather obvious (though they may never acknowledge it) at least one set of roles that composes their identity. Some couples far prefer positions of equality (lying both on their sides, for example); others eschew intercourse altogether, because of its symbolic significance, the male "inside of" the female, "invading" her. But there is nothing right or wrong about this viewpoint. Symbols mean what they are believed to mean, and for some couples this is what they mean. And there is nothing "natural" or "unnatural" about such views either, in so far as there is nothing "natural" about symbols and their meanings.

Touching itself represents intimacy to us precisely because we are so cautious about it. A salesman's slap on the back or a co-worker's pat on the butt is not intimacy but intrusion, and it is because we so guard our bodies that sex itself remains a matter of personal privacy and so significant. The genitals remain the key to sex for most of us just because, not as a matter of nature but of custom, they are so rarely even visible much less touchable by other people. We can easily imagine it otherwise. Indeed, promiscuous people may well develop a sense of intimacy which largely ignores the genitals and emphasizes instead some part of the body and activities which are generally neglected: fingertips, face or even feet perhaps. Again, it is the symbolism that counts, the mutual roles that are acted out silently that constitute the heart of intimacy and the expression of love. Every touch is an assertion, and where and how is meaningful in terms of the role(s) in which it plays its part. A single touch can represent control, domination, even vulnerability, all at once. There are positions and actions which clearly symbolize vulnerability, "openness" and trust (although it is important to point out that this is obviously not the only way to express vulnerability and trust; as one of my critics has pointed out,[4] opening a joint checking account may be a far better expression of trust than any sexual openness). There are fancy ways of making love that represent co-ordination to a remarkable degree, plain and simple ways of making love that represent simplicity and tradition, outrageous ways of making love that represent eccentricity, daring, mutual creativity or rebellion. There are ways of making love that are explicitly subservient, self-consciously noncommittal, openly devoted. One might (if so inclined) chart all of these explicitly, in a sort of "how to" book of positions for the non-verbally inarticulate. But expression is whatever makes itself mutually understood, and a book of translations would be appropriate only in the most bizarre of circumstances (perhaps for Robert Heinlein's peculiarly "groking" creature in *Stranger in a Strange Land*, though he seems to have been successful enough without it).

Sex is central to intimacy as its medium of expression, though one can easily imagine or find cultures in which this is not the case. Intimacy in turn is central to love as that set of

[4] Janice Moulton, "Another Sexual Position," *Journal of Philosophy*, 1976, in response to my "Sexual Paradigms" in the same journal, 1974.

essentially private and personal roles through which we build a shared identity, although one can imagine and find societies which do not distinguish the personal from the public as we do, and consequently will not have either our concept of intimacy or our conception of romantic love. One might imagine romantic love without full-blown sex, without intercourse and heavy petting, perhaps, but one cannot imagine romantic love without some form of caress, if only with eyes and the touch of two fingers and an occasional kiss. Intimacy tends to be vulnerable, not because it is intrinsically confessional or an admission of weaknesses, but because it is essentially devoting oneself to roles and investing oneself in an identity which another person can snatch away, without warning, or with a clumsy statement or gesture, even a critical look. While we're playfully cooing, you can at any moment turn serious and "adult," reducing my remaining moment of childishness to mere foolishness. And as I act out my own sense of insecurity or trust or submissiveness or mock aggressiveness you can at any time raise the curtain on my private performance, by laughing at me, chastising me or, worst of all, dismissing me. It is not that our intimacy is itself built out of embarrassments, but intimacy as strictly private and personal roles and identity is by its very nature easily embarrassed, even if it is not in itself in any way embarrassing. There is nothing intrinsically embarrassing about sex, from which it does not follow that public performances are not shameful, including even public talk about it. But if we want sex to be a continuing vehicle of intimacy—which is to say, if we want to keep our conception of sensual sexual intimate romantic love intact (and this is always an open question)—then sex too will have to be kept under wraps, which is in no way to say a "dirty little secret," much less "repressed." But what romantic love, sex and intimacy share in common, and what allows them to function as they do in our lives, is precisely this common yet in each case unique sense of privacy, this completely familiar yet in every couple original expression, using gestures and organs equally available to every one of a billion-odd couples, in every case signifying something quite special.

21 LOVE AND THE TEST OF TIME ("DIALECTIC")

It is very romantic to be in love. But there is nothing romantic about a definite proposal. Why, one may be accepted. One usually is, I believe. Then the excitement is over. The very essence of romantic love is uncertainty.

OSCAR WILDE, *The Importance of Being Earnest*

Nowhere is our all-or-nothing attitude to love more evident than in that peculiar slogan, "Love is forever." It may have an impressive metaphysical ancestry, in Plato, St. Paul and the whole of Christianity, but in a plain matter-of-fact everyday interpretation it is not only false but absurd. Love comes to an end. Sometimes abruptly, sometimes quietly. Often it starts again, and not infrequently it actually lasts a lifetime. But no love has the assurances of eternity; all love is fraught with ups and downs and uncertainties, and even the marriage contract has its temporal escape clause—"till death do us part." We all know love to be risky, traumatic, a ragged road with cataclysm possible at every turn. So why do we say, "I'll love you always"? Sometimes, in the thrill of the moment, we even believe it.

As in other all-or-nothing dramatizations of love, such as "Love is everything" (that is, it is at times extremely important to us) and "You're the most wonderful person in the world" (I'm enthusiastic about you), "Love is forever" is an overly extravagant expression of an important emotional truth. It is a child's word—the Greeks called it "infinity"; it means "uncountable," a *refusal* to see the end, open-ended desire and continuity. Whether or not love is going to end, that ending is emphatically not built into or even allowed in its experiential structure. (One might contrast such emotions as hope, fear and the thirst for vengeance, whose end is essential to the emotion.) Couples beginning to live together or entering into marriage are loath to discuss legal agreements about what will be whose if they break up. Making contingency plans ("if it doesn't work out") is considered in poor taste, as well as proof that one isn't really serious. Love projects itself into the indefinite future, not forever, but as far as one can see—though sometimes this is not much more than a year or a month or two, or even a week or so. Love needs that opening. Many other emotions do not. Love is a process, a *dialectic*. It takes *time*. And not to give it the time it takes is indeed to be that much less in love.

Time is the test of love. Love that does not last is mere "infatuation," no matter how intense, how dedicated, how indistinguishable from "the real thing." Indeed, there may be no other difference between the two.[1] Of course the amount of time required to prove the "truth" of love varies from generation to generation; most of my friends seem to consider eight or nine months sufficient, some of my students a few days, my parents and their friends nothing short of a lifetime. But the point to ponder is that we do consider time as a test, since it is not so for most other emotions. One would not dismiss anger or jealousy if it lasted only five weeks, or even five days. Indeed, one can get truly angry even for a minute. ("I'm glad I got that out of my system.") Yet the idea that love could be

1 "Infatuation" is therefore not the name of an emotion at all, but a retrospective judgment about love. It is like the word "counterfeit," in that counterfeit money might indeed be indistinguishable from the real stuff, but nevertheless it is judged to be worthless.

satisfied the first time we make love ("I'm glad I got that out of my system"?!) or that love could be complete in a single moment—no matter how "marvelous"—is unthinkable. Thus the troubadours confused the beginning of love for its end, and Don Juan is a problem not because he loves for only a week, but because, what's worse, he knows this in advance.

Love and Death

> One of the bases for our civilization has been the idea of love. The idea of love was founded on our loving a mortal person forever. This brought us to terms with the idea of death. It is a way to face death. That is what makes it tragic and dramatic and precious—
>
> OCTAVIO PAZ

In contrast to the idea that love is "forever," that time is the test of love, the same tradition has promoted the dramatic connection between love and death. Octavio Paz suggests, as Plato did twenty-five hundred years before, that love is a way of *facing* death, a means to immortality. But in literature it is one of our favorite clichés to *end* a romance with the death of the lovers, thus saving the author the almost impossible task of spelling out how they lived "happily ever after" without passion fading away or getting lost in the clatter of domestic responsibilities. How would one have continued *Romeo and Juliet*, or written a sequel to *Tristan and Isolde*? But this literary device is not to be confused with the sometimes tedious exigencies of life, and the connection between love and death, for most of us, is again one of those all-or-nothing dramatizations which leads us to falsify and demean our own experience. Few of us are ever asked, much less expected, to die for love. And we are practical enough to look with pity, not admiration, at some young lover who dies of despair by his or her own hand. But this does not make love any less—perhaps only more circumspect, more in perspective. But again, this dramatic exaggeration of the life-and-death importance which we ascribe to love has its germ of truth, not only in showing once again the remarkable significance this emotion has in our lives, but also in proving how closely love and identity are linked to our very existence, so that cessation of love is often equated with death. But moving from metaphor to real love and life, we have to do what Romeo and Juliet did not—understand how love continues, day after day, how the dialectic of love goes on, the stuff of which comedies, not tragedies, are made.

When Denis de Rougemont published his classic if tendentious *Love in the Western World* some forty years ago, he tried to capture both "love is forever" and the love-and-death connection in a single theory, and with a single distinction. He distinguished what he called "conjugal love"—essentially based in a marriage and supported by the grace of God—and "romantic love," which he considered pagan, irrational, anti-social and essentially destructive, even fatal. Not surprisingly, Romeo, Juliet, Tristan and Isolde appear as paradigmatic examples of romantic love, and he takes their premature demise to be not a literary but an emotional necessity. Romantic love, which is intrinsically unstable, has no other possible end, unless, of course, it simply fades away and ends in disappointment, the less than dramatic but perhaps still tragic experience of us less than fictitious everyday heroes.

I think De Rougemont overstates his case, but he has recognized something quite essential which his many critics often prefer to ignore: that romantic love is not only unstable—or I shall soon say "metastable"—but a poor preparation for, even a threat to, the stability of marriage. Romantic love is not the anteroom to marriage but, in an important sense, its opposite (which is not to say that they are not complementary). As Kierkegaard argued in *Either/Or*, marriage is responsibility, romantic love is irresponsibility, the first a bedrock of civilized society, the latter a rebellious emotional attachment. I think that De Rougemont is right in pointing out the essential difference between a relationship which is based on obligations, expectations, the mores of society and, in marriage, a contractual "commitment" and a relationship that is based wholly on the contingency of an emotion. Now granted, in our day the distinction between love and marriage has broken down considerably; few people still see marriage as a lifetime necessity which they *cannot* ever get out of, but marriage (and often living together too) includes commitments and obligations which love does not. It is based on the *expectation* of staying together, while romantic love includes only the desire and hope. Although there may be some time when the two emotions are almost indistinguishable, the essential experience of each is distinctly its own.

It is the contingency of romantic love that concerns me here; "working out" a relationship need not have anything to do with love. Indeed, one thinks of Rodney Dangerfield's classic line: "We sleep in separate rooms, we have dinner apart, we take separate vacations–we're doing everything we can to keep our marriage together." Romantic love is essentially a tension. Marriages can be happy; romantic love must be exhilarating. This is not to say that one cannot have both, but it would be naïve to suppose that two forces moving in opposite directions "naturally" belong together, "like a horse and carriage." Marriages are made "forever," ended ideally only by death. Love, on the other hand, lasts but from day to day, week to week, an exquisite contingency which, like all uncertainties, chooses death as its metaphor. But it is a metaphor, like "happily ever after," that conceals more than it reveals, and hides the essential relationships between romantic love and time.

Love and Time

"Love me forever, if only for tonight."
—ANON.

Of course we want love to last. But here we may find one of those curious sleights of hand that Nietzsche once diagnosed as the "great philosophical errors," confusing cause for effect, wishes for causes. We begin by assuring each other that love will last. Soon we are taking love's lasting as the test of love and then it is no longer the desire but one of the structural components of love, love as a state which if real endures. But love, we keep insisting, is not a state.

We say love is forever but celebrate love for the moment. Indeed, lovers are notoriously reckless in the conception of time, in their impatience, in their view of the future. The moment is everything. But then, to confuse matters even more, we say, "I wish this moment would last forever." But it is the very nature of a moment *not* to last; that's what makes it a moment. So there seems to be confusion at the very core of our conception. We treat love as a state when it is rather a process, and treat love as a moment which might last forever. But love is neither of the moment nor forever. Love essentially involves a sense of time—indeed time comes to be defined by the relationship—but we do not need to refer either to the specious present or to unimaginable eternity in order to understand this.

To say that love takes time is to say that it is never just "for the moment"; love always has duration; because it is a process, it always looks forward to the future and back to its past. Love looks to the future, in fantasies of marriage, babies, a trip to Boston next summer, for it is in future plans and possibilities that our shared identity (like our individual identities) is largely determined. Our mutual expectations are as essential as our mutual admiration of one another, and here too the dialectical complexity of love becomes apparent: you tell me that you want to become a great musician, and I adopt your ambition as my own. You get insecure and have your doubts, but I'm now the one who urges you on, and indeed I have come to take your sense of the future as so much a matter of my identity that your loss of interest in it can be extremely damaging to my sense of my own identity, and thus to our love as well.

The future is not an infinite expanse of moments (an archaic view of time in any case) but a series of hypotheticals and contingencies ("what if . . .") whose significance fades asymptotically. Quite the contrary of love being concerned with the infinite, much less lost in the moment, it is rather absorbed in the immediate future. Sometimes it is the next ten seconds that seem to mean everything to me, or the next five hours, the next two days. It is the anticipation of your touch, expecting you to call, waiting for the movie to end or the bill to arrive. It is being hardly able to wait until we get home, or enjoying this weekend as if it were followed by an abyss, and preceded by one as well. Indeed, one sure way to threaten love, though inviting assurances, is to push such abstract questions as "What will happen when we get tired of each other?" and "What if you get bored with me?" Or even, more positively, watching old couples and hoping to be like them. Indeed, not only do such questions break the delicate webbing that ties the present to the immediate future—by stretching it too far—but they may even help bring about precisely the feared possibility that they seek assurance against. Love is not so much moment by moment as it is step by step. And in love as in Keynesian economics, "the long run" is often least important, and least real.

Love also refers to the past, sometimes in an obvious and all-consuming sense, for instance, in love that has gone on for years. The sense of a shared past can act as an anchor, to hold love together through an extremely troubled present and not very promising future. At least for a while. But even the beginning of love looks to the past, in a most curious way, desperately trying to weave together a temporal identity that has little basis either in past or present. "You mean you went to that Allen Ginsberg reading too? I wonder if we saw each other then, perhaps even bumped into each other in the aisles?" It is a frivolous enterprise but an essential one. If love is the temporal process of forming a self-identity, then the past is as essential as the present and the future, just as prone to fantasy (in this case retrospective interpretation) and just as much of an ingredient in the sense of a shared self emerging from two seemingly wholly separate selves. But because love takes time, it takes whatever time it can get, even creating time from random moments and memories. If life is art, then even short is long. (*Si vita ars est, ergo donc brevis longus est.*)[2]

Dialectic

> The essence of our relations with others is *conflict*.
>
> JEAN-PAUL SARTRE

Love is a process, a dialectic, a movement—toward what? Toward a shared identity, the creation of a shared self. But this is complicated by the fact, which we have not yet sufficiently emphasized, that this goal is impossible, unachievable, even incomprehensible. Two selves cannot become one, not when they start out so differently—with different origins, even from different cultures, with different tastes and expectations. And yet this does not mean that the goal is impossible to work for and to want even desperately, to *yearn* after. For this indeed is the famous *languor* of love, the play of contradictions reinforcing each other.

The paradox of love is this, that it presupposes a strong sense of individual autonomy and independence, and then

[2] The pun is from Gayatri Spivak; the Latin is from Jon Solomon.

seeks to cancel this by creating a shared identity. But this cannot be, for no sooner do we approach this goal than we are abruptly reminded of our differences. Perhaps you dislike a movie I love, or maybe I'm bored or insulted by one of your friends. Even in the most trivial differences, we are thrown back to our individuality, wondering how we could possibly "work" as a couple. But then, as we move apart, the self we have already formed together pulls us back; the separation is too painful; we have too much at stake, too much together, too much to lose. We *want* this, whatever the differences. Love is this process, not a state of union but a never ending conflict of pushing away and pulling together. In some couples the dialectic is wholly obvious, in that curious alternation of love and hate and sweet sex and battles and reconciliation that leaves other people looking on in perplexity. For others it is a subtle wave motion of relative independence and dependency, never so violent that either becomes a matter of desperation. But whether dialectic is violent or rather a soft fluctuation, it is alternatively adoration, minor annoyances, passionate joy, indignation, childish play, guilt, euphoria, shamelessness, shame, delirium, resentment, gratitude, indifference, gaiety, need and solitude, too easily summarized, after a few months or years, simply as "love," when in fact it's been a hundred other emotions besides, all as a part of love.

Because love is a process, it takes time. Because it has a goal, we can say that love is "going somewhere" even if that goal is ultimately impossible, and even if, in another sense, love has nowhere to go (Chapter 7). To say that an affair "isn't going anywhere" is to say that the possibility of a shared identity now appears to be impossible, though one can, of course, be mistaken. It is important not to assume, however, that progress toward a goal is necessarily "growth"—in the current laudatory term—an improvement, a betterment or "expansion" of self. Sometimes it is clearly the case that progress in a relationship involves individual degeneration or stagnation. Sometimes, the cost of shared identity might well be the withering of an autonomous and admirable self, or both individual selves. Our romantic mythology aside, romantic love is not guaranteed to make us better people, more creative, less violent or any of the other grand consequences that are supposed to flow from it. Indeed, the tension that keeps love alive may be severely damaging to other facets of one's self, depending not only on the intensity of the emotion but on the specific roles that the lovers adopt along the way. But luckily, it is not usually this way.

At first, particularly when two people have just met, shared identity consists almost wholly in fantasy, in projection into the future and a kind of ignorant idealization. Through time together, shared efforts and enjoyments—most importantly the various roles that constitute intimacy, including, presumably, sex—the self that is formed comes to be less based on fantasy, more on matters of fact and mutual recognition of real virtues, needs and foibles. The excitement can cool as well, but it need not, for it is a cynical view indeed that makes the thrill of love dependent on fantasy and novelty alone. Because love is a dialectical tension, it survives over time not only in its erratic and never completed progression toward shared identity but also in the sporadic counter-assertion of individual identities, in which we push apart and challenge those bonds but at the same time test and help strengthen them. Thus love continues by creating conflicts and differences as well as similarities, and the motive for doing so is not only the assertion of one's differences vis-à-vis one's lover but continuing the dialectic as well. Thus one becomes "the sloppy one" in part so we have something to fight or tease about, in part to assert our differences from, as well as to define, each other. The same differences and conflicts that at the time seemed to be proof of our incompatibility and the beginning of a breakup turn out to be precisely the movement that keeps us together.

Differences and conflicts have as much a place in creating the new identity as in threatening it from within, and here especially we can understand love as a dialectical process over time, not necessarily growth toward a goal but a dynamic equilibrium of tensions alternatively created and resolved, always with a sense of difference and contingency, but never losing that sense of identity that is no longer only one's own. Here too we can understand the role of such "negative" emotions as jealousy—which can be one of the most fatal threats to any relationship—as another way of preserving that tension, a simultaneous and extremely painful recognition of both the independence of one's lover and the powerful bonds of identity—now appearing perhaps as "possessiveness." But in small doses it is a force for cohesion as well as bitter conflict, and although jealousy itself may last only for an instant, it may be the violation that reminds us how much we value a relationship we may have come to take too much for granted.

Metastability: Master and Slave

> METASTABLE (chemistry) chemically unstable in the absence of certain conditions that would induce stability, but not liable to spontaneous transformation.
>
> RANDOM HOUSE DICTIONARY

Dialectic is tension, but a certain, distinctive progressive tension that supports and creates as well as threatens and destroys. One can imagine two dancers or wrestlers, pressing against one another with more than sufficient force to knock the other down, but because their force is balanced and properly directed the net result is that they hold one another up. Two teams of children in a tug of war lean back on their ropes so that they would surely fall down if each were not pulling just as hard in the other direction. Indeed, it is the most grievous crime for one team to suddenly let go, thus releasing the tension and letting the other fall into the mud. And unromantic as the examples (and the ones to follow) might be, they are good illustrations of the mutually supporting but at the same time opposed tensions and conflicts that make love as a process possible. Indeed, the idea of love as a simple stable "union" is as banal—and as false—as it sounds. Love is a struggle but, as in dance, a struggle that can be both beautiful and inspiring.

The fact that love is balanced tension explains why it should so often have the *appearance* of a state—sometimes for years. But love is always to be understood as what Jean-Paul Sartre calls *metastable*. It may have all of the appearance of stability, but the violence of the forces in balance are such that, should there be a single slip, a momentary imbalance, an ill-considered comment or careless act, that stability shatters into disaster. A homely example is the familiar experience of carrying hot coffee across the room. Four friends are visiting, and we are making the hazardous journey from the kitchen to the living room, five cups of near-boiling java and a small pitcher of milk balanced on outstretched arms. If all goes well, the tensions will disappear in a sigh of relief and the dangers be soon forgotten. But we know what happens at the slightest spill or loss of balance: one drop of hot coffee on tender skin causes a reflex action, perhaps only a minor twitch, which spills much more coffee, which makes us drop one of the cups; we instinctively grab for it and then—total disaster.

Love is like this too. We literally play with fire, evoking in ourselves and each other the most intense passions and extravagant expectations which we encourage with an uneasy sense of confidence. At first one can say almost anything, for nothing is at stake. Soon only the most precise answers are allowed, and only the most exact movements. Lovers are completely tolerant, but only within those delicate boundaries. (It doesn't much matter how much sugar is in the hot coffee.) One can become practiced as a lover as a host or hostess, and become adept at managing the dangerous tensions, keeping them in balance, avoiding or correcting those disappointments or discourtesies that all too easily lead to disaster. But the tensions and the dangers are always there. Unless of course one decides to play it safe by letting love cool until it is no longer capable of causing any pain. But then, unfortunately, it will be too tepid to enjoy as well.

Because love is always metastable, apparently in a state of rest but always bustling with tension and prone to disaster, it also tends to *move*—by breaking down barriers and allowing a relationship to expand its scope—but sometimes to degenerate too, causing new wounds and insecurities that keep a couple off balance for weeks. But it is the movement itself that is most important, not its direction; indeed it is only at the very beginning of a relationship—or at the very end—that the image of a direction to love even makes sense. It is the tension and the balance and the movement that constitutes love, the conflicts and accidents as well as the happiness. The idea of a real unity—as Aristophanes suggested—is only an abstract ideal. Love is this shift of needs and tensions, mutual fantasies, plans and ideals *within* the structures already formed by the ideal of shared identity. Dialectic is as often a switch as a progression, indeed it is sheer movement without an end—like quarrels without a point—that characterizes romantic love, not at all the ascensions into heaven that are preached so tiresomely and the "happily ever after" that ends our fairy tales.

The fairy tale or fable that seems to me to best illustrate the nature of dialectic is a parable that the German philosopher G. W. F. Hegel proffered in his *Phenomenology of Spirit* (1807). It is Hegel with whom the term "dialectic" is most often associated, and Karl Marx, for one, took it directly from him. The parable is called "master and slave," and although Hegel intended it as a general statement about a certain kind of interpersonal relationship, it can be adopted precisely—and has been, for example, by Jean-Paul Sartre—as a model for the dialectic of love. The story is simple: two people who are essentially equals (this is important) meet each other, size each other up and engage in a battle. What they are fighting for, Hegel says, is not riches or territory or peace or greed or selfishness or any of the other aspects of "human nature" that philosophers and political theorists have imagined, but simple *recognition.* Hegel calls the battle "for life and death," but we can say, less violently, that it is a quest for *identity.* Imagine two people on a first date, each trying awkwardly to impress and attract the other, not because one wants anything further from the other—let us assume they do not—but because each wants to be thought well of, as a good person, as intelligent, as interesting, as if (and it seems this way at the time) one's conception of oneself depended upon the recognition of this single stranger. But since each is looking for recognition from the other, each may be all too likely to ignore the needs of the other. So empty compliments turn into teasing, and teasing turns into an argument; the attempt to be charming becomes defensive—too much praise of oneself, too much belittling of everyone else. They are offended; they try to be civil. Or they are nervous, well on the way to being depressed, but they wait, hoping for some magic "click" that will end this awkward struggle and start another. So they start a fight. Or lose themselves at a party, or—more often—begin a sexual struggle, not so much out of desire as desperation. Sex provides the magic. Sometimes it becomes a way of seeming to lose oneself in an activity that is sufficiently overwhelming or familiar or both that the tension seems to have ceased, or at least becomes a far more exhilarating form of tension. Sometimes sex is magic in quite another sense, introducing the end of that civility that covers up Hegel's life-and-death struggle to allow a full outburst of indignation, an abrupt end to a "date" that wasn't going anywhere anyway—or something new to talk and argue about, which may end in frustration and irresolution but nevertheless marks the beginning of a tense and passionate affair. (Then again, some people do just manage to "have a good time.")

The struggle itself is just the first step in Hegel's little story; the best part comes in its aftermath. In Hegel's parable one person wins, one loses; the winner spares the loser in return for his subservience. The analog in love may not at first seem clear, but Jean-Paul Sartre works it out in some detail in his *Being and Nothingness*. Back in the days when sex was a man's demand and a woman's defeat, the identification of winners and losers, masters and servants was rather straightforward. Today it is not. But in a thousand subtle ways we recognize what it is for someone to "make a point" or lose one. Consider a couple beginning a quarrel. The point of the quarrel doesn't matter; there may not even be one. They are struggling for recognition, to be recognized as needed, perhaps, or as having carried the lion's load of the relationship. But here the notion of winning and losing makes perfectly good sense, whether or not sex is part of the battle, its cause or, often, its resolution. And it is here that Hegel makes his most exciting observation—namely, that winners and losers are always in a precariously unstable way; the winner, now faced with an awesome responsibility and the dependency of the other, finds him or herself even more dependent in return. The winning spouse in a marital quarrel breaks the other down to tears, wholly dependent on the next response, hoping desperately for an apology, or "I didn't mean it." He or she is racked with guilt and anxiety, no matter how angry a moment ago. The relationship is in one's hands, and everything now becomes focused on the defeated other. The loser, on the other hand, finds just the reverse: that this position of seeming dependency is indeed a position of tremendous power. It is the loser who feels free to think about something else, to reconsider the relationship and think, perhaps, that his or her self-esteem might well be better served elsewhere. The victor becomes the dependent one, the loser the more independent. But this state can't last either, for as that independence is asserted, as the "master" gives in to his or her anxiety, the roles are once again reversed, and the dialectic moves again—though not in any direction, perhaps even forever in a circle. It is this constant movement, expressed in as well as punctuated by sex in particular, that keeps the excitement of love alive.

The picture of love as a life-and-death struggle is overdramatized, for certain, and Hegel is quite clear (as Sartre is not) that this is not all there is to human relationships. But it is a model of the dynamics and dialectics of love that is more instructive than the idealized image of love as unperturbed and calm emotion, mixed with hostility only as a sign of "human weakness" and torn apart by our "tragic inability to love." Love itself is conflict, but a conflict which can be as constructive as destructive. Two people can never become one (though Hegel at times seemed to think so) and yet, as Aristophanes so rightly pointed out, we desperately want to do so. And in that impossible desire is the essence of love, a constant struggle between our sense of individuality and our sense of a "union." But this sounds more negative than it is. Perhaps the Hegelian-Sartrian parable is too brutal to capture the often tender and extremely enjoyable means we employ to carry on this conflict, but the battle for identity, sometimes indeed involving the sense of winning and losing and dependence and independence, is what love is ultimately all about.

Movement takes time. How much time? Certainly not necessarily a lifetime, much less forever. Some people can find in an evening of intimacy what others can't do in a year. In fact what we mean by "a good lover," our recent sexual technical fetishism aside, is predominantly the ability to inspire that sense of intimacy and familiarity quickly. For some people, intimacy seems to take nothing else *but* time; it is not so much an effort or an activity as mere presence, time spent together. For them, love indeed may require years and, even then, end with the tragic impression that "we never really got to know one another." But whether love takes a week or a decade, this much is clear: love is a process of transformation, a sometimes violent alteration of self that is always torn between our ideologically all-pervasive need for independence and autonomy and our equally all-pervasive obsession with romantic love and shared identity. And this takes time, whether the tension is developed through a gentle tender wave motion of alternative attitudes and identities or in the violent twists and turns of our grade B romantic novelists. Love takes enough time to allow for that famous *yearning* that Aristophanes quite rightly put at the very core of love, that impossible desire to be (re-)united in equilibrium with one's sense of oneself. It cannot be found in a moment; it may not last forever. But in between the moment and eternity, there is for love all the time in the world.

BEYOND SEX AND GENDER (LOVE AND FEMINISM) 22

"Love. Being in love. Yuck!" Val poured more wine in their glasses.

"Val hates love," Iso explained, a wicked smile on her face.

Mira blinked at Val. "Why?"

"Oh, shit." Val sipped her wine. "I mean, it's one of those things they've erected, like the madonna, you know, or the infallibility of the Pope or the divine right of kings. A bunch of nonsense erected*—and that's the crucial word—into Truth by a bunch of intelligent* men*—another crucial word. What the particular nonsense is, isn't important. What's important is why they did it."*

MARILYN FRENCH, *The Women's Room*

Is romantic love unfair to women? So it has been charged. There is an argument currently gaining wide acceptance, as evidenced, for example, by the enormous number of readers who have recognized themselves in Marilyn French's *The Women's Room,* which would undermine everything we have argued here, if it is sound. The argument, which I will call for convenience "the feminist argument" (see Chapter 8) says essentially that romantic love is a cultural concoction whose purpose is to delude women into rationalizing their own subservience.

The feminist argument is extremely persuasive, far more so than the murky pious praise and the alleged "need for love" that have been the topic of so many predominantly male theoreticians and theologians from Plato and St. Paul to Rollo May. The argument begins with the realization that romantic love, which has so often been promised to women (by men) as the key to happiness, is a myth, an illusion, a fraud. It does not, as promised, change one's life, turn the drudgery of housework and motherhood into joy, much less "forever." But not only that. It is the myth itself that has this as its ulterior motive; it is an illusion whose deconstruction reveals a political purpose. Love was invented by men as an instrument of a kind of culture—which might be summarized as "capitalist"—in order to "keep women in their place," or in any case isolated and dependent on men, and if not happy, then at least hopeful of love and complacent about their socially inferior but infinitely useful occupations. By preaching that love is always good and desirable, it is charged, men have convinced at least most women that love is more important than politics and power, thus limiting the competition to themselves. By teaching that love is "everything," men have convinced many women that it is also worth any sacrifice and, like generals in their luxurious tents behind the battle lines, they have succeeded in getting others to make the sacrifices without having to make them themselves. And within the realm of love itself, men have created an image of the "feminine," such that the virtues a woman finds or creates in herself for the sake of love are directly at odds with the virtues required for success in the world—soft, yielding, quiet, accepting versus hard, aggressive, outspoken and critical. A man can be sexy in pursuit of his career; a woman is sexy despite of or in contrast to hers (unless, of course, sex is her career). To be in love, for a woman, is to be submissive, and therefore, even within the relationship, disadvantaged and powerless, second class and degraded. And if the lover or husband also insists on praising her effusively, worshiping the ground she walks on or putting her "on a pedestal," that is just so much worse, for he is disguising the fact that, even while being worshiped, she is becoming the willing victim in her own political oppression.

This is not the cynicism of neo-Freudian male reductionists: "romantic love is nothing but sex," etc. It represents the personal outrage of a million minor tragedies, of an enormous number of women, only some of whom would identify themselves as "feminists" and few of whom would be able to articulate the precise mechanism by which they have been systematically shut out of power or what this has to do with love. And yet, though I disagree thoroughly with the conclusion—that romantic love as such is the machinery of oppression—there is so much in the feminist argument that we have already accepted:

- that much of what we believe about love is demonstrably false or obscure, mere mythology and pious illusion;
- that love indeed is not "everything" or "the answer" nor is love always good or desirable;
- that love often provides private compensation for public impotence or anonymity;
- that love is a cultural creation in a male-dominated society and so—we may reasonably suppose—it was indeed "erected by men," presumably not to their own disadvantage;
- that love consists of personal roles which, more often than not, cast the woman in the more submissive and subservient position.

There can certainly be no argument against the claim that the promise of romantic love has long been used against women, by way of compensation for political impotence, as an excuse to keep them in the home (and away from the public positions of power) and as a ready rationalization for social inequities in everything from politics ("women are too emotional") to changing diapers ("women are naturally better at that sort of thing"). And indeed there can be no objection to the charge that the "feminine" role in love makes it difficult for a woman to be both romantically desirable and successful in the male-dominated world of money and power. So what, you might well ask, is left of love to defend?

What fails to follow from these persuasive premises is the conclusion that romantic love itself is the source of inequity or an obstacle to equality between the sexes. It does not follow from the fact that there is much in love that is illusory that love is an illusion, nor does it follow from the fact that love is a cultural artifact that it is simply artificial, a "fiction" or a manipulative ploy. It does not follow from the fact that it was (probably) invented by men that love is disadvantageous to women (a man may have invented the wheel and the toothbrush too). It does not follow from the fact that romantic love is often used to reinforce submissive and subservient women's roles that those roles are intrinsic to romantic love as such, and, most important of all, I want to argue that these supposedly "feminine" roles have no essential connection with women and no essential place in love.

If, as the feminist argument charges, romantic love *required* in its structure a division into distinctly male and female roles, strictly corresponding to what has traditionally been called "masculinity" and "femininity," then I would agree that love and the loveworld constitute archaic emotional structures that we had better leave behind us. But if, as I have argued in a preliminary way in Chapter 15 and will argue more thoroughly now, romantic roles are fundamentally sex-neutral and presuppose a significant degree of equality, then the much-abused neo-Victorian crypto-caveman scenario of macho "me-Tarzan" and passive submissive lovingly house-cleaning Jane is not at all a paradigm of love but at most one of its less likable historical curiosities.

The Argument Against Nature

The key to the feminist argument is to be found in an initial attack against "nature," not against the birds and the bees, that is, but against the word, and what has been done with it. "By nature"—that is, as a matter of biological fact—women have vaginas and uteri instead of penises; women tend to become pregnant, have children and nurse them. Women tend to have smaller frames and more predictable emotional cycles. The innocent conclusion is that men and women are different "by nature." But then the argument runs wild. It is argued that women are "naturally" more passive, men more aggressive. It is "natural" that women should stay at home, be more emotional and find in themselves an overwhelming "need to love," nature's preparation for perpetual motherhood. It is argued that women have naturally submissive sex roles, an argument often backed up by dubious analogies to the mating habits of certain fish, a couple of birds and a peculiar species of spider. The psychologist Albert Ellis writes in *Cosmopolitan* that men are "naturally" more promiscuous and so women will "just have to put up with it," and a common argument even among feminists is that women's love is "naturally" unconditional and more "accepting" than men's because of their motherly instincts. A recent book in "sociobiology" (*The Evolution of Human Sexuality* by Donald Symons, Oxford, 1979) argues on the basis of evolution that women are "naturally" choosier than males, "naturally" more concerned with their own physical appearance, "naturally" less combative, and "unnaturally" concerned with orgasm, which is "a by-product of selection for male orgasm."

Against this horrendous tradition of genetic fallacies and casual extrapolation from some detail of nature to grand hypotheses about "human nature," the feminist argument rightly objects that virtually everything about men and women worth our attention, apart from those concerns peculiar to gynecologists, urologists and designers of toilet fixtures, is not a matter of "nature" at all but of culture. This is especially true of romantic love. In her book, *If Love Is the Answer, What Is the Question?* Uta West rightly comments that "we no longer have instincts; what we have instead, is *myth.*" It is an overstatement, but no matter. Romantic love is indeed better understood as a myth than as natural instinct, and the differences between men and women are part of that myth as well.

This might be a good place to develop that distinction which has become immensely important in recent literature but is often confused or ignored in more volatile arguments on the subject. The word "sex," in addition to referring to that complex of physical desires, feelings, activities and processes that we call "sexual," also refers to that very distinctive set of biological differences that allow us to distinguish "the sexes," male and female. But "sex" in this second sense must be distinguished in turn from "gender," which involves differences in roles and behavior rather than in physiology. The contrasting terms here are "masculine" and "feminine," not "male" and "female." All of this is typically tossed together in a set of simple equations: that males are masculine and have distinctively ("natural") male sexual desires, and females are feminine and have distinctively female desires, which may or may not (depending on the theory and the period) include sexual desires. But whether or not gender has a natural (biological) basis in sexual (physiological) differences, gender is essentially a cultural category, and so, for the most part, is sexual desire. Sex itself may be biological, of course, but to say that sex is biological is not to deny that we *make* sexual distinctions and that *what* we make of them—like racial differences or differences in height or facial features—is a cultural matter.[1] And to say that gender is a cultural category is to make quite explicit the sug-

[1] A differ*a*nce, the current French philosopher Jacques Derrida calls it, a difference whose only difference is to "differ," i.e., to *make* a difference.

gestion that genders differ, along with their significance, from culture to culture, even to the point at which a culture might well come to expect what we call feminine behavior primarily from males, and what we call masculine behavior primarily from females. Or a society might come to deny the relationship between sex and gender roles altogether, in fact do away with gender roles and relegate sexual differences to the oblivion of utter unimportance. This last possibility is now commonly celebrated as "androgyny," and we shall talk about it in some detail later in this chapter.

The feminist thesis, now recast in more specific terms, is that sex differences are—or should be—a matter of indifference. Gender roles, which typically function in such a way that women are considered less capable, more emotional and therefore unable to wield power, are wholly a matter of cultural creation, artifacts, like electric can openers and putt-putt golf carts, and consequently both unnecessary and wholly dispensable. But at this point it is important to slow down the feminist counterargument long enough to emphasize that cultural creations are not therefore easily dispensable or unnecessary; some are essential to the structure of a particular society. And whether or not sex and gender distinctions are now dispensable, it does not follow that romantic love is so easily done away with, unless romantic love in fact depends upon those gender roles, which is what I shall deny. Indeed, my point is that romantic love is both sex- and gender-neutral, which means that love between lesbians or between male homosexuals is just as much romantic love as love in the traditionally heterosexual married couple.

As far as sex is concerned, what love requires is sexual *expression,* not the efficacy of species preservation, and this is just as possible between unreproducing lovers as it is between fertile and baby-ready protoparents. Indeed, it has recently been argued, by Masters and Johnson, for example, that homosexual couples—both male-male and female-female—tend to be more expressive and consequently more mutually satisfying in sex precisely because they are free from the traditional sex models. It is true that, even where there are not male and female roles (in a homosexual couple) there is nonetheless a tendency to bifurcate into masculine and feminine gender roles, one dominant and aggressive, one submissive and more accepting. But, first of all, this should only confirm our distinction between sex and gender (without leading to the conclusion that homosexual couples are thereby "trying to be like" heterosexual couples) and, second, it should not be supposed that dominance and submission, or any number of other complementary roles in sex and love, are the same as masculine and feminine gender roles. Comedy teams tend to bifurcate into complementary roles too, but not necessarily by sex or gender. (Every couple needs a "straight" role sometime.) But the main point, of course, is that romantic love does not require any couple, hetero- or homosexual, to distinguish themselves by either sex or gender roles. Love is shared identity and mutual expression, and there is nothing about shared identity—including reciprocal sexual identity—that requires male and female or masculine and feminine roles. Indeed, a man who feels that he has to assert his "manhood" in his personal relations is rightly suspected of being *less*, not more, of a lover, and a woman too eager to be dominated by men should quite rightly wonder, not about love, but about the ease with which she accepts the role of passivity. There is nothing in the structure of love as such that requires or even suggests that women ought to be cast in submissive "feminine" roles and men ought to act aggressively "masculine."

I have argued at length that romantic love does indeed serve an important function in our society, one not easily replaced. But at the same time I have argued that love is not necessary, that other functions in our society meet the need it serves, sometimes equally well; yet it does not follow, because it is not exclusively needed, that it is not needed at all. Indeed, when one looks at the distant utopian solutions proposed by some of the feminists, romantic love seems far more preferable, at least more practical, and far more easily improved than replaced. Uta West rightly criticizes one of these utopian fantasies—the all-female lesbian society—as simply shifting the abuses of romantic love from one domain into another. Her own neo-Aristotelian solution—friendship *cum* sex or "balling buddies" (an odd as well as vulgar locution)—seems to ignore rather than deny the emotional connotations of *any* sexual relationship, treating sex as essentially release and recreation. Shulamith Firestone, on the other hand, proposes a grand posthistorical fantasy à la Marx and Engels which, like their own "classless society," gains most of its appeal from its utter obscurity. And then there is the more common tragedy of resignation, refusing to give up what one knows to be a fraudulent hope and rejecting it at the same time.

What makes the feminist argument particularly viable at this particular time in history is the fact that, in only the last generation, the linkage between women and biology, the easy equation between sex and pregnancy, marriage and love has been thoroughly broken, by pharmaceutical breakthroughs and corresponding changes in custom. Women are no longer, to use the common phrase, "trapped by their biology." Neither are they subject to the vast array of fallacious arguments about what's "natural" and "the difference between men and women" either. For even where these arguments are not fallacious they have now lost the premise on which they have always been based. The "natural" differences between men and women, suddenly, make no difference at all.

There is an innocent sense in which biology remains at the basis of love, of course. Romantic love is essentially sexual, and one cannot imagine sex in any sense between disembodied spirits. But no particular sex, size or shape of the requisite bodies is required by love—only that there *be* two bodies, sensuous, expressive bodies that can do whatever needs to be done.

There is nothing essential to romantic love that requires the requisite bodies to host genitalia of the "opposite" sexes; in fact, there is nothing about romantic love—or sex for that matter—that absolutely requires genitalia at all. Genital sex is not the exclusive or ultimate expression of love. Genital sex is not the purpose of love either, as biological reductionists are prone to believe. None of the roles that make up romantic love are firmly bound to genital sex, nor to heterosexual genital sex. Romantic love is utterly neutral with regard to biology; however sexually obsessed we may be, there is nothing "natural" about it.

Love and Power

Even if romantic love is utterly neutral with regard to sex (that is, male and female and what most prominently distinguishes them), it does not yet follow that it is similarly neutral with regard to gender. Indeed, what would become of our romantic literature without *her* soft and dutiful gaze, waiting for *him* to return from the battle and give her a hard and possessive embrace? But in our no longer warrior society, in which the day's battle is more than likely a screaming telephone battle with the local tax office, we can switch the above pronouns all that we want, delete as well the adjectives "soft" and "hard," dispense with the roles as well as the sexes. Yet it is part of the history of romantic love, and so part of the feminist argument as well, that masculine and feminine gender roles have played a large part in this emotion and, consequently, in our respective gender identities as well.

Many years ago, in one of the more virulent classics of the genre, Shulamith Firestone argued in her *Dialectic of Sex*[2] that

[2] A book easily maligned and too easily dismissed *ad feminem* as "fanatic," on the basis of its venomous prose and bewildering contradictions as well as its sometimes silly Marxism and a relentless diatribe against men—as "robots," "sadistic manipulators" who are, of course, "incapable of love" and "oppressors." The arguments, however, are often insightful.

it was precisely the "liberation of women from their biology," not now but several generations ago, that brought about the distinctively male invention of romantic love:

> Romantic love developed in proportion to the liberation of women from their biology. . . . Male supremacy must shore itself up with artificial institutions or exaggerations of previous institutions (p. 165).

Romantic role models, she argues, the gender distinctions of "masculine" and "feminine," are developed *in place of* the no longer essential distinction between male and female. Gender depends not on nature but on culture; thus the question, *for what purpose*, and *for whose benefit*, has gender been created? The answer is not long forthcoming.

> Romanticism is a cultural tool of male power to keep women from knowing their condition. It is especially needed—and therefore strongest—in Western countries with the highest rate of industrialization (p. 166).

Romantic love is thus to be understood in terms of *power* and, so viewed, the main difference between masculine and feminine gender roles becomes obvious. The argument, interestingly enough, is traced to Freud. Freud is usually considered the nemesis of feminism, but Firestone rightly credits him "as having grasped the crucial problem of modern life; sexuality" (p. 49). But where Freud takes sexuality to be a psychobiological problem, Firestone sees it as a political problem. Where Freud mysteriously talks about the powers of the libido, Firestone talks concretely about *power* itself. And where Freud talks murkily and unconvincingly about penis envy and castration fears, Firestone substitutes the tangible fact of family power relationships, the all-powerful father and the privileged sons (p. 53). Penis envy becomes privilege envy, and Firestone quite plausibly suggests that the young girl who is said to envy her brother's curious genitalia is more likely feeling deprived because she is not allowed to play her brother's rough-and-tumble games. And with this switch on Freud, the theory can begin: romantic love is the extension of this power game into adult life, a more subtle way of depriving a woman of "male" roles and at the same time flattering her as a "lady." Promise her anything, but offer her only love.

What Firestone is arguing, from Freud, is what Freud and many neo-Freudians prefer to ignore—the institutional nature of romantic love and its functional role, not only in the individual psyche and the family but in the power structure of society as a whole. Firestone's argument is that, now that female sexuality as such is of much less importance for survival, the institution of romantic love serves the function of introducing femininity as a matter of emotional significance, as a way of continuing archaic male-dominated institutions and power structures. Femininity, in a word, is *impotence*. Masculinity is *potence*. And to reinforce the roles, femininity is isolated in the home, as soon as possible, while masculinity gathers further power in the market place. Women, in turn, find themselves seeking approval—the test of success in their feminine roles—entirely from men, while men gain their support and approval as well in a variety of friendships and business or professional relationships.

There are a number of arguments that run together here, all with the same conclusion but quite different all the same. First, it is said that romantic love has been foisted upon women as a way of perpetuating archaic and distinctly inferior household roles, once based upon biological necessity, now simply so that men can retain their traditional dominance outside the home. Second, the argument is that the privacy of romantic love and its marital aftermath is such that it keeps women isolated from each other and wholly dependent upon the approval of men, thus reinforcing their archaic and inferior positions within the home by making them the only possible source of personal self-esteem. Third, there is a kind of proper suspicion that, since romantic love was obviously invented by men, they did so to their own advantage, in order to perpetuate women's roles. And, fourth, it is argued that romantic roles as such are essential to love and cast women in submissive, inferior positions.

I have already agreed with the first of these arguments, that romantic love has been *used* as a way of continuing to encourage women to retain once biologically necessary roles that are now unnecessary. But it is clear that our society in general, not only feminists, is becoming fully aware that the once easy equation between sex and gender, the identification of the biological necessities of tribal life and the cultural niceties of Victorian courtship rituals, is no longer viable. The next step is to remove the supposed necessity of gender identity from romantic love as well, which is just as archaic and now unnecessary as the biological complementarity of the sexes.

The isolation of women and the exclusively male-dominated world of power are starting to break down, extremely quickly on any reasonable historical scale, and this changes at least one of the key connections among romantic love, gender identity and power. Much of the power that was once the exclusive domain of males had to do not only with the fact that they had power but with their variable sources of recognition and approval as well. Men were not solely dependent on women for their sense of self-esteem as women were entirely dependent upon men. But now, as women aggressively find themselves friendships and alliances—even to the extent that a current popular argument maintains that only women are even *capable* of friendship—and are beginning as well to find professional, political and other sources of self-esteem, this source of power is opening up to them as it is to men. Thus in this sense it has become evident that it is not romantic love or gender roles as such that determine one major traditional source of asymmetrical women's dependency, but an entirely distinct set of inequities which might be summarized as unequal access to approval and self-esteem. This isolation of women is now coming to an end—I would argue. (Even the reactionary countermovement, the "total woman" syndrome, has the ironic outcome of helping to bring about the public visibility of women speakers and "women's issues," thus destroying this sense of isolation.) Romantic love, consequently, no longer remains a woman's sole source of self-esteem, a burden which, in any case, no single emotion could ever be expected to sustain.

The argument that romantic love was invented by men, as popular as that may now be, is as much paranoia as history. And in any case it is very bad history. If one considers Plato a male author of *eros,* what is most evident is that he used this conception not as a way of casting women in inferior roles but of dismissing them altogether, as not worthy of love. Women were inferior, yes, but not because of love. If we follow the scholars and date the origins of romantic ("courtly") love in the chivalric spirit of twelfth-century France, we might attribute the "invention" of romantic love to the wandering knights and their poet accompanists the troubadours, but regardless of who "invented" love, it is clear that the women who were loved were more than willing to co-operate, since the new role of "the feminine" was not a form of oppression but of liberation for them, the first step in the individualization of women as well as men, the first recognition that a woman, any woman, was more than a household convenience. She was no longer merely an object for interfamily barter, a mother, a mistress and, literally, a possession.

It is often argued, for example by Firestone and more recently by Linda Nicholson, that romantic love is essentially a product of capitalism, a creation of industrialized market society. This is clearly not true. Shakespeare gave a rather complete description of romantic love in his sonnets, well over a century before the Industrial Revolution in England. Indeed, romantic love appears on the European scene centuries before the first versions of capitalism and, in so far as there is any parallel at all, this is not due to the rise of a market economy but instead due to the presupposition of capitalism—namely, the idea of individual autonomy and the severing of feudal ties according to which every person was locked into a rigid system of obligations and allegiances. Linda Nicholson argues, for example, that the market society destroyed the old conception of women as "creatures before God" and began our current capitalist insistence on evaluating people according to what they're "good for," but the truth seems to be that under feudalism women in particular were "worth something" only according to what they were "good for," and it was with the rise of a less regimented and household-centered society that individual worth "as a human being" came to mean anything at all.

Love may or may not have been "erected by males," but it does not follow and is not true that they did so—if they did—to continue the subjection of women. But this leaves the fourth argument, and to my mind the most crucial—namely, that romantic roles, in which the woman is essentially submissive and inferior, are built right into the structure of romantic love. Even if we reject the now outdated biological arguments, even if it is true that the isolation of women is no longer the issue it used to be, and even if romantic roles were once—eight hundred years ago—a liberating influence, it can be charged that the straitjacket of "femininity" is today a source of oppression and a still powerful psychological rationalization for the continuing exploitation of women, in the name of "love."

Beyond One-Dimensional Love ("Androgyny" and More)

My answer is that "femininity" and so-called feminine roles have nothing essential to do with love. But before I argue this, I want to consider briefly an argument that would seem, if successful, to make this answer unnecessary. One feature of romantic love, which has been often neglected or distorted in current controversies, is the essential *privacy* of love and the loveworld. There can be no conception of romantic love, I have argued, without the crucial distinction between public and private, and a personal sense of "who I am" over and above—in fact sometimes opposed to—my social status and public image. But this means that, in so far as masculine and feminine roles are part of love, they need not enter into public life at all. The roles one plays in love, and the roles one plays in public life, need have no essential connection. Thus one answer to the feminist argument is that we can and should indeed do away with our concepts of femininity and masculinity in the public sphere, but not therefore in the personal sphere. But this answer is not sufficient, and for at least three reasons. First of all, distinct as they may be, it is difficult to imagine that they would not affect each other, and that a change in public status would have no effect on one's personal self-conceptions. Second, this would still be disadvantageous to women, in so far as *attracting* a lover, as opposed to already living with one, requires a public display of romantic availability which makes the woman's public role thoroughly schizoid. There can be no exclusive relegation of love to the personal, except in very restricted cases, and then only after the relationship has been initially formed. And, third, even if such separation were possible, it would still relegate the woman to subservient status *within* the relationship, however powerful her roles in public. It is therefore the concepts of femininity and masculinity themselves that must be rejected.

There are at least three ways of doing this. Two of them have become popularly known under the camp word "androgyny." The word is often confused with "bisexual"—which is only one of its variations—but in any case I tend to agree with feminist poet and author Mary Daly when she writes that "androgyny makes me think of Farrah Fawcett and John Travolta scotch-taped together." The first form of androgyny (or "androgynism") insists that masculine and feminine characteristics exist together in everyone, and so it is unnecessary, the argument goes, for everyone to feel that he or she should develop only one set of sex-bound characteristics. In the public sphere, the argument is appealing, since what it says, in effect, is that everyone has the same potential and so should have the same opportunities. Its effect, in other words, is to deny the difference between men and women and to provide a single ideal of rights and potential for all, which leads one author, Joyce Trebilcot, to call it "monoandrogynism."[3] In the personal sphere, however, the same view leads logically to the idea of bisexuality; if we each have essentially the same masculine and feminine characteristics, then it would follow that we each also have the same masculine and feminine desires. This sounds like Freud's well-known bisexuality argument, but it isn't. For Freud, this was a sexual matter, a fact about biology; for the monoandrogynist, it is a matter of cultural potential, not biology at all. But here we see a problem with this simple view too; as a theory about *potentials,* it slips too easily between the idea that the various roles that we call "masculine" and "feminine" *can* be developed in everyone (whether or not they should be) and the idea that these roles are *already* lurking somewhere inside of us, waiting to be developed but, alas, in our society only one of the roles ever is, frustrating the other. But the recognition of the cultural origins of these roles ought to lead us to a more radical conclusion, not that they are "there in everybody" but rather that they are unnecessary, unreal; they do not exist except in so far as we *will* them.

The second form of androgyny is more radical in just this sense; it denies the simple duality between masculinity and femininity and emphasizes the wide variety of gender roles, including any number of combinations of the two "pure" extremes, masculinity and femininity. In effect, this breaks down

[3] "Two Forms of Androgynism" in Vetterling-Braggin, Elliston and English, eds., *Feminism and Philosophy* (Littlefield Adams, 1977), pp. 70–78.

the extremes as well and refocuses our attention on particular traits and roles rather than on the monolithic extremes, and opens up the possibility of a large variety of roles which are neither, traditionally speaking, masculine nor feminine. (Because of its pluralism, Trebilcot calls this "polyandrogynism.")

But this second form of androgyny or androgynism suggests a third possibility, which escapes the man-woman etymological orientation of "androgyny" altogether by dismissing masculinity and femininity as essential roles, particularly where romantic love is involved. What we have been allowing without comment for too long is the idea that these two roles define, if not all, at least a large part of our romantic tradition. In fact they had no place in Plato; there the crucial distinction was one of age and experience, the lover as teacher, the beloved as pupil. The notion of masculine-feminine may have played a significant part in courtly love, but the notions of chivalry and attractiveness were matters of historical context, and not necessarily essential to the concept of love as such. And as one looks at the structure of romantic love—apart from the grade B novels—divisions according to sex and gender have had very little place, even where sex itself is concerned. Indeed, romantic love consists of roles, private roles which are only occasionally or coincidentally played out in public. But the point now to be made once and for all is that few of these roles have anything to do with sex or gender and, in so far as they do, it is not *because* they are male or female or masculine or feminine roles but only because they contain roles that are usually associated with sex and gender, such as domination and submissiveness, aggressiveness and passivity. But what happens in love is that these roles are continuously redefined, and whatever might be expected on the masculine-feminine model, what we actually do in love is something quite different. Indeed, this leads to the unexpected conclusion that masculinity and femininity are, in fact, public roles, and not private, and that love requires the overcoming of these roles rather than the realization of them. Indeed, as soon as one begins to list the huge gamut of roles through which we are intimate with one another—not only the thousand varieties of sex that need have nothing to do with gender, but cooking, talking, walking, dancing, looking, scratching, fighting, driving cross country, feeding the squirrels, confessing, celebrating, crying, laughing, knowingly nodding to each other in a room full of people, sharing the events of the day, consoling one another in defeat, studying German, staying in bed on Sunday, reading the funnies, bitching about the weather, whispering and occasionally whimpering—the emphasis that puts so much stress on a single set of asymmetrical roles, "masculine and feminine," becomes nothing more than embarrassing. Indeed, people who are too caught up in their "masculine" and "feminine" roles are not infrequently, after the initial attraction, disappointing lovers. This has nothing to do with sexism but only with boredom. How can you build your life around a one-act actor? How can you identify with a movie poster?

Beyond sex and gender means beyond *androgyny* too, beyond that one-dimensional set of man-woman identities that too many bad movies and sado-masochistic Freudian fantasies have set out for us. Love is a multiplex of personal roles of all kinds, which are being continuously redefined and re-enacted, which need have nothing to do with sex or with those simple stereotypes of gender. In fact to think of love in terms of masculinity and femininity is like having a conversation in which each party is assigned in advance the same (one of two) single speech. At most, one can expect a predictable performance, instead of the "anything's possible" exhilaration of love.

Why Blame Love?

One of Marilyn French's refrains in *The Women's Room* is, "But of course, she would never think of blaming love." It is the presupposition of her novel, the structure of the tragic parade she sets before us. Men are unfeeling and selfish jerks, women are victims, but it is love itself that is the illusion that binds the two together. It is the illusion that gives rise inevitably to dis-illusion-ment, and the appeal of that illusion that keeps women hoping for love, that single wonderful stroke that will make life meaningful.

Is love an illusion? No. I have argued at length that love is essentially fantasy, but fantasies, unlike illusions, are not self-deceptions and so not prone to disillusionment. Love has its impossible ideal, of total "oneness," but an unreachable goal does not an illusion make—unless one also believes that the goal is possible, even, perhaps, easily achievable. Our conception of romantic love does indeed include a number of tragic illusions—the idea that love if "true" will last forever and make life over in a flash, for instance—but these are detachable from the emotion itself, which is not an illusion but a perfectly ordinary, if extraordinarily delightful emotion. If love often fails to "work out," then perhaps we have to re-examine what we think we are "working for"; but it is our expectations, not love itself, that ought to be revised or rejected.

The danger of confusing love with illusion is more than the personal unhappiness it causes; its cost also includes creating a serious obstacle in the public fight for women's equality. Even if one assumes that the battle for equality will entail antagonism with men on a public level, it is sheer folly—if it is also unnecessary—to carry that antagonism into intimate relationships which, despite certain utopian hopes and radical experiments to the contrary, may well be indispensable in our society—at least for the present and the foreseeable future. The argument goes beyond this too, for if, as I have argued, romantic love actually *requires* a sense of equality, then love provides, rather than works against, the ideal of feminism. Historically, romantic love (and Christian love too) were powerful forces in breaking down the old hierarchies and roles. But today, too, that conception is still at work, in spite of the continuing overemphasis on sex and gender roles and despite the fact that too many feminists see love as the problem, instead of as part of the solution. Indeed, here as elsewhere in politics, projecting one's personal disappointments onto the world as cynical "realism" is not the way to win adherents. Romantic love between men and women, from its very inception, has always been the primary vehicle of personal and, consequently, social equality. It has always been "feminist" in its temperament, whatever mythologies have sometimes been imposed on top of it. Romantic love and feminism are neither incompatible nor antagonistic; in fact I would argue that, for the present at least, they should not try to do without one another.

23 WHAT'S SO GOOD ABOUT LOVE? (LOVE AND SELF-ESTEEM)

After seven years of marriage Pierre had the joyous firm conviction that he was not a bad man, which he had come to feel because he saw himself reflected in his wife. In himself, he felt all the good and bad inextricably mingled and overlapping. But in his wife he saw reflected only what was really good in him, since everything that was not absolutely good was rejected.

TOLSTOY, *War and Peace*

We began this book with a question, not out of cynicism but rather curiosity—why is love so important to us? If love is one among many emotions, each of which consists of its own self-defining meaningful world, why have we so singled out love, romantic love in particular, as "the meaning of life" and "the ideal of human existence"? We can't imagine without criticism a person dedicating his or her life to anger or envy (though many do), but we not only imagine but celebrate those who live (or give) their lives for love. Why? Why do we think, as Walker Percy puts it, that "the only important, certainly the best thing in life, is ordinary sexual love"? (*Lancelot*, p. 12).

What is so good, so praiseworthy, so admirable and exhilarating about love? It is often said that love is "good in itself," "intrinsically good," even the standard by which other values are measured; but this isn't an answer, first, because it is clear, even in our romantic society, that love will not excuse *every-*

thing, that love is not *always* desirable (for example, when one is already in love with another person). Second, I would argue along with a great many philosophers (John Dewey, for example) that nothing is "good in itself"—not pleasure, not life, not sex, not even happiness. (God, perhaps, is "good in Himself," but nothing follows from this about us.) And, third, we have already covered considerable ground in showing that the desirability of romantic love can be explained, can be accounted for in terms of both the place it fits in our society in general and its internal definitions of self and identity. In this chapter, what I would like to do is to bring these explanations together as an answer to the question, "Why is love so important to us?" In other words, "What's so good about love?"

The first part of the account is cultural, and we have stressed throughout this book the importance of appreciating the social preconditions and presuppositions that are necessary even for love to be possible. In particular, there must be a high degree of mobility and individuality, such that the more "natural" bonds between members of families and communities are systematically severed, sending individuals "out into the world" to "find themselves" and each other. And there must be a general distinction between the social public roles an individual plays and the personal private life he or she leads, with a stress on the personal and private as the realm of a person's "true" identity. Thus we can begin, in a very general way, to explain the cultural significance of romantic love by pointing to the interpersonal gaps that are perpetually created in our society, waiting to be filled, and the need for relationships which will give form and structure as well as content to our personal as opposed to our less personal public lives. But we should not make too much of this "external" cultural account. It explains, as too many theorists fail to explain, the socially created "need" for love and its cultural peculiarities—not as an ideal of "human nature" but rather as the invention of certain kinds of societies. But preconditions and presuppositions only provide us with the framework within which love finds its place. Given the interpersonal gap to be filled and our emphasis on personal rather than professional relations, our alleged "need" for love could just as well be filled with friends and extended families. The special significance of romantic love does not follow from the fact that there is a definite place for it in our society, for it is a place that can be filled by other, less exclusive and less complicated emotions as well.

One might argue that what love provides that friendship and extended family do not is intimacy, sex too perhaps, but this seems to me to be wrong on several counts. First, it is an emasculated view of friendship and family too, perhaps, that assumes from the outset that these cannot be intimate, at least. Secondly, it remains to be seen what is so good about intimacy, just as we need to pull together our answer to the question, "What is so good about love?" And, third, however good that might be, it seems to me that discussions in terms of *need* are in any case mistaken. If we need romantic love and intimacy, these are *created* needs, and then the question simply moves one step further along—why are they worth creating? What do they provide for us, in addition to the fact that they fill a gap in our social lives which might be just as well fulfilled by staying with our families, moving in with an uncle and aunt, forming new friendships at work or "just hanging out with the boys/girls"?

The key to our answer, which we have kept hammering away at for the last dozen chapters, is SELF. It is sometimes said that love is "selfless," but this would indeed render love a mystery, for what would then serve as its motivation? But the essence of love, we have argued, is precisely the formation of self, a shared self, and here, in the realm of self-identity, we shall find the answer to our question.

Self-identity is the structure of self; the value of this structure, on the other hand, is called *self-esteem.* Every emotion forms its own self-identity—in anger as self-righteousness, in resentment as the oppressed, in envy as the deprived and in faith as the faithful. Every identity gives life a certain meaning —as unfair, offensive, competitive, hopeful and so on—but not all meanings are of equal value. Some meanings, one might say, are *de*-meaning. Others tend to maximize self-esteem, roughly, "how good we feel about ourselves." This in no way implies any lack of consideration for others or any desire for their disadvantage, unless the emotion itself is antagonistic or competitive, as in hatred or jealousy. In love, in particular, the maximization of one's own self-esteem goes hand in hand with the maximization of the lover's self-esteem, since, as we have argued, they involve one and the same shared self.

The reciprocity of romantic love explains not only its importance as an interpersonal bond but its value for self-esteem as well. Whereas many other emotions tend to be antagonistic or competitive, romantic love intrinsically includes mutual reinforcement and encouragement. Emotions such as anger, resentment and jealousy, which turn another person into an offender, an oppressor or a trespasser, tend to maximize one's own self-esteem (which they do quite effectively) but only at the risk of setting someone against us, who in return is anxious to knock us off our high horse, humiliate us and substitute for our self-esteem his or her own. In love, since this sense of self-esteem is constituted mutually, it is entirely in the other person's interest (even in unrequited love) to think well of us and encourage us too. It is a simple but powerful difference, and in this difference the significance of romantic love becomes apparent to us; it is the one emotion (or at least, one of a very few) that enlists other people as wholehearted support for our own sense of worth, in return for which they earn our support too. And since the world—the loveworld—within which we carry out this mutual support for self-esteem is by its very nature an essentially private world, within which no one else's opinions are even allowed, the mutual maximization of self-esteem can indeed be astounding, virtually without limits —at least for a while.

The Psychology of Self-Esteem

The literature on self-esteem tends to be split into two warring camps, ever since Freud argued quite clearly that love was an attempt to assure self-worth through what he called "identification." On one side of the dispute it is argued, for instance by Freud's disciple Theodor Reik (1944) and more recently by the social psychologist Elaine Walster (1965), that romantic love is an attempt at compensation. This means that people with low self-esteem, who are "down" on themselves, are more likely to fall in love than those whose self-esteem is not so threatened. On the other side, such theorists as Abraham Maslow (1942), Carl Rogers (1965) and Alfred Adler (1926) have argued that people with "high" self-esteem are more capable of love than those with "low" self-esteem. Of course there are reports of patients by the hundreds and experiments by the dozens to support both theses, but here as elsewhere in the social sciences one might be wise to consider first British philosopher Peter Geach's warning, that "no experiment can clear up a confusion of thought." For it is evident even in this brief statement of positions that it is none too obvious what is being argued, what is meant by "self-esteem" or what is meant by "love."

In one sense, the apparently conflicting claims about love and self-esteem are about two completely different phenomena; the tendency of "low" self-esteem people to *fall* in love is quite different from the alleged ability of "high" self-esteem people to *be* in love, that is, to sustain a more or less long-term relationship with a minimal amount of neurosis and dependency. Moreover, a reading of much of the literature on love and self-esteem shows the correlation with "low" self-esteem people to be not about love at all but merely about "romantic liking" (Walster), mere "attractiveness" (Dittes, 1959) and "acceptance" (Sheerer, 1948). Seeking approval and becoming infatuated are both much less than love, and except for the psychoanalysts (Reik) there is virtually no mention of "identification," the earmark of love, in any of these authors. This leaves us with a rather limp set of hypotheses: (1) that people who feel down on themselves are more likely to seek approval from others and (2) that people who feel good about themselves tend to sustain better relationships than those who do not.

The intricate connections between love and self-esteem are not going to be captured in such crude correlations. First of all, as Elaine Walster has correctly argued against her colleagues, such talk about "high" and "low" self-esteem *people* ignores the obvious—that we all fluctuate in our sense of self-worth by the day and by the hour.[1] Second, although it may make sense as a kind of convenient generalization to talk about "feeling good about oneself," our self-esteem, like our identity, is context-dependent, and it is a common enough experience that we find ourselves extremely self-critical in one social or personal context immediately before or after feeling extremely good about ourselves in another. Tolstoy's Pierre is a classic example; after a life of dissipation, whores and scoundrel friends, several political and religious conversions and his stint as a prisoner of war under Napoleon, he comes to see himself through Natasha's eyes, not to the exclusion of all of these other identities, but by way of escape and compensation from them—or so, at least, Tolstoy tells us. His self-esteem, in other words, concerns that self which he now identifies with Natasha, not self in general—if there could possibly be such a simple monolith in such a complex character.

[1] In her experiment she "produced" low esteem in her undergraduates by giving them a personality test from which they emerged "immature"; she then had them asked out on dates (hardly a test of love).

Within this context, however, does it make sense to talk about love and self-esteem as the psychologists and psychoanalysts do, in terms of compensation (love for low self-esteem)? To be sure, a person unsure of him or herself will be far more receptive to the approval of others, but *loving* them is another matter. Furthermore, one might render up the hypothesis that self-esteem virtually *always* goes up when one falls in love, whether or not this is also complicated by problems of rejection or anxiety and subsequent collapse of self-esteem. Indeed, the structure of love is such that it *begins* with the recognition that mutual identification and reciprocal support are improvements over one's present solitary or in any case loveless identity, but it does not follow that low self-esteem is the precondition of love, as Reik suggests. It may be true that someone who feels sufficiently "down" on him or herself will be literally "hungrier" for love, but an increase in self-esteem is always a potential motive for emotion, and this is true of "high" self-esteem people as well as "low," in our best moods as well as our worst. But as a mutually reinforcing relationship it also follows that the liabilities of one personality will inevitably become liabilities for the other as well, and when two insecure and self-contemptuous people form a romantic identity, it is easy to see how their reciprocally inflated self-esteem is prone to collapse. Two relatively strong personalities, on the other hand, need not spend so much energy in mutual support, since each is already capable of holding up his or her own identity. Thus the psychological correlations reported in the literature are two not very significant manifestations of a much more complex set of emotional structures and tendencies.

But all of this is still too simple; to talk about self-esteem, even so qualified and relativized to contexts and relationships, and mutual support and reciprocity, in the formation of shared self-identity and heightened self-esteem, is to ignore the huge variety of mechanisms for mutual self-esteem that we find in romantic love, which are by no means to be reduced to the simple psychological catch-all, "seeking approval." Romantic reciprocity can be parasitic, symbiotic, a question of simply providing a context, or a challenge, or competition, or mere association, as well as identification, approval and sheer shared enthusiasm. To think of any one of these processes as the sole source of mutual self-esteem is to turn the fascinating complexities of romantic relationships into an artificially one-dimensional exchange that would not even work in a grade C novel. Which does not, of course, lessen its popularity as a psychological theory.

The Sources of Self-Esteem

Self-esteem, we should emphasize, is not the same as what one *thinks* about oneself, though no doubt this will always be both a factor and a reflection of self-esteem. But a person who accepts an ideology of oppression or egalitarianism or class superiority may well think quite differently than he or she actually feels about his or her self-worth. Thus what a person says about self-worth must be taken critically too, and what seems far more important are such indirect indications of self-esteem as the extent to which a person feels compelled to make excuses or apologize (Sheerer). Neither does self-esteem mean self-acceptance or high regard for oneself; a Christian martyr, if we may borrow an example from Nietzsche, might have remarkably high self-esteem even as he despises himself; indeed it is his self-contempt on the one hand that is the source of his remarkable self-righteousness on the other. But of course one can find another martyr for whom martyrdom is indeed an expression of and a reconfirmation of his sense of self-contempt and inadequacy, whether or not this is frosted over with self-congratulation and righteousness. And since people in love quite often act the role of martyrs ("self-sacrifice" and "devotion" and all that), the comparison is not out of place. The moral, however, is that there are no easy tests or dependable platitudes on this extremely delicate topic of self-worth.

Self-esteem is often summarized, as Pierre summarizes it, as the feeling that one is a "good" (or at least "not bad") person. This is not always the case. In our rebel society, in which criminals are often our folk heroes, "bad" can become a curious word for virtue, and a person's self-identity and self-esteem may well turn on seeing oneself as "the baddest" or even as "evil." (Certain witches and gang leaders come to mind.) But this makes it clear that self-esteem, like self-identity, does not pertain to some omnipresent entity called the self as such but rather to the various roles and qualities that constitute our sense of self-identity. And these roles and qualities might be almost anything whatever, surely not necessarily "good" or desirable from someone else's point of view. One person finds his or her identity in cruelty, seeks a partner who will tolerate that cruelty and finds his or her sense of self-worth heightened accordingly. Another seeks a submissive identity, free as possible from responsibility and defined as much as possible by the status of *victim,* finds a suitably oppressive partner and, in degradation, heightens self-esteem. But if this is so, in what sense can we talk about "high" or "low" self-esteem at all, if self-esteem can be raised in degradation or by sadism and, we might add, can be lowered for some people as soon as they find themselves in a position of respect or responsibility? Our answer, again, is in terms of self-identity; this is a role that they will *work* for, a role that they *want,* a role that they will *choose* from a number of alternatives, including its seemingly more savory opposites. One might point out that wanting such roles betrays a serious problem in self-esteem to begin with, at least in some cases. But what this shows is not that self-esteem cannot be elevated by degradation or lowered by responsibility but only that, once again, self-esteem is not a simple singular attribute but a complex sequence of senses of self-worth which may in many cases play off against one another, as our identities do too. But the point of romantic love is precisely to try to simplify this complexity and narrow down the sequence of senses to what usually at least begins as a more manageable set of identities, with one person, selecting out those identities and roles whose fulfillment seems most desirable, whatever *we* (looking in from the outside) might think of them.

Some of the mechanisms of self-esteem to be found in romantic love are not so romantic at all. For example, romantic love typically begins with a *challenge,* an appropriate conception of "courting" in terms more usually reserved for games and war, "winning" and "losing," making a "conquest" and strategies such as "playing it cool" or "playing hard to get." Marilyn French, for example, in her book, *Bleeding Heart,* is obsessed with this paradigm, which may indeed have its place in the initial phases of love, but as one among many metaphors and mechanisms and not as the definition of love itself. But though this sense of challenge is not itself sufficient to explain the mutual reinforcement of love, it does provide an initial impetus, an opening appreciation for the affections and approval of the lover and the first requirement that one must think somewhat well of oneself if one is to play this sometimes most serious game at all. But the challenge soon ends and love begins. Or, if the only source of self-esteem turns out to be the challenge itself, love soon ends as well.

A second and more enduring source of self-esteem in love is the simple fact of being admired or approved of by someone whom we admire and approve of in return. This is not, as some cynics might suggest, merely a matter of tit for tat, "I'll say something nice about you if only you'll say something nice about me." It is true that our estimation of others tends to increase remarkably when we find that they think well of us, but it is hardly ever true that our estimation of others, and consequently the importance we attribute to their estimation of us, lies wholly in the fact that we expect their approval in return.

But notice too that this source of self-esteem is not peculiar to loving and, indeed, is sometimes more effective when it is not part of love. Being complimented by a stranger is often far more of an ego boost than the now familiar compliment of a friend or lover—thus giving rise to "Arenson's Law of Marital Infidelity," that mutual approval is subject to the law of diminishing returns, and self-esteem is boosted less and less by those from whom we come to expect praise and approval as a matter of course. The law has a corollary too, that rejection and disapproval from those we love is far more devastating than rejection or disapproval from any stranger or mere acquaintance. But this, of course, serves as a source of inhibition and fear, not as a source of self-esteem. On the positive side, however, diminishing over time or not, mutual admiration and approval, though far from providing the whole story, are obvious sources of self-esteem.

To a certain extent, love raises self-esteem by mere *association* with another person whose virtues or accomplishments we admire. This need have nothing to do with their approval or admiration of us in return. The man who feels good about himself because he is with a brilliant woman is a clear example of such association, and the woman who feels good about herself because she is with a famous artist is another. Notice that this source of self-esteem, like the others, is not peculiar to love and might well be true without it. Notice too that this source presupposes nothing in return, though presumably the lover too has his or her motives for sharing the virtue so enjoyed by the other. Again, this is just a small piece of the picture, but it is obviously another source of increased self-esteem, through association with another person who has virtues that we ourselves may not have. (Again, even in unrequited love.)

A much stronger source of self-esteem in love that is easily conflated with the last is *identification* with the other. In association, one claims some sense of worth by being *with* the other person; in identification, one comes to claim the other's virtue as in some sense one's own. A friend of mine who is a mediocre violinist fell in love (and is still in love) with a woman who is an outstanding concert soloist. He *shares* her sense of pride and accomplishment, indeed feels (and she agrees) that it is partly his own, owing to his constant encouragement and support. This source of self-esteem is accordingly far more central to love than the others we have mentioned, because it is the first to presume some sense of shared self, virtues held in common, self-esteem that is not only reciprocal but shared. Indeed, what is crucial to my friend's sense of esteem is the fact that he does share his wife's sense of accomplishment and at no time wishes that it were his own instead. To do so would be envy, the very antithesis of love, for in that competition and opposition the sense of shared identity is inevitably lost.

And yet competition itself may provide a source of self-esteem in love. A classic example would be the old Spencer Tracy-Katharine Hepburn movies (*Adam's Rib, Woman of the Year*) in which they play lovers always at odds, in which their mutual appreciation of each other and their sense of self-esteem is boosted by regular competition with each other. This is not the same as the "love as war" or "love is a game" metaphor we first discussed, for it is not their love itself which is the subject of the competition. This is crucial. In so far as love itself is a matter of competition, it is not yet wholly love, for it is the distinction between selves rather than their identity that is primary. But in so far as love and shared identity are already established to a certain degree, competition in other matters can be a powerful source of increased appreciation and self-esteem —and perhaps, an antidote for Arenson's Law as well.

In the same way, the *idealization* of the other person in love raises one's own self-esteem, for in rendering one's lover ideal one is, if indirectly, idealizing oneself by implication as well. What must be true of me if I am loved by the most wonderful person in the world? I too must be quite wonderful, no? Thus

Pierre sees himself reflected in the eyes of his wonderful wife, who is all virtue, and so he too, at least in her reflection, is all virtue too. It is an innocent deception that serves an important function in a society that praises humility and discourages us from praising ourselves—namely, it allows us to congratulate ourselves indirectly, through our lovers. But perhaps too it is just this sense of "being used" as a vehicle for self-praise that leads many women, in particular, to complain about their men "putting them on a pedestal." Indeed, what they are really doing is putting them behind a mirror.

Love, Roles, Virtue and Identity

The sources of self-esteem listed above are collectively significant, but even all together they do not begin to tap the tremendous resources of romantic love and self-esteem. These "superficial" sources may be obvious, but they have therefore been overemphasized by many theorists just because they are so obvious. What is much harder to describe, and almost impossible to measure, is the extent to which self-esteem is boosted in love by the complementary roles that we are able to play with one another, the identities we are able to assume in private, often at odds with or the exact opposites of the roles we are called upon to play in public or family life. A man who has an inferior job as subordinate during the day compensates by acting the confident lover with his wife; the businessman harried with responsibilities enjoys a submissive role free from the burdens of control with his lover; the tough and successful businesswoman retreats from her daily need to be "businesslike" and totally independent into a relationship in which she can act wholly the child, all emotion and playfulness. Here the sense of shared identity lies not merely with some specific quality or accomplishment, which one lover shares with the other. The identity lies in the often asymmetrical playing of roles, in which one declares the self he or she would like to be (if only in contrast to other roles). And self-esteem follows from the playing of these roles, whether or not one would consider the role itself virtuous or in any sense an achievement. In a society where we tend to think of our "real selves" in terms of such private and personal roles, finding someone, in love, with whom to play them provides an all-important, perhaps the most important, source of self-esteem.

Perhaps most complex of all is the extent to which certain virtues are themselves created within the relationship. The key word here is "virtue," not simply a role or an identity—which in themselves are value-neutral. A virtue is by its very nature a source of self-esteem, but what is peculiar to most or at least many of the virtues is the fact that, while one cannot simply designate oneself to be virtuous, there is no settled factual basis for virtue either. Virtue is constituted by the agreement of other people. Examples would be courage, honesty and, more generally, "being a good person." Whether one is courageous or not depends upon what is expected of one by others, and to what extent one satisfies their expectations. No act is in itself courageous, whether it be facing up to a marauding grizzly bear (which might just be considered foolish), or standing up for one's convictions (which in a conformist society would be considered merely anti-social behavior). And so it is that within small groups the virtues are defined with but minimal reference to standards that hold for other groups, and within the smallest of groups, namely, a two-person relationship, virtues are defined by just the two of us. If only you believe that I am generous or trustworthy I am, and if only you believe that I am a "good person" I am that too. And in this context (whatever one thinks of it), we can see how important the personal privacy of love can be for our conception of ourselves, in terms of not only the roles we play together but the virtues we define for each other as well. And what counts as a virtue, too, might be wholly within our private domain. Thus kinkiness, wickedness, silliness, slovenliness, bitterness and coquettishness may not be virtues in the public domain, but we all know cases in which, within the confines of a relationship, they take on the aura of cardinal virtues, sources of pride as well as mutual admiration.

In addition to shared roles, identities and mutually created virtues, there are shared values and attitudes toward the world, shared enjoyments and happiness. Any value shared is thereby reinforced; an enjoyment shared is thereby approved as indeed "enjoyable." Happiness shared is thereby less likely to be mere foolishness. Thus one of the more obvious but by no means "superficial" sources of self-esteem is this sense of shared values, attitudes, joys and happiness. Loving someone is often said to be "wanting to share one's happiness"; one might also say that wanting to share one's happiness—or, for that matter, the lover's happiness—is itself a powerful reason for loving. Happiness shared is happiness made more real.

In addition to the various identities and roles that combine to form a relationship, there is an all-encompassing identity in being "a couple," which may in some cases be more important than all of the others. Pride in one's (shared) self *as a couple* involves attributes not applicable to either person alone, for example, "having been together all of these years." Indeed, people who take little pride in themselves as individuals may both take pride in their relationship as such, not because of any virtues or attributes which they share with the other in the senses we have discussed but rather because of just those attributes that they have created together as a couple. Some people are incapable of identifying themselves primarily as a couple, which does not make them incapable of love but means rather that their sense of shared identity and self-esteem remains first of all a matter of individual qualities and achievements, no matter how extensively these are also shared. On the other hand, some people are incapable of taking pride in themselves as individuals but can take great pride in their relationships, which tend therefore to be the prime ingredient in their conception of themselves.

Finally, one cannot underestimate the sheer importance of *having an identity,* any identity, no matter what it is. In most societies, family place and public roles define personal identity quite unambiguously, except for occasional and usually tragic conflicts as in *Antigone,* who was forced to choose between sisterly loyalty and civil obedience. In our society, in which self-identity seems forever indeterminate, romantic love provides one of the most ready sources of self-definition, and thereby the esteem of having a self-identity, even if that identity turns out to be demeaning. It is better to be the village idiot than to be no one at all. It is better to be loved as a fool than not to be loved and better to have loved and lost than never to have loved. And in our bewilderment about the multiplicity of romantic identities and the way in which lovers so often demean one another, it is easy to miss the most obvious fact of all: that having an identity is itself what is most important. Only then does one begin to negotiate for the better roles in life. The virtue of "first love," in fact, may be not so much its innocence or its unbridled enthusiasm as the fact that it takes whatever it gets and, for lack of comparison, can consider itself wholly satisfied.

So, what is so good about love? Love provides us with identities, virtues, roles through which we define ourselves as well as partners to share our happiness, reinforce our values, support our best opinions of ourselves and compensate for the anonymity, impersonality or possibly frustration of public life. Lovers not only by mutual agreement but by way of self-interest pay heed to what is best in each other, ignore what each would like ignored, provide support where others will not and provide fantasies where reality lags too far behind desire.

Love is not "everything," perhaps, but it gives us, in this society anyway, much that we might not otherwise obtain. It gives us a source of self, in particular, which is more free—if sometimes more insecure—more variable—if sometimes more uncertain—more intimate—if often less community minded—more exciting—if sometimes more dangerous—than any other we are capable of imagining. Indeed, it is hard to see how we could reject love—in theory or in practice—without rejecting an essential conception of ourselves. We are a romantic society, and given the alternatives suggested by its critics, I would hardly prefer any other.

EPILOGUE: ROMEO'S REVENGE, PLATO'S *SYMPOSIUM* REVISITED

Hang up philosophy,
unless philosophy can make a Juliet.
SHAKESPEARE, *Romeo and Juliet*

PERSONAE:
Socrates, Romeo, Agathon, Alcibiades, Aristophanes, others.

SCENE:
The House of Agathon, toward the end of the evening.

SOCRATES: [*Drunk as a boot*] Thank you, Agathon. I can see that I was indeed foolish in agreeing to follow you in praise of love. Well, I won't compete with you. You praised love in every way possible, regardless of the truth. Strange, isn't it?—how *eros* sounds so familiar—young, pretty, poetic—anyone I know? [*He laughs, bows, spilling honeyed wine down his thigh*] Phaedrus, I prefer your *eros*, old and wise, much more suitable to the present distinguished company. And, Pausanias, I like what you said about our obligations to educate and enjoy the beautiful youths. I'm glad to hear that my efforts have been appreciated around here. Aristophanes, I can see that you take love to be a comedy, like everything else, but you are simply wrong—if you were being serious at all—about love being the search for one's missing half; love is much more than that, as I shall prove to you. But now, if you'll pass the wine, I'll take my turn, in pretentious pseudo-dialogue form of course, and sing the praises of love in my own wise-ass and belligerent so-called "Socratic" way. That is, if you can stand to hear the *truth* about love. Can you?

ALL: Yes, indeed, Socrates.

SOCRATES: Good. Now, young Romeo, you haven't said a word all evening, so you'll serve as my "yes-man" for this dialogue; let's see how many short affirmatives you've got on hand with you.

ROMEO: Okay, Socrates.

SOCRATES: Good, now. [*Croons*] "Love is better, the second time around . . ."

PHAEDRUS: Come off it, Socrates.

ARISTOPHANES: Well, he said he'd sing the praises . . .

PAUSANIAS: Shut up, Aristo.

SOCRATES: Okay now, seriously. Let's look at love: Take my wife Xanthippe . . . please. Hey, there's a gadfly in my wine. Yuck! [*Throws the remainder of the cup across the table at Eryximachus*] Pass the wine again, will you? Now, Agathon, I wholly approve of your approaching the question by asking, "What is the *nature* of love?" That seems like a good place to begin our dialectic, whatever that means.

ROMEO: Indeed, Socrates.

SOCRATES: You agree, young Romeo?

ROMEO: Yes, Socrates.

SOCRATES: Once more.

ROMEO: Yes, Socrates.

SOCRATES: Well then, let me ask you whether love is of something or of nothing? By the way, where'd you get a name like "Romeo"? Anyhow, I know the question sounds unintelligible, but let me clarify it with a couple of tautologies before I hit you with my whammy. If I were to ask you if a father is the father of something, you would have no trouble answering, would you?

ROMEO: Uh . . .

SOCRATES: Of course you would say "of a son or a daughter," right?

ROMEO: Yes, Socrates, of a son or a daughter.

SOCRATES: Brilliant, you luscious young thing. And you would say the same of a mother?

ROMEO: Very true, Socrates.

SOCRATES: And would it not also be true that a brother is always a brother of something?

ROMEO: [*Puzzled*] Uh, yes, Socrates, but . . .

SOCRATES: And how about a sister?

ROMEO: You're warming up to something.

SOCRATES: Answer the question.

ROMEO: [*Impatiently*] Yes, Socrates, but what's your point? I have another engagement.

SOCRATES: So I now want to know, and I'm asking you, whether love can desire that which love already is.

ROMEO: What?

SOCRATES: That is, does the lover possess, or does he not possess, that which he loves and desires?

ROMEO: Well, that depends on what you mean by "possess. . . ."

SOCRATES: Don't be stupid, a man can't desire what he already has. Whoever desires something is in want of that something, and he who desires nothing is in want of nothing. That, in my judgment, is absolutely and necessarily true. What do you think, Romeo?

ROMEO: What does that have to do with the word "father" referring to the fact that a man has a child? Or, for that matter, what does that have to do with love?

SOCRATES: The very word *eros* means desire, don't you agree?

ROMEO: Yes, in Greek.

SOCRATES: So *eros* is the desire for something, right?

ROMEO: Right. I want Juliet . . .

SOCRATES: But if it is the desire for something, it cannot itself already have that something, right?

ROMEO: I guess so, Socrates. But . . .

SOCRATES: Look, I can't say that I wish to be rich if I'm already rich, can I?

ROMEO: No. But that's trivial and uninter–

SOCRATES: So if love is of something, it must be something wanting to a man, right?

ROMEO: Do you mean . . .

SOCRATES: Hush, kid. Now is this something that is wanted not beauty?

ROMEO: On that, finally, we agree, Socrates. Yes, she is beauti–

SOCRATES: And we have already seen that love is something which a man wants and has not?

ROMEO: Are you saying that *I* can't be beautiful because I love Juliet who is beautiful too?

SOCRATES: [*Ignoring him, addressing the rest of the table*] Then love wants but has not beauty.

ROMEO: [*Irritated*] Sometimes you say "love wants"; other times you say "a man wants"; *love* doesn't want anything: *I* want Juliet. Now what are you talking about?

SOCRATES: *Eros,* of course. Pass the wine again. Now would you call that beautiful which wants but does not possess beauty?

ROMEO: [*Disdainful*] Of course not.

SOCRATES: Then would you still agree with Agathon that love is beautiful?

ROMEO: That's a different question. Juliet is beautiful and love is beautiful but that doesn't mean . . .

SOCRATES: You and young Aristotle, always hung up on particulars. I thought we were talking about the nature of love, not just bragging about lovers.

ROMEO: [*Sulking*] Okay, Socrates. [*Impatient*] Isn't it midnight yet?

SOCRATES: Now I want you to answer one more question—is not the good also the beautiful?

ROMEO: No! Mercurio is good but he isn't . . .

SOCRATES: You're supposed to say yes.

ROMEO: No! You're right that *eros* has certain connotations of nobility, but I'm not going to let you shift the whole discussion into ethics.

SOCRATES: But that's where I'm best. I know all the arguments about virtue.

ROMEO: But not, evidently, about love. No, the beautiful is not the same as the good, even if beautiful people are sometimes good, like Juliet.

SOCRATES: You're really cramping my style, kid.

ROMEO: We're here to talk about love.

SOCRATES: Well, I don't know about you, but I'm here to drink. The idea of talking about love was the Doc's over there, to slow us down in our drinking.

ROMEO: Doesn't seem to have worked.

SOCRATES: Doesn't matter. Anyhow, where were we? Oh yes, and you agree then that, in wanting the beautiful, love also wants the good?

ROMEO: No. You cannot ignore me, Socrates.

SOCRATES: Let us just say that I ignore the truth, for young Romeo cannot be easily ignored.

ROMEO: Let's see where you were going. Okay, suppose I give you your "Yes, Socrates"?

SOCRATES: Say it.

ROMEO: Yes, Socrates.

SOCRATES: Ah. Now, if love is of the good, and the beautiful, and also, of course, of the true . . .

ROMEO: Hey, wait a minute . . .

SOCRATES: Then the lover is, in short, a lover of wisdom. And following our strange friend Pythagoras (who didn't know how he could both come and be here at the same time), we can call the true lover "philosopher."

ROMEO: Are you trying to tell us that philosophers make the best lovers?

SOCRATES: The *only* lovers, kiddo—the rest is just poking around.

ROMEO: You really are trying to argue that philosophy is love, and philosophers lovers. I don't believe it.

SOCRATES: And I've proved it. . . . More wine, please. . . . You already agreed that truth and goodness are the most beautiful things and, since love seeks beauty, what is more beautiful than wisdom, and who is more wise than a philosopher?

ROMEO: I don't believe it. Damn your philosophy; I want my love.

SOCRATES: And now I will take my leave of you, and rehearse a tale of love which I once heard from the wise woman of Mantineia, called Diotima. Of course, I won't tell you when or where this was, and you may well suspect that in doing this I'm just expressing the opinions of my scribe Plato. But in fact I am doing it so that you can't pin me down for my opinions.

ROMEO: In your other dialogues, you feign ignorance.

SOCRATES: Same idea, different technique. Anyway, here's the tale, told through me by Diotima. [*To the table, in a high-pitched falsetto voice, with a pronounced lisp, as Diotima*] "So, my dear Socrates, since humility forbids you to say this yourself, I shall speak through you, as the spirit of love, which has

blessed you philosophers above all men, where the true beloved is truth, and you, poor henpecked lout of a libertine, so eagerly pursuing this truth, are the happiest of men."

ROMEO: [*Astounded*] You really are a clown, you know. A buffoon.

SOCRATES: [*With a wink*] An *ad hominem* argument, kid, an elementary fallacy. You'll go far in this philosophy business.

ROMEO: That's not my ambition. Besides . . .

SOCRATES (as Diotima): [*Assuming an extremely effeminate posture*] "Address the goddess, if you please."

ROMEO: Okay, Diotima, why then are all men not lovers, since all men seek the true and the beautiful?

SOCRATES (as Diotima): "You left out the good."

ROMEO: And the good.

SOCRATES (as Diotima): "Most men are misled by their desires and their passions."

ROMEO: [*Ironically*] You mean most men are poor lovers because they are misled by their passions and desires? I thought that love is a passion. And you already argued yourself that *eros* is a desire.

SOCRATES (as Diotima): "Socrates argued that, not me, and he's taken his leave."

ROMEO: This is insufferable.

ARISTOPHANES: But fun, you must admit.

SOCRATES (as Diotima): "Hush. I don't mean that mean-spirited desire that drives you, Romeo, so obsessed with a single beauty—and a mere *girl* at that—but that true passion, the love of wisdom, which sees through the follies of fleshy desire and the endless pursuit of a beautiful body."

ROMEO: You've been known to pursue beautiful bodies yourself, Mr. Philosopher.

SOCRATES: [*Normal voice, offended*] I'm an educator, and the beautiful learn better.

[*Guffaw from around the table*]

SOCRATES: How dare you profane a Platonic dialogue. Besides, I'm seventy years old.

ROMEO: A dirty old man.

SOCRATES: But pure in my thoughts. Let's get back to philosophy.

ROMEO: You mean love?

SOCRATES (as Diotima): "I say that love is a philosopher at all times, an enchanter, a sorcerer, a sophist."

ROMEO: I'm surprised to hear you call yourself a sophist.

SOCRATES: [*Normal voice*] That's Diotima, of course.

ROMEO: Of course.

SOCRATES: Anyway, love. (As Diotima): "Love is not mere desire, that is, desire for bodies and beauty, love is the desire to see past these fleeting desires and passions, to transcend ourselves . . ."

ROMEO: You mean to deny ourselves, and our lovers too.

SOCRATES (as Diotima): "No, I mean transcend ourselves, forget about these ugly bodies . . ."

ROMEO: You mean *your* ugly body.

SOCRATES (as Diotima): [*Annoyed*] "To see ourselves as something more than transient existence among corruption and decay."

ROMEO: "Corruption and decay"? She's only sixteen!

SOCRATES: [*Normal voice*] You just wait.

ROMEO: I will, but with Juliet.

[*There is a loud commotion at the other end of the table. A lizard fouls the tunic of Aristophanes; Plato's revenge for* The Clouds.]

ROMEO: Why do you have to pretend it's all for a "higher" purpose? Why can't you consider your desires themselves noble, without having to rationalize them? Does love need your philosophy as rationalization?

SOCRATES: I believe that they are indeed "higher." Diotima will explain it to you. (As Diotima): "And is not the possession of beauty and wisdom in love conducive to happiness?"

ROMEO: No, being with Juliet is happiness, wisdom be hanged.

SOCRATES (as Diotima): "And is it not true that all men seek happiness and the good life?"

ROMEO: I'm happy now. Besides, given the Greek word for "happiness" (*eudaimonia*), that's a tautology. Yes, whatever men seek as the good life is to be called "happiness." That's just what the word means.

SOCRATES (as Diotima): "And is not enduring happiness better than merely fleeting happiness?"

ROMEO: Well, more is better, if that's what you mean. I hope that Juliet and I can spend a lifetime together.

AGATHON: [*Softly*] I wouldn't set up a retirement fund just yet.

SOCRATES (as Diotima): "And so the love of the eternal, which brings everlasting happiness, is far better than love of mere men, which is only transient?"

ROMEO: It's a woman I love, I'll remind you, and where did "love of the eternal" come from?

SOCRATES: That is what love is.

ROMEO: Would it be fair to say that the core of your argument, Socrates, is that love is better without another person to foul it up?

SOCRATES (as Diotima): "Diotima."

ROMEO: Diotima, you do prefer the impersonal, the eternal, to the virtues of particular persons and personal beauty.

SOCRATES (as Diotima): "Mere trifles."

ROMEO: Trifles, perhaps, but they're all we've got. And they're enough.

SOCRATES: [*Normal voice, impatient*] Look, do you agree that one loves a lover for his beauty?

ROMEO: "*Her* beauty," yes. Though I know this is not the company in which to praise my Juliet.

[*General chuckle*]

SOCRATES: And that what makes one person beautiful may make another person beautiful as well?

ROMEO: Yes, but there is no one . . .

SOCRATES: So then the reasons for loving one person apply to another?

ROMEO: If beauty were the only reason for love, which it's not. Every lover is different in some respects.

SOCRATES: But they're all beautiful?

ROMEO: Indeed.

SOCRATES: Well then, the reason for each is beauty, and what you seek is beauty; do you not agree?

ROMEO: Socrates, that's the best argument for promiscuity I've ever heard. But you have no conception of love at all, which is nothing if not for a particular person, not a type, not an abstraction.

SOCRATES: Why not seek Beauty itself, instead of any one of these trifling instances? Divine beauty, unclogged with the pollutions of mortality?

ROMEO: "The pollutions of mortality!" No wonder you have such a jaded view of love. You're right, I'm hung up on particulars: Juliet, my one and only, her particular body, her particular beauty. I'm not after Beauty. I'm not after Woman. I want Juliet, nothing more.

SOCRATES: Nothing more?

ROMEO: Nothing more.

SOCRATES: But you must want something more, for what is desire without a goal, without a state of satisfaction, and why should anything satisfy you short of eternal happiness?

ROMEO: I have my goal, my satisfaction, my happiness. Love is happiness. Who needs eternity?

SOCRATES: What else could be satisfying, in the eyes of eternity?

ROMEO: But I don't have the eyes of eternity, and neither do you. A passion is satisfying because it transcends eternity, in the only way we can transcend any of your metaphysical pretenses, by being indifferent to them, by being wholly absorbed in life, by being in love. Besides, the point of desire is not its satisfaction but its prolongation. When you're happy, you don't need eternity. Why do you need it, old man?

SOCRATES: How can you choose a life of mere repetitive and momentary pleasure? There are higher desires, you know.

ROMEO: And what makes them "higher," except for the fact that they fit into your moral theories? Besides, I don't lead a life of pleasure. I'm in love. And I'm in love with Juliet. Why do you keep talking about love as an abstraction, when there is nothing more tangible and personal in the world?

SOCRATES: How can you call that "love"? A mere passion.

ROMEO: And what else could love be?

SOCRATES: I think you just want to *be* in love. Juliet doesn't matter. It's just the passion you crave.

ROMEO: But she *does* matter; she counts for everything. Even if you're right that I want the passion, it doesn't follow that it isn't Juliet I want too. And what I want even more is to be loved in return. That's just what's wrong with your whole damned theory, that you pretend to love only that which cannot return it—the eternal forms—and so you've got no responsibilities. And my family calls *me* irresponsible! You take your lovers for granted—young Agathon, for example, while you babble about "love." For me, it is the love that is everything, not the idea of love. I don't use my Juliet as a medium to the absolute.

SOCRATES: I do prefer philosophy, but . . .

[*There is a loud crash, and much shouting. Alcibiades stumbles into the table, drunk and roaring, supported by a flute girl, whom he is fondling clumsily. His head is entirely covered with flowers.* (*He had, we later learned, just knocked the genitalia off half the statues in Athens.*)]

ALCIBIADES: Well, what are you waiting for?

AGATHON: We've quite started, thank you, but please join us.

[*Alcibiades virtually falls on top of Socrates, dumping the heap of flowers around the philosopher's head, making it difficult for him to either see or speak.*]

ROMEO: Well, that's one way to shut him up. Thank you.

SOCRATES: Mmmmph.

ERYXIMACHUS: Hey, Alcibiades, are we to have neither conversation nor song when you come in, but simply to drink as if we were thirsty?

ALCIBIADES: Let's sing then, much better than the drivel I heard in here before. No, on second thought, I'll say my piece on love as well. I shall praise my friend Socrates here, for he is a raunchy old hypocrite and the dirtiest old man in Athens.

ARISTOPHANES: Yes indeed. He gave me fleas last week.

ALCIBIADES: [*To Socrates*] Now tell me, Socrates, you will not deny that your face is that of a satyr?

SOCRATES: Mmmph. Mmmth.

ALCIBIADES: And do you not play a marvelous flute, to charm the young girls, and do you not play your wonderful wit as a musical instrument, to seduce the young boys? And even war heroes and army commanders? [*He chuckles to himself*] And isn't your idealistic philosophy nothing more than a cover-up for your own life of past raunch and a flimsy justification, I would add, for your rotten marriage? You're always falling in love, you raunchy rascal, and you'll have rogered half of Greece by the time the law catches up with you. You should be tried for hypocrisy, you know. You lose the most noble idea at the mere hint of a fleshy thigh. And afterward you jump into a fit of abstraction the way we jump into the baths. You are indeed a lover, but hardly of wisdom. Like us, you love a good party.

ROMEO: Ha!

SOCRATES: Mmmpth!!

ALCIBIADES: [*Waxing eloquent*] Stronger than the walls of Ilium is your outrageous and self-righteous stance of ignorance, which no one can refute. Yet you battle incessantly, and will no doubt be happily chattering at dawn when the rest of us have long since given in. But then it's probably better than going home to Xanthippe, where you never get a word in edgewise. Oh, Socrates, you're a satyr, and a cocktease besides. Let me move closer to you, and hold you in my arms!

[*He passes out, on Socrates' lap*]

SOCRATES: [*Pulling the flowers off his head, looking at the unconscious Alcibiades*] Well, that's another way of being irrefutable.

ROMEO: You're being upstaged in this dialogue, you know.

SOCRATES: Well, I can't win them all. But he's right, you know, I'll bet that I am the last one left standing.

ROMEO: Braggart.

SOCRATES: No, I'll let Plato tell it for me.

ROMEO: Why not write it yourself?

SOCRATES: Because it's the face-to-face encounters I love, more than the philosophy.

ROMEO: You know that, thousands of years from now, scholars will be picking apart your arguments with tweezers, making up arguments where you leave them out and adding embarrassed footnotes about what they'll call your "pederasty."

SOCRATES: I can never find the argument myself. It's the *inter-*

course that I love, quite literally. I could teach you a thing or two, young Romeo.

ROMEO: Thanks, Socrates, but I have to see my chemist.

SOCRATES: You're missing a first-rate education.

ROMEO: Do you think the scholars will take notice of your lusty desires? Do you think they'll realize how much you enjoy these games, and how playful you are?—which is your own expression of love. No. I'll tell you what they'll make of you: a moral prig. They'll accept your arguments against the flesh and your repudiation of desires. They'll turn your pretense of eternity into a rejection of life itself and love besides. They'll call you a "sodomite," and a "pagan," and reinterpret you as a proto-Christian.

SOCRATES: [*Flabbergasted*] That's not possible. What's a Christian?

ROMEO: In fact, do you know what the ideal of love will be? The sexless adoration of the divine. And do you know what they'll call it? "*Platonic* love." You won't even get the credit.

SOCRATES: Should I sue? Call in one of the wasps, Aristophanes.

ROMEO: That's what happens when you keep blabbing about "transcendence." Besides, people will make of you what they want to make of you. When it suits them, you will be a pagan and a pervert. And when it pleases them, you will be the father of philosophy and the hero of the truth.

SOCRATES: But that's not fair.

ROMEO: That's what happens when you don't publish.

SOCRATES: But you're nothing but a fiction yourself.

ROMEO: I'm actually a fantasy, but—I'd rather have me as a fantasy than you.

ARISTOPHANES: [*Very drunk*] If I may interrupt you there, I've been wanting to protest all evening that none of you, particularly you, Socrates, ever seems to take me very seriously. (I suspect you don't appreciate poets, myself, but perhaps I'm just being hypersensitive.) But what you failed to take seriously tonight was my perfectly serious argument, that shows just why love is so serious, not because it is eternal but because it answers an essential metaphysical need. It's serious, in other words. Seriously. [*Collapses*]

SOCRATES: How can we take you seriously, when you present us with a fable that is so at odds with all of our established myths?

ROMEO: But they are all myths, including your tribute to *eros;* the difference is that Aristophanes' wonderful myth tries to capture the experience of love, especially that exquisite *yearning* that goes beyond sexual desire and that desperate need to be together. That's just what your famous philosophy leaves out entirely, Socrates.

SOCRATES: But how are we to understand that nonsense? It can't be the literal truth.

ROMEO: How can you not understand it? Juliet is my other half. We were made for each other. And what difference if that isn't true? Surely you must know the experience; you just don't talk about it. Indeed, Aristophanes was the only one here tonight, except me, who has understood love at all; the rest of you have just been muddling around in metaphysics. This is a poor dialogue, Socrates—you've done much better.

SOCRATES: Yeah, I know, but there really isn't much to say about love. It's not like the theory of knowledge, or the theory of justice, where you can be hardheaded and argue about precise hypotheses. In fact, Eryximachus, I think your idea of talking about love is simply dreadful, and I'm glad Plato isn't here to write it down and publish it for posterity.

ARISTOPHANES: [*Sleepily*] I have no objection to my little tale going down in history. I rather like it, in fact.

SOCRATES: Well, no one would understand what I've been saying anyway. I'll tell you what—why don't we talk about virtue for a while?

ROMEO: Not me. I'm exhausted. And I have a full night ahead of me.

ARISTOPHANES: Ciao, Romeo.

SOCRATES: If you want to redeem yourself, Romeo, tomorrow we're going to enjoy a long harangue about justice. Want to come along?

ROMEO: Not my kind of entertainment. Ciao, Greeks. [*Exit*]

SOCRATES: [*To Agathon, who is asleep again already*] Who invited him here tonight anyway?

[*Agathon half opens his eyes and with great difficulty rises to join Socrates on his couch. But then a band of revelers enters; great confusion ensues, and everyone is compelled to drink large quantities of wine. By daybreak everyone is asleep or has gone away, except Socrates, Aristophanes and Agathon, who are drinking out of a large goblet which they pass around. Socrates is lecturing to them, saying something about the need for a writer of tragedy to be a writer of comedy too. Aristophanes obviously disagrees, but is too tired to argue. Agathon nods his assent, too sleepy to understand Socrates' meaning. And when they both have dropped, Socrates puts them to bed and goes off to the Lyceum for a bath. He never speaks of Romeo again, but he vows, if ever again should anyone speak of love, that it should be far more mysterious and obscure than anything he said tonight.*]

Index

INDEX